# BEYOND THE DUNES

*This anthology is dedicated, with admiration and firm confidence,
to the burgeoning young men and women writers of Saudi Arabia.
In their hands lies the sure continuation of their country's literary tradition,
itself the cradle of the rich Arabic literary heritage
from time immemorial.*

# BEYOND THE DUNES

## An Anthology of Modern Saudi Literature

EDITED
BY
MANSOUR I. AL-HAZIMI,
EZZAT A. KHATTAB, *ET AL.*

English Edition edited by
Salma Khadra Jayyusi

I.B. TAURIS
LONDON · NEW YORK

Published in 2006 by I.B. Tauris & Co. Ltd,
6 Salem Road, London W2 4BU
175 Fifth Avenue, New York NY 10010
www.ibtauris.com

In the United States of America and Canada distributed by Palgrave Macmillan
a division of St. Martin's Press, 175 Fifth Avenue, New York NY 10010

ISBN: 1 85043 972 9
EAN: 978 1 85043 972 1

A full CIP record for this book is available from the British Library
A full CIP record for this book is available from the Library of Congress

Library of Congress Catalog Card Number: available

Printed and bound in Great Britain by TJ International Ltd, Padstow, Cornwall from
camera-ready copy edited and supplied by the author

# CONTENTS

## Part I
### POETRY

### I. THE PIONEERS

### II. THE INNOVATORS

# Part II
## SHORT STORIES

# Part III
## EXCERPTS FROM NOVELS

# Part IV
## PLAYS

# Part V
## AUTOBIOGRAPHICAL LITERATURE

# Part VI
## BIOGRAPHICAL INFORMATION

# Dar al-Mufradat
## Academic Committee

# Preface and Acknowledgments

There have been two major cultural events in Saudi Arabia in recent years. The first fell on the Hirja date of AH 419, on the one hundredth anniversary of the founding of the Kingdom of Saudi Arabia; the other occurred in A.D. 2000 when Riyadh was designated the "Capital of Arabic Culture." The cultural, educational and media institutions of Saudi Arabia played an active role in promoting these events, not just locally and in the Arab world, but also internationally.

The Academic Committee of the Dar al-Mufradat Publishing House played its part in marking these two occasions by publishing a ten-volume compendium of modern Saudi literature. The Committee then sought to expand its efforts in this field by recruiting specialists to translate sections of this literature into English.

In this anthology, we trace the literary and cultural development of modern Saudi Arabia from the period beginning with King 'Abd al-'Aziz Al Saud's conquest of Riyadh in 1902 up to the present. There are, roughly speaking, four stages of literary and cultural development during this period. The first stage, the beginnings, spans the first twenty years or so of the Kingdom's modern history from 1902-1923. The second stage, after 1923, was a period of experimentation and growth. By 1954, with the advent of oil revenues, literary culture was bolstered by the development of institutions of education and learning. During this third stage of development, which stretched up to the mid-70s, there was not only a marked revival in the old inherited genres such as poetry, but also an innovative audacity and a desire to experiment with new genres, hitherto little developed in Saudi literature, such as drama and fictional prose. The dialogue between modernisation and tradition continues up until the literature of the present day, the last stage in this volume. Needless to say, these phases, each of which is around a quarter of a century long, cannot be separated discretely from each other, but are connected and overlapping. However, each phase had its own characteristics, which played an important role in changing the forms of literature, thought and culture along the way.

This volume is intended to introduce the Western reader to modern Saudi literature. We have been lucky enough to have Dr Salma K Jayyusi working on the English edition. Dr Jayyusi is the director of the prestigious Programme for the Translation of Arabic literature (PROTA). Dr Jayyusi and PROTA's track record of producing translations that are both authentic and accessible to Western readers speaks for itself.

We are grateful to HRH Crown prince Sultan Ben Abd al-'Aziz Al Saud for all the support which made the translation and publication of this volume possible. We are also grateful to IB Tauris for including this innovative literary volume in their prestigious programme of publications.

*Dar al-Mufradat Academic Committee*

# INTRODUCTION

## I. LOCATION

The Kingdom of Saudi Arabia constitutes the largest part of the Arabian Peninsula. Perhaps the oldest documented evidence of the name of the Arabian Peninsula is the Hadith (tradition) of the Prophet: "Two religions shall never meet in the Arabian Peninsula." This label is mentioned after this in the books of Arab geographers, as in the title of the book by Al-Hamadhani, *The Characteristics of the Arabian Peninsula,* as well as in the commentaries and lexicons of various countries.

The oldest mention of "the Arabs" is an inscription of the Assyrian King Shalmanesar III (858–824 B.C.) referring to the existence of "Arabs" with a king called "Jundbou" (Jundub), whose people allied against him (i.e. Shalmanesar) and were defeated by him. No one is sure whether this meant the Arabs generally or merely the Bedouins who took part in the war against Shalmanesar. Most probably, the Assyrians meant an Arabic "emirate" or "Shaikhdom" that ruled the northern parts of the Arabian Peninsula.

The Kingdom of Saudi Arabia is located in the south-west corner of Asia, giving it a unique location at the meeting point of the continents of the old world: Asia, Africa and Europe. It occupies almost 80% of the Arabian Peninsula. Its geographical features vary, therefore, in terms of geological structure and rock formation, including all types of igneous, sedimentary and metamorphic rocks. Saudi Arabia is bordered by Jordan, Iraq and Kuwait in the north; by the Gulf, Qatar, Bahrain and the United Arab Emirates in the east; by the Sultanate of Oman and the Republic of Yemen in the south; and by the Red Sea in the west. The Kingdom is located between 25 00 North and 45 00 East.

Sandy and non-sandy deserts extend over a large part of Saudi Arabia, which was covered in water during prehistoric wet periods. Its waters were some of the first to dry and leave deserts behind, most famous of which are the Empty Quarter, Al-Dahna' between the Empty Quarter and Mount Tuwaiq, Nafud Al-Dahna' to the north west of Mount Tuwaiq, Al-Dahna' al-Sharqiyya to the east of Al-Majma'a and Al-Zulf, and Al-Nafud Al-Shamaliyya which lies between Mount Shammar and Dawmat Al-Jandal.

Perhaps because the coastal mountains of the west and the south stop the rain-bearing winds from coming inland, Saudi Arabia is mostly dry and hot all year round. Yet those arid plains have been a fertile breeding ground for social, cultural and political movements that have influenced the region, and the world.

## II. HISTORY

Pre-Islamic Saudi Arabia was a place of clans and conflict, of rampant commerce, and of poverty. The Prophet Muhammad was born in 570 A.D., into a merchant family in Mecca. He was actively involved in the social life of Mecca at that time before he received a revelation from God, known as his "calling." Although he was involved in inter-tribal politics and mercantile enterprises, he embarked on fasting and contemplation. And it was during one such fast that, according to Islamic belief, the Angel Gabriel recited to him God's commandments for mankind.

It was several years before Muhammad proclaimed his mission publicly. He incurred the wrath and enmity of his tribe, the Quraysh, and the hostility towards his followers became intolerable. He ordered his companions to emigrate to Abyssinia, and subsequently had to emigrate himself to Medina. Medina became the capital of the Islamic world, and things stayed like this throughout the era of the first three Orthodox Caliphs.

The expansion of Islam in the Arabian Peninsula took place against the backdrop of The Byzantines' military defeat of the Persians in 622. The subsequent expulsion of Persians from Greater Syria meant that the Arabian Peninsula became the new frontline for the ongoing rivalry between these two great empires.

During the caliphate of 'Ali ibn Abi Talib (656-660 A.D.), the centre of the caliphate moved from Medina to Kufa in Iraq. When the caliphate subsequently passed to the first Umayyad caliph and founder of the Umayyad dynasty (660-750), Mu'awiya ibn Abi Sufyan, he made Damascus the base for his rule and the capital of the Islamic state.

After the caliphate had passed to the Abbasids in 132/750 and they were safe from the rebellions of the Shiites (those affiliated to 'Ali Ibn Abi Talib), the Arabian Peninsula took an increasingly minor role in the politics of the Islamic world. The Abbasid caliphs paid little attention to it except during Hajj season, such as in 845 when, after Bedouin tribes had wrought havoc in Medina and its environs, the Abbasid caliph al-Wathiq sent his leader, Bagha al-Kabeer to ensure that such activity was curtailed for the duration of the Hajj.

As Abbasid power declined, a number of independent states appeared in the Arabian Peninsula. After the fall of the Abbasid caliphate at the hands of the Mongols in 1258, control of the Hijaz passed to the Mameluke sultans, whose state had been established in Egypt in 1250. After their defeat of the Mongols, the Mamelukes ruled Greater Syria and Hijaz. They ruled Hijaz through the appointment of 'Alawi ashrafs (dignitaries) as princes of Mecca.

By the beginning of the 16th Century A.D., the Muslim world (of west Asia) was divided between three empires which competed for leadership: the Safavids in Persia, the Ottomans and the Mamelukes.

Clashes developed, eventually, between the Ottomans and the Mamelukes in Egypt, Syria and the Hijaz. The Ottomans defeated the Mamelukes in the battle of

Marj Dabiq in 1516, and the Mameluke empire subsequently fell to the Ottomans who entered Egypt in 1517. The Emir of Mecca, Sharif Barakat the Second, sent his son Abu Nami to the Ottoman sultan to declare his loyalty, and Hijaz thus submitted to Ottoman rule. Among the manifestations of this were the offering of prayers for the Ottoman Sultan during the Friday sermons, obtaining the Sultan's approval of the Sharif's new governorate, the presence of a representative of the Sultan to participate in the running of Medina, the appointment of the Shaikh of the Holy Mosque in Mecca, and a share in Jeddah's customs revenues.

## III. THE SAUDI STATE

### SOCIO-POLITICAL DEVELOPMENTS

The history of the Saudi state can be divided into three chronological stages. The first stage began with the historic meeting between the religious reformer, Shaikh Muhammad ibn 'Abd al-Wahhab and Imam Muhammad ibn Saud in 1744, when they pledged to each other to spread Islam. This stage ended with the defeat of the first Saudi state in 1818 by the Ottoman Turks led by the Wali (ruler) of Egypt, Muhammad 'Ali Pasha. The second stage began with the rise of Imam Turki ibn 'Abdallah ibn Muhammad ibn Saud in 1820, and ended with the Saudi rulers' exit from Najd upon the Rashid takeover in 1891. The third stage began with the struggle of King 'Abd al-'Aziz ibn 'Abd al-Rahman ibn Faisal ibn Turki Al Saud to regain his ancestors' crown in 1902 and the establishment of the modern Saudi state.

It is the third stage which provides the most relevant context for understanding the literature of this volume. King 'Abd al-'Aziz unified the Saudi state, and set the foundations of a vast country on the ruins of the Ottoman Empire out of myriad principalities and tribal leaderships across the Arabian Peninsula. He did this through a combination of military prowess and political acumen.

Great Britain was a major world power at the time, and it stood on the northern and eastern borders of the Peninsula, as well as in parts of the south. The King realised he either had to fight the imperial superpower or come to an arrangement with it. He skilfully persuaded Britain that a united Gulf under Saudi rule would offer a secure link with Britain's colonies in Asia. A series of treaties culminated in the Jeddah Accord in 1927 in which Britain acknowledged the independence of Hijaz, Najd and their adjoining lands under the sovereign rule of King 'Abd al-'Aziz.

Although this pact with Britain gave 'Abd al-'Aziz a huge advantage in his conquest of the kingdoms and principalities of the Peninsula, many of them also had foreign protectors of one kind or another. Where he could not achieve military defeat, Saud co-opted, offering the leading families financial incentives and status within the emerging state.

What King 'Abd al-'Aziz had succeeded in gaining control of was a patchwork of illiteracy, poverty, illness, violence and underdevelopment. There were no advanced urban centres except for a few cities such as Mecca, Jeddah and Medina. In order to develop the desert and the society, and to build internal security, the King embarked on an ambitious modernising and state-building programme.

King 'Abd al-'Aziz worked to settle the desert people and to replace their itinerant life in continual search for water and pasture. He established what became known in Saudi history as the *Hujar*, which were small villages or towns built around wells for the Bedouins to settle in. He provided the Bedouins with social facilities such as schools, health clinics and agricultural centres. This encouraged the desert dwellers to opt for a more comfortable life and to give up their nomadic lifestyle. Comprehensive awareness programmes in religious, social and economic matters accompanied these moves, and some kind of commercial exchange developed between these regions, the *Hujar* settlements and cities.

When King 'Abd al-'Aziz entered Mecca in 1925, he reviewed the administrative organisation of Hijaz used in the bygone days of Ottoman and Hashemite rule. He realised, however, that the region he ruled needed to face the challenges of modern times with a new administrative structure. One of the first steps towards re-organi- sation was the founding of *the Majlis al-Shura* or Shura Council (Consultative Council). He invited learned men, Shaikhs and merchants of Mecca to consult among themselves and to choose a select group of qualified men. This led to the election of the Shura Council which held its first session in Mecca in February 1925. Though the first council was dissolved the next year, subsequent councils undertook much of the administration of local government, with a special emphasis on the application of Shari'a (Islamic) law.

Tribalism dominated life in the desert and in the village. Within their walls, towns were exposed to all sorts of political discord. Furthermore, bandits threatened the trade caravans travelling between the towns.

Life in the desert was hard. Drought, epidemics and locust raids all brought great misery to its inhabitants. Perpetual conflict between warrior tribes meant that, even without the natural conditions to contend with, life was insecure.

Those who lived in villages probably had the easiest life in the beginning of the 20th century. Villages were based around oases and the outermost parts of valleys where running water was available. Livelihoods were earned from agriculture, trade, grazing and local craft making. The village acted as an intermediary between merchants in the town and Bedouins in the desert, providing both societies with its own products and those of the other.

Saudi urban society had its cities on the western and eastern coastlines. Their inhabitants work in trade, craft making, fishing and pearl-diving. There were also cities inland in agricultural regions such as Qaseem and its environs. Urban life was not uneventful and did have its fair share of excitements. It relied on the *Hajj* (pilgrimage) seasons; its foreign trade was prone to piracy; the sea was unpredictable and the movement of ships often handicapped by political factors. Agricultural produce depended on rain, which was irregular, and the movement of imports and exports was influenced by supply and demand and other problems.

Once conditions were settled, opportunities for work and trade multiplied, particularly after oil had been discovered and industrial cities had sprung up attracting people from every direction. This led to the formation of new, more homogenous communities. Many changes in social culture followed.

In order to cement stability, the government began to invest its natural and human resources and to move towards the development and expansion of its social and cultural services. This era started in 1953 and continued through the reigns of Kings Saud, Faisal, Khalid and Fahd, all of them sons of King 'Abd al-'Aziz Al Saud.

Saudi Society was disconcerted by this transformation, the force and pace of which it could not control. One aspect of this phase was increased emigration from both the desert and village to the city, where there was greater opportunity for work, earning money, education and a more comfortable life. Another new development was the entry of women into the public arena for the first time, working in the new economy. This increased economic participation was reflected in a new presence in public discourse and writing.

During this phase the atrophy of the old social values, traditions and customs was felt most keenly. The need for foreign educational and technical experts, as well as labour resources, had opened Saudi society to an unprecedented degree of exposure to international influences. As the disparate polities and landscapes of the country became gradually homogenised under the rule of a single authority, within each area new economic and cultural stratifications sprang up. The old communities were breaking up as a result of new economic opportunities and imperatives – new divisions of rich and poor overlaid the old divisions between tribes and clans. All these factors came together to create a collective sense of internal dislocation and confusion which has become almost a cliché in Saudi Arabian studies.

## EDUCATION AND CULTURE

The two holy mosques in Mecca and Medina have been beacons of learning throughout Saudi Arabia's history. Starting in Ottoman times, they became locations for the holding of study circles, which were frequented by pilgrims and citizens alike. Besides the study circles, there were some state schools in the *wilayet* (administrative district) of Hijaz which were run according to the educational system in other Ottoman districts. The civil education during the late 19th and early 20th centuries comprised elementary, intermediate and secondary stages, each constituting three years. There were also industrial and agricultural schools and teacher training colleges. The Turkish government made efforts to raise the level of education in the *wilayet* of Hijaz after 1908. Alongside the government schools, there were private schools in Mecca, Medina and some other cities in Hijaz. There was however virtually no system of formal education outside the Hijaz in the first quarter of the 20th century.

Libraries and printing presses during the late Ottoman and Hashemite eras were found in the two holy cities and in Hijaz more generally. Private and public libraries were essential features of the spiritual life in Mecca and Medina. Muhammad Labeeb Al-Batanouni, the author of *The Hijazi Journey* spoke of several libraries which he found in these two cities when he visited them in 1909.

Through the mosques, some works of scholarship were published. Newspapers such as *Al-Qibla* disseminated writings to a wider audience. Literature did not play a prominent role in either the Hashemite or the Ottoman publications. A modern conception of literature did not develop until the start of Saudi rule as the country became more and more exposed to world-wide intellectual trends and as a state education programme made it possible for a new generation of Saudi writers to discuss these new trends with one another.

A Directorate of Education was formed as far back as 1926, during the second year of King 'Abd al-'Aziz's rule in Mecca. Twelve schools were opened initially, and the number rose after ten years to 27 schools throughout the country. At first, the Directorate faced a shortage of qualified teachers in elementary and intermediate schools. Accordingly, it started the Saudi Educational Institute in 1927 to address this shortcoming. A school was started up in Mecca in 1935 with the specific aim of bringing Saudi students up to international standards to enable them to complete further education in other parts of the Arab world, especially Egypt.

The first group of Saudi students was sent to Egypt in 1926. The Second World War interrupted this policy, although it was resumed in 1942, when Saudi schools became larger and better organised. The number of Saudi graduates of Egyptian institutes and colleges reached 34 students between 1946-1949, rising to 192 in 1950, not to mention those studying at Egyptian elementary and secondary schools. A government report on Saudi students abroad says there were 19 students studying in the U.S.A. in 1951.

Education then during the reign of the late King 'Abd al-'Aziz made major advances and was not restricted to Qur'anic, elementary and secondary schools.

Turning to journalism, another important cultural factor, we find that during its infancy (1924-1953) it amounted to a few newspapers and magazines, which none-theless played an important role in terms of literary development, as well as in attracting intellectuals of all persuasions. The first of these newspapers was *Umm al-Qura* which replaced *Al-Qibla* in Mecca in 1924. Although it was, at the outset, an official newspaper, it was nonetheless full of articles of a literary, historical and social nature. It also played a pivotal role in the revival of the literary movement. Another paper, *Saut al-Hijaz* was published in 1932, with a literary role no less important than that of *Umm al-Qura*. Moreover, *Saut al-Hijaz*, as emphasised by its proprietor, was "the voice of the Hijazi literary revival." Alas, it did not stay in print for long, like many other newspapers; it ceased publication because of the paper shortage during the Second World War. When it re-appeared in 1946, it was under the new name of *Al-Bilad al-Saudiyyah*. After *Saut al-Hijaz*, another paper *Al-Madinah* was published in 1937. Not only did this paper focus on matters literary, but it was also covered social and historical topics. It also focussed on local news and the internal affairs of Medina.

Alongside the above three newspapers, three magazines were also printed during the same period: *Islah, Al-Manhal* and *The Muslim Call*. The first, *Islah*, was published in Mecca in 1928 and was described as a "religious, scientific and social newspaper." It was run and edited by Shaikh Muhammad Hamid al-Faqi, a notable Shaikh from the Azhar and the then head of the Printing and Publishing Department in Mecca. The second magazine, *Al-Manhal*, was published in Medina in 1937. It was a monthly magazine that "served literature, culture and learning." It was owned and edited by the renowned writer 'Abd al-Quddous al-Ansari. *Al-Manhal* showed particular interest in new literary forms such as novels, short stories, literary criticism and translation. In contrast, *The Muslim Call*, which was published in Mecca in 1937 was described as a magazine for "religious, social and historical affairs." It was published monthly in both Arabic and Malay and was managed and edited by Mustafa Andarqiri.

The next phase in the development of Saudi literature was the "renewal phase," spanning from the accession of King 'Abd al-'Aziz's son Saud to the throne in 1953, to the era of King Faisal in 1970. This period saw an intensification of state education programmes. The first Ministry of Education in the Kingdom was formed in 1953 and was followed by the opening of various schools, institutes and colleges across the Kingdom. The Ministry created administrative posts to supervise the newly established technical and administrative units, and it also started specialised departments for planning, as well as independent administrations for elementary and secondary education. It divided the Kingdom into 21 educational regions and gave its managers considerable administrative and financial powers to enable them to supervise their respective schools in each region.

The most significant development of this period however in terms of literary progress was the expansion of higher education. Higher education in Saudi Arabia began with the establishment of vocational colleges such as the Teacher Training College in Mecca in 1952, which was later transformed to the College of Education. In Riyadh, the College of *Shari'a* opened in 1952 and the College of Arabic Language in 1954. These colleges were later to become the nucleus for the University of Umm al-Qura in Mecca and the Imam Muhammad Ben-Saud Islamic University in Riyadh. With the increase in the number of high school graduates and the need for a workforce with specialised qualifications, the idea of establishing a national university arose. The University of King Saud in Riyadh opened in 1957, first with a faculty of arts, and later expanded into other faculties such as sciences, pharmacology, commerce, engineering, agriculture, education and medicine.

In 1961, the Islamic University was established in Medina, and it included the faculties of *Shari'a*, propagation of the faith, origins of religion, Holy Qur'an, Islamic studies, Arabic language and Hadith. The Higher Institute of Law was established in Riyadh in 1966. The establishment of other universities followed: King 'Abd al-'Aziz University in Jeddah in 1967, Muhammad ibn Saud Islamic University in Riyadh in 1974, King Fahd University for Petroleum and Minerals in Dammam in 1975, King Faisal University in al-Ahsa' in 1975, and later, King Khaled University in Abha in 1999.

The first modern industrial publishing houses were established during this period, producing newspapers such as *Al-Yamama* and *Riyadh*. Of the magazines, there was *Al-Yamama* and *Al-Jazira*.

The development of these new media was enhanced by the efforts of the General Administration for Radio, Press and Publishing founded in 1954 (later the Ministry of Information). The body channelled resources into the development of press and broadcasting, and brought a new professionalism to them.

During this time, Riyadh also witnessed the building of libraries such as the Saudi Library, the National library and the Library of King 'Abd al-'Aziz Foundation. These were not just libraries, but cultural establishments which produced leading work throughout the year such as specialised seminars, conferences and the publication of books and specialised, modern studies.

Much of this new modern knowledge industry was directed at illuminating Saudi Arabia's cultural past, and many of the landmark books on Saudi Arabian proverbs, colloquialisms, folklore and mythology were published in this period

'Abdallah ibn Khamees's ground-breaking *Popular Literature in the Arabian Peninsula* (1958) in particular brought the diverse oral and written literary traditions of the country together for the first time, and had a huge impact on future generations of Saudi writers.

The modernization period (1970-2000) is the richest and most complex in the Kingdom's history because it was in this era that the pace of social change exploded, mainly as a result of the oil boom in the 1970s. In the literary sphere, the education programmes instituted during the renewal period started to bear fruit.

As well as an expansion of internal education, it was in this period that large numbers of Saudis started to receive education internationally. Between 1975-1985 there were around 20,000 Saudi students studying in the United States, most of whom have since returned and embarked on careers in education and in the cultural sphere.

This period also saw an expansion in the number of public libraries in the country. There are now 68 libraries across 66 towns, with an average of one library per city, save for Riyadh, which has three. This excludes the libraries of universities, institutes and research centres.

In the mid-1970s, the state began to sponsor literary performance evenings. They were intended to replace private get-togethers, which were usually held in the homes of prominent writers. There are currently fifteen of these literary "clubs" nation-wide and they are one of the main conduits through which the government seeks to make contemporary arts accessible to the population.

Thus the country, once characterised as an inward-looking cultural wilderness, has come to be an intellectual hub of the region, producing world-class novelists, poets and dramatists. Writers from the past 30 years show a particular awareness of international political and cultural trends. But for all their cosmopolitanism, the writers included in this volume share a sensibility that is distinctively, irreducibly Saudi.

## IV. INTRODUCTION TO MODERN SAUDI LITERATURE

### POETRY

Towards the end of the Ottoman era and during the Hashemite era in Hijaz, the provinces of Najd, Hijaz and Ahsa' saw the emergence of some celebrated poetic voices. Their popularity led some literary historians of the period to refer to them with admiration and appreciation and to describe them as milestones in modern Saudi literature.

One of those voices was the poet Ibrahim al-Askoubi (1848-1913). He was one of the *imams* of the Holy Mosque in Medina, and was known for his travels to Syria and Egypt, as well as for his links with the writers and leaders of the Arab Renaissance. Al-Askoubi wrote a poem in his last days in which he criticised Ottoman rule and its Caliphs and in which he highlighted the weakness afflicting the nation as a result of its move away from Islam and its teachings. The poem was unprecedented in its daring criticism of the Ottoman state, and was immediately popular.

In addition to al-Askoubi, we should mention 'Abd al-Jaleel Barradah, Othman al-Radhi, 'Abd al-Muhsin al-Sahhaf (1874-1931) - the poet of the Arab Revolt in Mecca, Anwar 'Ishqi, 'Abd al-Wahid al-Jawhari al-Makki (1861-1893) who only left some writings on love poetry, and Muhammad al-'Umari (1848-1931) who was born in Algeria and lived in Medina. He was seemingly one of the most talented poets in Hijaz during that period. Although we have only a limited number of his poems, they, nonetheless, demonstrate a fluency of style and innovation in content.

Al-'Umari expressed political views in his poems that were relevant to the events of his time. He was one of the poets who criticised heavily the Arab Revolt and the European allies, in light of his own experience in Algeria under the French occupation.

One influence of Shaikh Muhammad ibn 'Abd al-Wahhab's mission (*da'wa*) in Najd was the revival of poetry written in classical Arabic after years in which colloquial poetry prevailed in the region. His mission also helped to expand religious content, not just in Najdi poetry but also among other poets who were influenced by and later supported this call in Yemen, 'Aseer and what became known as the United Arab Emirates. This eventually led to the birth of a new religious poetic trend. One of the most famous of those poets was Sulaiman ibn Sahman (1853-1930) who was born in the province of 'Aseer and travelled as a youngster with his father. Ibn Sahman is considered to be one of the most famous of the *da'wa* poets and the most combative.

Another poet influenced by the call of Shaikh 'Abd al-Wahhab was Ahmad ibn 'Ali ibn Mishrif (?-1868) who lived in Ahsa'. He lived through the second Saudi state and knew Prince Faisal ibn Turki. One section of his *diwan* contains a few poems in the form of fables where the characters are birds and animals, that aim, through their exchange, to encourage honourable conduct and high morals.

The poets of Ahsa' during the period of the late 19<sup>th</sup> century included a number from families famed for learning, such as Mubarak 'Abd al-Qadir, and al-'Alji and a few others. Their poetry was characterised by being free of affectation through the frank portrayal of their lives and conditions. It avoided defaming others and was not aimed at financial gain. It was also marked by a nationalistic dimension which accompanied some of the political events in the Gulf. An example is the poem written by Shaikh 'Abd al-'Aziz ibn 'Abd al-Lateef al-Mubarak (1893-1925) when Shaikh 'Issa Al Khalifa, the ruler of Bahrain, was ousted and his son Hamad appointed in his stead. In his poem, al-Mubarak expressed his fears about growing European ambitions in the Gulf. This is a long poem which condemns the British and their policy in the Gulf, particularly in Bahrain. It has a genuinely strident tone, and it warns people to prepare for the impending danger by heightened awareness and solidarity throughout the region.

In Qateef, there were also prominent poets such as Hasan al-Badr and 'Ali al-Jashi (1886-1957). They retained the traditional forms of heroic and elegiac poetry about the Prophet's family and in religious occasions. Their poems were notable for their genuine sense of regret, despite their traditional structure.

In summary, the poetry was not completely free of the shortcomings of the time: colourless in style and poor linguistically, playing around with words, repetition of traditional topics, and recycling of old styles and ways of thinking. On the other hand, there were a few poems which were in tune with the religious and political events of the time. We have already referred to the influence of Shaikh 'Abd al-Wahhab's calling *da'wa* on poetry, as well as the influence of political events in Hijaz and the Gulf. The poets of this period could not touch upon the other concerns of their societies, such as those manifested in the harsh lives they lived because of ignorance, poverty, fear and insecurity under the volatile political situation.

The first signs of the literary renaissance appeared in the Hijaz during the first quarter of the 20<sup>th</sup> century, in common with the rest of the Arab countries save for Egypt and Greater Syria. The latter two countries emerged from their political and intellectual isolation at an earlier stage, during the early 19<sup>th</sup> century, by opening up to Western culture via different channels such as study scholarships and the arrival and subsequent presence of western societies and missions. Some historians and scholars of this period see the publication of the first newspaper in Hijaz in 1908 as a sign of literary renaissance. That said, the greater event was that of the Arab Revolt in Mecca in 1916 and the founding of *Al-Qibla* newspaper as its official mouthpiece in the same year.

That year, many of the leading literary, intellectual, academic and journalistic figures who were supporters of Sharif Husain ibn 'Ali's revolt came to Mecca. Among them were: Fu'ad al-Khateeb, Muhib al-Din al-Khateeb, Kamil al-Qassab and 'Umar Shakir. They sought refuge in the revolution in Mecca from the oppression of the Ottoman ruler in Damascus, who had tightened his grip on them because of their active resistance to "Turkification" and their struggle against the suppression of the Arabic language, heritage and identity. These men were prominent literary figures and distinguished writers in both intellect and style. Their writings and poems, which were published in *Al-Qibla* prompted a new consciousness among the youth of Hijaz, who used to read the paper's articles avidly and were greatly influenced by them. In this way, reformist and enlightened ideas found their way towards Meccans, some of whom later became pioneers of poetry and literature during the Saudi era.

It was not long before the fruit of this interaction manifested itself in the book *The Literature of Hijaz, 1926,* which stands at the forefront of modern literature in the Kingdom. The writers and intellectuals of *Al-Qibla* were a major influence on the book, with their call for national reform and literary renaissance. The book contained poetry and prose written by a young generation of writers whose style and thinking was formed during the Hashemite era. It was edited and introduced by one of the most prominent pioneers of the period, Muhammad Surour al-Sabban. He also put up the funding for the book. He was one of the most enthusiastic supporters of reform and enlightenment during the dawn of the literary renaissance. In his introduction, al-Sabban refers to his sorrow at the state of literature in the Hijaz and its backwardness in comparison with the rest of the Arab world.

The poetical section of the book contained writings by authors who would later become influential, such as: Muhammad Hasan 'Awwad, 'Abd al-Wahhab Ashi, Muhammad Sa'id al-'Amoudi and Muhammad Surour al-Sabban himself, whose work was notable for its remarkable poetic sensitivity. It is also obvious that the book was influenced by the ideas of the literary renaissance in Greater Syria, Egypt and the *'Mahjar'* (i.e. in North and South America where emigrant Arabs had settled), which encompassed poems that were influenced by those of the Lebanese-American poet, Mikha'il Nu'aima (1889-1988) and the Syrian poet, Badawi al-Jabal (1906-1982). The writings were generally influenced by the style and thinking of the *'Mahjar'*, as well as by Fu'ad al-Khateeb and his pioneering companions of the Arab literary awakening. The writings have a strong rhetorical tone, especially when speaking of reform and exhorting people towards progress and development. Most of the writings were critical of the prevailing circumstances at the time and of the underdeveloped conditions in literary and social terms. There was also an early attempt at literary criticism. Historically speaking, the book is an important literary and intellectual document for the study of early modern Saudi literature.

Another book entitled *Declared Thoughts* appeared in 1927 and it added to the already strong criticism of the state of literature and poetry at that time. It was written by Muhammad Hasan 'Awwad (1902-1980) and was originally a collection of articles which had been previously published in the press. 'Awwad paved the way for the appearance of the romantic trend through his fierce attack on traditionalism in his famous article "Literature in Hijaz." Critics find a similarity between *Declared Thoughts* (1927) on the one hand, and, on the other, *The Diwan*[1] (1921) and *The Sieve*[2] (1923). 'Awwad was indeed an admirer of al-'Aqqad (1889-1964) and emulated his severe style of criticism. His writings also leaned towards irony, similar to Mikha'il Nu'aima's criticism of the arcane. On the other hand, `Awwad was influenced by and on friendly terms with the Egyptian poet, Ahmad Zaki Abu-Shadi (1892-1955). He was also one of the voices in Hijaz that advocated the ideas and theories of the "Apollo" school of romantic poetry.[3]

Before we get onto the features of the renewal movement that began to appear in Saudi poetry through various influences and through the literary schools such as The *Diwan*, the writings of the 'Mahjar' poets and critics, and of the "Apollo" group, we should point out that its timing coincided with the revival of a more traditional poetry in both content and style. Two of the most prominent representatives of the latter were Muhammad ibn 'Abdallah ibn 'Uthaimeen (1854-1944) and Ahmad Ibrahim al-Ghazzawi (1901-1980).

Although influenced in different degrees by the old style of poetry, the new poets still composed in the old style, especially as far as eulogies were concerned, in the construction of the overtures to the poems, and in the use of words, structure, style and imagery. Ibn 'Uthaimeen has poems that begin, according to the ancient poetic style, with stopping at [imaginary] ruins and inquiring after the abode of the beloved before riding off on his camel and heading towards some glorified destination. His poems reveal a deep-rooted knowledge of a very old cultural heritage and a broad familiarity with old poetry. This however made his poetic lexicon laden with obscure terminology and idioms that were far removed from our day and age. On the other hand, Ibn 'Uthaimeen could also be likened in some respects to the Egyptian neo-classical poet, Mahmoud Sami al-Barudi whom critics consider to have been the earliest poet in the Arab world to restore full classical strength and virility to Arabic poetry.

Al-Ghazzawi was known as "His Majesty's Hassan"[4] because of his close companionship with and praise of King 'Abd al-'Aziz. Al-Ghazzawi lived long enough to write eulogies about 'Abd al-'Aziz's sons, Kings Sa'ud and Faisal. His poetry is characterised by his evident skill in structuring the opening, by his uncomplicated language, and by a poetic lexicon shaped by urban culture.

As we have already said, Muhammad Hasan 'Awwad was one of those influenced by romanticism and its approach to literature. Through this influence, he sought to combine poetry and critical analysis. This was something that singled him out from his generation of innovators. In fact, 'Awwad represents a special phenomenon that may not be repeated in Saudi literature.

Right up until his death, 'Awwad possessed a youthful spirit that was always open to and striving for things new. This was the key to his personality and the secret of the respect which his students and admirers held for him. His book *Declared Thoughts* contained many of his views and ideas about the need for innovation in poetry and literature. He was also fiercely critical of the prevailing way of life, and he derided some of the customs, traditions and social practices in Hijazi society, which he described as backward and frozen in the past. For him, literature had an important and fundamental role in terms of bringing about transformation.

With regard to poetry, 'Awwad called for the use of myths and he embraced free verse and prose poetry, in accordance with the Apollo school. His poetry reflected this. He wrote poems about topics that called for revival and reform, and he tried to write in new poetic forms, bringing together, for example, more than one rhyme in some of his poems. Although his attempts at the use of myths and at breaking from traditional styles may not have been completely successful, they encouraged others to experiment in this field.

The limitations of 'Awwad's poetry derive from his well-known personal disposition towards argument, debate and the triumph of reason. Moreover, he elevated rational thinking and philosophy in poetry at the expense of imagination and emotion. This led his friend in Egypt, Ahmad Zaki Abu-Shadi to describe his verse as the "poetry of philosophy." Moreover, 'Awwad did not take the time to polish his language or to revise his poems, which may explain the prosaic nature of much of his poetry and the dullness of his vocabulary. The importance of 'Awwad in the history of Saudi ideas on literature, therefore, supersedes his position as a poet. His courage in attacking tradition, his enthusiasm for innovation, his honesty, candour, defiance in defending his views and his well-known support for young talented writers all gained him a unique place amongst his generation.

Some features of romanticism began to appear, albeit timidly, in the poems of a number of 'Awwad's companions such as: Husain Sirhan, Hamza Shihata and Muhammad Hasan Faqi. To a different extent, these features were also to be found in the poems of the following: Ibrahim Hashim Filali, Tahir Zamakhshari, 'Abdallah al-Faisal and others. We should make clear from the beginning that a literary trend, be it romanticism or something else, takes on the colour and characteristics of the country in which it appears. What brings the Romantics together is revolution against hackneyed traditions in poetry. As to the nature and shape of this rebellion, it differs from one poet to another, even within the same country. This is because of the various psychological and cultural factors and objectives as well as the environment with which a poet must comply and to which he must adapt. In this respect, Saudi poetry is no exception.

In addition to the theories of the Diwan school and the Apollo group, the poets of this era were also influenced by other major romantic Arab poets such as: Bishara al-Khouri (1884-1968) in Lebanon, 'Ali Mahmoud Taha (1901-1949) and Ibrahim Naji (1898-1953) in Egypt, al-Shabbi in Tunisia (1909-1034) and Iliyya Abu-Madi (1890-1957) in the U.S. The prevailing mood of romanticism in the Arab world during the thirties and forties influenced them equally, and their poems were marked by an air of sadness and pessimism, full of questioning and perplexed contemplation about life's enigma. They directed their passion and their worries towards women and nature, and their poems were full of pain, alienation, loss and despair. The emphasis on personal suffering led some poets to an inflated state of self-importance and narcissism, at the expense of human and national pain. That said, this period also witnessed serious attempts to get away from the classical vocabulary. Thus, the language of poetry began to break free from unnecessary complexity and artifice and to become full of stirring rhythms and emotional promptings. There were many poets of this era who spanned generations, and there are differences in the extent to which some took on the characteristics of romanticism and freed themselves from classical influences. Their poems, therefore, mostly blended traditional and romantic trends and were used in the cause of reform, as well as in the wider political and intellectual debate, including issues of concern to the whole Arab world. The educational and moralising elements remained, and the nature of their topics demanded purity of style, linguistic magnificence and a distinctly oratorical tone.

We mentioned earlier the names of some of the reformist poets. We shall now mention some new names to enlarge our area of study in order to encompass more than one generation and one type of experience: Ibrahim Fouda, Muhammad Sa'id al-Musallam, Muhammad Sa'id al-Khunaizi, 'Abdallah al-Jashi, Hasan Sairafi, Mahmoud 'Arif, Majid al-Husaini, Ibrahim al-'Allaf, Muhammad Hashim Rasheed, Hasan al-Qurashi, 'Abdallah ibn Idris, Muhammad al-Fahd al-'Issa, Hamad al-Hijji and Thurayya Qabil. If we look at their poems and compare them to those of others, we find that some in this group give expression to an attitude to life and a vision that distinguishes them from others. It is indeed this group which brings a new element to the poetry of the era.

Within this group, we should mention Husain Sirhan (1916-1993) whose poetry reflected the influence of the older generations in terms of style, imagery and structure, but this traditional prologue can often lead, after a few verses, to a novel content.

Husain Sirhan was continually asking questions, and his obsession with death was expressed repeatedly in different images in his poetry. By the age of fifty, he began living as a recluse in a state of psychological turmoil. A sad and tormented tone dominated his poems, which was fed constantly by his excessively gloomy reactions and philosophical reflections on existence, life and the fate of man. Indeed, Sirhan's voice remained honest and distinctive in all the subjects he tackled.

With Hamza Shihata (1910-1973) the Saudi poem reached a high point in terms of language, composition and vision. Like Sirhan, Shihata is of the older generation which spanned more than one era and which used new content within traditional forms. The image of the woman as treacherous, untrustworthy and a creature to be scorned, is constantly repeated in his poetry. This negative image did not stop at women, however; rather, it became part of his philosophy in life. He saw that this core of unfaithfulness and lack of fidelity ruled all human relationships. He was a poet who went on a continuous search for analogies which he never found. He constantly spoke of the loss of values, described his feelings of estrangement and the randomness of life. Shihata managed to express his philosophy in a rich and powerful language, free of affectation and full of vitality.

The poets of this era were not just many in number; some were also prolific in output. Of them, we should mention: Muhammad Hasan Faqi (1914-2004), Tahir Zamakhshari (1914-1987), Hasan 'Abdallah al-Qurashi (1926-2004) and Husain 'Arab (1930-2002). The greater quantity of output adds nothing in terms of variety in the content, for content usually remained the same, and was repeated over and over again. The oeuvre of one poet would normally contain a number of totally unrelated subjects. Furthermore, their view and approach were rarely revised. Apart from a few exceptions, the same form is found in more than one poem, without the reader gaining any insight into the standpoint or anguish of a given poet.

The oeuvre of Muhammad Hasan Faqi is laden with confused and confusing reflections, and it has an excessive focus on the self. The worries expressed had little relevance outside the poet's own misfortune in life. These feelings kept on recurring in his works without crystallising into something more profound, in a way that might have amalgamated personal and collective pain. Had he achieved this, his vision might have transcended his narrow circle to encompass man and the reality of the human condition.

The language of those poets was refined, powerful and flawless. That said, it was not used in support of any distinguishing causes or matters. Instead, some works were merely soulless echoes of Arab voices outside Saudi Arabia. If you read the oeuvre of Tahir al-Zamakhshari, you will find that most of it revolves about local or Arab occasions. The poetry also reflects a passion for nature; it emulates al-Shabbi in choosing forests as a topic; it is about grievances which are quickly pacified by patience, hope, regret and repentance. Although al-Zamakhshari seems talented enough to have avoided pomposity in his poetry, his choice of subject matter did not serve to distinguish him from the other poets of his time.

Hasan al-Qurashi is one of the many poets of that time, although his voice is barely heard amid the mass of romantic poets, both old and modern, who influenced his work. He made an important experiment with the poem's metre, notwithstanding the limitations of the form, and wrote on various subjects as was the habit of the poets of that era. His poetic talent is most evident when he follows his instinct and his optimistic love of life. As for Ibrahim al-Filali (1906-1974), his is another voice which is distinguished by its rhythm from the other poets of his time. His long stay in Egypt and distance from a conservative environment both contributed to freeing up his writings on women and wine, in the spirit of al-Khayyam and the famous Abbasid poet, Abu-Nuwas (146/763-198/814). That said, he did so without triviality or exaggerations. His early writings that he published in Egypt contain longing and yearning for his people and his country; they also describe his suffering abroad and his lack of funds. This was a real experience to him, and it was expressed with obvious spontaneity and strong emotion.

With the emergence of the romantic movement's second generation, there were some poets who were not known for the quantity of their poetic output. Indeed, scholars of Saudi poetry might have overlooked their names. They were poets with an original flair for creating new contexts and avoiding clichés. A good example is 'Adnan al-Sayyid al-'Awwami (b. 1937) who focuses on the new poetic image and strives to capture everyday human reality in clear and carefully chosen language.

In his collection entitled, *Shati' al-Yabab* (shore of devastation) 1992, al-'Awwami reveals a local flavour which carries the smell of the earth and of the place, portraying a picture of the environment, its inhabitants and their interrelation with each other. In his poetry, one can find moving expressions on the places and towns with which he was acquainted or in which he had lived in the Eastern part of the Kingdom. This is a notable feature, which is also shared with a number of poets hailing from that part. Another feature of al-'Awwami's poetry is the frequent use of such words as *'abaya* (cloak) and *qina'* (veil), both of which reinforce the poet's attachment to his environment. His love poems and stories about women are often framed in a narrative style which gives these topics a lively and vital dynamism.

In 1960, 'Abdallah ibn Idris released his book *Contemporary Poets of Najd*, which is one of the first of its kind featuring poets from Najd. The book contained works by: Nasser bu Haimid, Muhammad al-Fahd al-'Issa, Muhammad al-Sulaiman al-Shibl, 'Abd al-Rahman al-Mansour, Muhammad al-'Amir al-Rumaih, Sa'd al-Bawardi, 'Abdallah al-'Uthaimeen, Hamad al-Hiiji, 'Uthman ibn Sayyar and Ibrahim al-'Awaji. The book reminds us of the earlier work *The Literature of Hijaz*. Not only does *Contemporary Poets of Najd* publish works of Najd's first poets, but like *The Literature of Hijaz* its texts also point to a new phase in the history of Saudi poetry in both content and style.

With regard to content, the thinking seems to be clearly influenced by the Egyptian revolution and the Arab nationalist tide, the international call for freedom, the realist movement in literature and the use of literature in support of national and Arab causes. This does not mean that all the texts in the book were free of all romantic spirit, with its tone of regret and melancholy. As for style, the book offers us the first attempts at the abandonment of the traditional form of poetry, at writing free verse, and poetry in prose. There are also signs of the Western influences of symbolism, surrealism and translated European poetry. Changes during that era in form, content and vision are clearly manifested in the collection, *Qalaq*, by Nasser bu Haimid (b. 1930).

Before we get to the modern poets of free verse and rhymed prose, we should mention religious poetry, or rather what is categorised as Islamic poetry within Islamic literature. This latter requires writing from an Islamic perspective about how the world was conceived. It also included poetry which attacks trends and ideas deemed dangerous to society and community, in its bid to protect Islam and its principles. Current representatives of this school include: 'Abd al-Rahman al-'Ashmawi, Ibrahim Abu 'Abat and Habeeb Mu'alla al-Mutairi.

As for the poetry of political protest and criticism of the Arab world, the two voices that are most heard now are Usama 'Abd al-Rahman and 'Abd al-Muhsin Hilleet Musallam.

## FREE VERSE AND PROSE POETRY

We need to distinguish between the early attempts at free verse poetry on the one hand, and the technical level it reached in other Arab countries. Many poets tried to write free verse poetry e.g. Muhammad Hasan 'Awwad, al-Qurashi, Mansour al-Hazimi, Muhammad al-Fahd al-'Issa, Ahmad al-Fasi, Nasser bu Haimid, Muhammad al-'Amir al-Rumaih, Sa'd al-Bawardi and others. Their attempts did not venture far from the traditional style, either in form or metre. As for content, it remained romantic for the most part. Thus, free verse poetry in its modern form (with its use of symbolism, myth and tradition, and its language and metaphors) did not appear until the late 1970s and early 1980s.

We pointed earlier to the influence of Western intellectual thinking and literary schools such as existentialism and surrealism. Moreover, the Arab world, indeed the world at large, witnessed events such as the June '67 War, the Camp David Peace Accord in 1979 and the Israeli invasion of Lebanon in 1982. The 1970s also marked a jump in the Kingdom's fortunes which greatly influenced the social and economical structures. The generation of the seventies thus found in free verse poetry a form capable of accommodating the emerging feelings and of expressing their worries about the pace of change and modernisation.

Before we explore this generation, mention should be made of two prominent poets, Ghazi 'Abd al- Rahman al-Qusaibi (b. 1940) and Muhammad al-'Ali (b. 1940), both of whom write both in the two hemistich verse and in free verse, contributing greatly to the development of free verse poetry. The poetic experience of al-Qusaibi dates back to the 1960s. His voice is an independent one which distinguishes him from many other poets. His language is rich, coherent and highly evocative. The personal tone of al-Qusaibi's poetry did not obscure his foresight and perceptiveness in dealing with general Arab issues and the causes of the Arab world.

Muhammad al-'Ali's experience also dates back to the 1960s. However, his poetry has yet to be collected in book form. It is possessed with angst and human anxiety. The influence of traditional structures is evident in his language, especially with regard to the purity of his vocabulary and the integrity of his diction. Al-ʿAli's poetry depends heavily on the rich traditions of the Arabian Gulf, and he uses them to focus and deepen the vision of the poem and to enrich it through suggestion and meaning.

The 1970s and 1980s have seen an effusion of modernist poetry. Breaking free from the traditional metre served to broaden the scope for poetic statement, thereby creating more variety and permitting poets to experiment continually, with the birth of new names and generations. Saʿd al-Humaideen was the first poet to publish a book of free verse poetry, *Drawings on the Wall* in 1977. Other attempts by a number of young poets followed. They included poets loyal to the free verse structure and those ranging between the latter and the two hemistich poetry. Some examples are: ʿAli al-Dumaini, Muhammad al-Thubaiti, Ahmad al-Salih, Muhammad Jabr al-Harbi, ʿAbdallah al-Saikhan, ʿAbdallah al-Zaid, Hasan al-Sabʿ, Khadija al-ʿUmari, Thurayya al-ʿUrayyid, Latifa Qari, Ashjan Hindi, Fatima al-Qarni, Jasim al-Suhayyih, Ahmad Qiran al-Zahrani, Salih al-Zahrani, Ibrahim Miftah, Husain Suhail, Ibrahim Saʿbi, ʿAbdallah al-Rasheed, Ibrahim al-Wafi, Ibrahim Zouli, Muhammad Musayyar Mubaraki, Husain al-ʿArwi and ʿAbdallah al-Khashrami. Before we discuss the characteristics of free verse poetry, we should point out that the two hemistich poem written by this latter group represented a break from the conventions of traditional poetry because it reflected a contemporary outlook and a language that was new and free of oratory and rhetoric.

Some critics argue that themes have disappeared from free verse poetry and were replaced with what can be called ideas or "points of view." There are stances concerning man's destiny, women, love, death, ideas and ideologies, conflicts and philosophies, causes of the homeland and the community, separation from one's city and village and all things that constrain man's freedom.

Saudi free verse poetry is preoccupied with these issues, and they give it its identity and distinctiveness amongst similar voices in the Arab world, for these poets employed technical tools such as symbolism, local imagery, historical and popular figures from the Peninsula, colloquial vocabulary, elements from the desert environment such as caravans, sands, melodies and rain, musical instruments such as the *rababa* (a single-stringed fiddle) and folkloric dances and tunes, and the deep connection of the above techniques with the consciousness of the inhabitants of the Peninsula. Religious traditions were also employed in the form of references to religious stories, to events and personalities in Islamic history, and to the use of religious terminology. Dramatic poetry with multiple voices came into being, as did poetry that simulated the folktale in its use of dialogue and narrative.

With regard to diction, there was a renewal of the poetic lexicon which now eschewed complex metaphors and excessive musicality; instead, it became marked by sweetness, by the eloquent choice of words and by the use of colloquial and popular expressions to reflect daily realities and the lives of ordinary people.

Today, there are a number of prose poets in the Kingdom including: Fawziyya Abu Khalid, Ahmad al-Mulla, Muhammad al-Dumaini, Muhammad 'Ubaid al-Harbi, Mansour al-Juhani, 'Abdallah al-Safar, Ibrahim al-Husain, Ghassan al-Khunaizi and Huda al-Daghfaq. As in the rest of the Arab world, some critics in Saudi Arabia view rhyming prose poem as being too vague and mysterious, and as nothing but an attempt to burn bridges with the past and to let in, through the back door, those with no poetic skill.

In any case, the rhyming prose poem did not supplant either the two hemistich poem or free verse poetry. It emerged within a period of intense intellectual and historical activity to establish its own poetic style. Short in length, rhyming prose poetry relies on an intense focus on an idea, on symbolism, suggestion and the sparkling conciseness of poetry. It is also based on peculiarity, dissimilarity and perplexity.

## THE SHORT STORY

The first attempts at story writing in Saudi literature began between the two world wars as part of the reformist literary movement. They were published by newspapers and magazines on a large scale in the main towns of Hijaz. Here, as in other Arab countries, short stories did not emerge out of a traditional convention and art forms such as folktales, the assemblies (*maqamas*), poetry competitions (*munazara*) and night time literary exchanges (*musamara*). There weren't specific writers whom one would think of as pioneers, as were Edgar Allan Poe, Guy de Maupassant and Gogol in the West.

Translation played a major role in gaining the interest of Arab writers in Egypt and Greater Syria in modern narrative and dramatic styles. The art of story writing evolved gradually and in the context of the reformists' rhetoric which called for progress, advancement and modernisation. In general terms, it was the rhetoric of "journalism" which propagated various new forms, styles and ideas.

Some critics have shown that the essential first attempts at writing stories shared common ground with the "journalistic essay" in general and the "literary essay" in particular.

Essay writing represented the spirit of the times and spoke on its behalf. It also played a critically important role in renewing styles of expression and composition and in making a break with the second rate literature of the preceding phases of decline.

Those who led the movement of renewal and modernisation in poetry and story writing were some of the most prominent writers in the daily newspapers and in the weekly and monthly magazines. Some were professional journalists for much of their lives, in managerial and editorial capacities. These men of letters were the pioneers of the emerging cultural elite in a society which had just seen the spread of schools, printing houses and publishers. Their society had just begun to interact with the modern world after centuries of cultural isolation.

The ideas that caught on during the phase in which essay writing became "established," developed in outlook and vision over the years. This owed much to the varied efforts by pioneering writers in the initial phases of a new cultural movement in a society that was similarly undergoing its own process of social development. The following writers wrote essays, poems and short stories: Muhammad Hasan 'Awwad, Muhammad Sa'id al-'Amoudi, Ibrahim Filali, 'Abd al-Quddous al-Ansari, Ahmad al-Siba'i, Muhammad Hasan Faqi and Muhammad 'Ali Maghrabi. Some also endeavoured to write novels and plays. At the same time, most of them held senior posts at newspapers, magazines, printing houses and schools, all of which were mushrooming in Hijaz. It would be wrong to expect that any of these writers had a profound knowledge of the finer techniques of story writing, however. This new and attractive art form was still in its infancy in Saudi Arabia and had not fully matured even in Egypt, the country whose writers were seen as "role models" for our own young writers.

Modern story writing during this earlier period was not yet firmly established, unlike poetry and essay writing. The former is deep-rooted and revered in our collective memory; the latter gained ground quickly, thanks to its relevance to the emerging medium of mass communication represented in the press at the time.

It is no surprise then that story writing during the "foundation" years seems to us today to be flawed, mixed with sentimentalism and dominated by ideas. As Mansour al-Hazimi describes, these stories ultimately remain "another type of social essay that aims at reform but does not abide by the rules and fundamentals of story writing." The story was not, in itself, the final goal as an artistic expression, but was rather seen as a medium that had its own appeal to writers looking for new forms and to readers looking for enjoyment. The readers were also probably seeking an escape from the shock and surprise of political developments that had seen overnight changes in allegiance. Most stories of the time contain features which support our contention. We find, for example, that the distance between the writer, the text and the reader was less than it should have been, because writers often manipulated the story line and the characters in order to put their own personal view across. Muhammad al-Shamikh and Mansour al-Hazimi showed this in a detailed and analytical study.

We find a significant influence of some elements of modern story writing in authors such as Ahmad Rida Houhou and Muhammad 'Alem al-Afghani. If we attempt to understand and explain this phenomenon, however, we would be venturing outside the local socio-literary context. Ahmad Rida Houhou, for example, was Algerian and fluent in French, in which he probably read sophisticated works by the likes of Edgar Allan Poe (in translations) and Guy de Maupassant, both of whom were pioneers in story writing in the western literary context.

One indication of the influence of Western literature on Houhou's stories is his discussion on the end of literature and art in an age of "science and scientists." This notion is connected with Hegel's thesis which was alien to the general context of

Arabic literature at the time. Back then, writers were the elite who pioneered and dominated culture in Hijaz, as in Egypt and Greater Syria.

On the other hand, Muhammad 'Alem al-Afghani hailed from Afghanistan, and although we know little of his biography, one can probably infer that he was fluent in Urdu and English. He might therefore have come across the works of Gogol and Chekhov in their English translations, the two pioneers of this field in Eastern Europe. What supports this assumption is the element of optimism and realism in his writings. In his story "Two Birds Flying to the Moon," al-Afghani seeks integration and interaction between "literature" and "science," not opposition and contradiction. It is as if he was responding to Houhou's story "The Last Writer."

When we come across stories written at the time by local writers with strong language, good analysis of the protagonists' emotions and thoughts, or an obvious use of sarcasm, it is probably due to the writer's creative talent. It also reflects their view of their work as a serious and meaningful endeavour, not just a passing fad or money-spinner.

We think that these matters deserve more research and investigation, something which the scope of this study does not allow. The same applies to the relationship between the story and the essay during the early history of literature in the Kingdom. The most important question that deserves thorough research using modern comparative techniques relates to the pivotal role of *Al-Manhal* magazine (founded Spring, 1937). It served to create awareness and add appeal and validity to story writing, for both the generation of pioneers and their successors. From its inception, this literary magazine made sure that a slot was allocated in every issue for a short story under the title "Springtime of Stories," or "This Issue's Story" as it became known. In each edition one would find a story written by a writer from Hijaz or by a correspondent who worked in other parts of the Kingdom. *Al-Manhal* was, in fact, the only magazine that was dedicated to literary writings at the time. On top of this, we also find reviews of the stories which had been published in previous issues. This marked the beginning of the critical study of story writing, the analysis of which broached technical matters such as style, structure, elements to attract the reader's attention etc.

On the other hand, there is no doubt that the owner and editor-in-chief of this magazine, writer and linguistic researcher 'Abd al- Quddous al-Ansari was one of the writers with the strongest sense of critical awareness as to the importance of story writing in modern literature. He expressed this clearly in the introduction to his story "The Twins," considered by some to be a leading work in the art of story writing in Saudi literature.

We can understand the desire of al-Ansari and Houhou, two of the most prominent editors of this leading literary magazine, to publish a great number of translated works from Urdu, Turkish, Russian, French, English and Japanese. This reflected their personal commitment to this new art form as well as its appeal to readers. The translated works provided an ideal opportunity for the writers of that generation and their successors, as it enabled them to read and discuss stories which were more artistically developed and intellectually mature than their own works.

In summary, the stories of that early period represented the phase of "unawareness," as Najib al-'Aufi described it. We call this phase "the lure of the story form" as a distinct literary genre with its own characteristics and structure. If it lacked in story content, it amounted no more than an essay poorly aimed at social and emotional issues, often with no linguistic artistry, no uniqueness of subject, no specification of outlook, no coherent structure and no meaningful analysis of the protagonists or description of events. That said, the lack of these elements may be partly compensated for by the richness of the vocabulary, a strong style and grammatically correct phraseology in the works of that generation, when compared with the writings of the following generations.

Awareness of the characteristics of the story as a distinct literary genre developed gradually among the 1960s' generation who benefited from the efforts of earlier writers, both directly written or translated. This generation also benefited from the effective continuity of the creative works of fiction in much of the Arab world, which were becoming very popular. During this period, short stories in the Arab world reached a new pinnacle, thanks to the works of Yusuf Idris (1927-1991), the quality of which was superior to that of the former generation of the Egyptian, Yahya Haqqi (1905-1993), and the Nobel Prize winner, Najib Mahfouz (b. 1911). These new works were also accompanied by a new critical discourse represented particularly in Rashad Rushdi's book *The Art of Story-Writing* (1959). This showed the potential of this literary genre as the most suited to the expression of individual awareness in an unstable Arab world, in which general awareness began to re-evolve after the Second World War. Patriotic and nationalistic speeches of the time played the most important role in bringing about and describing this transformation, in particular after the revolution in Egypt in 1952.

This made story writing of the new generation an end in itself, not divorced from its general social and cultural context. Rather, storywriters became more aware of the characteristics and structural elements of the short story which could be used to enhance their stories' powers of expression and their potential to wield influence on the readers.

Perhaps the best indicator of this new awareness was represented in the anthologies of writers such as Ibrahim al-Nasser, Ghalib Hamza Abu al-Faraj, Sa'd al-Bawaridi, 'Abd al-Rahman al-Sha'ir, 'Abdallah al-Jifri, Luqman Younis, 'Abdallah Sa'id Jam'an, Siba'i 'Uthman, Najat Khayyat and others.

This phenomenon which we witnessed at the same time in the Maghrib, Greater Syria and Iraq had various key dimensions. Moreover, it reinforced the transformation or "development" from the phase of "unawareness" to that of "consciousness" of the technique of story writing, meaning that both writer and reader were aware of the specifics and prerequisites of this narrative art form.

Writers became aware of the importance of "professionalism," not so much devoting themselves exclusively to writing short stories, but dedicating more time and effort to this appealing yet difficult art form. Writers could no longer treat it as a casual hobby. To publish a collection of short stories, writers needed to be confident that it was worthy of the attention of others. Most importantly, a good writer had to show that he could identify with the new genre.

Hence the term "storywriter" developed a specific cachet as with the labels of "poet," "playwright," "novelist" and "critic." Increasingly, people were aware of the contrast between form and rhetoric, and not just with regard to short stories.

Doubtless, any critical reading of the works of this generation would reveal great differences in writers' abilities to transform their intellectual consciousness into an artistic vision through their prose. Without doubt, too, the stories of this period were, on average, better than the earlier attempts. In the works of Ibrahim al-Nasser, 'Abdallah al-Jifri and Hamza Bogari, the stories have a single theme or influence, a limited number of protagonists, a coherent timeframe and place setting, and a cohesive structure. The same is particularly true in the writings of Siba'i 'Uthman and Najat Khayyat, who are considered to be the best examples of their age. Moreover, we find that most of these elements are present in the stories of amateur writers such as Jamil al-Hujailan, whose story "After Sunset" shows definite promise. The language is concentrated and inspiring, and the events are intense. The experiences presented in his text are deeply rooted in the human condition, which is full of paradoxes and can only be observed and laid bare by a truly creative writer.

Another early feature of this time appears in story writing which fluctuated between different intellectual and stylistic trends. For example, the realistic trend is clearly evident in stories by Ibrahim al-Nasser, 'Abd al-Rahman al-Sha'ir, Sa'd al-Bawardi and 'Abdallah Sa'id Jam'an. Stories by al-Qurashi, 'Abdallah al-Jifri and Jamil al-Hujailan come under the "sentimental and romantic" trend. As for stories by Siba'i 'Uthman, Najat Khayyat and Hamza Bogari, they are realistic but with a significant addition: they contain a symbolic ingredient broader and deeper than the rather direct meanings contained in traditional, realistic works.

It might be said that all these trends result directly from the continuity and interaction of our writers with the prevailing trends in Arabic and international literature. This does not mean, however, that these trends do not reflect awareness of the self and of the world, as well as the growing aesthetic and existential expertise of these writers. It would be useful, therefore, to examine some of these cultural-literary trends, and to follow up their progress. This can be seen in the pioneering study of 'Abdallah 'Abd al-Jabbar, in which he deepened our understanding of the issue through his structured and intellectual approach to the topic, which the rhetoric on fiction avoids to this day.

Over the last two decades, story writing has seen such dramatic changes that permit us to speak of an aesthetic and intellectual schism between the writers of the "modernist generation" and the two preceding generations. There is a complete system of concepts relating to the art of short story writing, the meaning of which has changed in order to accommodate the writers of this generation. Specialist critics may uncover this, as may the readers of the stories of Muhammad 'Alwan, Husain 'Ali Husain, 'Abdallah Bakhashwain, Sa'd al-Dosari, 'Abdu Khal, Noura al-Ghamidi, Badriyya al-Bishr and Laila al-Uhaidib, to name but a few.

The outside world is no longer restricted to what our senses realise of the manifestations and links within which lies our immediate reality. Instead, the senses have evolved to include the invisible, the distant and the metaphysical which have long dominated traditional legend, whether factual or mythical, official or popular. The inner world, on the other hand, is no longer restricted to memories, imagination and contemplation that could be consciously controlled. Instead, it now includes "all" that is stored in that "unknown continent," or the unconscious as Freud called it. Indeed, it has become the role of modern writing to expose, and perhaps to celebrate our desires, delusions and obsessions, as symbols of the darker side of our existence which affect our behaviour.

The notion of "crisis" was no longer restricted to certain places or localised in a textual context to the plot itself. Instead, it became evident from the whole text. It was as though one individual's anxieties had combined with the general tensions to turn the crisis into a mental and psychological state through silence, speech and writing. Perhaps this state was made acute by multiple levels of meaning, which is what brought about the feelings of alienation, from which most of the central protagonists in the stories of this generation suffered. Mansour al-Hazimi referred to them as the "strangers' generation." This use of terminology was in line with the kind of consciousness mentioned previously, as it was in line with modern writing more generally.

Moreover, the language of the short story also developed, becoming more concise, more vivid and faster moving, which reflected most writers' awareness of the dangers of digressing and padding the story with verbiage. Some writers began to invest in unspoken linguistic devices such as spaces and punctuation marks, as if these were a magical language appreciated by both writers and readers.

As for the short story form, it began to interact with other art forms such as poetry, drama, cinematography and oral renditions. It also responded to artwork, which has become more present in some story collections, as though it were a "parallel text" to be read and appreciated for its literary quality alongside the written narrative. Muhammad 'Alwan managed to blend the poetic ingredients with the story, revealing seriousness and depth and emphasizing the merger of these two forms, not just in the vivid language employed, but also in respect of the art of story writing more generally. Sa'd al-Dosari and Shareefa al-Shamlan went on to use elements of drama, both theatrical and cinematic. They used segmentation, restructuring and the merging of details in order to turn the story into a "scene" where visual signs played an essential role in the construction and delivery of the message.

'Abdallah Bakhashwain and Jaralla al-Hameed used the rhetoric of madness to dismantle the outline of the story and to portray people with illnesses and illusions living on the margins of life, and unable or unwilling to fit into a seemingly strange and aggressive society. 'Abd al-'Aziz al-Mishri, Maryam al-Ghamidi, Turki al-Nasser, Sultana al-Sidairi and Hasan al-Ni'mi tried variously to borrow from different oral history forms which allowed the modern story form to blend with inherited tales and old stories of the *majlis sha'bi* (social or tribal gathering). Jubair al-Mulaihan is one writer who loved and mastered the art of the "snap shot" or "short story," as he would refer to it. In this case, the text comprised a group of abridged passages and short, vivid sentences, each of which could be read on its own. The sentences could also be incorporated into each other by virtue of spatial progression and proximity until they formed a story more in keeping with prose poetry than any other form of traditional story writing.

Whereas the previous generation was influenced by the likes of Yusuf Idris, Yahya Haqqi, Chekhov and Maupassant, this generation was influenced more by the writings of the Syrian short story writer, Zakariyya Tamir (b. 1929), one of the foremost in the Arab world, the Egyptian 'Abdu Jubair (b. 1948), the late Moroccan Muhammad Zafzaf (1945-2001) and the late highly original Egyptian writer, Yahya al-Tahir 'Abdallah (1942-1981). One can also detect Kafka's influence, which is unmistakable in the stories of 'Abdallah Bakhashwain. The notion of "influence" deserves some scrutiny in this context, because it no longer encompassed the same traditional messages that were addressed by comparative studies, or by the "French school" in particular.

The writers of this generation no longer resorted to imitating others out of mere reverence. Instead, they began to write "like" them, because they could see that the language and technique of these writers, and their view of themselves and of their world agreed with their own intellectual and artistic vision. In other words, these writers were becoming part of a general Arab front facilitated by global communications and by the push towards modernisation all over the world.

Story writing in this phase is part of a general discourse in literature and culture. More than this, it is a manifestation and expression of the impact of modernism, which may be both negative and positive in its effect. It is also a reflection on individual, national and humanistic attitudes.

We may need today an in-depth critique of the "ambiguity of modernism," away from the heated and simplistic debates thrown up by personal and ideological rivalries. The latter added nothing of intellectual merit to our cultural discourse. The impact of modernism is not merely found in just a few poems, stories and journalistic essays. Instead, it is to be detected in the initiatives aimed at comprehensive modernisation which were represented by the development plans and the consequent radical changes across the board. To this day, we remain incapable of analysing and representing these initiatives, as our own cultural debate appears to be incapable of renewal!

Another phenomenon worthy of careful in-depth research is the gradual decline in the language of storytelling in the works of the later generations, compared with the works of the writers of the founding generation. The language used here does not enjoy the same strength of vocabulary and structure. Indeed, there are sometimes errors in semantics and grammatical usage. As for punctuation marks and editorial symbols, they are often used at whim, with no appreciation that these unvoiced signs are part of the skill of modern writing.

Some modern critical studies sought to restrict the narrative styles of contemporary Arabic story writing to limited patterns. One such example is found in the work of the Egyptian, Salah Fadl, who simply speaks of "lyrical," "dramatic" and "cinematic" styles, because of their widespread use in Arabic novels. Despite the usefulness of this description, we still believe that expanding the area of study within a larger number of texts and narrative styles, can further enrich theoretical concepts, depending on textual content and research topics.

Starting from here, we identified and analysed four styles in the writing of Saudi fiction, and the reader will be able to see their distinguishing characteristics and differences by reading sample texts contained in this volume.

1.  The first of these styles is the "didactic realisitc" narrative which leans towards discussion, description, analysis and documentation. It emphasises the realism or "objectivity" of story writing. The whole text revolves around an "external event," and writers try to concentrate their efforts by representing this event with as "neutral" a hand as possible, i.e. one that sets the event in its proper perspective and focus.

2.  The second style is that which borrows from "lyric poetry." It is strongly expressive of the writer's own being, in a narrative which revolves around subjective feelings, emotions and personal thoughts. Reality and objectivity are only present when they are used as a pretext for the outpouring of emotions in the text.

3.  The third style is that of the "stream of consciousness," which depends on liberating pent-up thoughts so that they appear in the text as vestiges of desires, dreams, nightmares and hallucinations, without any apparent logical order. This transforms the whole event into a chain of verbal and physical behaviour outside the readers' normal expectations, and which cannot be understood without a certain suspension of disbelief.

4.  The final style is the "multiple-dialogue." This is characterised by a multitude of voices, a diversity of accents and conflicting views which the writer seeks to blend together, without any one voice dominating the other. According to Mikhail Bakhtin, this style is represented more in fiction, but modern short stories may accommodate many of its techniques, as in the case of stories by 'Abd al-'Aziz Mishri.

The central issues and their general cultural indicators can be grouped into two main camps, with everything else branching off from here.

1. The first camp is represented by the predilection of some writers to express matters of "external reality," be they of a local or general social nature. This predilection dominates the work of the founding generation, and it was directed towards reform. Many stories belonging to the renaissance generation adopted the social realistic mode. They were preoccupied with notions of progress, unity and social justice, which were popular in both national and socialist rhetoric, and which dominated most Arab circles from the end of the Second World War to the seventies.

2. The second camp is represented in writings that looked into the world of the "self." It reflects the suffering of creative writers who lived in a society that did not understand their ideas and ambitions for freedom, justice and progress. Writers in this style were introspective, believing that it was the only place where they could identify with their own personalities and writing. Indeed, it was very common in the stories of the generation of renewal, which latter had suffered the disappointment of the failure of the "big dreams" promised by previous generations. Instead, they lived the daily reality of the "impact of modernity" which was manifested in fast-changing lifestyles, work relationships and means of communication. The impact also instigated an intense migration from the countryside and the desert into the big towns that were built after the "oil boom" and during the implementation of the five-year plan, with all the psychological and social reactions this migration introduced. This generation did not make up their sense of "alienation," nor did they write about it simply because they had read the works of other writers. Instead, they lived this estrangement and suffered its trials in their life and work. This prompted Mansour al-Hazimi to refer to them in one of his critiques as the "generation of alienated writers." This is appropriate, since one would not normally expect otherwise sensitive and rational writers to feel comfortable in a new world whose technology, news, images and values had overrun their traditional society which had had no substantive contact with the outside world until recently.

It is important to reiterate what we mentioned earlier about our specific national discourse. This literary rhetoric is part and parcel of a general cultural dialogue that is still in its infancy. The only way to develop this dialogue is through awareness of the importance of research, creative experimentation and willingness to take risks, and not through over-confidence. We call this way the "only" way because no achievement or change is possible without both "theoretical" awareness and practical "endeavour" which embodies these theories in the text itself.

## THE NOVEL

In chronicling the art of the novel in Saudi Arabia, we seek to make it accessible to ordinary readers. We also try to interpret excerpts from scripts which may be more than seventy years old and which differ in language, style and technique to modern creations. Perhaps this was the aim of the introductions which we have given in this anthology to all the other literary genres. The art of novel writing differs from other genres inasmuch as it is more introverted, more constrained and lacking in distinguishing literary characteristics than is the case with poetry, essays or short stories. This may result from the novelty and difficulty of this literary genre; the novel may also demand a certain degree of forbearance and broadmindedness towards the other. If poetry has a long history in the Arab literary tradition, and essays and short stories have parallels in the old epistles and rhythmic prose (*maqama*), the novel is primarily the product of the modern age, with all its conflicts and tensions. This is notwithstanding classical Arabic history's stories and long narrative accounts.

'Abd al-Quddous al-Ansari's novel *The Twins*, which was first published in Damascus in 1930, is considered to be the first Saudi attempt at this genre. Other efforts followed, such as *The Temperamental Revenge,* by Muhammad Nour 'Abdallah al-Jawhari (1935), *Mecca's Maiden,* by Ahmad Rida Houhou (1947), *An Idea,* by Ahmad al-Siba'i (1948) and *The Resurrection,* by Muhammad 'Ali Maghrabi (1948).

We can see the limited number of novels and their modest artistic achievement in this initial phase, which stretches back to the beginning of the second half of the twentieth century. The writers of that time did not seek literary enjoyment; instead they made it their aim to write about matters of educational and social reform. They often emphasised their objectives on the covers of their novels, in dedications and introductions.

The 1950s and the 1960s witnessed some important new changes in the Kingdom of Saudi Arabia, which encouraged the emergence of the novel as an art form, distinct from the didactic novel of the previous period. On the educational front, the number of schools multiplied and colleges and universities were established. On the social front, the Kingdom drew closer together, and the main towns began to attract many Bedouins and villagers, not accustomed to city life previously. On the economic front, revenue from petrol began to flow and to enhance individual income and the life of the community. If Europeans connect the emergence of novels in Europe with the emergence of the middle classes, the spread of education and the flourishing of printing houses and the press, the emergence of the novel in Arab societies is not much different. In his book *The Development of the Modern Arab Novel in Egypt,* Dr 'Abd al-Muhsin Taha Badr ascribed the emergence of the novel as an art form in Egypt in the early twentieth century to the life style of the Egyptian middle class in the wake of Turkish feudal rule, the growth of nationalism and the desire for independence; the novel was also, in part, a revolt against stagnation and tradition.

Although the conditions in Saudi Arabia were different, it is notable that the first artistic novel that appeared, *The Price of Sacrifice* by Hamid Damanhouri (1959), was based on a portrayal of the businessmen of Mecca. Along with some government employees, they represented the vanguard of the middle class at that time. In this respect, Damanhouri's novel resembles Muhammad Husain Haikal's *Zainab*, which was the first artistic novel in Egypt to portray the Egyptian countryside at the turn of the twentieth century. The landlord's son plays the lead role in this novel, combining cultural awareness and aristocratic bearing. Ibrahim al-Nasser's *A Slit in the Night's Attire* appeared soon after Damanhouri's novel. It also depicted reality, albeit a different kind of reality with specific features relating to the east of the Kingdom.

This artistic trend which first appeared in the above two novels deals with the notion of living with reality and concern for it. It was achieved either through a process of reconciliation, as in Damanhouri's novel, or through rebellion, as in al-Nasser's work. Depiction of reality in both ways is generally considered to be one of the great achievements in the history of the novel and in the history of art and human thought. In *The Price of Sacrifice*, Damanhouri describes the local environment in a period of transition, which began with education and the growth of an enlightened middle class. It came to an end with the expected conflict of generations, between the old and the new. Ibrahim al-Nasser portrayed the same transitional period with all its contradiction and conflict, but he shifted it all into a similar extraneous environment. It did not take him long, however, before he transferred the novel's setting to a local reality. Indeed, the concern about the setting and the portrayal of social transformation illustrate both writers' awareness of the importance of the artistic tension on which the novel is built.

This trend required both writers to widen the base from which this tension or generational conflict could be illustrated. The base here is not simply spatial; it is not a mere expansion of the area in which actions and events can be inserted as they are in novels of adventures; it is an extension of the time in which the characters are allowed to develop. If *The Price of Sacrifice* transported us from Mecca to Cairo, and *A Slit in the Night's Attire* transported us from the village to the city, they did so in order to illustrate new and extraneous factors. These factors deepened significantly the conflict in the principal protagonists. Both writers could have managed without this change of setting, had they wanted to do so. They could have resorted instead to remembrance or what is known as internal "monologue."

The broadening of the base in the artistic novel should not be confined to just one or two main characters around whom events revolve, and who are given the role of the hero or heroine in other narrative genres. Indeed, it is vital to expand the picture frame to include the group of characters and types representing different human relationships, all of which combine indirectly to embody the idea which the writer is striving to define and expose. In Damanhouri's and al-Nasser's novels, the characters have been carefully chosen to achieve this. *In The Price of Sacrifice*, for example, the writer selects a Meccan business family comprising a child, a young man and an old man. This choice does not just indicate the paradoxes of age; it also records differences in mentality and in intellectual and emotional capacity.

The main dilemma in the plot lies in the marriage of a university graduate to a woman who is less educated than him. This, of course, was a true point of weakness in Saudi women over half a century ago, but it is no longer the case today. The writer seeks to deepen the conflict in the character of the hero by choosing for him to become emotionally and intellectually involved with a university graduate from a different place. What is he to do now? Should he sacrifice his cousin with whom he is united in kinship and marriage covenant? Or is he to sacrifice his new girl with whom he is united in intellect and love? The latter is, after all, the ideal wife that he yearns for and wants. This is the balance between emotion and reason. Eventually, he chooses the first woman, who becomes the price of his sacrifice.

Ibrahim al-Nasser does the same in his novel *A Slit in the Night's Attire*. The family he chooses for this story also represents the middle class, business folk who cling tightly to customs and traditions. The family first undergoes social and economic change in the village, then moves to the city, with all its temptations, delights, freedom and problems. This subjects Haj 'Ammar's conservative family to the risks of collapse and break-up. The tragedy lies in the main protagonist, the eldest son of this conservative rural family. He becomes caught in a web of contradictions: the village community versus the dislocation of the city, paternal strictness versus maternal compassion, the deprivation of the home versus the rich variety of society. These factors combine in the character of the hero to bring about rebellion and ruin.

As some researchers noticed, *autobiographical* traits became evident in some of the novels that appeared during and after the 1950s in the Kingdom and in other Arab countries. Possibly, Ahmad al-Siba'i was the first writer in Saudi Arabia to try to incorporate his personal experiences into a written narrative. He did so in his autobiographical story "Abu Zamil" (1954). Later, he renamed it *My Days*, which was probably influenced by Taha Husain's *The Stream of Days*. In this work, al-Siba'i draws from the memories of his childhood and youth in Mecca in the latter days of Ottoman rule and during Hashemite rule in Hijaz. Characters and human types jostle in al-Siba'i's mind, and he paints them as they were preserved in his childhood imagination, not as the mentality and maturity of manhood might have caused him to categorise and formulate. Most of the characters are real people, known to the author through his family, his neighbourhood and the small community he lived with.

Hamza Bogari's *The Safa Sheltered Quarters* which was published in 1983, is perhaps closer to a novel than al-Siba'T's *My Days*. In this novel, Bogari reveals little of his private views, shapes events in a new way and creates a lively, humble hero who grows with the events, recording, watching and learning. Bogari was deeply influenced by his teacher al-Siba'i, particularly when he talks about the *kuttab*

(Qur'anic elementary school), his schooldays and certain prototype figures. He greatly reduced the amount of personal autobiographical detail although, like his teacher, he was attached to the old Meccan life.

In his novel *No Shade Under the Mountain* (1979), Fu'ad 'Anqawi clarifies his motivation in writing it at the beginning. It is a personal and sentimental motivation in which 'Anqawi seeks to recall his childhood and youth in Mecca, as al-Siba'i and Bogari had done in their novels. 'Anqawi describes his work as a "social novel." He emphasises his eagerness to provide the basic elements of artistic writing in terms of structural integrity, dramatic events, character portrayal and depth of conflict. However, his interest in documenting the past and reviving folkloric traditions spoiled what he himself declared in his introduction was his resolve to give priority to artistic merit. Characters were chosen for their portrayal of prevailing customs at that time and events were orchestrated precisely to show and document the many festivities, chants and well-known folk songs of the old Meccan life.

The autobiography has become a feature of the artistic novel during the renewal phase in the 1950s and 1960s. In large part, the autobiography is a longing for the time and place of one's childhood and youth, if not a simple desire to resurrect the past. This romantic/factual trend, which was also at times a critical trend, continued into the modernisation phase with some storywriters. The following novels appeared late in the revival phase, but they still followed an autobiographical style: *The Young Maiden* by 'Isam Khouqeer, *The Husks* by 'Umar Tahir Zaila' and the *Flat of Freedom* by Ghazi al-Qusaibi. If the novels of Damanhouri, al-Nasser, Bogari, Zaila', 'Anqawi and al-Qusaibi have enriched the renaissance phase and given it some mature works, there are many other works which do not make the grade. Indeed, they are more like thrillers, for light entertainment. In such novels, the setting, the characters and the plot all disappear, and all that remains is a series of emotional events and violent incidents which are used as the writer wishes. Edwin Muir calls this type of novels "the novel of the event" because they have little artistic merit, but are nonetheless the most popular with the masses. The works in this genre are mostly historical novels, detective stories and tales of love, war, crime and sex, which latter is always the preferred subject for films, radio and television programmes all over the world.

Most works produced by novelists in both the phase of revival and the modernisation phase are of this emotive type. Examples include: *The Slaves* by Muhammad 'Alem al-Afghani; *My Wife and the Friend,* by Muhammad 'Umar Tawfeeq; *A Night in Darkness* by Muhammad Zari' 'Aqeel; *The Sun has Set* by Muhammad 'Abdallah al-Mulaibari; *Samra' from Hijaz* by 'Abd al-Salam Hashim Hafiz; and the novels of Samira Bint al-Jazira. Despite the differences between them in subject, language and style, all these novels are similar in being light entertainment, with stirring themes, completely unrealistic and lacking in character development.

Coming to the modernist phase, which began in the late 1960s and early 1970s, according to most researchers, modernism is not an issue of time, but an attitude of mind and an open-minded approach to art and culture. Most researchers associate the defeat of the Arabs in 1967 with the defeat of Arab heritage, values and old inherited principles. Through modernism, they aspired to a new way of thinking which would, it was felt, rid Arabs of accumulating misfortune and restore some of what they had lost.

The same realism which we celebrate in Damanhouri's and al-Nasser's work is to be found in the new novel. It has been turned inside out. In this realism, relationships and feelings are intertwined, and a huge and complex network of cultures, events and times is blended together in its folds. It is well-known that the "new novel" as it was at the hands of Alain Robbe-Grillet and Nathalie Saurrate after the Second World War, broke all links with previous conventions. The new novel, for which Joyce, Proust and Kafka paved the way in the first quarter of the twentieth century, relied on experimentation and the creation of new and obscure worlds. According to Grillet, the novel is a search for a reality which only exists after writing has been completed. For Saurrate, writing is a continuous quest to uncover the unknown and to bring about an unknown reality. The Saudi novel has not reached this complex standard in the modernist phase, but it has undoubtedly benefited from the new narrative modes, as can be seen particularly in the novels of Raja' 'Alem, 'Abdu Khal and 'Ali al-Dumaini.

Perhaps 'Abd al-'Aziz Mishri in his novels *Al-Wasmiyyah; The Clouds and the Tree Plantations;* and *The Conditions of the Land,* is the novelist of the modernist phase who is most at home in his environment. Indeed, he is the most aware of place, especially the village. In these novels, Mishri succeeds in creating a new world of nature, man and mythology that we had not encountered hitherto. Muhammad al-Shanti noted Mishri's interest in feeling the pulse of change in the social structure of his village as a result of its contact with the town. This contact has brought about a great amount of disturbance in the old social fabric, causing conflict between generations. Mishri is not after the artistic quality of the old novel in depicting an elaborate and developing episode. Instead, he aims at calmness and change in a number of chapters or in sections which unfold continuously towards a vision that weaves in and out with its threads. Hence the vision meshes into an integrated structure by means of characters with artistic presence who are governed by a single movement in time and space."[5]

'Abdu Khal writes about his village in Saudi Arabia in his novel *Death Walks Here,* as other writers have done, but no writer has written about his village in quite the way Mishri did. It seems that the past has been resurrected and has taken over the writing of the New Novel. Some researchers have noted this, including Husain al-Manasira: "We stand before a new narrative genre: the autobiographical novel. It's a genre which requires us to formulate its aesthetic characteristics, especially after such narrative work began to lead the way for new writing in the 1990s. It may also play an active role in the next century." Al-Manasira includes both *Adama* by Turki al-Hamad and *The Asylum* (al-'Asfouriyya) by Ghazi al-Qusaibi in this genre."[6]

The novels of Raja' al-'Alem fall into this same autobiographical framework, despite their folkloric and mythical medium and the overlapping of time, language and characters. The framework covers description, suggestion and argumentation as well as memories, personal matters and poetry. 'Alem describes her novel *The Silk Road* as a journey, although we do not know whether this journey is factual or fictional, by land or by sea. It can be inferred from the beginning of the novel that the journey is coming from the Sahara in the west, and is heading towards the Arabian Peninsula via Egypt or Sinai. Later, we discover that most of the events of the journey are written through remembering or internal "monologue" in Mecca. The novel describes the family of the narrator, and in particular her grandfather, Ahmad al-Bukhari, who came from the East via the famous Silk Road. It also describes many forgotten Meccan customs and traditions, such as "Qais"[7] wedding parties and old folksongs. Moreover, this is a journey in time and into the unknown, in which the reader encounters numerous historical and mythical characters, such as Ibn Khaldoun and Mansour the Chess Lover. In this world, humans mingle with jinn, speech is weird and amazing, the letters of the alphabet are counted numerically and superstition reigns.

In the novel, the journey starts in 1372, around the eighth century of the Hijra and during the days of Ibn Khaldoun. The novel stretches into modern times. It might be more appropriate, therefore, to say that it is a journey which conjures up old spirits and mixes up times, ideas and characters.

*The Silk Road* is full of memories and personal recollections, but it is a marvellously exciting novel in structure, language and style of writing. It is also laden with traditional texts and verses from the Holy Qur'an, alongside the historical and mythical characters mentioned previously. The chessboard on which Mansour and Ibn Khaldoun are playing, controls the events of the journey. It can also summon numerous historical characters. The board can be likened to *mandal*-type fortune telling that was known to Meccans in old times for its ability to unravel mysteries.

Finally, there are some other new novels which were written in the 1990s, and which have been pored over by the critics. Such examples include *The Adama*, *Shumaisi* and *Karadeeb* by Turki al-Hamad, as well as his latest novel *East of the Valley*. Other examples include *The Leaden Cloud* by 'Ali al-Dumaini and *Wasted Paradise* by Laila al-Juhani. These novels combine the setting with the autobiography. They also adopted the tools of new narrative modes in novels. Whilst we cannot examine each of these remarkable works, we prefer to conclude this modernist phase with two small novels, neither of which is more than eighty-four pages in length. The first is *Raihana* by Ahmad al-Duwaihi, a novel which has no chapters, numbers and titles. It is written in the modernist style, with overlapping chronology, dialogue, characters and recollections. It says nothing in particular and jumps around scenes and reflections. Apparently, it is set in a village called "al-Jubaila" in the south of the

Kingdom, as it contains descriptions of the nature, animals and peasants of this remote place. As for the title, *Raihana* is the name of the hero's lover, if indeed there is a hero! In the first page of his novel, al-Duwaihi writes of Raihana as "lighting the fire to show the way for the newcomers."

The second novel, Laila al-Juhani's *Wasted Paradise*, is small in size and intense in style. In some chapters, it is closer to poetry. The chapter titles tell their own story of emotional grief: "Air suffocates," "Details of anguish," "Another continent sinks," "The fall of the flower," "Sensitivity shall not cry on balconies" and "Severing of Souls." The story tells of the tragedy of Saba, the heroine, who falls for 'Amir and becomes pregnant with his child. 'Amir later abandons Saba for her friend Khalida, whom he eventually marries. The story is first narrated by Saba, explaining how she fell into this disaster and mentioning her abortion attempts when she realised that 'Amir had left her to marry her friend. When she dies during or after the abortion, the story is then taken up by Khalida, who now knows of the tragedy from the letters that Saba had sent her before she died. The last chapter seems to be narrated by the writer herself, as she addresses the city of Jeddah and remembers its history and its present.

*Wasted Paradise* contains much of the narrative style of Algerian born novelist Ahlam Mustaghanimi in her novel, *The Memory of the Body*. In Mustaghanimi's novel, the events are first narrated by the heroine, and then by some of the other characters. Al-Juhani's novel also borrows considerably from the famous Palestinian poet, Mahmoud Darwish. There is also a tendency to use myths, especially folktales about the city of Jeddah, such as the one that tells how Adam [peace be upon him] met Mother Eve in 'Arafa, a well-known place on the Hajj (pilgrimage). Eve's grave lies still in Jeddah, as the traditional storytellers tell us.

## DRAMA

Although the difference between theatre as an intellectual endeavour and performance theatre has diminished with the advent of modern technology, the former appeared in the Kingdom before the latter, as was the experience in the rest of the Arab world. Many of the earlier plays, however, had the potential to be performed on stage because of the diversity of subject matter and multiplicity of aims.

Although the emergence of theatre in the Saudi kingdom was late in comparison with other Arab countries such as Syria, Lebanon and Egypt, it is fair to say that the Kingdom today shows significant interest in theatre at both the official and the popular level. It views it as an essential tool for cultural development and the achievement of a robust literary renaissance.

The origins of theatre in the Kingdom lie in nightly social gatherings and end of term performances in which students would perform comic sketches as well as historical and educational plays which were declamatory in tone. Theatre began in schools, al-Najah school in Mecca being the first to experiment in this genre during the early days of Saudi rule. Other schools followed suit in staging their own concerts and festivals. Subsequently, universities contributed to this process by making theatre an important activity in their cultural programme. Many of the leading figures of Saudi theatre in recent years had their first training at university. King Sa'ud University in Riyadh was one such institution. These universities promoted theatre through financial and technical support, student training, and appointment of well-qualified directors, as well as through organising inter-varsity competitions at the end of the academic year.

Thus, the reading of plays preceded the birth of theatre in the Kingdom of Saudi Arabia. The following plays were written in the early thirties and were published before the rise of Saudi theatre: *He who wrongs himself*, 1933; and *Buthaina's Jamil*, 1942 by Husain 'Abdallah Siraj; *The Migration*, 1946 by Ahmad 'Abd al-Ghafour 'Attar; *Uncle Sahnoun*, 1952 by 'Abdallah 'Abd al-Jabbar and *The Bygone Night*, 1970 by 'Isam Khouqair. The plays were written in classical Arabic and were to be read, not acted. In contrast, writers after the 1970s began to write plays in the local dialect that were acted and not read. Classical Arabic, however, remained the language of theatre in schools and universities.

There are a number of different trends in playwriting in the Kingdom. First, the historical play appeared at an early stage in Saudi theatre. One example of this is *The Conquest of Mecca* by Muhammad 'Abdallah Mulaibari, which was specially commissioned for the opening of the Quraish Theatre in 1960. The theatre was founded and sponsored by Ahmad al-Siba'i, one of the most interesting early Saudi writers and a pioneer of Saudi literature. Alas, it did not live to see the light of day. The other play was *Musailima the Liar* by 'Abdallah al-'Abbasi. Both plays drew upon historical sources and set out to articulate historical themes through events, dialogue, structure and depiction of characters. The two plays also aimed to instil in the reader the principles of faith and pride in Islam. The link between the present and the past was thus used as an important device in the renaissance, especially in the early days. Ahmad al-Dubaikhi's *Oh Mu'atasim!* portrayed the Mongol occupation of Baghdad and their subsequent defeat at the battle of 'Ain Jalout. Mulaibari's vision of history is replaced by the critical viewpoint of al-Dubaikhi, who managed to avoid the tedious by relying on the variety of historical data instead of moralisations.

The historical trend did not preclude other theatrical trends, in particular social comedy, which kept up with the fast-changing Saudi society and the financial boom of the 1970s. Furthermore, history is often used in Saudi theatre as a means of guidance and exhortation, of which the Saudi reader already has a surfeit in his daily life. Meanwhile, other trends pursued aesthetic satisfaction, steering clear of sermonising which can be boring in a context such as this.

After the historical play, we can talk about the social play which addresses the issues and problems of society. The social playwright differs from the writer of the historical drama inasmuch as he needs to have a more lively and fertile imagination. Whilst history is a script which is already written, social playwrights gleaned their words from the social detail of events, plot, characters and language. Scripts which were about Saudi society and its many issues include: *The End of the Adventure,* by 'Abd al-Rahman al-Sha'ir, *A Palm Fibre House,* by Nasser al-Mubarak, *Who is Complementing Whom?* by *Muhammad Rajab;* and *Dumb Devils,* by 'Abdallah 'Abd al-Jabbar. These plays address local issues and problems such as marriage, the rise in dowry payments, unemployment, the collapse of family ties and local and Arab politics.

Social and economic changes led to what is known as the drama of real estate, nepotism, bribery and the drama of exile and alienation. Those who were most prominent in laying the foundations of this trend in their plays were: Ibrahim al-Hamdan, 'Abd al-Rahman al-Sha'ir and 'Abd al-Rahman al-Hamad. It may be that social comedies such as the "real estate comedies" emerged out of the economic and social upheaval and the subsequent transformation in values of large sections of Saudi society. Prominent examples of the genre of social comedies include: *A Doctor by Mish'ab,* by Ibrahim al-Hamdan, *The Deaf,* by Muhammad al-'Uthaim and *Under the Seats,* by Ahmad al-Dubaikhi.

The third trend in Saudi theatre was that of the "self" and the "mask." After the economy and society, the next most significant element in the consciousness of creative dramatists, was the drama of masks and symbols. Writers' imagination developed from direct discourse in real estate dramas and social comedies to the drama of the mask, which resorts to reflection on a psychological and social level, including the drama of folklore and social symbols.

In *A Slap in the Mirror,* 'Abd al-'Aziz al-Saq'abi looks with a critical eye at the strange transformation in society and expresses his reflections on his inner "self" as it exists now in unusual social situations. Rashid al-Shamrani adds a folkloric dimension to his plays and uses traditional literary forms, as in *Ibn Zuraiq Limited; The Groom of the 19th;* and *Shaddad ibn 'Antar.* He also uses to advantage the symbols of collective memory in *The Kingfisher.* These symbols were portrayed in different forms as in *The Blue Watermelon* and *The Slender Years* by Muhammad al-'Uthaim.

What these playwrights had in common was dissatisfaction with direct discourse. Hence their adherence to symbolism. Nevertheless, they bear witness to the psychological, economic and social changes of the time.

Raja' 'Alem's plays are a fine example of the drama of the "self" and the "mask." Her play *Actor's Last Death* is closer to a poem. It is set in an unspecified location, although some events take place in Mada'in al-Hijr in the desert. Despite the fact that the characters are listless and unreal, they carry a bright symbolic energy and unambiguous meaning. The play is more like a "monologue" i.e. a drama with a single voice, and it expresses the yearning for freedom and liberation from the shackles of oppression. The language pulsates with suggestiveness and dazzling ideas. Not only is the dialogue full of meaning, but it also transports us to a magical place. The "self" in 'Alem's work is armed with creative thoughts and symbolism in order to capture the essence of life and freedom.

Children's theatre has advanced in leaps and bounds in recent times. The idea of using theatre for education of upcoming generations, and its commitment to protect young minds through the portrayal of good characters overcoming evil, was a milestone in gaining acceptance of this new literary genre. It succeeds as an educational cultural tool by creating situations and dramatic devices which reach out to a child's mind, to his emotions and to his conscience, and it works through performance and not through direct discourse.

Without doubt, children's theatre in the Kingdom has shifted from a moral and educational tone to a joyful and entertaining one. 'Abd al-Rahman al-Muraikhi's play *The Son of Adam is Coming* reaches out to children through the use of fairy tales about animals in a lyrical style. The story revolves around man and beast. The son of Adam arrives uninvited in the jungle and uses his intelligence to reign over the jungle. He becomes the symbol of good against evil, which is symbolically represented in some of the animals. Al-Muraikhi adopts an educational approach appropriate for children, in a way that does not detract from the play's artistry. The influence of the Umayyad book of fables, *Kalila wa Dimna* by Ibn al-Muqaffa' can be seen in the play, as it pairs drama with fable in a successful work that uses allegory through a symbolic story.

The poet Husain 'Abdallah Siraj is considered to be one of the most important pioneers of poetic theatre in Saudi literature. He worked on the poetic play, which is seemingly more readable than the prose play. In *The Passion of Wallada* he dramatises the life of Andalusi poet Ahmad ibn Zaydoun and his celebrated love for the Andalusi Umayyad princess, Wallada Bint al-Mustakfi. The play's centre of attention is Wallada herself. Siraj managed to work his poetic talent into the historical material to produce an attractive poetic drama. In this way, he contributed to the development of Saudi poetry to the point where it could express the objective, the dramatic as well as the emotional and lyrical, much as the famous Egyptian poet, Ahmad Shawqi (1869-1932) did.

Husain Siraj wrote another play *Yearning for You*. Alongside the dramatic style of the good Arabic poem (*qasida*), the play also has a tangible dramatic sensitivity. It is a potent portrayal of characters, dialogue and plot. Not only is Siraj master of the (*qasida*) poem, but he also shows flexibility in his prose, which enabled him to write a play that is based on both poetry and prose. The play has an emotional and sentimental theme which is exemplified in love and revenge. The events of the play are set in the north of the Arabian Peninsula and in the modern day cities of Beirut and Cairo. Although it is crowded with characters, Siraj focusses their performance by use of both poetry and prose in order to give us a full picture of the play's location, time, characters and plot development.

Siraj's poetic language is at its highest when expressed in a coordinated and melodic style through the use of constants in the dialogue, whilst expatiating upon the feelings, emotions and objectives. Thus, his control of the fabric of the poem and his tailoring of it to suit each character were supplemented by the importance he attached to the portrayal of character and plot through his prose preamble.

The criticism which has been directed at Ahmad Shawqi's work i.e. the predominance of the lyrical over the dramatic, especially in themes dealing with love and emotional intrigue, also applies to Husain Siraj's plays.

What remains to be mentioned at the end of this brief introduction to the various trends in Saudi theatre, is what is known as experimental theatre. Playwrights endeavour to free themselves from the prevailing forms in order to devise new plays in which they experiment with the structure, with the portrayal of ideas and characters, and with the formulation of dialogue and styles.

Fahd al-Harithi's *The Train* is an example of this experimentation. The play is an allegory to life's constant movement, with no fixed setting of time or place. The subject is man and his universal relevance. It is a dream which transcends time and place. Sometimes it turns into a mirage, but it does not end with the end of life itself. On the contrary, "new trains" carry forward this dream, and the mirage rises again from ruin to form a new dream. People wait for the "Train" which comes laden with good things, and it surprises them when it appears on the horizon with its whistle blowing and smoke flying, because they had thought it would never return.

The play comes in six tableaux, and because the nature of the dream is hazy or unclear, its characters are presented as numbers, without names or distinguishing features. The director of the play weaves his way between these characters and moves them, much in the same way that words become effaced in dreams and pictures and shapes become accentuated. The play is a production of the Saudi Arab Society for Culture and Arts, which is the foremost theatrical body in the Kingdom. The Society stages plays in national and international festivals.

The other experimental play is *The Masks* by 'Abdallah Bakhashwain. It is closer to a police play because the main event revolves around an illusive crime or prank. The play is acted first by the "policeman," involving the first and the second actors. Next, one or two spectators jump on to the stage to take part in the plot, or one of the principal actors leaves the stage to converse with the audience so that they too can take part in the same theatrical game.

Role-play is the central theme of *The Masks,* which states, in the introduction, that its aim is to explore the actors' capacity for enjoyment and give them pleasure. It also recommends the cast's participation in filling the gaps which the writer left in the original script of the play.

*The Masks* is a well knit and excellent play which is based on the mathematical and logical relationships of its characters. The relationships alter as in a game of musical chairs, however. The roles rotate between the three main characters. Whilst the first actor plays the witness, he assumes the role of the judge at a later stage. The second actor plays the attorney general, while also still playing the suspect. The third actor plays the policeman, switching subsequently to the role of the lawyer. The role of the audience remains marginal for the duration of the play.

The script is divided in two acts, in which both classical and colloquial Arabic alternate, thus creating two opposing rhythms. Similarly, metaphor or imagery confront the truth in the structure of the play and the change of scenes. Thus, what is written in the script as fiction is treated as if it were true, and truth becomes fantasy and hypothesis.

Bakhashwain's play belongs to the theatre of the absurd in the relationships of its characters with the plot. The script is originally a theatrical one, in which crime and murder comprise its central plot. The police enter to interrogate a supposed witness. The body of the victim begins to fidget, then rises to protest at his interrogation and suggests that a fair trial would entail role reversal. The theatrical game now switches from one text to another and from one game to another. The playwright bluffs his way by using masks and one character becomes two. The theatrical game continues to change back and forth using a mocking tone which laughs at life and how its roles resemble the ones played out on stage. The play ends as it begins, with role playing. The work is finally concluded with a game of musical chairs, which is the essence of the original text.

## THE AUTOBIOGRAPHY

Autobiographies are the weakest part of Saudi literature and possibly Arab literature generally. The genre still faces difficulties which have been overcome decades ago by the writers of novels, short stories, poems and plays. It may be useful, therefore, to clarify the genre's most important manifestations and general parameters.

From a social and cultural perspective, it is not straightforward or appealing to speak of oneself as different and set apart from the rest in a traditional society in which tribal and clan structures play such a powerful role. This applies in everyday life and in the prevailing system of values, ideas and norms. A good or honest person represents the collective personality, the general stereotype, and abides by his original identity. This identity is normally centred on "symbolic literature" to which the sense of belonging is ascribed and through which relations of kinship are strengthened. The logic of "know thyself" which has long been celebrated in philosophy, both old and new, is met here by "know thy ancestors." Herein lies the foundation of genealogy, a system long revered in Arabic culture and tradition.

From a religious perspective, we know too well that speaking of the "self" has long been connected with notions of superiority and abandoning group unity. The group is thought of as one nation and one body which follows one path in life, a path which guarantees a happy fate. If an individual were to deviate from this path, then he would be condemned to eternal damnation in hell, just like Satan. After all, Muslims remember to this day Satan's utterance of the word "I "before God, which they quickly follow by saying, "We pray that God protects us from uttering the word 'I'"!

From the perspective of history, it is recognised that the person who is aware of his individuality and of his right to differ is a new phenomenon in many societies. It is a phenomenon which is connected with the establishment of big cities, the growth of the middle classes, the spread of education and the various professions and careers that depend on individual merit. Liberal, democratic thinking has evolved into a set of laws which determine the relationship between the individual and society and state, on new terms which elevate the status and interests of the individual. This enlightened thinking played a vital role in shaping these changes and contributed to modernism in a historical fashion. It was in this context that the autobiography began to emerge as an independent literary genre, as known by literary historians today. It was possibly to be expected that the autobiography would remain a marginal literary genre with no significant influence on Arabic literature, given that the modernisation process in Arab societies did not make a serious start until the twentieth century. This was even more true in traditional societies such as those of the Arabian Peninsula, which began the development and modernisation process only a few decades ago.

The first part of Taha Husain's, *The Stream of Days*, was published in 1926 and was the first work of this literary genre, according to Ihsan 'Abbas[8] and others. This notwithstanding, the second and third parts of this autobiography were not published until later in the twentieth century. The specific conditions of the literary scene in Egypt can only be appreciated when one is outside this context. For example, factors which hindered the progress of autobiographical writing were beginning to wane, in part at least. We cannot compare the Saudi model with the Egyptian one, therefore. More importantly, we are yet to find in Saudi literature any autobiographical work which matches Husain's *The Stream of Days* in literary and intellectual terms. Why, and how? We shall endeavour to address this in the following paragraphs.

Scholars of Saudi literature agree that the first attempt at this art form was *My Days* by Ahmad al-Siba'i, the story behind its writing may establish the validity of what we said in the previous paragraph. Al-Siba'i first published the text in 1954 under the title *Abu Zamil*, and he intended it to be "a portrayal of the life of a whole generation." We cannot find any autobiographical components in this earlier text. Twenty years later, however, al-Siba'i decided to add some material from his own life. He revealed stages in his own self-development during his education and his work as a businessman and teacher, and ending with the moment when he became aware of himself as an auto-biographer. This owed much to the work of the Lebanese-American writer, Jibran Khalil Jibran (1883-1931), whom al-Siba'i admired greatly. The re-worked text was entitled *My Days*, and it is this later version which establishes al-Siba'i as a pioneer of the autobiography in Saudi Arabia. Alongside his personal experiences and his developing self-awareness, al-Siba'i strives to adopt a bold critical vision which pervades the whole text, from the dedication at the very beginning right to the end. Al-Siba'i also writes sarcastically about various aspects of traditional culture which he had experienced at home, at the *kuttab* and at school.

This autobiography commands attention to this day because of its courageously critical and sarcastic perspective. Al-Siba'i did admit the powerful influence which Jibran had had on his critical consciousness and on his writings which railed against prevailing customs and traditions. Taha Husain had an equally important influence on al-Siba'i, for sure. Not only is the new title bound to make us think of Husain's *The Stream of Days,* there is also that profound doubt over the validity of traditional culture in the modern age. Al-Siba'i does not enunciate this doubt, however, possibly to avoid the sensitivity of conservative readers who, to this day, are disaffected with the works of the Egyptian writer. After all, Taha Husain was well-known for his fiercely critical views on many aspects of Arab Muslim culture, old and new.

When we examine autobiographies from the 1970s to the present day, we cannot find anything as inventive as al-Siba'i's *My Days.* Muhammad 'Umar Tawfiq's *46 Days in Hospital* (1954); Hasan Kutubi's *My Life* (1956); and Hasan Naseef's *Memoirs of a Student* (1956) all fall short in artistic terms. Moreover, they reveal little change in terms of self-awareness, and they lack any criticism of the self, society or the world at large. These autobiographers are stereotypical in approach, traditional in their style of writing, and of no value other than as a historical record. No new biographies were published between 1960 and 1969, good or bad. This illustrates the confusion in writers' minds, as well as the lack of interest in autobiographies by both writers and readers alike.

Substantive change only occurred over the last two decades, during which thirteen autobiographies were published, including three works which constitute a true addition to al-Siba'i's work, even though they do not match it artistically or intellectually. 'Aziz Dia' published *My Life with Hunger, Love and War* in 1984. The language of the book is precise and sophisticated, with an underlying honesty. The writer, who came from a bourgeois family from Medina, narrates his experience of events during the First World War which destroyed his family, and from which he suffered for the rest of his life. The second writer is 'Abd al-Fattah Abu Midyan, whose autobiography *The Story of the Young Miftah* (1996) concentrates on his early childhood in Libya, where he was born into a poor family. He was forced into doing hard work in order to make ends meet for himself and his mother, and he was denied any education until he emigrated in his teens with his mother to Hijaz. His circumstances began to improve, thanks to the support of his maternal uncle and to his diligent approach to education and work.

The third writer is Mansour al-Khiraiji, who published his auto-biography *What the Job Description Didn't Tell* in 1997. In the book, we encounter an attractive literary narrative which speaks of the difficult childhood that the writer experienced. He returns with his family from the Syrian Desert to Medina and then begins to pursue his education, again with the support of a relative. He also tells of his travels to the

United States of America to pursue higher education and of his return to work as a translator in the royal palace. If numbers are anything to go by, the interest of Saudi writers in this narrative art form was growing. Indeed, these three works can be seen as indicative of the serious development which autobiographical writing underwent during this particular literary phase.

There are other autobiographies which are distinctive in style and which were written by authors about their own creative attempts at writing literature whether poetry, stories, or novels. Two of the most prominent works in this category are *A Poetic Biography* by Ghazi al-Qusaibi and *Revelations of the Sword and the Flower* by 'Abd al-'Aziz Mishri. These two works are not autobiographies in the artistic sense; rather, they shed light on the writer's consciousness, his view of creative writing, and the sources which enrich his experiences. The typical readership of incomplete autobiographies such as these includes students of this genre; it also includes young, upcoming writers wanting to learn from this creative endeavour. Hence the "educational objective" is ever present on the biography scene. The most conspicuous sign of the negative impact of traditional culture on this still fragile, new literary genre is the absence of the autobiography in traditional Saudi literature.

There are a number of distinguished female poets, storywriters and novelists whose creative output has a strong following in the Gulf and other Arab countries. In spite of this, not one of them has risked writing her own autobiography to date. The autobiography can only flourish in an atmosphere of open-mindedness and social tolerance and where there is recognition of individual rights. It is the absence of these facts which reflects on the lives and the writing of women, more than any other group in society. Patriarchal, male dominated cultures have become accustomed to promoting a set of ideas and values which are biased against women. This state of affairs is normally reinforced in the name of religion, even though it may have nothing to do with ideas which are rooted in pre-Islamic tribal culture. A few years ago, one well-known cultural magazine convinced an excellent writer and poet to publish an autobiography which she had written some time before. After publishing six serials depicting her childhood and formative years, the magazine stopped the serialisation for social reasons that were not declared but were nevertheless known to readers. The writer had not written about anything which might have provoked religious sensitivities, nor had she intended to publish anything which might have clashed with family values. She was from a well-known family, and she chose to publish her autobiography in a widely read conservative local magazine. In spite of all of this, the remaining excerpts were not published, and the text awaits a fundamental change in the socio-cultural situation. Other female writers have addressed this problem and have called for removal of the obstacles which still stand in their way. These are people who have become authors, doctors, businesswomen, and university professors. Women achievers can no longer accept the same prejudices which their more traditional sisters may still tolerate.

All Saudi writers face problems in writing autobiographies, but more so in the case of women. All the works of this genre which we are looking at avoid talking about adventures of passion, although they are normally faced by everyone at some point in their youth, when impulse and natural desire are striving to express themselves in so many ways. Furthermore, these autobiographies lack any ideological stand against the establishment, even though criticism, protest and rebellion are normal for any well-educated writer, whose ambitions and ideals transcend their immediate reality and the existing conditions of their society.

Intellectual angst is similarly absent from these works, although that is what often drives writers to question their existence and their beliefs, which they then try to interpret from different perspectives. Many Classical Arab writers have suffered this conflict against an absolute certainty of belief, and some of them became symbols of Islamic thought, like Abu Hamid al-Ghazali (d. 505/1111) Such topics do not necessarily mean being swept away in the literature of "bold confession" as in the work of the Moroccan Muhammad Shukri (1935-2003); nor do they fall under the literature of radical political opposition or genuine religious doubts. They would simply reflect a degree of honesty in writing which is both realistic and truthful. In other words, the very issues which make a biography stand out aesthetically and intellectually are unlikely to be found, because of most writers' compliant attitudes towards the norms and values of their conservative society, with which they have no wish to clash.

We find considerable awareness among some writers, nevertheless, who normally addressed these issues in their essays, as did the rebellious writer Ahmad al-Siba'i, the distinguished writer and poet Hamza Shihata from Hijaz, and the great reformer and researcher Hamad al-Jasir. The latter is considered to be the pioneer of informed, cultural renewal in the central province of the Kingdom. Writing about such sensitive issues in general articles of a theoretical nature is different, however, from writing about them as a personal experience in an autobiography. We went into this subject in some detail in the long introduction to the volume about autobiography in the Arabic edition, and we recommend it for further research. In this context, we should point out that echoes of intimate human experiences are commonly found in the fictional writing of authors of all generations. Perhaps the reason behind this phenomenon is that imagination gives the writer, male or female, opportunities to express their otherwise silent experiences, without fear of the likely repercussions from any direct clash with the establishment. In other words, it is acceptable so long as the characters are imaginary or "creations of pen and paper."

Does this mean that the autobiography has no standing in Saudi literature by comparison with other Arab countries, or even compared with the fictional narratives by the same Saudi writers? We do not think so, nor does the above analysis support such a conclusion. We simply seek an objective understanding of the structure of published biographies and the ways of writing them. At the very least, these written accounts have a documentary value, especially for modern critical appreciation. After all, the best way to analyse texts and discover their messages is through informed and in-depth dialogue looking at what the text says, what it omits what it forgets or ignores. Therefore we must evaluate artistically those autobiographies which utilised the turn of phrase and sarcasm to advantage and which have hidden depths, through their use of rhetorical and stylistic devices.

Next, there are those autobiographies which speak about the experience of study trips to the West, especially to the United States of America. These works are heavily influenced by modern critical awareness, where the image of the "other" is held up as a mirror in order to expose to the reader the shortcomings and weaknesses of his own society and culture.

Hamad al-Marzuqi's intellectual biography, *The Exodus* is definitely the most notable. The writing is transformed into a two-pronged criticism of the "self" and the "other," where the latter belongs to an attractive and modern culture. However, his political stances towards the Middle East and the Palestinian cause in particular, give grounds for repugnance and irritation. What makes the paradox stronger is that al-Marzuqi belongs to a new generation which works hard to promote modern Western thinking and values in their own society. However, the bias in favour of the Zionist state and towards the greed of major companies is bound to weaken the author's moral and intellectual standing, strengthening, at the same time, the position of conservative and traditional forces which reject any form of modernism, especially when the message is linked to Western thinking which itself had brought about the loss of Palestine from its native inhabitants, reflecting the attitudes of the United States, which still supports this colonialist project.

Although the writing of autobiography has already achieved a place in Saudi literature, it is still in its infancy as a modern narrative art form. However, the mere quantity of works produced in the past three decades reflects the autobiography's increasing acceptance and growing appeal. But although the principal elements and structural components can readily be found in many texts, they still suffer two fundamental flaws. Indeed, the fate of this particular genre will be determined by how aware writers are of these flaws and whether they will succeed in overcoming them.

The first flaw is the individual's inability to be independent of and different from the traditional collective entity to which most people still adhere. With the exception of Hamza Shihata and Ahmad al-Siba'i, most writers strive to prove that they are good citizens or decent members of a healthy society.

The second flaw is the lack of realism and honesty in these works. Writers are eager to forget more realistic and intimate experiences, so that neither their text nor their subject would clash with the prevailing traditional culture.

In order not to put all the onus on either the "writer" or "society," we should point out that the notions of what is "shameful," "forbidden" and "prohibited" still hold sway over both writer and reader. The public tacitly colludes by staying silent about these issues and about sensitive social, religious and political subjects. Critics who subscribe to these conformist terms may consider their silence as part of the "deal" over the writing of autobiographies in Saudi Arabia. They do not have to justify this stand, however, since the function of informed critical discourse is to contemplate, to analyse and to explain things from as rational and objective a perspective as possible.

Biographies written in Egypt, in the Mediterranean Middle East and in Morocco have overcome these obstacles without necessarily becoming base tell-all accounts or personal exposés. Indeed, the distinguished autobiographical works of prominent Arab writers from Taha Husain and Ahmad Amin to Shukri 'Ayyad, Ihsan 'Abbas and Fadwa Touqan are the closest to our deep-rooted literary heritage. These writers did not refrain from addressing all kinds of issues in order to be more honest with themselves and with others. The point here is that such honesty is not a simple imitation of Western literature, as some critics might lead us to believe.

Accordingly, it is likely that biographies will become more daring in their portrayal of the life of their writers, not just as reclusive or unusual beings, but as ordinary people with both a weak and a strong side. Their views may be correct, but they may also be wrong. Similarly, their past actions were not perfect; otherwise it would turn our writers into the stuff of legends and stereotypes, totally implausible. From this standpoint, we should expect to see more biographies by women in the future. The absence of contributions by women in this field cannot be justified, intellectually or logically, by blaming it on their lack of awareness or their inability to express these feelings in an artistic form. Quite simply, we have to address the massive pressures which the conservative culture imposes on their lives and on their writing.

It is most probable that more realistic and intimate experiences will flow increasingly into this genre. For the present, the autobiography still hides behind the mask of fiction writing, without concealing some characteristics of the biography in terms of documentation and recording, as can be seen in the works of al-Mishri, al-Qusaibi, Muhammad 'Abdu Yamani and 'Abdu Khal, to name but a few.

The prospect is indeed that biographies will become increasingly realistic, because biographies are already widespread in world literature. The biography is also the field most suitable for female writers in the future who might need to express their experiences, opinions and dreams with honesty and depth. At this time the greatest fear is that they can become embroiled in direct confrontation with the ideas and values of their society.

This is exactly what we find in the many fictional biographies which take such risks in this direction. While they may not be available publicly, these works have nonetheless been widely read and covered in articles and studies in the national press. The greatest challenge to biographical writing is certainly of a social nature. However, it is clear that conditions have begun to change.

*Translated by Reem Kelani & Christopher Somes-Charlton*

---

1. The book of avant-garde criticism written by 'Abbas M. al-'Aqqad (1889-1964) and Ibrihim 'Abd al-Qadir al-Mazini (1890-1949) in which the neo-classical school headed by Shauqi was viciously attacked. Attacked as well was the two poets' old colleague and associate 'Abd al-Rahman Shukri (1886-1958) whom they grievously ridiculed. Despite this, Egyptian critics (followed by other Arab critics and literary historians), harking back to their old close association, grouped the three under the name of the Group of the Diwan.

2. The *Sieve* or *al-Ghirbal* is an avant-garde book of critical articles by Nu'aima, one of the leading writers of the Arab émigrés to North America, published in 1923 in Egypt. It was, however, not dependent on anything written in the *Diwan*, as most of its articles had already appeared in the second decade in North America.

3. Founded by A. Z. Abu Shadi, it made quite a movement towards poetic renovation in Egypt, making contacts also with rising poets in the rest of the Arab world. Its major achievement was the publication of the famous, but short-lived *Apollo* magazine (1932-1934). Its weakness lay in the fact that it was not headed by great poets whose verse could be a genuine example of avant-garde poetry in the thirties.

4. Hassan was the Prophet's poet, who defended him.

5. Muhammad al- Shanti, The Art of the Novel in Modern Saudi Literature, 1990, P.116

6. Husain al-Manasira: "The Auto-biographical Novel," *Al-Jazira* Newspaper, issue 9341.

7. A folklorish song used to be performed by women in Mecca, during the three days of Hajj (pilgrimage), mocking any man they see loitering in the streets instead of being outside the City doing the Hajj rituals.

8. A Palestinian academician and scholar.

# Part I

## Poetry

# I.
# THE PIONEERS

*'Abdallah al-Faisal Al Saud*

## ILLUMINATION

As when light shines on the horizon
   glides over green meadows
As when lush pavilions are filled with fragrance
   And shed their perfumes like mists
So hopes shine in my breast
   And dreams stir my youthful brightness
I feel existence is my possession
   I forget all its worries and pains
The hours, as they fly past so quickly
   almost beat the speed of a mirage's light
It is my life, I want its footsteps to be bold
   So my youth will endure
But so long as you are near me, my love,
   I wouldn't care where life took me
Love, do you feel as I do,
   the tremors of our exultant love
Answer me, are you an alien phantom
   in the world of people, if you comfort me in my exile?
Love, are you like me, ever heartbroken
   Seeing nothing in life but a mist?
And when your eye meets mine would you think
   The world is a garden of love?
Speak out, do not fear any accuser
   Our love was never smeared with hypocrisy and lies
It's the covenant of two hearts that thrive on loyalty
   Rejecting the treachery of the wolf

The covenant of two hearts confident that love
   Is nobler than trickery and doubts
Leave me not to silence that inflames a heart
   which has no place left for burning
Do not leave me distraught with my doubts
   Some doubts have the sharpness of spears
Don't say: enough for you what your eyes tell you
   My eyes might be blind to the truth
Don't be coy, you know how earnest my love is,
   how pure my desires,
Say, even in whispers "I love you, cherish
   your sweet and noble aspirations."
The heart of the deprived needs the confession
   of lips, it is a sin to deny him.


Translated by Bassam al-Hilu with Alan Brownjohn

# *Muhammad Saeed al-'Amoudi*

## QUARTETS

Is the end truly a return to the past?
   I have misjudged and now I am grieving
Do we hope that to-morrow we shall reap
   sweet fruit where now we reap only despair?
Who'll forgive me for being enthralled by
   Enchanting words of eternal love?
He errs who succumbs to illusions
   And does not heed the lessons of life.

A world of freedom is a mirage,
   How can the thirsty be satisfied by a mirage?
The East is a barren space
   How can one take refuge in a wasteland
There's no good in the West, there is
   No good in then East, both are ruined worlds
The West in its greed is just
   Like the East in its enslavement of people

Sweet dreams that we shall with love
   Climb, and not with hatred and misanthropy
Great is power, if only it could eliminate rancour
   and those who grudge.
Knowledge is fantastic, it disseminates
   Wisdom, not frivolous thought.
Sweet are dreams and genuine, if only they
   Were not illusions for the dreamers.

Translated by Bassam al-Hilu and Alan Brownjohn

# Muhammad Hasan 'Awwad

## SECRET OF LIFE AND NATURE

What secret lies in the winds
blowing north and south
bringing rains

What secret lies in the sea
one day calm, another day tumultuous

Chasing the full moon, and the stars
in its ebb and flow

Why does the earth revolve around the
sun, forever and ever going

Why do the stars shine at night
and the sun at day, dazzling the eyes

Why does the eclipse of sun and moon
appear one day, and other days hides away

Why is Neptune inscrutable to us
We cannot see the stars around it?

Why are we willed to live on earth
Not choosing, and spend our lives
uncertain of the world

Why is death, like life, decreed upon us
it robs the soul of its potency and grandeur

Have philosophies, science and religion
been a minaret for people?

Did they awaken our minds from slumber?

Have we torn out he curtains of uncertainty?

Like the ancients we live our course
Then others come after us to do the same

And life, sun and stars, and night and day
Revolve as ever before
Life's secret must remain inscrutable.

Translated by Laith al-Husain and Alan Bownjohn

## Muhammad Hasan Faqi

### QUARTETS

**1.**

I traveled life in search of tranquility
But the journey amplified my sorrow and qualms.
From so much suffering I feel as if
I've inhabited this space for centuries
What is it I want? I do not know my pursuit
Is it glory that I seek? Is it pleasure?

Yet hardship has its contentment
I have grown,
for all of life's jolts
More tender still.

**2.**

Yes, there's something called luck,
but part of luck is to strive and seek.
Life doesn't deter those who commit
to their quest with resolution.
Resolution might founder but, if persistent
will rise again.
Responding, turning this will of fate
will draw you nearer to remote desire.

**3.**

I ask, I, who collided with despair, who has
suffered profusely, experiencing life
not finding pleasure in either
misery or bliss,
I, like a drowned man, am tyrannized by
the waves. I sink into the dark deep; yet,
having been redeemed by suffering I question,
will I go to heaven or to hell?

**4.**

I wandered in life to get comfort,
 but in those wanderings
my sorrow and woe increased. The sheer suffering
has stretched for centuries, it seems.
What do I want when I do not know my quest?
Is it glory, is it enchantment?
Yet in times of hardship there is some kind of bliss
For from so many disasters
I've become a more tender man.

**5.**

Mist-clouds passed by the garden saying
"From me come your flowers, your fruit,
without me springs will not flow,
nor will the trees stay green!"
The garden laughed and said,
"Without the earth, nourishing rain
will not succeed in burgeoning the plants.
It is from us, both of us
That lovely flowers flourish."

**6.**

Dear little butterfly I thought you were
A piece torn from the papers I've thrown away.
But, you became a thing of life after all,
full of radiance.
Oh, little butterfly, your beauty fluttered
In my hands, but I did not keep it.
How often did my hands hold similar
Beauty, yet I, out of much love, set it free.

**7.**

Brother, here is my hand,
Clasp it in yours.
My future, should you question,
Is tied to yours.
The fate of all our brothers,
Hinges on yours.
I have abandoned dreams in my slumber-bed,
Therefore, abandon them in yours.

**8.**

Sleep and rest, what a losing deal.
that has vanished from my hands.
They're gone away, and plenitude, even if all gold,
has no more value.
And wisdom? Oh! They've both illuminated
my future, and annihilated it.
I find tranquility and dreams are greater
Than all knowledge, than all power.

**9.**

Had I been forced to choose, my soul would be less lonely,
And the journey of my quest would not have felled my will.
Why care for glory and its light!
The mountain slope might be happier than the summit,
There where one could find contentment, but I have none.
All I see perturbs me.
How the ambitious man regrets his long vigil
While a contented man is happy with his sleep.

**10.**

I had wished I were a rose in the bud.
Its fragrance and beauty, a fascination.
What is the world without gardens,
And its springs to tempt the eye?
Souls pine in the wilderness, thirsty, caught up
By the dearth of fate.
On this earth there's an abundance of lush edens and arid deserts,
And we are the paradise; we are the hell.

**11.**

How often I wish I were a shining star.
A pilot that steers the perplexed in the passage of life,
Soothes the in the pitch of black night,
where darkness intimidates even lions.
How I wish the lone traveler can see my rays as a friend, a guide
and after walking in the pit, can happily reach the plain
Wishes we desire, if they should happen,
We might prefer that which once we abhorred.

**12.**

Vicissitude shaped friendship between us.
How well we met them, what patience and what pride!

You never asked for mercy in the presence of evil,
Knowingly, with your own eyes, you witnessed death.
And while I met with one catastrophe,
You met with scores.
There are men shaken by time's disasters, but
Here is a man who shook the disasters of time.

13.

I yearned one day to reach the heights,
Instead went plunging to a bottomless pit.
Alone I dug hard in the abyss
Seeking the rare friend
Instead in the hollow, I stumbled on
Rare treasures of glory and honour.
Had I sought my quest in heights
I'd have only found glitter.

14.

Light gleamed in the pitch black night.
One day, I did not see it; I was blind.
When the caravan roared nearby, I asked why,
There was no answer.
I was alone the seeing eye, for my
Conscience was not blind,
Nor was my heart deaf.
A blind man may see truth clearly
When a sighted man sees only delusion.

Translated by Laith al-Husain and Patricia Alanah Byrne

*Ahmad Al-Fasi*

## SHE AND THE LIGHT

The light embraced her body
In love with her
Folded her with tenderness
Wrapped her, kissed
All that was revealed of her
Precious beauty
Enveloped her
Cradling an calming her frightened breasts
The befuddled moon
Ran silver waves over her cheeks
And came to rest on her hair
In a riot of colours
Silver one minute,
The next a golden glow
A riot of twilight
Ecstatic

As the light shone out of her
She was a portrait of enchantment
A heaven
no longer mortal
In the Eden of chrysolite
the mirrors of
marble
the dancing light rejoices
reflecting its coral beauty.

And the light slept embracing her
and she slept,
an enchantment
awakening love's
multitude of melodies.

Translated by Bassam al-Hilu with Alan Brownjohn

## *Ahmad Qandeel*

## A SCREAM

Don't bind my steps
With what you call
Traditions, or a system of life

Don't wipe away my tears
With all your gifts
of advice

Don't fell my will
With what you insist
is rationality and commitment

Do not belittle of my escapades
With what you readily number
As sins or mistakes

Let my feet walk freely on the path
my sighs exhale bitter sorrows
and my ideas decide the verdict clearly

Give me the right to do things openly
He who lives in chains is not alive in the world
Birds have their wings, rocks have their solidness
Water goes stagnant when it's blocked by dams
We were born for the flow and ebb of life.

Translated by Bassam al-Hilu with Alan Brownjohn

*Hasan 'Abdallah al-Qurashi*

## SHORT POEMS

**1.**

My lady,
I came to you lamp in hand
But no light,
Yesterday's wound aching in my breast.
I could hear your stifled whispers
In my dream
It was as if my love were suffocated.

I came to you, not fearing despair,
Not asking the shore its secrets,
I came on wings of pain,
A subdued question hovering on my lips:
When will we meet again?
I shun impossible promises.
So leave them for tomorrow, there's no luck today.
There's no cup in our hands
No flowers to sing our love
I'm no more that enchanted lover,
Nor are you that intoxicated rose.
Your fragrance has been lost in the valley
Leaving bitter agony behind
For my wailing heart.
Just leave the fragrance, and leave
the frightened river to run its course.
Neither the singing of birds,
nor the charm of scenery
will ever return to us the fruits
of life, and rekindle the fire of the heart.

**2.**

My dear, our plans are disheveled,
Lost on the road.

Since our second spring, since I sublimated my April
For your love, and you ran
to discover in me the fountains of the past,
the night lodged in my veins
And numbed me. No song revives me
I am not I and you are not you.
Each of us goes astray on the road of the past,
drunk from the fountain of despair,
storing memory after memory
for a false celebration,
painting illusions, covering delusions,
but the mirror will betray
the sleepless nights.

3.

My dear,
I am the one who complains, and here
I've poured forth my pleas
And when I knocked at dawn's door
It did not heed my pain
But laughed, like a wolf it laughed,
And I returned to my prison.

4.

My dear,
I pierce the wall of my seclusion
With my nails,
I drag my dreams in the paths of night,
scatter my flowers, and alone
I read my story in the glow of fire,
The story of a tired man who lived
Between the fangs and the nails,
Alone, full of doubts, feeding only
On crumbs of memory,
Pouring my heart on papers
with no one reading my poems
No one visiting me.
The wall of my dumb seclusion
I pierce with my nails.

Translated by Bassam al-Hilu and Patricia Alanah Byrne

## *Husain Sirhan*

## BREAKDOWN OF THE BODY

My body is worn out, all its strength gone,
   today my life span is diminished
As if I am about to see
   the hand of death, blessed be this hand
It's called me to extinction and my soul
   has answered the call with quick delight
Throwing away heavy bonds
   happy to wake up from sleep
And float on the wings of space
   no time limit, no direction
Liberated from a finite place
   from a time bound by my own footsteps
Released to where the river of love flows
   where its Eden extends a welcoming hand
He sees things forbidden to others
   a beauty other eyes fail to perceive
No longer imagining bliss but feeling it
   wherever his wishes beckon
Oh soul that has endured with no rancour
   is now in eternity blessed with its hopes
Remember your body thrown in a grave
   with stubborn stones and hard earth
You'll find its remains gravely reminding
   the heedless of what they had forgotten
You'll find them in flowers full of fragrance
   the dew dancing in the buds
You'll find them in the roses protected by thorns,
   but still retaining their scent
The remains of an emaciated body
   devoured by death
Earth dissolved it and recovered it
   to give nourishment to the plants
People asked, 'has he really died?'

Yes, and sorrow has also died with him
Friends who'd grieved for him have now forgotten him
   Old loves who'd cried for him, now neglect him
And laughter now rings joyful after the grief
   The clouds have dispersed
Condolences given place to felicitations
   Each person minding his own life
Nothing left to the dead
   When the world is bereft of their singing
Each heart that once embraced him
   now consigns his phantom to discarded memories


Translated by Bassam al-Hilu with Alan Brownjohn

# II.
# THE INNOVATORS

*Usama 'Abd Rahman*

## MOTHER OF HISTORY

Was it fated that a whole nation
   should disintegrate into fragments?
That it should be slain on every road
   and sail in the depths of misery?
That a night of conflict should envelop her
   and darkness follow on darkness?

Do not ask about chastity
   Honour is eroded
Gardens are now deserts
   Never visited by clouds
And the proud homestead, the old Bedouin tent,
   is no more that tent
Wisdom has turned counterfeit
   Is no more the old wisdom
Oppression lashes my nation
   But I dare not challenge it
Oppression condemns me to death
   And I obey, I do not reject its orders
Oppression feeds poison to me
   I take it in submission
Oh my country, land of the proud
   Why do you no longer care?
Blood is shed profusely
   But the wounded do not fight back

Wounds carry no swords
   Cannot attend summits
Make important declarations
   and indulge in great intrigues
No call for revenge has sounded
   No calamities have called on courage to prevail
Chivalry has not warned us
   With the blazing fire of its alarm.

Mother of History! Answer me
   Is this a decree of fate?
That the sparks of honour should be snuffed out
   That conscience should be banished
That an Arab should kill a homeland
   Sell his people to the enemy
leave his mother in a river of tears
   mourning her offspring

If only the sword edge was unsheathed
   If only repressed men divorced their peace
Then victory would be on the horizon
   The winds could not prevent its embrace
And shame would disappear
   and the blemish would be effaced

If it were fated then
   That we suffer a multitude of disasters
We would not fail if we met them
   with the power of our will and our courage.

Translated by Bassam al-Hilu with Alan Brownjohn.

## *Fawziyya Abu Khalid*

## TUFUL: NOONDAY RAINBOW

I open the book of poetry
  Or the valves of the heart
What poem can contain
  The gentle waving of your
Little hand at the school door?
What rhythm can retain the movement of your little feet
And the swishing of your uniform
  As you flit
Between the street and my heart?
The noon sun kindles your hair
your chestnut hair kindles the noon sun
with rainbow colours
You throw the heavy school bag off your little
shoulders
like a branch getting free of its weight of apples
And I can hear the fluttering of the feathers
on the wings,
You take off your school shoes
And a river of holy ink pours on the slate of my fate
  You come near…you jump
you give me a kiss that pours the anxiety of poets
  in my veins,
etches the miracle of the scene
fleeting like a boundless colt.

Translated by Ruanne Abou-Rahme (with the help of the editor)
and Patricia Alanah Byrne

# Two Little Girls

I hang on the tail of her dress
as a little boy
hangs
to the thread of
a rising kite
  I climb her braid
as a squirrel climbs
the branch of a hazelnut tree
We hop in the open deserts from one world to the next
Reroute ourselves with every gust of air
  like birds just freed from a cage
Move from one game to another
And she teaches me
  the names of flowers
  the seasons of rain
  the love of country
And I teach her
  obstinacy and mischief
We share one apple
  and innumerable dreams
We paint with the desert a paradise of questions
sprinkle each other
  with mirage water
  and befriend a fleeting gazelle
and when sunset surprises us
the doors open their jaws like ogres
in the inscrutable twilight

And who can solve
The mystery?
Which is the mother
Which the child?

Translated by Jinan M. Coulter (with the help of the editor)
and Patricia Alanah Byrne

## FIRST FLAVOUR OF DEATH
## FROM THE *REMAINS OF MEMORY*

A coffin gleams
Crowned with thorns and laurels
Who was that queen
*Kohled* and perfumed
Who'd stretched her legs like
An amber river
And boldly lay on the
shoulders of men
as they carried her across
distance and time.

Who?
Who was that queen?
In vain I search for the memory
Nothing remains but the lingering
taste of grief
Impenetrable and sharp
That touches
The depth of my heart
Recklessly

Translated by Ruanne Abou-Rahme (with the help of the editor)
and Patricia Alanah Byrne

## An Experience

She mingled the acid of ink with the salt of the sea
  and the wounds of the heart
She merged them
Etched her wings and wrote
  her longings
  on the harshness of the desert
  and the mercy of paper

She tried to fly…

## After Time

I line up the bottles of time
Hour by hour
Day by day
And begin
Filling the years of life
with this terrifying void
A little poetry…a little love
A big weight of sorrow and
numerous agonies of yearning
I shake the burning acids
and drink the remaining draught
by myself.

Translated by Laith al-Husain and Patricia Alanah Byrne

*Faisal Akram*

## A MOMENT OF DREAM

It's a moment in life
which we know
is not ours
we sleep a little in
the innocence of childhood
in the beginning of awareness
the mystery of an early dream
the biting of tender lips, the whispering to the stars
We have passed on, or time
has left us and we did not know.
Oh stubborn Time: can't we have, in your
eternal heart a place
to rest
or some space
for hope?
Will sleep
arrive after the years of travel,
to return to just a few of us
a little memory?
Our hopes are now myths
in a climate of dry thought,
hard dialogues, and words clashing by night
But life has two windows
One to the sun of childhood, the time of light,
And one…but this is a long story,
and might lead us to tears.
Our autumn drowned in a setting sun
And in our boats
The spring of time would grow
– the time we choose chooses us itself –
On its edge, we walk alone or in groups
And it embraces us. We flee from it
into the winds. The winds

have two deserts: a small desert we
explore, exposing its secrets,
and a vast desert
which explores us and exposes our secrets.
It's a moment that time passed without
extending its years, but extending ours
It's a moment of time we know is not ours
but we drink from its flowers to gain time
in which to play our tune
Those on illusory roads fear for us
as if we arrived and yet never arrived
and
because we ignored our weaknesses,
our desires diminished and our fire ripened.
Said the one who thought himself a winner
It's a moment in the depths of my memory
the silent one
the forgotten one,
draws a picture with features that were ours.
The tired ones search our sleep
Invade the recesses of our night
 in the depths of the darkness
and the tremulous moment
removes the chains from our approaching death
It's a moment in life which we know is not ours.


Translated by Jinan M. Coulter (with the help of the editor)
and Patricia Alanah Byrne

*Muhammad al-'Ali*

# WHEN I WRITE OF LOVE

Dust covers the water
These frothy stars in the cup
are treacherous
and treacherous is this morning, still drifting backwards
and those branches
breaking loose in the winds.
Yet the heart did not falter
Promises did not abandon it
The land, that whorish beauty, is brighter in the distance
Fountains pour into it, abandon it
But it stays where it is.
Oh time of decorated thorns
Rocks have tamed us
Whenever we approach
the foot of the mountain
we start the climb again
But we will tame them
Have you scrutinised my face inhabiting the waves
Oh blue little girl that has not yet learned
to speak?
We came to you with the palms
With the trees that shimmer in the heart
Come, drink the goodness of these clouds
or throw stones at the palm trees
one tree after another.

Love humiliates
Yet we have loved
Those lying awake through nights never know
the wound the sea creates
Oh poet Abu al-Tayyib![1] Stop a while
And read your poems about the wounds
With which you left Egypt

Your steed was the night
It slipped away without neighing
and you plunged your wound into poetry then.
But how are we to cure the
agony of a blue little girl that has not yet
learned how to speak?
I bless your eyes
If you should grant me some of your
Pearls
This frenzied Gulf has lost its oysters shells!

Take me to your voice, Fayrouz[2]
Then break it on the sea
The waves have turned the key in the lock
And buried their joy
Then emigrated,
left me alone
and emigrated.
But your voice is the wings of those who come
From every direction
From the sands, the waters, and the palms
From every source of darkness
From all that I will mention
When I write of love

Oh, but when can I write of love?

Translated by Laith al-Husain and Alan Bownjohn

*'Adnan al-Sayyid al-'Awwami*

## THE ROBE

You came, the robe undulating around you
And I felt my heart leap

Where are you going, end of all desires?
I'm a poet, camouflage for me is beyond me

If some eyes are bind to you
Mine are wide open

Had I been bolder
I would have stretched out my hand to touch you

And broken through this protective wall of silk
While my heart leaps into temptation.

***

If I could reach it, I would embrace it
If space would disappear, I would gather it into my arms

There would be no harm in embracing
This billowing robe and the body it envelopes

What harm if my hands should rest
On its enchanting fabric?

You chose a black velvet robe
Oh the loveliness of black velvet!

In an enclosure of night
a star is enveloped

Such elegance in the dress!
as it quivers, enchanted by your beauty

And the road flows with fresh love
Giving out fragrance and dew.

Translated by Bassam al-Hilu and Alan Brownjohn

*'Ali Bafaqeeh*

# 'URWA THE OUTLAW[3]

**1.**

His words grew ripe in the eyes
Among those who lived
In the deepest poverty
'Urwa traveled with the swift lightening
Slept a thousand years in its incandescence

Salma calls him but he hears the horses
Salma calls him but he hears the palm trees
Salma calls him but he hears a vast wilderness
He casts the slanders onto the free wind

All the Abs tribe slept while 'Urwa recited his poems
    To the distant stars
As the night stretched on
'Urwa would etch a wilderness
And gather it to his heart

**2.**

The caliph's messenger whispers in 'Urwa's ear:
"Our chief wants your sword and your words.
Come with me
The cauldrons of food are delicious
The wine jars are full."
And 'Urwa still gazed in the face of a thousand years.

Translated by Laith al-Husain with Alan Brownjohn

## Ahmad Bahkali

# NADA (POEM TO HIS DAUGHTER)

Nada…Nada
The dew on the rose of life
Nada…Nada
A smile adorning the lips of dawn
Nada…Nada
My dream of blossoms
Incomparable fragrance
Bouncing rhythm of poetry
Nada, you are the hope sprouting from rock

O innocent eyed beauty
This mouth glowing with light
smiles
I fear for it, my little one
I fear this sweet smile
Will wither
In this hard age
This barren age
This time of war

Nada…I call you
Will you heed the call
The sign of your innocence
rekindles our own

My little one
When I see you my joy is reborn
I feel a fountain of happiness
Wells in my heart
Rippling with love
But, my little one, I fear
I fear, my little one,
the time of drought
The age of terror

Plunder and loot
In this time of war

My child
lucid as mist
Like every child on earth
In your presence
Melancholy lifts,
in your presence
I feel my heart grow tender
My ribcage a cage no longer
But large like space
a space for one heart
yearning
for a million hearts
longing to embrace all creation
to its breast
But the worst of my fears
are for you, radiant innocence,
in this worst of all times
in this time of oppression and distress
In this time of war

Nada, my little one
Because I love children
I fear for them
Pity them
I pour out my dark mood on paper
Before the deluge
Perchance he who ignites the fuse with a flash of his eyes
will awaken to the lisp of a beautiful child
a refugee
suffering in Lebanon
lost in Iraq and Iran
or in the Afghan valleys
and instead set his fuse to the wick of a lantern
in a milk factory
not in the factories of war
And in place of a bomb
a thousand stalks will flower

***

Nada, inhabitant of my heart
Your father carries
Propitious tidings
to all lovers of kids
and warning to those
who steal their happiness
For life and splendor,
are the birthright of children
They are your birthright, Nada

\*\*\*

My precious pearl
hope whose roots strike deep into my heart
May the Merciful God guard you
Sleep, my little one for you are safe
Under His wing
O child of peace
Child of peace
Child of peace.


Translated by Bassam al-Hilu with Alan Brownjohn

*Sa'd al-Bawardi*

# REBEL AGAINST LOVE

I offer her peace
she offers me war
I give her ease
She extends to me
Hardship.
My heart lamented
Over her piercing eyes,
She perfected
her fatal gaze.

The night is somnolent on her breasts
And in my eyes,
Despite their drowsiness,
It knows no sleep
The sea, the magic, the waves
Are in her glance
A wilderness that stretches
Across distance
And time.

***

I extended her my heart
A gift she rejected
All the while
I knew
cold hearts' intent
is to defeat the heart.

In song and music
I laid down my love
She felled down
the love and the music
In whispers
I searched for her touch

The nectar of her love,
She returned my whispers
In dire tones
And I
Was overcome with grief
*Woe to a lover destroyed by the*
*Cruelty of love!*
I laid my love in her protection
remembered her as a dream,
And my dream grew old
Never knew youth

Translated by Ruanne Abou-Rahme (with the help of the editor)
and Patricia Alanah Byrne

*Nasser Bouhaimid*

## OF WHAT DO YOU DREAM?

What do you dream about?
You loiterers
Hungry and tired
Your eyes full of supplication
a question
hovers on your lips
On the pale foreheads
Something unsaid,
What do you dream about?

      ***

You hungry hordes
You who set out at nightfall with no light
Crossing the plains with no baggage,
What do you dream about?

      ***

O you melancholy shepherd
Seeking shade on sand dunes
Your wasted fledgling children
Roaming the sands,
What do they dream about?

      ***

You who are vexed
Furious at the earth
Seeking help from the mists
Following in the tracks of mirage,
What do you dream about?

      ***

This world of abundance
Of water and shade

The bread of the hungry
Entreating the heavens
Fearful for their lives
These are the dreams of men
Who labour
Without cease
Who hew their homes
Out of rock, of mountains
You who loiter
Tired and hungry,
Of what do you dream?


Translated by Bassam al-Hilu with Alan Brownjohn

*Lulu Buqshan*

# WOMEN AND A CARAVAN OF PAIN

**1.**

Women in a caravan
Their faces reveal fatigue
Dust conceals their wrinkles
An old woman extends her arm
to embrace me
dashes words of fire on my face
Another flings on me roses that
wound me
Then vision wanes
I resort to tears…a poem of pain.

**2.**

And you come…leading your hostages of women
to their deadly end
in your hands
a firm chain
which settles on the parting of
my hair.
Laughter and songs
Reach my ears
A chill numbs me.

**3.**

You came to receive me
Your treasures arriving one
after the other
Your sacrificial beasts
Slain at my feet.
And I drown in blood
While wedding henna covers me
stains my skin
as if I've just been butchered.

**4.**

The women in the caravan continue their march
A prey to anguish
A suckling baby boy cries
But you still laugh
because the child is
yours and from you.

**5.**

And I succumb…to pain?
No…to fear
Because bewilderment
resides in my bosom.
I tremble
I panic
Whenever your gaze wanders
and your smile turns to frown
I am gripped by
A persistent spell of pain
Because this little girl
sleeping in my lap
is from me
and that little boy
playing with the sand
is from you.

Translated by Jinan M. Coulter (with the help of the editor)
and Patricia Alanah Byrne

## *Huda al-Daghfaq*

### ECHO

Sometimes I weep for this moon
Climbing our room
What fault that its hands, like a clock, should shine?
I commit it to loneliness every evening,
it grants me its amorous eyes

### A LITTLE TREE

Those rocks embracing themselves
Their calm tears at me when I listen to it.
They are gathering their volcano for eons.
Their silence is a will.
Those rocks embracing themselves
have a little tree in their guts
which does not appear now.

### From: WOODS

1.

The sparrow
A branch that flew
Gone flying
Flying
So the tree
Populated its trunk.

**2.**

> Let your latticed shades relax,
> And flow on, you tender trees
> Drown out the pavement,
> Your outpouring will sniff off the sun's burner.
> But my eyes will light up as lamps,
> Their joy is in your soft whispers that
> dances in night's tranquility.

**3.**

> The Tree… One branch only
> Crying, crying, crying,
> Its tears becoming a wood.

**4.**

> The leaf, green, calling me.
> The leaf, when *I* call it, is yellow.

**5.**

> The green branch
> Approaches, approaches the black face
> of the earth,
> approaches. Why??

## TENDERNESS

> His palms caress the white loaf
> Its face inflates.
> The loaf is now red,
> Its appetizing aroma
> is the baker's love.

## DEPARTURE

> The clock of this house
> Is a deaf ear, its two hands
> A mute mouth that does not confess

even to its own silence,
Dust has deflated its wings

*** 

The clock of this house
Is a mummified butterfly.
Loneliness has hung it
On the blind wall.

# FAREWELL

You used to comfort the vines of my days
With your promising reminiscences
Ah, my tender friend,
Your voice would listen to my remarks
And how often I saw you,
Yield with affection
When you heard the disturbing words
As they boiled in my mind.
So now, you rare friend,
Words, gilded, fly to you.
Oh grief!
I've bidden farewell to your eternal moon.
My friend,
Why did your foot trip off the table?
I keep chiding you.

# WHY DO THE PLACES LEAVE ME

Dust visits the place
The seats are collapsing
The tables turning on their axes
The flowers wilting on the walls
The windows closing now
Part of me is closed too
The stars
Have handed me over to the darkness

How am I to leave this place!
When this place is really time?!
The spirit of this time is a portrait,
With a hidden face.


# REALISATION

She dialed his number
For a year he had not answered
The simple building…no longer inhabited
It had grown old
The reel alone was entranced by that ringing
Once, the wind of longing raged
And enveloped her and the reel,
Enveloped his voice
And the reel kept turning.


Translated by Laith al-Husain and Patricia Alanah Byrne

*Fawzi al-Dahhan*

# DREAMY SONGS IN THE TEMPLE OF SILENCE

Here I am, playing dreamy songs
In the temple of silence
the silence of a stone.
In my temple I remembered the eyes
of those maidens who had chased me
then fled, taking refuge in the night,
and left me alone to hold communion with the moon.
On the face of night I learned
the love of exiles
And how I cherish my estrangement
during the nights of travel;
when the nights sleep in my temple
and block out all vision in the eyes
of those sleeping
in time of repression.
I've learned
How to cherish sorrow
During the nights of madness
How to play the melody of silence
On the strings of the lute.

Translated by Laith al-Husain with Alan Brownjohn

## 'Ali Al-Dumaini

## THE SIGNS

**1.** *The Sign of Dust*

Dust has its dwellings
And signs have their tribes
Should my sight be blinded
their beginnings will touch me.
A night in the lap of a pregnant woman
And I not the agent:
 if a boy it be, then he is mine
And if she gives birth to
"an enchantress"
then it is hers.
A bunch of suitcases saturated with dust
Woman of cities, she in whose halls the daylight filters
Love's hammock swings down here, rises there, so neither is water
drunk from its embers
nor voice borrowed from its silence
A horizon of hands the color of Turkish coffee,
Tatar in form
A rose of iron
Another of palm leaves
A third one unyielding…
So you who are about to rise up from the moss over the grave
How do you mend up the emptiness
And heal the wound of young maidens
And repair the vessels disintegrating on death's tracks.

**2.** *The Sign of the Crayfish*

I chose not to fight the enchantress of my youth against her wishes
and volunteered to rest
near the wall of wounded words.
I repented from resisting a song
which violates the dew
and gives license to

rain, to the branches of the
branches of the winds.
I chose not to teach my child that creation is of two kinds:
Woman and man
Man and woman.
Lineages of wine imbibed by creation
beam with signs
so gardens moan from the weight of bracelets.
I chose not to speak until I saw
Cities within villages
Coffins of silver taken and not bought
I chose not to see that which should be seen.
In the dream of one doleful from indiscretion
In the un-avowed pain between two intimates
I gave up trying to prevent my love from crying out:
only what is right, is permissible
in a time when the storm has forewarned of war!

**3.** *The Sign of the Virgin*
The carnation of morning said to its neighbor:
Master of the age of foliage
give me the rope, the cane and the harnessed wine jars
To ascend the horizon however difficult,
go up its ladder,
I, tree of love, am the flute's marked wind
turned part star, part medal
turn me into a young maiden and recreate me
Time has made room for the cloak of the dead
My own cloak is not soiled
I mend its braids across the horse's halter,
meet mariners
The country throws the talisman of
festivals into my lap,
I suckle it
And set it free
And in its birth refuse my death.

**4.** *The Sign of Children*
Morning's silence hung its lantern over the arch of the city
But I do not pass
I and the dust
And a glass of mud I fermented for two nights
Beautified with the yellowing of trees

We share this time its melancholies
And console the stone.
As evening approaches
And a woman who does not smile appears
Children in their beds sleep between notebooks and ink
Waiting for the paling of Thursday and the face of "news"
the dust and I fought over the waves
I let go so it can depart
And depart so it can diminish
But it settles over my fruit!

A First dance
Artery of cities
You have bargained with me
With the metal loaf
And the milk of slumber
So drink blood now
To your fill.

**5.** *The Sign of Eve*

A portrait on the wall, gathering her jewels, tempts me
away from autumn's supper
I protect half of her with my shirt,
her loosening veil burns me
an Eden, eyes lined with tormented sweetness, its colors
drawn from a familiar time
How do I set up her crown in the vessel of dust, how?
I choose her, she surrounded by foot soldiers
between fire and deceit

**6.** *The Sign of the Arch*

I count the bracelets in your arms, and distill silence so it can sprout
Prepare feasts for the travellers
And lift from the saddles of the wind:
what ever, and whenever
The flasks heave within the soul in awe
And the evening spreads
Perchance I might choose you at the end of a lifetime, a youthful archer
brooding like a female
Who beats on the shells with her gold
So the houses flow with their compartments
As sorrow turns song deaf
Perchance I will choose you towards my end,

and perchance we will
exchange with this dust its guilt
horse by horse.


Translated by Laith al-Husain and Patricia Alanah Byrne

## *Muhammad al-Dumaini*

## Roses Sleeping in Baskets

The one with the warm heart and the silent figure
invades the hall with his acid mood
Complains of the sea to the sailor
and runs through the freshness of water
towards her
who searches the heart slowly.
What wind are you,
You who are free as anger?
Slumber is tired of two eyes that
Amuse themselves with sleep
While the garden cats
Shake the joy of the grasses.
There are fires on the roads
But no fire can
Extinguish this fire.
Leave me then
in this village that
wanders through me
Leave me
to die willingly on the ashes of childhood
like a priest who has broken free
of his frock,
and hung his medals
on the breasts of soldiers and women of allure.
Carry your baskets, son of my mother,
And restore to shape
your lovely female
The roses have slept in the baskets
And the wall has reclined on the twilight's splendour
And there are no roses any more
No evening
No closets.
Your endurance is great.

# DESPAIR

Without reticence
Without fear
my neighbour raises an axe
And I bend my head to him
Content with you, my heart,
You tyrant with no hope

Without reticence
Without fear
Without even a cigarette
Without a twig of jasmine
I take my heart
And bury it, listening
To approaching footsteps
That have
No purpose
Only the smoke of boredom

Translated by Laith al-Husain with Alan Brownjohn

*Muhammad Habiby*

## TRACES REMAINING

My friends wore many different faces
And hurried away towards
many other places
I spent a lifetime here,
paying homage
to the silence of their absence
my tears were no kind of a reprieve
my longing did not
fill the emptiness.

***

I am like a palm tree without
any branches
No water around it
Its fruits shriveled
The trees mocking me.

***

I remain here alone
Singing of the crumbling houses
Mourning many departed faces.
Where can I find a face
as steadfast as my mother's?
I said to my life
Do not pass so quickly and expose my secret!
And life stood still
But by that time I was old.

***

He said one day
"Isn't it time to collect all those words together
words left idle like the leaves of your life?"
I said,

"But where is Ru'a
Do you only like what you see in images?"
"Oh my son,
Ru'a has become a tall tamarisk tree
She did not wait for you."

I slept, hugging my sorrow.


Translated by Laith al-Husain and Alan Brownjohn

*Sa'd al-Hamazani*

# A PEN

He wrote out all the numbers
Until they were overpowered by sleep
He wrote down the days until
He found himself
unobtrusive in his day of exile

He wrote and still writes the names
On every page
On every mountain
On every wall
Then he wrote water
On water
And the sea went on reading.
As the sky hems in a forest,
he chased the demons of action
and besieged them
And in the polished valleys of the sun
He recorded, with tranquillity, deep roots
spun by the nipples of the moon light.
He was strong when he wrote down those letters
Scattering them in the unyielding wind to sprout,
Flinging them into the sea
to dry up and swim back to him
like the eyes of fish.
He multiplied in the mirrors of space
like a sail.
Wearily, his shores,
waiting for something,
drew closer.

From a flame that stretches out in the dark
He will this time
Draw for a drowning man

whose lined hands he examines closely
two pieces of paper
which he leaves behind on land

He wrote everything that was outside himself
And still went on
Until consciousness
Gave birth to
a female swift as light
Leaving her scent behind her on the summits of his ripened years,
Seizing his eternal ink,
And, in the instinct of darkness,
Those stars hung in the pit
Scatter
Where the glitter
like the blood from the amplifier's wounds
drops dry unintentionally.

Translated by Laith al-Husain with Alan Brownjohn

## Muhammad 'Ubaid al-Harbi

## THE ACCURSED YEARS

Love was our unarmed child
On the usual days we offer it our windows
And
because houses
falsify our existence
we lavish on it our sensations
and disappear:
You to the blackboard of the road
　Wrapped up in gossip
and the ignorance of the schoolgirls
and I
to the ever-watching eyes
and the breasts that take in the chaff of words
What terrified years!
Years shorter than an elegy.

From which we return
to sleepy words in the sitting room
while we try to open the box of the sun
But the freezing wind alone prevails, conceited
Speaking about hope
Borrowing our condemned feet
then resting if it succeeds
in producing some warmth

Oh, what frozen years
Years longer than an elegy.

Translated by Laith al-Husain and Patricia Alanah Byrne

*Salih al-Harbi*

# NIGHT'S LONELINESS

In the Loneliness of Night
the grasshoppers
Gnaw at the chambers of my heart
The blood vessels seem to burst
The moon vanishes

In the loneliness of night
The streets are crowded
With white flowers
their pungent scent
fills the narrow places
They are plucked, then wilt
in human hands

In the loneliness of night
the clouds gather
the stars vanish
Only one face remains
followed
by rain showers.

Translated by Laith al-Husain with Alan Brownjohn

*Ashjan al-Hindi*

## MOON WARS

His moon is waning
and mine is full
What the sky chooses for its moons
will be final
We'd be eclipsed
if they brought us down to earth
We'd wane
We'd uncover
the vices of the world
get familiar
with earth's sins
Then we'd swear
that love up there
was purer
And when my footsteps tired
I'd let him carry half the earth's
burden of sands
we'd go together
prisoners of our mistakes
suspicious
falling into each other
dazzling
But utterly exhausted.

I'd ask him
About the nectar
of the question
how the secret kindles the mind
how it revolves on embers
how it is savoured
in the cups of the greedy
I'd ask him
whose fault it is
that we should be dragged

into the agony of fire
ourselves ablaze
and whose fault it is
in the slumber of the seas
who is the torturer
that laid the fire
who released the night among the tents.
Truly, love's face is clear now
Pour out your passion in the spirit
Or bid farewell to patience
Let's return to the road of crescents
if you like
And if you don't
draw the wound out of its sheath
And rest on its edge
Reason out with the dubious
The secretive,
The candid,
suppress the breasts of the suspicious
Release the siege from the clouds
And should you accuse me now of erring
I would not wonder
Would not weep
Would not go away
to waters other than that of the galaxies
I won't drink
from your tears
Why does my heart tell me
while the caravan is
behind the remnants of darkness
that questioning is my doom?
that you and I were neither fair
nor treated fairly
were not satisfied
with what the Bedouin moon has given us
and what we drank of its barrenness
and that we did not celebrate
what we had poured into its heart
and exposed of its faults
I ask myself
Why did the full moon tell me
that you are still loyal to its love
and that my accomplishment

cannot screen
the moon's full brilliance in your eyes
the magic of its power
because you are of the moon
you go back to it
and because I am the fruit
of oppression, barenness and clouds
of war and peace,
of dream and wakefulness
because I am crooked
the apple of temptation
the basil leaves of sin
when I am touched by oppression
I'll beget
only seeds of temptation
that invade your good seasons
defiling your hands
sharing with you the fertile flame
Because God has created me from my own fascination
from the yearning of your soul for love
and fashioned me
from the hunger of your spine for
sin
Thus God has fashioned me
Because I am from you
I'll come to you with all the grace
God has fashioned me with
With all that I've never revealed
never spoken
never obtained
I'll come to you from my grief
From my nothingness
From my pain
From my regret
My arms
My feet
Choosing from my own impetuousness
what I choose
and tempt you until evening
whimpers
and seek your temptation until you are
intoxicated
and the sins of men

dance and prance around you
and I'll slay them
planet
after planet.

Translated by Laith al-Husain with Alan Brownjohn

*Ibrahim al-Husain*

## WHENEVER THE MEMORY NEIGHS

Since roses left
My hand has remained exposed
Naked
to the world
Neither the waters
Nor the suns
in my depths
Were enough.

*** 

My soul shrivels
Whenever roses pass
that soul which once
was kindled by roses
leaving no shade
for anything else.

But for the roses
A short distance away
There is no meaning
For any plant
That lights up the depths.

In the pitch black darkness
Of night
A branch passes
Tempting our bodies' roses
As if roses were
The ecstasy of those drowning
Night flowing into night
As if we were weeping.

We are those whom dreams
Intoxicated,

We are those thrown into
Their vapour
With nothing but the margins
For our days
With nothing but the trunk of pain
For our fields.

So let the roses be
our minaret
Those roses which awoke
before us
leaving but the trail
of their fragrance
and shirts of sorrow.
They befriend now
our bed of tears,
the meal we prepare
for the harshness of night,
Against the petulant waves
Let them be
the merciful helm
We had bared our hearts
Our imperfections were
The only light.

Evening…
Between one distance and another
They prod on now
With smiles
Interspersing the valleys of silence
With cigarette ash
Decorating their eyes
With the wrinkles of their life
And resting.

Whenever the memory
Neighs in their soul
They rise,
Saddle their tears
And flow.

Translated by Ruanne Abou-Rahme (with the help of the editor)
and Patricia Alanah Byrne

## ONE DAY

Perhaps because we did not
Draw curtains around our dreams
Perhaps because we left them
exposed
Because we kept them
unprotected
just like this
that now, if we
should stretch our hands
at the limits
To our breasts
We'd find them
Empty.

## TOWEL

Midnight begins
I hold a large towel
And wipe the windows of the whole city
Go back to my room
Throw my body on a seat
Near the window
And face the night alone
Waiting for the scream.

Translated by Laith al-Husain and Patricia Alanah Byrne

## Hashim al-Jahdali

## BLOOD OF INDISPUTABLE EVIDENCE

- *Impulse*
In the bend of a lone branch
A child stuttered as he expressed his secrets
to the poem.
In a rose that dwells in the wind
There was my hiding place…
…
Why then shouldn't you be my sky?

- *A song*
At the sea, a child mends his dreams
A little girl kneads
from the earth of the dream
a horizon for rain
On the waves a pelican craves to scratch
the face of the horizon
On the young pelican some blood
…
On the sea there are also
The witnesses of my death.

- *A Life story*
Silence burns away
The old man comes and
the sea stabs him
obliterates his names
then forgets him
taking refuge in the salt
the iodine and the water
clad in nothingness
…
One day, death shall burn

- *Aloneness*

Alone and lonesome I was
In my speech there was agony
And I discovered
That I belonged
To the suns that shine
At the end of your days.
…
Alone
But you inhabit my blood.

- *Creation*

My girl, who blossomed from my ribs
has contained me at last.

Translated by Ruanne Abou-Rahme (with the help of the editor)
and Patricia Alanah Byrne

## *Nayif al-Juhani*

## AMBER AND GRASS

**1.**

> When light is obscured
> I am consumed
> By
> Images
> Fields
> Songs
> Returning
> From the day of water and
> The last land.
> This rain comes
> Like a bird
> From an open space
> Reducing me to nothing
> In degrees of silence
> Between one branch and another,
> Growing
> Like a vast wilderness between friends
> Like a wide distance stretching
> Through the caravans of history
> And its gleaming heap

**2.**

> Alone
> He was alone
> When song
> Burst out of him
> He was alone
> When he vanished
> Calling to the
> Distant wall

**3.**

> What the threads of the wind
> Have left
> to the doors
> I pledge to your face
> What names and
> Mirages
> Have seized
> I dedicate to your death.
> For my sorrow over you
> I pose my questions,
> Untangle the mist of lover's letters.

**4.**

> When the wind spreads shadows
> Behind the walls
> I am free to fall
> I am free to weep
> Or choose the water
> behind the barricade
> I am free to write
> Or abandon the words
> Crawling over the platform
> Of fire.

**5.**

> Now
> Here you are
> Hair coloured
> in henna[4]
> Squeezing
> Life from a
> Turbulent autumn
> Stirring
> The calm of things.
> Here you are
> Trying
> To give the
> Secrets of the earth
> To the water.

Translated by Laith al-Husain and Alan Brownjohn

*Ghassan al-Khunaizi*

## WOMAN OF LINEN AND COTTON

Was I still sleeping
When you dressed the balconies in the gift
of all those linen and cotton clothes?
There you were,
The moment day arrived,
Spreading out all those soaked garments,
the dew hovering on your hair, tied up and black,
Then you plunged into the darkness of the stairs.

In the sinking sun the shadows bend
and whisper to you
a flock of butterflies glides
You bend on the washing line embracing the sheets
Then turn in a half-circle
Towards the stairway.

Translated by Laith al-Husain with Alan Brownjohn

## SHADIYA

And you were asleep
I remembered that your father and mother
Married in Lebanon
Like mine who inhabit
the bliss of an old life
I never saw them together
and do not know
if a wedding picture
ever held the two of them
I never heard of the blind singer

Who sang for my mother on that day
I remembered,
Then realized that my mother's heart
Is a very deep chest

And you're asleep
Many birds twittered outside
And your face
lit the morning
I remembered that we talked
About what we have done
Remembered our life with quiet tenderness
Such great tenderness
How we contemplated a little boy
With the glow of your face
We were raising him, pampering him,
Waiting for him to speak

And you were asleep
I patted your face twice
And lit the house with the grace
Radiating
Wherever I went,
From one room to the next
A translucent light penetrated the place
I felt my soul emitting light
Where I touched you

And you were asleep
When my hand brushed your shoulder I knew
How I ache for you, for me
So I left you,
Went exploring myself
What lines had emerged
What I used to love in me
And where I counted my yearnings,
Arranged them,
Remembered how I collected each of them
And where in my body they had settled

And you were asleep
I remembered I was light

Like a shadow or a phantom
About to melt away in life

Translated by Jinan M. Coulter (with the help of the editor)
and Patricia Alanah Byrne

# EXPERIENCING THE SENSES

Beauty
Is lifted to the highest places that have visited us
And were gentle
In our ecstasy and in our song, and
In that intense numbness of the body:
The hand I know
The waist I have
The weeping when existence sways
Between light sleep – the deprivation from awakening-
and the distraction when awake.

Strange proximity!
As if the body flies a little
As if its bewilderment embraces all that's near
A slight elevation is too much for it
And the voice
Is bigger than the daze that had made
Its day long, very long.

No descriptions are whispered
Nor was weeping an alternative
To singing the praises of the body
When pain was tender and shocking
And time froze, the sensations explored
And the body is assailed by soothing water
When passion was a balsam against pain.

The body when it grieves,
And gets old from grieving,
Its joints turn blue

Groaning,
And at the height of pain
It recalls its youth and its pleasures.
Lo the hand that seeks to relieve
The body's decrepitude
Or when it stretches for a book
The hand that mourns.
Does death crawl over the fingers
When the body neither loves nor is loved?


Translated by Jinan M. Coulter (with the help of the editor)
and Patricia Alanah Byrne

*Ghaida' al-Manfa*

# For Open Cities,
## for the Sun and Lovers

The stream of my anger grows like a curse in my eyes
It colours all the distances around me
Drowns me in the naïve love showing on my face
And yet I remain
Myself, a night roving through the leaves of the world
Myself, sands lost under the tread of feet
And I remain
Enthralled by my love for you
Madly reflected in your eyes
An open city, for the sun and for lovers.

                    ***

This violence of mine ravishes the peace in my eyes
The flow of life captivates me, and I kneel and pray:
"Set me free from this silence imposed
around me
so I can run in the field of rejection,
speed my steps towards those outstretched hands, toy with
those that come to the shallow pond of my soul
but your love remains
those chains
that absolute presence.

                    ***

And always, I make a compact with myself
never to bury my dreams in the hollow of black rock
in the depths of the sea
in the anger of water
in the void of days, torn from the history of the living
For I live…a pain resting in its shroud
or a hope
dwelling on the horizon, in the folds of the clouds

an ambition which blows the horn of what will come
That is I
precursor of my time
I carry the knapsack of tragedy on the shoulder of day
Hide it
like a passion smothered in my face
buried in my eyelids
crucified
between the rhymes of my poems,

my name inscribed
in the corners of all the secret papers...

\*\*\*

I testify that I have loved hundreds of times
miscarried hundreds of times
That my children are dead
buried alive
I testify that I loved you like a wound washed in blood
bandaged with tragedy
Silence on my lips...a cactus plant growing
Breeding in the words of the settler in my desert
He who stole all the places where I would stop
Who chases me breathlessly into all the corners of my life
and I fear that my voice shall grow stony
that my papers shall be burned
And my million-fold love for all things shall be torn apart.

\*\*\*

But, despite refusal crying out across the horizons,
despite the pain proclaimed in your eyes, in so many eyes
Love will remain, though we hide it
a grandchild to death, orphaned,
And my love shall remain
a pulse in my letters, my words
and in my face, as it lies under the waters!!!

Translated by Bassam al-Hilu with Alan Brownjohn

## *Muhammad Sa'd al-Mish'an*

## LAILA

You ask me who I love but she is
    Beyond description
She's like the sun, yet the sun does not have
    Her tenderness
She's like water
    But its drinker is never satisfied
She's a consuming fire; my heart
    Lives on her love and burns in her love
I complain of her love to her and she
    Complains of my love to me, what mutual suffering!
We're on the two banks of a river of longing
    Each seeing consolation on the other bank
We wake up to anguish, we sleep with distress
    God! Hasten Thou our union or give us reprieve
Oh Laila, it is to God that I complain of those nights
    In agony like the nights of famous lovers.

But do not despair at this long separation
Time might design a meeting place for our love.

Translated by Bassam al-Hilu with Alan Brownjohn

*Ahmad al-Mulla*

# THE ROAD

He stopped me and said
A foot
That does not read carefully
Has no right to be
Proud of where it is going.

# WOOD

The tree that walks in the night
Is wounded
When people come out
it hides
in its own shadow.
Who will keep it warm?
Who will shelter under it?
Who will lean against it?
…
A wood, crying in the fields.

Translated by Laith al-Husain with Alan Brownjohn

## *Khalid Mustafa*

## RHYTHM I

Like a fresh heart we prepare
ourselves for some air to
breathe, but find the air
bribed also.

## RHYTHM II

The idea is neither obscure
Nor unwieldy
The damage is

In your head.

## A HEARTFELT PRAYER

In a state like this
When desire like heat rises
To the top of the room
Handel arrives with fingers
That make the cords yield, and
With a little tenderness,
Prepares the place for prayer.

Fall-Down
They're the ones splattered on leaning walls: our words
And in the scanty corridors
There is screaming
Somewhere a simple prayer is carried near us

We are not yet ready
To block it off.

The earth in its slow sliding
Announces that
Corruption
Is the ladder
To KNOWLEDGE.

Translated by Laith al-Husain and Alan Brownjohn

## 'Abd al-Rahman al-Qa'oud

## A FORGOTTEN FRAGMENT OF NIGHT

When I was still a child
and had not yet mastered the arts of expression
nor savored words
had not yet been ensnared by the caravan of poetry
or overwhelmed by the perplexing babble of the twentieth century
when Hegel's dialectic had not whetted my appetite
When I was still a child
All lips
Teeth still too weak to meet in a kiss or to bite with;
A child unable to calculate differences in numbers.

Cunningly, my mother
Spun one tale after another
To keep sleep hovering over my head
In the hope that my eyelids would droop with the first tale
She wipes from my face the remains of the dying day
And, spinning to prepare for the chill of winter,
Says
"There was a time, O apple of my eye, a noonday long ago
When the fiery orb was driving people to delirium,
When the burning sand was sticking to their feet
And the only water was a salty sweat,
A man laboring in the desert
Spotted a forgotten fragment of night
I don't know, said the storyteller,
Or was it an exiled fragment?
Was he a media expert my son?"
"I don't know, Mother, but in the story teller's time
All the broadcasts
Were blaring white lies that could amaze even a genie
So, go on Mother, with the story of the abandoned fragment of night."
"O Son, are you still not submerged in the sea of dreams?"
"No, mother

I am enamored of words
So do not forbid me what is quite allowed."
"I shall not
I shall not, my son!
The night became fractured
And forgot its fragment
The fragment still lay there by itself
I know nothing of the night except that the storyteller said:
The night was invaded
At its weakest point
By a fragment of light
And they are now in combat with each other
As for its fragment of night
It has turned into an ogre
That makes the devil's hair stand on end
It seeps through the crack in the door
Everywhere
And threatens anyone who would embrace and love
Or flirt with the morning light
and wrap the darkness around his amorous yearnings."

At the sound of the last syllable
My eyelids closed and all was absolute oblivion
except for that one forgotten fragment

The years chased each other
The dark painted my memory
A question stabbed my mind like tongs
That greedily searched and rummaged
And found no answer.

One blue winter
with night fading
The voice grown weary
deep in the heart of silence
My oars floating in the stillness of time
A dream tore off my cover and revealed to me
a path where my father knelt in prayer
And there!
A fragment of light appeared
A flaming ball rolled
And with incredible speed
Disappeared round a bend beyond my praying father

I woke up and remembered
That forgotten fragment of night
And I recited a brave verse:
If any time in my life,
 The night is forgotten
A fragment of light appearing
In a dream
Will remind me of it again.

Translated by Bassam al-Hilu and Alan Brownjohn

*Lateefa Qari*

# WHICH OF THE TWO IS ME?

Does my sorrow move you?
Then speak to me in words that will soothe my madness
and rein in my doubts
the air screams with my sins
fixes them into the pores
of my skin
throws them onto my eyes
The air sways with me
slaps me
undermines my certainty
Does my death disturb you?
Then wrap yourself in the farthest stars
Scare away the darkness of windows
Prepare
the Pleiades of the night
for my heart
And shatter my calm
I never lost myself in the eyes of a stranger
I never melted like wax
My words never made bracelets for my heart
How can my words create bracelets
to adorn a female wrist?
And how could my words dissemble love
in the clothes of a woman!
How did the moments leave me like birds
To peck the eyelashes
Of a woman?

Numb expressions frighten me
I never made peace with
Dreamy words
I never succumbed to the temptation of words
Never savored their frivolity

All the mists in my hand, I never drove them away
All that came out of me was strange,
Its meaning was strange
What wilderness should I seek out?
which of the two am I, my friend,
Which face have I betrayed?


I am the sin and sin is part of me
When I write poems heavy with nectar
My spirit is loud with complaint
I am driven by insatiable thirst,
My song sparks in my veins
I embrace the shades
That reveal the jasmine hidden in eyes like glass
A sea surrounds me
And a sharp world fit for the times
To which I don't belong
How can I leave my world, live in it like a stranger?
And how does it abandon me
Suddenly
When I forget it for a while?
And how do I pray
And walk on earth dazed with my communion?
Kneel down to absence
I never got drunk with words that tempted me
with words that I did not deny.

Strange climate, strange sorrow
As if the edge of my soul were thick with clouds
Let my pain be inscrutable like an echo
Let my yearning be shattered
Let my sighing choke
I'm tired of hiding behind a cloud of dust
I am tired of my breaking down altogether
I lean on the wrist of a woman
And say: expose my desire for madness
What will be will be.


Translated b y Bassam al-Hilu with Alan Bownjohn

## *Fatima Al-Qarni*

## RESISTANCE

Nocturnal habit that was her
ritual began
with thoughts, then moved
to the moon, then to poetry,
And in the end to the peacefulness of worship.

Since the face of the universe revealed
No colour, its blackness covering all,
Since the laws of futility dominated,
Since scorching flames were generous,
the hopeless dream, now remote, embraced
Its own neutrality,
She no longer adopted anything.
She no longer knew how to bury
vacuous tear in the folds of her pillow.

## MY DREAM

My youthful dream is still in its prime
Still young, and preserves life's ecstasy:
My celebration of living, my songs, the echoes of my heart,
of my whole being,
And all that has deviated and remains with me.

Why shouldn't I approach that tender lonely echo
If I remembered that I
Am still a female,
A woman unlike any other.

# A CITY

They counted a thousand streets
in it. And when I came to it, I
Walked every night those thousand streets.
How is it that I did not find...
That life did not abandon its harsh vigilance
And allow
Our footsteps to meet?


Translated by Laith al-Husain and Patricia Alanah Byrne

*Ghazi al-Qusaibi*

# THE MOON AND THE GYPSY QUEEN

Here am I, prostrate
experienced in defeat
Watching misshapen spiders
Weave their web across my ribs
Watching morning and evening
Continue their sterile journey
The sun – my sweet generous sun –
Refuses to light even a candle
in the cellar of my soul…one single candle
And the night? – where is the old intimacy? – envelops me…as if I were a
crime
And where is my favored childhood companion
Who so closely shared my tale on through the night
my sibling moon?

       ***

Laid down am I on the earth
Watching the gypsies
Walk through the fields, consuming all they see
even the flowers, and the birds
Laid down am I on the earth
Salma's robe a stain of
blood and flies
beside me
searching for my manhood
watching the gypsies
ascend to the sky with their lances
to tear up the moon
divide it among them
turn it into an earring to adorn
the gypsy queen.

       ***

Lover of cornstalks and flowers
what did you do when the locust arrived?
what will you reap in the harvest seasons?
Companion of the night, is there
after the funeral of the moon
anything left but to keep watch into the night?
No! I was no coward
I wrote a few words
in the wake of the flowers
a few words
about the martyred moon
and tomorrow I shall craft an epic
about the return of the birds
and our new dawn

***

My manhood
Shall remain…even if the gypsies shear away
my manly hair…
shall remain…even if the gypsies violate Salma…
even if her purity
is trodden down

***

"Life will triumph"
Since ancient times,
poets have said
"Right that springs from the will to live shall triumph
the words shall triumph
because they believe in life."
so write poems of struggle,
write! The age of miracles has not passed
Even inanimate objects might become angry
Even soil, water, plants might rise up
against the invaders

***

I see her from afar
old and graying like the devil…deformed
like the night of the frightened,
Salma's ring glittering
on her hand
my moon burning around her ear

while writers cry out in warning
"life shall triumph"

      ***

Moon, I wonder…will you ever return?
Will you return if
after your departure
we plant candles
in our vacant breasts
on our ribs
if we water them with the
tears time has left us
will you return if we pledged ourselves
to believe in
the right of each to say what they will
to be what they will?

      ***

Moon, how will you return
when we are not repentant
when we have lost faith?


Translated by Bassam al-Hilu with Alan Brownjohn

## *Hasan al-Sab'*

### LONGING

"I have a longing"
I know for what and I know why?
A longing for a palm tree which
when the desert dries
it waters it
with a thousand small desires.
A palm tree, the greenest, boldest
of all trees,
A palm tree burnished by the noonday sun
A palm tree which stretches most boldly of all
A palm tree, its head in the sky
Its sorrows deep in the sands of Arabia.
I have a longing for it....
And I know why.

### MOON OF SEVILLE

Star of Seville
In whose presence language falls to its knees
My heart was lost to me on the road
I search now in the glances of the women who watch my silence
for eyes as bright as a moon
The corners that escaped
the hot breath of the desert
the corners which left us drunk
this was where poetry
captured its lovers.

I search in the glances of the women who
watch my silence
for the eyes of a moon

A tourist from New York, laughs in the palace courtyard
  While my heart searches the palace stone
  for its longed-for past
It was right that I should yearn.

      ***

If only I had Scheherazade's imagination to escape the trap
Don Quixote's madness to fight the world's windmills
The Trojan horse to crash into the space of justice
Baudelaire's lips to pluck desire from the narrow curves
  of the city
The freedom to write verses of love
to a distant woman.

Translated by Laith al-Husain and Patricia Alanah Byrne

'Abdallah al-Safar

# THE MEAL OF STRANGERS

**1.** *We Did Not Know*
> We did not know
> That nights were heavy
> We did not know,
> That we were only counting the days
> We did not know,
> That our bones were breaking,
> Their echo shaking the wilderness

**2.** *Broken Image*
> You will go and the road
> Will be crowded
> The road will be crowded
> And you will go
> The road will be crowded
>
> And the passage will be
> A splintered image
> Shrouded with our bones

**3.** *Bring Forth The Knife*
> He did not try howling
> Did not saddle the horse of temptation
> – Why are you adorned with regret?
> Bring forth the knife
> Here is the neck
> That yearns for it
> And a ready mat
> For what do you wait?

**4.** *The Meal Of Strangers*
> Where is the open road?
> Where we can sit and complain,

Exile dispersed us
Now, ice is the meal of strangers.

**5.** *A Boorish Wilderness*

Was he translating his heart
When he granted his blood
To the road?
Snatching the lamps
in a boorish wilderness
They did not ask
About their oil.

**6.** *A Song*

The song shakes the windows
Reawakens the road
But our putrid blood
What do we do with it?
Do not call out, there is
No one there

Translated by Ruanne Abou-Rahme (with the help of the editor)
and Patricia Alanah Byrne

## 'Abdallah al-Saikhan

## A MYTH

The Time: A time that's passed
The Place: Our village, lying on the sandy hill
The Occasion: A woman from our village called Laila who fell in love
The Actors: The village chief…some village men
They said: "This beauty brimming in Laila's eyes…
where did it come from?
This beauty tattoo, glittering always in the palm of gypsy women
Who painted it on her hands?
This anger clear in the faces of the village men
Who grew it in her eyes?
Who taught Laila to dwell in the breast of a man?
To mix with his breath?
 To forget a woman's modesty?
Who taught her
To draw this passion coming down from Rayes to Abha?
In this place we hide our faces
behind our hands if
Love is mentioned
Or if some lad asked what the colour of love was
What, village Shaikh, must we do?"

Standing in the middle of the circle the chief said
Why not cut out the roots of love
and be saved?!
There stands its tree planted on the road of the village
Cut it down to its deepest root
So that no other Laila
Can ever emerge
 to dwell in the breast of a man.

The narrator said:
A branch of that tree resisted
and grew,
Laila,

in the heart of the night,
would slip out,
to water it
with the love that dwells in the pupils of her eyes

And it grew and grew
Until it became a tree
Its branches stretching
From that village
To cover the whole earth
Whoever eats from it
is afflicted with love
Whoever sits in its shade
falls in love with the first girl
he meets
of all the girls of this earth.

Translated by Bassam al-Hilu with Alan Brownjohn

*Ahmad al-Salih*

# NIGHTMARISH DREAM

A vision stopped me within the dream
I never saw a dream like this before
I saw, my dear:
   That I stood at all the doors
   Where people were laden with questions
and answers
Feeling deep fear,
I tried to open the first door
But ended as I started
I neither entered,
Nor got out
   And at the last door
   I had already forgotten
   My camel's saddle
   My village
   A picture of my village
   A verse of poetry I'd written to my love
   My friend's sword
   And a wise saying I'd learned from my father.
Day continued and I turned round
And asked all those who had passed
On the road
One by one
The road said
   One…onn…onn…
I got frightened from this repetition
   And woke up
Looked right and left
   But there was no one…no one
I looked behind my back
My eyes failed me
I walked…my camel could not return
And the horizons
Kept forcing the mirage
With more mirage.

I threw out all my worries
in the thickness of clouds
  Oh wise friend!
  My journey which was aborted
  Oh wise friend!
And whatever wisdom it contained!
For people, during these days of relapse
Suspect even their clothes.
The heart, Oh dear friend,
Is the victim of grief.
I remember my love, for only her tenderness
gives me warmth,
her words falling on the ears, full of anguish,
like soft, generous rain.
  I remember her silence waiting for her love
In the shade of a palm tree
My beloved has abandoned slumber.

I looked onto the horizons
  Waited for her voice…her light
  Waited for her shadow stretching to the sky
  Waited…waited
  I waited for someone coming on a Buraq[5]
White as the morning,
  With open wounds
  Who would enliven the dead
Oh dear one, still I stand on the ruins of the camps
So please give us your notion
  of what you see
  You'd be trustworthy to consult
  For with you all visions end. Tell us!
Truly we are frightened of this dream vision.

I opened my palm to be read,
I tried this once or twice
But could find no answer for the nightmare
I then closed my palm and thought
  And got no answer
  The expression eluded my thoughts
I tested my wisdom, in case…
  But found no answer still…only your knowing suggestions

But doubts intermingled with fears
I gave the wine seller to drink from
  His own old urns
I bought all residual drinks
I broke the pitcher of wine
Poured it on my vest
And did not bathe after
Then I came to you…full of rain
Lovely maidens pushing me
away from temptation…I came to you
  When the landmarks had lost the way
With you…all words end
All dreams open up their secrets
And the curtain is drawn.

## from CONFESSIONS

I concede now
That grief mixes in children's joys
That it peels off the down of apple peels
Tears off the flowers' crowns
I concede
  That I have melted my passions
  On the petals of roses
Like drops of dew
  Sang rhythmic poems
  Opened the doors of the heart
  Where we could embrace
But found that the doors
  were too narrow for our love
  they could not endure what we hid of
  desire, and so we would return
  to tidy up our losses.
I confess now that I experienced love on
the hills of snow
And over the fire's flames
That I know nothing
That I cannot explain
The mystery of the universe
I do not know

How rain can kill our village's threshing grounds
How they can devour the goodness
   In young people's looks
How it can kill the smile
   In the eyes of lovely women
And in the dance of the feasting crowd.

I confess now
That whenever I open my eyes
To look at someone else,
I see you in the face of every lovely maid
And I embrace you.
…
I confess now that
Before you
I was a letter on a mute lip
That after you
I've become a verse of poetry
Sung by desert caravans
…
I enter our enchanted world
Sometimes savage like a Tatar prince
Who'd break the most precious things
I confess now that in you
I have avenged the wound
   So stubborn to a cure,
That in your hands
I am the worshipper and the sinner
Oh mistress of this love
A poet's love is taboo
In Bedouin tradition
And I am that tradition,
A reaper of all sins.

What does it mean
Oh you who have the right to command
   and to forbid
that the lover should confess
should spread his notes to others
should announce the secret of his love
What does it mean
That he should recite
To people in pain

His poems of warm words
Spread among them his poetry
The sin of one sin after another
Do not blame me…I shine
   within the awe of poetry where the tragic dwells
Oh how I yearn, my lady,
For our love to become my tragedy
Where I will hang onto the fringes of lightning
And enter the depths of the waves
And begin my voyage across the twilight
stretching over the horizons
   but I fear
Oh my inspiration
   That intimate moments shall reach their end with you
I confess now
   That I have exploded the time of anguish
So give me your lips
   Let's sow the seeds of longing there.


Translated by Laith al-Husain and Patricia Alanah Byrne

*Husain Suhail*

## VOICE AND JOURNEY

Prepare some tales…
Gather the young maidens
Tell them the story of the child
  Who had wearied of waiting.
Don't worry now
  Tell them he was a sail, reaching high
The grey time that once was
has receded into yesterday…
when the night was paralyzed, and the sun's sword
was slaying the day.
Gather all the young maidens
Tell them how that child
  has disappeared across the face of the deserts
…
raising love
  A lighthouse and a slogan
Tell them he's lived in the sea, and loves the oceans
That he's unwavering
like the sea when waves heave and toss
That he is deep and patient
like a rooted tree
standing firm in the wind,
that even hurricanes
fail to bring him down.

Translated by Bassam al-Hilu with Alan Brownjohn

*Jasim al-Suhayyih*

## MY FATE IS WRITTEN BY YOUR COMB

My life is the journey of your Bedouin hair when you comb it
Stretching from the beginning of the desert to the end of cities
 I count it, its richness that besieges me, its ageless span
I am chained to its braids, a pawn to them
They swim on your shoulders and I am the ship
That arrives through the waves to discover their buried legends,
transcending the frost of a monotonous life
bringing warm surprises
Never betrayed by longing, I live by its steady pulse
The pearls on your brow let loose the precious gems
Tell your hair to limit its distance when you comb it
For behind it my life follows the sad road of night
Have pity on the comb, give it serenity
That's not your hair, that is the secret you do not understand
The world is disorder in my eyes when you spread it out
and order again when you tie it up
And when you curl it I see the wrinkles of my life
It's not your hair, it's my fate which you write with your comb.


Translated by Bassam al-Hilu with Alan Brownjohn

## *Ahmad Sa'd al-Tayyar*

## LANGUAGE

What enchantress
Veiled me behind her tresses in my youth
Then let me part with her scent
At the advent of autumn?

What moon
Gleamed in the bosom of darkness
So that my first steps
Would falter
into the trap of love?

What dream
Beckoned me to its details
To let me be wiped out by
the sun of awakening?

What impulse gripped me
To plant my flowers
In front of the distant shores?

What yearning surprised me
then flew far with me
away from the city walls?

What fields of language I invaded
To yield for me
the summer fruits
in the season of ash?
And what sun bathed me with its fountains
So I remained alone
Drifting at the edges of the orbit?

What harbour
Whispered in the hearts of those

passing through it:
"You'll never return?"

What little vessel
Toyed with the waves
to become a unique history for the storm?

And what warm tear
Fell tonight
to turn the valleys of life
a cascade of weeping?


Translated by Jinan M. Coulter (with the help of the editor)
and Patricia Alanah Byrne

# Muhammad al-Thubaiti

## SANDS

He embraced me
Then stopped me in the sands
Called me: Muhammad
And shone clearly to my eyes.
He said:
"You're twin to the palm tree
You've embraced the lonely star
And heightened the tidings
They've acquiesced to the secret of parting
And revered the commandments."
Fruit of the poor
Fruit of poets
You exchanged drinks:
innocent and blessed magic
"You're twin to the palm trees
This which the medals claim
And that which the orchards covet
That to whose virgin orbit you entered
And that in whose virgin limbs you abided
Autumn expectations
Spring completion
You're twin to the palm trees
One recurs between seasons
The other repeats in songs:
I befriend the streets
The sands and the orchards
I befriend the palm trees
I befriend the town
The sea and the ship
and the beautiful shore
I befriend the nightingales
The opposite house
Music and birds' twitter

I befriend the stones
The illuminated square
and the long season.

"You and the palm trees are two children
One a witness among men
And the other depicting beauty
You're twin to the palm trees
You've become their mate
And they've become your hands
You've become a cover to them
And they've become your sky
They've seen the Pleiades sink
And you've seen the crescent rise
Blood flows from their clusters
To the veins
The language of lightening is revived:
What rhythms do you perfect?
What ink do you seek?"
"My master is no more master
My hand is no more my own."
He said:
"You're far as water of the sky!"
I said:
"I'm as near as the dew."
Space and cities,
Wilderness and scarcity
Fruits and orchards
Cactus and patience
The bride of ships
Night and sea
Verse and prose."
He said:
"Oh Palm tree!
Weak trees slander you,
The meekest pegs malign you,
But you still stand high in God's space
With mythic fruits
And great patience."
He said:
"Oh Palm tree!
Do you elegize your times
Or your place?

Or did your heart defy you
When passion took hold of you
And you rebelled
And in the heart of Mecca you wrote
Those penetrating words
with crescents glowing around your face
and poems a splendid trap in your hands
With night a sea of apprehension
And day a poem which belongs
only to its creator
the creator of the music of the spheres
Oh you who've gone deep into exile
Be safe
If your foot should trip
Be safe
if the eyes of those following
your footsteps
should find you
I gaze deep into Medina
but do not see you
there's nothing but
the smell of the araak tree.

*The Second Text:*

I go straight to meaning signified
I squeeze the nectar from the fire
And get my fill
I sip from the water of blame
pass between roads and dangerous places
where's no sea to gather my scattered sails
no horizon to contain my strewn wings
no trees
in which my doves can take refuge
I go to the gist of meaning
Between my fingers
The roads entwine
and the times merge
the mirage takes leave of the drink
my shadow
is thrown
in front of me
I deflower the virgin stars
Accumulate worries

And relish the thrill of fear when
it moves from the numbness
of the veins
to the bones.
I roam the wilderness of night
Until I am blessed
by the sunrise of the mind
while still sleepless
and thirsty.
– I've seen… Haven't you seen?
– My eyes were abandoned by sleep
the Canopus star has thrown
its heart in the hand of the sun
and left
The Pleiades is invaded by
a full moon
from Damascus.
Ah moon! You guide to the mind
And its pride
Love of its inner secret
Its colt
The sanctuary of the tribe
its hair
the length of the braids.

In the place of pitfalls
Between renegades and warring ships
My patience
protested
my stay
became anxious
And I went to the core
Of the meaning
Gazing closely
At the features of the beloved
To give her a name
But the names were no match
For her traits
I found she was my homeland
The thrill of her voice gives
Me throbs at my heart
Her glorious presence is my wish
Her pure nectar

My wine
I looked into the eye of the sky
And the sparks of thirst abated
My clouds opened to pour with rain
To those who sleep
with hunger
Those who announce
That which had been folded
To those who look forward
to the palm trees
to the sandy dunes
to the northern wormwood
to the breezes from the Saba winds
to the birds from the verdant hills
to the sun
to the mountains of Hijaz
and to the Tihama sea.


                        Translated by Bassam al-Hilu with Alan Brownjohn

*Ali al-ʿUmari*

## A MIRROR

You bend every night
See the coarseness that has afflicted your face
Touch forgotten years on your shoulders
Determine who you are
Then slip outside, leaving words
That shimmer in the blackness of the room.

## COCK

What has stirred your soul
To make you shriek at this hour of night
Where the neighborhood has eroded of its people
And sleep pervades through iron windows
And no one
but you
Vibrant with shrill melody?

Translated by Jinan M. Coulter (with the help of the editor)
and Patricia Alanah Byrne

*Thurayya al-'Urayyid*

## QUESTIONS

"Your mystery compels me to ask you questions:
Are you still you!
Enveloped in longing
hemmed in by a near horizon
by perpetual thirst
and, like a bee heavy with honey
still unyielding?
Will you die standing
raging
still looking for your homeland?"

Here you go, laying down questions like incense
assailing me:
How can a woman
– crushed by the ramparts of myth-
how can a woman
dare to differ?
How can a woman who
– even before
you pour out all your fears about her
you pour out all your proud passions-
say that which is never spoken
say it without trembling!

You're the homeland?
But you drown in old conventions:
Haya's glimmering lips
'Abla's tents…the vicissitudes of Khawla's camp[6]
the pomegranate breasts of a naïve lass

Laila…and Laila…and Laila[7]
Laila who did not say "yes" to him
And Laila who forgave but never confessed

And the other who had no flavour
The other who had no face
The other who had no name
The other who had no words
Who now dared
To take another path.

But here we women are
In our long silence
We now hear a choking
a wailing of winds
console ourselves with a song of parting
and do not stop
to ask
Him whom we knew as our own
whom we called love and home
where do we stand with him?

Are we satisfied
With the eyes in which sleeplessness found a home?
With the holes we patch in the houdah's curtains
During the heat of the storm

We ask
Who shall burn or be burned?
It was not given that I,
or her, or her, or her
could choose the firestorm
or the road that winds around the neck,
which narrows to the footsteps
along the route of those
who go astray
We can't read the horizon, but
we ask it:
when will the rains come
And how do the storm winds blow
the birds fly high, or drop and settle?
And how do the roads tell all these tales
And murder our words in the telling?

But I do not exaggerate
And I do not lie when I
complain

of the yearning in the hidden desires,
How can birds forget the dizziness of exile?
…
Enough for you that silence announces its season
And enters the battle
time trembles between lips and sinking waters
abolishes our features in the mirrors of reality
and in masks.
Scruples are deaf to the details,
deaf to words,
Scruples believe you are walking in the dark:
"And how will you return
When the night is pitch black and you
Have no companion?
You'll get lost between love and sleeplessness
Night bears the secret of burning
On the crossroads."

Are you humming a song on this morning of departure?
between me and me and the splinters of my soul
Distances turn restless
A locked moment devours our dreams
We plant our feet in reminiscences about what was,
About the days of longing and the days of lament
The melody of a woman in chains
droning a song in retreat.

I am not celebrating a woman in whom I burn.
Is the moment of death like oblivion?
Is it like awakening
Like running in the pulse of the homeland
And its stunning ecstasy?
Am I braver than you
To remain on this murderous field?
If we are the death of the echo in the echo,
the narrowing of the road,
do not fear
that I cross the distance of silence for you
to accept it.
Everyone is tired, and words
are torture
I plunge the dagger of truth
in the answer
and spill the blood of the ignorant.

I have this one question
I have this question for myself alone:
When will you wake up
When will you know
that you are all the meanings and their shadows
all the imagined thoughts?
Answers do not have their definite moment
It is time I close the register of suffering and questions
I will,
Most certainly I will
Return proud,
Assured of a homeland,
The echo of the coming moment
Rooted in you.


## Name it What You Like

Were this that exists between us
Not there between us,
Name it what you will:
A dialogue between the butterflies and the flowers
a child's desire for the universe
Sand grains dissolving in water

This, that at a distance
possesses us…inhabits our dreams
An apprehension sweeping through us
Directing us
As our bodies are
Surrounded by the earth
As our spirits, drunk with joy,
Reach for the sky
Were this
that is larger than you and me
Larger than our reason and our calculations
Than the knowledge of the caravan leader
Than our convictions
Than our features and the burdens engendered within us
Masks that we wear
But which don't mask us
Our songs in the morning
our hymns at night

This strange sensation,
this wondrous
Solemn
Awesome sensation
we know it so well
and, into ecstasy take
the whole universe into ourselves
so that we ourselves were here
before time was here
so that what is distant is also near
so that any stranger
is also the beloved
nearer to us than ourselves
overflowing within us
bursting with desire
with tenderness
calling out
If this feeling
That you are of me and I am of you
Was never there,
My friend,
What would remain of us
Such as we are,
Husks on this earth
At which emptiness eats away at us.

Translated by Laith al-Husain with Alan Brownjohn

### 'Abdallah Salih al-'Uthaymeen

## LEGEND

When I was a boy
I would listen, enchanted, to legends
I was not the only one to listen enchanted
To legends
Every child in my country
Listened to his grandmother
repeating strange legends
and believed. them
Everything grandmothers said
the children believed
bats that turned into lions
snakes becoming pigeons
she was not trying to deceive us
with pretty words

*** 

I traveled across all the years of my life,
stage after stage
and even now,
with the hair on my head
nearly grey
I still sometimes hear strange legends
And tales retold
To make me believe.
For almost twenty years
I have been listening to over and over to fictions,
And strange tales,
Allegations turning wrong into right
Turning oppression into justice
Almost twenty years ago
They were telling me
That Israel was wrong

So I advanced into the arena
to wrestle for my rights
except that
each time I retreated,
I was denied victory

And once again I listen to the elders
Revealing to people the secret of the defeat
With words that concealed
half the truth
One day they would say: treason
the next day they called it: intervention
recently they mentioned casually
That I am off to an honorable battle
assuring for future generations
dignity, a glorious victory
reclaiming the land and justice for my scattered people

Like a ravaging fire
I advanced into battle
Except that
after I wrote as history
legends of my steadfastness
And the signs of my victory heralded the dawn
They stopped me in my tracks
And with Kissinger's devices
Plunged a dagger into my back
Began talking of peace and compromise
My transparent rights
now betrayed
Yesterday's wrong is today's right
Yesterday's liar today's honest man
Yesterday they said:
No peace
With the enemies of the Arabs
Today I sing
the praises of
The peace proposals

Yesterday they said...
Yesterday they said...
Everything said yesterday has changed
All the things they said

Were only legends retold
And I
am forever submerged,
caught between
my grandmother's legends
from my boyhood
and the elders' new legends for today

All that has changed is
that once upon a time
I listened to legends enchanted
And now
I listen to legends
with dismay.


Translated by Bassam al-Hilu with Alan Brownjohn

## *Ibrahim al-Wazzan*

## AWAKENING

I will come to you
as a witness,
clad in clouds
To kindle a hope
of harvest
in your eyes,
To awaken in you
an answer
that vies
with all questions
impossible
for words
or patterns
to describe.
In the past
Or the future
There is nothing
But
One
Single
Utterance
Beloved, you
Are existence itself
Against the treachery of
Time!
I will raise my head
abandon myself
vision,
mind,
and soul,
to become in you
that young and innocent heart.

Translated by Ruanne Abou-Rahme (with the help of the editor)
and Patricia Alanah Byrne

---

1. Abu al-Tayib al-Mutanabbi, one of the greatest Arab poets in classical times. He had to flee Egypt when his relationship with its ruler, Kafour, soured.

2. A famous Lebanese singer, very popular in the whole Arab world. uiuhui

3. 'Urwa ibn al-Ward, from the 'Abs tribe, was one of the most famous outlaws of pre-Islamic times, known for his courage, sense of social justice and selfless generosity "I divide my body in many bodies." He would go on raids, then divide the spoils among the poor and hungry. He was also a fine poet. Salma was his wife

4. From time immemorial, men in Arabia used henna to colour their white hair.

5. The Buraq is the mare described to have flown the Prophet Muhammad on his nocturnal journey from Mecca to Jerusalem to the heavens where he saw and spoke to God. Then mare became here the symbol of speed and achievement.

6. These are names of women. Classical Arabic poets sang about the lovely maidens they saw and loved in the various migrating camps. Much of the poetry, in the poem's overtures, spoke of those various maidens: Khawla, Laila, Abla, Mayy, Asma' etc. who disappeared with their tribe moving in search of pastures. The memories evoked by the vicissitudes of the abandoned camps were a fixed convention in the old poetry.

7. Laila is the most symbolic name for a loved woman in Classical Arabic poetry, particularly in cases of failed, unrequited or intercepted love.

# Part II

## Short Stories

*Muhammad 'Alwan*

# That's How the Story Starts

The wind burrowed deep into the sand, swept through trees bare of their leaves. The wind – the wind beat down the faces one by one. The sun moved far off, hid itself behind a cloud, and the cloud itself raced away. Lifting up its rims, it scudded off, gathering its last raindrops to let them fall over the sea.

A drop escaped from the barred face of the cloud, which fled the desert noon to restore life. It revived ecstasy in the earth, spreading green in a bush that had waited a thousand years.

The desert: a place born from everything. The land, the sand, the bush. Through a hole in a lizard that had died of thirst, the sun returned once more. The mirage areas burned, the visions mixed one with another. Then they all rose, so very slowly, above the fractured horizon, as if mounting toward heaven. The footsteps tramped down, no warning given – just like this desert's storms. The camel dropped at last, bereft of food; of the track, of vision. No one was left there in the yellow circle, except for a lost man and a pregnant woman.

Two tongues wooden from thirst. The smell of death approached the exhausted bodies. The desert widened – became narrow. It narrowed, smothering the hope in the eyes, leaving nothing but mirage. The shadow of a distant tree stood up like the headstone on a black grave. The bare feet trod the burning sands. The sun felt the vast sky too small for it, choosing, instead, to enter the head of the pregnant woman. The eyes were weary.

The woman felt her swollen belly. Then she wept, sinking to her knees and raising her arms.

"What has he done wrong?" she cried. "What has he done wrong?"

The thick sand, the waves of sand, the bare trees quickly swallowed up her cry. A tear trickled down on to her cheek, reached the edge of her lip, and the wooden tongue was stuck out to take hold of it before the sun could drink it.

Place became void there. Time became void. The vicious circle had no end. The sky moved off as if nothing was left any more but loss, and the sand.

She could walk no further. The man tried to help her, but it was useless. She dropped to the ground, then cried out, terrified:

"Hold me up. I've no heart left any more, no human hope left – no longing left, of the thirsty earth, to drink in water. Hold me up. Is this wretched child to leave one grave, only to enter a wider one? Hold me up!"

The man made a jerky movement. He took hold of the woman who was clutching at him, gazed at her as she thrashed this way and that, eating the sand, seizing hold of the ground with a hand that shook and sweated, desperate to keep a hold. She looked up at the sky, searching for the shining sun.

"Rain," she cried, "stop! Rivers, stop! Waters thirsty for the times of love, stop! I'm being purified, in this desert, from all past sins and all sins to come. I'm drinking from my thirst."

The woman turned, and the man looked towards the corners of the desert. He tried to whisper something. Nothing returned but the echo. The bush was receding. The camel had fallen, the woman had fallen, and the man was alone, scouring the distances through a single eye. Taking hold of the woman's dress on one side, he began to drag her. He strove to reach the bush. All day he walked, carrying his burden, his wife and the child stirring inside her. The thirst reached his eyes, sucking the water from them.

The moment had come. The flagship was adrift. The moment, undetermined by time or place, moved in an unknown orbit now. The man cried out. The child cried out. The mother, the earth, sank in the rain of a dream, watered by unseen rivers.

The man held the child as he would have held a fish pulled from the water. The child was turning, crying out, looking for a full breast. The man was still dragging the dead woman and carrying the child. The child uttered the cry of life in the lonely desert.

The breasts of the sheep and camels were full. He felt his face – the hair on his head. He tried to swallow, but he couldn't. The smell of earth filled every part of his body. He remembered the child, and the woman in her tomb in a desert cave. He remembered himself. And then he fainted.

He felt water on his lips. Coldness swept right through him. He couldn't open his eyes. Was this death? Was it life? How dreary they were.

The phantoms leapt. He heard a whisper. Slowly, all visible things began returning. He saw them all. They had healthy faces, all of them, as though they were all basking in bliss. They were laughing. One of them burped. The others were racing behind their horses.

The tomb – the cave – the desert. The man leapt up and tore himself from their hands. He stared at the faces all around him.

"Where's my wife?" he cried. "Where's my child?"

The corners of the desert responded. The people walked the distance of illusion, of the probable. When they reached the bush near the cave, the father – the killer and the killed – walked in. The woman in the cave was just half a body now, full of milk for a hungry baby thrust out by death into life. One eye looked at the husband

– the killer and the killed – then closed. The body was laid into the ground, into the sand. A heap of sand met eyes filled with amazement and fear.

In a big house, the fat man pressed the TV switch, turning off the set. He gazed at the body of the woman lying on the bed. Night embraced the house. The room embraced the guard.

"I had too much to eat and drink tonight," the fat man said.

He burped. Then he winked at her, with lust in his eyes. He moved towards her. "Do you believe that story?" he asked.

She winked back at him.

"Let's forget about all that," she said. "Turn off the light, and let's start our own story."

*'Abdallah Bakhashwain*

# EARLY AWAKENING

He found himself suddenly sitting up in his bed, his head clear, not a hint of sleep in his eyes. He stared at the alarm clock in astonishment. It was still not past five o'clock. He screwed up his lips, confused and surprised to have woken at such an hour.

Thinking perhaps the alarm clock was wrong, he put his hand under his pillow and reached for his watch. He looked at it, and saw he really had woken early.

He felt fresh and energetic as never before; he was filled with a lively sense of security, and his mind was clear and alert. He sighed with relief, happy at his present state, after so much hardship and sleeplessness. He stretched, not lazily. "Oh God," he said, "how generous You are! Your beneficence is timeless."

He could scarcely believe this sudden zest, compared with the normal effort it had always taken to wake early. The insistent urge to take a bath convinced him this morning was unlike any other.

"Praise be to You, God," he said. "You separate morning from the dark night."

He got straight up, took off his pyjamas and headed completely naked for the bathroom, a shiver going through him as his feet touched the cold bathroom floor. He stopped, hesitating for a second, then reached for the tap and turned it on. The water streamed out, and he drew away, shivering as the drops splashed his feet. He turned off the tap, and, still shivering, went back to the bedroom without taking a bath after all.

Ecstasy filled him. He lay there on his bed, happy and excited as he gazed up at the ceiling and thought of the night that had just passed. When had he fallen asleep? How had he come to sleep so soundly? Usually he'd lie on his bed racked with insomnia, tossing and turning. It scared him that he couldn't remember anything.

All of a sudden he closed his eyes and surrendered to sleep, feeling at peace with himself and utterly secure. No insomnia, no worries or apprehensions, no nightmares.

Nothing remained to remind him of the night that had passed except this lovely morning, with all its vitality, clarity and liveliness. Taking a deep breath, he filled his lungs with the dew of the morning breeze, which washed his naked body for the first time in many years.

He pulled his hands out from beneath his head and tossed comfortably in his bed, thinking: "Praise be to You and Your timeless beneficence." Then, lying there on his back, he let his eyes wander around. Long years had passed since he'd slept so pleasantly or woken feeling as he did now.

Regret had spoiled the beauty of his days, turning him to a hulk. Life had lost its sparkle, and he'd become filled with infinite loneliness and longing for home.

When he left his small town and came to the city, he'd been treading the banks of a wondrous dream. Thousands of kilometres he'd crossed, almost flying to reach his goal. He wanted to enter the dream city, see all his blocked abilities come gushing out. He wanted to enter the city and find fulfilment.

When he did arrive, he found himself standing on a pavement, bewildered, not knowing where he'd come from or where he was to go. His confusion left him defeated and embarrassed. Afraid, he wanted to go back where he'd come from, but the distance he'd crossed was greater than his ability to retreat.

He picked up his bag and began to walk aimlessly. Finally, exhausted, he sat down to rest in a café he'd stumbled on and ordered a pot of tea; then he looked around perplexed, not knowing what to do. He gazed at the faces of the people in the café, seeking help, but was shocked to see everyone concerned with himself or whoever he was with.

Regret tugged at his heart, wrenched at his nerves, turning him at last to a hulk, knowing himself utterly alone, without family, friends or relatives.

A stranger – a stranger. A stranger! The truth struck him with a sense of shock. It filled him with terror, making him feel like an orphan. Unable to hold back the tears welling in his eyes, he began to weep. The waiter, noticing the state he was in, came up, tapped him on the shoulder and asked in some surprise:

"What's wrong, brother?"

Trying to speak, he sobbed and covered his face with his head cloth.

"I'm a stranger, brother," he said, his voice breaking. "A total stranger. I don't know anyone here. I've come – I've come from a place a long way off – so far off! I'm confused, brother – confused. I've not the smallest idea what to do. Help me, brother, please. Help me! I'm – "

He couldn't go on. The waiter tapped him on the shoulder once more.

"Don't upset yourself, brother," he said, trying to comfort him. "Don't upset yourself. We're all strangers here."

Becoming calmer at last, he explained to the waiter his reason for coming to the city. The waiter told him of a place where he could spend the night, and gave him the name of the street where the labour office was. He also directed him to the quarter where he'd be able to find a place suitable for an unmarried man to live.

He had no difficulty finding a job, and he found a suitable place to live in the quarter the waiter had told him about. Even so, the ironic situation he found himself in raised problems far greater than he could handle.

Back in his small town he'd lived as part of one great family. Now he found himself surrounded by a loneliness over which he had no choice and which he was unable to bear. A vast throng of people, and yet no one – no one.

Alone and a stranger, in a strange place that must perforce become his homeland. His true homeland was deep in his heart and soul; and yet there was no homeland. Disappointment surged through him. Regret seemed to have fangs and claws that sank deep, without mercy, into his heart.

He lost his mental balance, the ability to think and act rationally. A fearful rope was coiled around his neck; bonds of loneliness, homesickness, regret encircled it. He strove fiercely to throw off those bonds. He wanted to go far away, so far away, but stumbled in the attempt. There was, he knew, no way of getting loose, of going any further than the length of the rope. Fear settled in his heart; he felt himself engulfed by some awe-inspiring force. His life was like a void, which he orbited in utter surrender and submission.

Each morning he'd be late for work and hear his boss reprimand him. More than half the day he'd spend sitting at his desk, doing nothing of any note; for the rest he'd wander the streets, passing the shops without the smallest curiosity or interest. He'd gaze at the things around him, barely seeing them. His eyes would be looking inside himself, seeking the dreams that had vanished so suddenly – after he'd grasped hold of them, or supposed he had.

Things would pass before his eyes like the recording of a film, which he'd watch with wide-eyed amazement, trying to work out what this thing was, which he'd grasped hold of, and had then become somehow lost. He'd scan the faces of passers-by, the windows of the shops, but his gaze would just rebound back on him, broken and disappointed.

Night would descend on him abruptly, and the city would surround him with its bright lights and late night cafés. But he'd walk back to his home, lonely and sad, and there surrender to the memories, apprehensions and nightmares.

His night and his day didn't feel like any other. He'd toss between the two, as if lying on the flames of his loneliness and his longing for home, bereft of despair, or hope, or ambition. He was sick at heart, sick in his soul. He swayed between the night and the day, and there was nothing – nothing but disappointment and bitterness; no hope and no expectation. All these feelings filled his soul, then came flooding out.

All night he'd be prey to apprehensions, seeing things he'd never seen before, things that couldn't be seen. The stillness of his room was shattered by vast tumult. The fear that took hold of him was beyond anything he could bear.

Snakes and scorpions would creep over the hot bed where he'd be tossing still, and he'd try to flee from them, till at last sleep would hand him over to the dreadful nightmare world from which only the ringing of his clock would deliver him. Then he'd leap up, startled and full of fear, would throw on his clothes and hurry to catch the car that would take him to work. As he walked, he'd set his head stiffly on his shoulders, thrusting out his neck like a hyena, not looking left or right to see what was around him. He'd wave his hand like an imbecile, greeting everyone he met, without expecting anyone to return his greeting.

In his haste and awe, he never once tried to look at the faces of those he greeted. He'd enter his office, wish his colleagues a fearful good morning, then sit down behind his desk, gazing into space, waiting for the work that might or might not come.

For six hours he'd do nothing, taking no part in any conversation with his colleagues, who'd spend their time talking. Never once did he try to find out their names, and if he should chance to meet one of them, he wouldn't even recognize him.

His eyes were gazing outside, rebounding back inside, with a sense of bemusement. From the moment he'd wept at the café on the day of his arrival, an odd sensation had swept over him. He felt, deep down, that he'd somehow never chosen to come to the city, that he'd stumbled on the place by mistake, while on his way to somewhere else. He riveted his eyes on an endless void, striving to work out the place he'd been heading for. To his growing confusion and shock, he found he could remember nothing at all.

A year passed, two years, three, four. It felt more like a hundred – as though time had stopped the moment he got out of the car that had brought him to the city. There he was still, standing alone on the shore, disappointed, unable to believe what had happened.

A great throng, and yet no one – no one. The city had broken him, destroyed him with its inhuman rush. Alone – alone. Unable to stand, unable to run without some reason, unable to retreat.

He'd wandered many streets, without once trying to learn their names or where they were. He knew only the name of the street where his office was, and the name of the quarter where he lived.

He walked without focus. He had, it would seem to him, meant to do something, then, all of a sudden, forgotten what it was. He remained in a state of constant bafflement, trying to remember what it was he had to do.

In the evening he'd close the circle, heading off home exhausted, no progress achieved. He'd open the door of his house and sigh with regret. Wearily, he'd take off his clothes, having earlier turned on all the lights in the house, so as to sense some company, and to drive out the darkness and the ghosts.

The stranger, though, could find no comfort or rest by night. The stranger's night was a fertile field for apprehension, illusion and nightmare. Nothing to compensate, no oblivion. How, just how, was he to find sleep?

All night he'd stay fearful, with the sense that someone was watching him from a corner of the house. He'd sit in his bed, his mind working, then gaze around him, trying to fix the corner where the watching eye was; and this would leave him more fearful, more confused and anxious than ever.

He'd pray, then close the door of the room and lie down on his bed, feeling more relaxed. Then, as he was about to yield to the stillness of his weary body, the thought would come: had he locked the door properly? He'd leap up, to make sure the door was locked, then return to his bed.

The night was long for the lonely stranger. Long indeed. Still he went on, dragging the night's lengthy rope. Might he perhaps fold it, or wrap himself inside it, and find sleep?

Sleeplessness would leave him battered. He'd feel tired, but still the night went on, and still he found no sleep. He'd close his eyes for a while, then open them once more. Again he'd look at the door. Perhaps the watcher had slipped into the room, at the instant he was trying to lock the door; and now there he was, watching him. He'd sit up in his bed, gazing at the walls of his dumb room, coming to no certain conclusion.

The night of the stranger was lonely and long. The sleeping apprehensions would wake and turn his night to hell.

Say: "I seek refuge with the Lord of the People,

"The King of the People;

"The God of the People,

"From the evil of the slinking whisperer,

"Who whispers in the breasts of people,

"Both *jinn* and men."

Thus he'd recite from the Holy Quran, till at last he'd grow calmer, feel safe. He'd close his eyes and wish for sleep to come. Yet, the moment he turned on to one of his sides, he'd imagine the watcher standing there on the other. Then he'd turn and look to the other side, praying as he did it.

He'd toss and turn, able to rest only if he lay on his back and kept turning his head, right and left, in a kind of loop. But it was all useless.

He'd only go to the toilet if really necessary. He'd get up, slowly and hesitantly, turn the handle of the door with care, as if afraid someone might hear him. Then he'd close the door quietly, fearful of making a sound, look outside and hurry to the toilet.

Once there, he couldn't relax. He was constantly on the alert, as if afraid a snake might spring and bite him. His eyes would swivel between his legs and the door, for fear someone might creep in while his attention was wandering.

He wouldn't go back into his room straight away; he'd stand by the door, looking inside, cautiously searching. Abruptly, he'd look behind him to see if the watcher he sensed should be standing there, behind him. Closing the bedroom door, he'd lie down, feeling safe. Then he'd look at the alarm clock, and remember his working hours, and the endless reprimands of his boss, and the deductions from his salary.

He'd close his eyes and beg for sleep to come. But the splinters of light would dance inside his eyelids, assuming dreadful forms. He'd open his eyes in fear, and stare, confused, at the ceiling. Flashes from his past life would pass before his eyes, and he'd watch them without any great emotion, till the images of mother and brothers and sisters appeared.

At that moment, pain would squeeze his heart, his bed would seem to fall into a deep well. Dizziness would overcome him, and he'd close his eyes, surrendering himself to the Almighty, Whose eyes never sleep and Whose eyelids never close.

One year had passed, two years, three, four; and still he'd felt the same. But this morning was different from all the other mornings he'd known. There he was, lying naked on his bed, filled with a peace, and a vitality, unknown to him since he'd come to live in the city. It was truly a new day, like the days of everyone else. "Praise be to You, Whose beneficence is timeless. Praise be to You."

For once at least, other people would see him without his swollen face and his red eyes. They'd be surprised to find him behind his desk, first thing in the morning and in a good mood, returning their greetings with heartier ones, looking them straight in the face; the mask removed behind which, without wanting to, he'd hidden for so many years. He'd seem to them as if born anew, or as if they were seeing him for the first time.

"Praise be to You. Praise be to You."

He leapt from his bed and stretched, not lazily. He put on his socks and shoes, his head cover and headband. He stepped confidently towards the mirror by the door, and looked into it as if seeing his face after a very long time. He fixed his head cover and headband, then rubbed his hands, feeling a sense of inner pride. Finally he headed towards the street.

When he got outside, he felt a cool breeze on his body, and this increased his sense of freshness and well-being. The wind, it seemed to him, was entering through the pores of his skin and washing his very soul.

He walked slowly, lightly, across the street, his steps confident. He gazed at the shops, their windows still closed, as if seeing them for the first time. How lazy these shopkeepers were, he thought, to be still sleeping at this hour, instead of getting up and enjoying the morning breeze!

The only place open was the one serving cooked beans; there was a solitary man sitting at a table outside the shop, busy eating his breakfast, only his back visible.

Before he reached the place, he noticed a man coming towards him on the other side of the street. The man stopped when he saw him, then stared at him in amazement; hesitated for a moment, then looked away. The man hurried past, saying: "I seek God's help against the devil!"

He looked at the man, surprised, then walked on, screwing up his lips. Reaching the place where the cooked beans were being sold, he waved his hand.

"Good morning!" he said loudly.

The shopkeeper turned away.

"Oh God!" he said. "The man must have gone crazy!"

The man eating his breakfast spat the food from his mouth and turned away too.

"God," he said, "have mercy on Your people. Shield us from disgrace!"

He passed slowly on, paying no attention to what they were saying. What other people said had absolutely no meaning for him. The curiosity inside him had died, nothing that had bound him to other people remained, except for greeting anyone he might see on his way. And he never expected a reply.

Even when he bumped into other walkers, he'd hear their curses without emotion, as though the words weren't directed at him at all. He'd meet their attempts to be quarrelsome with smiles, then walk on without any apology.

His sense of loneliness had cancelled everything that bound him to other people. He'd cancelled other people. Nobody remained except his boss, who reprimanded him and made deductions from his salary.

He passed from the side street where his house was, out on to the main street with its expensive shop windows. He considered walking on to his office, so as to get further pleasure from the cool breeze that had washed his body, had made him feel so light and graceful he could almost fly.

The office was far enough away, though, to make him fear one of his colleagues might get there before him; and so he stopped on the pavement, his back turned to the window of one of the big shops, and waited for a taxi.

A number of taxis passed, and each time the taxi would stop in response to his signal. Then the dumbfounded driver would give him one look and the car would speed off again.

Surely, he thought, the way these drivers were acting was very odd, quite uncalled for in fact. He just screwed up his lips and said aloud to himself: "What's the matter with everyone on this lovely morning?" Then he returned to looking for a taxi to take him to work.

Finally, bored with waiting, he crossed his hands behind his back and started walking back and forth, in front of the gleaming shop window. He lost count of how much time passed while he was occupied in this way.

Then, at a particular moment, it struck him he saw something strange reflected from the glass, and he stopped to take a look. His gaze was quite vacant at first, but then his eyes widened.

The reflection was familiar enough to him. It was his own image, reflected and looking at him as he stood there, his hands behind his back, staring back at the image in his turn.

There he was, with just his head cover, headband, socks and shoes. Completely naked otherwise, wearing nothing else at all.

*Fawziyya al-Bakr*

# A Paper Life

I'm the woman from the lands of scorching heat, and of sharp freezing cold that twists the bones. Night falls early within the limits of my small village, and all living creatures take refuge inside their own skins. I'm the woman who has nothing, in her world, but the chance to stand secretly on tiptoe, gazing at the world outside through cracks in the small window. The narrow cages that shut life in haven't stopped her eyes from looking up – with an aimless gaze sometimes, it's true – towards some undefined future.

Oh, I feel I could gather my village to my heart, let it feel the warmth it's given me.

The young men of my village seem like pieces of felt floating on the water's surface, with nothing to anchor them. You can read the bewilderment, the aversion in their eyes. They like to speak of tedium; but here we live with our fields and vineyards, with our green fodders that nourish all the small creatures, even those that crawl unseen.

How many things there are here that we simply love! We can't help loving, deeply – loving even those cracks in the walls of our old mud houses, even that light hardness tanned with brown, in our faces, after the toil of so many days in the sun.

How captivating to see the old houses, sleeping in the lap of our small village, when I go myself to the roof to sleep. There we gather, we and the mosquitoes and the scorching heat. We're all friends, inseparable, none of us tired of the other – even of the mosquitoes' whine, which relatives on visits from the city complain of so endlessly – irritating, they say, and bringing harm. To us it seems normal enough. We hardly notice it, as it merges with the rustle of the cypress trees from behind the hills: those trees that protect the village from the onslaught of the fierce sands.

Moonlight, at the time of half moon, now fills the horizon, and my small brothers and sisters are leaping over the beds. In the midst of us sits our venerable father. How venerable he looks, indeed! He's the centre of the circle; all the threads come from his hands, and he it is who decides on everything.

We've had no rain, he says. There's a drought on the way.

"Let's hope," my brother answers, "for some summer rains."

"What rains? If the winter's been dry, then summer's going to squeeze us dry too, to the last drop. The trees – they're pale now from lack of water – told me once they were going to stifle, and that would be the end of the village. We'll be carried off, like some old left-overs, to be swallowed up in the belly of the city."

Strangers in an old city quarter. There they call it the "old quarter." I pictured the red sands opening their jaws and swallowing the vines, stifling, without mercy, all the green grasses stretched out before the eyes. The whole flow of life will stop, and the canopy, from the protecting father, will drop to the ground. The laughter around the cups of green tea will die, my father's strength, remarkable though it is, will be snuffed out, and he'll end like some statue, forgotten in a buried castle. What strength? I banish the thought, hoping the disaster won't happen, stroking the green grasses in the hope they'll stay alive.

Yesterday I plucked the fruit, reaped a harvest from the good earth. Someone passed by: one of those weary, lost young men who wander between city and village. He gazed at my hands, bloodied by a thorn. I looked at him, from my swarthy face and my calm eyes.

"That's how life is," I said.

He smiled.

"And what a life!" he said. "Thorns make the hands bleed before fruit can do it."

"Isn't there ever any cruelty in the city?" I asked. "Aren't you ever overwhelmed by its thorns?"

Gazing away into the distance, he plucked a dry twig from a tree and put it carelessly between his teeth.

"Sometimes," he said. "But here we've become like old tools inside grandfathers' chests. Our faces, our lips have shrunk. We can't laugh the way we want to, because things are on the edge of collapse."

Later I recalled his words. And I remembered, too, one of the city's advantages: what they call "the school." But is that life? The small school house in the village is still the one we know best. It was a new world we found there, when I thought I'd start attending. I walked there in good time, in the early afternoon, accompanied by the soft breezes. As I went in, my head felt as though it was bursting, I couldn't settle my eyes on anything. I saw the plantation girls sprawled out on the floor, laughing softly together, dressed in their simple peasant clothes. Their curiosity, their wonder and eagerness to talk – that was what had lured them along. Among them I saw her. She was wearing a dark dress, and had glasses over her delicate nose, and a crop of hair in the fashion of city girls. She was talking quietly to one of the peasant girls, while the others watched nervously, till the girl contrived to answer. We felt we were in the presence of high expectation. To begin with, I was filled with a sharp sense of strangeness, an urge to run off.

My anxious eyes couldn't settle, my hands moved with obvious tension. She looked at me, and I felt my heart beating in my chest. Then I smiled, and a great wave of tenderness came close to overcoming me. I gazed at her, lowered my eyes, listened like someone hypnotized. Raindrops were falling, one by one, over the dry earth. Little by little, the enchanted world began to reveal itself.

After that it became familiar to run to the school house in the early afternoon. Here was the world come to us at last. Here was a new enchantment, seeping into our blood. We weren't just weary bodies any more, and fingers torn by reaping. But was that true life? We had to go back to the toil; we had no choice. There was the field again, and the harvest again, and the thorns – the thorns making our hands bleed before the fruit could.

Often, at night, I like to whisper to the moon, to count in the moonlight all the things I love: the palm tree, the small water spring, the hanging vine. Yes, I do meet with the moon alone; love it, and give what a woman can give when she loves. Give, to the moon.

The light insists on being master of the moment. It's over every tree, every plant. But is that life?

Return to the land is destiny, and I'm the woman of the thirsty earth. Is that life?

That enchanted world revealed from behind her sleepy eyes, behind the eyeglasses, calls us, drowns us without our knowing it. But is that life?

*Badriyya al-Bishr*

# THE SCHOOL CARETAKER

The quarter woke to Um Sulaiman's footsteps as she pushed open the door, leaving behind her the smell of coffee with cardamom and cloves. The damp mud walls of her house had sticks of incense wedged in the cracks, and the old man leaning on his cane uttered a prayer while waiting to sit down with the other old men and pass the time.

Wrapping her thin veil around her ears, Um Sulaiman focused her sharp eyes, intent on picking up the details of the road ahead. She wound her *abaya* around her long arms, balancing on her head the bundle filled with things the schoolgirls might buy.

At the end of the quarter, by the asphalt road, the yellow bus stopped, and Um Sulaiman thrust open the two panels of the door to climb in. The girls answered Um Sulaiman's morning greeting, which carried prayers and blessings with it. She knew all these girls, knew whose daughters they were, where they lived, and their mothers' requirements for their grooms.

Abu Saad, the driver, called out:

"Haven't you found me a bride yet, Um Sulaiman?"

He winked, his lips parted, waiting for an answer.

"These schoolgirls don't want a man with a wife, Abu Saad."

He raised his voice as if in anger, so that everyone in the bus could hear him:

"There's nothing wrong with a man, so long as there's plenty of money!" And with that he slapped his pocket.

The girls' laughter subsided as they waited for Um Sulaiman's answer. She was the one behind many of the girls' marriages, and many of those still left had pinned their hopes on her to find their new prince, in her worn-out notebook.

One of the girls on the back seat let out the secret word, and her eyes peered through the rear windows of the bus in search of a familiar car following them that morning – a car from which the smell of Arabian jasmine spread, filling the air and lingering on her exercise book. From the car's cassette recorder a sigh of love could be heard.

\*\*\*

Um Sulaiman sat in the yard of the school, with its two floors of mud brick and its cracked ceilings through which the rain leaked in winter. She was sitting on a multi-coloured blanket, which she sometimes used to pray on. She arranged the sweets, the white and coloured ribbons, the small combs, the exercise books and rulers. The lipsticks she hid in the left-hand pocket of her outfit, ready for the secret word the girls would whisper in her ear once they knew themselves come of age.

Um Sulaiman had had the privileged role of finding a husband for the school headmistress. She'd talked this headmistress around, telling her how short life was, and how unmarried women soon ceased to be eligible. As for brothers, she told her, these would change once their wives started playing on their minds. Education (Um Sulaiman went on) was a mere scrap of paper, not to be compared with the joy of having children, and a husband who'd come home to bring freshness to life at the end of the long hot summer days. Um Sulaiman came to be in high favour with the headmistress, and was actually her official companion for the three days after the marriage ceremony, celebrated during the summer vacation.

Hussa sat alongside Um Sulaiman during the prayer break. She complained, impatiently, of the many lessons she had, of the chalk dust, of having to study at the same time she was washing the dishes and preparing the house and the dinner for her brothers.

Um Sulaiman pressed her lips together, then took the *diram* stick and wiped her lips and yellow teeth with it. Sighing, she said:

"Too much studying, child, takes away your youth."

"And if we don't study," Hussa said, feeling a sense of the long, endlessly empty days, "what do we do then?"

"Get married!"

Drawing closer to Hussa, Um Sulaiman whispered a couple of words, opened her small notebook, then said:

"Write down your home telephone number."

Munira passed by without a greeting. Um Sulaiman had once offered to find her a fiancé, and had almost had her things flung all over the schoolyard.

Um Sulaiman stood in front of the mirror and moistened her dried lips by the *diram* stick. She put on her red dress striped with gold thread and tied the wrap around her waist, just as in the old days. She opened the jewel box, took out the gold chain and carefully put it on. She set a nose ring on the right side of her nose, then turned to open the door, the fragrance of henna spreading from her hair.

The old man was asleep, curled up under his *abaya*. She opened the door and headed for the bride's house.

\*\*\*

Um Sulaiman was now the first lady at the bride's house. She wasn't the school caretaker any longer. The bride's mother was waiting for her anxiously, asking her, for the tenth time, about the customs of the groom's family, and whether everything was as it should be. Um Sulaiman stood waiting by the door, along with the bride's mother and the other women of the school, who were holding the censers, ready to greet the women of the groom's family.

Um Sulaiman made sure everything was set in order: the proper number of coffee pots and cups, and the teapots. She whispered to the young schoolgirls gathered there a number of recommendations if they wished to be lucky in the future. Then she went into the bride's room to carry on with these.

"Hussa, my child, don't raise your eyes from the floor, so they'll think you're immodest. If the groom says anything to you, don't answer him. Don't let him touch your dress, don't let him touch your veil."

Drawing closer to Hussa, she whispered some further words that made Hussa's knees tremble as the groom walked in. Um Sulaiman greeted him with a great show of affection, making his face glow with happiness.

"Congratulations, Muhammad," Um Sulaiman repeated, three times. "Hussa's the daughter of a very good family, and you deserve her." Um Sulaiman went on praising the couple till Muhammad took a thousand riyals from his pocket, which she quickly snatched, happily and proudly too, and put in her left-hand pocket.

Next morning, the red striped dress had disappeared. The gold chain was back in the jewel box. She put on her everyday clothes, got in the bus and told the girls a host of stories about the previous night.

In the schoolyard Um Sulaiman spread out her goods, and, as Munira passed by her, said in a loud voice:

"Hussa sends you her regards, and asked me to tell you she's through with studying!"

*Hamza Muhammad Bogary*

# THE DARK ALLEY

One winter night, in the hallway joining the only two rooms of the house, Hassan sat with a book clutched to his chest, as if afraid it might run off. Next to him was the lantern his sister had set on a wooden chair, so that its light would reach both rooms. He opened a page of the book in front of him and skimmed through it. Then, turning round, he looked towards the ladder opposite him, which led to the roof where he'd been half an hour ago, before night had fallen. He'd had to come down from the roof – he couldn't take the only lantern in the house and leave his sister in that frightening darkness. He'd come down and seated himself between the two rooms, next to the lantern. His sister kept moving back and forth between the rooms, with a broom in her hand, trying to clean off the dust the long day had left on the mat laid out on the floor. Abruptly, his eyes returned to the book, and he became engrossed in his reading. He didn't notice the dust his sister was stirring up with her sweeping, which was blowing into his nostrils. Even the face of the lantern was growing murky from the whirling dust, but still he went on reading, his expression growing tenser or more relaxed, following the sentiments of the writer. Every now and then he'd clench his fist, as if he wanted to smash something, but then he'd let it rest on the floor of the hallway. So he stayed till ten in the evening,[1] when his sister was already asleep in the room to his right. She was a little girl still, not ten years old, and she was tired from working all day – that's why she'd fallen asleep. Now, waking again, she started shouting at her brother and scolding him, because he hadn't gone as usual to his father's shop, to help him serve beans to the customers. He'd go to the shop in the early morning and stay there till eight o'clock, before leaving for school. Then, in the evening, he'd be there from dusk till ten o'clock. No wonder his sister was so surprised to see him still there with her – she knew well enough what was in store for him. But he only answered that reading was better than dinner. She, of course, didn't understand what he meant. Shaking her head and closing her eyes, she just said: "It's up to you!"

The book in his hand was none other than an issue of *Iqra'*, or "Read," which had just that day reached his school from Egypt. He'd hurried to the library supervisor, who was a high school student, and begged him to let him borrow the book before anyone else took it. According to school rules, students had to return monthly magazines the next day after they'd been lent out, and Hassan couldn't bear to have to give it back before he'd read everything in it. That was why, several times a month, depending on the number of issues the school got hold of, he'd miss going to his father's shop. This month's issue was about the great philosopher Socrates, whose life so appealed to him that he lost all thought of himself, of his waiting father, his sister lying in the next room, or the dinner he was going to miss. None of these things seemed remotely important.

He stayed like this for a while, only taking his head from the book when his sister's snoring grew louder, or when she raised her head and asked him in a faint voice, made still fainter by sleep, whether he'd gone to join his father.

The minutes passed, till at last the time reached eleven o'clock. He closed the book in his hands, then opened it once more and skimmed through the pages, fearful he might forget a single word of what he'd read. His father was due to return, and he knew what would happen if his father found him there at home. He'd have to leave the house, at least till his father was home and asleep. He opened the door and sneaked out just like a thief, fearful of the creaking noise it made. A blast of cold air drove him back for a moment, then on he went once more, walking aimlessly along. Hazy images kept passing, even so, in front of his eyes. The image of his father sitting in his shop, a dark pot in his hand, which he was holding out to one of the customers. Images of his sleeping sister with the weak light from the lantern, the mat on the floor, the ladder leading up to the roof, the school, Socrates and his wife who used to beat him, and the poison Socrates had drunk rather than betray his ideals. Slowly, little by little, something began stirring inside him, something he was always afraid of and had been trying not to think about. He was starting to feel hungry, on account of the cold weather. Still he walked on, with no kind of aim in mind, till he reached a quarter where great mansions had been built, a quarter swimming in lights, as if on a wedding night. On he walked; then, from the left, he smelt something. His feet stopped, as if they'd reached their goal. Turning, he walked down the alley from which the smell was coming. The light from the great building opposite reached into the alley, and there he saw something he'd never seen in his home or in the homes of any of his friends. He saw a delicious dinner. He didn't think about what he was seeing, he didn't try and ask himself where it had come from. Just to sit and fill his empty stomach was enough. Alongside him, in the darkness, a shadow moved. For a moment he trembled; then he felt calm, sensing the fellow-feeling that linked those who were wretched and poor. He didn't, even so, think of speaking to the other person. At last he licked his hand, stood up and walked a few steps. The lights engulfing the great mansion flashed in his eyes. Lifting his face towards those lights, he prayed for the owner of the mansion, who, so generously, had thrown away so much food, to make a dinner for him and his poor companion.

*Sa'd al-Dosari*

# THE MIRROR

The mirror covered the four walls. But for the wooden door, she would have found herself quite under siege from the sharp glass.

Shivering still more, she gazed towards the door, the only thing not to send back her image. The thing too which, when it moved, would presage mysterious things – things of whose beginning, and end, she had no notion.

The mattress sent out a smell of newly fluffed cotton. Why, she asked herself, was it so big? She drew her legs up to her chest, then sank down into the mattress, laid so carefully there on the floor.

She could barely distinguish any one smell. The air was filled with the vapour from the different bottles – bottles like the ones she'd seen, just now and again, inside the box of the saleswoman who'd call unannounced, knocking on people's doors in the morning.

The memory of one of those mornings came back to her. It was the time she'd peered cautiously out from behind the wooden shutter of the window, to see him leaving his home.

He was such a very smart young man – and –

She swallowed – so very handsome.

The children's voices began to fade, the girls' whispers were hushed. The laughter of old women could be heard, the sound of their pious invocations audible from inside the house.

Her ears were peeled for noises outside her room, but she found only silence, ringing in her ears. She strained to make out any sound from round about her door. What if he were to come in now?

The sound of plastic shoes beat inside her like a drum. She placed her hand on her chest, pressed down hard. Her dry lips came apart, her face began to quiver.

The knob on the door turned, the rusty hinges creaked. Her knees began to shake. The hairs on her soft skin – the few her mother hadn't been able to remove – stood on end.

An old woman came in.

"What's the matter with you? This is God's will. Who does a woman have but her husband? Remember God, and don't let me down with your mother. The groom's family think a lot of your mother, and of you too. If he comes close to you, move away. Keep hold of your clothes. Don't smile at him, at all. Don't answer him, at all. The more you resist, the more he'll respect you. The man doesn't know anything about you."

The door creaked, and the deadly sound of silence returned once more.

She heard the sound of feet, more than two. She made a swift count. Four. The door opened, and two people came in.

He sat down beside her and greeted her. She made no reply.

The old woman poured him a cup of coffee. He took the cup and drank the coffee. The old woman poured a second cup and offered it to her.

"Coffee, daughter?"

She didn't answer.

He smiled. The old woman returned the smile, her own as wide as his. He told her to give him the cup of coffee. He drank it, then gave both cups back to the old woman.

"That'll do."

Taking a big leather wallet from his pocket, he pulled out two notes and held them out to the old woman, who took them with a false show of reluctance.

"God bless you! Congratulations! From you the money, from her the children."

The old woman picked up her things, where they lay wrapped in a bundle in a corner of the room, and left.

He finished the evening prayer. Then he took off his *ghutra* and lay down next to her.

He tried to touch her face. She moved away. Suddenly her eyes struck the mirror. She found herself alongside a fat, ugly man, his clothes streaked with sweat, his lips flecked with spittle.

She turned her head away again, and began to weep.

*Khaleel al-Fuzai'*

# AWAY FROM HOME

The rosy dreams I'd embroidered through all the moments of waiting – waiting to reach the beloved village; the longing for the warmth of meeting, nourished by the countless, wondrous feelings inside me; the intimate memories playing with my thoughts. All these things were to no purpose. All was turned to hands stretched out in hostility, bitter and clear, toward the returning stranger.

My paper horses had wandered far, toward limitless spaces. The dreams were shattered, the surging tide of the sea had vanished, a great mountain of rejection left in its place. Why (people were asking) had the traveller returned, after twenty years among the allies of the unknown?

Those old nights in the village square were filled with dew. The tales slumbering inside us were repeated, in all their detail. The Quranic verses of al-Fatiha and al-Kursi protected each one of us as we went back to our homes, after sitting up in the moonlight, or by the light of the lantern we provided in turn. We were young. We'd drink in the moonlight; we'd travel to lands unvisited, to lost worlds. And yet we'd find ourselves, at last, still in the village square, still talking, with the night almost over. Could time blot out all those beautiful memories?

One day I left as others had done; I said goodbye to the village. For a time I'd return every now and then. Then I travelled somewhere a very long way off. No news of me ever reached the village, no news of the village came to me. But harder than being cut off from home was the isolation in the heart. And by the time I did go back, everything was changed. Had the change been physical only, it would have been easier to bear. But it was people's hearts that had changed, in a way I'd never conceived.

Just one person hadn't changed – he met me with his usual smile. The passing years had made no impression on his features.

"You're still alive?" I said.

"I've found out the secret of life," he answered. "I don't see death coming near me."

"So, what's the secret of life?"

"If I told you, it wouldn't be a secret any more."

"I want to live the way you do."

"You can't."

"Why not?"

"Because your generation doesn't believe in life the way we see it."

"What do you mean?"

"I'll tell you. I've lived over a hundred years, as you can see. I've known over a thousand women, and I still want more."

I wasn't surprised at this. I'd known for twenty years past of his passion for women. Still, I couldn't see the connection between these words and the secret of life he'd talked of before.

"But you can't," I said, trying to provoke him.

"That's what you think! I tell you, I'm dying for a woman. Do you know what my father told me? 'If you want a long life, then keep looking for women.'"

I caught his meaning well enough.

"But that's all wrong," I said. "Are you going to pass those notions on to your children?"

"They won't listen. They make fun of sayings like that. You know what one of my sons said? He'd read once, he told me sarcastically, that being with a woman might make your beard grow longer, but it won't add anything to your years. I did my best to convince him. If it makes your beard grow longer, I said, then it can make anything else grow too, your age along with the rest. But he wasn't convinced."

There was one question I was dying to have an answer to.

"Why," I asked him, "are they all giving me such hostile looks?"

"Why don't you ask them?"

"They won't talk to me."

"When you deserted them, they needed you. Now you've come back, and they don't need you any more."

"What did they need me for?"

"The village needed all its sons, when the flood destroyed it. Everyone came back, except you."

"I had my own struggles, somewhere else."

"Any struggle should be for the village."

My love for my village had never grown cold. My bond with it was my whole life. How could anyone desert his own life? How could I prove to these people that I worshipped the land, that I longed to kiss the earth, to rub its very soil into my face?

Some boys were gathered around, staring at me in astonishment, as though I were some creature from another planet. I tried to talk to one of them, but they all bolted, like wild horses. Had I stayed, one of them might have been my son. Had I stayed, I could have spoken to them with affection. Anything might have been possible had I stayed.

The walls of the village were filled with a sense of isolation. Hostility filled the air. I felt it. I could touch it. It was heavy and real. But I'd never leave again.

*Maryam al-Ghamidi*

# THE MAD GIRL WHO TRIED TO CHANGE VILLAGE TRADITIONS

I woke to the smell of coffee being roasted on the stone stove built in the middle of the living room. The smell found a way into my small nose, then on to my whole breathing, where I took it in ecstatically. I stretched where I lay on my small straw-stuffed mattress. It was rough, but held me in with its warmth.

My mother was starting her morning routine. The hot coffee beans were being ground in the stone mortar. The small beans would fly around, trying to leap from inside the mortar, but down would come the strong pestle to crush them. My mother's flat palm, which she used to knead great lumps of dough in a big bowl, kept the edge of the mortar covered, blocking every exit, making sure the beans would be crushed and make that wondrous, revitalizing drink for all the farmers and shepherds, and for the owners too, who worked the land with them, starting off a day that would be weary with bustle and anxiety till night fell at last.

"Get up, girl!" my mother shouted. "The sun's up. The shepherds have already gone out to graze!"

I rose languidly. The winter frost seared my body where it was covered with the gown my mother had woven from my sheep's wool. That day, I remember, I'd spoken out against it. How, I'd wondered, could sheep stay warm if their fleece was sheared?

I put on my hat – without washing my face. And I didn't comb my hair either. My feet were shivering from cold and fear, and I buried them in wool to guard them against the chill that lay in wait for them, beyond the old, creaking door. My mother coated my face with cow's butter – the wind would soon be gusting over my cheeks. I stuck out my tongue, trying to lick any butter I could reach, and my mother scolded me.

"Butter's precious, girl! We'll make a lot out of it when we sell it."

I begged her to put just a small piece of butter on my tongue, so I could suck it slowly, making the taste last as long as I possibly could.

I took with me my share of the delicious bread my mother had made. It had passed its night on the ashes of the stone stove, covered by live embers. I'd watched my mother the night before, as she sat by the shadows of the dancing fire, made from dry leaves and kneaded with her big hands. I thought of how my mother's hand would have kneaded the great lump of dough, how that hand must have fashioned the mighty loaves! How marvellous my mother was!

I opened the door to the barn. My sheep were gathered there, by the door, waiting to be let out to the green pastures and the laughing sun behind the mountain; waiting to get moving, to leap in the meadows, on the mountainside, full of mischief and fun. It's winter, you sheep! The sun's in its winter home. Even when it does shine on us, and on our fields, it still looks sleepy. We're going to hide away in the mountain caves, or between the rocks. We'll sing the song of rain and sunny weather.

The barn was cold and dark. The damp, and the lack of room, were oppressive. The small lamb leapt on to its mother's back to catch a sight of me. Then it called out to me. I let the grey light embrace them from beyond the walls.

My sheep and small lambs, and my other animals, came joyfully out; I could sense their unbounded freedom and release. I went into the barn and cleaned up the manure they'd left behind on the floor. I managed not to stop my nose! I gathered up the manure and put it in my wrap, to carry off this priceless treasure we'd use to fertilize the fields; it was the sap that flowed in the roots of the plants. I carried it with the greatest care, making sure – "so my father taught me" – that none of it fell on other people's fields. I didn't bother, afterwards, to wash my hands. I just thrust my fingers through the wool of one of the sheep, sticking them into the warm wool.

The usual walk began, the sheep and small goats all assembled. One of the animals jumped about to get warm, feeling happy and free. My dog barked, to warn me of a small lamb being left behind. The mischievous animal leapt madly, then stumbled against an acacia tree in the field.

We reached our valley, and I set my precious load down, in a secret spot my mother knew about. Then I heard a loud cough. It was my father, who'd gone down to the valley as usual after early morning prayer. There he was, standing like a lofty mountain, with two blinkered oxen. Now and then he'd run along between them, singing a traditional song, to spur the oxen on to go faster. The dawn was still hiding its face, in the embrace of darkness. I gazed at my father with admiration, and his tender smile embraced me, bringing a sense of relief to my frozen body.

Poor father! He was standing by the well – the dangerous well. The one that had lured my brother on one morning, as he was lovingly sowing the valley with seed. He'd been standing by the edge of the well, trying to fix the reel on which the rope of the bucket was fixed. The two oxen approached my brother, smiling at him. His foot slipped, and he fell into the well's embrace, sinking into its depths. He never came back that morning. And when they pulled him from the well that night, he wasn't the brother I'd known. The perilous well had made him drink its magic potion, till he was robbed of his senses.

I cried out that day, I shouted: "Let's leave this place! Let's abandon that well, that whore who opens her arms to her victims, lures them ever closer, till they're besotted with her and die!"

What was this? This mad girl was trying to change the village traditions! Leave our fields, our home, our well and our valley? Now I've grown up, I've learned to love the well. Whenever I've gone to my small village, sleeping there in the lap of the mountain, I've passed by the well that embraced, to the point of death, all those I've loved, and could ever have loved.

*Noura al-Ghamidi*

# UP MY GRANDFATHER'S LONG SLEEVE

When people saw my grandfather, they'd bow to him and hang about his person. They'd feel the heavy clouds of the Hijaz approaching with their thunder, along with the smell of clover and the whistling of the ulayya opening the hearts of the palm trees.

You wouldn't dare look into my grandfather's long face, with its henna-coloured beard but the moustache clean-shaven, as he lifted his arm like some leaden giant that was all lotus honey inside, and thrust out a chest his womenfolk swore was made from gardens of basil and cashew. He'd raise his hand and push you out, telling you not to come back till you had a back of iron and a hand of thorns.

People knew how Saqr – my grandfather, that is – had shaved his moustache after he'd defended his home against the onslaught of the Turks and Ottomans, but hadn't been able to protect his neighbours, who'd all been burned along with their dwellings.

Saqr's belly had been burned, and so had his thigh and two hands, as he stuffed the mouth of the Turkish leader with hot ashes. His face covered, he'd seized the leader's rifle as well. Luck had played its part: the troops had fled, dragging the head of their dead leader with its ashes and shame. Saqr, though, felt guilty in spite of that, because his house had survived while his neighbours had died. So he shaved his moustache out of shame, as the house slept by the dead bodies and woke to the stench of decay. The men of the tribe, hunger and fever etched on faces that clung to life, consulted together. The final decision, outweighing all other answers, was to leave the place. For all his burned and weakened hands, Saqr walked along with the rest, taking with him his Ottoman rifle and his meagre Hijazi provisions. The prayers and counsel of his father lit his way, guarding him against the painful days:

"My son – My son, don't cross the sea."

That had been eighty years ago, longer even, and still my grandfather Saqr shaved his moustache, though with soap and a razor now. And still you could hear him from the highest corner of the house.

"If you just work like a slave, and then you're satisfied, you'll never amount to anything." That was the lesson Saqr began instilling in his sons, as he urged them to leave, to move to God's spacious domains and make their living from their own hands. He had no time for those who were content with what they had; that, for him, was a kind of surrender. He'd urge his sons on, with reproaches, to keep working, never to give up, and so become just what Saqr wanted them to be: rich men. He wasn't disappointed. The house became almost empty as he shouted at the last son to leave. "Are you waiting for the crumbs I'll leave you?" he yelled, just before the son left. "Get out of here! God's lands are vast!"

He'd get up in the morning, alone, and take a piece of white cloth from his wooden trunk. He'd spread it out on his thighs, then, bent over a pot of water perfumed with cashew, he'd start washing it with all the vigour of a young man. This he did every day, letting the cloth dry, then folding it and putting it away. He'd point at one final son, who had a deformity in his mouth, and hadn't left like his brothers. Actually, Saqr tried to make him leave; and the son, for his part, was thinking of going off and seeking his fortune, as his father had taught him. But what was to be done in this case? Day after day Saqr would scold him with his famous words: "You'll never be anyone as long as you're satisfied doing the work of slaves." It was slaves, so Saqr firmly believed, who ploughed the earth, fetched the water from the well, ground the seeds, hand-fed the camels and oxen, guarded the fertilizers that were the life of the tilled land, and guarded the crops against birds. This son, disabled though he was, liked to guard against the birds, and did it often. But what was he to do? He was disabled. His brothers had all gone off, to various parts of the world. Two of them never sent back any news. His eldest brother had gone to the Sudan, where he worked as a wandering trader along the Sudanese and Ethiopian frontiers. He was the only one who'd send gifts, with a merchant from Hadhramaut who lived in Jeddah. According to news reaching them from the fourth brother, he was in al-Ihsa. Saqr was convinced, even so, that his sons would all come back. He spent many nights awake, his arms raised towards heaven; and, whenever he looked and saw his disabled son close by, his cheeks would glisten with tears.

Despite all this, Saqr would often spend the final part of the night fixing a round disk inside an old telescope he kept hidden inside the deep hollow of a wooden pole, in the middle of the guest room. The sight of this telescope left the people of the house perplexed. A number of times Saqr had assured his sons, in an audible voice: "I've nothing to leave you." With that he'd struck the floor with his hand, telling them to go and plant the earth, and not to lean back against the wall, waiting for something to come from him.

The sons never believed him. Everyone knew Saqr was rich. Wasn't that clear enough from his house, with its two storeys, which he'd built so long before? It was the wonder of its age. People from Yemen, and from cities and tribes throughout the Peninsula, would come to see that house. Building it had cost Saqr a fortune, not to speak of the many slaves who'd died beneath the huge rocks that had rolled from the mountain top when the explosives were set. The builders would detonate the explosives and start work; then they'd find themselves surprised by the rolling rocks, which killed a good number. The old building was constructed so as to have the ground floor as lodging for the slaves, storage for grain and a furnace. It had windows twenty centimetres by forty, which let the light in and the smoke out. This ground floor was crowded with slaves, camels, cows and two oxen. The upper floor served as quarters for the family, and it had a wing for guests, which would be filled with wayfarers. The rooms were built side by side, on three sides of the house, while the fourth had the staircase, built from stone mixed with clay and painted with the green clover leaves that gave it its pale green colour.

Opposite these upper rooms was a spacious balcony surrounded by wooden fencing, through which Saqr could see the inner yard of the house, unsuspected by all, even when he was lying on his bed. One day Saqr saw one of the slaves stuffing the mouth of a camel. Saqr took hold of him, gave him a kick, then pointed to the camel.

"That's your money there," he said. "Take care of it, and it'll take care of you!"

The things my grandfather Saqr said would set small wars raging – wars no one ever heard of, but the kind, even so, that set hearts ablaze. Saqr would feel a deep pain down in his chest, he'd feel heat coming from his ribs, painting his ears the colour of blood.

"My money's for you," he cried. "For the tribe and the slaves."

"No," replied his son, who'd just returned with bags of hay and tins of fine dates. He tried to find some explanation for what his father had just said to the slave.

Saqr turned his face away from his son.

"I swear to the God of Mecca and Medina," he said. "Be quiet, son, please, and take away whatever you've brought with you. It's yours, from your own hard work. I don't want it – I don't want any part of it."

With that he pulled an old document out of his ancient trunk, a deed for a large piece of land. He gave it to his son.

"Take it! It's yours, bought with my own clean money, in the land of Hijaz, where the sun gives birth to rocks and the wells swallow the lightning."

The son opened his mouth. Just what was clean and dirty money? His mouth stayed open, but Saqr's was closed in silence now.

Saqr put his old lunchbox on his horse's back and picked up his Ottoman rifle. Then he woke his disabled son and forced him out into the wide world.

That same day, the eldest son broke the last link binding him to the Sudan. He moved swiftly towards the south and became the wealthy owner of vast areas of palm trees and pomegranate, and the head of a small family. But he still needed a son to carry on his name and inherit his life's work.

Two of Saqr's sons lived in huge cities, and they'd return home loaded with goods, speaking a strange language and wearing strange clothes.

Saqr kept silence before all these things. His sons, for all their resources, could find out nothing to establish their rights, nor could they even tell any stranger how large their father's fortune was, or how he'd come by it. He was proud that he could turn his back on any envious eye. That back, he knew, was protected by five men, and a valley full of livestock, and twelve horses, along with a substantial house with thirty slaves.

He felt secure in the knowledge that the money his grandchildren would inherit was clean money, earned through their own fathers' toil. All that remained for him now was to make ready his own shroud, and turn his horse's head to Mecca to perform the pilgrimage, having first distributed his money among the poor of the tribe, the slaves and the women, with a portion left for his disabled son.

He was followed by his four sons, each of them wearing a belt full of money and praying: "God, You are the Friend in matters of wealth, family and children."

Saqr stayed silent, peering narrowly at his four sons. The eldest was the one nearest his heart, and the one who resembled him most closely. He was also the only one of his sons who raised no objection to his father's decision, to give his money to heirs outside the family, against the established prescriptions. His father, he realized, must have some powerful reason for this, and he only wished he knew what that reason was. Many times, seeing his father's compassionate gaze on him, he tried to cajole the secret out of him; but Saqr, in his wisdom, would just change the subject. Then the son, laughing, would glance towards the old telescope Saqr kept so carefully hidden in his lunchbox. And Saqr would laugh too, and nod his head, as if sure his son had understood everything. They seemed to understand one another. Did that old telescope hold something more profitable than the small craft that had brought him back from Sudan to Hijaz?

Laughter would burst out, followed by dignified prayer. "We submit to Your will, oh God!"

What the son had brought back with him was a story in itself. It was the same tiny boat that had witnessed his adventures and the beginnings of his fortune. He'd filled its interior with clay, planted it with basil and flowers, and set it at the entrance to the house. This boat of the son's, constructed in Sudan, was something to be proud of; that was why it had been set there, with the basil and flowers sprouting from it.

Scratching his nose, Saqr gazed at his lunchbox, then carefully pulled out the old telescope which, earlier in his life, he'd never abandoned, never let anyone know of, never spoken of to anyone. He'd brought it back with him when he returned to Hijaz, the place he'd once left with burned hands, hungry and bearing the burden of his whole future. That day of Saqr's return had been unforgettable. His father had slaughtered the ox, the ox he used to plough the unfruitful earth that only lived at all by the work of the beast's hooves.

People had been stunned by this.

"The old man's slaughtered the ox!"

"To celebrate Saqr's safe return!" the old man had said.

That disturbed my grandfather. He clutched his throat in fear. Then, covering his eyes, he moved slowly off – there was no place for him, he felt, in Hijaz. His father's happiness had drowned him in tears. What could he do now, returned, empty-handed, after three years? All he had was the telescope, passed to him as a gift by a man so tall his head reached the clouds. It was the only thing the man had possessed, and he'd given it to Saqr when recovered from a sickness during which Saqr had attended him for three whole nights. This telescope had a strange disk which, when pressed, allowed the user to see Mecca and its roads, the holy plains of Mina, Muzdalifa with its pure stone, the steadfast region of Mount Arafat and the stone of al-Aqaba.

For two whole months, Saqr had been held enthralled by this amazing device, there on the island of Sumatra, which was the first and last place to which he'd travelled – following the rich Indonesian pilgrims, who'd take money out from under their tall hats and fling it into the hands of the water sellers, and the poor who lived near the holy places of Mecca.

It so happened that Saqr had returned at the time when robber bands were attacking pilgrims, and highway robbers were vying with one another out on the rims of the Peninsula. Pilgrimage had its dignity, and its secret, terrifying stories too, and its special journeys that people rarely came back from.

Saqr decided to make his fortune. For five days he stayed in his room. Then, on the sixth, he announced he could whisk people to Mecca and Medina in the twinkling of an eye. If anyone wished to perform a pilgrimage, or a half pilgrimage, he had to pay five Arabic riyals for the first and five French riyals for the second. The person also had to "follow" Saqr across the Jiyad pass, a narrow, dark pathway between two great mountains – a place whose inhabitants had always attacked and harmed the people of the village. There would often be fires inside the pass, and fetid smoke would rise up, so that people believed it to be inhabited only by evil jinn. Every returning pilgrim would tell of the horrors of that road, and of the things those in the pass would do to block the road to pilgrims. Some pilgrims had taken part in the jinn's weddings and battles, and many young pilgrims had played with those jinn who were kind and gentle.

Once alone with my grandfather, the pilgrim would pray to God to give my grandfather long life and to bless him. It was Saqr, after all, who'd spared the pilgrim the hardship of travel, and of absence from home for a number of months, with all the risks of hunger, sickness and death, violent or otherwise. The pilgrim would follow my grandfather quietly. They had their doubts. Could Mecca and Medina really be seen through this man's hand? Still, they'd say: "That other person did it. We'll do it too." And so the pilgrims started following Saqr, who'd designed a special robe with two wide sleeves. Whenever he reached that narrow pass, he'd choose a dark spot, then ask the pilgrim to look inside his broad sleeve. The pilgrim would stick his face into the sleeve, where the telescope was set under Saqr's armpit, directly facing the pilgrim. Then Saqr would turn the disk with his other hand, and, in less than ten minutes, the pilgrim would see all the holy lands. When my grandfather heard the pilgrim gasping, he'd shout: "Pray, you pilgrim. Pray!" He'd start reciting prayers and reading from the Quran, and the pilgrim would repeat after him.

All this would happen in the greatest comfort and ease, and the pilgrim would go back to his family, shave his head and slaughter a sheep to celebrate his safe return.

The good thing that sprang from my grandfather's deeds was that jinn no longer dwelt in the pass. Perhaps that came from the reciting of the Holy Quran; for, as the pilgrims repeated the prayers after Saqr, they drove the red jinn from the pass for ever.

In the same way, the slaves, after growing rich, left my grandfather's house and followed him to Mecca and the Ka'ba. The telescope was quite forgotten.

*'Ashiq 'Issa al-Hadhal*

# THE BROKER OF DONKEYS

Despite all the things he was going through, he didn't get upset when his father called him to afternoon prayer.

"I'm up," he answered. "I'm awake. May you be rewarded, father."

Raising his head from the pillow, he glanced despondently around his humble room next to the front door. The books were all mixed up with the magazines – a problem long unsolved, calling to his mind those people who sold magazines on the pavements. The clothes were hung anyhow on the old rack; his head cover was hanging down from his headband, touching the floor; the ashtray was groaning, with ash clinging to its sides; the matchbox lay, like a lazy sentinel, on top of the cigarette packet. His gaze fixed itself, finally, on the small cupboard where he kept his things, including her letters – the things that had, until quite recently, been his most precious possessions.

He looked moodily away, shifting his body in an attempt to ease the pain that had returned. He turned on the radio, only to hear the song: "My heart favours you." Angrily, he switched the radio off again, then rose to perform his ablutions and pray. He found the tea there in his room; he always drank his tea in his room, so as not to bother his parents with his smoking. He poured himself a cup, took a sip, then lit a cigarette and placed his left hand under his armpit, as if striving to make a stand against some stubborn enemy. His gaze focused on the ceiling. He looked as though he was reading:

"I was dreaming," he said to himself. "Dreaming life was going to give me all the things I wanted. It was an illusion. Oh, I'm just empty now."

His hand slipped and touched the radio.

"Even you," he spat out furiously, "playing 'My heart favours you.' Go to hell, you and whoever made you, along with the singer, yes, and her too."

Irritably, he got up and opened the cupboard. His long, sweaty fingers reached for the letters and started ripping them up. The sight of the torn paper brought him some relief. He looked to see if there were any big pieces left, that hadn't had their full share of tearing. He found a piece that seemed to be challenging him. Before tearing it, he read: "It's not in my hands, my love." His grip loosened; he held the paper close to his heart, then placed it under the pillow.

He lay down, feeling utterly depressed.

"Whose hands is it in then? In your father's, you'll say. He managed to persuade you and your brother, who said he was a friend, to get shot of me – all because of money. That was what made him take against me. Even the way he apologized was stupid and cheap: 'She wasn't meant for you.' As if your father was the one who decided fate and destiny! What is he, anyway? An imbecile and a fool. He never made a proper success of anything. What has he achieved? Just what? The money turned his worthless head. He's a loafer. And what was he before? A broker of donkeys!"

He heard his name being called out:

"Go to 'Awad. He'll write out the purchase agreement for you."

There was a rap on the door, and he got up to open, cursing his wretched neighbour, the owner of the real estate office. "Am I his slave?" he said to himself. "Why doesn't that pampered son of his write it for him? Oh, of course, he'll be busy driving his new car."

He wrote out all the cheap things the agent asked him to write.

The cool autumn breeze soothed the sitters better than any electrical appliance. He made an effort not to smile. His mother, seated next to him, had a serious air, as if ready to open a heated conversation. His older sister was busy trying to shine her gold bracelet, the only one she had, with a lock of the long dark hair that added a touch of grace to her average beauty. Her young brothers and sisters were hiding behind her, trying to conceal their childish games.

A windstorm blew up, knocking over the plastic bucket and making a noise, inside the house, that made the children laugh out loud. Their sister looked at them and bit her lower lip, as a sign they should be quiet.

Their father sighed.

"It's autumn," he said. "God grant us a good end, and make us leave this world as Muslims."

'Awad stirred.

"You'll live long, God willing," he said. "We'll get you married," he added, laughing, "if mother lets us."

"Why don't *you* get married?" his mother broke out. "You're the urgent case. We don't know what you're about, now you've been turned down by that ill-fated father of donkeys. If you like, I can look for someone better than his daughter. But you won't talk, and we don't know anything you're about. What do you say?"

"I say, let's leave marriage till later."

"How much later?" his father said furiously. "Aren't you done yet, with being a bachelor? You've been good enough to us now."

"Father, I haven't done anything for you that I need to be thanked for. It's the least I can do."

Heavily, the father rose for the evening prayer. His gaze was fixed on 'Awad, who got up too, not hearing what his sister had whispered to her mother:

"They say the father of the groom's waiting outside."

He lay down on his bed. The heavy question marks lined up there in front of him, approached, then burst into peals of derisive laughter.

He took the small piece of paper, wrapped it in tobacco paper, then lit the cigarette and began, slowly, to smoke.

Next morning, he went off to work feeling drained. He sat down at his desk and started looking around him. A thought came to him, then drifted off again. Oblivion – oblivion. As he gazed in front of him, he heard the office boy say the manager wanted to see him.

"Why were you late, 'Awad?" the manager asked.

"I wasn't very late – just a quarter of an hour – the traffic."

"Yes, a quarter of an hour here, and another quarter of an hour there. I don't like the way you've been acting lately."

"In what way?"

"You're constantly late. And you've been getting careless." He thrust out his thin white hand, then added: "It's everything, all together."

"I don't know – what can I say? Is it just bad luck? Or something else?"

"I'm asking you about being late for work," the manager broke in. "Not about the philosophical thought for the morning!"

*Husain 'Ali Husain*

# THE DEPARTURE

Hamid left his work at the workshop and went off to the city. None of the other labourers realized Hamid was leaving – he hadn't told anyone, had shown no sign of stopping working. Deep down he'd known he must act on his own initiative. He knew exactly what he wanted, so why discuss it with other people? Still, being a good-natured man, he went to see the owner of the workshop and, as he took off his tattered khaki outfit, told him he was feeling unwell. He had a lean, dark body, full of furrows from countless strange maladies, for which in the past his mother had sought the help of charms and prayers. The owner allowed him to leave. Hamid, he was sure, was a good, decent man, who took his working hours seriously and wouldn't have left had he not been genuinely sick.

But where, the owner suddenly asked himself, was Hamid intending to go? The question, once awakened, stayed in his head like the buzz of a stinging bee. He grappled with it till he could barely think any longer. He took off his spectacles and set them slowly down on his desk. He spat on the black floor covered with oil, tar and tools scattered here and there.

He took out his tobacco box and rolled a cigarette. Then he inhaled deeply and took a sip of cold black tea, doing his best not to think about Hamid. "He must have had his reasons," he told himself. "He wouldn't have left his work otherwise, at the busiest time of the morning." That was just what puzzled the owner. He stretched his legs unsteadily, then stepped out of the workshop.

The cigarette was still between his lips, the cup of tea stuck firm in his long fingers, like a premature baby in a powerful midwife's hands. Once outside his shop, he walked a short distance, then suddenly stopped and gazed down the length of the quiet street, trying to fight the unsteadiness and inertia in his tired old limbs. He could leave the workshop and follow Hamid, but the two lads he employed couldn't be trusted. They couldn't cut an iron bar unless he was there, watching over the one who was holding it. So he told himself, as he dragged his steps back to the workshop. The sun was getting stronger, and most of the blacksmith's shops had spread their drapes, stained with oil and powdered iron, over the street.

A few moments later, Hamid was knocking on the door of his house. His old mother, her face sombre, opened the door, lifted the grubby black veil from her face and shot him a look filled with sarcasm and blame, more painful than anything she could have said.

Hamid, though, refused to give in. He thrust open the door, then his heavy footsteps resounded on the earth floor. When, he wondered, would all this suffering come to an end? "Strength comes," the echo answered, "from those whose will is strong." But, he told himself, it was no longer a matter of strength of will. There was no other way; he must leave this place. If he stayed any longer, his sickness would come back. He washed his feet, hands and face, put on his best clothes and went out. His old mother was still looking at him critically. "What a world we live in now," she mumbled. "He's going to leave, no doubt of it."

"What a world we live in now!" He heard the repeated, fractured mumblings, but there was no other way. He had to leave.

Hamid re-crossed the road, clutching a bundle of documents. He wasn't really clear what these documents were, only that they were for his identity card. The employee wouldn't have misled him, wouldn't make out anything else. He absolutely needed an identity card. Now he had the documents under his arm, and all that was needed was the signature of the mayor. After that the agony would be over. His mother ought to appreciate him. He couldn't stand the situation any longer. All his money went on doctors, and the illness only got worse. Her temper, too, was growing worse by the day, and he couldn't do anything any more to satisfy her. There was no other way. He had to leave.

Just a few more minutes now and he'd have the small pink booklet, and all his dreams would come true. He reached the identity department, mounted the stairs one by one and handed the documents to the employee, who checked them over, then asked:

"Where's your father's identity card?"

"He's dead," Hamid replied.

"But you need his identity card."

"Give them back to me!"

Such was the brief exchange between Hamid and the employee at the identity department. When the employee placed the documents on the desk, Hamid took them without a word, then stumbled down the long staircase. He'd lost, he realized, all hope of leaving now. How could he get a license and start up his own place? He knew his mother had his father's identity card, and that she'd never let him see it. Resigned to enduring his torture, he headed back toward the workshop, the documents still under his arm.

*Umaima al-Khamees*

# SALMA THE OMANI

It was told in ancient tales how, if a beautiful witch from Oman lived in the trunk of a palm tree, the trunk would become hollow and fly off. The site of Oman was hazardous, overlooking the ocean, the sea of darkness, where closed bottles filled with genies have nestled for centuries on the sea bed.

In Oman, too, the sugar mixes with cardamom to make round sweets just like Salma's rounded cheek. The slave women of Oman are warm like the dates stored for winter, shining like the silver frames of the mirrors in palaces, and submissive like the flame of a lantern at dawn. This was why the merchants trading in slaves would have to pay out their last penny to enjoy the bracelet hung around an Omani ankle.

Mothers would terrify their daughters with tales of "Abu Dostain." He lived in the mountain caves, was thin as a snake and wary as a lizard; and on dark nights he'd come down from the mountains to seize young girls, carrying them off to distant places, or perhaps devouring them. Shepherds would often tell of human remains on the mountains peaks, of scattered necklaces and bracelets made from coloured beads.

Perhaps he existed, perhaps he didn't, like the genies or the magic carpet. No one ever saw him, yet everyone talked of him. People carried him inside themselves, and they avoided him as they did the devil. When this century began, the very mention of Abu Dostain's name would send the young Omani girls inside their homes, where they'd sink into a terror of night footsteps stealthily approaching.

The marble mountains of Oman were splendid and silent, as if held in an everlasting gasp in the presence of the sea. Um Salma chose the narrow sandy stretch between mountain and sea to build her cottage, beneath a great *ghaf* tree, and around it she raised her goats and hens. Her two daughters, Salma and Moza, would, with delight and excitement, pursue the waves and flee from the tide as it flowed toward the mountain crags. Glittering on the sea were the flags of countless venturesome sailors, who'd devoted the sails of their ships to wayward ambition, and were afterwards destroyed by the sea storms.

Salma, slim and slender like the mountain goats, dreamed of magical cities beyond the mountains. She'd fling the bucket into the well, and the bats hiding there would go flying off. Then she'd look down into the well at her reflection, and behind it she'd see the clouds scattered in the sky. The hens would cackle around her and fight their daily fights among themselves. She used to wonder about the daily alliances made among the hens. Carefully, she'd pour the milk into earthenware pots for drinking in the evening. The mountains knew her footsteps and watched her with affection from their soaring heights.

Boundaries were wide open, and the tribes feared the cities. When a Bedouin entered a city, they knew, he'd lose the desert and so lose himself. Frontiers were contentious at the start of the century, and the whole place was restive, hesitant between tribal tradition and the constitution of the state.

Salma's cheek remained round, like the sweets made from sugar and cardamom. To this day no one knows who spoke of her to Abu Dostain. Was it the mountain? The seasonal Indian birds? Or was it mere chance that decided how things should end?

It was a Tuesday evening, and the sea was breathing out its warm heavy breath on the shore, while shells slipped beneath the feet and the stars gazed down hard on the troubled waves.

Um Salma would tremble each time she heard of the Beluchi girl who'd vanished some days before. It was the talk of the whole village. Accounts differed, but they all centred on Abu Dostain. Inside the cottage the air was humid and stifling, and the three women brought their bedding outside, trusting to the protection of the mountains and the village dogs. The fence of the goats' yard was locked securely, and the lights went out in the village. Salma dug her hand into the sands of the damp beach, finding them warm and moist. She made small heaps and decorated them with shells.

He came down from the west side of the mountain, the seashells cracking beneath his leather shoes. He almost tripped, but took hold of a small mountain *samar* tree that scratched his hand. Salma, meanwhile, fell into a deep sleep.

He came closer, followed only by his shadow. The large body was the mother's. One of the smaller bodies then. Right over Salma's head, he bent down, and, first putting his hand over her mouth, swiftly took off his headscarf and used this to stuff her mouth. His headband he used to tie her hands, as he'd do with game he hunted. And before the next wave could break onto the beach, he'd put Salma in a *zanbeel* bag and was on his way to the west side of the mountain.

In the morning, the mother found one of the dogs killed, Moza trembling from a fearful nightmare, and Salma gone. As for Salma, she knew now that beautiful Omani women didn't just vanish inside a hollowed palm trunk; they were carried off, too, in a *zanbeel* bag and taken to the west side of the mountain on the way to Najd. As the smell of the sea receded, and the desert opened onto its far-reaching pathways, she began to scream. She screamed in agony, her voice breaking strongly out, then fading slowly away like the whine of a bullet, only to start as strongly once more.

Salma stopped screaming only when she found Faddah in another *zanbeel*. She embraced Faddah, who looked like Moza, and gave her some dates. Faddah whispered to her that a group of knights would come suddenly from the sea to rescue them, and they'd return to Oman. Salma was silent, listening intently, but all she could hear was the sound of the camels' hooves and the hubbub of Abu Dostain's men. And all the while she saw the rocks grow pale and the trees become fewer, till they reached the first edges of the hills of Najd.

There, Salma became like pieces of gold lodged in a secret pocket in Abu Dostain's belt. Her first night she slept in the palace, in the room of a huge black slave woman with great sagging breasts. She'd been the main wet nurse for many of the palace children, and enjoyed a very special status. Salma began to scream once more when told this woman was her new mother, that she should call her Mother Luwaila. Salma was strong-willed and hard to manage, and she'd never agree to take orders.

Salma never saw the sea again. She'd dream of the sea, but the sea would vanish along with the waves and never come back. She imagined her mother's heart being crushed with grief, like the beans of coffee when they were crushed in the grinder. She wanted to tell her mother she was alive, that the human remains and beads found in the caves were nothing to do with her.

She remained wilful and headstrong, till at last everyone in the palace began calling her "Salma the water scorpion." As the years passed, Salma knew many intimacies. But her children would die a few days after their birth, so that the other women advised her to wear charms, to protect her against those who bore children away. She suffered, too, from constant seizures, and this made people in the palace fear her and say she was possessed. At last old age found its way to Salma. The silver rings darkened on her lean fingers, and her mistress began to look for the chance to set her free. Salma's freedom came as the fulfilment of a vow her mistress had made, concerning the return of her son from Iraq.

Mother Luwaila was long dead now, and the seizures had increased apace. Everyone feared her, and no one dared approach to wipe away the white spittle that gathered around her lips when the seizures surprised her. When Salma was still not fifty, and when she had stayed three days in her room with no one daring to approach her, the driver Mubarak took her to the home for old people, where Saif the Omani was guard. He'd travelled for many years, before settling into his present position.

Every morning Salma would wait to hear the sound of Saif's plastic shoes in the garden; and, through talking with him, she regained the sea of Oman drop by drop. Oman: the rapture of the seashores, the glitter of the marble mountains with the shining moon, the slim goats that looked like deer, and the bewitching jinn of the palm trees.

As the talking and the standing by the door went on, the people at the home decided Saif should marry Salma. Saif was happy, and took a joyful part in all the preparations. Salma wept for a long time on Saif's old shoulder, telling him how her mother's name was Sa'ida and her sister was called Moza.

One night Saif sang for her an old Omani song. The music, the mixture of drum beats and strings, raced through the night darkness, recalling, deep in the heart, the forsaken land covered with incense and henna. Saif sang to her, dancing joyfully: "My moon, carry our daughter." And Salma clapped her wasted hands with their blackened silver rings, and said:

It bore her away and departed!
It bore her away and departed!

*Najat Khayyat*

# ONE DAY THE SUN WILL RISE

One day the sun will shine on this stagnant lake of mine, wipe away all the sadness and cleanse the silt in the depths. One day the sun will rise; so my mother's told me time and again. And it will give me strength to carry on along my life's dark road.

The sun will rise. But when? That's something buried deep in the unknown. Everything around me tells me to wait. But how? How can I wait?

Others live their lives day by day, hour by hour; but my life's like dry autumn leaves. At any instant the wind might gust, carry off a whole part of my life in its fearful swirl. The long days pass, and still I repeat, absurd and abject: "One day the sun will rise." Yet I've never asked myself, never wondered, how the sun will rise, where the dawn will spring from. Was there, somewhere, a rift in my darkness, through which the light might creep in and find me? Would my hand find some way to dig and let the light creep in?

This question I left within myself, unanswered. When a shock comes, everything's paralysed, the springs of life are clogged. You don't ask what's happened. You just plunge into distress, then, once the numbness is past, you start to question yourself. But the numbness was still with me. I wasn't asking questions, just waiting to be free of the darkness of so many things dragging me down: a way of life I'd followed from the moment I came into this world, outdated traditions we'd inherited from thousands of years, which we dragged behind us for all their cruel weight. A husband above all – or should I rather speak of him as worms crawling into the darkness of my grave, to eat from my body? And a dusty, run-down home where everything recalled the life of centuries past, filled with misery, backwardness and hardship.

Those dusty shutters seared by the hot sandstorms, the ceiling where horrible insects grazed, a great fat jar (our twentieth-century fridge), and an old Indian sofa, its ends ragged from use by two generations, who ate, drank and slept on it all their lives, till they had to leave it and be buried at last.

That sofa seems to be staring at me now, sadly, mourning my lost years. As for its corners, worn down by time's ravages, I can only wait for them to tumble on my head and bury my short-lived hopes.

My mother's life had been wretched and burdensome. Yet, one day, she came to me smiling, and I asked her anxiously: "When will it rise, that sun you promised me?" She gazed at me with a mother's affection, then said: "If I could, my darling, I'd redeem you with my soul. If my whole being could burn, so that the sun rose from it, I'd burn myself for you. Don't lose hope, daughter. The sun doesn't shine on those who lose hope. Be patient; patience always brings its rewards."

I murmured something, feeling inside me a suppressed revolt that shook my very bones. Did I have enough years for patience? Or would the happy ending come when I was buried and my bones mouldering?

A voice screamed out inside me: "Are you any better now than you will be then, a body in a dark grave? Death would rid you of the pain, be more merciful perhaps. The husband – the worms living with you now, silting up your lake – this husband provides your bread and butter, but he takes a double price in return, from your mind and your life." Oh patience, help me. Isn't it time, you sun, to rise on my black horizon, and take pity on me and my pain? The stench of my silted lake repels me. Why, sun, won't you wash away my anger and make my waters clean? Rise, sun, and melt my chains, let me feel, for just one moment, that I'm a human being, living a worthwhile life in all the freedom God granted to Adam's children.

Oh sun, rise. My night's been so long, my eye's grown blind from the pitch dark. Rise and delight my eyes, with the splendid colours of your dawn. Warm the blood in my veins before it dries. I'm so weary of all this talk, helplessly crushed here in myself. I close my eyes, sadly, on two burning tears.

Here's the husband, the grimy worm moving its head this way and that, in search of a tasty meal to defile with its trace. Like a dark nightmare he crawls on my breast. My blood goes cold, my breath's cut off. I scream, but no one hears. My body rebels, but the nightmare comes down on my face like a fist, a warm liquid flows over my lips, to stir up my feelings and set my nerves on fire. I rebel, and gouge countless wounds into his flesh.

The worm stopped eating my flesh. A shining thought passed through my mind, the first thread of the sun. The numbing clouds vanished from my thoughts, and I started asking myself, why? Why had I lived so long under the tyrant slave master who owned every part of me, while I owned nothing of myself? Why had destiny flung me into the arms of this black, malicious worm? How could I have endured it, to live in this dark grave? Why had my eyes remained there in the darkness? Why hadn't I rebelled? And the answer came to me. None of us can travel life's road as we wish, so long as a higher will dictates our steps.

I felt at rest, as this final truth dawned on me. But I saw a giant, vast and looming like a raging storm. Stretching, yawning, then rising to stir the depths of my stagnant lake. The waves raged, as if some spring had uncoiled far below, sending the murky water racing off. Light came to my dry eyes. I stared at the worm with disgust, felt like throwing up all the bitter bread inside me.

In a single moment all those questions rang in my head. As the light shone in my eyes at last, the giant scowled at me, moved towards me to make an end of me, put out the light in my eyes, crush my humanity under his feet.

An instinct, long dead since my husband took possession of me, was reborn in my blood: the instinct to survive. I stood there in front of the decrepit wooden shutters. Then, with a swift movement, I slipped from his hands. His weight struck the shutters and they fell together.

Why was my head squeezed between these bandages? And why did my eyelids feel heavy, as if weighed down by stones? I groaned, heavily, and I felt the pain tearing my ribs. Slowly I opened my eyelids. The place was dark and warm. A calendar hung on the white wall, and a beam of light, finding its way through the door, cut across the calendar.

The darkness scared me, and I stirred in my comfortable bed. I wanted to call for help. I wanted someone to reach out to me. I gave a loud cry.

The door opened, and the beam of light grew broader. Still my eyes gazed at the light, falling there on the floor of my room. I didn't feel the hand that was touching me, or hear the soft voice that was talking to me.

My eyes were hungry for light. I could still hear the voice, but I wasn't taking it in. All my focus was on the light. I wanted the light. Let the light engulf the place, let it come in to bathe me, to heal my wounds and wipe away my pain. Let it be. I screamed: Let in the light!

The hands around me quivered, then they pulled apart the dark green curtains. The light came in and engulfed me. I smiled peacefully, then lost consciousness.

I woke. When did this radiant face greet me, with a smile warm and filled with promise, with soft, compassionate words that calmed me even if I didn't grasp their meaning?

I spent days lying on that white bed. Each day a man in a white gown would come and tear a piece of paper from the calendar, announcing the birth of a new day; and I'd lose a day of my life like everyone else. But there was no storm each hour, to come and blow part of that life away. Every day the light engulfed the place where I was, and I felt it deeply. Every day the sun entered my room and cleansed my wounds.

I began to wonder where I was, why parts of my body were wrapped in white and drawn together. I felt my face and head, and found they were wrapped in bandages. A man, the doctor, came in and put an end to these thoughts.

"Where am I?" I asked him.

He patted my cheek and smiled. We'd almost lost hope, he told me, that you'd still be able to think. Good, you can still think, child. You're in hospital. The shutters of your house collapsed.

He stopped, and his expression grew sombre. Later I found out the reason for this. It was the worm, my husband, call him what you will. He'd been killed when the shutters fell. I didn't want to know how it had all happened. My thoughts went far off, towards the unseen horizon, to the long awaited dawn my mother had painted.

My mother came that evening to see me. "Thank God, my darling," she said, with the deepest gratitude. "You're able to think again."

I replied, utterly happy.

"Mother," I said softly, "it's the day of the sun. The sun's risen, just as you promised me it would. The dawn's so splendid, it smells so wonderful. Mother, the sun's risen."

I leaned my head on my mother's breast, and she embraced me with her hand that had tailored a whole life for me. Always after that, whenever I was asked my date of birth, I'd give my answer without the smallest hesitation. I was born, I'd say, the day the sun rose.

*Fahd al-Khilaiwi*

# THREE EPISODES

*First Episode*

Hunger, tedium and the sad sea of Jeddah. A dead dialogue went on through what remained of the heart. The stench from the sea sand felt bitter in the nostrils. The men scattered, then gathered like insects in the wet asphalt squares.

Jeddah's an estranged city, whose tears never cease to flow. The phone rang. It was Laila. Her husband, it seemed, was out of the house, bent on his abandoned, meaningless courses. Her voice was deep, made beautiful by some coquettish womanly touch, gained, no doubt, from memories of her girlish childhood. When they were courting one another, her husband used to say her voice was like the sound of a violin.

As she talked, a deep sense of nausea went through me. Still, I wanted to fulfil my dream: of declaring to some woman how I hated all women.

"Laila," I said, "I hate women."

She gave a mocking laugh.

"Liar!" she retorted. "I swear to God you're a liar – you son of – "

Hunger, tedium and the sad sea of Jeddah – a magic flowing in the blood.

"The holiness of suicide."

"Liar! I swear to God you're a liar – son of – "

Her voice was transformed to a piece of gypsy music that danced deep inside my head, then spread to my body.

"Don't read so much," she said. "It'll drive you crazy."

She was just imagining things, I thought. Reading, for me, didn't mean true salvation. Even writing didn't lead to putting things right. Often, indeed, it was a mere suppressed overflow, out on to paper.

"Women," I said, with immense satisfaction, "don't serve women's own real goals."

That surprised her.

"You're complicated," she remarked. "And sick."

A savage roughness overcame my tongue, and Laila started crying.

*Second Episode*

A grey mouse, pregnant to all appearances, passed close by me. I shuddered and spat. The street was dull, and into the people's features sank a kind of lazy worry that overlay their natural wrinkles.

I looked far into the distance, and I could see the street, like a belly within which human beings were struggling, as they persisted in living out the worst kind of existence.

The mouse crossed the street, heading for the bathroom of one of the houses. Then it vanished.

*Third Episode*
*Fragment of a Dream*

The shadow spread beneath the mountain like a crooked line. The crowd of thirsty people, come in from the desert, were talking. They looked mournful and sad.

The shadow quivered around the people and the mountain. Their footsteps buried themselves in the deep sand. An unarmed man appeared, exhorted the hungry people. The master of the mountain laughed loudly, eyeing the crowd.

Thick blood spread, then congealed inside the forest; it was turned to a solid object, which was flung away and formed a lonely cave. The man appeared once more. He smiled to the crowd, astonishment anchored on his lips.

*Hiyam al-Mifleh*

# CRAZY MINUTES!

Tick – tick – tick –

If I hadn't been home alone, and if I hadn't had an urgent appointment for five that afternoon, I would never have put that noisy alarm clock next to me.

I flung my weary body down on the bed, like some old log. Every muscle in my body strained hard against its sister muscle, refusing to loosen. I'd never known such a hectic day as this one.

Ceaseless work – meetings – visits – discussions that kept resonating in my head, even though the working day was over.

Tick – tick –

I even ate my lunch at top speed. Then I set the alarm clock for four o'clock precisely.

Tick – tick –

I closed my eyes, waiting for the shadow of sleep to bear me off to its sombre caves. I longed for this, for the repose I could now drink in perhaps, to keep my blood flowing through those tense, exhausted veins of mine.

Tick – tick –

I had just a single hour ahead of me, from three to four. A single hour to relax my mind and body, before getting ready to go for my appointment.

It was to be my first literary evening. I could feel fear in every part of me. Restlessness shook my body, set off a wakeful alertness through every cell in my brain.

Tick – tick – tick –

That stupid alarm clock was heightening my fears, setting my nerves tingling, making every cell in my body, it seemed to me, explode. My pulse began to race, and that led to a brutal sensation in my forehead. It was like an electric current in my head, ready to tear away my very soul, at any moment.

Tick – tick –

The story I was going to read that evening was a symbolic one. I needed to be utterly calm, to concentrate closely as I read it, to be sure the audience grasped its full significance.

Tick – tick –

My heart pounded at the very thought of those hundreds of eyes, on the verge of devouring me as I read the story. My tired mind was filled with the terror of confronting that audience.

Tick – tick –

The crazy minutes were running on, and still my body found no vestige of rest. Time was drifting away, and with it my dream of an hour of good sleep to wipe away my nervousness, take away the black circles from around my exhausted eyes.

Tick – tick –

If only those ticks would be quiet, just for a few seconds – let time pass quietly, silently.

Tick –

As I read the introduction, I thought, I'll keep my voice low. Then, as I reach the climax, I'll raise it.

Tick –

When I answer the audience's questions, I must concentrate on what they've asked.

The crazy alarm clock rang. It was four o'clock!

I grabbed the clock furiously, and hurled it – with all the strength I had left – right across the room. It hit the wall opposite, fell down on to the carpet, then spun around and came to rest facing me. To my great relief, it didn't sound as loud now.

I returned to gathering the pieces of my self, scattered this way and that by the ticking of the deadly alarm clock. It was four o'clock now!

I had an hour to get myself ready, then go and hold the evening. I was still exhausted. The ticking of the alarm clock had irritated me, adding to my torment. My head was beating from the ticks.

I just couldn't drag myself out of bed. It was going to take five minutes of the hour to collect my restless self together. There was no time left for sleep. I could only try and charge myself with some enormous energy, without sleep.

How about some yoga, I thought? That was said to be good for body and soul alike. Why, I wondered, hadn't I done some yoga right at the start?

I took a deep breath, then held it. I stopped the pulsing in my veins, the angry flow of blood surging through them. I let my hand rest by my side. Then, slowly, I breathed out. All the noises, clashing inside my head and numbing my body, fell silent.

I repeated the process, a second, third, fourth time. My body felt charged with energy now. I moved my hand and my foot. I opened my eyes.

I could feel a powerful force taking me over. The blood was coursing into my cheeks. I stretched with pleasure, I yawned, then sat up in bed, giving thanks to whoever had invented yoga. Here I was, ready and prepared to hold the evening.

Recalling that infuriating alarm clock, I looked at it where it lay on the carpet. I could see its hand shining brightly; it seemed to be putting its tongue out at me.

I leapt towards it, as if I'd been stung. Then I brought it so close to my eyes, I almost pushed it through them. The luminous hand was pointing, obstinately, to nine o'clock precisely.

*'Abdallah al-Nasser*

# MUZNA

"Oh, how my heart enjoys tiring itself out!"

"Tiring itself out?"

"How can a heart go on tiring itself like this? Loving may be a problem, Hammad, but the worst thing of all is not to be loved. I love this village so much. But it doesn't understand now, how I love it. How deep my feelings are."

"Calm down. These things aren't so very important. They're just passing fancies – they bear down on the heart sometimes, make you feel that way. Then off they go like the wind – when it passes over the plants in the fields, say, or over the reeds. It sways them this way and that, breaks them down, then away it goes again. There's just stillness and silence left behind."

"No, Hammad. You're talking of things you know nothing about. Or maybe that's just personal to you – some rush of feeling comes, grips you for a time, then you calm right down."

The scent of palms and dewy grass, filling the valley, woke a painful longing that suffused the heart. It was like some perfume, imbuing the soul with a mingled passion: sorrow and happiness, longing and yearning, hope and pain. It was a beautiful thing with its own mystic pain; a kind of sting. Yet there was a glow too that lit up the soul and filled it with a dewy fragrance.

He let the tips of his fingers play idly with the cold, soft sand.

"Two weeks I've been here now, Hammad. I can't find what I used to find, and I haven't met the people I used to meet. I haven't found what I was looking for. I used to carry this village in my heart – in my baggage and the corners of my memory. It was the sweetest memory I had, the loveliest thing in my whole life. My village was a candle that stayed with me wherever I was: in cities, villages and streets; on trains; among snow-covered mountains and landscapes covered with green. The place is a monstrosity now! Look at those concrete houses, stuck up alongside the mud ones. Those great pylons rearing over the palm trees. The paved streets, the big satellite dishes jammed on the tops of roofs, the cars blocking the roads and squares. They've taken the heart right out of me. Oh, Hammad!"

Hammad had been with him there as a young boy, working on the farm. He'd reaped the crops and fed the cattle, filled the pool with water, helped out his employer, carried the lunch from the village, made the tea, and, alongside Nasser, watched for the birds in the harvested wheat. They'd chase off the birds, there together in the heart of the tamarisks. Burned and sweating from the midday sun, they'd drink from the pitcher slung up in the vineyard, and swim in the pool. Just before sundown, they'd walk down the valley and on to their home, where they'd eat their dinner and pray the sunset prayer. Then they'd sit with their relatives, or play in the moonlight, in the square in front of their home. Or else they'd go on down the valley and romp in the sand, getting up to boyish mischief – digging holes in the road, then covering them with bushes so the cars wouldn't see them. Or else they'd steal grapes and pomegranates, or cucumbers and tomatoes.

Finally, tired out from such evening tricks, they'd creep back to the southern end of the roof on the big house and sleep till sunrise, when the palm tree would cover them with its cool shade.

Hammad was married now and owned a house in the village. He sold cattle and provisions. As for Nasser, he'd come back from Europe, to a good official appointment in one of the government services. He'd had dreams of returning to his childhood, of reviving the old times if only for a single night. He'd thought it all out carefully. He would, he decided, spend his holidays in the village. He'd meet Hammad again, and they'd talk and arrange to meet up with other childhood friends. They'd go to the same places as before, try and do the same things. He was searching for the taste and smell of the old days.

They did all the old things. They dug holes for the cars, they stole watermelons, then cut them with stones and put them in the sand to cool. But something was missing even so. After two weeks in the village, Nasser realized he'd just been playing a stupid role. There was no point trying to reconstruct things, the way they'd been once. Actually, things had just happened then. They'd been part and parcel of childhood life, of its natural laws, with no strain or acting involved. However hard he strove, those days would never come back.

Sometimes, in the old days, Nasser would sit by the water before sunset. There'd once been a pool, over on the west side of the valley, and to the east and west of this there'd been palm trees. In the summer, square and valley alike would be filled with the tents of nomads, who came every year to pick the dates and gather in fodder for their animals from the nearby farms. Just before sunset, the grazing cattle would come down from the pastures and gather at the pool to drink. Young girls and women, too, would cluster around to fetch water in their pitchers, while others would bring their clothes to wash at the water's edge.

Where Muzna had come from, or where she'd been born, he had no idea. She'd just landed, like a migrating bird. Her body was tender like a pomegranate. She was tanned and slim, and in her large black eyes was gathered all the sweetness and delight of desert life. She had an angelic, smiling face, fair but just a little tanned, with a subtle radiance that touched the heart.

From that angel's face shone a hidden, mystical beauty, beyond words to describe: the desert beauty woven from dawn and moonlight, from magical flow and morning dew. He saw her as she was filling her pitcher with water, her mind elsewhere, and she leapt like a startled deer. Shy, embarrassed at the sudden meeting, she stayed motionless and said nothing, while he simply stood there, stunned and marvelling.

He didn't sleep at all that night. There was a tension in his heart, and a sense of void too. He'd place his hand on his chest, keep tossing around in his bed. Then he'd curl up, leaning his head forward towards his knees, striving somehow to close that void in his chest. But still he couldn't sleep.

That entrancing beauty had stolen his heart and taken over his mind. Still he turned in his bed, gazing out at the heavens, asking a glimmering star where she was, what she was doing, if she was asleep or awake. Was she speaking or silent? Was she thinking of him? A delightful thought – how marvellous that would be, if she was thinking of him! He started telling the star all about his feelings, all about his secret. If only it could have carried a message from him! He would have told Muzna of his feelings; he would have sent them through the lustrous glow of a planet that shone just as his own heart was shining, from the spell of that bewitching girl.

Next morning he made a round of the tents, watching her from a distance. Dogs barked at him, faces scowled at him. In the afternoon, he sat beneath a palm tree, bathed in sweat. He cast his eyes over all the tents. Perhaps he might see that angel, draped in her tattered clothes. But he had no experience in these matters, and lacked courage too. And so he was left quite bewildered, tense, a prey to aching perplexity.

"Hammad," he said, "my heart's been stolen. Muzna's destroyed me, Hammad!"

"You love her, Nasser?"

"I swear to God, if my love for her landed on a rock on the Tuwaik mountain – it would turn the rock to ashes!"

"Talk to her, Nasser – "

"I can't. If only I knew whose daughter she is."

"You idiot!" Hammad said. "I'll find out about her for you."

"I'm not an idiot. If you'd seen what I've seen, come to know what I have, you wouldn't, I swear to God, want to eat or drink again!"

Hammad laughed. Blindness, he said, was in the heart, not in the eyes at all.

"Don't talk like that, Hammad," Nasser said. "Just show me her tent and tell me whose daughter she is."

"All right," Hammad said. "God willing, I'll find out about her."

One day, after sunset prayer, Hammad pointed with his hand.

"That's her father," he said. "That man there."

"Her father?" Nasser exclaimed. "You really mean that grubby, white-haired man's her father?"

One day, while she was drinking her morning coffee, Nasser's mother Tarfa addressed her husband, Abu Nasser.

"Your son," she said, smiling and handing him a cup. "He's a man now."

Nasser, unable to keep his feelings secret, had told her the whole story.

"What do you mean, Tarfa?"

"Your son's in love. He wants to get married."

Abu Nasser laughed, then winked.

"You mean he's grown up?"

She laughed too, then gazed down at the ground.

"Who is she?" he asked.

"I don't know," she answered. Her tone was anxious.

Abu Nasser covered his mouth with his hand, trying to hide his laughter.

"Well," he said, "where's the problem? I'll see them married, then they can go and live in the fodder room."

Soon after, Abu Nasser, Nasser and Hammad were sitting under a fig tree, drinking their morning coffee.

"So, Nasser," Abu Nasser said, barely able to hold back his laughter, "your mother tells me you want to get married."

Nasser trembled, his heart leaping. He was thunderstruck.

"It's all right," his father went on, in a bantering manner. "No need to be shy. Just tell me who she is."

Nasser said nothing. His face was covered with sweat, his body quivering to the very tips of his fingers.

"Come on, no need to be shy!"

But Nasser simply froze. His heart was pounding, and he couldn't get out a word.

"Tell him," Hammad said. "No need to be shy."

Abu Nasser turned.

"Do you know who she is, Hammad?" he asked.

Hammad drew back, laughing. His smile was a shaky one even so, nervous and tentative.

"Come on," Abu Nasser said. "You tell me. Nasser's too shy."

"Shall I tell you? You won't be annoyed?"

"Annoyed? Why should I be? Where's the problem? Marriage isn't a thing to be ashamed of. Nasser's grown up now. If he doesn't get married today, he'll get married some time."

"Abu Nasser, your son loves Musained's daughter."

Abu Nasser leapt up as if he'd been stung.

"What? What did you say? Musained? Are you drunk, or crazy, or what? You, Nuwaiser, get up, curse you! You think I'm going to let you marry the daughter of some wandering blacksmith? A man who works with pots? Are you crazy? I swear to God, if I hear another word about it, I'll break a log of wood over your head.

And you won't be my son any more either – I'll disown you. Get away from here, curse you! You want to marry a blacksmith's daughter, you grubby scoundrel?"

The wretched lad took the cutting words in silence. You might have thought he was a mute, or some lump of lead. He held down all his emotions, all his fine and noble feelings. It was as if he had a heavy rock inside himself, as if he was sinking under the weight of his feelings, helpless as a prisoner fettered with heavy chains.

He shut out his love, his feelings, even from himself, lying sunk in a kind of unconscious pain. His young emotions, his fledgling feelings, were like his tender body, ready to break under the fearsome assault. Helplessly sensitive as he was, he shattered at the first blow, his heart broken and prey to suffering. His smiling youth and joy were gone.

His links with Hammad were severed too. The pair drifted apart, no longer seeing things in the same way. Nasser, pale and quiet, had become an enigma, while Hammad, completely excluded, had no idea what to do. Nasser had become a riddle no one could read; no one could reach him any longer. All he ever gave out were gestures, or else a few abrupt, meaningless words that fell the way the pale autumn leaves fall to their quiet death.

"Tell me, Hammad," he said once, racked with pain and sorrow, "don't people who work with iron have a God too? Aren't they the children of God?"

Um Duhaim was a woman in her seventies. She was tall, and, as she walked, seemed like an upright palm tree. Sometimes, too, she'd sway just as a palm tree sways when a strong wind blusters against its trunk. She was a friend and neighbour of Um Nasser, an older woman who stayed by Um Nasser's side in times of trouble.

She was sitting with Um Nasser now, a pot of coffee between them. She had a tender face, red and full, with a big nose that curved forward on account of her age. Her features had begun to droop, for all the smiles and vestiges of beauty. Lowering her head, she began toying with the gold rings that turned easily now, especially the one on her little finger; either the finger had grown thinner or the ring had loosened with the years. That ring, she'd tell people, had been handed down to her from her grandmother Heila; it had been her grandmother's wedding ring from the late Sultan, who'd bought it when he was a sea diver. She put down her coffee cup, still twisting the ring, then spoke in a voice low but full of self-assurance.

"God only knows, Um Nasser," she said. "Maybe the boy's bewitched. Maybe the blacksmith's girl's put a spell on him. Those people cast pebbles and write charms. I'm afraid the boy's fallen under a spell."

Um Nasser was leaning forward attentively, her hands folded, her fingers twisting in and out.

"What can we do, Um Duhaim?" she asked. "What do you think?"

Um Duhaim closed her eyes and put her right hand on her henna-dyed hair.

"The only one who can help," she said, "is Um Khlawi in Manfuha. She can melt some lead and undo the spell."

"But what about Abu Nasser? He might not agree."

"Leave it to me. I'll take Nasser myself. We'll pretend you didn't know anything about it."

Um Nasser pleaded, wept in her son's arms, kissed his head and cheeks. Finally he agreed to go with Um Duhaim.

In a dark room filled with blue smoke, a strange smell and soft whispers, Nasser sat on an old pillow, feeling frightened and confused.

A pot was placed on his head and some lead was trickled into it, making a bubbling sound as the lead met the water. While Um Duhaim held the pot firm, Um Khlawi made mysterious movements and whisperings, then took a dark-coloured rooster with a big comb, slit its neck and let it loose. The rooster leapt around, beating its wings against the walls of the small room, letting out strange sounds and cries. Um Khlawi, meanwhile, was uttering prayers, repeating special phrases and throwing her hands into the empty air. The rooster fell and began fluttering its wings on the floor, thin sounds of death coming from its breast. Then, at last, it was still. Um Khlawi took the rooster's blood, still warm, and used it to paint Nasser's face and head. Nasser saw a man sitting in the corner of the dark room. His eyes were shining, his hands fettered with iron chains.

After a time, Um Khlawi poured a bucket of cold water over Nasser.

"Get up," she told him. "The evil's left you. The spell's gone away."

Um Duhaim placed thirty riyals in Um Khlawi's bosom, and Um Khlawi gave her a small bundle containing a potion that Nasser was to take at sunrise and sunset. But no dog should be barking when he took it, and no donkey should be braying.

Nasser left the dark room and went out into the light. Once there, he rubbed his eyes, cursed Um Khlawi and Um Duhaim, and flung away the potion. He looked thin, and seemed sad, pale and shocked by all the things that had happened.

He grew ever thinner and weaker, like a bird struck by a bullet that had failed to kill it, a bullet it still carried in its body. Hammad would take him off to the farm, doing his best to amuse him and draw him out from his silence; and still Nasser remained stunned and apart, like a Sufi who'd renounced everything, even talk. At the end of the hot summer, Nasser stood watching the truck, as it raised dust and noise all around it. The tent was torn down, the cattle were loaded into the truck. There he stood as they left, watching them from behind a cloud of tears.

On the first day of secondary school, Abu Nasser went to the teacher with his son.

"Mr Fahd," he said, "the boy's in a bad way. He's infatuated with a blacksmith's daughter – they say she's cast a spell on him. We helped him get rid of the spell, but he's still just the same. You can see for yourself. Curse that blacksmith!"

The teacher told the father to leave matters in his hands. It was just young love, he said. It would need a good deal of patience and careful handling, but, by God's grace, all would be well.

The teacher was known as a wise, resourceful man, and for the clever, tactful way he handled things. He was renowned, too, for his patience and powers of persuasion. He had Nasser take part in sports and showered him with books, presenting him with a copy of the *Thousand and One Nights*. Slowly time passed, and the gash Nasser carried began to heal. Even so, the effect was much like the blow of an axe on a tree trunk, where the mark becomes bigger as the trunk itself grows taller.

Nasser grew up, maturing beyond youthful impulse; and still that angelic face was imprinted, burned even, on the walls of his heart.

He travelled and visited many cities. He lived in modern cities, settling in one by the sea, full of beauty and delight and allurement, the ocean lying beneath its feet along a shoreline curving this way and that. At the city's back were green-sloped mountains, their peaks covered with snow. The houses in the valley were harmoniously built, with roofs of red tiles like beds of red roses. Houses lay scattered among the mountains as if asleep in the heart of forest and greenery, while springs tumbled from the mountain tops, flowing into the city and its suburbs.

A prosperous city, overflowing with the faces of lovely young girls, which looked themselves like clear springs of water. Here, in this city, Nasser discovered things he'd never thought of or even dreamed of. At the university his female classmates were skilled in making themselves beautiful and showing off their beauty. Everything amazed him, everything suited and tempted him. Yet it had no allure.

The village, fringed with palm trees and sleeping in the heart of the valley, stayed as a living picture in his heart and mind. He bore it in his soul, like a sweet dream from which he never wanted to wake. When that village, that magical genie, lifted her veil, every city tumbled down in front of him.

"This city of yours," he once told his colleague George, "is the most beautiful city there is."

"I know it is," George said.

"And yet my village is more beautiful still."

"A piece of paradise, I suppose," George said mockingly, "dropped down on the hellish sand!"

"No, it's a village surrounded with seas of sand and mirage. It's a village burnished by the sun, washed by the moon; the mirage wanders around it and the stars twinkle at it. It's a small heart in the vast desert wastes. A small heart beating with love and friendliness. My village is a dark secret, like the dream of a virgin, wrapped in phantoms."

"Really! I never knew the desert foxes had a magical paradise like that."

"Foxes? Us? You son of – "

He poked him in mock anger.

"Listen, my friend," he went on, "your beautiful city's a marvel, but it's like the rhythm of some electric musical instrument, or one made of copper. It's like a noisy band, and coloured lights, and feverish dance. My village is like the sound of a sad flute, carried from far away by the night breeze."

\*\*\*

The night breeze was blowing on the valley as always, the moon casting its gleam on the sleeping palm trees that were like young brides. Nasser's hand was playing with the cold, soft sand. The valley was empty of people, the village squares were empty apart from the rows of parked cars blocking the ways in and out. The streets were empty apart from the faces of the foreign workers and the sounds of the satellite TV stations, mostly foreign too, to be heard from the windows of the houses.

"Hammad," Nasser said, his hand still grasping the sand, soft and cold, "Hammad, the village has been deformed. It's alien now. You can't see the face of that young lover any more."

The wind was carrying the sound of the water in the pool, as it lapped gently towards beasts and people who'd long since abandoned it. Nasser's spirit flew through the corners and shadows of the old, simple village: the farms, the shadows of the palm trees, the flocks of birds, the singing of the peasants, the mud houses, the faces of the good people; and that angelic, bewitching face.

The village he'd carried with him to all the foreign cities, to which he himself was a stranger now – this village didn't know him any more. Or perhaps it didn't love him any more.

But the beloved face of Muzna, and the picture of the peaceful village, still watered his heart with the nectar of love; and in his blood still ran the love and longing for his village.

*Hasan al-Niʿmi*

# FOOTNOTES TO LAILA'S HISTORY

*This is a symbolic story lamenting what the author regards as the absence of love on earth in modern times. Laila is a legendary figure, the prototype of love in Arabic culture, whom Qais loved till he grew frantic and died. The Umayyad story of Qais and Laila has endured through the centuries, and crossed over to other countries, languages and cultures, as the symbol of pure love par excellence.*

It was a different morning for the village, a morning that wept from grief over Laila. Now, what do you know about Laila? They said many things about Laila's life. If she'd died, they said, then weeping over her death would have been right and proper. But where was she? Then what had once been a burning question faded gradually in the course of life.

Qais was one of her lovers, Laila's lovers, and such was his desire for her that he wandered great distances, searching, seeking to find what had become of her. One day they took his Laila from him, they led her away, till she turned to a bloodless dream. Standing at the margins of the desert, gazing at the line where earth and sky met, Qais wondered: on which part of the earth might Laila be now?

No one said outright that he was mad, but they all agreed he was strange.

"Where's your Laila?" they'd ask him.

And he'd reply, with angry disdain:

"Say rather, where's your Laila, our Laila, Laila of those coming before and after us."

"Don't you feel her loss?" Qais asked them once.

"Indeed we do," they replied, "but we've grown used to her absence. She lived in a luminous age, but now she belongs to history."

Laila was the space and the sky. She was the symbol of motherhood. Laila, who lived a vivid dream, had faded. Even those who vied in butchering her wept and covered their ill-doing, for fear of a tyrant's iron fist or the sarcasm of some insolent person. Laila's history became a secret told only by the closed whispers of the heart, within the vaults of darkness.

Only Qais went out in search of Laila and what remained of her life. The day of his departure made history. He smiled, promised the people he'd find Laila. He could feel her pulse in his heart, in his arms, in a fierce strength, in an overwhelming courage that took hold of him whenever he thought of her. At a certain place on this earth, he stood tall before a vast building where great numbers of people had gathered. For them Qais was a myth in human form. His request was a simple one, or so it seemed to him. And when he was granted permission to speak, he revealed his love by asking about Laila.

An old man asked him:

"And who are you to go in search of her?"

The question saddened him.

"She is the sole desire," he answered, "that prompts me to go on with my life. I've lived through her, and I'll go on living in hope of her return. She is purer than the whole face of this earth."

"If only I knew where she was," the old man said.

While walking another road, his question turned to brain-sickness. He'd ask those who passed: "Have you seen Laila?"

He feared the seed of despair he felt growing inside him. He shook his head, like a drunken man striving to muster his strength.

"Should Laila not be a living creature," he asked himself, "could she not be a supernatural one?" The notion left him thunderstruck. Yet it was a truth in his search for Laila. "May it be God's will," he said, as he knocked on the genie's door.

"Who are you?" he was asked.

"I am one who believes in Laila's existence."

"And how does that concern us?"

"You are mighty and powerful."

"Each person has his own Laila. Whoever loses her is unfortunate. Search for her."

Despair began creeping into his heart. As he made ready to leave, a harsh voice stopped him, asking him to stay till the night. "I'll wait a further night," Qais said to himself.

When night fell, he was taken to a dark room with a small window through which a dim light shone, lessening his solitude somewhat. He drew nearer, then gazed with fear and trepidation. What was that he was seeing? He was quite dumbfounded – surely the sight before him was some kind of miracle, in an age void of miracles. He could see Laila. She was lost, destitute and oppressed among people. He saw her as a body, quivering with fragile life. The sight left him desolate. Worn down she might be, yet for him her existence was precious above all. "Did Laila," he wondered, "once have strength in those legs of hers?" But, however that might be, the present was the important thing. So he viewed the matter.

Through that small opening, he saw what he'd never in his life seen before. He saw people weeping over Laila's state, people ever more believing in her existence.

Still the belief in Laila grew, turning to a thing of untold dimension. Qais was astonished to see the change in the love of Laila. Was he dreaming? Was it akin, perhaps, to waking from a nap on a hot afternoon? No longer was he the sole person in love with Laila. She, who was a mere wisp of air, had become the focus of overmastering love, living in the blood of others. People awaited her arrival, from near and far. That had no importance, for her presence was overwhelming. Even those who didn't love Laila felt her presence, and felt the coming peril that would reveal their secrets. Suddenly, Qais leapt up. He shrieked till the place echoed with his shrieking. Somewhere on earth he saw how tyrants were plotting to kill what remained of Laila.

*Laila al-Ohaidib*

# MOVEMENT OF A STATUE

That evening (before she died) she talked to me a lot.

"I can't believe I'm dying!"

"No one can bear the thought of their own death – "

"Do you think those false children will feel sorry when I'm dead?"

"Even the maid will feel sorry."

"And then they'll meet new people?"

"People can't stop being human. Whatever happens."

"But I've done so little. I don't want to die now!"

"We all say that, right at the end. But people still have to die."

The street, in the morning stillness, had a hazy look. My eyes were fixed on the door. I was watching to see if anyone went in or out.

A stout man was going out (not looking behind him). The cars were driving slowly by. The street was still shimmering in the sticky heat, but the stout man hadn't left yet. He came back inside. Then he went out for the third time. He noticed we were there (he turned to look at us). She loved to wait, she said; it was her favourite game. But I couldn't stand that hazy heat. (She was in the sun, and that upset her, it made her feel down.)

A man with a beard passed by. He shot us a quick glance, then walked on. Another man left. He was wearing a dark suit with a red tie, and this made me feel even hotter; it made me surer than ever she was waiting just to annoy me. Not that I cared!

The stout man got into his car. He was searching in his pocket. He was watching us, I was sure of it. He didn't make any movement. He was just passing the time.

The street wasn't hazy any more; things had cleared. The stout man had vanished. In the short time I'd been talking to her, everything around us had woken up – the shops, the garbage van, the cars motionless in the parking lots. The men would get out, stifling in the heat, unable even to look. Others had puffed faces, you could see the sleep still there on their dry lips. And still he didn't get out.

It was five to nine in the morning, the weather was hot and close. And still he hadn't come.

\*\*\*

I could feel the sun still burning on my head, the stickiness passing through the waves of my hair, as if the edge of my hair was ablaze. I set light to all the settled ideas, but she put them out again! I brought her into my madness (nothing matters).

I made a joking remark about my hair, but she said nothing. She was as tired as I was, and that young boy didn't concern her anyway. She poured the ointment on to her chest and the drops scattered.

That sun was just about killing me.

"Hey – You've just about killed Camus' stranger!"

"I don't blame him. I swear to God, if he appeared there in front of me now, I'd scratch him with my nails."

No reply.

"How much longer do we have to wait? I'm tired of this game. Maybe he'll come, maybe he won't."

"Godot will get here, I'm sure of it. I'm sure he'll come."

"Who's Godot?"

"The one who never comes!"

I woke alone. There wasn't a hand touching me, the alarm clock wasn't ringing next to me. I felt as though I'd slept a lot, much more than I should have done; I was still tired and heavy-headed. I tried to get up. I touched the edge of the bed, but the bed was spread right out – there was no edge and no side. The room was a black block, with the yellow light from the bathroom standing faintly out from behind the half-open door. I went back to sleep. I was frightened. Why was the house so quiet and dark? Where were the others? The children? Where was the sound of the television? I tried, again, to find the side of the bed, so I could get up, but still I couldn't find it. Catching sight of someone, in the dim light, I closed my eyes tight. My God, how frightened it made me to look towards that door! I was afraid, if I moved in that darkness, so many things would move to threaten me. Carefully, I opened my eyes. There she was with her knowing face, standing right by the door, in the black room. If I could only have crossed, from the bed to the light switch! But the bed had no sides, and no edges.

Afraid, I moved to switch on the light in the room. Not sure if she was there, I ran to the first floor. The staircase was dark, the way was dark. The hall – the kitchen. The house was asleep and the rooms were dark – all but my room, and myself.

***

"Are you certain that's the door?"

"There's only one door. The windows, though – they're as many as there are women in the world. The door's half open, kept that way for girls with a lot of questions. Every time that wicked girl went near the door, she'd see things that tempted her, but never the whole thing. Whenever she tried to go in through that door, the hinges swung and jammed shut, and the windows lit up, in such a tempting way. But whatever came in through the window went out again. Those were the rules of his kingdom. It was the game he played."

"You've really seen them?"

"Yes. Real, whole women. I knew them well enough, but I didn't look like any of them. He'd chosen them from different times and cities. They all gathered, around his gate, but no one ever came in, and no one ever left."

"What about him?"

"He can't control them all, that's why he made sure not to lose them. Nothing ever had a clear conclusion (why not?). It was never one thing or the other."

"So what are you waiting for?"

"To understand the game."

Today's my birthday. My mother died giving birth to her – not giving birth to me. From the time my mother died, they say, she's been perverse and quarrelsome, condemned by everyone. I never quarrelled with them; they were good people, I knew that. She was stubborn, went into black moods; didn't look like them at all. When they made the family tree and hung it in the hall, they drew a woman with a sickle next to her. She never came back after that night. I suspected they'd killed her, because she killed my mother the day I was born. I was happy she wasn't there any more. She was prettier than I was, she looked different from everyone else. I'd win against her in my dreams, but I never really beat her.

She was strong and didn't care about things. Everything looked false to her, not serious the way she was. When she felt herself choking, from the things she'd done, she'd brandish her motto: nothing really matters. She'd call them the false children, and she knew how to make them confused, how to condemn her childhood in front of them. If a child did something against her, she didn't hit back. Instead, she'd choose the right one to stab. She'd disappear, to get over her confusion, then come back with a dagger in her hand, to paint her future wound for them. I don't know that game, I couldn't play it the way she did. I'd just cry and decide to forget.

She might cry too, but she didn't forget. She'd come like some soft innocent who couldn't be managed. She acted differently, in a way to provoke them. Or so they always said. I was different too, but my ways could be moulded, just like clay.

"Are you alone? Cross the darkness, come over to the light. That's where they are, celebrating because she's leaving them. She was – I don't know what – and her death was a white cloud. They're suggesting going out, to some different space, so go out with them, dance away your pain – singing in a voice that comes out defeated, frightened by the beating of the drums, which have just been taken down from near the fireplace. Dance for what was left of her life, of her heart, her tricks and her bad moods, the white clouds she used to move away, stealthily, so she could shine. Shake off all her defeats. Those faces that surrounded her for so long, till they killed her at last – let them feel the ecstasy of your dance. Dance, dance, and let her tumble off from you each time the earth shakes under your feet, each time your shoulder rubs against one of the dancing backs. Get her right out of you – she made you so wretched for so long! Get her out. They killed her yesterday, and tonight they've been celebrating, with white clouds to cover her sinful memory."

"Laugh, pour your sadness into coarse jokes. That wicked one, the one who made you suffer so much! Don't move too far from the fireplace. Don't go back to that stupid role. Don't let them cry alone. Drink from them. They're coming towards you. Do you like singing alone, on his chest, under a roof you're able to hang from, without falling? They're coming towards you. Leave him, and leave her with him. Celebrate with them, dance on one foot, for the white clouds covering the memory!"

"I was condemned for something, always."

"I have to bale out the river of life, from something!"

"But they're false things."

"I was fated to be condemned. Every bond I had with people, with myself even – they were all brought to nothing by that woman."

"You're still talking about how she was?"

"And I think she was just myself – no one else at all."

"But you're different."

"I'm different, according to different men. But the betrayal's never any different. It starts with a man who doesn't care, and ends with him. Both acts are condemned."

***

I saw a ghost once, that looked like her crazy image. It was crossing in the darkness, coming towards me as that half-open door swung. I prayed, I recited verses from the Quran, but the ghost didn't go away. It was a human being, with a shadow! Perhaps she's come back. But why would she come back? She wasn't afraid of anyone, and she never loved me, so why would she come back? This time I decided not to shut my eyes, to get a good look at her. She was standing like a statue, some way off – as if she wasn't seeing me, and never meant to frighten me. As I moved towards her, the door banged loudly shut.

"Our story's a house made of sand. Isn't it?"

"Things aren't that bad."

"Well, how much longer can we stay like this?"

"Think of God."

"Do you trust our tomorrow?"

"I can't even control tonight."

"Will you build another house of sand? Together with me?"

"It will only vanish. The way it did all the other times we've met and been afraid."

"Will our story live on?"

"Our story of tonight?"

"No, our story of tomorrow."

"I don't know – "

"What am I to do?"

"Think of God."

***

Disco fever, a nervous jerk of my limbs, as I lay there on the pillow. Alone! I knew that. But what was I to do, on a long, hot summer night, but move my limbs to the rhythm of the music you like. He likes everything with balance, that's why he always chose Fayrouz. And when I told him how quickly I grew tired of her singing, how I didn't like listening to her, he got upset, told me he was shocked at my taste. He didn't really like Fayrouz, I was sure of that. Only, he saw her as the proper banner for people like him to carry. I respected Fayrouz. I just didn't like her singing.

I respected Fayrouz, I just had to try and convince him of that. But all he said was: "It's just a matter of taste."

I saw the ghost, wandering by my half-open door. I prayed. It was her. Her features were clear this time, but there was nothing to frighten me, seeing her like that. My mother had to die giving birth to her; and I had to live; and she had to go away, after everyone had condemned her. I nearly went up to her. But she vanished as I was pressing the button on the tape recorder. Next time, I thought, I won't let her go away. I wasn't frightened of her any more.

***

It sounds ridiculous, the way I'm talking tonight. That doesn't matter. It's my night after all; besides, the whole house was asleep and I'd just woken up. Yesterday morning's sun, in that hazy street, was still burning in my hair. What did I do yesterday? At nine forty-five in the morning, that is? I didn't want to spoil my mood too much, because nothing mattered at all. Even so, the rhythm, of that loud music, provoked all those sleeping in my memory. They were banging on the door. What did those false children want? I surrendered my body to the music of the song, I saw myself dancing, I saw them all around me, dropping down one by one. My head started ringing, my skull couldn't take any more. The heat of the sun was still steaming from every part of my body. I was dancing, and the world, with all its worries, was running off, down my shoulder. I danced, and I saw them dropping down. I'd trample them with my foot, singing loudly with the singer, as they gathered around me. Hot blood rushed to my face, and with it rushed all the nights I used to spend in this wretched state. (I was dancing, seeing them drop down around me.)

"Are you alone?"

"She used to wake at this time, alone. She looked enticing, alluring."

Come in. I'm here with him, alone, my head hanging down and my face made of clay. I'd hold his hand and say (that woman wasn't me): Come in – No one's going to know you've come back, no one's going to have to admit they were wrong. Plant your pain in my heart, let my hand seize its burning fire. Let me enter your blind fires, blindfold. It's through your madness I live!

Come in, choose whatever kind of tiredness you want for meetings with me. Block his path. Tell him all about what happened, while he was away. Tell him I got free of the mud that put out the light of my seven moons, that I'll shine on you (the light scattered, the way I want it). I'll open my heart to your kingdom's destruction. And when I tumble down, into a dark part of your memory, I won't mind that, because the fall will be like me. I'm a woman of turbulent mood. I want utter confusion, with no line or full stop to change its form. When I drop down, I'll be alone, and the clouds will stay white!

*** 

In total darkness, I saw her – she looked pale and sad, downcast and whispering (that woman wasn't me). She came closer to you. You sensed her standing next to you. She looked more desirable in the dark. She came closer to your face, and the night, with all its worries, came closer too. The face was clear, beautiful and real. She came closer. She almost came in. The loud music stopped. The door banged loudly shut. They parted.

"Did they kill you?"

"A black mud formed, it blocked out the light of the seven moons."

"Did anyone see them?"

"She was the only one who saw me. My other half, the half that was cast out."

"Did you feel pain?"

"My place of rest still isn't dry."

It was one thirty in the afternoon, they were gathered around the table for lunch. The din they were making tore the sleep from my head. The door of the room was half open. How can anyone eat that red meat, in heat like this? It was two o'clock, and the sun was hot, right overhead. Could I, I wondered, have that heavy soup with them, with the sun beating down on my hot, wet head – just as if I hadn't left it by the door of the room? I decided I'd die properly this time.

*'Abdallah al-Salmi*

# STORY OF A BRIDGE

I had nothing to do that morning, and, as always, I left the house and went off to the bridge. The weather was cloudy and grey. The sight of the passing clouds filled me with distress; no rain fell any more, even though clouds covered the sky each day. I recalled those days when raindrops big as lemons would fall, while we played, half-naked, in the cold water. It was then, I remembered, that the bridge had been built. People had smiled a lot in those days, and exchanged cheerful words. The bridge, it was said, would change the face of the land; the water would run gloriously beneath it, and vast fields of violet spikes would shoot up.

I joined in the happy atmosphere then. We'd put off whatever work we had and go off to the bridge. Actually it wasn't a bridge yet – that was just the name we gave to the long gap that had been carved out. In utter astonishment, we watched those huge machines, and the great army of labourers, as they widened the water course, extending it in a new, unfamiliar way. And, as the water course grew in size, so the smiles on people's faces grew wider too. As time went by, some of the men abandoned their work altogether, and just spent the whole day watching the bridge. Even the women, under pretext of looking for their children, would go to the bridge and spend long hours talking about it and watching it.

Before the bridge even took shape, rumours abounded. One old man said one evening, marvelling, that the bridge was a sacred, mystic object, one that would bring benefit without end. According to another wise man, it was a carefully crafted machine that captured the clouds, then poured the rain into its great channel, to be spread out on the land. Some men saw the bridge in their dreams, where it took on strange shapes. And, when they recalled this next morning, they took immense pleasure in the astonished looks of their good wives.

And so the bridge became a mystic, undefined thing, one that grew in a fictional, almost mythic way. I used, myself, to think a lot about the bridge. The desire to see the other face of things would keep me awake. Once or twice I very nearly asked one of the workers about it. But they spoke a foreign language I didn't understand, and in any case their boss was a savage type who brandished his whip all day long and wouldn't let anyone near the place. Tired, finally, of thinking to no purpose, I simply watched the bridge's progress, as bewildered as the rest. It took a long time to build, I remember, and during that time the people spent what they'd saved over long years. Since the men rarely did any work now, being happy just to watch the bridge, they didn't go to sleep early, and the children multiplied almost like flies.

At last the great day arrived. Braving the beating sun, we gathered to see the bridge complete: a great grey block joining the two banks of the water course. It was a truly wondrous sight.

There was silence for quite a time. Then the celebration began, in red and green and silver. The men danced, the women ululated. We danced on the bridge, far into the night – some of the young men didn't leave till the morning. Then we waited. What happened, though, was incredible: the rain stopped falling, the clouds would streak away from the great water course. From time to time, we'd see small cars speeding across the bridge.

The people, grown quite desperate, stopped visiting the bridge. Then, little by little, they forgot about the bridge altogether and went on to dream other dreams.

But I didn't forget; I kept on with my visits. Gazing down into the deep space beneath the bridge, I saw the trash and garbage gradually pile up. Then I saw great numbers of maggots crawling around, eating the litter, multiplying apace. In the course of time, the creatures, finding nothing more to feed on, began eating the poles of the bridge. Often I'd see their steely teeth as they gnawed on the iron and cement. The bridge, I was sure now, had become nothing less than a trap, and I wanted to say so. But the speeding cars never stopped. Then, one morning, I found the maggots had eaten right through the poles of the bridge.

As I sensed disaster approaching, I saw a big, bright-coloured car and heard the sound of rhythmic clapping and laughter. I ran, waving my hands and crying out, to warn them of the impending danger, but they didn't hear my voice – or perhaps they thought I was trying to hitch a ride. Soon I saw the bridge collapse like a heap of sand, and heard how the sound of laughter became mixed with weeping.

'Abd al-'Aziz al-Saq'abi

# Your Night Isn't Mine –
# and You're Not Me!

He closed his eyes, surrendering to slumber; he became lost in different worlds. She looked at him, thinking what a fool he was. Did he know what the coming days had in store for him? He didn't, and neither did she.

She thought of waking him, of bringing him back from the grip of pleasurable sleep, which she'd learned to hate from the moment she married him. She loathed sleep. What was it, after all, but a kind of flight into nothingness?

She gazed at the white hairs on his chin. Suppose she were to fetch the razor and shave that beard of his while he was asleep? When he got up, he'd look for the beard he loved so much, and he wouldn't find it. And then he'd kill her, because she hadn't kept watch, to see the beard came to no harm!

She tried, fruitlessly, to blot out these illusory thoughts. All she'd been able to do was roll in the mud, float on the surface of shallow swamps – to live as frogs did. Let all the stars converge, she thought, then be swallowed up amid a surging sea!

She'd seemed cheerful and light-hearted once; indeed she had been. She was a child robbed of her youth – she was, she felt, growing a hundred years older. Day by day she was aging, her hair turning white, her eyes dimming and weakening, leaving the world before her as dark as her own days.

She was searching, in a time forever lost to her, for something called love. An old man would come and bemoan that love in a lament that only served to strike such feelings dead. For a time she'd sleep, then she'd wake to find the old man sleeping there beside her, tossing restlessly, this way and that.

Nor was his sleep noiseless. He'd cough – then spit into a black cloth next to him. He'd ask her to get him his various medicines, which he'd then gulp down; and she'd hold him in her arms, fearful he might go, leaving her alone.

Once a little girl had been playing in a small alley with some young boys. She'd seen how the big house in their quarter was filled with decoration, how, when night fell, it turned to a great halo of light. There were some men carrying incense burners, while others gathered curiously by the entrance to the house, to see the young groom.

The little girl had been curious too, standing alongside those men to catch a glimpse of the groom as he arrived. The groom had come with a large escort, wearing gleaming white clothes, so clean they seemed washed like a cloudless sky. The little girl hadn't grasped the meaning of purity. Nor had she known that this groom would, in the course of time – when life had endowed him with weakness, and ill health, and a great fortune – become her husband.

In a different time from this, someone had told her how childhood existed as long as a person was alive. He'd asked her to remain a little girl for as long as she lived, because he'd loved her as a child when she'd played with the young boys, never dreaming she'd age while still so young. He hadn't realized aging was like a plague, its victims more numerous than those who died in car crashes.

The old man took a few pills, drank a glass of water, then returned to his other world.

For a time she wore black, leaving the black days behind her. She went back to the one who'd asked her to remain a child. She wasn't as beautiful now, or as slender; but she still nourished great hopes of returning to her childlike state, and playing, so very innocently, with the other children.

She was, people told her, being too eagerly hopeful. "If loving life," she answered, "is being too eagerly hopeful, then let death come!"

That person with the dark face returned, to win a faint smile from her and ask her to become his partner in time to come. But she refused, preferring to remain a child. She'd known tragedy once, and had no wish to know it again. She felt innocent and pure.

In the whole world, she felt, there was just one person, and that person was herself. So, let her remain alone. The one she'd wanted to share her life with – the very one now asking her to share his life with him – lacked the strength to stay by her side.

She wanted to sleep. She felt her whole body aching. She wanted to leave, but didn't have the strength.

You, who could once take ecstasy from the fragrance of the moment – you're quiet now, and filled with pain. I don't understand why you can't be part of me. Is it because I feel you piercing me day by day, subjecting my body to invasion?

You fail, in spite of all the wealth you own. You think this possession makes me more submissive to you. But I'm wrapped around with a cold that makes my body shiver and ache.

"Look," I told the waiter, "I don't want chilled juice. I want tea. Do you understand?"

Apprehensive, he brought me a cup of tea. I hate getting irritable, but I don't think I can act any differently. So, please forgive me if I called you a child, an imbecile even.

I said it on the spur of the moment: "Here I am, offering you all my respect, looking to find an ideal in you – in an age when the ideal's out of reach for everyone." Perhaps you find me ridiculous.

How can I look at what's left of a woman married by force, to a man her father's age, a man who died and left her pain and sorrow over the youth she'd wasted?

Perhaps you don't know anything about me. It's enough, isn't it, to know how good-hearted I am, how decent and how young?

It's so very long since I saw you. I still remember, though, the time you were a little girl, I remember how I asked you to remain a child. Now I'm asking you, if you're still a child, to play a game with me, serious and yet innocent. Will you agree to play "bride and groom"?

You won't agree, will you, that we remain children? You don't know how pure children's feelings are, when they love.

What do you expect the little boy to do, when he loves the neighbour's little girl who plays with him? Can't he keep her for himself, keep her with him? Is he, a child, too weak to marry her? When a person leaves a place he loves, he usually goes back, even if it's a long time after; just like the birds, which leave the shores as winter sets in, to return the next summer.

And here I am now, returning to the shore. You're my shore. Will you accept my return?

His words fill the air, but only he can hear them. She can't hear his words, because she'd rather stay asleep and never wake.

*Khairiyya Ibrahim al-Saqqaf*

# AND THE STEP CHANGED

When the dawn broke, and the sun cast its gilded braids on the breast of the fertile land; when the dew-drenched birds shook their wings and made ready for a day spent darting this way and that; and when the crowing of the roosters announced the new morning and the new awakening – that was when she rose.

She was used to being the first to wake. She'd pray, then put the coffee on a fire with which she'd kindle the first log of endless love. The firelight would spread far and wide, lightly heralding the coffee he'd drink in.

That's how I feel too, she thought to herself. I'm the one eternally there beneath his skin, the one who flows in his veins, always, and mingles with his blood.

She'd prepare a slice of bread and cheese, then take it to him along with the coffee. Then, after that, he'd start a long day filled with toil and struggle. These, for her, were the pivots of his manhood, tokens of steadfastness, confidence and loyalty. A hardworking man, she thought, who's loyal and runs in my blood.

He wasn't any richer than those who lived around him, in the modest local quarter in one of the suburbs of Jeddah. In Jeddah, the city sleeping in the lap of the sea, were buried the secrets of their two hearts, away from the envious eyes of the local people. Everyone's talking about us, she'd say to herself. Then she'd spit to the left and quietly utter the traditional formula: "I invoke God's aid against the devil."

Saeed would spend the whole day working, non-stop, and an hour or more in the evening on top of that. The moment she saw him, she'd forget the questions she'd been planning to ask him all day long – about all the details of his own long day. What had he been doing? Who had he been talking to? What kind of work had he been doing? How she wished she could live with him, through words at least; penetrate the moments of his day through the things he described, find herself with him in the pores of his skin, in the pores of his day. And yet, the instant she saw him coming, she'd forget everything she'd meant to ask. It would be put off to a second day, a third, a fourth, indefinitely. His face, she thought, makes me forget every question. In his face, there are my moments, my evenings, my nights and mornings.

He'd bring her nothing but his weariness. He never saved more than one or two dirhams, over the whole month. She never, though, asked him for anything for herself. She was satisfied to live through the whole day getting ready for him, and all her cares would be forgotten the moment she caught sight of him. Even if her dress got a tear, she'd sew it or patch it, without letting him see. Many times she'd loosen the hem of her dress and walk barefoot, till she had her shoes back from the cobbler's shop on the edge of the quarter.

One day, seeing her walking barefoot, he asked her why she wasn't wearing her shoes. She laughed.

"I heard," she answered, "what people in the city say – that feet need fresh air. They need to touch the earth. Our barefoot ancestors knew the wisdom of that, didn't they?"

He shook his head.

"How clever you are!" he said "If only I had a quarter of your cleverness!"

Often she'd spend the night by his side, especially when he complained, in loud tones, how tired he was. Fearful of touching his head, she'd put her own head on his chest. I can hear his heart beating, she thought. And those beats will touch my own heartbeats, and my heart and my senses. If only I could read heartbeats. If only I could understand the language of the heart!

Sometimes he'd laugh, the way everyone did. Just an ordinary thing, but for her a day when he laughed was a day of deep happiness, because he was the whole world to her, and everything else was commonplace, not worth her attention. She'd express her feelings straightforwardly, normally, with simple emotion.

He was the hope that filled her, giving her a sense of fullness she'd never known before. He was the confidence that held her firm, where before she'd been like a feather blown away and landing among the mountain crevices.

In the course of her life with him, she'd sold every valuable thing she'd owned: the two gold bracelets, for example, that her father had given her as a wedding gift, the silver ankle chain her mother had given her, and other items too. Material things – except for him – meant nothing.

Her confidence in him grew ever greater; it bore him to the clouds. It helped him climb to the peaks of mountains, to trample every weakness, and humiliation, and fatigue. He rose higher in everything, grew more educated. He became a person of education! He rose to be a high-ranking employee, then, after some years, graduated – while she sat up at night, quietly making him coffee, serving him with dates and love. She nursed him with eyes that poured out all the affection a person might need on his difficult journey.

Saeed became the first in his quarter with a degree in education. One day, she sat looking at him as he read a book. I can see the letters in his eyes, she mused. I'll climb the pages of books on the lashes of his eyes. I'll plunge into the heart of understanding, moving with his thoughts. Oh, how splendid you are, Saeed! You've turned the light of the lantern to electric light, the one and two saved dirhams to tens, hundreds, more than that even – "

One morning she saw him off as usual. He'll be back at noon, she thought. He comes back at a different time too. Together we've saved time. He doesn't come back in the evening any more. We've cut down on time. Our life's become a wondrous rose, on a strong, green stalk, its perfume a delight.

He'd be back at noon, and there she'd be waiting for him. The moments, the few hours, the time saved – they were all gathered up in his footsteps.

"Aida – Aida."

"Saeed! You're smiling, I see. Good news?"

"It may not make you as happy as it does me."

So, she thought, what the women in the quarter said was right. He'll be going to the city. He's been offered a house there, and a car and a driver.

"Why not?"

"Because you won't understand."

"Understand what?"

"That I'm moving to the city."

"Oh! You're moving to the city."

"Alone."

"But what about our life? Our life together? Why can't I come with you?"

"You wouldn't be able to cope with city life."

She remained sunk in her tears, for many days before he left. A strong current's driving us, she thought. I was rowing against myself. I didn't know the river had side streams, till I saw them there in front of me. There's a surging current all around us, with its waves and waterfalls. The current's stronger than we are. I was rowing against myself.

As he left, she stretched out her hand to say goodbye.

"You'll have to go to your parents' house," he said.

At her parents' house she wept. The palms of her hands dried up from the warm tears that tore her heart, her mind, her cheeks.

While she was waiting, still, to hear some news of him, her father gave her a letter.

"Father," she cried out, laughing, "I can't read."

"If only you could. If only you'd taught yourself to read, instead of rowing against yourself."

"What does he say? Does he want to see me? Has he made a home for me? Is he waiting for me?"

Her father went back to where he'd come from. She could read the failure, realized the river had dried up.[2]

Dried up. She never knew she'd dug so deep, and that all the river's water had been taken away.

Her father didn't let her sink helplessly, in the dried river bed. He made many attempts with her, sometimes kindly, sometimes forcefully. It was a shame, he told her, for a young woman to dream of a man who no longer existed in her life. Who no longer owned her!

The harsh suffering took hold of every last part of Aida's body. Saeed, for his part, was growing acquainted with life in the city, and what the people there were made of; with the hard struggles, in all their various colours.

The days passed. One day her father came hurrying in.

"Aida!" he said. "Tomorrow you're to marry 'Awwad."

The lights were lit. People laughed and played drums, the children shouted happily. Some of them carried the carpets outside the traditional house, others cleaned the ground and sprayed it with water.

On her wedding night, the wet earth was mingled with the tears coursing down her cheeks. 'Awwad had possession of her hand, but not of her heart. As she turned her back on her father's house, she was trampling the last part of that heart that was still alive.

The wind, filled with her father's smell, blew the last vestige of the earth's tang under their car. Looking back, she fixed her gaze on the car's rear window.

She thought she saw him. She saw him, physically there, standing next to her father. If only, she thought, she knew what they were saying to each other. The wind carried his voice along with it, and she looked back once more.

The car moved on; the voice faded away and the shadow vanished. He became a phantom. And she never knew just why he'd returned.

*Ruqayya al-Shabeeb*

# THE APPEAL

Here, within this large square space, the final sentence of death might be pronounced – or perhaps I'd have to wait for it to be pronounced later.

The three judges sat there in a line, the bell making a fourth. Or were they four judges, with the bell making a fifth? Or did the truth maybe lie somewhere between?

I burst into a laugh that resounded through the hall, making the judges' eyes pop out. Then I was overcome by a fit of weeping and bitter sobbing, which softened their hearts. Next, I succumbed to a fierce attack of dry coughing. My intestines and craw were, I felt, being torn apart; then I recalled that – being a human being and not a chicken – I didn't have a craw.

There was no witness to events, no witness for the defence even. You might have thought the hall itself was the one being tried.

I felt an urge, almost overpowering, to leap from the dock, chained though I was, and embrace the judges. The smell of the first judge recalled my father, while the middle one looked to be wearing a shirt with a dirty collar. Perhaps, I thought, he'd quarrelled with his wife the night before, and this inelegant appearance was his reward. Looking towards the third judge, I saw he was asleep.

The bell rang, and the judge with the white hair instantly took on a most solemn air; he was in a hurry maybe. The hall appeared empty. Being the sole accused, I should, I calculated, specify the charge against me to the honourable judge, then make a powerful speech in my defence. I made to raise my forefinger, then hastily thought better of it.

I breathed a prayer, then, in a husky voice, furnished the judge with an account of my tragedy. I had, I told him, entered this prison through a single door. The sons of Jacob had entered through twelve doors, but the bird, cut into pieces and scattered over various mountains, was back and flying high. The judge called me to a halt. I felt the force of his stern gaze.

"Go on," he shouted finally.

I let out another laugh. It was the weight of my burden, I realized, that had led me to begin in this way. I'd felt such sorrow last night, before coming to be tried for my life in this hall that was empty apart from the judge and myself. He banged his gavel, then took a sip of water with evident enjoyment – as if, it seemed to me, he was drawing in the breath of the woman he loved. But I held back my sudden laugh. There was, I saw, the scar of a deep wound between his eyes, Perhaps, I thought, he was a former war hero; then I remembered judges don't become heroes in wars. I gulped, feeling as though spikes were piercing into me and drawing my blood.

I passed my fingers through the locks of my dark hair. The judge, it struck me, had a feverish air; he was lightly quivering. I seized the chance to waft some of my perfume towards him, to draw him into a silent admission. It occurred to me, suddenly, to measure the distance between us. How many feet were we apart? I moved towards him, and his eyes widened. I drew nearer, and his breathing quickened. I drew nearer still, and his hair moved. Then, as I approached still closer, the swords of his eyelashes thrust out to repel my attack!

The time had come, I felt, to confer with him; he had, after all, to bring the session to an end. I laughed. There were, I told the judge and his colleagues, just four feet between him and myself.

He brought the gavel crashing down, then rose. He was huge and tall, like a mountain. Then, sitting down once more, he told me to be quiet, and I acted accordingly. He was, I realized, studying the corners of my mouth, assessing how full my lips were, as I went on gazing at him.

He relaxed in his seat, fully ready to pronounce final sentence in this pending case. There was perspiration on his brow. I started answering questions left unasked.

The bell rang. The hall was empty apart from myself. His fingers, pressing hard on the bell, seemed like the faint threads of a spider's web.

I, though, wouldn't go along with him. I insisted on a full confession, long and detailed, and he had no option but to listen – with his ears, that is, even if his eyes were elsewhere.

A sudden desire flooded through me to sign some treaty or truce – as if it was somehow the proper thing to make peace in the presence of His Honour the Judge. He stood up, banged his gavel, rang the bell, then sat down again. Leaning back in my chair, I outlined my four conditions for acceptance of the sentence. He had to assess the sum lost in the war and pronounce when the dollar would be defeated; to ensure there'd be no other judges beside himself; to release all Arab armies; to give up his territorial ambitions, warning all comrades, in the light of modern conditions, that they'd be stoned and should therefore not think of building a house of glass. Finally, he had to pronounce that everything we saw would fade away, that the human race would die off from starvation, and that water couldn't be stored up in bottles. He had, further, to issue a sentence banning all radio stations. I'd then accept any ruling he made in my case.

"Your Honour," I said, "I call on the justice symbolised by your robe to come over to me at once – with no ringing of bells, no sips of water, and no whispering of your colleagues.

"Your Honour, my speech – during which I haven't uttered a word – is over now. I'm confident, though, that you've understood it; that you've had to take off your glasses and examine my case with your own eyes, with a view to coming to a decision. Don't bother to ring the bell. The world's asleep around you; there's no one but the judge and the accused. Come closer. The sun's still round and shining, the moon will always be a crescent. Next year the Arabs will agree on a single date for the feast; famine won't destroy us, rain will tumble abundantly from the sky."

The judge suddenly burst out laughing. Then he coughed loudly, before spitting into his white handkerchief. I went on with my speech. Sickness, I said, wouldn't strike us. The Arabs would fight with a single wooden stick. What did His Honour say to releasing me, so I could use his decision to fight on?

He took a drink from his glass, then turned to his colleagues, hearing their snores for the first time. Then, laying his head down on his desk, he joined them in their sleep, cautioning that he shouldn't be woken up unless the light poured out from the windows of the hall. I felt the urge to laugh all over again. I pointed to my chains. But he was fast asleep.

Before falling asleep, though, he pointed out that I'd laid down more than four conditions. Also, I should remember that the testimony of a man was equal to the testimony of two women.

"But what about my chains?" I asked.

There were three of them, and the bell made a fourth. The smell of their easy breathing came across to me.

I would, I decided, snap my chains and creep out into the light, before the judges woke. I would, I decided, wedge myself into my life jacket, and lay down no conditions at all. Let the judge convict me *in absentia*!

And so I made to escape, taking the judge's bell with me; that way he'd never again be able to ring it against a convicted woman. I took his glasses, too; that way he wouldn't, any more, be able to magnify the letters and count the teeth of women who smiled at him.

But before I could flee, I was assailed by a deep sleep – laid my head down on the dock and curled up. I soared in my dreams. The place appeared rectangular, and I had no limbs, just broken wings.

"How can I fly," I said to myself, "with broken wings?"

I still haven't woken up. As for my judges, they're floating in a different world. The pages of the calendar have fallen, a year's ended.

And the appeal still hasn't been heard.

*Shareefa al-Shamlan*

# SCENES FROM A LIFE

*First Scene*:
I'm twenty years old. I'm sure of that. My mother died when I was ten. I was seventeen when they brought me here. I used to count the years of my life. Every year I'd plant a palm tree. I've spent three years here, I know that, because of my father's visits. He visits me every Ramadan. Three visits.

Another Scene:
Today's the eve of the Eid. Tomorrow's Eid. They decorate our place here, not for the Eid, but because a big official's going to visit us.

I asked for a pen and paper. I wanted to write a long letter to my mother, and a greeting card for my father. They wouldn't let me have them. They were afraid I was going to write a complaint to the big official. That made me laugh a lot, deep down. The fact is I don't know how to write.

*Another Scene*:
I couldn't stop laughing as I looked at the Director. He was fat – really, ever so fat. The nurses lined up on the two sides, looking clean and shiny. As he came up to me, the head doctor whispered softly in his ear. "She's dangerous," I heard him say.

I tried to touch his *abaya* with my hand. He smiled.

"What is it you want, young lady?" he asked.

"I want to touch your *abaya*," I said.

"And why's that?" he asked

I asked him to come closer, so I could whisper in his ear.

"I want to see," I told him, "how much your *abaya* would be worth if it was sold. Would it be enough to buy sweets for the children in my village?"

He laughed, then moved on. The head doctor was afraid. His eyes were bulging out.

*A Retrospective Scene*:
I always laugh when I see the head doctor. He has scratches I made on his face, with my own nails. One day he tried to break my pride, so I did my best to break his nose, only I couldn't. So I just coloured his face with his blood.

*A Small Scene*:
The orderly handed me my meal. I didn't ask her anything. She, though, said without my asking: "I've given the meat to the neighbour's dog. He's hungry."

"It's right for him to have it," I told her.

*A Passing Scene*:
The nurse came up with the injection as usual. She didn't inject my arm, instead she emptied the medicine into another bottle. Then she thrust the bottle in her bosom. I didn't care. The injection takes me to beautiful places, I know. To a vast world. But later it leaves me in a dark world, with a horrible headache.

"Do you think," I said to the nurse, "you could get me a lot of palm leaves?"

"Why?" she asked warily.

"I want to build a fence around my bed," I told her, "so my stomach won't get swollen."

I squeezed her stomach. She swallowed hard, wrapped her apron tight around her, and went away.

*A Painful Scene*:
Once my father bought me some bracelets. That made me happy. I showed them to my friends. My stepmother bought a chain, and anklets, and a lot of bracelets.

I wasn't concerned about them. I was happy my father was rich. I sat looking at my bracelets. They shone, glinting in the sun. I heard a loud noise. A big machine was digging up the orchard. It was coming close to my palm trees. I screamed. I ran and sat in front of it. My stepmother dragged me off.

"We've sold the orchard," she said. "They're going to build a road here."

I pulled her hair and scratched her face.

"Didn't you ever ask yourself," she said, "where the bracelets came from?"

I flung the bracelets under the big machine. It was after that I was brought here.

*Final Scene*:
"They've written about you in the newspapers," the orderly told me.

"Why?" I asked her.

"The Director's sent sweets," she said, "to the children in your village."

"Did it make the children happy?" I asked.

"Yes," she said, "and they've sent the Director a note, thanking him."

*Hussa Muhammad al-Tuwaijiri*

# MY HAIR GREW LONG AGAIN!

*I dedicate this story to every young woman in my country who believes that married life is simply a matter of friendship joined with co-operation, love, sacrifice and support.*

"Do you need anything?"

"No, nothing at all."

"What's the matter? Are you annoyed with me?"

"Not yet."

"But you're not saying anything."

"That's more like it!"

"What do you mean?"

"You ought to know."

"I'm getting tired of this. You're not making yourself clear."

"I never thought of you as stupid."

"Stupid? Who said so?"

"No one did."

"Why are you out of breath?"

"I'm not."

"And yet you don't want to talk?"

"Maybe not."

"OK. I'll see you then."

"Goodbye."

He slammed the door and left the house.

I looked around, contemplating his chair. His cigarette was still lit in the ashtray; he hadn't taken it with him. That was a habit of his. Whenever he felt angry, he'd rush out of the house and forget everything else. He just wanted to escape! Sometimes he'd forget important papers and come back an hour later to pick them up, and I'd avoid seeing him. At other times he'd send the driver to pick them up. Mostly, though, he wouldn't bother to do anything. I sat gazing at his chair. My eyes fell on the daily newspaper that hadn't even been unfolded. He hadn't touched it. I went on contemplating it. Why hadn't he read it through today, as he was drinking his tea?

Then I remembered. I hadn't made his tea, handed him his tea, this morning. I also recalled how it was the first time such a thing had happened since we started our life together. I'd felt an urgent desire to get out of the daily routine. I was suffering from the way my feelings had become frozen, and he must have felt that. Or maybe he'd joined me in the feeling that everything was coming to an end.

I got up to leave our living room, utterly convinced a resolution must be reached. Life with him was growing tedious and stagnant. There was nothing new about this. We were constantly disagreeing over so many things.

The odd thing was that we were different from other married couples. We never discussed our problems aloud, nor did we argue. We just took to silence, and the silence between us was growing by the day.

He'd tried to remove the wall that separated our life, but he wasn't good at solving problems. For my part, I tended to get closer to the things that separated him from me; and so I never cared to co-operate in resolving the issues, never tried to discuss our petty problems with him. Often I avoided having any contact with him.

I heard his steps in the hallway when he came back at noon, but I didn't hurry to meet him as I normally did. I made no attempt to set a counterfeit smile on my lips. The acting was over. It was impossible, I was sure now, to go on acting for further years. More than ever before, I was resolved to reinforce my confidence with courage, and decide to do whatever I wanted.

I sensed his footsteps had stopped, and I heard him call my name in a trembling voice. I had no desire to answer him. I just smiled and said to myself: "let it happen as it will." There was nothing worse, after all, than living without affection. There was no greater agony than living with a person you couldn't depend on.

His footsteps stopped at the door of the balcony, where I was lying on one of the seats, gazing at the jasmine tree that covered the balcony's opposite wall. I could feel his looks hanging on my back, as he stared at my hair that I'd cut that morning, to a little above the shoulders.

He rushed up and stood in front of me. I saw his polished shoes. I tried to look up quickly, but I needed some more courage to do it, and I remembered the challenging attitude I'd decided to take. Suddenly, my looks shifted from his shoes to his face, to find him looking at me with a mixture of astonishment and pain.

He came closer, took hold of a lock of my hair. Then, in a weak voice, his looks confused, he said:

"What's this?"

I replied quickly, trying to ignore the implication of what he had said.

"Nothing. Just my hair."

With that I got up, turned my back on him and left the balcony without looking behind me. I went on to the living room, sensing his footsteps right behind me. Before I could reach the chair, I felt his powerful hands on my shoulders, pulling me strongly around. My soft hair flew and covered my face. I jerked my neck to get rid of the locks of hair that stopped me seeing him. Our eyes met. He shook me fiercely, then shot out:

"Why did you do that?"

I shook myself free from his strong grip and rushed breathlessly to the nearest chair. Hardly knowing what I was doing, I put up my hands and made to fix my hair. He came closer. I expected him to do something stupid. I expected him to slap me, because I knew how much he loved and admired my hair. I'd decided to give him the chance to do it, but instead I saw him go down on his knees in front of my chair, gazing at me in misery and despair. Then he sat on the edge of the chair, his head in his hands. I waited for him to say something, and finally he did. Lifting his head, he started whispering sadly, as if talking to himself:

"Why did you do that? Why did you cut your long hair? You don't know how beautiful it was!"

I moved to the other side of the chair and, for the first time, spoke in a challenging voice:

"I'll do whatever I like. I'm tired of your control over me. You treat me as if I was a doll, just there for your convenience. But you were the stupid one. You never thought I might have a will and feelings. I've come to hate myself, because all I do is follow your orders, without having any views of my own. From today everything's going to change. I've cut my hair, and it was my right to do it. And another thing, I'm starting work and I'm going on with my studies. I'll have my own say in this house, even if it's just for a couple of days. I want to feel that I can use my rights."

I got up to leave, and went to sit in the study, as I usually did when I felt miserable. Knowing that, he didn't try and come in, and as usual we never discussed the matter any further.

The night passed in silence between us. In the morning he went to his work, and I didn't say goodbye to him. I'd decided to stop doing what I didn't want to do, and to stop acting. In the evening he came back to find I'd left the house. I'd decided to break the chains of my simple life. Life was too short to be spent in misery. We only live once, so why should we keep suffering? We make our own happiness. Because happiness isn't a pill we swallow to rid ourselves of the bitterness of despair, but something we work for and earn.

He tried hard to get me to return to an abject life, but I refused and did what I'd always wanted to do. I went on with my studies and started working. My hair grew long again and this time I never thought of cutting it!

*Qumasha al-ʿUlayyan*

# DAYS WITH NO HOPE

In a daze akin to submission, I heard the judge's verdict. His strong voice resounded through the hall, piercing with poisoned barbs to my very heart.

"They are to be separated," he said, in a tone of careless indifference that made me bleed, "on the grounds of general good."

I looked at my husband – or rather at the man who'd been my husband just the day before. He was gazing at me silently, all the sadness of the world there in his eyes. He tried to speak, but couldn't get the words out. I had the message even so, from those expressive eyes: "I'll never forget you."

For all the noise in the hall, the stern faces around me, the restraining hands of my brothers and father, I let out a burning sigh, from a heart filled with words I was given no chance to say: "I'll love you till I die."

Was death the true separation? Or was separation in life harder and crueller still? The one who was to leave for ever was like a man who'd died. Neither would ever return to life.

Our gazes, wrapped in sorrow, embraced. Then I was torn away from him by my brothers and taken to the car. My father sighed.

"Don't be sad, daughter," he said. "What I did was for your own good. For your future."

My future? My eyes were filled with tears, and my whole being screamed with pain:

"Does my future start by separating from my husband? My love, my soul mate, my very life? Has divorce been the beginning? Or has it been a painful ending, then a dark future and an everlasting grief? Was it just, father, that the love of five years should end like this, with such tyranny?"

The singer's voice came over from the car radio, to disperse the lonely dreams of my future:

"I loved you in summer – I loved you in winter – your eyes in the summer, my eyes in the winter – "

The tears streamed down my cheeks as my life with my husband unfolded in front of me. I hadn't known him before we were married. I'd only heard of his qualities from my father, been shown his picture with my mother, learned about him from my brothers. But the reality was more beautiful by far than the image. In him I found just what I'd always wished for: a distinguished manhood, overflowing with affection and imbued with modesty. He was my Prince Charming, who mounted his horse each night to go with me on a fantasy trip to a world of dreams. He was my love, my husband and my companion. I loved him with the depth of my affection, and he loved me in every sense. The days passed, the months hurried by, the years rushed by, but without our seeing any fruit of our love. Our questioning eyes met. I said first, before he could say a word himself:

"I'll go and see a gynaecologist tomorrow."

"But – " he began anxiously.

"We have to find out," I broke in. "What is there to lose?"

We tried any number of doctors, but the result was always the same. There was nothing preventing pregnancy. Everything was normal. The husband ought to be tested. After much hesitation, I said what I'd been keeping inside me.

"Don't worry, my love," he said cheerfully. "I'll go and see the doctor."

It struck with the force of lightning. My husband was sterile; there was no hope of his having children. I shrieked in the doctors' faces:

"Hope's in God's hands alone. You've no right to deprive him of hope!"

One of the doctors shook his head.

"I believe in God," he said. "But if a pregnancy came, it would be a miracle from God."

Despairing, we held one another's hand, while hope, like flocks of birds, flew off from the home. My husband wept, while I stood there, fearful, striving to get a grip of myself. His tears snapped the final thread, and I plunged into the depths of despair.

"You're free, Fatima," he told me brokenly. "You've the right to ask for a divorce and marry another man, who'll be able to fulfil your dream of children – You're – "

"I love you," I interrupted him. "You're my son, my husband and my love. You fulfil my dreams by being alive."

My world brightened with happiness, but the happiness was contrived. Like a paper wall that crumbled the instant I was faced by the first question people asked:

"Why aren't there any children? When are you thinking of having children? Whose fault is it?"

We'd go back to our empty home, all alone, taking nothing with us but the sorrow that tore at our hearts, and a question that kept ringing in our heads: "How much longer?"

How could the marriage last without children, in the face of other people's hurtful looks? My mother wept, begging me to go and consult a doctor, while I tried to hold back my tears. With a mother's instinct, she understood everything. "Love isn't enough," she told me gently.

I raised my head, and she turned to wipe away a tear. My husband grew worried, suffering more by the day. He was being cruelly torn, between his love for me and his duty towards me. I noticed how tense he became when he saw my young nephews. I felt his pain, as the eyes watched and waited. I sensed how lost he was becoming, as the whispers around us grew, and the words turned to deadly bullets and poisoned barbs.

We weren't left to our suffering, to our despair and tears. The family, with my father at the head, gathered and pronounced their sentence of death on me.

They told me I must separate from my husband, since he couldn't have children. As any strong warriors would have done, we refused in the name of our strong love. They took me to the judge, who pronounced my death sentence. I wept, but my father turned to me.

"It's not the end of the world," he said. "There's a distinguished young man who wants to marry you, and we're all in agreement."

Preparing for this new marriage, I lived out a fearful nightmare. I felt as if I was being sent to my grave, not to a new life with a new husband. On the night of my wedding, it came home to me how things stood: a new husband, different from my husband and my love. How could I look him in the face, when the other man's image was still right there inside me? How could I love him, when my heart was filled with my first love? How could I be faithful to him, when the other man's love flowed through my veins?

I cried out loud. "Mother," I said, "I beg you, please. I don't want this marriage." She looked at me disapprovingly.

"Stop this nonsense," she said. "Your husband's almost here."

I collapsed, weeping, as the sun abandoned my world, and I was left with a moonless night, a darkness where nothing was to be seen now but the ugly truth of my plight. I decided, through my tears, not to follow my parents' will, even though I was physically in their hands. I wouldn't become a prisoner to a mortal body. They could burn my body if they wanted, but my will was my own; my heart, my mind, my whole being were my own. I'd be a body to my new husband, but no more. I'd live with him without feeling. I'd respect him and feed him, but my heart – no, a thousand times no.

Married to this other man, I was surprised by his kindness and felt shame on account of his deep respect for me. His modesty made me feel inferior, his noble character made me feel small and meaningless. The days and months passed, but still I couldn't love him. The image of my first husband, implanted in my heart, stood between us. Still, if I had no hope of loving him, my hope of children grew. My mother and father would ask, but the waiting went on; the dream folded, and, by slow degrees, hope began to fade.

"I don't want to embarrass you," my husband said to me one day. "But I do wish you'd tell me why you were divorced from your first husband."

My eyes filled with tears.

"He was sterile," I whispered. "He couldn't have children."

He gave a sigh of fear. I looked at him. His face was pale. His eyes were unfocused, filled with pain and sorrow.

And – before he could say a word – I began to weep bitterly. I didn't need to ask. He was sterile too.

*All short stories were translated by Dina Bosio and Christopher Tingley*

---

1. Literally "four in the evening," following a different Arabic system. Other times in the story are similarly adapted.
2. The paper, it is implied, is a divorce paper sent to her address.

# Part III

## EXCERPTS FROM NOVELS

## Hamza Muhammad Bogary

# FROM THE SAFA SHELTERED QUARTERS
(saqeefat al-Safa)

*Hamza Muhammad Bogary tells the story of a young man who grew up in Mecca between the two world wars – before, that is, oil had changed the whole tempo of life in Saudi Arabia. His novel* The Safa Sheltered Quarters, *basically an autobiographical account of the life of the main character Muhaisin al-Biliyy, provides a full description of the social and educational life of Mecca at that time: the school system, the condition of women and their isolation, the life of the freed slaves of the rich, and of Mecca's madmen, and the many customs, beliefs and superstitions which dominated the life of the individual. The novel opens with the death of Muhaisin's stepfather, a loss that immediately raises the central character's status within a household now comprising just his mother and himself.*

*Bogary's depiction – graphic, vivid and abounding with a rare humour – of a way of life now irreversibly changed gives the novel a special importance in Arabic letters.*

\*\*\*

Mother decided to dispense with the services of Misfir, the man who carried water to our house in two cans slung either side of his shoulders from a bamboo rod. It was, she explained, improper now for Misfir, as a young man, to call at the house of an unattended widow. He was replaced by an elderly Nubian, 'Amm Bashir, who brought the water not in cans but in a skin. But mother hadn't perhaps realized, when she deprived herself of Misfir's services, just how many various chores he'd taken on for her. He it was who'd carried mother's wooden tray of loaves to be baked at the public oven, who'd killed the rooster or the hen when a special meal was to be prepared. He it was who'd cleaned the carpets and bed covers during the last ten days of Ramadan, and who, when the fast was broken, had distributed alms – both for himself and in other worthy cases. And, on top of all that, he'd ground the corn, carried anything heavy around the house, even gone to buy in provisions from the local grocer and butcher. With Misfir gone, some of those duties now fell to me; they were simply too much for 'Amm Bashir, who wasn't just old but half blind as well. He didn't carry a knife in his belt – he couldn't have killed an ant, let alone a chicken – and he was one of those water carriers who spent every afternoon sitting on what our quarter called the "slaves' bench," because the men in question had been freed only after they'd grown too old and feeble for proper work.

When 'Amm Bashir joined our household, I became curious about this bench and its associations. The bench was strictly reserved for the group of water carriers, who had their own chief. They spoke an African language of which I understood not a word, and they had memories of a past rooted in a village in Black Africa. They could all recall a whole series of masters, men who'd bought them or sold them for this reason or that, and some could even remember a son or daughter who'd been sold off one day, vanishing without trace. And there was one other thing they all shared: each was skilled in telling stories, tragic and comic alike, about events in his past life.

I found out, too, that the bench had its own particular set of rules; anyone breaking one of these was liable to the appropriate punishment. Most offences, as far as I could gather, involved behaviour at the well where they drew their water. If one of them failed, let's say, to wait his turn, or made insulting remarks, he was tried, at the bench, after noonday prayers – the chief sitting with the elders grouped around him, the accused man forced to squat. The charge would be read, then witnesses would be summoned and heard; after which the accused would be required to admit his guilt, then take the invariable punishment: a flogging from a leather belt the chief wore across his chest. The victim would receive just three light strokes, as he lay stretched out on the ground, and not even that if the accuser pardoned him, or if some officious person flung a bunch of green clover or leek into the middle of the circle. This latter would be a signal for the court to adjourn, and the accused would be reprieved – to the great annoyance of the presiding chief, who'd be utterly furious at the one who'd interrupted the proceedings. Interventions of this sort were mostly made by local hotheads like Sufyan. I never found anyone able to explain to me the symbolic significance of that green bunch flung into the circle. Perhaps there was some remote link with the olive branch in the Biblical account of the Flood.

As I kept returning to the bench, I heard more and more of the stories told there, most of them about masters selling or freeing their slaves. Often, I gathered, the masters would have irregular liaisons with their female slaves, regarding these last as their personal property. Then, if a girl became pregnant, he'd marry her off to one of the other slaves of the household, so as not to have to acknowledge the parentage – and thereby accord the child a right of inheritance. 'Amm Bashir had a fund of stories like this, speaking of Mahsoun, say, or Saeed, or others, who were actually not sons of the slaves at all, but of their wealthy masters. There were many tales recounted about the women of their masters' households, all of them unsavoury. I'd like to think they sprang simply from 'Amm Bashir's imagination. If they didn't, then I'd have to admit that the moral behaviour of those times was no better than what I see around me today.

\*\*\*

Our quarter had its set of madmen. In this it was just like any other quarter in the world, no different from the Reeperbahn quarter in Hamburg, say, or the Montparnasse district of Paris – apart, that is, from the name we conferred on those of feeble mind. In Paris they're commonly called "artists" or "bohemians"; we, for our part, refer to them as imbeciles or people touched by God. That apart, they behave in much the same way, and they wear the same tattered, patched-up clothes. In Paris, indeed, they often patch their new clothes with pieces of old cloth, in various colours, to match the latest fashionable style. This serves to fulfil an old prophecy of mine: that one day wearing patches would become a mark of the age.

Some of the deranged in our quarter had a passion for drawing, but, finding no great encouragement, they'd focus their efforts on the walls of houses. Getting hold of artistic materials was never a problem – there was more than enough charcoal around in those days. Some of the drawings might have been seen as illustrating the existential modernist school, since most of them depicted humans who didn't cover themselves even with the proverbial fig leaf. Others might have been dubbed expressionist attempts, the crazed minds of the artists producing a degree of exaggeration in the anatomies of the creatures represented. Then, when they'd finished their works, they'd ask some schoolboy to write, under the drawing in question, the name of one of their fellow madmen. Often, though, the mischievous scamps would write a different name altogether; and this would result in a fight between the madman (the artist, I should say) and the person whose name actually appeared. Mostly the fracas would end with this latter person insisting the madman should wipe out his name, and the madman insisting the name wasn't the protester's at all but someone else's. "Can't you read?" he'd taunt his opponent. "Are you crazy?"

The worst of these fights involved a madman well known for his good nature, and also for a body so vast you might have thought he came from another planet, like those creatures who've begun to invade our world over the past few years. This madman produced an obscene drawing of a couple quite scandalously intertwined, then, following the usual practice, asked a schoolboy to write in the name of a particular imbecile underneath. The schoolboy, though, wrote in the name of a notorious local thug, one of the quarter's most noted hotheads. The moment this man set eyes on it, he seized the madman by his back hair, swearing he'd force the man to wipe the signature out with his tongue. The madman put up a heroic resistance, and the result was a brawl between the two of them. A crowd swiftly gathered, some cheering on the madman, urging him to flatten his opponent, while others cheered on the well known thug. Meanwhile, the quarter's more level-headed element (a numerous group) kept intoning: "There is no power or strength except in God." The two fighters ought rather, they said, to be guided by reason. How, though, was a madman supposed to follow the dictates of reason?

A solution was found at last when another madman volunteered to lick off the writing in return for a couple of *halala*s, to be paid him by the man accused; for the price, that is, of a glass of a cold drink made from steeped raisins, of the kind sold before fizzy drinks were around.

One of the quarter's best known figures then was a madman who bore a double mark of distinction: he was blind as well. He was commonly known as "the bomb" – this being a time before rockets were known. The odd nickname sprang from the lightning speed with which he walked along (blind or not), his stick thrust out in front of him so that he ran into everything: people, animals, and, above all, the vendors who set out their goods in a long line in the middle of al-Tafran Square.

Whenever he bumped into obstacles, or into people, he'd yell at the top of his voice: "What's the matter with you? Are you blind?" This he'd say, indiscriminately, to inanimate objects, or people, or animals. Then on he'd go, veering right or left according to the particular position of whatever he'd collided with. However many cuts and bruises he suffered in these accidents, he never changed his ways. Presumably the warning system, which most people have built in, was lacking in his case. He vanished, finally, after running into a donkey belonging to one of the quarter's more prominent citizens. This was due not simply to the accident itself but to its aftermath. The donkey, it seems, took the matter violently amiss, and its assailant, in return, almost bit off the beast's ear. The donkey's owner then lodged a complaint with the corporal at the police station, and the corporal thereupon hauled the offender off to the local asylum and had him locked away. We never heard of him again.

If we'd had a news agency then, or newspapers, the whole thing would have made a splendid story. It isn't every day, after all, that you find a man biting a donkey.

That recalls a somewhat similar story we had wind of, about a reverend clergyman who bit a dog. This was considered distinctly newsworthy – you would, after all, rather have expected the dog to bite the clergyman.

For all the occasional mishaps involving the madmen, these men were on mostly friendly terms with the quarter and its inhabitants; they were in fact part of the fabric of daily life there. Indeed, some of them provided its entertainment, being responsible for forming our first musical group. This they did through the improvised use of empty drums and cans that had once contained various liquids imported from abroad. Each afternoon they'd assemble in the square and beat the drums with their sticks.

There were three of them, and, having decided they ought to branch out, they made up a circus troupe and performed various acts. The three men would climb up on to one another; then, when they were standing upright, the one on top would cry out: "God give him the victory!" No one was sure what this meant. What was really comic about the feat (if you could call it comic) was that the hoisting didn't follow a rational plan, with the strongest man holding up the other two. It was the other way round, with the strongest man on top. They were utterly crazy. The instant the performance was over, the one on the bottom would start shrieking at the top of his voice, uttering threats against the pair who'd been up on his back.

He seemed, even so, to derive some obscure pleasure from carrying one or other of them in individual acts, set apart from the group programme. Often he'd carry them, one after the other, from the square to the well, a hundred metres almost, running if he could manage it, and viewing it as a triumph if he could only get safe to the well without tumbling over. If he didn't manage this, then the failure would be the fault of the man riding on top. Those madmen were simply amazing.

And yet we couldn't have done without them. No one, for instance, was ever unable to honour a vow; they were always ready to attend votive feasts. They took alms when the Ramadan fast was broken, and they ate whatever was left over from weddings and funerals. They were employed to carry things around, like bags of rice or chests of tea. The only things they were never allowed to carry were the furnishings for weddings – either for fear of damage, or on account of the superstitions surrounding these items. The traders used the men too, to supply information about their rivals. "Does such-and-such a person have more customers than I do?" they'd ask. Or: "Does he have any goods left over?" And they were used to carry out acts of deliberate sabotage – a clear indication that international terrorism, and blackmail, are instinctive in mankind.

There were two especially notable pieces of sabotage during our time, involving two new vendors who'd moved to the quarter from outside, and were threatening the local traders with unfair competition and eventual loss of their livelihoods. The injured parties used two of the madmen to counter this danger. One received instructions to walk behind a vendor who was carrying a tray heaped with yoghurt and cream. Then, when they reached the dark, narrow depths of Saqifat al-Safa, the madman suddenly pinched the vendor and made him stumble. His goods came crashing down, and most of the yoghurt dishes were smashed and their contents spoiled. The madman, meanwhile, just stood there a few paces away. "There is no power or strength except in God," he intoned. The vendor, he advised, shouldn't come back, since the quarter was inhabited by malignant spirits and jinn.

The second occasion saw a madman (at the instigation of another vendor) hurl a bucket of dirty water into a deep pan of hot oil prepared to fry *maqliyya*, a popular evening food with Meccans. Never before had I seen a grown man send out agonized wails, over the loss of part of his capital, or all of it very likely. The oil and the dirty water flowed together, and everything was spoiled, including the dough prepared for the evening. The ploy worked. The vendor went back to his own quarter, leaving the local man with a monopoly in his particular trade. As a result, though, the quarter was deprived of the benefits of commercial competition. As they say: "When horses compete, the riders are happy!"

***

When I returned home to tell Mother I'd been appointed as a teacher, her shriek of joy was more like an ululation at a wedding. She ran off to take a mouthful of water, then squirted it out all over me (as was customary in those days, to protect a person against envy even from those closest to him). Next, she announced, she was going to hold a small party to celebrate the occasion. I was to go to Aunt Asma's home to invite her to lunch, then to the home of another lady whose name I forget now; I only remember she was from the Turabi family. After that I was to go and say the noon prayer, prostrating myself two extra times in thanks to God, while she prepared the food for the lunch.

The four of us ate the meal in the main room of the house, the only surprise being that the grand lady of the Turabi family remained veiled during the meal, in recognition of my status as a grown man now.

Aunt Asma was furious at this formal behaviour.

"What do you mean by it?" she cried. "He's just a child still. He's younger than your own youngest son."

She, though, insisted on keeping on her veil, and the strained atmosphere from this left me embarrassed in the three ladies' presence.

My first days of teaching were difficult and tiresome beyond anything I'd ever known. I hardly recognized myself, as, each morning, I strode along in my turban and cloak. It took me several minutes in the morning to get my turban adjusted to the proper angle, endlessly astonished by the sight of that other person staring back at me from the mirror. I looked, Mother insisted, just like Father in these new clothes of mine. I, for my part, felt quite out of place in my new role, having no relish for the picture I presented. Nor did I feel remotely comfortable standing or sitting in front of a set of pupils. What if I'd been transformed from someone receiving knowledge to someone transmitting it? I still felt, deep down, like the pupil I'd been such a short time before.

What made matters worse was that the headmaster insisted on sitting in on my classes for the first few days, to assess my skill in the teaching role he'd assigned me to. There he'd sit, at the back of the room, listening intently to every word I uttered; and, from time to time, he'd make a sign with his forefinger to show I'd done something wrong or made some inadvertent grammatical error. The only benefit I gained from his presence was the silence in the classroom; no one, while he was there, dared call out, or taunt the pupil next to him, or disrupt the class. During these classes I seemed to see the mischievous Sufyan there in front of me. Who, I wondered, would be his successor in this particular class? At any moment I expected a *nabq* stone to come flying at me, or at one of the pupils. The headmaster's presence, though, was enough to ensure nothing like this ever happened.

Sitting in the teachers' room made me feel no more comfortable than I felt in the classroom. All those people there had been my own teachers, and I wasn't used to sitting and talking with them. I'd simply say nothing. Then, as soon as the duty official's whistle blew for the start of the next lesson, I'd be the first off to the classroom. My whole day was spent scurrying to and from the classroom, or else rushing off home at the same top speed, hoping no one would see me in my official garb. Any moment I expected to come across one of my old, mischievous comrades from the quarter, ready to greet my appearance with a loud mocking laugh, or launch some sarcastic comment at me.

One day someone slipped a piece of paper, neatly folded, into the pocket of my cloak. I had no idea what was on it till I reached home and opened it. It was just the kind of thing I'd been expecting. The note comprised one short piece of verse:

*Turbaned, we see a monkey's leers.*
*He leaves it off, a pig appears.*

I read it, then went into the toilet and burst into tears, first in a stifled voice then in a loud wail for all to hear. Mother, startled, came rushing to see what had happened, and a strange sight I must have presented, standing there in the narrow space where people go to relieve themselves, fully dressed and sobbing out loud, while Mother vainly patted my shoulder. Seeing the distress I was in, she took off my turban, then my cloak, and led me off to the roof so that I might (as she put it) get some fresh air. All the while she was intoning prayers invoking God's aid and power, and His protection against the devil's wiles. She asked me, over and over, just what had happened, and still my flow of tears wouldn't stop. I grew quieter at last, ashamed of the way I'd been acting in front of Mother. But what was I to tell her? She was so proud of my profession. How was I to explain my misery?

For lack of any other recourse, I ran off to the Holy Mosque, always my refuge in times of trouble. I started to circumambulate the Ka'ba, seven times by seven – I finally lost count of the number of circuits I'd made. Then I took some warm draughts from the bucket at the Zamzam Well,[1] till I was so full I felt my ribs almost splitting apart. Only then did I calm down at last. I hurried back home to reassure Mother everything was all right, and things returned to their normal course.

Meanwhile, I made an effort to work things out, trying to guess who might have put that piece of paper in my pocket. I went over, in my mind, all the things that had happened up to the time I discovered it. I tried to recall the exit from the classroom after the final class, the crush at the door, the pupils milling around – including one whose face jumped out at me now, someone moving in my direction and pushing the others aside. Yes, he'd done it – it must have been him. But why?

I thought carefully back over my six years at the school. He and I had, I recalled, been in the same class together during our first year there. Then he'd dropped back, having to repeat the year, while I went on successfully to the second year's work. I hadn't seen him since, till now, without any warning, he'd just appeared there in front of me. What year was he in now, I wondered? I resolved to find out. Before that, though, I had to devise a strategy for the next day. I'd need to see him. But what course should I take? Report him to the headmaster? Or summon him to the teachers' room, demand that he explain himself, then reprimand him? Would I be capable of that? I could almost picture myself afterwards, trembling from fear of him. To make matters worse, the rest of the staff would come to hear about it, and I'd have to read that piece of verse out to them. Suppose one of them burst out laughing, there in front of the guilty pupil? That would bring me further shame.

No, I told myself, that wasn't the way to handle it. I'd have to resort to something quite different, tried and trusted from my own personal experience: namely, tactical planning. The first tactical manoeuvre I'd learned, over many long years, was to try and disguise my true intention by pretending to do something else. I forced myself, accordingly, to put on a pleasant smile when I met the lad next day, during the few minutes between classes. I even patted him on the shoulder, the way someone of experience might do to someone younger (even though he was actually older than I was, and stronger in build too). Then I stretched my hand out towards his ear, in the affectionate way a father might to his naughty child. "Still up to mischief, are you?" I said. Then I asked him, with a friendly air, what year he was in now. I hadn't, I said, seen him for some years.

"I'm in the second year of upper school," he answered.

"Well, then," I said, "next year, when you've finished your studies, I'll recommend your appointment as a teacher. And then *I'll* put this piece of paper in *your* pocket."

He hung his head in shame, and I simply walked off, leaving him there. But I have to say, those few moments of confrontation had left me drained. I went into the teachers' room feeling like someone who's survived an unarmed encounter with a giant or a wild beast!

***

The moment the headmaster stopped sitting in on my classes, all hell broke loose, with pupils shouting and generally taunting one another. Each day brought its fresh problem, and I tried to counter the situation by following the advice the headmaster had given me when I was first appointed. I tried to classify the pupils into the three groups he'd suggested. But my plight was made worse by my relations with the other members of staff. I couldn't form any bond with them or behave as though I was one of them.

In the end things grew so unbearable that I went to see the headmaster and asked him to release me from teaching and assign me to some administrative duty. He, though, refused. The school, he said, didn't need any more administrators. Instead he asked me to talk my problems over with him. Perhaps he might be able to help me solve them.

"It's the other teachers," I said. "I don't feel I'm one of them."

"That's only natural to begin with," he replied. There were, he went on, lunches from time to time at their various homes. He'd invite me to his own home the next week, and there I'd be able to meet some of the staff socially, outside the atmosphere of school. His suggestion turned out to be a good one – further indication of what a wise, resourceful man he was.

I was able, in this way, to see how different people were with their heads covered or uncovered; and this was something that hardened into a general principle with me as years went by, whether the person in question was accustomed to wearing a turban, a fez or a foreign hat; the principle has, in fact, been borne out on numerous occasions. These teachers, bare-headed, weren't the same as they'd been in their professional turbans. They joked and made barbed comments. They even made fun of one another with comic anecdotes, whether true or not. The dinner served the purpose of making people relaxed, of making sure they didn't become mentally exhausted or stuck in a groove, as had happened with some former teachers who'd grown to be serious the whole time.

When the food arrived, they started tossing a particular part of a sheep at one another, burying it, finally, under the layers of rice on which a whole lamb was laid. The only one who didn't take part in these antics was *Mawlana*[2] – the only teacher to be accorded this title. *Mawlana* was tall and portly, and he wore such an air of dignity you hardly dared look at him. But even he, though he wouldn't deign to join in our frolics, took his turban off like everyone else, and this lent a degree of humanity to a face naturally austere.

I was, I found, able to join in the general hilarity of this small Meccan group. I wasn't too shy to tell one or other of them some amusing story, or provide a satirical anecdote to match his own. I went so far, even, as to cut the tongue from the sheep and put the larger part of it in front of *Mawlana*. He gazed at me, smiling, then duly ate the tongue without the smallest show of anger or irritation.

Headgear and clothing, we may well suppose, tend not just to disguise people's physical form but to hide a good part of their inner self and basic personality. The particular type of clothing, too, and the amount of stiffening in it – all this helps give people a quite deceptive air. The false appearance clothes provide quite possibly lies behind a practice of the ancient Chinese, who are traditionally associated with wisdom. "If," they declared, thousands of years ago, "you wish truly to know a man, then talk with him in his nightclothes." In other words, in his pyjamas. This is because a person's likely to be truer to himself, less inclined to affectation, than when he's in some official garb. A man dressed up will admire his reflection in the mirror; he'll be conscious of his social status, or his wealth, and behave in accordance with these rather than show his true feelings.

Europeans, in northern Europe especially, have taken a forward (or backward) step regarding this maxim about nightclothes. The best relations or agreements, are, they've found, those arrived at in a sauna, where people take off not just their headgear but everything else too. The most traditionally inclined will, it's true, retain a very scanty covering. The rest are content just with the steam.

Returning to the question of headgear, we may note how it was once customary to say of such-and-such a person that he'd "uncovered his head" – meaning, he'd made his true intentions clear. The expression was used, very probably, to mean that a person had dropped all caution or reserve. If a woman made open show of her desire, people would say she'd unveiled her face, the female head covering being a veil rather than a turban. In the present age, you'll see a European man raise his hat when greeting a lady, as a mark of respect or consideration; and, if he visits another person in that person's home, he takes off his hat the moment he enters, as if to say: "Here I am, hiding nothing."

There was a saying among the common people: "Better to lose your head than your turban." In other words, taking off the turban stripped the wearer of his aura and revealed his true self to others. Following this dinner at the headmaster's home, I grew so excited about the revolutionary change in my relations with my colleagues, and the way we'd truly uncovered our heads, that I made a suggestion to the headmaster. Why shouldn't I invite them all to my own home the next Friday?

"Don't rush things," he advised me. "Don't invite anyone till you've eaten in all their homes first. Then it will be your turn."

I naturally complied with this, and came to realize how sound his judgement was when the other staff members started pressing me to arrange the next Friday lunch at my home, even to fix one for the following week. I had an answer to their solicitations.

"Anyone who gives on Saturday," I told them, "will receive on Sunday. Most of you haven't given an invitation yet. What right do you have to demand one from me?"

***

The sizeable salary I drew from the school created its own financial problem, resulting in what's known as a cash surplus or budget imbalance. I had to give constant thought to the various ways I might spend the money, or part of it at least. It could even be that the later inflationary crisis sprang directly from people like myself, whose income had suddenly shot up. I was palpably perplexed when my monthly salary came in; I simply didn't know what to do with it. Where should I put it? How could I hide it? Mother, of course, provided the best possible financial guidance. As I stood there in silence, she'd take the ten riyals, swiftly close her hand over them, then rush off to the innermost room to hide them in a safe place.

Mother also thought of ways we might better our standard of living. Her first step in this direction was to start using the services of one of the so-called African women who'd go around the streets of Mecca calling out: "We'll wash the dishes! We'll sweep the stairs!" She employed one of them to do just these things, by the day or by the week as necessary. The hallway became spotless as a result, while the upstairs sitting room, in contrast to its old state, was kept fit for the reception of pilgrims. As time went by, she came to give extra tasks to these hard-working women, trusting them with the clothes wash each Tuesday – that being the day, according to popular tradition, on which the mountains were created. Mother had her own system with these African women (or *faqeeha*s, as they were called). She herself would prepare the tub, filling it first with quantities of ash and then with water, then leaving the wash to soak. (In those days, before the arrival of detergents, ashes were used as a rough and ready means of removing stains and dirt.) The *faqeeha*s would then carry out the first two washes, which were the heavy labour of the operation, while Mother kept the final wash for herself, adding starch or bluing as necessary.

That isn't to say, though, that we'd had no dealings with the *faqeeha*s before that time. The fact is that, in earlier centuries, every family had used their services. Who else would have pounded the wheat for the soup preferred by Meccan families, which was the main dish during Ramadan? The job was carried out, each year, in the second half of Sha'ban. The women would walk out into the streets of Mecca carrying wooden pestles a metre high maybe, and crying: "We'll pound the wheat for the soup!" The women of the quarter would then hurry to call them in, haggling over the appropriate fee for the job. It was all very orderly, even though (according to rumours flying about in those days) these African women belonged to the Namnam tribe, who were cannibals. The rumour was in fact borne out some centuries later by a certain Emperor Indasa, who demonstrated the practical aspects of cannibalism by cooking and eating one of his ministers for lunch – before the minister could have the chance of eating his Emperor for dinner.

The extra help she received meant that Mother now enjoyed a good deal of free time, which she had to find some way of filling. She set herself to her loom for hours on end, or else she embroidered our handkerchiefs and drawers, this being fashionable among the notables of our time. She devoted extra thought, as well, to preparing our meals – an effort reflected not only in the excellent quality of the cooking, but in the variety and amount. This prosperous life was, in turn, reflected in our two figures. Our clothes no longer hung on us loose but were moulded to the shape of our bodies.

But Mother's household management went further than this: she acquired a whole range of new domestic appliances, articles and pieces of furniture. This she did whenever she felt an itching in her palm – a sign, according to common belief, that it was time for people to spend whatever they might have in their pockets in preparation for what Providence had in store in them.

One appliance that never ceased to delight me was our home ice-cream maker. This was a most useful device. You placed a certain amount of crushed ice in the outer part, and a cup or two of sweetened lemon juice in the inner part; then you turned the handle. When the juice was close to being frozen, it became ice cream, ready to eat.

Mother (I'm not giving away any family secrets here) had a cheerful nature, and would croon quietly to herself all day long. Her favourite song was the Syrian one:

*Sway, sway, O sycamore tree.*
*How sugar sweet are the apples of Syria!*

There's one secret, though, that I disclose with more reluctance. Once, a long time back, Mother had bought a gramophone, or "singing box" as it was called then. How she'd bought it, and who she'd bought it from, only she knew. She'd put it in the back room, then soundproofed it by stuffing rags inside, for fear the neighbours should learn of her secret. It was discovery of this that had led me to realize, for the first time, that the things our parents did weren't automatically above suspicion. All she'd wanted to do was spread a cheerful atmosphere about the house. Even so, that gramophone made me so nervous that I went around constantly on edge, sure of some disaster if anyone at school learned we had it. Only one thing relieved my painful anxiety on this score: namely, *Ustadh*[3] 'Umar's advice that I shouldn't be concerned about it. There was nothing dishonourable, he assured me, in owning a gramophone. He himself, he confessed (so as to reassure me), owned one, and he could see nothing wrong in it. More amazing still, he offered to lend us some of his records, on condition we gave them back when we'd finished with them. This (as Mother put it) placed him – that freemason – on the same level as herself – such a retiring woman as she was. She was astonished!

***

I went on giving Jameel his lessons in Arabic grammar, though I brought in a number of changes to liven them up. This I did after first consulting the *ustadh*, telling him I thought we needed to improve Jameel's reading ability – he'd get little benefit, I argued, from grammatical rules in isolation from a proper text. The best way to encourage Jameel to read was, I discovered, to write down for him some of the simple stories I recalled my mother telling me up on the roof, under a mosquito net, with the insects whining around us. In this way I think I managed to pass on to Jameel at least a solid body, if not all, of the folklore passed on down the generations. The sole difference in our case was that the tales were passed on not in the usual way, by a female, but by a male. Again and again Jameel's jaw would drop, as a particular development in the tales took him by surprise. It was a disconcerting sight; the impression was less one of simple-mindedness than of total imbecility!

The tale that gripped his imagination most, making his eyes glint with delight, was the one about the Rabbit's Wood, which I made up for him and wrote down in his exercise book one day, when the fount of my mother's tales had finally dried up. It was a simple story about a colony of rabbits in a remote wood, who lived together in perfect harmony until, one day, a dust-coloured rabbit arrived among them and began sowing discord in the community, inciting one group against another till finally they began fighting and devouring each other. Eventually only one rabbit was left, and he, having devoured so many of his comrades, was now so enormous he no longer looked like a proper rabbit at all. All the bulls in the world (I ended) were descended from this selfsame rabbit, and that's why they like to eat clover, just like their rabbit ancestors.

My story pleased Jameel so much he read it many times, finally learning it by heart. I took advantage of his enthusiasm about my bull-rabbit to have him make a grammatical analysis of the words. Was "the bull" definite or indefinite? Was "the rabbit" masculine or feminine? I think he learned more Arabic grammar during these days than at any other time, mainly because he got so excited about the rabbit, and because he wanted to analyse any sentence where the word cropped up.

I wasn't prepared, even so, for the odd question Jameel sprung on me one day. If all those rabbits, he said, had fallen in the battle, then just where had our present rabbit species come from? I pondered the matter, then answered that these rabbits were descended from a herd of bulls who'd been overtaken by famine and want, till, at last, their bodies had shrunk to the size of the rabbits we have now. This additional episode only increased his delight in the tale.

The *ustadh* was overjoyed with the regular progress he noted in his son, and repeatedly thanked me for my efforts. Even so, his face clouded over with sadness when Jameel read him the story of the rabbits, and the cloud grew more sombre when the lad went on to relate what had happened to the hungry bulls now shrunk to the size of rabbits. He realized clearly enough that Jameel wasn't of normal intelligence, and that neither my efforts nor anyone else's would ever succeed in bringing him out of his backward state. Still, the *ustadh* encouraged me to go on.

"If," he observed, "Jameel can read some of the books in this library one day, then he might be able to live a half-normal life, the way a lot of others do."

One day, as I was leaving the room where I taught Jameel, *Ustadh* 'Umar stopped me and invited me to join him in a cup of tea. He'd arranged this especially, so as to present me with a surprise gift: a small book entitled *Common Expressions in the English Language*. I thanked him for the book and made to leave.

"If only," he said, "my daughter Jameela was a boy. I would have asked you to tutor her. It would have brought excellent results. She's highly intelligent – in fact she seems to have taken her brother's share of brains along with her own."

I thanked him for his concern over my endeavours with his son Jameel, and for his anxiety over the poor results, despite all my best efforts. As for his remark about Jameela, I didn't give it a second thought. It was, I supposed, just his way of showing his appreciation to me. In fact, I'd derived some enjoyment at least from the lessons I was giving Jameel.

But the subject of Jameela cropped up once more.

"It's such a pity," *Ustadh* 'Umar observed on another occasion, "that there aren't any schools for girls. Because of that, Jameela's been denied the chance of an education, however much she deserves one."

Why, I asked him, hadn't he sent her to the girls' *kuttab*,[4] where she could at least learn the *'Amma*[5] of the Quran and become acquainted with some of the Quranic *sura*s, which she could then recite as she prayed. He'd already done this, he assured me, and she'd memorized most of the *'Amma*. That, though, wasn't sufficient. She was capable of so much more.

He fell silent again, and, unsure just how to react, I remained silent too.

"But for tradition," he went on finally, "I would have asked you to give her lessons, the way you do with Jameel."

Finding me still silent, he didn't pursue the subject, and I went home. On my way I reflected on what he'd said about Jameela; and, during the few minutes' walk between our two homes, I decided the Freemason must have been implying something beyond the mere wish that there should be schools for girls. A few days later, my suspicions were confirmed.

"Isn't learning a duty for all Muslims?" he asked me. "For men and women alike?"

Yes, I replied, it was.

"So how," he pursued, "are we to fulfil this religious duty?"

I didn't answer. Then he asked me, point blank:

"Would you be prepared to teach my daughter, the way you do Jameel?"

I showed some hesitation over this, but he went on to assure me she'd be accompanied by her grandmother, and, of course, by Jameel. I was to divide the lesson between the two.

I was shocked, indeed panic-stricken, but he gave me no chance to express my inner feelings.

"She'll be veiled, naturally," he went on. "And she'll spend the first few lessons just listening to what goes on between you and Jameel. She won't take any active part. That will come later. You can use the same stories and tales you've written down for Jameel. Once she's mastered reading, you can go on to use the school reader you learned from yourself in the lower school. It's unfair, surely," he concluded, "to leave her in a state of ignorance, when she's capable of acquiring knowledge."

Jameela was younger, by two or three years, than her brother and myself. It was a very long time since I'd last seen her – since she was five or six, in fact. After that she'd started wearing a veil, and so vanished for all intents and purposes. Indeed, I'd quite forgotten she existed till her father started talking about her.

"What must be, must be," as the saying goes, and Jameela accordingly came along for her first day, accompanied by her old grandmother – to her brother's marked agitation, and to mine too. I kept looking around me, afraid someone might see us. I came close to losing my grip on the situation when Jameel shouted: "A girl! A girl! How can she be allowed to sit here, with us?" To make matters worse, her grandmother kept begging, audibly, for God's forgiveness. She, it seemed, didn't agree with these developments either. But she'd submitted the matter to God, and in accordance with the firm instructions of the Freemason.

Jameela was a strange, inscrutable bundle. You couldn't see anything of her at all, wrapped as she was in a *jama*, a large woman's cloak that enveloped the whole form. The only openings were two small slits for the eyes, through which the wearer could look out on the world.

Her body seemed to be small and slender, in contrast to the much bigger frames of Jameel and myself. At first she'd sit stock still in a corner, throughout the lesson, with her grandmother alongside. Then, when the lesson was over, she'd leave silently, the grandmother following behind. She didn't once speak to us or greet us.

When the time came for her to take an active part in lessons, *Ustadh* 'Umar attended personally, followed by a servant lad carrying the tea tray and a plate of the cakes housewives always made during the pilgrimage season. *Ustadh* 'Umar took absolutely no part in the class. His very presence, even so, created an aura of confidence and trust that helped us all, and because of this I was emphatic he should attend all the lessons thereafter. He couldn't always come for the whole class, but even then he'd look in once or twice to make his presence felt. In time the grandmother became persuaded that what we were doing – albeit quite without precedent – wasn't really overstepping the mark to any great extent, and this new attitude was reflected in the greetings she started giving me when she came to the lesson. Initially her entry had been marked by silence. Then she started saying: "Peace be on you." A few weeks later this had been lengthened to: "Peace be on you, son." Finally, with time, she actually started exchanging a few words with me, asking after my mother and expressing admiration for my appearance in cloak and turban. Gradually things reached the point where she was asking God to protect me from the evil eye, till finally she went so far as to ask God to send me generous recompense for the lessons I was giving her grandchildren.

By now, I had no doubt I was accepted by the whole family, the clearest indication of this being when the *ustadh*'s wife came to one of my lessons herself and listened to her daughter as she read out one of the stories I'd written down for Jameel earlier.

While the grandmother was experiencing her psychological transformation, two other things had been developing hand in hand. One of these was the progress made by Jameela, who was a good deal more intelligent than I'd been expecting. She simply devoured the stories I gave her to read, one after the other. Then, having been through them once or twice with me, she'd review them during the day till she knew them by heart (including the final vowels), with no faults of grammar, even though she had no direct knowledge of grammatical rules.

The other development was inside myself. I grew so used to that low voice, with its soft resonance, that I started missing it during the day and making an effort to remind myself how it sounded. That was the only clue to her personality. Otherwise Jameela remained a screen of clothes, enigmatic and impenetrable. There was just that childlike voice, which, little by little, she began to raise as her confidence grew.

I hadn't then read the story "Love of the Blind," which describes how love comes to grow between the blind person and another, on the basis first of voice, then of touch. But, if I wasn't familiar with the story itself, instinct prompted me to work along the kind of lines set out there. Familiar now with her voice, I found it began to fascinate me; I grew attached to it, even though I knew nothing of its owner. I was inspired to re-read the *diwan* of Majnun Laila,[6] and I found myself, in my free moments, murmuring some of its celebrated verses to myself: the one, for instance, where Laila's eyes and neck were compared to those of the gazelle – even though it would be many years before I was to have sight of Jameela's eyes. I was led to reflect on people's tendency to become fond of things, in others, by virtue of mere repetition and custom.

Jameela began to occupy my thoughts. I started conjuring up a mental picture of that mysterious, slender bundle sitting there in front of me, basing this image on the three people I already knew: the grandmother, *Ustadh* 'Umar and Jameel. I'd place the nose of this one under the forehead of that other one, then add Jameel's frame, but making it more slender. In this way a composite picture of the veiled girl sitting there before me began to take shape in my mind.

The grandmother played her own special role in deepening my relationship with Jameela's voice. Many times I'd complain of not being able to hear what was being read, at which the grandmother would say: "Speak up, Jameela. Let Muhaisin hear what you're saying. He's only like your brother," she'd go on. "He's about the same age even."

Several months passed, with no conversation of any kind between teacher and female student. But Jameela's astounding progress meant that her education had, following consultation with the *ustadh*, to be broadened in its scope. It was decided, accordingly, that I should introduce first arithmetic, then grammar. These subjects needed an occasional exchange of words, followed by questions, answers and discussions. "Greeting," as they say, "leads on to conversation." Matters never, even so, went beyond these aspects.

Jameel had stopped complaining about his sister being there. There was, after all, less pressure on him now that I had to divide my time between two pupils. In fact he finally started enjoying the discussion, and the introduction of questions and answers. He'd even, from time to time, volunteer an answer to a question not put to him at all. What's more, he embarked on spirited discussion with his sister, and this afforded me the chance to feed his brain cells, which were now being stimulated to some extent.

*** 

The dawn prayer on Friday in the Holy Mosque or *haram*, especially the *sajda*,[7] induced a sense of immense spiritual uplift, both for me and for many others living at that time. Indeed, this is probably still the case with people living in Mecca today. It was a source of positive rapture for a man to be able to arrive at the Mosque an hour or so before the call to prayer, so as to set his mat in the front row, immediately before the Ka'ba. He'd then engage himself in the night prayers, or in circumambulating the Ka'ba, till the muezzin gave the call. This was all part of a tradition handed down, whereby sons, even before the age of puberty, went to the

Mosque with their fathers. So it became the custom with them, as it had with their fathers before them, and they in turn handed it on to the following generation.

On one of these pre-dawn journeys I caught sight of *Mawlana* beneath a portico of the Mosque, alone and saying the night prayers, accompanied by Quranic recitation so lengthy it seemed he'd never be finished. I stood at some distance, watching him. Then, when he'd finished his prayers at last, I went up as though I'd just that moment seen him and had felt I should come to pay my respects. In fact I did briefly sit and greet him, before moving on to the place where I usually said my own prayers. I forgot all about this encounter, but *Mawlana* evidently didn't.

At the school he taught religious jurisprudence, and also the principles of Quranic exegesis – all this was quite apart from his role as an authority on Arabic philology. He even, amazingly, had some knowledge of Syriac. He was a pious, highly respected man, reputed to be a mystic and founder of a mystical order with a following mostly in North Africa. Still more, he was said to be marked out by special spiritual powers. Were he alive today, this might eventually have brought him under investigation. Indeed, I don't quite rule out the possibility that he *is* still alive, since he was a giant of a man and possessed of remarkable strength. He would, though, be well over a hundred now.

One day, not long after our dawn encounter, *Mawlana* invited me to his home for an evening meal. This left me perplexed, since it was something quite separate from the regular dinners with the whole teaching staff. Having dinner alone with *Mawlana* was no easy matter. Just what was the right subject to bring up in conversation? You had to wait till he spoke himself, or started plying you with questions. He invited me a second time, and a third; and still I had no idea why, though he must, I assumed, have accepted me. On the fourth such occasion, he told me the food we were eating had been prepared by Ameena. Then, very gradually, he began telling me about Ameena, First he spoke of her piety and her memorization of the Quran. Then he moved on to a physical description of her, while I, confused and embarrassed, just went on smiling imbecilically. Finally, after drinking the cups of green tree he gave me, I realized that Ameena was his daughter and that he was offering me her hand in marriage. He didn't, it's true, say this right out, but his hints were enough – at any moment I was afraid that, in the customary way, he'd ask me to stretch out my hand, while he uttered the standard formula: "I have given her to you in marriage. Say that you agree." In fact he didn't say that. He merely remarked:

"Next time you'll see Ameena. It's desirable to see a woman's face before the marriage takes place. Indeed, it's essential."

This suggestion had the effect, on me, of surgery carried out on someone bereft of sight, to bring him to awareness of objects and people. Up to that day, the thought of marriage had never occurred to me, nor had I devoted any thought as to who my lifelong partner might me. It was my mother who took the lead in all matters of importance, and she'd never even broached the subject.

As I went home, a picture of Ameena, as conjured up before me, began to take shape in my mind. And, for some odd reason, the image of Jameela appeared alongside that of Ameena – the second very tall, with a fair skin and a full figure, the first small, slender and brown-skinned, like most Meccan girls of her time. My short journey home was enough to clarify my mind; Ameena's phantom going with me, through the dark alleys of Mecca, till I felt I could almost reach out with my hand and touch her. Her face wasn't a welcoming one. It was stern rather, having, built into it a good deal of *Mawlana*'s grave aspect and overpowering character. By the time I'd reached home, I was gripped by a fear of the shadowy likeness being translated into reality; a fear that I'd be condemned to spend the rest of my life with her. Mother showed no surprise at my account. Nor did she seem frightened at the vision I'd conjured up.

"Where's the problem?" she rejoined. "Fair-skinned, tall, a full figure. What more could a man ask for?"

"But I don't want her," I answered.

"How can you know that?" she said. "You haven't seen her yet."

"It doesn't matter," I observed, "whether I've seen her or not. The very thought of her, there next to me – it terrifies me."

"Don't reject God's bounty."

"And just what kind of bounty," I inquired, "are you talking about?"

"Don't be so childish," retorted Mother. "A revered shaikh like *Mawlana* offers you his daughter's hand, and then, instead of rejoicing, you're a bag of nerves."

"But I've always lived quite happily here at home. How can I suddenly start living with this Ameena?"

"Men always talk like that to start with," she said. "But once they've tasted the nectar, they soon get the appetite for more."

"Let's forget about honey, shall we? I've never even thought about marriage, and you've never suggested anything of the sort either."

"If I didn't suggest it," she said, "it was for fear of losing you. I'm all alone in the world. Even so, when your due portion comes along, I don't really think you should turn it down."

"When the right person does come along," I said, "I hope it'll be someone else. Not Ameena."

"You mean," she said in amazement, "you have some other woman in mind?"

"I might," I replied.

Our "discussion" was more like a dialogue of the deaf. Finally I was exhausted. In the course of our talk, though, I realized something for the first time. If I really had to have my "due portion," then I wanted it to be Jameela. She, and not that towering phantom, was the one I visualized standing there in front of me. I felt attracted to her, and repelled by this other creature I'd never even seen.

In the end it was Mother who settled the matter.

"Marriage," she said, "is the lot of everyone, ordained by heaven. Go to *Mawlana* and let him introduce Ameena to you. If you don't want to marry her, no one's going to force you. Say the prayer for guidance before you go. Ask God to make your choice for you."

"And suppose *Mawlana* stretches his hand out to me, and says, 'I have given her to you in marriage'? What do I say then?"

"Tell him: 'There's no need for haste, *Mawlana*. Let me talk it over with my family.'"

But when I prayed for guidance in the Ka'ba, behind Ibrahim's shrine, I didn't ask for God's help in making my choice. I prayed to Him to deliver me from Ameena.

The dinner at *Mawlana*'s house had the usual rich food – quite unlike the one we had at home, which was mostly cold dishes. The talk went on as usual, without any mention of Ameena. Indeed there was no mention of our previous conversation at all. Then, when the meal was over and the servant had taken away the *mafatta*, there was Ameena, bringing in the tea tray with the cups and pots, with the same servant following behind with the other things: the samovar and the small stand for the utensils.

"Peace be with you," she said. Her voice was clear and strong, with no hint of shyness.

She sat down and poured the tea into the delicate cups. Then she returned the teapot to its place on the samovar. Next she put two cups on a small, silver-plated tray, rose to her feet and came towards us. Approaching *Mawlana*, she leaned forward, placed her left hand on her breast, then extended the other hand to him with the words, "If you please, Father." She approached me in a similar fashion. Then, finally, she went back to her place in the corner of the room and began sipping her own tea, apparently indifferent to proceedings. I shot a furtive glance in her direction (being careful not to let her see me doing it), and I noticed, once or twice, that she was striving to get a glimpse of me, in an effort to take my measure. She didn't strike me disagreeably. If she was tall and plump, she had a cheerful face, with a glint in her eye, and her movements were graceful like a child's, lacking in any affectation.

*Mawlana* took up the conversation he'd begun at dinner, telling one anecdote after another about this pious person or that, describing the divine help they'd been accorded in time of distress. Not all the virtuous people he spoke of were Muslims; some were from other religions. He had an extensive fund of stories about those living before the Prophet's mission; about the times of Noah, Abraham and Moses. Just once he raised his brows and put a question to Ameena, about a book by al-Tanukhi. His aim, perhaps, was to show me how educated or well read she was. Or maybe he'd simply forgotten the title of the work and wanted to make use of her young memory. It might have been either of the two.

Our evening together lasted longer than usual. Too embarrassed to ask if I might leave, I just stayed where I was, now sitting cross-legged on the floor, now squatting on my haunches, constantly cracking my knuckles to relieve the tension. I was the shy one, not Ameena; I was the one, I felt, who was being submitted for approval. I found myself covered in confusion, while she remained composed and sure of herself. When, finally, she left, carrying out the various tea things, I took my leave of *Mawlana*, my eyes downcast, and off I went.

I tried, on the way home, to piece my thoughts together – I was well enough aware of the stream of questions Mother would have waiting for me. I dawdled along, seeking any excuse to delay my progress. I asked, myself, several times: "So, Muhaisin, what's it to be? Yes or no?" At last, unable to find an answer, I quickened my pace home. There was Mother, on her feet just as I'd expected. She'd evidently been pacing round and round the house. She didn't even give me the chance to catch my breath. She tilted my head straight back, as if intent on reading my face for the impression the crucial encounter had left with me.

"What's the matter with you?" she asked. "You're pale. Did it go badly?"

I said nothing. She repeated the question.

"Just a moment," I said. "Let me calm down."

"Calm down from what? Is she beautiful? Did you like her?"

"I don't know."

"You don't know?" she exclaimed. "What do you mean, you don't know?"

"I told you. I don't know."

"What a strange lad you are. Why don't you know? Tell me, how did you find her? Is she fair-skinned, and tall, the way her father said?"

"Yes," I said, "she's fair and she's tall."

"So you liked her?"

"I didn't say that."

"What are you talking about? If she's tall and fair, she must be beautiful."

"But Mother, just because a girl's tall and fair, she doesn't have to be beautiful."

"So she's ugly then. Does she have a bad complexion?"

"No, there aren't any visible faults."

"What a strange lad you are," she said.

"Mother, believe me, I can't say exactly how I feel about her. Maybe I need to see her again, to get my feelings clear. Maybe," I added without thinking, "the matter isn't as simple as you think. Perhaps she'll be the one to decide, not me."

"I never heard of such a thing in my life," she retorted. "The man's the one who decides, not the woman! What does she need to decide anyway? There's nothing wrong with you. Any girl would be happy to have you as a husband."

"Let's wait and see," I said, turning towards the stairs to end the discussion.

The days before my next invitation to *Mawlana*'s found me still perplexed, uncertain as to what I should do. I tried to read his face, to see if it shed any light on my situation. How, I wondered, should I proceed? Who should open the conversation, and what was I to say to him if he asked the expected question? I began to feel that, if thinking about marriage posed all these knotty problems, then I ought perhaps to wait, till I could make my decision without so much painful anxiety. In due course I was reminded of our next dinner engagement (not that I'd forgotten the date). This time he scanned my features with unaccustomed intensity, and spoke in a disjointed manner quite unlike his usual speech. At any moment I expected him to stretch out his hand and say: "Do you agree to take Ameena as your wife?"

If I said "yes," she'd become my wife there and then. He might even ask me to take her home with me; she'd now be regarded as mine, after all. I nearly cried out aloud, at the thought of the matter being taken out of my hands; of being forcibly married, as it were. And yet, why shouldn't I marry Ameena? What was wrong with her? This man had heaped generosity on me, opened his house to me, given me his daughter. All of a sudden I heard his deep voice:

"Muhaisin, my son, it's the tradition that, if a person should come along of whose religious practice you approve, then you give him your daughter – or other female dependent – in marriage. I approve of your religious practice."

There was a brief pause. Then he continued.

"Marriage is something ordained by God, not by man. We may be willing, but God does as He wills. Were the matter up to me alone, I should have no hesitation in my decision. But Ameena has the right to choose, or at least to give her consent to my own choice. So far she hasn't given me her agreement."

He fell silent at this point. Then he noticed the glazed way I was looking at him.

"Don't be sad," he went on. "It may be God has someone more suitable appointed for you. It may be He intends Ameena to be bestowed on another, in accordance with His own purpose."

Then, with a view to consoling me, he recited some verses of poetry routinely quoted to assuage grief or counter a sudden shock.

"You mean," I said, when I'd finally regained control of my emotions, "that she refuses to have me?"

"She hasn't given her consent," he replied.

Once more I dawdled on my way home, trying to come to terms with events. In those few minutes I came to realize what a strange, contradictory person was living inside me. I'd earnestly begged God to deliver me from her. Now, when He'd done so, I had no sense of thankfulness. In fact what I felt was overwhelming disappointment. Perhaps I felt shamed, humiliated by the fact that she'd rejected me – even though I'd been quite ready to refuse her, without any thought to her own feelings, her own sense of humiliation and disappointment.

Mother was there at the door as always, waiting to question me.

"Well?" she said. "Did he suggest a date to recite the *Fatiha* and make the marriage final? Has he fixed the time for the marriage? I hope he's not thinking of having you go and live there with them!"

"We agreed," I contented myself with saying, "to put things off till his daughter's a little older."

I couldn't reveal, even to my mother, a situation where I'd been rejected, rather than being master of the situation myself.

"Maybe it's better that way," she said. The remark surprised me. Why she said it, I don't know.

Soon the whole matter no longer preoccupied me on any conscious level, and in time it was wiped from my mind altogether – basically because *Mawlana* showed himself to be a true man. He went on with our special relationship as though nothing had happened. The invitations to dinner, the austerely cheerful manner, the inquiries after my mother – all these continued unchanged. The way he behaved was an enormous comfort to me, allowing me to forget how I'd been insulted in his house, by the one closest to him.

*Hamid Damanhury*

# FROM *THE PRICE OF SACRIFICE*
(thaman al-tadhiya)

*This work, published in 1959, is regarded as the first Saudi novel to comply with the genre's technical requirements in terms of actuality, character and appropriate standpoints in the context of the dramatic action. The basis lies in its description of the commercial quarter in Mecca, and of those who, along with certain government officials, then made up the vanguard of the middle class. In this respect* The Price of Sacrifice *somewhat resembles Muhammad Husain Haykal's novel* Zaynab, *the first technical novel by an Egyptian, which describes regions of rural Egypt in the early twentieth century, and whose hero, the son of a landowner, is both educated and aristocratic. The love stories in the two novels show remarkable similarities: in both cases the focus is on a female cousin within a conservative society. In Haykal's novel, she is the beloved but remains out of reach on account of tradition; in Damanhury's novel, by contrast, the hero is compelled to marry the cousin, and the educated girl he meets and loves in Egypt becomes the victim. Both novels give a meticulous portrayal of reality, though Haykal's reality is beautiful and romantic (for all the degree of poverty and misery involved), while reality in Damanhury's work is the actuality of the old, conservative Meccan society that combined piety with entertainment, and kind-heartedness with cruelty. But the author is also describing the local environment during a transitional period – following the Second World War – which began with education and the growth of an enlightened middle class and ended with a predictable conflict between generations, between old and new. Cairo is the main location within which the character of the hero ripens, along with those of his youthful friends who have come from Saudi Arabia to enroll at very different Egyptian university faculties. They become familiar with numerous causes and ideas, and are introduced to many of the leading personalities of whom they have only read previously. All these new elements clearly have their influence on the personality of the hero, and on the personalities of the other young men who come, like him, from a conservative environment.*

***

Ahmad sat at his wooden desk, facing his bed, while 'Isam sat at another. Each was holding an open lecture notebook, studying in an intent silence broken only when a question occurred to one of them, or a word of inquiry from one received a brief answer from the other.

The room was simply furnished: just two iron beds, two wooden desks with some books and references on them, a bookcase by the door, a sizeable cupboard for clothes and a medium-sized Arabic carpet over the floor. On the walls were some photographs and some Quranic verses in elegant frames.

This was the room of Ahmad and 'Isam, in the house they'd rented along with their two fellow-students Husain and Ibrahim. There were two other rooms, one apiece for Husain and Ibrahim, while the fourth served as a reception area. The dining table was set in the foyer, in the middle, between the four rooms.

This house they'd chosen, after a search that had taken days following their arrival in Cairo, in a building along al-Hakam Street in the Duqqi district close by the university. For all their different academic bents, the four students had remained bound by their old high school ties, and by their common sense of alienation in Cairo. And so they'd decided to live together under the same roof.

Their relations had deepened over the three months since their arrival in the city, until now they were like a close-knit family, each knowing a good deal about his friends' affairs – things which would, before, have been seen as private family matters. Gradually, day by day, the barriers had begun to fall between them, and increasingly they were discovering common viewpoints and aims.

So, different though their characters were, they'd slowly got to know one another and ended as a domestic unit, with each having his own importance in this new family life. The differences, they realized, had nonetheless to be taken into account in the running of the home. They differed, often, over details of food: the quantity and kind of food, and how to cook it. Ahmad and 'Isam were inclined to moderation, while Husain was for saving and economy. Ibrahim, on the other hand, liked plenty of white meat, shying away from lentils and the like.

They'd finally appointed Ibrahim to see to the food, advising him to be careful what he spent. They'd be watching him, they told him. And, if he'd been entrusted with the task, that didn't stop them showering him with reproof and highly critical remarks if he showed signs of spending too much.

He paid little enough attention to all this, meeting it with tolerance and a wide, bellowing laugh, reminding them regularly of the favour he was doing them.

"Have I run away from my marriage ties," he'd shout, "only to find myself responsible for a pack of children? You don't appreciate the sacrifice I'm making for you. I've left a proper home in Mecca, where I wasn't responsible for a thing, and now here I am, landed with the job of seeing to your food, filling four stomachs that could digest stones. And where? In a weird place like Egypt, where we're all away from home! Just leave these things to me, don't tire yourselves out worrying about them. I'm the one who's responsible. If you want to economize and save money, there are other ways of doing it, besides food. I'm studying economics, at the

College of Commerce, don't forget that. I'm quite capable, believe me, of applying what I learn to things in the household."

Early on that bitter January night, with the darkness slowly falling and spreading its dark shadows over the silence, Ahmad, sitting at his desk, could feel the cold piercing every part of him, even through the woollen *abaya* he was wrapped in. His face was clouded with an unaccountable depression, only deepened by a silence so profound the house appeared quite empty of people. The sound of public vehicles passing in the main street, some way from their house, caught his attention. He listened intently, imagining the people riding in them, their noise, the voice of the inspector, the ting of his whistle. Then he returned to his notebook, only for the sound of some other vehicle to reach his ears and distract him once again.

Every so often he turned to 'Isam. But 'Isam was intent on his notebook, as if he was cut off from everything around him, having no part of Ahmad's feelings or the pleasant visions breaking in on his friend.

As this unsettling state of affairs went on, Ahmad's disquiet began to mount. He felt he had to talk, about anything, just to break the heavy silence. He got up, went to sit on the edge of his bed, then leant on his right arm on the pillow. 'Isam glanced at him in silent inquiry, and Ahmad, sensing this, didn't wait for 'Isam to voice any question.

"It's really cold tonight," he said, folding his arms tight over his chest. "I can't take it. I can feel the cold running in my bones. It's like water coursing around in there."

He paused, then added:

"It'll be warm in Mecca. And where's Mecca now?" He sighed, without waiting for an answer. "God bless her days!"

'Isam looked at him, laughing, then intoned a verse:

"Nostalgia after just one night?"

He grew more serious.

"You've still years to go," he went on. "You're a long way from Mecca."

"That's what makes it so wretched," Ahmad answered sadly.

"What do you mean, wretched?" 'Isam said, with disapproval. "You should thank God it's the College of Medicine you're enrolled in. You'll be here for a long time. I'm here for four short years, then it's back to work. A life of responsibilities, and duties, performed, oh, so respectfully and respectably. I can already feel the weight of it – all those heavy duties waiting for me, not too far away now. It's so lovely, student life! We won't really appreciate it till we're plunged into working life. Till we've tasted its bitterness, then drunk it down, one cup after another. And yet we'll have to keep smiling, accept things, put up with things, ration our words, our fun, what we think, how we move. We'll have to change the very way we live, the way we think about everything.

"How tedious it's going to be, to give up our kind of life and take on one that's weighed down with so many problems. Everything so carefully planned by other people, the lines laid down so clearly. Society's going to make us walk inside those lines. No turning aside, left or right. No looking farther ahead than our noses."

He paused.

"That's the future," he said, with an air of boredom. "Why are you trying to bring it closer?"

Ahmad laughed.

"Well, there is an answer. Go on studying for a few more years."

"Are you asking me to fail on purpose?" the other man asked censoriously. "I can't believe you're serious."

Ahmad became grave again.

"I'm only joking. I know how you feel about life, what your views on it are. You're too brave to take the coward's way out."

'Isam smiled, pleased by Ahmad's words. He had respect for the other man's views, and the deep comfort he took from the conversation was reflected in his smile, and in his agreement with everything 'Isam had said. These words between them had wiped away much of the depression that had taken hold of him earlier that evening. He felt more comfortable now he'd given 'Isam the chance to air his views. And he was keen, in any case, to keep talking about things like that. The four friends had, after all, been utterly sunk in the practical matters of living, and in their studies, for the past three months, since they'd arrived in Egypt. Their discussions had centred on household and academic affairs, mostly the first, and on how different things were here. They'd talked about the problems of studying, compared impressions of the new life they'd set up together; about a new kind of society, particular traditions and approved ways of thinking, which they'd had to go along with and get used to. They'd suffered and they were still suffering, trying to come to terms with the ways of this new life.

Ibrahim, though, had been the first to blend in with the new environment. He was prepared, by temperament, to accept all the changes that sprang up in his present way of life, to merge into all the new circles. And so, within those three short months, he'd been able to make a number of friends of different kinds – a source of amazement and a topic of discussion among his friends. The three of them were genuinely surprised at Ibrahim's ability to assimilate the new atmosphere, to adapt so readily to this society he'd moved into. They admired him and wished they could be like him. Each debated the matter within himself, and ended up feeling sorry he couldn't keep pace with Ibrahim.

None of them shared Ibrahim's social gifts, and yet each fell short in a different way. Ahmad was the least sociable of the three, reserved and inward-looking, as though he liked to talk to himself continually, or uncover things hidden within himself. Most of the time he was silent; and when he did take part in some conversation, it was on neutral subjects, especially with people he didn't know well.

His debates took place solely within the four walls of the house, and with his three colleagues. He seemed as if lost in some long dream, and his introverted nature made him, as he realized, unfitted for this new life of his. He hadn't made any friends among his university colleagues, as if completely satisfied with his three fellows who'd moved with him from Mecca to Cairo.

All he'd been able to achieve was a superficial acquaintance with just two other students at college. It had all started when one of these borrowed his notebook, and they'd come to know one another's full names and country; and then this student had introduced him to a friend who accompanied him to college each day. Even then Ahmad had set certain limits on the friendship.

The first was called Mustafa Lutfi, and he was from Tanta, where he'd studied up to high school. Then his father had been appointed to a judicial post in Cairo, and Mustafa had moved there with his family and enrolled in college. The second friend, 'Izzat Badr al-Din, who'd been a fellow-student of Mustafa's in Tanta, had come to Cairo alone to attend the university.

Ahmad was proud of the effort he'd made in acquiring these two friends – though in fact he hadn't put in any effort at all. The friendship had been born through those two related circumstances that had led him to get to know them.

As for 'Isam and Husain, they came somewhere between Ibrahim, with his gift for making friends, and Ahmad at the bottom of the list.

Ibrahim never stopped boasting about all the many friends he'd made during his short stay in Cairo. He sought out all kinds, though he made a point of choosing those who had some special quality, so he could boast all the more whenever the subject came up among the four friends.

"You're living in a closed shell," he'd tell them repeatedly. "You've brought your old way of life with you to Cairo, and you'll be no different when you go back – no store of memories, no new thoughts. Whereas I've studied this new way of life, through these friends I've made, and I'll make more friends too. There's a vast world out there, and you can pick and choose as the fancy takes you."

That night, 'Isam and Ahmad had a long talk, feeling a degree of closeness and affinity with one another. As the talk went on, Ahmad felt his depression of the early evening begin to fade. Finally, 'Isam returned to his notebook, as if to make clear his wish to resume his studies, while Ahmad continued to recline on his bed, swirling around in a cascade of his own thoughts.

After a while they heard taps on the door. There was Ibrahim, dressed in a new navy blue suit and a smart blue tie, his hair carefully groomed. He greeted them, and they returned his greeting together, in a whisper almost. Ahmad shifted a little and gazed at him with awe, as if eyeing some film star: the tall, compact body, the tanned face that seemed fuller and brighter than usual. Ibrahim pulled up the nearest chair and sat down, radiating pride and confident self-assurance.

As for his two friends, they were less troubled by his air than filled with curiosity. Ibrahim was, they knew, good-hearted, not in the least arrogant. Many a time his friends had advised him not to set too much store by appearances, but he'd simply give a loud laugh.

"I dress to fit the occasion," he'd say.

Tonight, apparently, he was wearing his best clothes, ready to spend a thoroughly cheerful evening. The other two young men gave rein to their imaginations, wishing he'd invite them to go along with him.

"There'll be new faces," they said to themselves. "New kinds of people and talk, beyond this little circle we live in. How lucky Ibrahim is, being able to live day by day. And how miserable we are, living like recluses in this monastery, away from the whole wide world outside."

Ibrahim, as if aware of what was passing through their minds, invited them to go along with him. 'Isam excused himself, while Ahmad said nothing, hastily reflecting on the matter.

Ibrahim repeated the invitation. Still Ahmad seemed to hesitate, and the other man began spurring him on.

"I've invited some other students," he said. "To see this marvellous film that's showing at the Metro. It's called 'The Past Never Comes Back'. Have you heard about it? It's a big hit. Let's go, I'll introduce you to my friends. You'll like them. They're from high society."

'Isam laughed, while Ahmad nodded in agreement. He got up to dress, taking a towel from the rack and going off to the bathroom. As the door closed behind him, Ibrahim got up and started pacing the floor. A long silence ensued, making Ibrahim feel embarrassed. He turned to 'Isam.

"You're too serious," he said in a bored tone. "And you study too hard."

"One madman's more than enough in this apartment," 'Isam rejoined, laughing.

Ibrahim returned to his chair, ready to argue the matter.

"You're the madmen," he said. "Studying, looking for knowledge, sitting up late poring over books. What sort of life's that? I've gained a whole lot more, going out and meeting people, than you've gained from the university."

'Isam went on laughing.

"We've come up here to study at the university," he said, "not in those social circles of yours. The truth is, you've got nothing out of your studies, and now you want to bring us round to your way of thinking, make us believe you're right. But Ahmad won't be able to keep up with you. I know him."

He paused for a moment. Then he asked:

"Why don't you move to the School of Literature? There are nicer people there than you'll find in Commerce. Milder people."

"Later on maybe," Ibrahim said, laughing. "For the moment I can do without any more complications. I'm an emotional type, and I can't take too much niceness or mildness."

"If you were that emotional," 'Isam laughed, "you wouldn't have backed out of your engagement in Mecca. Why didn't you go through with it?"

Ibrahim's manner grew more serious now.

"I thought hard about it the night Ahmad was betrothed, and I decided the time wasn't right, especially as her parents were against me leaving the country. Anyway, you did well enough out of my decision. Just imagine this household without me! In the end, marriage is a matter of fate. It's destiny. Maybe I'll go back to my fiancée when I've finished my studies."

He reflected for a moment, then said, with a bored air:

"Why talk about it now? What's past is past. I've brought my parents enough trouble. I've caused a rift between our two families, even though they're related and so close to one another. But it'll pass in time."

"Provided the reasons for the rift are removed," 'Isam put in.

"If, that is," Ibrahim went on resentfully, "fate allows it."

They both fell silent. As Ahmad came into the room, the towel over his shoulders, Ibrahim asked 'Isam:

"What does Ahmad think about it?"

Ahmad turned to them.

"About what?"

"Marriage," Ibrahim said.

"I'm married already."

"I know that. I mean, what do you think about marriage?"

"It's something every young man has to do," Ahmad said, surprised. "As for what you decided, I believe everyone should think and act according to what suits him best. My own viewpoint's clear enough."

He moved over to the mirror, then added:

"My engagement to my cousin was what I'd been dreaming of since I was a child. She's a part of me. I simply can't wait for the day our marriage is consummated."

The other two gazed at one another in silence, while Ahmad proceeded to dress. When he'd finished grooming himself, Ibrahim remarked:

"You look smart. You've shown good taste in the colours you've chosen. You'll like the group tonight."

Ahmad looked over his clothes, then took a last glance at his face – it was clear, he noted, and just a little rosy.

"I'm not keen on meeting high society people," he declared, "but I thought I needed a change of scene. Earlier this evening I felt depressed, all of a sudden. And I've heard how great the film is that we're seeing."

They said goodbye to 'Isam and started for the door, Ahmad with his slim, medium-sized frame, Ibrahim with his tall, compact body and tanned complexion. They made a contrasting pair, even in their feelings about the outing. Ibrahim was glad to have Ahmad alongside him; he felt proud and superior, at being able to introduce Ahmad to some of the new friends he was always boasting of so much in the house. Ahmad, for his part, was indifferent. He was only going out at all to try and lift his depression and painful sense of anxiety. Getting to meet new friends had never been a priority for him.

As they passed through the door, 'Isam stood behind them, wishing them a pleasant evening.

***

It was eight in the evening, and the three friends, Husain, Ahmad and 'Isam, were gathered in Husain's room. They'd opened the windows looking out over the street to the north. Husain was reclining on his bed with his feet on the floor, and 'Isam was sitting on the other side of the bed, while Ahmad sat on the wooden chair behind the desk, where he'd put a tray with a teapot and some empty cups.

They'd drunk their tea, and now they were chatting about various things, recalling old memories that sent them into fits of laughter; memories that came to them invariably during these meetings of theirs. They'd adopted the habit of meeting every day at the same time, going again and again over their memories of some particular incident, presented constantly in a fashion that was fresh and new. Then they'd start laughing all over again, as if discovering some new comic angle to arouse their hilarity.

Memories they could put a date too and others they couldn't. Happenings as old as their bygone childhood, of their school days in Mecca, and bizarre incidents from the six months they'd been in Cairo.

There was the student who'd asked Ahmad:

"Do you live in houses like ours, or do you still live in tents?"

And then there was the other one who'd asked Husain:

"How many oil wells have you dug in your house?"

Even so, it wasn't anything like the same without Ibrahim there. There wasn't the same joviality they usually felt when he was around. He was mostly out at this hour, though he did occasionally manage to get back to take part in these cosy gatherings, where they'd recall the past and discuss bizarre incidents from the present. Usually Ibrahim would bring the gathering to a close by describing one of his recent new experiences, as if he was reciting pages from an open letter. And they'd doubt whether it could be true, laughing and winking at one another; to which he'd respond with a bellowing laugh that would be louder than their two laughs put together.

Tonight they were saying how close the exams were – just two months away. It was mid-March now, and that feeling of tense apprehension students have shortly before being tested was making itself felt. They were aware how little time there was left, and how intensive their professors' lectures had become following a student strike. Those strikes had, though, given them time to make up for missed classes, or to look at their regular assignments more closely.

Over the past six months they'd led a closely organized life, regulated by the hour and hardly ever varying. Each morning they'd leave for their colleges: Ahmad and Husain for the Pre-Medical class, 'Isam for the Faculty of Law and Ibrahim for the Faculty of Commerce. They'd return home as their college timetables dictated, gather at five o'clock, then study for an hour or two before supper – all except Ibrahim, who'd usually be out.

Time passed quickly through those months, with its minor incidents and changing scenes, and the four young men found themselves almost imperceptibly changing, in different ways; in their reactions, for instance, to the new society and environment they were living in.

"I wonder if Ibrahim's prepared for the exams," Ahmad remarked. "It seems to me all he's interested in is those new friendships and activities of his."

"What he's keen on studying is the different social classes," 'Isam answered, laughing. "He's collected a set of samples now, from every class."

Husain sat up in his chair.

"I think," he remarked, "Ibrahim will pass the exam."

"He's planned a big programme," 'Isam said, "to cover all the faculties. It's all mapped out, taking in all the different colleges. He's often talked about it. He's started with commerce, and next year he'll study literature or law, and go on till he's where he finally wants to be. Wherever that is."

He paused, then added:

"He's told me all about it. From what he said today, he started studying music a month ago. He's been trying out all kinds of instruments and can't fix on the one he really wants to play. All that before he's learned to read a note! I'm afraid he'll end up playing the *somsomiyya*!"[8]

"And then," Ahmad said to general laughter, "he'll find himself a living at the *tundubawi* and the grave diggings. That's not a bad idea. He'll find it useful for the future."

Their talk was interrupted by the creaking of the outer door. Then came the voice of Ibrahim, welcoming in someone he'd brought with him.

There was a tap on their door, then Ibrahim appeared, smiling broadly and ushering in a broad-shouldered young man who had the air of a boxer or wrestler. The friends held their breaths, exchanging perplexed glances. Ibrahim turned to the guest and introduced him to his fellow-students, who rose as one, welcoming the man and shaking his hand.

Ibrahim introduced his friend.

"Samir Rushdi, the musician," he said.

Afraid of bursting out laughing, 'Isam hurriedly left the room. Ahmad and Husain greeted the man with a show of interest, but their looks expressed little enough confidence in his musical skills.

A moment later 'Isam returned and invited them into the reception room. After they'd taken their seats and told the houseboy to make tea, their eyes glinted with the hope of discovering what lay behind this new surprise of Ibrahim's. The day before he'd brought along a scrawny friend and introduced him as an athletics champion. And here, today, he was bringing them a further specimen: a giant, built like a bullfighter and introduced as a great musician. It was pretty odd. He'd left his studies to go to ruin, taking a different way altogether, completely aimless.

Ibrahim, sensing what his friends were thinking, smiled to himself. Then he indicated the musician.

"The professor here," he said, grinning, "represents a new school in music. Its tendency is to dig deep, with a view to identifying the people's true characteristics and portraying their pure spirit in musical terms. I've been studying with him recently, and, with his help, I've been pretty successful, even over this short time."

'Isam laughed inwardly.

"Well," he remarked, "after Sayyid Darwish,[9] traditional eastern music needs someone to revive it. Maybe Professor Samir's destined to succeed him."

The musician's face relaxed. Happy at receiving such high praise, he looked at his student and said proudly:

"Ibrahim has the makings of a good musician."

Ahmad, though, just laughed.

"Ibrahim's tastes are in western music," he said. "He doesn't much like the eastern kind. Unless, of course, he's changed now."

Mindful of his old preferences and changing views, Ibrahim answered the remark.

"If I've changed," he said, "it's all down to Professor Samir. He's the one who's shown me the great things there are in eastern music. The delightful melodies, which represent our true spirit."

'Isam gazed at him.

"After the exams," he said, "when, God willing, we're celebrating our success, we'll celebrate the birth of the budding musician too, Professor Ibrahim."

This recalled Ibrahim, suddenly, to the exams so close at hand and the way his friends had gone ahead of him by studying while he was losing so much time in pursuit of some vague aim. This futile search would probably go on, he felt, unless divine providence saved him. A fellow-student, he remembered, had promised to get him the notes for the lectures given over the past two weeks – the period during which he'd become involved with music and musicians. He'd been missing classes and studies for so long now that college affairs were the merest scrambled picture in his mind. He felt as though he was waking from some deep sleep. What would happen if he failed his exams?

"Did anyone bring a notebook for me?" he asked casually. "While I was out?"

Ahmad answered in the negative. Ibrahim thought long and hard.

"It's mid-March now," he announced at last. "The exams are only two months away. I haven't a hope of passing."

"There's still hope," 'Isam said, "if you start studying straight away."

Ibrahim felt as though some hidden force was driving him on to think of himself and his future. He realized, suddenly, what a gulf there was between him and his friends.

"Isn't it time," he said to himself, "that I started being like the other three here? What's my father going to say, when the results come out and he hears about them? How's he going to feel, when he sits with his friends in Mecca and can't be proud of his son?

"'Ahmad, Husain and 'Isam have all succeeded,' he'll say, 'but he's a failure. And why? Because he spent his time learning how to play the harmonica, and the hand-drum, and the tambourine, and the reed, and the *somsomiyya*.'

"What do these instruments have to do with our country's future? And what kind of childish behaviour have I led myself into? I've fooled myself, and my friends, into thinking Samir's a musician. But I can see, from the looks on their faces, they know how things really are."

The truth was revealed now, the straight, bitter truth about the delusions he'd been nursing, and he began to despise himself. With a worried glance at his watch, he got up and took his leave. The guest did the same. Once the two of them had left the building and reached the street, Ibrahim said goodbye to the other man, then hurried over towards the Giza district, heading for the home of the fellow-student who'd promised to provide him with the notes. From that night on, he rejoined his hard-studying friends, trying to catch up with them and so prepare for the coming exams. It was a new page in his academic life.

*Turki al-Hamad*

FROM *AL-ADAMA*
(Al-Adamah)

*The title of this novel denotes a quarter in the city of Dammam, in the east of the Kingdom of Saudi Arabia, where the author/narrator lived until almost eighteen. Having graduated from high school, he moves to Riyadh to enroll at the College of Commerce at King Saud University. Al-Adama is the first part of a trilogy by Turki al-Hamad, the two subsequent novels being Al-Shmaisi (a quarter in Riyadh) and Al-Karadeeb. The three works have, as overall title,* Phantoms of the Abandoned Alleys; *the phantoms, that is, of the old streets he remembers.*

*These novels are, then, autobiographies, fusing the imaginary and the real. Al-Adama contains numerous allusions to historical events lived through by the author: the defeat of 1967; the coup in Libya; the rule of Gamal Abdul Nasser; the rise of the Syrian Baath party; and so on. There is observation, too, of the spread of Marxist thought, and of the secret organizations and pamphlets that aroused the students and spurred them on to rebel and to adopt elements of banned leftist thought. But the narrator also records aspects of the personal life of the hero Hisham, and of his family life: notably that he is an only son whose parents doted on him as a child. Eager to please them and abide by their rules, he nonetheless lives out a personal life filled with daring and adventure, as seen, for instance, in his immense zest for reading officially banned books, his joining of dangerous political parties, and his secret romances with Nora, the girl next door. The narrator records, too, some of Hisham's experiences in Riyadh, when he goes there to seek admission to the university. But the experiences of his first city had already essentially moulded his personality, in terms of his courage, his broad knowledge, his revolt against tradition, and his love of adventure.*

\*\*\*

Through the window of the train from Dammam the buildings of Riyadh began to appear on the skyline, like a vague dream in a summer nap. On that August day, the mirages blended with the sandstorms sent spinning up by the breath of jinn from the Dahna desert, giving Riyadh the appearance of a talisman from the tales of Sheherazade, or of a demon of King Solomon or King Sayf Ben Dhi Yazan.[10] One of these would appear suddenly, then vanish in an instant: a mystery saying both much and absolutely nothing – a tale of an island of Sinbad or a lake of the bewitched king.

The din mounted and the bustle quickened, as passengers went about gathering their belongings ready to leave the train. They were vying feverishly with one another, as if every moment was supremely important – though in fact their whole lives meant nothing to most of them. Perhaps the long haul between Dammam and Riyadh, those seven hours of expectation and tedium in a hot tin box, had led to a sense of excitement now, from the mere fact they'd soon be leaving their magical confinement.

They were all lost in utter hurly-burly, with laughter here and yelling there. Here was a man scolding his wife, and checking, for the first time since he boarded the train, on where his children were. There was another gathering up his belongings. Some women were adjusting their *abaya*s[11] and veils, others checking inside their handbags. He alone remained seated, staring through the window at the specks of dust breathed out by the desert jinn. He looked at everything, seeing nothing, as though nothing had any meaning for him. Yet, if he scanned the view outside without interest, his breast was heaving.

A young man, eighteen years old, lean and short, with a tanned colour and a freshly shaved moustache, pearly teeth inside a small mouth, thin rosy lips, a straight nose, a wide forehead, long hair showing black as night through his cap and head-dress, eyes long-lashed and topped by thick brows, gazing through glasses at everything yet finding interest nowhere, a pointed chin set in a pointed face. All these features belonged to a certain young man who, coming into the world, had been given the name of Hisham Ibrahim al-'Abir.

***

As the train neared Riyadh station, the passengers crowded at the doors. Still, though, he stayed there in his seat, gazing at place without limits and time without confines. He'd just graduated from secondary school, his grades not especially high or low, though he was, for all his youth, highly intelligent and educated. Hisham had come into the world with a single interest and a single enjoyment: reading anything and everything that came his way. All through primary and middle school he'd passed with flying colours. Once he'd even been promoted from the third to the fourth class in acknowledgement of his distinction – a feat that had made his parents proud, especially his father, who could talk of nothing else but the brilliance of his only son; a source of annoyance to some of his listeners, whose sons were below Hisham's level. Everyone, though, had recognized his excellence and predicted a bright future for him.

After starting secondary school, he'd become much attracted to political and philosophical writing; a friend of his father's had given him a copy of 'Abd al-Rahman al-Kawakibi's book on *The Nature of Tyranny*.[12] As a result of this, he'd begun spending his evenings reading Marxist, nationalist and existentialist literature, along with texts from other philosophical schools and political tendencies. He'd take them out from local libraries, and, later on, had even managed to acquire some books that were officially banned.

His mother, entering his room late at night and seeing him engrossed in his reading, would smile affectionately, supposing he was busy revising his school texts. "You study too much, son," she'd say. "Why not rest for a bit?" And he, for his part, would smile lovingly back and say: "In a little while, mother – I still have a few pages left." At that his mother would smile again, close the door and start praying for him. She would, though, return with a glass of hot milk and put it on his desk, insisting once more that he should rest.

"Drink this milk," she'd say. "It'll help you sleep."

He'd smile at that, as if in surrender, and say:

"How could I refuse anything you ask me to do?"

She'd stay in the room even so, till he'd drunk the milk. Hisham would submit, drinking it quickly down, and she'd leave, persuaded he'd soon go to sleep. Then he'd go on with his reading of *The Story of Philosophy*, enchanted by the cascade of men and their thoughts. And on he'd go still, till he was roused by the voice of the muezzin calling to the dawn prayer.

*** 

The train entered the station, and the commotion of the passengers rose still higher. The smell of packed human bodies spread in the air, blending with the kind of dust speck found only in Riyadh. Children screamed, men shouted and the women grumbled irritably because the bustle and pushing showed no respect for their veils and the sanctity of their bodies. Amid all this, Hisham appeared to be in a world of his own.

At the secondary school he totally neglected his studies. He wouldn't, indeed, have studied a single page but for fear of wounding his father's pride and his mother's heart – would have plunged himself totally into the study of forbidden texts. For a month or two before final exams, he'd force himself to revise and gain some partial understanding of the textbooks, so as to stumble through somehow. He didn't, though, pass with distinction the way he'd done before; just enough to save his face in front of his parents and others. His parents were surprised to see his grades slipping, in spite of his endless reading and constant studying, and the surprise was mixed with deep pain; but this was better than utter failure that would have led to embarrassment in front of others, to shame and heartache. One day his father quizzed him on why he was dropping back, and Hisham came up with various flimsy excuses and justifications. But he knew they hadn't convinced his father. As for the father, he preferred not to take the argument further, putting everything down to critical changes as the boy left the innocence of childhood for adolescence. His only recourse was to ask God to bestow success and guidance on his only son.

History was Hisham's favourite subject at secondary school, and he was deeply attracted to a young history teacher called Rashid al-Khattar, newly returned from America and fired by the enthusiasm and energy of a young man intent on making a mark. This teacher stayed fixed in his memory for many years, encircled by a halo of respect and idealism, even though the man had taught history for just one year before going off to settle in one of the Gulf Emirates, where he took citizenship. Hisham had been profoundly shocked by the news of Rashid's suicide straight after the Israeli forces had invaded Beirut in 1982. This happened fourteen years after their last meeting, when Rashid was an ambassador for his new country in a European state.

Hisham was entranced by the study of history, and entranced by his history teacher, who admired him in return. He loved the lessons about the Industrial Revolution, the French Revolution, the Napoleonic Wars and the conflict of ideas in Europe, together with their reflection on the Arab world in the wake of the French campaign in Egypt, and the effect of this on Arab political and intellectual life. He was entranced by ideological and political conflicts of all kinds; wanting more than the official textbook courses, he went everywhere in search of suitable books, till he became well known in the few libraries in Dammam. Professor Rashid would lend him books on the subjects in question, then he'd take what was available from the local libraries. These, though, were never enough to satisfy his passion for his newly found world; and so, throughout every holiday with his parents, to Jordan, Lebanon or Syria, he'd gather books not permitted in his own country; and these would become his source of knowledge till the next trip. No one, in those days, had any knowledge of London, Paris or New York. Few people had even been to Cairo, which for them was something akin to a dream, a fantasy world like the old Baghdad of Caliph Haroun al-Rashid, or the old Damascus of Caliph 'Abd al-Malik; a dream rather than a geographical place. Cairo, in those days, was the capital of the Arab world, a focus of longing for writers, intellectuals, politicians and society at large.

Hisham brooded painfully on the way he deceived his parents during those holidays, spending all his pocket money on Marxist books unavailable in his country, notably the works of Ernesto Che Guevara, Regis Debray and Frantz Fanon, along with Marx, Engels, Pleknanov, Lenin, Trotsky and Stalin – these were his main intellectual sources. He was deeply affected by the works of Guevara, which found an echo in his inner self. These books, and other literary writings and classic novels, were sold cheaply in 'Amman, Damascus and Beirut, on pavements and on wagons very much like vegetable carts. During his trips and afterwards, Hisham would devour, as special favourites, all of Maxim Gorky's works and the classic Russian novels in general. He read Tolstoy's *Anna Karenina* and *Resurrection*; *Crime and Punishment* and *The Brothers Karamazov* by Dostoevsky; and the *Quiet Don* of Sholokhov. *The Mother*, by Gorky, stirred in him a mixture of intense emotions wavering between anger and zest, sorrow and compassion, cruelty and tenderness, and this led him to re-read it several times. He wept often, too, with Uncle Tom in his cabin; lived with Wang Lang and his wife in *The Good Earth*; and sympathized with Madame Bovary as much as he hated Scarlet O'Hara. He'd snatch long moments to read Alberto Moravia, and Balzac, and Emile Zola, not out of any love for their writings but to find here a scene of sexuality, there the description of an intimate affair, imagining himself, in his daydreams, as the hero of these encounters. As for the enchanting description of social life in these books, it failed to arouse his interest; Russian literature he judged to be the best in this regard. He also read some of Charles Dickens' books, finding much enjoyment in *A Tale of Two Cities*. This, along with *The Mother*, he felt to be the finest fiction ever written.

Much of the money his parents generously gave him was spent on such books. When the time came to return to Dammam, he'd gather them up, giving his parents to understand that he needed them for his studies, so as to get the best grades. They'd help him devotedly in clearing the books through customs, unaware of the explosive material they contained. Cheered though he was by this, he felt he was behaving meanly – that he was, by any standards, a cheat and a liar. And this painful sense would grow stronger as he considered how he was doing these things to the two people closest and dearest to him: his own parents. He'd try, sometimes, to persuade himself he wasn't lying or cheating. These books did, after all, contain learning, views and culture, even if the subjects weren't mentioned in the school textbooks that so failed to quench his thirst for knowledge.

***

His new readings thrust him into a vast world, of excitement and fervour; into broad spaces where the whole world held his interest, with no boundaries and no restrictions. He'd become filled with a new spirit, which aimed to transform this world into an earthly paradise where everyone could live happily, free of tyranny and injustice, enjoying equality and justice. The whole globe was his homeland now; his city had become a mere point in the world's sea, his country a mere part of the humanity to which every true human being should belong.

Once he'd been reserved and aloof, known solely to a small circle of friends. Now he adopted a vivid, dashing style of behaviour. He took a regular part in the fiery political and ideological debates at school, siding with this group or that, never a member of any one party. The school was typical of the political and ideological currents then swirling about in the Arab world: there were Marxists, Baathists, Arab Nationalists and Nasserites, debating and clashing openly. A Baathist student would pass a well-known communist and yell "Red!" And the other would furiously retort "'Aflaq!"[13] It was a way of exchanging insults.

Hisham remembered one debate with the teacher of religious studies, about Darwin's theory of evolution. The teacher had described this as cursedly irreligious and atheistic, calling Darwin a Jewish conspirator against Islam and Muslims. In fact, Hisham had told the teacher, the theory was a product of science, and science was master of the modern world; Darwin might be right or wrong about the particular origins of man or other species, but evolution itself was a self-evident reality. Nor, he added, was Darwin a Jew, on either his father's or his mother's side. As a result the teacher had became hostile towards him, referring to him as "that immoral person." Hisham, though, didn't care in the slightest, now that he'd found a new world of vivid freedom.

After that argument Hisham was famous in the school, and still more so after the headmaster had summoned him to his office one day and threatened to report him to the authorities – saying he was a pagan if he refused to withdraw what he'd said. He backed off for a while, but the other students had begun to take an interest in him now, and so had some of the left-leaning teachers. Every group wanted him on its side in the political and ideological struggles, in a school where the pupils had no choice but to join this faction or that.

He began to write zealously for the bulletins arrayed on the school walls. He wrote fiery articles, calling for solutions as radical as possible. After two of his articles (one in support of the communists, the other in support of the Baathists) had appeared on a bulletin board, the headmaster summoned him once more. The first article was about the 1967 disaster; about its causes and about the role of the western countries allied with Israel to destroy progressive forces in the region. The aim of the war, it stated, was to put an end to any attempt at cultural renaissance on the part of the Arab nation. The second article attacked the British teachers at the school, and their uncivilized behaviour, even though they claimed to have come to teach culture and civilization. The headmaster took a sheaf of papers from his desk drawer and tossed them on to the desk.

"These pamphlets," he said, trying to keep his voice quiet and severe, "were distributed today in the school. They call for opposition to the government, and they're signed: 'The Democratic Front.'"

He paused, watching for Hisham's reaction. When Hisham remained silent and unperturbed, the headmaster added:

"Their style's similar to the one you use in your articles. I suspect you had something to do with it."

Gripped by fear, Hisham felt his stomach tighten painfully. He wanted to defend himself, but the headmaster was too quick for him.

"Not a word," he shouted furiously. "I'm not looking for an answer! This is a second warning. I swear, by God, if you don't put an end to these clandestine activities, I'll report you. And I'll say not only that you're against religion but that you belong to secret organizations."

The lad tried to say something, but the headmaster dismissed him forthwith.

"Not another word," he said. "Just get out of here."

Hisham left, feeling as though someone had drained him of his blood. A cold sweat broke out on his hands and face. He was stunned by the reprieve he'd been given. He was actually guiltless of the charge laid against him, but he'd heard often enough that a mere accusation was considered evidence of guilt. As he left, he heard the headmaster muttering: "Curse you all! You're trying to get us into trouble – "

As he left the office, Hisham almost bumped into the school overseer, Rashid 'Abd al-Jabbar, who'd been there in the office, though Hisham hadn't noticed him. Rashid had a habit of mingling with the students; in fact he looked more like one of them than he looked like one of the teachers or other staff. He was young, no more than twenty-two years old, short, extremely thin and dark-complexioned, with small eyes, a sharp expression, a tiny mouth with thin, dark lips, small regular teeth yellowed by smoking, and a thick black moustache below a small snub nose. The whole formed an elongated face for which the students nicknamed him "Goatface."

As the two left the office, the overseer took Hisham's elbow with an air of encouragement.

"Don't take too much notice of the headmaster," he told him. "He's a good man really. If he'd wanted to do you any harm, he could have done it without calling you to his office or threatening you. Don't let his threats get you down, all right? You're a splendid young man with a bright future ahead of you. Remember the old saying: Keep going, and you'll get there in the end."

He looked hard at Hisham, accompanying the look with an enigmatic smile.

Hisham took little notice of the overseer's words. From the moment the headmaster tossed those pamphlets down in front of him, he was haunted by the picture of his parents. He dreaded the idea that something might happen to him. What would that do to his parents? He decided to put an end to all his activities and return to his old, preferred solitary life. Tormented by his misgivings, he walked back to his classroom and sat down, completely unaware of the words and glances around him.

*Laila al-Juhani*

# FROM BARREN PARADISE
(al-firdaws al-yabab)

*If* Barren Paradise, *by Laila al-Juhani, covers no more than eighty-two small-size pages, the intensity of language is such that some of its passages almost resemble the writing of poetry. Even the chapter titles transmit the passionate grief to be found everywhere in the novel. We hear, for instance, that "the air dies strangulated," of "the details of anguish," "the stenography of the soul," and so on.*

*Events take place in Jeddah. We are told of the tragedy of the heroine, Saba, in connection with 'Amer, the young man she has loved and to whom she has given herself. When she becomes pregnant, he leaves her for her friend Khalida, to whom he becomes engaged. At the beginning, the heroine reveals how the tragedy has occurred; how, when she learns he has jilted her to marry her friend, she tries to lose the baby. Next, Khalida takes up the narrative. She has, she said, learned of the tragedy through the papers her friend sent her before her death. The last chapter is narrated by the author herself, addressing Jeddah, and noting its ancient history and its present state.*

*The novel's narrative method is strongly reminiscent of that used by Ahlam Mustaghanmi in her novel* Memory of the Body. *There are, too, numerous quotations in the novel, especially from the famous Palestinian poet Mahmoud Darwish,[14] and there is also a marked tendency to utilize legend with a view to deepening the novel's ties with place. Jeddah was in fact formerly called "Jaddah," and this name ties in with the traditional belief that Adam had come to know Eve on Mount Arafat (where pilgrims stand during the pilgrimage season) and that Eve was eventually buried in Jeddah, where a tomb still bears her name. Indeed the true heroine of* Barren Paradise *is, as we finally learn, Jeddah itself. This is the spoiled, or abandoned, paradise of the title.*

\*\*\*

When Moses, peace be upon him, called out, the sea parted and each parting wave was like a mighty mountain. And now here you are before the sea, longing to make a sign to the waves and cry out: "Open up, Abu Khalid!" You'd see the damp sand, the seaweed whitened by the ebb, the fish leaping, the lobsters and tiny sea creatures that leave their frail prints on the sands. You'd move your finger over these prints, and they'd fade and vanish. That would make you feel sad. What you yourself were going to leave behind you was, you'd reflect, a mere flimsy mark to be erased by the waves and the footsteps hurrying along the sand. It would all be so swift that no one would be aware of you, lying as an illegible line amid all this clamour.

"Open up, Abu Khalid!"

Not to flee the Pharaohs of today, but to cling to the sand, indeed to write about the sand; about Jeddah, sunk beneath the sea. About Eve's footsteps, which she left on these sands so many ages ago as she walked towards Adam who longed to see her. Almighty God had her walk to him from Jeddah, and they met on Arafat.

You'll return to the beginning. Jeddah will bring you back not only to her own beginning, but to the setting out of this weary world, which writhes around you like a trapped fish struggling on the hook.

And what of you? Are you still resisting? Do you still dream?

A flock of gulls appears in the distance. It seems far off, so far as to be some indistinct dream, lost between water and clouds.

You scatter the sand with your nail, you write your name and Khalida's name. You sketch a small dove and entitle it "Jeddah." You draw a rose, with no colour beyond that of the sand, then write there some lines you've borrowed from Mahmoud Darwish, leaving these unadorned by roses or stems:

*I no more have a present*
*So as to pass tomorrow*
*By my yesterday.*

He seems alone on the sand, facing the waves; but when these ebb, there will be sketches of him, and ruins. You stand over them and weep. Oh Saba, you grief-stricken Arab, all those centuries past, all the defeats and disappointments – they haven't changed you at all.

"Open up, Abu Khalid!"

Fortresses will emerge, and citadels and sunken ships, and mermaids and the bottles of Solomon; and Jeddah perhaps will take you from your past to her own remote past; to all those who passed through, left behind their wounds, and were no more.

Do you love Jeddah?

Sometimes, as you wander through Jeddah, you feel you're searching for your own self, for your details and secrets strewn about its streets and its houses, its sidewalks and markets. Jeddah will seem to you like a book. You'll be afraid of death striking, suddenly, before you've read it through to the end.

Jeddah. Just how alluring can this city be?

Now, what brought up this subject of allurement? A dramatic, suggestive word they prefer not to use openly; and you're enamoured of everything they're averse to. You stand there aloof, beyond their boundary walls. Jeddah emerged many years ago, from her walls and fortified towers, from her moat and from her nine gates: Bab Mecca, Bab Jadid, Bab al-Yaman, along with six other gates on the waterfront.

These things have stayed behind; in history books and in the memory of ancestors. Perhaps Jeddah called out one day, "Open up, Abu Khalid!," so as to leave her boundaries for a place where no boundaries exist. She may have come out from you, too, leaving you to the questions you ceaselessly form and wrestle with.

How alluring, how bewitching can Jeddah be?

Your query springs more from love than from doubt. There's nothing new, Saba, in what you're saying. You know already that the things we love have greater power to bewitch us; but doubt spurs us to walk far, to run sometimes, and you've run through the alleys of Jeddah to the point of love. And now here you are at the edge of the sea, your thoughts running away with you, even to the point of creating writings that are painful, sometimes frustrating.

Writing about Jeddah will doubtless be like Jeddah herself: there she is, clamorous, madcap, changing her face each day, without once looking behind her at the walls, and the gates and ditches.

Now, can Jeddah really go off like that, without looking behind her?

The sea dampens the hem of your violet skirt, and loneliness grips you as you watch the wetness make its raid, the way night raids the remnants of the day. You think of Khalida, the dreamer, but not so deeply as to bring you pleasure, or anguish sometimes. There's a strength in her you don't yourself possess; she surprises you perhaps with a certain bluntness, and yet it's the bluntness of truth that enchants you. How many times you've wished to be like her, you with your utter brittleness that frightens you sometimes. You've always nursed a sense of imminent harm.

But what led to talk of your brittleness, amid all this talk of Jeddah? Swim out just a little way from the beach, from Jeddah and her nine gates, each guarded by two sentries who ask every comer for the password. Each gate has a password; sea, open your waves, clouds, open your eyes. Jeddah, open your gates. The lovely, wounded mermaid, abandoned by the waves, lay atop the rocks and closed her eyes, so Jeddah would emerge. The rocks sank, the body turned to soft sheltering sands defending the sea, and to a wilderness hugged by the water of the sea from which you emerged. We've all, in some way, emerged from humble water.

Look where Jeddah takes you! You haven't seen her wall, or her moat, or her nine gates. When they tore down the wall, your mother was a mere child. She has no memory of it either, beyond the small tales people pass on about the world that once huddled behind the wall; of the straw houses, the reeds, the huts of blacks and Bedouins, and the European cemetery, holding only Jews and Asians who left their far-off lands to die at the borders of Jeddah. Your mother hasn't told you about the cemetery, perhaps she never knew of it. But now you can take it from the crossways of your memory, to reflect on it by the side of the sea, while a cold sense of solitude creeps through your heart; for death's gone, and so have the cemeteries and your papers scattered in drawers: clippings, letters, magazines, pictures, jotted notes, all the neglected drafts you hardly ever check, think sometimes of tearing up to start again from the beginning – the beginning suggested to you by Jeddah, each time you think of her.

Oh Jeddah! What is Jeddah? It's the glint of tiny packed memories, like mosaic tiles in the corridors of your soul. The memories you've failed to emerge from, just as you've failed to lessen the shrillness of their piercing calls. The memories that pile up daily, layer upon layer, like the layers of the earth uncovered by archaeologists; each revealing its fossils and slabs of clay unknown till now, the footmarks of people unsuspected by all but you. You, who constantly abuse dreams, even while walking alone amid the crowded city. When an age has passed perhaps, you too will become one of the fossils of Jeddah, or a carving younger than a Thamoudic[15] carving entombed so very long in the Buweib valley, imploring Kahel, the deity of the tribe, to preserve the people entire.

And you, after a stretch of ages, what will you pray for in a wilderness that has nothing but the sea before it? Or even the sea perhaps won't be there. Perhaps Jeddah will have called out, one evening: Open up, Abu Khalid.

"Open up Abu Khalid!"

Yes, even the sea dreams of eternity and borrows its name; and you know, for all that, that you're closer to mortality than the scent of a flower, when it sends out a little fragrance then fades unnoticed. Is there still, around you, someone who's aware of these small things whose loss you constantly note? The lights gently moving away?

Who cares about Jeddah now?

Jeddah isn't the only one to change her face, her lineaments, each day. You too, however subtly, change your face and lineaments daily, but you're conscious of what's happening to you. You resist. Even with solitude, and perhaps with the futile rage that burns your ribs, yet forms no barrier between Jeddah and your raptness at her changes. Many times you resist, the countless dreams cascading like the droppings of doves, that begin hot and soft, then end cold, calcified, on window ledges and terraces and hallways, unnoticed by anyone.

You close your eyes. The waves leave you constantly dizzy, and the hot wetness rises to your knees, weighing down your clothes. For an instant you feel yourself standing behind some thick barrier of glass, which mutes the sounds of horses, mules, donkeys, camels, motorcycles passing swiftly behind you. The horns of cars and ice-cream carts, all these sounds approach you like a dream, like music from a radio in a back room – bringing in the world's voices but not the world itself. The mounting clamour behind you brings in the voices of Jeddah, not Jeddah herself. Here come your questions again. What is Jeddah?

Yes, why is it that when you think of her, and write of her, she thrusts you down, down into your own unquiet depths? What secret wraps this city around and wins your love?

Al-Jubail,[16] too, lay over the sword of the sea. A compact coastal city you never liked, despite the sea itself. In the compound where you stayed with your family, you had nothing better to do than pace the paved alleyways between those small residential units, with their endless windows and their curtains motionless because no one was there behind them. The compound was almost empty, just some Americans in the far buildings. You knew that from their cars, with the small flags on the glass, and from their brisk, staccato speech. You'd watch them sometimes when they went out to play tennis in a nearby yard. No one ever waved to you; they didn't really see you were there. They didn't notice things. Then your solitude would spur you on, to run through the alleys behind the sound of their speech, and the butterflies, and the doves that cooed sometimes on the ledge over the wall; and the birds that landed on the trees in the alleyways, pale like al-Jubail, the city you never truly grew used to, never loved perhaps.

That same evening, you felt you would have liked to leave this city which filled you with a sense of tedium and solitude. Everything seemed as usual. You never thought al-Jubail would so soon leave you stunned, before the door of the unit your family had rented. The door was quietly creaking, and the trees were rustling gently and sadly. You went about, beating the asphalt with a bare branch. Then, suddenly, they appeared in the alleyway. You heard their voices. Then you saw a lad, his face furious and a bright red cap on his head, the girl behind him. He was striding along, carrying a small case with a cord dangling on the ground. She was standing behind him. "Joe," she was calling, "Joe, wait for me!"

Her words tumbled out into the space around her, like floating butterflies you could never quite grasp. The girl – around fifteen years old, she looked – was pounding the sidewalk, letting out a torrent of burning admonishments you busily strove to translate. You kept moving the words around your head, but it didn't need a translation to understand. She ran after the lad. Then, when she caught up with him, there they were right in front of you, still unaware of you or anyone else. She started kissing him and hugging him, repeating an apology over and over again, loud, panting and coarse – so you told yourself when you'd grown up. When your senses came back, you saw they'd passed beyond the nearby sidewalk. The bare branch had fallen from your fingers. You were fourteen years old; you had no lad to pursue along the planted alleyways, to catch up and noisily kiss, apologizing all the while. The kiss, that was no part of your own life; just something you'd seen in video films and come to accept as a mere gentle violation. You laugh now, but that day you were astonished.

A few days ago you were astonished once again, though not so much. There was no kissing this time. It was a din that arose in the coffee shop where you sat sipping your coffee at one of the small tables. The waiter had hurried forward to welcome a herd of girls – you couldn't call them gazelles, because gazelles don't shout. The waiter wanted to usher them in, but they ushered him instead. They passed by you, and a couple of them started whispering about you, as if saying you were bound to be waiting for someone. You thought of smiling, but changed your mind, let the din pass by and returned to your coffee. Unluckily, though, they sat down at a nearby table, and, the moment they settled, one of them started tapping on the wooden table and the rest started to sing:

*Send my greetings to one who's absent*
*Send him my greetings*
*Oh how my heart melts!*

A chorus of clamour, wanting to be noticed; if only, this time, by the waiter, who hurried over to ask them to keep their voices down. But they weren't ready to quieten down yet. Soon they took up another song:

*Lately you've grown above yourself.*
*I speak but you don't answer.*
*You've forgotten the mountain house,*
*The many nights of snow and cold*
*You spent there with me.*

"It's just a lot of FM noise," you told yourself. Irritated though you were, you felt unable to blame them. Perhaps you pitied them. You recalled birds in their cages, how sad it made you feel when they went on singing, ever more loudly and crazily. When they got up to leave, one of them waved to you.

"Hi, sweetheart," she said sarcastically. "You might as well go home. There's no one coming. He's forgotten his date with you, he's got too many others."

She let out a nasty laugh, but that didn't bother you so much as the reason she could possibly have had to show you such cruelty. After those barbed words of hers, you recalled seeing her winking at the waiter and rubbing her hand on his. When their shoulders came together, she didn't move. As for the man, he moved desperately this way and that, begging God not to let the fire burning in his body burn his reason too, and spur him on to some mad indiscretion. Still you held yourself back from shooting any cruel, hurtful words at her. You were thinking of all the bitter things that made her rebound her wretchedness on to you. She (as she thought) the pure creature and you the tainted one, because you were sitting alone in a smart coffee shop, sipping your coffee and waiting for someone who existed only in her suspicious imagination.

Oh God! You see just how far Jeddah's taken you? You thought you were dispersing her details, and all the while she was dispersing you. And now she's taking you from al-Jubail, into yourself. For a period in your life, perhaps, you too thought it was just al-Jubail's way, to treat you cruelly. You thought it wasn't meant. You didn't have the experience to be able to forgive. And there in the coffee shop, when you did have the experience, and the ability, bitterness overwhelmed you because you knew the cruelty was meant. For a second it seemed to you the girl had been driven to cruelty. You weren't convinced, but you considered it. Cruelty, you said to yourself, comes from cruelty – not always, but sometimes.

Khalida spoke to you once about cruelty. "Cruelty," she said, "can almost take the skin from people. Those who aren't cruel to others are cruel to themselves. Look at them, the way they drift through life without a thought for anyone or anything. They run after money, BMWs, Marina Bs and plush weddings, where they're entertained by some top woman singer, or some super-handsome male superstar, who, the moment he appears, sets all the girls sighing out loud. That same super-handsome star was targeted, cruelly, by four girls who invaded his room in the vast hotel where he was staying, and they raped him there amid the carpets, sofas, chandeliers and – Almighty God!"

Khalida blurted this out, and you fell silent, just gaping at her.

"Khalida," you said at last, "that's unbelievable!"

"It's easy enough to believe. I don't suppose, even so, they would have behaved in that cruel way if they hadn't been treated even more cruelly themselves. Don't misunderstand me. I'm not justifying what they did. No, I'm explaining it to myself, to stop myself falling apart."

She fell silent once more. You hadn't reflected on what you'd heard. You were trying to pull yourself together, to stop yourself being swept away by a flood of despair. What's left for an Arabian mare except despair? You ask without waiting for a reply, you've no desire to enlarge on cruelty, a subject without end. But here's Jeddah now, playing the game of discovery with you, peeping through the keyholes of ornate doors. It fills you with the details that were piling up before your eyes, spreading haphazardly over the carpet of the sea, perhaps because neatness robs things of their spontaneity and offers them up for pigeon-holing.

And, when you write about Jeddah, you won't seek neatness either. Words, things, events, faces, names, all these will pour out on the paper. It will leave your conscious and subconscious mind, will clothe itself in words, then stretch into lines on the paper. You won't write a history with a view to making everything neat; rather you'll write and sketch the Jeddah you've known and know: the awe; the longing and frustration; the shrubs planted along the sidewalk of King's Avenue; the boys running between the cars at the traffic lights, waving boxes of napkins and sprigs of different jasmines. Small, tanned girls pacing the avenue by the beach, holding bags filled with firecrackers. They walk loosely and without sound, needing just a small gesture to move forward or hold back. You'll give these things, and so many others, the freedom to cover the pages with words that don't praise or criticize, justify or explain. Words that will take on humanity in an age where humans are close to perishing with no one hurrying to their rescue. Words akin to a small picture, where the old is mixed with the new, the authentic with the contrived. You'll pick it up in your fingers, ponder it, then you'll lay the pictures one alongside the other, with no point of resemblance, no link between this one and that. But they'll all make up Jeddah and speak of Jeddah. You won't know if you've succeeded or failed, but you'll make the attempt. All life's a trial, no more or less; and when we come to comprehend it at last, death will be there at the door.

Try then. Write about this city, but don't make a history. No, you won't do that, because you have no interest in a history that's brought pain to your heart. Let history be kept inside books, and behind the walls and houses of the Jeddah that the soldier Hasan al-Kurdi tore down; tore down to rebuild and fortify Jeddah against the raids of the Portuguese, who spread their sails on the sea and ventured out to discover the seven paradises, the islands of spices, pearls and silk, and the earth that gives birth to women knowing neither age nor despair. Those Portuguese ships cruised the seas, and Hasan al-Kurdi destroyed Jeddah to fortify her. A logic you can't accept – to defend by destroying! But you've no right to dismiss such a logic; nor to accuse the man of cruelty, when a builder was late for his work and al-Kurdi built the wall over his body, leaving him to die slowly beneath the mud and stone. He died so Jeddah could remain alive, he died so the wall could rise and surround what was left of a city. A city built that lofty wall from its stones and trees, its birds and people, so as to leave nothing for the foreign conqueror.

Oh Jeddah, when will the universe end? And, when it does end, will people ascend to its sky from Jeddah, which was witness to their descent?

You pick up a small shell, and, the instant it settles between your fingers, the jelly-like life takes shelter inside it. For a second you marvel at the fragility of the life which takes refuge behind those shells scattered along the beach. Just behind you are the colossal buildings, and there, within your fingers, rests the small jelly-like creature, behind the walls of a shell spotted with tiny specks, white and just a little in relief. You contemplate its interlocked colours, and scattered specks, while the memory in your fingers stores up the soft touch you'll remember when you write. From the touch of many other things, the touch of the spotted shell will stand out; not for its softness but for the way it can be recalled whenever you touch rose petals, or velvet, or coloured pictures, or smart book covers, or sleek paper, or the silk shirts hanging in your cupboard. You'll shake these last, and their printed roses will shake too, and so will their butterflies and birds, filling the closet with the voices of the universe, coming from every place; even from a sea you often sat in front of, where the spotted shell and its touch came to you. Now you return to it as to a dream. You live its details, and you know it's just a dream.

Jeddah. How could you say about her all that you want to say, when, in the midst of your attempts, you become absorbed in writing of yourself – of all the things you didn't want to say or write about yourself – and all because writing about them is so futile? But Saba, who are you, callow and headstrong as you are, to judge what's useful in writing? What have you written up to this moment, to fit you for those naïve judgements of yours? What have you ever known? How many years is it since you left your mother's womb, a piece of red flesh crying out for food and warmth, like any animal in the wilderness – except, of course, that animals don't bawl?

Close your eyes now, let Jeddah come out, oh so slowly, from the cells of your body. And, as time passes, you'll come to see that it's you who've come out from the cells of Jeddah. You'll see, too, how you've come out with the same number of chromosomes that Jeddah holds, the same structure of her DNA. You'll come to see you've started to be Jeddah, herself, because your bond with her is so complete. Didn't your mother say it? "Lovers grow to be like one another."

Your love of Jeddah spurs you on to folly; but then, what love has no foolishness in it? You used to cry out: "She's the loveliest of all cities!" But, now you've grown up, you've learned there are no superlatives in beauty, or closeness, or wretchedness. There's only our love, which gives things their features, their names and colours. Love has ripened, and I hope you'll grow ripe too. Yes, love's ripened, become worthy of writing now. It's worth recording that Jeddah isn't her crowded streets, or her bridges, buildings, markets, gulls and sea. She's not her people with their dreams, and their hopes and woes. No, Jeddah's much deeper than that, so much so that you can never encase her, you'll never reach her. She's the spirit that suffuses you when you stand on the balcony of your house, not seeing the sea but knowing where it is. You know, too, what a din there must be in Gold Street. You can almost see the limousines speeding through the streets, the drivers veering suddenly without any signal, as if there were no cars in front of them. Then comes a shriller voice, the sound of sudden braking that pierces the ears like a scream in a dark night.

You know there's no time in Jeddah for contemplation, even though everything in her calls out for it. Here you are now, by the sea, contemplating her as you do your own anxious soul. You're eager to write about her, to have her set down on paper, in words and lines; but is it possible to set down the soul? To reduce a rose you've set on your window ledge then left for a time – returning to find it a mere blot of blood on the forlorn asphalt of the street?

But Jeddah isn't a rose, and writing isn't a balcony. And now, as you face the sea, you're no more than some minute detail in a vast painting. Someone, maybe, will contemplate you so as to write about Jeddah as he knows her.

Go back to Jeddah, then. Go back to your digging, in search of what there is of her lying hidden beneath the sea. Go back to the sea.

"Open up, Abu Khalid. Open up, Abu Khalid. Open up, Abu Khalid."

*'Abdu Khal*

# FROM *DEATH WALKS HERE*
(al-maut yamurru min huna)

*This novel by 'Abdu Khal differs from those of the previous Saudi generation in being modern in tone, with little adherence to the familiar rules of the traditional novel. It comprises a number of chapters, some short, some long, each dealing with a particular aspect of the story of the Sawadi, the village ruler noted for his tyranny, cruelty and corruption. These chapters are recounted by various oppressed persons, the identity of the narrator changing from one to another. One chapter is assigned to the Sawadi himself, who (having been up to this point an enigma shrouded in mystery) at last reveals his personality explicitly. The chapters effectively lead into one another, as in the* Thousand and One Nights, *and they abound in the legendary and the eerily strange. The title* Death Walks Here *is indicative of the novel's main subject: a death that occurs in a southern village of the kingdom during Turkish rule. The inhabitants of this village, al-Souda'a, are impoverished peasants suffering from nature's cruelty and drought, and from the tyranny of the Sawadi, who usurps their lands and deploys his spies so as to be informed of anyone thinking to disobey him. The citadel in which he lives is notorious for violence and terror; nor does he himself hold back from murder and every kind of evil, including the rape of beautiful girls. The novel is, from first to last, a description of the misery that envelops the village, and of attempts at revolt that mostly end in failure and punishment. 'Abdu Khal has clearly grasped the importance of place in the narrative structure, and his work reflects a systematic sociological viewpoint: that the analysis of text should emerge from the text's inner environment, and from focus on a plurality of voice and language, as noted, for instance, in his dialogues between two sisters.*

*I was sculpting life.*
*When I was done, I found the wall was blind.*
(Ra'na Sabra)

***

I bear towards him all the rancour of the earth, and my only cure will be to kill him.

I bear towards him my old hatred and the wounds he sowed in my life. He'll never flee from me; and even if he should, I'd follow him to the very heart of the tomb. Yes, I'm going to kill him, chew on his entrails to heal my grief. No. No, I'll rather hang him up and make his belly swell like an animal in its death agony. I must slit his belly, so the people of the village will smell his rottenness, knowing then they could have killed this everlasting serpent themselves. And when they smell his reek fouling the air, then they'll know their nightmare's dead. This time their eyes and their noses won't deceive them. In the past, whenever we smelt something bad, we'd rejoice and sing, supposing he was gone at last from inside us. Then, when we started preparing for his burial, we'd find it was a dog that had died, or a donkey; and we'd leave the corpse to the swooping kites, so they could lift from our noses the rottenness that came from his carcass.

Yes, I'm going to kill him. I'm sure God will reward me for the deed. This serpent lived on and on, till at last time itself grew weary of him, fitting him with a pair of wings to soar beyond his old boundaries, making him like Hanash Abu Jawhara.[17] He's the devil that was granted full life to destroy us. Day and night this village prays to God to be saved from his evil; but our prayers go unanswered, his face is still there in front of us. The village is inured now to secret loathing of him, and to seeking God's deliverance.

I used to murmur those prayers too, till he burned my life, made it unendurable to see him taunt me over my pain. I'll go beyond helpless, secret prayer, and be delivered from his evil. I'll kill him, because only his extinction will bring mercy to those hearts that beat in terror, or else stop beating, at the mere mention of his name. With his death, those bowed embalmed bodies will stretch up their necks and find release in God's broad spaces, able to raise their heads high.

Killing him would bring so much benefit to the land, to its crops and livestock –

He's the venom that creeps through every vein. The instant he blends with the air, fruit dies and water seeps down into the earth. He's a prodigy of the devil, who assigned him the rule of the earth, then sank into sleep, leaving to him the task of seduction, and agitation, and covering our bodies with fire. In this village, which now thinks only of obeying his commands and creeping under the soles of his shoes, people vie for the honour of having the Sawadi[18] trample their heads. And who can blame them? Life's painful and hard, he holds all the water and food. He rules over necks, leaving them secure or else cutting them off. Fear of him has become a drug now: to rebel would be like rebelling against life itself. This unquestioned master has only to bat his eyelids and hearts will sink, begging, abjectly, to be blessed by this devil. If I could only kill him, these people would, I truly believe, come after me thirsting for my blood. Where, after all, could they find a better refuge than under his shoes? Submission's taken root in their lives. They'd be free, all of a sudden, to think, eat, sing, just as they pleased. The village could never cope with a situation like that; it's always lived under his sway, and with his death the sway would be gone. Stability, for them, means hanging endlessly in space, their heads spinning with fatigue and vomit. It's a state they're long inured to, and anyone ridding them of it will have to be slain. They're like bees, pursuing their mother to kill her. They place their lives at the service of others, produce honey for people they've never met. They can't endure the sight of their mother among them; that wise bee who, even if she'd lived, would have seen her foolish sons squandering their lives still, for the sake of those who take pleasure in jailing them and tearing out their bowels.

How the serpent was able to use those bowed bodies, to pass through them, I don't know. That tiny handful who wouldn't abase themselves were still within range of his fire and torment; he slit the bellies of their livestock, slept with their women, confiscated their fields, thrust them into the lightless dungeon. This cursed creature once had dreams of making my womb a nest for his venomous offspring; but I stood firm and tall before his lust. I wouldn't be the repository of his whims, and so he swore to stalk me for ever. He tried long and hard to creep towards my belly, and, when he failed, he turned to my offspring. I've seen his marks on Saliha's bosom. As Jibril was questioning her, beating her, I felt with every stroke a mounting desire to kill him. Still Jibril kept lashing my daughter, while I wept inwardly, my rancour beyond all bounds. I begged him to have mercy on her, to turn the whip on the serpent whose soft body creeps to twine itself around every neck.

As Jibril was lashing Saliha, and she was writhing this way and that to change the places where the strokes would fall, I wanted her to die under the whip; and then I'd pick up my scythe, storm his citadel and slit his belly. And I wanted, all over again, to slit with my scythe the bellies of all the village people who'd gathered to gloat over our scandal. Often, indeed, I'd absolve the Sawadi himself from all he was inflicting; I'd rather indict those conquered eyes and bowed bodies. Hadn't the Sawadi found, there in front of him, men more like donkeys, offering him their backs, happily bending their necks? It's the abjectness of men that creates Nimrod, who rules the earth and fills it with destruction. This Nimrod, this beast, would think twice if he ever faced a real opponent; someone who'd force him to stay his hand, hold it back from beating necks, plundering money and driving the meek down into the pit.

It's the craven weakness of the village's menfolk, I'm sure, that gave rise to this deadly creature, plunged him so deep in his crimes that it's somehow improper now not to heed his orders, not to let him enjoy whatever he desires, not to bless his spittle whenever he spits. We've turned into tame animals, with no other goal but to swallow our food and loll around.

Quite often I picture the Sawadi as he lords it over the women's bodies. He tells their men to put their hands over their eyes; and, as he gasps to his feet, the women wipe the dust from their hair and clothes and get up weeping. Then they take hold of the passive witnesses of their ordeal, and they shake them. "Why," they cry, "did you let him sport in your fields?"

"That's what he told us to do," the men answer, stammering foolishly. "But we outwitted him. We took no notice."

"What do you mean?" the outraged women cry. "He mounted us as if we were beasts."

The men give stupid, weak answers, inflaming any patience still left in the women's breasts. "We put our hands over our eyes," they say, "the way he told us to. But we left gaps between our fingers, and so we saw everything. You're free women."

Each man tries to approach his spouse, but she thrusts him away with reproaches. The women cry out, in unison: "Shame on you, men!"

This is the nearest I can come to portraying the acts of this serpent in our midst. Even in his moments of carnal enjoyment, he makes no attempt to hide what he does. Indeed, he heaps humiliation, whenever he can find some way of degrading us in front of the men so fearful for their bowed necks. And they take positive pleasure in letting these necks sink down over their chests, they close their eyes to anything that upsets him. That's why the village has become a soft bed for this dog. They even quote him.

"Why should I marry," they echo, "when all the women are there just for me?"

He can make them tremble with fear of him. They rob themselves to win his love. They fear the thought of hating him – he might hear of it and have them beheaded. They fear being separated from their necks; he'd bury the headless bodies, leaving the heads hanging on the gates of the mosque, staring at the village till the eyes glazed over and the heads grew dried and skinless.

That's what's given him the right to bark, deadening other voices, the right to stretch his limbs, while other hands move the fans to chase away his nightmares and bring him quiet sleep. If he lapped from someone's pot, that person would feel honoured to use it, without first washing it clean.

Everything's limp here except the Sawadi's voice; he's the death that's escaped from time. If our good health should vex him, he comes to run in our veins. Then, when his plague's infected us, he moves off, relishing our groans and letting us drop, like an ageing bird in a cage tight shut, which knows no face but its owner's. The owner opens the door of the cage, and the bird, shunning freedom, falls dead. We're imprisoned in our bodies, still loyal to our fear of him; and, when death comes knocking at our souls, we find life holds two kinds of death.

We could lament our grief in secret. But he'd know soon enough what we were weaving in our dreams, and he'd bring us harm. We'd go down, to the cracks in the earth, searching for tombs to hide our bodies from the ravening dogs that roam everywhere, standing with their limbs over the carcasses, over our very breaths. Like rotten fruit we'd seem, crawling with maggots, while time tramples our bodies and creeps into our veins. Without vestige of resistance, we yield to him limply, and, when he's sipped and swallowed down the nectar of our lives, he lets our lives spoil, leaving just a foul smell in their wake.

He, it seems, is the only one to have flown from time, finding refuge in its might. He watches us fall like hacked palm trunks. And, when time's scythe leaves us, there he comes, buttressed by his arrogance, while we're crucified on the soil of exhaustion and death. Then he'll crop our heads and line us up in front of his sofa, so as to spit on us when the *qat*[19] swells his cheeks; and we take it all in meek silence, still abject, bereft of any hope that our ceaseless wails will rid us of him.

This serpent's found a way to creep right inside us, and there water the tree of terror that grows so fruitfully in our limbs. And when we seek out our beds, he's there before us to muddy our dreams. We wake and count the storms, read the message in the heavens, assailing us with dark eclipses and long nights. Then we shake the sleep from our eyelids and hurry out to work in the fields.

And so we live beneath his supple, stinging cane. He's become life itself. Only when he's asleep does life take on delight, for, when his eyes close for a time and his breath grows shallow, we race to our beds strewn with dreams, expel him for a time and breathe in peace.

No one knows anything about him, beyond a few stories passed from one to another with fear and trembling.

He was never an infant, they say. The old Sawadi came upon him when strolling among the groves. The young one was lashing at the trees and sands with his stick, and uprooting the wild plants; and when he felt thirsty, he'd stretch his lungs and breathe in the air till he was sated. The old Sawadi took a fancy to him, liking the character he showed; and so he adopted him, showing him how to uproot heads rather than plants, to lash bodies rather than flying earth. Others, though, say he was found wrapped in rags in the yard of the Ra'i al-Qadaba, and that no woman could foster him or nurse him because, in his very infancy, he killed a number of women. To begin with, one of the old Sawadi's bondwomen had taken pity on him and asked permission to foster him; but, the moment she gave him her breast, he bit off the nipple, leaving her breast awash with blood. She died at once; and the same happened with further bondwomen who offered to nurse him. The rumour spread then that he must surely be some divine master, because such do not drink a bondwoman's milk. And so they brought him a free woman of honourable status, but her nipple too he bit, and she died before she could wean her own son. There was nothing for it but to carry him back, to the yard where he'd lain for a full year. After that some people saw him throw off his wraps and walk towards the dome; and these witnesses swore he was already circumcised. No one ventured to approach him again, and the old men decided the infant was descended from Ra'i al-Qadaba, that his mother had sinned, and God had punished her with a son having the heart of a serpent, who'd bite everyone near and far.

In some of the neighbouring villages, people told a somewhat different story. According to this, he'd taken off his wraps and gone to the dome, where the tomb of Ra'i al-Qadaba had opened and the master had come out to greet him. They'd talked for a while, then the infant had raised his voice in insult towards the master. The master had then returned to his tomb, asking God to hold the infant apart from death and from all hearts, so that he'd be solitary for ever, cared for by no one. Then, when he longed for death, he wouldn't find it.

The boldest story about his origins was told by a man who died before he could finish the tale. This man told how the old Sawadi had been sterile and impotent, and how his wife, a rebellious and lustful woman unwilling to accept her fate, had sought out the beds of the slaves. Then, when she conceived and her labour began, she'd sought the help of Raʻi al-Qadaba; after which she'd given birth to her child. News of the birth had spread through the village, and the mother had pleaded with the old Sawadi to adopt her son. He'd agreed, but she'd died the moment she began nursing the baby.

The women embellished this story in various ways, gossiping about it before they went to bed. Their version was as follows:

When the old Sawadi learned the child was a bastard, he decided to kill him and blot out the memory of his wife's adultery. He carried him off to the depths of a grove, took out his knife and killed him – as he thought. Then he saw a mocking smile on the infant's face. Furious now, he hacked him about and buried him, while the victim's veins were still throbbing. A few days later, a heavy rain muddied the soil and germinated a boy, who was later found lashing the earth and drinking the air.

Around that time the old Sawadi was assailed by fearful nightmares. A serpent, he'd dream, was coiled around his neck, and, whenever he killed a part of it, a new serpent would sprout, till at last he despaired of ever killing it and wished only for death. He put his mouth close to the serpent's, and it turned to an instrument making delightful music. He'd wake in terror, and the soothsayers warned that the child's enmity would bring countless problems. If he wished to remain master of the village, they said, he should cherish the child. He'd gone out to the fields, brought the boy back and begun addressing him as his son.

From that time on (the old women continued), father and son were not seen; this was in accordance with the soothsayers' advice to stay out of sight. They began, in the rainy season, to go to the groves, where they'd shed their clothes, bathe in the rain and wallow in the mud. Then, before returning to the citadel, they'd go to the dome, draw blood from one another's veins and smear it on their skins to preserve themselves from death.

Others maintain the old Sawadi never knew death for another reason. Once, it was said, he'd forgotten to smear the blood on his skin. At that the ground had swallowed him up, and now he was ruling those in the depths of the earth.

The Sawadi remained an unsolved puzzle for us. According to yet another story, his mother, when he was a baby, had left him to attend a friend's wedding. While she was away, he'd become soaked in urine. He'd cried till his throat was parched, but the maidservant hadn't woken. At that his cries had turned to shrieks, piercing the calm of the night. There was (it was added) a fairy with a sick child that awoke, disturbed by the Sawadi's shrieking, and asked his mother to go and smother the noise. As the fairy stood over the Sawadi's head, she felt an urge to choke the child. She blocked his mouth and began to squeeze, but then stopped short; she'd seen his cunning expression. His face relaxed, he curled up his toes, put his two hands around her face, then chanted some meaningless words that made her laugh and hold back. She then fed him from her breast, leaving him happy and calm.

The village people swear he rules jinn and mankind alike, because he was fed on the milk of jinn and human masters. The jinn then gave him wings to fly wherever he pleased – this was why he was able to move, like a thunderbolt, from one village to the next. Nor (people went on) could his enemies strike him, because bullets and daggers had no power to pierce a body that held an iron-skinned giant within.

According to one of his aides, a tribesman of the Bani Sayf was once bent on killing him, and stalked him constantly till he found him unguarded at last. He stabbed him in the chest, then almost fainted with shock as he saw his dagger rebound back, its blade bent. In his panic the man stabbed himself, with the crooked blade, but the Sawadi instructed his jinn to place themselves between the man's chest and the stabs he made, and so frustrate his purpose. The man fell dead from pure terror, amid peals of laughter from the Sawadi.

It's said, too, that the jinn asked him to choose between them and his human kin, and he chose the jinn over his own people. But, to keep his heart empty and his position strong, he invited his relations to a feast and offered them poisoned milk, after which they died instantly. The jinn then knelt before him, becoming his eyes and ears. He, though, wasn't satisfied even with such power as this. He went on uncovering their hidden secrets till he'd mastered their knowledge and disarmed them of their powers – then made them his abject slaves, quite powerless to resist him. They could never rid themselves of him and ceaselessly plotted his death, but in secret, for fear he should learn of it and do them harm.

"He stands over a pool of blood," my grandfather told me once, "because he's built his tyranny on our weakness, grown ever taller as we bow. He knew how to drive us and so become our master, how to mount us in humiliating ways. He's ruled us with the lashes of his whip, cut down anyone who tried to stand straight. The jinn bring him news, I'm sure, because he knows every movement of our eyes. He's the agony inflicted on us for ever, till the Day of Judgement comes. At the turn of every age we expect his death, but he rises in our veins once more, like an undying fire! Every time he sinks inside us, and we begin to shake him off, back he comes like an agonizing sleep; and we yield numbly to him, go with his nightmares any way he wishes. Once, in a single day, he killed all the best people of the valley. His crier had announced jinn were set to carry off every person who had no red dye on his head; and so the people of the valley hurried to mark their foreheads with that colour. Next day, the Sawadi ordered his slaves and soldiers to search every corner of the valley and bring in all who had no red dye on their brows. They captured large numbers of men, and he summoned his headsman and had them all beheaded. Each year, my grandfather went on, the Sawadi would look closely at the people around him, and, if he found anyone had begun to use his brains, he'd have his head cut off. The red dye was just a test to search out those awakening brains and do away with them, before their owners could stand and confront him."

He'd tell his aides to spread particular rumours, then wait to see how the villagers reacted. If he sensed murmuring and complaint, he'd deliver a speech in the mosque, calling on people to help him seize the rebels, and offering a camel as a reward for anyone able to catch one. As a result, many came to own camels, and many homes grieved for their dead.

The Sawadi grew to be a colossus, feared by all the villages. No one knows for certain if he has any kin on earth; we only know he runs through us, alone, like death. Our elders tell how his tribe was swept by a flood while living at the head of the valley. His supporters claim he's descended from holy men, and that only one out of these remains alive through all times. Very few know the secret of how the rest of the Sawadi's family was wiped out. According to some, his father had advised him to kill all his kin, telling him:

"Blood, my son, is a killer. If it doesn't cut you down with its sword, it will kill you with its love or weakness. Preserve no blood but your own."

They go on to tell how he ordered his crier to announce, through every place, that all his kinsfolk should come to him. "Any of our kin," he was to cry, "merits our charity."

Many came to him, some true relatives, others seeking charity. When they were gathered there before him, he summoned his headsman and had them all beheaded. Their blood flowed in great quantities, drenching the parched soil, so that the year came to be called the year of the streaming blood.

Another group of people claimed that the Sawadi would die only when a certain man appeared, a man who had seen the holy master in his dream and been taught by him to utter a certain word, which would kill the Sawadi instantly. The man would be marked by a swelling vein in his chest, and this would shrink into the word he uttered as he faced the Sawadi, bringing instant death. Then prosperity would return to the valley and its people. But the people still await this person. The Sawadi had evidently heard of this, for he began gathering the citizens in the field in front of his citadel, then arranging displays of dancing, horse-riding, racing and dove hunting. At the end, all those taking part would pass in front of him with bared chests, so he could smear them with scented aloes. Those with the scars of wounds on their chests would then be called to duels with the Sawadi's men; and, responding unwillingly, they'd be killed there and then. Those with scars in other villages would be taken to the citadel and made away with in secret.

So it is that the Sawadi's remained a phantom beyond reach, even as we've watched him sporting with our lives, according to his whim.

*\*\**

As, time and again, fear finds its way to your heart and strikes at it, you become hardier and stronger. Your inner self shakes off its fright and welcomes death without fear.

I've nourished fear from my first childhood on. It's been part of me; if it were to leave me for a moment, I'd feel death creeping into my limbs. Since my youth, I've sat with fear and learned how to conquer it. I recall how, when I was a burgeoning shoot in our house, I was hostage to terror and turbulent nightmares. Again and again that dream would come — it still sticks in my memory, after all the lean years that have swallowed me up; remains stubbornly, ever present, in my imagination.

In my dream I'd see the sky split open, then ropes raining with blood would descend from it, and spread themselves over my face. There'd be crowds of people around me, laughing and winking, as I strove to take the congealed blood from my face. But my hand would fail me as a huge spider crept over it, locking my fingers together with stiff, numbing threads. I'd cry out, imploringly:

"Oh, Saviour from destructions!"

Still I'd shout, beg, but the spider would only be quicker in weaving its web. Then it would crawl over my body and urinate in my mouth. Next, it would stretch out its legs and weave its webs over the mouths of the people crowded around me, turning them to tiny worms that would gnaw, greedily, at my limp body. My eye, the only moving thing, would be focused on my chest to keep watch over a rooster, a bird and a hen, which would come to my aid and start eating the worms so avidly gnawing at my body. The spider, though, would advance and cut off the hen's foot. Then the rooster would nip the spider, which would sting him in return, dumping him on my chest where he'd kick till life drained from his veins and my chest became his tomb. Then my heart would be cut in pieces, and lowered down the blood-soaked ropes. My eyes filling with tears, I'd implore feebly:

"Oh, Saviour from destructions! Save us!"

Sensing my utter weakness, the spider would snap off the bird's head. At that I'd throw off my helplessness, begin biting at his thorny legs and breaking my teeth. He'd catch the bird by the neck, and I'd scream, then wake, my chest heaving and cold sweat streaming from every pore in my body. I'd open my eyes to find my mother there beside me, saying in soothing tones:

"God guard us from all evil."

Then she'd take me in her lap, wipe away my tears and pat my cheek.

"What's the matter, Ra'na?" she'd ask. And I'd sink sobbing into her lap.

Every night this dream came, encircling my head whenever I slept. My mother's friends were sure I'd been struck by an evil eye or some malignant wind.

One morning, they were gathered there in our house, and my mother was talking of the dream that kept tormenting me. She beat her breast in her fear for me, and one of those good women patted her on the back.

"Maybe Ra'na's under an evil spell," she whispered. "Take her to Shou'iyya bint Murjan to cure her."

Next day, accordingly, my mother woke me early and tied a rope to a black ram to take along as a gift. She was taking me to Shou'iyya, and reminded me I should kiss her head when we arrived.

"Perhaps you'd like me to kiss the heads of her bondwomen too," I said. "I'm not a slave, remember."

My words made her angry, and she struck me on the head.

"You stupid girl!" she cried. "This woman's related to the jinn masters! You have to kiss her head."

She pulled me along with her, murmuring her prayers there in the open air. Then, before we reached the step of Shou'iyya's house, she took a sharp knife and slaughtered the ram. As its blood gushed out, she took a pot she'd brought with her, filled it with the red blood, then poured the blood over my head. Then we stood there, waiting to be invited into the house. To begin with, the woman sat there without moving. Then, when my mother made to throw some earth over my head, Shou'iyya rose to her feet and came towards us, tremulously rubbing her head and swearing she hadn't given me the evil eye. I stepped forward, the blood seeping into my back and breast, so that I longed to take off my soiled clothes. I moved towards her, trying to kiss her head, but I was too short to reach its lofty height. My mother was coaxing her, pleading almost:

"Please, rub my daughter with herbs. She's going to die."

She swallowed hard, then resumed her plea:

"Think if she were your daughter, Khamisiyya. Would you let Khamisiyya be harmed?"

Shou'iyya bint Murjan was still unwilling, insisting her eye had never done me any harm. The more she swore this, the more my mother pleaded, her voice breaking. At last the woman responded. She led me inside, laid me on a sofa, then took out a mixture of sesame oil, saffron and some wild herbs I didn't recognize. These she rubbed into all my limbs, then she massaged my body. Her lips sent out strange mutterings, and after each of these she'd spit into a glass of water nearby. After she'd passed her fingers over every nook and cranny of my body, she sprayed the water containing her spittle into my face. Before we took our leave, my mother thrust a wad of money into Shou'iyya's bosom. Then, having split the belly of our slain ram and cut a tress from the tuft on his forehead, she led me happily out. Once home, she ordered me to eat the raw heart, blessed me with the tress, and sat me down, assuring me I'd never have the nightmare again. But the moment I closed my eyes, the nightmare came back to mock me, to every last detail: my journey among the masters, the cauterizing blades, all the old pains and nightmarish tears.

Then, out of the blue, an old woman from a gypsy tribe came over. She was adept in throwing cowrie shells and uncovering secrets by driving away the evil spirits. That day, my mother greeted her enthusiastically. She sat her down on my father's chair, cooked her a splendid meal, then gave her an account of that nightmare of mine that had drained us all. The old hag gobbled up the food, gave a heavy shake of the head, then, stuffed full, gave a fetid-smelling belch which she masked with a cup of rich coffee. Then she straightened up, untied a tiny bundle and took out some coffee beans, which she splayed in her right palm before raising them to her lips and blowing on them. Next, she began to drive away the evil spirits. She stayed silent, her narrow eyes glued to my small face. Each time she'd pick up the beans, gather them in her hand, then splay them on her palm in different forms – wide apart or close together. At last she rose to her feet, kissed my head, and said:

"Tonight you'll sleep."

She went out, my mother behind her. I saw them whispering, then my mother's eyes stood out with fear; she struck her breast and began moaning softly. When she came back, she hugged me and burst into tears; nor, for all my questions, would she tell me what the old woman had said. After that, whenever I broached the matter, she'd change the subject, so that I never did learn what they'd been whispering about. She stayed silent till her death, and with time I forgot about the dream and the hag's whispers.

Yesterday that same dream came back. This time, though, I was bolder. Fighting free from the spider's web, I picked up a sizeable stone to crush the spider, but he sensed the danger and hid behind the rooster's back. My hand lost its grip on the stone, and the rooster fell dead, gasping weakly. I woke in terror, and soon after heard the dewy call to dawn prayer. I got up, made my ablutions, prayed, then dressed myself in the clothes I use for my work of daubing dung. I mounted my donkey, then went to a wet field, where I filled two cans with mud. Next, I went to a refuse tip and collected some cow dung. Then on I went to 'Abdu Hasan's home, to daub his new hut. I began work on it two days ago, setting a large divan in the middle of the hut, then building up a number of smaller benches on it; beginning with a large one at the base, and following with smaller ones moving upward like a pyramid. As I built higher, I secured the structure with ropes made of palm fronds. Each time I moved up a stage, I'd first make sure it was stable. Then, for greater safety still, I bound a strong rope around my waist and fixed it to the top of the hut. The whole business then became exhausting, as I gazed up at the rounded top, which wasn't finished as it should have been. I'd be seized with tremors and bouts of dizziness, threatening me with falling and turning everything in front of me to sharp yellow spots. I couldn't stop the work, even so, in case 'Abdu Hasan claimed back the advance sum he'd paid me. I'd had to implore him for the money, which I'd used to mend our tattered drapes.

To finish my work, I had to stay hanging there, over five benches, my body covered with dung and stains, and racked with exhaustion. I'd stay like this from dawn till sunset, when I'd go back to my home and children, my limbs aching. I'd fling myself down anywhere and sink into a deep sleep. Then, in the morning, I'd agonize over those little hearts I'd neglected the night before. As one they'd gather silently around me, stretch out their small hands to touch my limbs very gently, but I'd have to leave them, though their eyes expressed such longing to talk to me.

There was no way I could find out of my exhaustion; no way I could stay at home to play with them, or tell stories they could memorize and happily retell to their friends – "our mother told us such-and-such." Every day I had to tire myself out, so they could get up and face the sun beating down on their heads, and have something to satisfy the fierce hunger gnawing inside them.

Each dawn I'd hang my body over those benches, having taken all my equipment up with me to avoid too many journeys up and down. I'd have to keep brushing away fatigue, hunger, dizziness. When I first started work as a dung dauber for the village huts, I'd climb the piles of benches and tremble, horribly dizzy. For a long while I'd keep my eyes closed, ever more terrified of falling, and so I'd fail to finish the job with proper speed. This slackness became talked about in the village, and people stopped giving me work; it took a further period to restore their trust in me. But the fear of falling never left me, because a fall would mean a broken neck or broken bones, as happened to Jubrana. She broke her leg and suffered appalling pain, till at last the bone setter was summoned, and he had to amputate her leg. Her wounds, though, festered, and through all her moans the agony grew worse. She died, and at her burial people had to clamp their hands over their noses to keep out the putrid smell of her body.

Today, as always, I secured my waist with strong ropes and daubed the walls of the hut with mud, filling the gaps between the sticks and the dry poles, smoothing out the walls as best I could. Doing this again and again, I felt the earth spinning around me and saw those yellow specks widening. I felt myself sliding into a deep abyss. Clutching at a wedge nailed to the top of the hut, I closed my eyes and began weakly praying till the dizziness subsided at last. I breathed a quiet sigh, then sat down on one of the benches like a child whose mother's left him to face a fall alone. I was afraid of being flung down inside the house, like a tattered umbrella no longer able to give its owner shade.

While I was sitting there, 'Abdu Hasan's wife Laila came on me. I became flustered, then jumped up, almost falling. I resented her false attitude: she'd thrown aside all her solemn disapproval and haughtiness, but the smile she'd struck on her old face was cold. Unable to give out a fresh, hearty laugh, she contrived a dry, croaky one. Her air of forbearance was even worse, as she said sharply:

"Come down, Ra'na. Come and have something to eat. Put something in your stomach."

Her insistence irritated me. I pretended indifference, giving the impression I'd rather finish my work first.

"It'll soon be sunset. I'll have supper with my children."

"Come down, I said. I want to talk to you."

I don't like talking to this woman, who weaves a conversation with silken threads, speaking in an affected way, eyeing you with haughty, indifferent looks as though gazing at some stray animal. But her insistent attempts to lure me into a talk made me fear some disaster afoot.

"Has something happened?" I asked fearfully. "Something you want to tell me about?"

"Oh, God help us! What's the matter with you? Nothing's happened. I just want to talk to you. Come on down."

I tightened the rope around my waist, then climbed down, making all those piled up benches creak and shake.

"Careful!" she said sharply. "Don't let those benches fall down on top of us!"

I felt myself choking.

"Are the benches," I asked bitterly, "more important to you than a human being?"

She gave a false laugh. Her face was suffused with false concern.

"Let the benches go hang!"

As my feet found firm ground, she pushed me gently away.

"Wash your face and hands before we talk," she said.

"Laila," I answered, "there's something up. What's happened, for God's sake?"

She stretched her mouth in a short laugh, then jokingly struck my breast.

"Nothing's happened. You always exaggerate everything."

Her eyes seemed very wary, but she softened things by sending out a harsh laugh from her flabby lips. I gulped. My throat went dry, and fear ran riot in my imagination, planting all kinds of dark possibilities. I went up to her, kissed her forehead, begged her to tell me the truth. She went outside, leaving me to my dread, to my trembling and prayers, as I leaned there on an old wooden crate. Then she came back with a pitcher of water. She made to wash my face, but I snatched at her hand.

"Have I lost one of my family?" I shrieked, panic-stricken. "Is someone dead?"

Her full lips sent out an eerie laugh. Her hand lightly pinched my cheek.

"How you build things up! No one's dead. There's no crier announced any death."

"So?"

Her expression grew warier still, her air of unwillingness at odds with her running eyes. I asked her in God's name to tell me. She fidgeted, then fearfully uttered the words:

"Don't panic, there's nothing wrong. It's just that 'Abdu was coming back from the Sawadi's house, and saw Saliha with her clothes all torn. When she saw him, she ran off weeping."

A hot fear gripped me. I grabbed hold of her and shook her.

"What's happened to her?"

She wriggled away from my clutch, and shouted at me, as a reminder that I'd forgotten my proper place as a mere working woman.

"Have you gone mad?" she yelled.

Then, suddenly controlling her anger, she gave a brief, lukewarm laugh.

"'Abdu said he caught up with Saliha and asked her who'd torn her clothes. She made a gesture towards the Sawadi's house."

"By God and His holy book," I cried, "if he's beaten her, I'll cut off his hand!"

She moved closer and whispered in my ear:

"Your daughter isn't a virgin any more."

I gave a mad shriek, cursing everything with a hatred overflowing. I walked through the village, weeping silently, torn between my agony and fear, my helplessness, hate and weakness, and his power. I was afraid the news would come out, and she'd be buried like some swollen, rotting animal.

"God!" I cried. "Save us from scandal!"

Who could I turn to? I went running, blindly, through the alleys.

'Abd al-'Aziz al-Mishri

# FROM THE BASTIONS
(al-husoun)

*In his novel* The Bastions, *as in his other novels, 'Abd al-'Aziz al-Mishri displays considerable interest in the southern village, representing as this does both his birthplace and an old world now in decline, invaded by the new urban life that has transformed so many features and upset so many certainties. In* The Bastions *itself, it should be said, there is no trace of this invasion, but it is much in evidence in his other novels, notably in* The Clouds and The Springheads of Trees. The Bastions *focuses on the traditional land: it comprises a collection of artistic tableaux demonstrating the old life through a dialogue between the "friend" and his "narrator," who are neighbours and close friends living in the same village. The friend's role is to unearth memories and raise questions, while his narrator, an old man embodying the memory of the village, provides the answers and enlightens him on many matters that are unclear. Among the tales he relates to the friend are "Abu Nakaa," "The Turkish Refugee," and the story behind a popular saying — "you're like the old men of the tribe, you fight on your bed" — along with the tales of "The Nobleman's Cow" and "The Slave Vendor." These anecdotes gain added vigour from the spontaneous interplay between narrator and friend, and from the actions of the children in the house. A tale in progress is characteristically interrupted by eating, drinking, prayer or sleep, before being resumed once more. The tales are also rich in sayings, stories and popular songs explained by the author, their particular language introducing the unfamiliar reader to the dialect of the village and its local traditions. Animals, birds and insects are given special prominence in these tales, but uppermost is the rooster with his red comb, his remarkable voice, his dignity — and, when cooked, his meat, broth and delicious taste. This recalls the novel's original title:* The Bastions: The Old Man's Rooster.

*Al-Mishri's novels represent a new phenomenon in the Saudi novel: seen, for example, in attachment to the land and in description of the ravages that have now befallen the old folk culture. In* The Bastions, *the writer has been able to fulfil his talent in vivid art, through scenes, wonderfully sketched, of the old village.*

\*\*\*

The country night was poured out, in all its stillness, over the small stone houses, weaving a pattern of expansive black sprinkled with distant silver stars; pure and sweet like the dream in a child's heart.

The small yards around the neighbouring houses were planted with upright, many-branched almond trees, striking fear in children who glimpsed them in the dark – a fear that grew still stronger if mothers and grandmothers should mention the demons of the night, and ogresses with long fangs. The chirping of crickets and the hum of insects turned to the hissing of snakes and serpents, lurking in the dark for any child coming near their holes.

The friend and his host the narrator, who had fed him with rooster meat, talked for a while of this and that, before sleep began to take hold of them. The host prepared his friend a mattress, along with an old pillow, a pitcher of water for ablution, and covering suitable for the coming summer weather.

The friend slept and dreamed, remembering the rooster. He saw the hens, without the rooster now, huddled against the wall, their heads bowed in fear and grief and remembrance. A picture came to him of the rooster chasing and wooing them; his broad wing was spread over them, but there was no head or comb to move this way and that.

When the muezzin gave the first call for the dawn prayer, the friend heard it loud and clear – remembering the call of the rooster which, till just the day before, had been the leader and mate for more than four hens: a muezzin who needed no alarm clock to rouse him!

Anyway –

The friend rubbed his eyes. The rooster, he told himself, was inside him now, digested, and what he'd seen was no more than a heavy dream. He rose, performed his ablution and prayed along with his host. Then, after a breakfast of coffee and dates, he took his leave of his host and narrator.

A few days later, he contrived to return during the afternoon hours and ask his host about the poet who, in the midst of the men's 'arda dance, had composed a poem to settle a peace between two tribes – a poem that had, over the course of time, assumed the force of law. What, he went on to ask, had been the reason for the conflict, and what had sprung from the talk carried on amid bullets and guns?

The narrator gave a detailed account of all the things he'd pictured. He described the clothes, the time of sowing and the kinds of plants sown; he told of the fierce weather, the ages of the people involved. He himself was, he implied, a notable, important witness: a man able to judge, decisively, about all the different matters involved. He carried within himself what the tribal poets had said of these events in their verses.

The friend, though, was – like all the others, among the villages and tribes, who passed on the remnants of the story – familiar enough with some of these poems. He made this clear to his narrator, the decisive judge:

"May God," he said, "guard your memory from failing. Could it be you've confused things a little? Remember what the tribe's poet said: 'We pay blood money for one slain.'"

The narrator struck his temples, and brought together the furrows on his brow – a habit of his when at a loss for words, or when he was searching for some important saying lost at the doors of his memory.

"Once," he said, "in a tribal village, there came a neighbour from the Turks who still remained, asking for refuge. In accordance with their traditions, he was given refuge and treated with every consideration, becoming like one of their own. This alien neighbour was, though, expected to be compliant and courteous in return. He had a fair rosy complexion, with a fez the colour of blood, and most handsome features; and you know, my friend, how rare such things are in our homelands. It so happened a woman from a neighbouring village fell in love with him, and there was a secret liaison between them. But, in due course, the secret came out. 'The honour of any one of us,' the tribesmen said then, 'is the honour of all.'

"And so a band was assembled to avenge the tribe's honour. The man was trapped, early one night, by the edge of the square, and there his neck was slit just as our rooster's was. As for the woman, she was spared the scandal. Even the village gossips have, to this day, no idea who she was. She actually married later, and bore some beautiful children.

"What injustices we commit, indeed! If a man among us falls in love, he comes to love everyone and keeps himself pure from evil – and we cut him off and chatter woundingly about his beloved. Meanwhile another lover carries everything on in the greatest secrecy, to keep people in the dark – and so he takes on himself the right to love and the right to forbid love to others among his kin. He forbids it to the ruddy-skinned one and permits it to the swarthy one – as if the swarthy one has a true heart, the other a heart of stone."

\*\*\*

The friend murmured something, the emotion evident in his tone. The narrator cleared his throat. It was as though he realized his friend's heart hadn't aged as his own had aged; that from somewhere, perhaps, springs still sent their waters into his soul.

Anyway –

Why did this sudden thought visit the heart, like dew visiting a flower? Paths led on to paths, and still more paths, and the friend asked his host how the incident had ended:

"And what, my skilful teller," he asked, "became of the tribe when the Turkish lover had been killed?"

The host went on with the tale.

"The sun's rays," he told his friend, "uncovered the hidden folds of the night. The villagers found their Turkish neighbour painted with his blood; it had turned dark, like the colour of his fez. He was carried – or dragged rather – from his lover's house to his own courtyard.

"There was uproar among the village people, who had no notion who the killer was. They swore by their beards. 'Whoever,' they cried as one, 'has done this to our neighbour has done it to us too!' Then, some days after, they learned who the culprits were and decided to avenge their neighbour, as one of their tribe. In this way they'd show themselves guiltless and preserve their honourable status among the tribes.

"Anyway –

"A vengeful fury stirred their souls, and war was declared by common consent. Guns resounded in the valleys, killing men on the two sides, tearing houses apart.

"A new morning dawned, and tribal villages made their alliances. There was killing everywhere, and such pillage that no one could feel safe any longer, for his property, his family or himself.

"And as you know, my friend, it was the custom of war, among the tribes, to carry things on daily from sunrise to just before sunset. Only a coward would hold back from playing his part. Who, even so, felt no fear amid a conflict that raged in the heart and fire and body? News of it spread to other, distant tribes, who sought counsel among themselves on their weekly market days."

***

"And they said – "

The narrator paused, listening, it seemed, to some cry from the far end of the courtyard. Turning his head very slowly, he saw his grandchildren running along the road to the house, spurred on by a tumultuous joy. They were barefoot, and one of them stumbled over a piece of glass that gashed his foot; and so he couldn't keep up with the others, whose small bare heads seemed like acacia trees strewn amid the night. They'd abandoned their toys, made from old tattered cloths, and small sticks, and almond and juniper branches, along with the other playthings left scattered through the yard. They were all there to announce their grandmother's arrival.

His host's wife, the friend knew well enough, had left the house a few nights before. The host had been complaining about her – she was getting older, he said, and that was giving her pains in every limb in her body. She'd complain of an ache in her joints, and the shaikh healer would prescribe an ointment; and then she'd come home and say: "No, the pain's in my head – in my back – " And with that she'd go off for a few days, to her family in the healer's village.

And now there was the grandmother, her head and breast veiled with a great white covering, sitting astride the jenny and trusting to God's providence. When she went to the shaikh's house, or came back from there, she'd let the jenny lead her on, making no effort to guide the beast.

Anyway –

This jenny was loved by every member of the household, young and old alike, and the narrator trusted her knowledge of the roads. There she was now, stopping when she reached the children, as if inviting some of them to join their grandmother on her back.

The grandmother, it goes without saying, would sweeten her meeting with the children with small square pieces of candy, or with sweets made from sesame syrup; or, if she didn't have these, she'd share out a few dates. All these things the children loved.

Once it had happened she didn't have anything with her that they liked. And so they'd furtively sipped, from a small silver vial, the ointment the shaikh had prescribed for her. The ointment was mixed with honey, lard, sweet-smelling leaves and other things, and it had the sweet taste the children longed for. She'd been furious, but she'd never come back again empty-handed.

Seeing his host was giving his attention to all this, the friend adjusted his head-dress and looked down at his discarded footwear. Then, turning to the narrator, he said he'd leave now, but that they'd meet again soon. He stressed the word "soon," as if he'd like to bind it fast with his tremulous hands.

Tonight there'd be no rooster or rooster meat; or, indeed, any sudden voices in the yard, apart from those of some small roosters who needed time to grow, and call for the pre-dawn prayer, and be killed with a knife.

***

After a day spent on personal matters, the friend returned for a further visit. His host, he was well aware, liked repeating the things he narrated, and he was curious to know how the story of the Turkish neighbour had finished. That red fez had been a symbol of the victim's arrogance and cocksure pride, and the friend was anxious to hear a fitting end to the matter.

Anyway –

He asked his narrator how long the conflict had lasted, and about the sayings of the poet who'd brought hostilities to an end with his verses, and how far the two villages had accepted the pact.

The host cleared his throat, preparing all his powers for the task of narration.

"I tell you," he began.

"The tribal shaikhs" (he went on) "debated the issue and decided to dance the *'arda*, during which the poet would recite verses imbued with wisdom; after which they'd act in accordance with his judgement and opinion. And so they did.

"It's the tribal custom, my friend, to respect a mediator and his opinion, especially if the conflict's grown fiercer and a good many heads have been struck from their bodies.

"The poet came, stood amid the circle of the dance, and recited the poem whose beginning you recalled to me. The Turk, he judged, was an alien intruder, who'd violated the laws of neighbourhood and caused war to flare up. Peace, here, should mean an eye for an eye, since he'd acted in a manner that broke the rules of neighbourhood, and he'd been killed for their sake. In view of this, no blood money need be paid for his death, nor retribution sought. The man had stood out against the traditions and paid the price.

"Then all those present cried out: 'War is at an end! Peace reigns!'

"And now, since you're so concerned to know how long the war lasted, let me give you the months."

With that he began to name the months, counting them one after the other on the tips of his fingers: Dhu 'l-Hijja, Muharram, Rabi' al-Awwal, Rabi' al-Thani, Jumada al-Oula, Jumada al-Thania, Rajab, Sha'ban, Ramadan, Shawwal, Dhu 'l-Qi'da.

The friend used his own fingers alongside his host's, counting the months with him one by one.

The back of the narrator's hand had a touch of beauty about it, some short black hair perhaps. On his finger was a silver ring. After he'd counted with his tenth finger, he stuck the tip of his tongue between his lips, and inclined his head, reverently, below his head-dress and the circle of the black cord.

At that moment, another, familiar voice intruded. Both men recognized the voice of Abu Rashid, who people hardly ever met except on special occasions, because he'd leave for his farm at dawn and return at sunset. So regular was he that the villagers set the time of dawn and sunset by him.

Anyway –

The friend and the narrator host answered his greeting cordially, inviting him to join their agreeable meeting. The man began to vent his feelings, about the lack of rain, and the thirsty plants, then he started explaining the proper times for sowing and reaping. He ended by sighing deeply, then saying, in a tone of patient complaint: "God's relief is at hand."

Abu Rashid had changed the atmosphere for the friend and his host. Still, they took in all they'd heard, paused, then both observed: "God's relief is at hand."

After that the host had to summon one of the boys in the yard and breathe a few slow, whispered words in his small ear. Soon the boy came in with a pot of fragrant tea, and Abu Rashid warmed his empty stomach with its hot, sweet tang, before returning to his wife and children at the top of the mountain. He didn't apologize for leaving so soon after drinking it; he had little skill at coining phrases, or even at listening and competing with the two talkers. He thanked his host profusely for the tea, then rose, standing upright like the sturdy trunk of a tree. He put on the shoes that stuck almost to the edges of his feet, then bent down and picked up the small shovel standing there on its handle. It sent out a puff of dried mud.

\*\*\*

The friend thrust his hand into the pocket of his robe and took out a white box, from which he selected a home-made cigarette. He slowly blew out the smoke, then asked his narrator about the ways of grey-haired men, who, as time passed, had become the subject of a saying: "You're like the grey-haired men of the tribe, who fight from their beds."

The narrator, as he was inclined to do when calling to mind some odd or amusing notion, let out a kind of cackle (if it had had a colour, you might have called it a light-coloured chuckle). It was very much like the clucking of an old hen after she's laid her egg. The close resemblance made the friend think, suddenly, of the rooster's voice, and his red comb.

Anyway –

Because things are so interlocked in the memory, each one calling another to mind, and further, similar things too, it was better to keep everything to its due time. For now he'd listen to the story of the old man, and the incident that led up to the saying.

The chuckle had clouded the narrator's cheerful, rather placid face. He said:

"I tell you. Once, during a fierce war between two tribes, there was a blind, bed-ridden old man who was constantly ranting and raving, threatening to mete out vengeance, through his people, on the opposing tribe.

"Then, after long negotiation, the two tribes decided on a truce. When the old man heard of this, his blood began to boil with fury. He turned almost white in his passion, refusing to hear any talk of truce or peace. Then a man of his tribe, one who'd been wounded perhaps, addressed him:

"'Uncle,' he said, 'a war fought on the mountains isn't like a war fought on a bed. Let's agree to the truce, for our own good!'

"And I tell you:

"Ever since that time, the saying's been passed down."

The friend had managed to control his wandering thoughts of the rooster, but now, in his turmoil, he started linking greyness with eggs. Once more he asked God to help him put an end to these comparisons.

And yet, having once taken in the details of the story told by his host, he found a further, insistent thought seizing hold of his fancy. He had the most vivid image of this old man. He imagined him rattling the slats of his wooden bed from sheer fury, flinging aside his head-dress to reveal a gleaming bald patch surrounded by a soft growth, white without a single black hair, waving his trembling hands in the faces of the unseen people before him. He visualized, too, visitors around the old man, who'd hung their rifles on the stone wall opposite, some of them rubbing against the earth that covered the wall. One of the men was quietly countering the old man's violent objection to his saying – that a war fought on the mountains wasn't like a war fought on a bed. That, the friend thought, was reasonable enough no doubt. But wasn't it cruel too, with no account taken of how wounding it was? Let the world, with all its burdens, be gone, and leave the old man there, burning with passion, with all that pain in his heart –

As these thoughts followed one another, the friend summoned up an image of the old man, wishing all the while to be rid of that momentary, wounded picture that tugged at his heart – the picture of the fighter giving that answer to the grey-haired man.

He began to fidget on his seat, cracking his knuckles, letting his eyes skim over the tree-like patterns adorning the cushion on which his host's elbow was reclining.

His narrator had joined him in this silent pause, as if wanting to indulge another fancy far removed from the fancies of his visitor.

And –

He cleared his throat, slowly and audibly, rubbed the skin above his eyebrows then looked his friend in the face.

"You know, my friend," he said, "I recall now that woman called Maryam, during the war of the 'Bastions'. She was busy as a bee, working and ululating with joy, sure of herself, awe-inspiring, winning every argument. I can still see her now, in my mind's eye. Her eyes were clear like a cow's, blackness was woven in that combed hair of hers – plaits dangling from a coal-black night. How well I remember her! She was pure, and, when she walked, she'd tread lightly, as if skimming the ground. No jewellery around her wrists – when she went off to the battlefield, she left behind her silver bracelets and rings.

"Her hair was tied with a red band – it adorned her head so beautifully. On her sleeve was some earthy dust, mixed with stains from the butter she carried around in a goatskin.

"Day after day she took the butter from her cow and carried it over to the battlefield, where, hard though times were, she'd hand it out unstintingly to the fighters, using it like a salve to clean their wounds.

"Yes –

"Life, in this world, deals out death. It takes no notice of any protests! When Maryam passed away, everyone said: 'Let's slaughter her cow and share out its meat, so God will grant her soul rest.' The cow was killed, and the villagers all took their share of the meat.

"But what was to be done with the hide that was left? Some wanted to work it into a strong rope, to bind around the backs of the oxen when they were drawing up water from the wells. Another said:

"'We'll make a drum from the skin, for our dances.'

"The others approved of this, and they had someone salt it and dry it in the noonday heat, to make a suitable drum."

The narrator was only semi-literate; he could read and do a little writing. But he'd memorized the Quran. He quoted:

"You will die and they will die too."

The friend, for his part, was well able to read and write, and he liked to gain knowledge from every book available. He'd memorized a substantial part of the Quran and the Hadith. He'd memorized some Arabic poems too, and would recite them even when he was alone. Now, once again, the rooster's long-drawn call rang in his ears, and he recited two lines he remembered reading, lengthening out the sounds:

*When the rooster crows,*
*Calling some of his family to the morning,*
*They will be unhearing and apart.*

## Ibrahim al-Nasser

# FROM *A SPLIT IN THE NIGHT'S ATTIRE*
(thuqb fi rida' al-layl)

*Ibrahim al-Nasser (like Hamid Damanhury, the author of* The Price of Sacrifice*) is regarded as a major pioneer novelist in the Kingdom of Saudi Arabia, where novel writing of this kind was unknown before the late 1950s and early 1960s. Novels before these two had chiefly been designed either to educate and maintain the traditional order, or else simply to entertain, with no thought given to compliance with the terms of the conventional novel as written in the western world, by writers like Dickens, Flaubert and Dostoevsky, from the nineteenth century on.*

*In this technically new kind of novel, which began to appear in Egypt in the nineteenth century, the focus of interest was on life as actually lived, portrayed through the characters and through their struggle against reactionary, backward-looking ways. In Saudi Arabia, however, while a minimum of literary performance might be permitted in terms of language and style, it was out of the question to touch on this actuality or openly to criticize conservative societies. Al-Nasser and al-Damanhury have, in fact, through the events described in their novels, moved on to a different Arab environment, one where there is more freedom and release.*

*The hero of* A Split in the Night's Attire *is by origin from Najd in central Arabia. Born in Zubair, he then goes to live in Basra, Iraq, where he completes high school. His father, Hajj 'Ammar, a religious man and a merchant by profession, is deeply conservative and inflicts cruelty on his family. The plot revolves around the conflict between the old traditions and the new urban life the family meets in the different atmosphere of Basra. This conflict the author reveals through a contrast between the father, who embodies traditional piety, and the son, who embodies the aspirations of a new generation seeking freedom and endeavouring to abandon the restrictions of the past. Initially the hero is portrayed in negative terms, on account of his total preoccupation with the girl he loves. Subsequently, though, the hero changes course, taking part, alongside his colleagues, in student protests. Following a period of imprisonment, the hero attempts to flee from Basra, but is unsuccessful and returns sadly to his family and the eyes of his beloved.*

\*\*\*

I came to know 'Issa in Z, a small town the desert embraced with a fervour bordering on devourment.

There seems, indeed, to be a clear likeness between the desert and the town, whose old mud houses have always been dusty like an old man's drab face, in spite of all the embellishments devised by the townspeople to brighten up their appearance: adorning the inner walls with coated plaster, painting the roofs in vivid colours, and other methods of primitive decoration, as opposed to artistic beauty.

Our house was in a quarter called al-Maragha, on the left rise of the town, where the desert's embrace has grown so fierce as to move the very ground beneath, shooting the bales of dust upwards in a bout of frenzied energy, then settling gradually over the roofs of the ancient houses – only to rise once more and cling to a sky sated with the many-coloured dust swirls. Not far from the quarter were a number of wells that would gather these swirls in, when they were exhausted at last with their frantic ascents or boisterous dances. The wells would, as it were, tap them affectionately on their backs, as though each were a mother welcoming home her quarrelsome sons. Then the swirls would grow calm, giving way to their mothers' ministrations, only to soar foolishly once more and strew their burning, gleeful specks over the benevolent town and its peaceful citizens.

I used, for some reason, to puzzle over something that gripped my mind strangely. Our town, cherished as it is by its maternal desert, has a most changeable climate. During the day it can turn to one long inferno, the heat bouncing from the walls and roasting the thin bodies of the people, leaving them to sweat ceaselessly amid the dusty, whirling clouds. And yet the winter's so bitter as to freeze the water and numb the normal to-and-fro of life. This is something quite accepted, as though written in the book of fate.

The strange thing I spoke of is that, when I gaze southward across the hills, and especially when I climb a knoll after the storm clouds have rid themselves of their dirt and rain, my eyes are met, caught indeed, by a thin green thread; and my fancy runs wild as I strive to make out what lies beyond it.

I'm spurred on to seek out the secret of that thread, adorned as it is in a way that makes the spirit soar, refreshes it with something which, if without concrete reality, exists none the less for the imagination and the inner eye.

So it was that I learned (and how I came to regret my question) that beyond that green thread that so caught my fancy lay a great city of legends and dreams. A city filled with mythical things that lead people of my kind – who have found a haven among the palm trees, in flight from a reality both fearful and disastrous – to find pleasure in those imaginary things planted deep in the impossible.

There was a river (so I was told) that ran through the city, dividing it like a line that crowns the head of a beautiful girl, parting exuberant bunches of hair that have just breathed in the very fragrance of life. Along the two banks of this river dangled branches loaded with luscious fruits, so interwoven as to make veritable forests and bowers, hiding the crystal face of the sky, with its bright azure hue. I hardly need speak of the scents rising from these fruits, borne on the mild breezes, to give you the full picture of this legendary city.

It was natural enough these scenes should entice my fancy and focus my thoughts, so that I truly imagined myself to be embraced by this strange city-paradise of 'Aad. I'd been flung into it by a wondrous wind, a wind that led me to become one of its citizens, living within its generous borders that held things melancholy and sweet alike. Still, though, the obstacle remained: how was I to converse with the people of this paradise? Were they human beings at all, or in a quite different mould?

But soon my fancy supplied a new, reassuring thought. These people didn't, perhaps, need to speak at all. Perhaps they needed just to nod their heads, or give some other simple signal, to summon the lads and pretty maidens who'd instantly perform whatever task was required. Weren't these, after all, their servants?

And so I grew calm once more, as though I'd solved some problem that gripped everyone round about. The chasm that gaped before me (swallowing up all serious thought of fleeing to that legendary paradise) was also a broad sea, leaving behind it whole layers of caked salt as the waters receded, heaped up over many months. This harsh salt world was, so I was told, the haunt of ogres of every kind, who'd devour boys of my age without a second thought, if they could only catch them unawares. The question sprang constantly to my mind: why had our ancestors chosen this arid, barren spot, rather than moving on just a little further to settle in that legendary city?

I was young then – too young for anyone to be interested in my reflections. My fellow-citizens were remote from any such thoughts sown by a heart thirsting to express what it saw and felt. They were lean people; you might have thought they'd taken a vow to keep plumpness, even good health, out of their lives. This made them seem taller than other people, and they'd walk along with their heads bent, like ancient philosophers of some kind. They mostly kept silent, and anything they did say would be wary and brief; they spoke to one another in a whispered, hurried exchange of words, as if too busy to have time for things around them. The dust storms were the baneful reason for this. They'd cough ever more, and talk ever less, and at last the truth dawned on me. They preferred not to open their mouths, so as not to have them filled with specks of choking dust.

I've told you now about the town that held me so long in its embrace; and I've spoken about my personal impressions of it and the memories that clung to my mind. Now I shall turn, in these pages, to what I know about the life of another young man, someone I've been acquainted with for so long that I've come to know almost all his private affairs. It wasn't so difficult, there in my town, to share life with others. There were, for practical purposes, no vast differences in people's lives; but for the conscious division of years into months and months into days, life there might have appeared a kind of seamless garment, with no distinction between yesterday or tomorrow: a single, long day, lived by strangers flung into just that spot, by fate, for a reason quite unknown to them. Only a stranger, longing for his homeland, would have sensed how deep the estrangement was. After the day of our migration, our lives became marked out by a series of events used by our mothers and grandmothers to record the progress of time. They, God rest their souls, never knew the meaning of years: they'd specify periods, mark phases and deaths, by, let's say, the day the Ottomans invaded the town, or the day these killed one of the leading citizens in broad daylight, or when a school was built, or the day electricity was installed in the house of such-and-such an official; and so on. All such events would make life pause for a moment, and men and women alike would remark on them, as marking unforgettable, historic days.

That's the way we give meaning to our past; so you must forgive me if I can't tell you exactly when 'Issa's story began, or anything about his family history. He himself knew little enough of his past life. All he knew – through other people – was that when his family migrated to the town he was a mere bundle of trembling flesh, unaware of what was happening around him, till the day he found himself living in a turbulent sea of paradox, which he sought to control with all his feelings and conscious thought. Outside his home, in society at large – the society of school and street and market place – many things were placidly accepted that 'Issa and others rejected at first; and in the end he too had to submit, rather than be accused, in the home or in the petty society around him, of crimes leading on to a charge of godlessness; of being branded, within the home at least, as someone utterly degenerate. But youth tended to swallow, straight, ideas that were set before it brimful of paradox, with no proper argument or analysis. Youth takes in and stores, avoiding clashes.

And so this period of estranged youth continued, warily, its thoughts uncertain and troubled. The situation was fraught with difficulty. Where, finally, could such a youthful mind turn? Should it turn to the family, strictly traditional as it was? Or should it move forward, take its place in a great outside world now freed, most disconcertingly, from the old traditions themselves? Finally those roots, of unreflecting, conservative upbringing, blocked off all liberation from traditional restriction. 'Issa still recalled (for instance) how his hair would stand on end at the sight of a female visitor entering their house. He'd start sweating all over, his blood would feel as if stoked in a furnace. To quench the flaming fire, he'd stare helplessly at the unnoticing visitor, in defiance of the virtue he'd been taught.

'Issa's real story begins from the moment he became consciously aware, and began to acquire some small discernment in the various matters of life. When he was nine years old, his father took him to one of the *kuttab*s, in a mosque where the Quran was taught; and there he stood before a turbaned shaikh with an imposing face, holding in his hand a long cane pointed at the top. 'Issa supposed the man must use this to support his weak legs, but enlightenment came soon enough when, after a few moments, he saw the cane come down on the children's feet, or poke them under their bellies, as they sat there in a circle in front of him. 'Issa's father told the shaikh he'd like him to teach his son the Quran. The shaikh eyed the boy suspiciously.

"Don't worry, Hajj 'Ammar," he said. "I'll make a real man out of him for you. Here, we turn boys into men."

Such was Shaikh Ibrahim, the rosy-cheeked imam of the mosque, humorous when not teaching, with downcast eyes that held a most attractive glint. He was quite an elegant man, with handsome features a young girl might have envied.

His assistant was Mullah Mahfouz, a middle-aged man with grizzled sideburns, curly hair and a ferrety face. As for *his* eyes, they'd take on a malicious gleam when he became angry. And he lost his temper easily enough.

Our friend 'Issa was the eldest of six brothers, a seniority that gave him distinction within the family, especially in his mother's eyes. He was listened to by everybody, and the smallest sign from him was enough to make himself obeyed. But, from the time he was enrolled at the mosque, he faced a new challenge; the hawk eyes of Shaikh Ibrahim and his assistant were constantly scanning the pupils' faces, following every twitch, every movement, of their own small eyes. A rude expression might sometimes be overlooked; but, if it was repeated, punishment would rain down. After a while 'Issa's feet showed the marks of a severe beating: clear enough proof that bad behaviour wouldn't be tolerated for long.

'Issa would touch his bloodied feet. Many a day they'd burn like fire. Then they'd grow icy cold. Only after years had passed, and his body had grown tall, did he really get over that torture. He recalled one particular incident, followed by the memory of those icy feet. He'd been beaten, on that day, for some reason he could no longer properly recall. Then, when he was home, his father noticed him limping about. He summoned the boy forthwith, in that loud voice of his. Then, without asking for any explanation, he tugged at 'Issa's foot as though he'd caught him red-handed in some crime. Seeing the swollen foot, his father nodded knowingly, then ordered 'Issa to get ready for a visit to Hajj Hasan, to have the rebellious foot cauterized.

'Issa paled at the very mention of the man the children called "the arch-torturer." He almost fell at his father's feet, dampening them with his tears and begging for forgiveness. Then he stood trembling before his father, imagining the red-hot spits that would sear his feet, wielded by that ignorant "doctor" who tortured children with the cauterizing he viewed as the sole remedy for everything, even the smallest wound.

Still trembling, 'Issa thought furiously. Then he decided to confess. His father's punishment would, after all, be far more bearable than Hajj Hasan approaching with the red-hot spits.

His father listened attentively to his account, saying not a word, his face colouring with his changing emotions. Then, at the end, he grew furiously angry. 'Issa stood there, like a shivering cat. At last his father relieved his feelings by slapping 'Issa's face.

"You brainless fool!" he yelled. "Your feet are swollen from a beating, and still you're not revising your lessons? You're no son of mine," he stormed on, "you son of a bitch! God damn your father, and your turbaned shaikh, and his black eunuch!"

He went on cursing him, the walls ringing with his words, till the whole house was drawn to the scene, headed by his mother, who seemed terrified of her husband's dreaded anger.

"Look at your stupid son," he said, when he saw her. "Look at that shining cleverness of his, that you're always praising. Do you need any better proof of how stupid he is? Better than his swollen foot, from a caning? God curse you, you stupid woman!"

'Issa threw himself on his mother, seeking refuge from what was about to come. But his father pulled him roughly away.

"Come with me," he roared, "you son of a bitch!"

The terrified mother could only murmur a prayer, begging God to save her son from the evils of his father's wrath.

Hajj 'Ammar walked with his son towards the mosque, knowing Shaikh Ibrahim never left before performing the sunset prayer. As the shaikh saw them approaching, his eyes gleamed, and he hurriedly ended the Quranic verse he was intoning.

When he'd finished the last prayer, Hajj 'Ammar sat down alongside him and began pouring out complaints about his punished son. He said 'Issa was stupid, and he also implied that the lessons had somehow been at fault.

Shaikh Ibrahim beamed, then answered in a mild tone:

"Your son isn't as stupid as you think, Hajj. It's just a matter of the way we teach. To tell you the truth, we drive ourselves into the ground to give these boys the best instruction they could get anywhere. Do you want us to go against our consciences, Hajj, and let your son fail in his lessons, without guiding his halting steps with a little corrective punishment? God save us from the anger that makes a tolerant man lose his balance – Don't worry Hajj, your son's on the way to becoming one of my best pupils."

Sensing Shaikh Ibrahim's honest candour, the father's anger began to ebb away – especially when he heard him say that 'Issa wasn't stupid. That statement alone was enough to make him see his rashness in accusing his son and casting doubt on the shaikh's manner of teaching. And he had to pay for it too! Shaikh Ibrahim was a shrewd, experienced man. He knew the right time to bring something up and what to talk about. He grasped the opportunity to start talking about his recent problems.

Because he'd taken up teaching (he told Hajj 'Ammar), the Ministry of Religious Endowments had stopped paying their subsidy. But these wretched boys (he went on) were dull in understanding their lessons, and his conscience would prick him if he showed any slackness. The townspeople had no notion of the problems he faced. And so it went on. Hajj 'Ammar took the hint: the shaikh was short of money, and he really ought to have helped him before this. His hand moved, and he thrust something into the shaikh's hand – 'Issa couldn't see what. The shaikh raised his beaming gaze towards heaven and prayed for the noble man there before him, while Hajj 'Ammar looked for some suitable way of ending the visit.

"But this wretched boy's foot, shaikh," he said. "Is it swollen or isn't it?"

The other man gazed at 'Issa, smiling benevolently.

"For your sake, Hajj," he said, "we won't beat him again for a whole week. But if he neglects his studies again, we'll remind him of his duty, and ours."

"But – is this caning on the feet really necessary, shaikh? Isn't there some better way of discipline?"

The shaikh's beam broadened. He clutched at his long snowy beard, then gazed sharply into 'Issa's mottled face.

"If your son stops his day-dreaming, then we'll stop the beating. If he revises well, we'll praise him. And if he should excel, then we'll make him a monitor. Can I promise any better than that?"

Hajj 'Ammar was profuse in his thanks. But the moment they'd gone out through the mosque's gateway, he grabbed hold of his son's robe and twisted his ear, as if to give vent to his anger at the large sum he'd had to pay on account of the visit.

"Go and find your mother, you mule," he said, shoving 'Issa in front of him. "She's longing to see you."

\*\*\*

So, was that sum of money paid to the shaikh enough to end 'Issa's problems? In fact it had the opposite effect. The boys, especially those who'd been close to him before, saw the careful way the shaikh began favouring 'Issa after the visit in question, and wouldn't have him with them any longer. So what were the different groups? And how had groups formed at all in a set of twenty pupils at most?

There were in fact two sets of boys: one set that was in favour with the shaikh and mostly received preferential treatment; and the other made up of boys who were lashed, constantly and without mercy, by the shaikh's cane. It need hardly be said that those in the first group came from rich families, where the fathers were influential and only too happy to help the shaikh financially.

As for those making up the second group, they were generally the poorer elements, and they'd try and take their revenge for the way they were treated, and show their general frustration, by annoying the shaikh and his assistant. For instance, they'd let a bee loose in the shaikh's robes while he was nodding and dozing, and he'd wake up in a fury and, finding no one would reveal the culprit's name, would start beating the boys nearest to him. This kind of thing was in fact the expression of hatred and protest, on account of the favouritism he showed.

Sometimes he'd get so angry he'd thrash some of the boys, or make them stand for several hours on one foot. Chastisement, as I said earlier, springs from the degree of vengeance sought; leniency will meet with leniency in return. If, though, most of the second group was punished, then secret meetings would be held to discuss the best means of revenge. If Mullah Mahfouz, the shaikh's shadowy helper, had meted out the punishment, he'd be dealt with in a simple but cunning way. It was his habit, after the sunset prayer, to relieve himself behind the mosque; more precisely, among the ruins of a once grand house whose owners had deserted it years before, leaving it to fall down. When Mullah Mahfouz sought out this lonely spot and lowered his under-garments, or when he'd started urinating, he'd be suddenly assaulted, from all sides, by a hail of stones; and he'd be reduced to yells and threats against his assailants, like a helpless trapped animal baring its fangs. The stones would shower over his head, wounding it to the point of drawing blood. The pain, though, hurt and infuriated him less than the darkness that had now settled over the place, stopping his short-sighted eyes from recognizing the attackers or from seeing where the cascade of stones was coming from. First he'd rant and rave, then he'd beg for mercy, till at long last someone would rush to his aid. The boys, meanwhile, would vanish, and next day Mullah Mahfouz would appear with a large part of his face and head bandaged.

This was the point of weakness in Mullah Mahfouz's daily routine, a routine he was powerless to change. Being a man apart, unable to marry and have a home to satisfy his private needs, he belonged to the open public mosque, and he was forced to urinate like some stray dog in a ruined, deserted house known to his devilish young enemies.

Shaikh Ibrahim's daily schedule had its Achilles heel too: his bathing daily, before the dawn prayer, in the mosque's pool next to the ablution area. This place had, unluckily for him, a dilapidated roof made almost bare by the winds. When the shaikh had taken off his clothes, bathed, praised God a number of times and started drying himself, he'd be assailed from above with sand, soil and dust, and – pretending ignorance of any foul play – would begin bathing all over again. Then, the moment he started dressing a further time, he'd be assailed by still more dirty sand and realize, now, that he was in danger of missing the call to prayer. He'd yell out, desperately: "Don't you fear God, you pagans? Let me put my clothes on and perform my prayer, you little wretches!"

So he'd keep raving, while the boys would go on making fun of him till someone came into the ablution area, or until the Mullah woke with a start and rushed off to rescue his chief.

Such incidents were readily magnified by wagging tongues in the small town, recast in some new, heightened way. Some would say the shaikh had come flying out of the ablution area completely naked and been seen chasing the boys; others spread the rumour that his body had been coated with tar; still others claimed he'd been scalded with hot water; and many more such novel embellishments of the kind our town invents with such ease. It all helped alleviate the town's essential emptiness. What else was there to do but pass around scandals about other people and their behaviour?

So secret were these campaigns of vengeance that 'Issa – following the change in the shaikh's relations with him – was excluded from meetings called to discuss them. When he came to a full realization of the shaikh's partiality, a question rose in his mind. Why did the man vent his anger on one particular group and take no notice of bad behaviour on the part of the other? 'Issa began to work out the answer by taking note of certain things: above all, that the boys forgiven for misdeeds belonged to rich, well known families, while the others were the sons of common people with shabby clothes and empty pockets.

'Issa realized now that his father had had him transferred from one group to the other, without asking him which of the two he'd rather be in. It hurt him to be thrust in with the rich boys he hated, on account of their arrogance, and the way they boasted of the attention the shaikh lavished on them, and their habit of looking down on the boys from a lower class. He wanted to express his dislike of belonging to the first clique, and of his alliance with the shaikh who'd humiliated him so often before, leaving the marks of this on various parts of his body.

He pondered deeply on his new, uncomfortable position: between a group he loved, but which treated him as an outcast, and a group he'd joined unwillingly, and whose members he couldn't stand. In the end he decided to bring grief to the shaikh single-handed, even if it meant forming his own "one-member-front."

Eventually he was ready to begin operations, and he set his revenge in motion in a subtle but fearsome way. What he did was noticed swiftly enough, by shaikh and pupils alike, and the shaikh at first inflicted even harsher punishment on the group that usually pestered him. Soon, though, the new style of campaign roused doubts in the shaikh's mind, and he was inclined to believe the fervent assurances of the other boys that they were innocent of the charges.

One of 'Issa's new methods was to make comic drawings on a large sheet of paper smeared with black ink, and stick it on the gateway to the mosque with the caption: "This is Mullah Mahfouz's face. The fire of hell has burned his features for torturing innocent children." Or else he'd write: "We, the avenging angels of hell, ask for the return of our colleague Mahfouz. He has had enough punishment on earth."

The castigation of Shaikh Ibrahim was carried out differently. 'Issa would steal his cane, take it home with him, dip it in molasses, then stealthily return it next day. This would attract swarms of flies to the cane, causing the shaikh endless vexation. At other times 'Issa would paint the cane black, or with henna. And he performed various other childish acts.

As misdeeds of this kind mounted, the shaikh's patience quickly ran out. One day he assembled the members of the "offending" group, and, his face distended with fury, ordered them to strip to their underpants, then started flailing them, while they, in their agony, protested endless innocence of the malicious pranks. But the shaikh refused to believe them. Didn't he have proof of their guilt, in his own hands? As he went on beating the boys without mercy, an odd feeling began to overwhelm 'Issa; his conscience, beyond all doubt, was pricking him, and he had to rid himself of the appalling feeling. He rose to his feet.

"My esteemed shaikh," he shouted, "I was the one who did it. These boys are all innocent."

As he fell silent, every eye was on him, staring at him. He began to sweat, feeling a cold sense of humiliation and shame. Then his legs gave way and he tumbled to the ground, his face pale, the sweat oozing from him.

The shaikh stepped towards him, his anger ebbing a little but his face still congested. He patted the boy kindly on the back, and said:

"God bless your pure soul! I absolve them, for your sake, from further punishment."

The boys began muttering and whispering, some remarking on 'Issa's loyalty, others accusing him of deception. The latter verdict cut him, hurting him deeply. He'd come forward to save his fellow-pupils, exposing himself to the shaikh's fury and retribution, and they'd repaid his noble motives with such ingratitude.

He'd now, he realized clearly, lost the affection he'd once felt for most of the other boys, especially the group exposed to punishment. He felt his loneliness stripping him of the compassion he'd once had for these. The solitude hemmed him in, till he felt himself stifled; it was as though some nightmare were squeezing the breath from him. He retreated to his home, where he found solace only in his brothers. But had the whole situation been imposed on him or had he brought it on himself? In fact, he decided, it had been imposed, and this sowed in him the seeds of a complex hardened by the other boys' attitude towards him. He took to beating his brothers, so as to assert a personality nullified by his fellow-pupils. His brothers wept and begged him, but still he went on beating them; the superiority this gave him was, he felt, reinforcing his personality and moulding its form. His mother's support increased his arrogance, making it all the easier for him to avenge his lacerated feelings. She made no attempt to stop him, nor would she let his brothers report him to their father.

After behaving like this for quite some time, his conscience began to prick him once more. Deep inside himself, he felt he was nursing a disastrous malice that threatened to destroy these innocent people around him. So he turned to piety: he started praying, asking for forgiveness and hoping for relief from the guilt he felt for mistreating his brothers. He started to memorize certain Quranic verses that enjoined mercy towards others. He even went so far as to ask some old women, who visited his mother, to tell him some of the old stories about the agonies suffered by the guilty in the afterlife. His mother noticed this distraction and change, on account of some of the thoughts and notions that would spring to his mind, with no one able to clarify them for him. After a time he started to lose weight, and his peace of mind was greatly lessened too. He began to suffer from nightmares, during which he'd shriek, and tremble, and weep, remaining in a deep sleep throughout.

By now his mother had come to realize the reasons for his behaviour, and especially the solitude he sought, apart from his friends. She took, accordingly, to bribing and cajoling these boys with sweets and candies, so they'd invite him to take part in their games. 'Issa, unaware of what was going on, wondered why the boys had started seeking him out and urging him to go with them. At last one of them revealed the secret.

"'Issa," the boy told him, "tell your mother to double the sweets, or we won't have you with us."

He didn't reproach his mother, but he held back from the boys and their games, feeling stabbed and bloodied to the heart. Those words had been like spears wounding his dignity. Once more he felt pain, along with hatred towards those boys. He even hated his parents for the way they'd cut into his dignity.

They were all of them responsible for the dreadful pain swelling up inside him. He noticed the great pleasure he felt now, whenever his father brutally scolded his mother. It was as though his father was inflicting 'Issa's own vengeance on his mother. And yet, when she began weeping, he'd find himself sharing her sobs and tears. Was there, he wondered, something abnormal about him?

Who could provide an answer to this question? No one. He himself, though, felt the complexes, the strangeness, in his personality.

'Issa spent two years at the mosque, during which he memorized the Quran and read it a number of times, with the question never far from his thoughts: Was there something abnormal about him?

That, and many other questions too.

*All novel excerpts were translated by Noura Halwani and Christopher Tingley*

---

1. Zamzam Well: The sacred well within the precincts of the Holy Mosque at Mecca.
2. *Mawlana*: Title of respect given to a learned Muslim religious figure.
3. *Ustadh*: A teacher or professor. The word may also, as here, be used as a professional title.
4. *Kuttab*: A traditional school for religious education for children in places where modern schools had not yet been the general vehicle for elementary education.
5. *'Amma*: The first part of the Quran, learned first by children.
6. This is the book of poetry by the famous Umayyad poet, Qais ibn al-Mulawwah, named Majnun Laila (the madman of Laila), who set the greatest example of chaste, unrequited love in Arabic culture.
7. *Sajda*: The kneeling of Muslims when at prayer.
8. A musical instrument similar to a guitar.
9. Sayyid Darwish: A noted Egyptian musician of the early twentieth century.
10. *Sayf Ben Dhi Yazan*: An ancient Yemeni ruler, of whom many legendary stories are told and who is the hero of the famous romance carrying his name. The romance has been rendered into English, part translation, part re-telling, by Lena Jayyusi for *PROTA*, Project of Translation from Arabic, and published by Indiana University Press, Bloomington: 1996.
11. The cloak worn, here by women, over their clothes when going out in public.
12. 'Abd al-Rahman al-Kawakibi: A widely influential nationalist Arab writer of the end of the

nineteenth century. His book, *The Nature of Tyranny* has been an eye-opener for aspiring Arabs fighting to break free of colonialism and internal tyrannies, and might have caused his death from poison in 1904.

13. A reference to Michel 'Aflaq, the Syrian Christian founder of the Baathist party.

14. A prominent Palestinian poet.

15. The Thamoud were an ancient tribe, or group of tribes, prominent from around the fourth century BC. Numerous rock writings and pictures of them have been excavated.

16. Al-Jubail: A Saudi industrial city.

17. Hanash Abu Jawhara: A mythical serpent.

18. The Sawadi is the tyrannical local ruler and the main character in the book.

19. *Qat*: A plant with green leaves chewed in Yemen as a narcotic.

# Part IV

## Plays

'Abdallah 'Abd al-Jabbar

# The Dumb Devils
(al-shayateen al-khurs)

*A One Act Play*

*Characters:*
NIDAL
NIZAR
SAFWAN
'ARJOUN
BAHLOUL
SALIM
MAYMOUN
THE PRESIDENT
THE SECRETARY
AN OFFICE BOY

*SCENE: A large hall. At the front is the desk of the* PRESIDENT; *next to him sits the* SECRETARY. *There are numerous chairs for the members. Employees come in and out. The atmosphere is sometimes very serious, sometimes facetious.*

*On the* PRESIDENT'S *desk are a blotter, a stamp, a bell and some scattered papers. He keeps putting on his glasses, then taking them off again. The* SECRETARY *has numerous papers in front of him, along with a large number of files. He is holding a pen; alongside him is his briefcase, which is bursting with papers.*

*Behind the* PRESIDENT'S *desk is an open window, with a recess containing a telephone. It looks out over many staff offices.*

SALIM: Your address, Shaikh Bahloul, was the jewel of the meeting.
BAHLOUL: Thank you. Thank you, sir.
SALIM: It was like a fresh bloom, glowing with poetry and fragrance.

'ARJOUN: A pearl is always a pearl.

SALIM: Truly, he's a great artist.

SAFWAN: Don't call him an artist, Shaikh Salim. Strictly speaking, you know, the word means "wild ass."[1]

SALIM (*breaking in naively*): He really is an artist, Mr Safwan, whatever you say.

BAHLOUL (*astonished and angry*): What was that?

SAFWAN (*to Shaikh* SALIM): Let's say, rather, artful, artistic, ingenious, versatile.

'ARJOUN: Mr Safwan, you really ought to be a member of the Linguistic Council.

NIZAR: Speaking of art, I beg leave to point out that the revered Council is in need of experts.

BAHLOUL: No need of experts, Mr Nizar. Or of rotten apples.

'ARJOUN (*addressing* NIZAR): Aren't we grand all of a sudden?[2]

SAFWAN: For my part, Mr 'Arjoun, I add my voice to Nizar's. The Council undoubtedly needs experts. Engineers, doctors, agricultural experts, and so on.

NIDAL: Not so fast. What have these people done, for you to be pensioning them off?

BAHLOUL: Pension? What pension, Mr Nidal?

NIDAL: Well, we're all pensioners now, aren't we? Why don't we hang a sign on the door of the Council, saying, "We feed you for the pity of God"?

SECRETARY (*nodding as he sorts through his papers*): Ha, ha.

PRESIDENT (*lifting his head from the perusal of an endlessly long legal document*): The Council is in session.

SECRETARY: The agenda.

BAHLOUL (*interrupting*): Didn't you hear, Your Excellency, what Mr Nidal just said?

PRESIDENT: What did he just say?

BAHLOUL: He said we're all pensioners here.

PRESIDENT (*smiling faintly, then putting on a serious face*): Mr Nidal's still young. He hasn't been seasoned by the years. He's only a recent member, like Mr Nizar. He hasn't studied the bye-rules, resolutions and regulations we've set up – to such general approval, may I say.

BAHLOUL: This is an insult, Mr Nidal.

'ARJOUN: You should apologize.

BAHLOUL: It isn't enough just to apologize.

PRESIDENT: Why not do things properly? He should sacrifice an animal for you.

'ARJOUN: There should be an apology *and* a sacrifice.

PRESIDENT: Let's take a vote.

MAJORITY OF MEMBERS: There needs to be an apology *and* a sacrifice.

NIZAR: I dissent from that.

NIDAL: You can decide what you like. Only, tell me one significant, worthwhile thing you've done.

BAHLOUL (*interrupting*): He's bowed to the decision, he's shown his agreement. Now, what do you feel like eating?

'ARJOUN: How about some *saleeq*?[3] After a pleasant evening like this one?

SALIM: What I'd like, Shaikh 'Arjoun, is mutton and rice wrapped in pastry.

BAHLOUL: Yes, that's the best. Especially with biryani rice.

PRESIDENT (*with mock severity*): Haven't you forgotten the mixed grill?

MAJORITY OF MEMBERS: Of course – of course – a grill – a grill – we're all agreed – we're all agreed.

MAYMOUN: We're all agreed.

PRESIDENT: Right, we're all agreed. We'll fix it for next Thursday. Please proceed, Mr Secretary.

SECRETARY (*still turning over his papers*): There are some new matters not on the agenda. (*Before he can go on, the* OFFICE BOY *enters with a tea tray and begins handing out cups of tea.*)

'ARJOUN (*refusing a cup*): Haven't I told you I only drink green tea?

OFFICE BOY: Certainly, sir. I'll bring it straight away.

BAHLOUL: The tea's bitter.

PRESIDENT: It's too sweet.

OFFICE BOY: Certainly, sir.

SALIM: The tea's too strong. Make it lighter. And don't forget the lemon for me and Shaikh Maymoun.

OFFICE BOY: Yes, sir. Yes, sir.

MAYMOUN: Why haven't you flavoured it with mint, boy?

BAHLOUL (*looking at his watch*): The time's flying. Let's start the meeting, Mr Secretary. I've an appointment with Dr Safargali at five.

SECRETARY: There are some new matters arising. I'll just enumerate the principal points. (*He begins to intone in time-honoured fashion.*) First: A complaint from one of the city quarters, concerning the admixture of barley in bread. Second: An appeal from the head of the porters' union. They complain of the bad quality of bread.

SAFWAN: I'll come in first on that point. Bread is, after all, the staff of life. The price of bread should be reduced to the appropriate level, and the government should punish those who exploit, who trifle with, the sustenance of the people.

PRESIDENT: Read on, shaikh.

NIZAR: This is a most serious matter.

NIDAL: Yes, indeed it is.

NIZAR: And one we need to consider.

PRESIDENT: Read on, shaikh. Read on.

SECRETARY: Third: A suggestion from a citizen that a sizeable zoo be set up in the country.

PRESIDENT: That's something novel. How about starting with that?

BAHLOUL: A most serious matter. Well worth considering.

'ARJOUN: It's a worthwhile suggestion. I say we should start with a compound for deer. They look so delightful when they're grazing and frolicking.

NIZAR: I say we start with a pen for monkeys, Shaikh 'Arjoun. (*There is some laughter at this joke.*)

'ARJOUN: Still making fun of us, are you, Mr Nizar?

BAHLOUL: You'd think he had a death wish.

NIZAR: I object. Do you care about animals and not men?

PRESIDENT: Yes, the peacock's lovely when he spreads his feathers. Those vibrant colours of his are so beautiful. Westerners, so they say, have modelled their most sumptuous wedding dresses on the way it moves its wings.

'ARJOUN: Giraffes. Don't forget giraffes, Shaikh Bahloul.

SALIM: Which is bigger, a peacock or a giraffe?

BAHLOUL: A peacock, I'm sure.

NIZAR (*laughing sarcastically*): If our city didn't have – I'd say, let's put a wall up round it. It would make the finest zoo in the world.

SAFWAN: All this only underlines the importance of taking up your suggestion, Mr Nizar – we need experts. If we'd only had an expert naturalist here, he would never have let you take God's creatures in vain. Mixing up birds and animals, and making out that a peacock's bigger than a giraffe.

NIDAL: Everything's upside down here. Big's small, small's big, animals are better than humans. There's an urgent, crucial issue at hand, and some trivial, petty subject's given priority. You ought to start by discussing this matter of bread.

BAHLOUL: I've an urgent appointment with the doctor.

MAYMOUN: We're agreed. We're agreed.

NIDAL: All you want, Shaikh Bahloul, is to end the meeting and shoot off, whether people live or die.

*The* OFFICE BOY *enters carrying a tea tray with sugar bowl, half a lemon and two cups, one green, the other red. He starts handing out the cups.*

PRESIDENT: Please read on, Mr Secretary.

SECRETARY: Fourth: A petition from the people of Malej to establish a school, a municipal centre, a health clinic and a police station, all of which they've long been without.

'ARJOUN: There's no call to add another penny to Malej's budget. The matter should be deferred. For another seven or ten years.

NIZAR: You could call it the Seven- or Ten-Year Plan.

BAHLOUL: I repeat the proposal's premature. Impossibly drastic. Let the esteemed Health Ministry supply the village barber with some emergency medicines. That would be enough.

SALIM (*laughing*): We could let him have a bone setter too. And a midwife from the village.

NIDAL: Why shouldn't their needs be met?

PRESIDENT (*angrily*): The matter's to be deferred. Deferred, I say! Read on, shaikh.

SECRETARY: Fifth: A young man has requested a permit to bring out a newspaper.

'ARJOUN: A newspaper. Ha!

SAFWAN: An excellent idea. I say we give a positive response.

'ARJOUN: Oh, yes, we must give a positive response, mustn't we? So all the young people can learn to get above themselves?

PRESIDENT: The matter isn't within our competence. Let's not waste time with all this babbling. Come on, Mr Secretary. (*He smiles sarcastically.*) What do you think, Shaikh Maymoun?

MAYMOUN: We're agreed. We're agreed.

SAFWAN: Honourable members, some years back I put forward a proposal to reform the prisons. The proposal was put on file. Would you agree to reconsider it?

'ARJOUN: Prison's a place for men, Mr Safwan. Give them a proper taste of pain and suffering. That way they'll be deterred from committing further crimes and misdemeanours.

SAFWAN: But those are old-fashioned methods, Mr 'Arjoun. They only harden people in their sins and crimes. Prisons are for reform, correction. We ought to turn them into schools, for reforming those who are depraved and lost.

SALIM: Prisons can only be reformed when prisoners are reformed.

NIZAR: And prisoners won't be reformed till the Day of Resurrection comes.

BAHLOUL (*looking at his watch*): I'm off. I can't stay any longer, my appointment's due.

NIDAL: All you care about, Shaikh Bahloul, is yourself. And all the passing, superficial things of life.

SALIM (*quoting an old saying*): "You packers, are you content with a single hazelnut?"

*Some of the members laugh.*

MAYMOUN: We're agreed. We're agreed.

'ARJOUN: The *sanjaq*[4] of Dawaran!

NIDAL: God bless those good old days!

NIZAR: Are you really saying, Mr Nidal, you're nostalgic for the Turkish times?

NIDAL: No, Mr Nizar. I was just recalling a free man who always used to say those words.

PRESIDENT (*angry now, pressing the bell and banging the table with the blotter*): Read on, Mr Secretary.

BAHLOUL: This has been a long session. We do have other appointments.

'ARJOUN (*to the* PRESIDENT): We've missed out the most important thing of all. The Council stands in need of repairs and furniture. We should draft a speedy request to the competent authority, for a thousand pounds for this.

PRESIDENT: Follow up on that, Mr Secretary. Write at once.

NIDAL: If I remember rightly, Mr President, we set aside funds for repairs and furniture six months ago.

SECRETARY: Those funds were spent on whitewashing the walls and painting the doors and windows.

NIDAL: You can't have spent a huge sum like that. Not if you whitewashed the walls with silver, and painted the doors and windows with gold.

SECRETARY: It's exactly as I said.

PRESIDENT (*looking up from the document in front of him*): Have you drafted the memo? It needs to be done at once.

MAYMOUN: We're agreed. We're agreed.

'ARJOUN (*whispering in* BAHLOUL'S *ear*): It worked. Well done.

BAHLOUL (*in a low voice*): Right, I'm off to the doctor's.

NIDAL (*seeing* BAHLOUL *is preparing to leave*): Where are you off to, Shaikh Bahloul?

BAHLOUL (*sharply*): Didn't you hear me say I had an appointment with the doctor? You seem to be in a bad way, Mr Nidal.

NIDAL: No more than you are yourself, Shaikh Bahloul.

BAHLOUL: I thank God, I'm able to look on the bright side. No dark thoughts.

NIDAL: You're in a chronically bad way. Suffering from the most dangerous illness, maybe, anywhere in society. You're not concerned about anybody. You only look to yourself, and how to make your wealth grow.

BAHLOUL (*preparing to rise*): I object. I object! (*He goes off to the editing room.*)

NIDAL (*continuing*): Yes, that wealth that's set up a broad barrier, an impenetrable dam, between you and people's sufferings. You can object or not, as you like. Your objection won't bury the bitter truth of what I said.

'ARJOUN (*to Shaikh* SALIM): He's boiling like a cauldron.

SALIM (*to Shaikh* 'ARJOUN): He's downright rude. His words touch a chord even so, deep down.

NIDAL (*falling into a fit of coughing, then going on to address the Council, as though delivering a speech*): Those pale faces, those toiling people, those empty bellies, those shrunken bodies, which don the mantle of the night for refuge against the winter cold, and feed on crumbs from the storehouse of tears and sighs, to ward off the assault of life and remorseless hunger. Tell me: have you any idea how they live? Tell me: are you ignorant of their story? Sirs, they reside not far from your revered Council, which was set up solely to look to the needs of splendid restaurants and tasty food.

SAFWAN: There is no succour except in God.

'ARJOUN: Ever since Mr Nidal became a member, our Council's gone downhill.

NIDAL (*continuing*): Look outside, Shaikh Bahloul. (*He looks around but fails to find him.*) Where *is* Shaikh Bahloul? Look outside, Mr President, and you'll see people like the remnants of the earth, using those slums as places to live in. If you don't know what graves are like, then just one visit to those slums will be enough to teach you. Graves are just what they are – except that the people inside them are alive. Oh, honourable President, distinguished members –

*The* PRESIDENT *looks up, but is soon immersed once more in the long document he has been examining.*

NIDAL (*continuing*): Do you know what kind of lives those people lead? The people living in those slums make do with a single meal a day. Haven't you heard how the children there go to bed on an empty stomach?

SAFWAN: To God we all return.

NIDAL (*continuing*): Haven't you heard of those who sleep on the sand, wrapping themselves round with it? They spend their nights starving, while, just a few metres away, the scraps from good food are thrown to the dogs. Haven't you sensed their bitter thoughts? Don't you know how the anguish, the deprivation they suffer makes each one of them wish a slithering snake would bite him in his sleep and turn him to a motionless corpse? So he could find rest from all this suffering and distress? (BAHLOUL *returns from the editing room.*)

'ARJOUN (*addressing* BAHLOUL): Haven't you left for the doctor's yet?

BAHLOUL: You've dragged the meeting out so long, you've made me miss my appointment. I've just called the doctor at his clinic, and I found he'd already left. I don't know what I've done to Mr Nidal, to have him treat me like this.

NIDAL: I don't mistreat anyone, Shaikh Bahloul. I'm a good-hearted man. I love those who love me, and I don't hate those who hate me. But I struggle against evil, and sin, and injustice. I rise up against those wherever they're to be found, in any heart or mind. My mother taught me not to be a dumb devil – to speak the truth, because it's the truth. Just because I tell the truth about you, do you think I'm being aggressive and hostile? I respect you personally, but what's crooked inside you needs –

SALIM (*interrupting*): – to be made straight, so as to follow God's path.

MAYMOUN: We're agreed. We're agreed.

BAHLOUL: You're blackening my good name, Mr Nidal. Nothing more or less.

NIDAL: Blackening your good name? Ha! A person's good name is like the musical
    ring of a real golden guinea. As long as that ring's there, your good name
    can't come to harm. (*Becomes animated.*) Strange, isn't it? Here we are, afraid
    of illusions, of words. It would be better if we feared our consciences, feared
    what was right, and feared God, Who knows what is revealed and what
    concealed. Every word's a bullet, every sentence a rapid firing gun,
    showering us with a hail of burning fire. An honest article, though – that's
    an atomic bomb, leaving nothing unscathed.

NIZAR: Calm down, Mr Nidal.

NIDAL (*continuing*): If what people say of us is true, then we'd better reform
    ourselves. And if it's false, then let's combat it, with cogent argument and a
    stream of good deeds. You're the people best fitted to be tolerant, because
    you – so they say – represent public opinion, and it's your duty to fight for
    people's rights. If you can't take criticism, then you'll be powerless to
    demand the rights.

'ARJOUN (*aroused by the sound of* NIDAL'S *raised voice*): An eloquent speech, sir. But
    we've strayed from the matter at hand. Why don't we go back to this zoo we
    want to build?

SECRETARY: Yes, we've strayed from the matter at hand.

SAFWAN: Oh God, isn't there some magician to roll up this carpet? Isn't there
    some new light to illuminate these souls? No human feeling able to suffuse
    these hearts? Strange, isn't it? That we're going to start all over again, with
    this charade about a zoo?

MAYMOUN: We're agreed. We're agreed.

SAFWAN (*continuing*): Isn't there some sacred flame, to burn away these ancient,
    worn out minds? Everything here's old, everything's worn out and frayed –
    all except these shiny new clothes we dress ourselves up in –

SALIM (*quoting a common saying*): "He broke his silence so long, to blaspheme and
    utter wrong."

BAHLOUL (*fidgeting on his chair*): Who's blasphemed? Why don't we leave all this –

PRESIDENT (*raising his head from the document*): Yes, shaikh, read on.

SECRETARY: The Council still hasn't decided on the matter of beggars.

BAHLOUL: Yes, that's urgent. It needs to be explored and discussed. This
    country's oozing shame from all those filthy beggars. They distort our
    civilized face to the world. They harass tourists and visitors, and people
    interested in ancient sites. They follow them around everywhere, as ugly as
    you like! They cluster round them the way flies buzz around in butchers' and
    confectioners' shops. We need to make firm representations to the Interior
    Ministry. They should take a hard line, a tough line, to combat this malaise.
    We need to fight these beggars the way we fight insects with DDT.

NIDAL (*sarcastically*): God save the small beggar from the big beggar.

BAHLOUL: When are we going to have an end to all these insinuations and
    insults? I object most strongly.

NIDAL: Don't get upset. We're all beggars here.

MAJORITY OF MEMBERS (*in unison*): We object!

SALIM: We object most strongly to the tone being taken.

MAYMOUN: We're agreed. We're agreed.

NIDAL (*continuing*): If the poor small beggar can beg scraps of food to keep himself
    alive, then we, the big beggars – we've used our "calling" to get hundreds,
    no thousands, tens of thousands even, for the houses and mansions we've
    built, for the grand rural estates we've got hold of. It's never occurred to us
    to set up a business, to give those wretched creatures work, to provide them
    with a livelihood, preserve their dignity, ward off the shame that – as Shaikh
    Bahloul says – disfigures our country.

SALIM: That's reasonable. That's reasonable.

PRESIDENT (*raising his head from the document*): Read on, Mr Secretary.

SECRETARY: Sixth: A citizen proposes we set up a popular theatre.

SALIM: Now that *is* a glorious vision! What could be better? It's an idea that's often
    struck me, gripped me even. Couldn't we have a popular playhouse, in the
    city? We could stage social and moral drama.

BAHLOUL: A playhouse! A theatre! God forbid!

MAYMOUN: We're agreed. We're agreed.

SAFWAN: It's a good idea.

NIZAR: Right, fine. But who's going to play the women's parts?

'ARJOUN: Yes, that's a point. Who's going to play the women's parts?

NIZAR: I know; it's simple enough. There are men who are more like women
    anyway. They can play the parts. They know how to mimic their voices and
    gestures. If they were to dress in women's clothes, and we put artificial
    breasts on their chests, and they used women's powders, red and white and
    black, then I'd say (*in a soft voice*) how beautiful they are, these lovely girls and
    pretty buxom lasses.

PRESIDENT: God – God – God –

*The majority of members laugh.*

'ARJOUN: But don't you think a project like that's going to meet a good deal of
    opposition and resistance? It would take a pretty daring body to see it
    through.

NIZAR: There's a simple solution. Our revered Council will perform the first story
    itself. Only, it should be a comedy.

MAJORITY OF MEMBERS: We object.

BAHLOUL: Is that how we're going to end up? As actors and actresses?

NIZAR: Why not? After all, this revered Council has been playing out tragedies for twenty years now. Why shouldn't it perform a single play to entertain people, and make them laugh just once in their lives?

NIDAL: Why should you be afraid of acting? We're all actors in this world, we play our parts on the great stage of life. There's no difference between the stage of life and the stage in the playhouse – except that on the stage of life we don't play out the last act, the one that starts in a different new world.

NIZAR: Your performance on the playhouse stage isn't as unpredictable, either, as the one on life's stage. The President will be director, and the Secretary will give you your cues. All you have to do is repeat exactly what he says, just the way you do here.

MAYMOUN: We're agreed. We're agreed.

'ARJOUN: In my view, we should start off with a play from Arab history.

SAFWAN: Let's make it the story of al-Hajjaj and Laila al-Akhyaliyya.[5]

NIZAR: Shaikh Bahloul would make a perfect Hajjaj.

BAHLOUL: God forbid! Me, play the part of an oppressive tyrant?

NIZAR: Don't get steamed up. I'll play the part of the tyrant, and you can play Laila al-Akhyaliyya.

*Everyone laughs.*

MAYMOUN: We're agreed. We're agreed.

'ARJOUN: Ha, ha, ha!

BAHLOUL: This is an insult, Mr Nizar. You should be ashamed of yourself! Me, play a woman's part?

NIZAR: Where's the harm in that? A woman like Laila's better than plenty of men are.

BAHLOUL: Please, spare me this nonsense.

*Milha 'Abdallah*

# THE SECRET OF THE TALISMAN
(sirr al-tillasm)

*Characters:*
AN OLD MAN
A YOUNG MAN
VOICES

*SCENE: A valley between high mountains, in the centre of which is a mountain peak straddling a cave with piles of rocks at its sides. The wind echoes between the mountains. To the right is a huge cactus plant, to the left a waterfall, its waters gushing out from among the rocks. In front of the waterfall is sitting an* OLD MAN, *extremely tall, with snow white hair. His hair and beard are both inordinately long, his hair falling over his brow so that only his eyes are visible. He is dressed in a white gown, peering into the waterfall, and as motionless as a statue carved from the rock.*

*The* YOUNG MAN *enters, swaying and clutching his shoulder. Blood is pouring down his clothes. He sits down in front of the cactus plant, obviously in pain. He seems exhausted. His eyes wander about him, and, catching sight of the old man, he crawls towards him; then, deciding he must be a statue, he rolls on to his back and falls asleep. The* OLD MAN *gets up and walks over, then stands over the* YOUNG MAN, *who lies there between his open legs.*

OLD MAN (*calmly*): It's high time you came to stand at the door of this old
    remnant. Many have come here. The difference is – you're alive.

YOUNG MAN (*terrified*): Who are you?

OLD MAN: That's not important. The important thing is, you've come.

YOUNG MAN: I had no choice, I had to come here. Bandage my wound first, old
    shaikh. (*He feels his shoulder.*)

OLD MAN: You're exhausted, my son, but –

YOUNG MAN: But what? My wound's bleeding, death's just a breath away, or
    closer even – and you just talk. Do something – anything.

OLD MAN: Have you been stung by a scorpion? Or bitten by a snake maybe? I've cures for anything like that.

YOUNG MAN: Stung, bitten, what do you mean? Just stop the bleeding.

OLD MAN: What's your name?

YOUNG MAN: Misbah, my name's Misbah. Did you hear? Help me, may God bless you.

OLD MAN (*scooping up some sand, which he puts in a cup of water and shakes, then gives to the* YOUNG MAN): Drink, drink, my son. This is a cure for scorpion stings.

YOUNG MAN (*drinking with disgust*): This isn't a scorpion sting! This is a deep wound, very deep. Just take a look. (*Shows him his shoulder.*)

OLD MAN: I'll climb up the mountain and gather some leaves for you. I'll boil them to dress your wound.

YOUNG MAN: No! There's no time! I'm bleeding, bleeding to death, don't you understand?

OLD MAN: Tell me first, how did you come by your wound?

YOUNG MAN (*crumpling up*): It was a – (*Hesitates.*) It was a bullet. A bullet struck me. The bullet's in my shoulder. Now do you understand?

OLD MAN: Fire will cure you. I'll have to cauterize your shoulder. Where are you from?

YOUNG MAN: Over there, from beyond the river.

OLD MAN (*feeling the shoulder*): This isn't an easy wound. There are a lot of rivers. Which one did you cross over?

YOUNG MAN: I crossed over the big river.

OLD MAN: Ah, that river's full of scorpions and snakes. How did you manage to avoid them?

YOUNG MAN: An old fisherman – Let me rest, father, give me some water.

OLD MAN: Of course – you'll rest soon. But tell me, don't you have a wife and children?

YOUNG MAN: God's mercy, aren't there any other human beings here? (*He cries out, his cry echoing back from the mountains. Meanwhile the* OLD MAN *trims some palm leaves.*)

OLD MAN: There's no one but me. I've been guard over this remnant for – for four hundred years, let's say.

The YOUNG MAN *leaps up in fear, then falls back on the ground.*

OLD MAN (*feeling the wound and singing one of his special songs*): The old fisherman, with the holed boat.

YOUNG MAN: Holed?

OLD MAN: That's when the crocodile struck the boat, holed it, and it filled with water – how did you cross over?

YOUNG MAN: Shall I get up and light the fire for you?

OLD MAN: The fire will be ready soon, you'll see – it only takes a few moments. (*Blood flows copiously from the wound.*) Your blood will soon congeal. I'll put a little of it over the fire, and a smell of grilling will rise – then you'll see.

YOUNG MAN (*shouting*): I'll see? The nonsense you talk! Please, stop the bleeding.

OLD MAN: No – no – don't move, the blood will scatter – what we need is a cake of blood, let it flow till it congeals. (*He kindles a fire, brings out a drum and a flute and begins playing to a special rhythm.*)

YOUNG MAN: Please, carry me to that boat, the boat with the hole in it, so I can cross to some place where there's life.

OLD MAN: Forget all that. Calm down, I said, you'll see. Did you look closely at that old fisherman's face?

YOUNG MAN (*writhing in pain*): Oh, I just heard his voice. But it seemed to me he was wearing a mask over his face, with bones coming out from it.

OLD MAN: That wasn't a mask, my son, let me assure you. That was a skull on his head. He's been carrying it for more than a thousand years.

YOUNG MAN: I told you to get me away from here. (*to himself*) A thousand years, he said. What was it brought me here?

OLD MAN: I told you. You'll see. They've been waiting for you to come since they laid their bodies down on the ground.

YOUNG MAN: Who are "they"? What do I have to do with them? I want to live. I don't want to die now.

OLD MAN: "Who are 'they'?" you ask! They're the ones lying there in the cave. If you'll climb up to the cave and peer in through its mouth, you'll see them there, all laid out side by side in their tattered rags; all you can see is their skin stretched over bones sticking out. Only their beards have resisted time. Those have grown to their feet, and every morning they're blown from side to side by the wind.

YOUNG MAN: How have they managed to keep the night animals off, here in these dark mountains?

OLD MAN: Dark mountains? Each night, the glowing fire of their eyes turns the caves' blackness to the mouth of hell. (*He takes a folded paper from the folds of his gown, smoothes it out very carefully, then sets it before the* YOUNG MAN.) Take a close look at the features of this young man.

YOUNG MAN (*in alarm*): What *is* this?

OLD MAN: Careful! Didn't I tell you to stay still, so the blood can congeal? What are you afraid of anyway? Relief's close at hand, for you and for both of us.

YOUNG MAN: Relief? Where's that going to come from? It's death itself. Tell me, how did you get that picture of me?

OLD MAN: For thousands of years we've been shackled, here among these silent mountains, waiting for you to come.

YOUNG MAN: "We," you say. Who are you, who else is here with you?

OLD MAN (*pointing to the cave*): They're here, and I'm here – the sentinel in this place for four hundred years, a thousand years.

YOUNG MAN (*shrieking*): You're a thousand years old?

OLD MAN: From the moment your feet touched the waters of the great river, these mountains have resounded to your echo. Listen. (*The echo of the YOUNG MAN'S voice is repeated. The YOUNG MAN seems almost unconscious as the old man takes the cake of blood and places it over the fire.*)

YOUNG MAN: The smell's filling the place – my blood's burning.

OLD MAN: The secret's all in this smell, and in this picture. (*He shows him the picture.*)

YOUNG MAN: The picture's burning. Who drew this picture, tell me? (*He becomes sleepy, laying his head down on the ground.*)

OLD MAN: A shaikh who passed by gave me this picture, when he saw them deep in slumber for thousands of years, with only me to guard them.

YOUNG MAN: I'm losing blood, I'll be joining them soon. Tell me, please, what's in that paper?

OLD MAN (*reading*): In time to come, a young man will arrive from beyond the river, in a holed boat, his blood gushing out. The blood will congeal over the flames of a fire, he'll pass over snakes and scorpions, yet live, so that the picture may burn and the talisman be deciphered.

YOUNG MAN: Show me the picture! It's burning in your hands, the way my congealed blood's burning over the flames! (*The OLD MAN turns over the cake of blood on the fire.*)

OLD MAN: When the talisman's deciphered – that will be my eternal dream.

YOUNG MAN: What are you saying?

OLD MAN: Don't worry – I've been waiting a thousand years, two thousand years maybe, or longer – I've grown weary of counting the dead inside this cave, and I've grown weary of counting the years.

YOUNG MAN: The dead?

OLD MAN: I'm their guardian, waiting fervently, passionately, for you to come. You are he.

YOUNG MAN (*nervously, to himself*): There's going to be one more of them after today.

OLD MAN: Try to read the secret of the talisman.

YOUNG MAN: You read it.

OLD MAN: I can't read well. But I do hold the secret of nations, the history of civilizations. I've been longing so much for you to come.

YOUNG MAN (*reads*): The two-horned one, he who bears the world on two horns – he who came from Macedonia, carrying the great dream. (*Thick smoke rises from the burning blood.*) Hulegu Khan and the victorious golden horde – the overlord of East and West, the great Nero, he who burned Rome. (*The fire flares up.*) Abu Qais who squats over the afflicted river hippos, Ibn Yusuf al-

Hajjaj al-Thaqafi, who harvests the ripe heads, Tamberlaine, Napoleon, Hitler, Mussolini. What are all these names? And what is this? He joins the names of every tyrant on this paper, which I read writhing at your feet. (*The smoke billows to the mouth of the cave, from which moans can be heard.*) What are those sounds?

OLD MAN: Their sounds. They're beginning to wake from their sleep. You're the one who's waking them, who'll save them. The cave will open now.

YOUNG MAN: Open? Are they going to destroy me? I don't want to die.

OLD MAN: No, you'll live and be reborn – look – but first finish reading, my son. The cave won't open yet. (*Sounds rise from inside.*)

YOUNG MAN: When I came here, I thought I was saved.

OLD MAN: Saved – yes, you are saved. But tell me, who do you want to be saved from?

YOUNG MAN: Sir, I'm a young man like all the young people of our city. Our spirits burned to transform the unequal state of things there.

OLD MAN: Unequal state of things?

YOUNG MAN: The state of things in our city grew worse, the hardships of life made us restive. I and my friends acted. She let fly a bullet, which lodged in his brain, and I fled.

OLD MAN: Who?

YOUNG MAN: The she-terror – the curse – she descends on our fields, swallowing up our grain, cutting down the white cotton – trampling the green beneath her feet. Then their legions attacked us, from sky and sea and land, and turned our green fields to waste land.

OLD MAN: What of the bullet in your shoulder?

YOUNG MAN: It's the fang of the she-terror, more venomous, more deadly than a sniper's bullet. That's what rests in my shoulder.

OLD MAN: That old fisherman with the leaky boat, he brought you over, then died. You came here rowing your boat with your own two arms.

VOICES: Misbah – Misbah.

YOUNG MAN: They know my name. How?

OLD MAN: Didn't I tell you they want you? That they've been waiting for you?

YOUNG MAN: Yes – yes (*in a loud voice*) Save me! (*The cry resounds through the mountains, and so do the* VOICES *from the cave.*)

VOICES: Misbah – Misbah.

OLD MAN: Look! (*They look towards the cave, which begins to gape as the smoke clears.*) They've woken. The time has come for you to enter their city.

YOUNG MAN: Will I be cured of my wound?

OLD MAN: You'll be reborn, and we'll be reborn with you.

YOUNG MAN: Let them come out then.

VOICES: We can't come. It's you who should come in to our city – and be healed of your affliction. (*A loud cry, its echo reverberates.*) Come, Misbah. Advance.

*The* YOUNG MAN *and the* OLD MAN *advance towards the entrance of the cave. The* YOUNG MAN *crawls to the opening, then collapses. The* OLD MAN *returns to sitting on his rock, gazing at the waterfall, as smoke thickens at the mouth of the cave. Darkness descends.*

*Raja' 'Alem*

# FROM *THE ACTOR'S LAST DEATH*
### (al-maut al-akheer li 'l-Mumathil)

[NOTE: The following list of characters (like the set of times and locations that follows it) is for the play as a whole. Since only part of the play is given here, some may not be applicable to the present text. – EDITOR]

*Main Characters:*
MAN REPRESENTING SHAMSHUN [SAMSON]: The main character, twenty-one years old.
ZARQA' AL-YAMAMA: A woman beyond the influence of time.
THE RUNAWAY CHARACTER: A changing character; escaped from his author to choose his own time and personality.
THE ONLOOKER: A man whose age has frozen at thirty.
THE PUPPET MASTER: A short man in his forties, who owns a factory for making wooden puppets.
THE SUPERVISOR/SCRIPT WRITER: His assistant, a man in his thirties.
DALILA [DELILAH]: A wooden woman, belonging to the Puppet Master.
THE VENDOR: Mother of Shamshun's Representative.
THE SHAIKH: An imaginary ghost that appears to Shamshun's Representative.

*Other Characters:*
A MAN, A PUBLICITY MAN, A POLICEMAN
A GROUP OF WORKERS, THE DRILLERS, THE ACTORS

*Time and Location of the Event:*
ACT ONE: The stage in the theatre.
ACT TWO: The stage, twenty years later.
ACT THREE: The stone cities of the desert.
ACT FOUR: The stage in the theatre.

ACT ONE
Scene One

*Darkness envelops the stage. To the left is a high balcony representing part of a factory for wooden puppets. A long line of puppets appears, these moving along a never-ending metal conveyor belt, which goes through the balcony wall and exits, still moving, at another point.*

*The features of the puppets are obliterated; they have a forehead that extends to a mouth occupying most of the face. Each puppet bears a serial number.*

*A large photograph of a woman – ZARQA' AL-YAMAMA – covers the walls in many copies. The photographs are spoiled and full of holes.*

*Part of the balcony is cut off by a wall. Linking the two parts is a small door in the separating wall. The isolated area overlooks the audience through a railing that is an extension of the balcony wall.*

*A large part of this isolated area is occupied by a statue of ZARQA' AL-YAMAMA, made of polished wood. The statue lies within range of a strong light that falls on it continuously, capturing it within its circle. The light exposes numerous thin pins stuck in the area of the statue's eyes, a thin thread wound around the neck, and the two arms pinioned to the body and the legs.*

*The light in the factory is strong. The movement of the puppets never stops.*

PUPPET MASTER (*voice rising from behind the stage*): Don't let the machines stop. Let's have the workers in shifts, so work can keep moving night and day.

*A man enters, short and in his forties, carrying a stack of newspapers. He is followed by a huge man, the SUPERVISOR/SCRIPT WRITER, who is carrying a box of small darts, moving around the PUPPET MASTER and offering his services. Behind them, at the entrance, the RUNAWAY CHARACTER appears, a thin man standing and looking on.*

SUPERVISOR/SCRIPT WRITER (*hands the darts, one after another, to the PUPPET MASTER, who throws them at the photographs of ZARQA' AL-YAMAMA on the walls*): But, sir, we don't need any overtime. Our track record's unequalled. Our products have flooded the markets.
PUPPET MASTER (*throws a dart towards a photograph of ZARQA' AL-YAMAMA; it drops near the RUNAWAY CHARACTER, who remains fixed in his place*): Make sure they stay in the towns – all the towns. Make sure my male puppets fill the streets, the houses, the air, everything. Tear down anything in the way.
SUPERVISOR/SCRIPT WRITER (*firmly*): Nothing to be in the way.
PUPPET MASTER: What about the people?
SUPERVISOR/SCRIPT WRITER: They've opened their doors. Each one's dreaming of a Zarqa' al-Yamama. This scheme of yours has leaked out somehow. Still, it's saved us money on publicity.
PUPPET MASTER: What a stupid lot! They need to be taught a lesson.

SUPERVISOR/SCRIPT WRITER (*rancorously*): And we'll make sure they don't wake up from it.

PUPPET MASTER: Do they think they're speaking the parts?

SUPERVISOR/SCRIPT WRITER: Of course they do, sir. And they play the parts of masters.

PUPPET MASTER (*sniggering*): Well, let them dream! Let's keep the work moving. They've got my big surprise coming their way – puppets that do as they're told. And this is the main outlet. Let's keep the work moving.

SUPERVISOR/SCRIPT WRITER (*with a mock military salute*): No let-up.

PUPPET MASTER (*stopping by a finished puppet with a serial number, examining it closely, then pointing to the line of puppets*): When will this consignment hit the markets?

SUPERVISOR/SCRIPT WRITER (*enthusiastically*): At once. Everything's scheduled. There are sets of serial numbers, in chronological order.

PUPPET MASTER (*snaps his fingers, whereupon the puppet begins to move, smartening up its appearance*): Magnificent! Real precision work! (*Snaps his fingers again.*)

*The sound of a recording is heard coming from the puppet.*

PUPPET: "Only numbers will bring about relative buoyancy. The earthly sphere, flooded by the waters, will take on its old form, before its present one. It will be just a great fish, in a boundless ocean that supports no life but fish."

PUPPET MASTER (*sniggering to the* SUPERVISOR/SCRIPT WRITER): You, Script Writer, let's think up something a lot brighter than that, for the livelier models. Up to four million of them. Then we'll work out a schedule of some sort.

SUPERVISOR/SCRIPT WRITER (*echoes obediently*): Something a lot brighter than that.

PUPPET MASTER (*using all his strength to throw a dart at the chest of* ZARQA' AL-YAMAMA *on the wall*): How naïve I've been!

SUPERVISOR/SCRIPT WRITER (*fawningly*): All this success is thanks to those clever plans you made. You're master of everything that moves, inside and outside.

PUPPET MASTER (*after flinging another vigorous dart*): On the other hand, a whole lifetime, just to make one rebellious puppet – what's that but plain idiocy?

SUPERVISOR/SCRIPT WRITER: But Zarqa' al-Yamama didn't –

PUPPET MASTER (*breaking in abruptly*): No one's to mention her in my presence. (*Sends another dart.*) No one's to mention her. (*His manner becomes authoritative.*) Make sure no one leaves this factory of ours without his number. Just numbers. No more names.

SUPERVISOR/SCRIPT WRITER (*repeats mechanically*): Each to have his number. No more names.

PUPPET MASTER: And make sure everything's scheduled exactly. We don't want any hitches, of any kind.

SUPERVISOR/SCRIPT WRITER: Don't worry, sir. Your schedules are on everyone's lips.

RUNAWAY CHARACTER (*standing by the door, intervening slyly*): And no more Zarqa' al-Yamama after today.

PUPPET MASTER (*gazing gloomily at the* RUNAWAY CHARACTER, *then repeating firmly*): No more Zarqa' al-Yamama after today. (*to the* SUPERVISOR/SCRIPT WRITER) Make sure all the doors are locked in her face.

SUPERVISOR/SCRIPT WRITER (*firmly*): Locked. And we'll harry her to the end.

PUPPET MASTER: To the end. You, personally. (*articulating each letter deliberately*) Make sure she comes quietly.

RUNAWAY CHARACTER (*to the* PUPPET MASTER): I don't see how you've made all this work. All these never-ending puppets, so utterly precise and obedient. And yet here you are, harking back to this Zarqa'. (*The* PUPPET MASTER, *giving no answer, moves gloomily off and enters the isolated section. There he stands gazing at the statue of* ZARQA' AL-YAMAMA. *The* RUNAWAY CHARACTER *follows after him.*) I must understand. (*The* SUPERVISOR/SCRIPT WRITER *exits.*)

PUPPET MASTER (*switching off the pattern of light surrounding the statue, then, as the room is sunk in a pale glow, addressing the statue*): It was an enlightened name. I was the one who gave it to you. Zarqa' al-Yamama. Zarqa' al-Yamama. (*He whispers the name, then repeats it.*) Why did I choose that for you, of all names?

*The voice of* ZARQA' AL-YAMAMA *is heard from behind the stage.*

VOICE OF ZARQA' AL-YAMAMA: I'm going out. (*The statement is repeated in echo.*)

PUPPET MASTER (*glancing malevolently*): Oh no! You're not going anywhere! (*He murmurs the name backwards*) Amamayla. Amamayla. Just leave all that, and come. (*On tiptoe, he climbs the short wooden ladder standing next to the statue and winds the thread yet another time around its neck. He climbs down, moves within the area, and returns with a censer filled with coals. This he raises to the base of the statue, gazing at the statue fiercely.*) We'll see. If reason doesn't bring you back, then my madness will. (*He listens, as if expecting an answer.*) Nothing to say? Good. You're learning. And we'll see how you do come back – more lively and obedient. Not powerless and listless any more, in the face of my wooden armies. (*He begins to kindle the coals, looking at* ZARQA''S *statue over his shoulder, making threatening gestures from time to time.*) You should have frozen right from the start. Outside, everything was getting complex, going round in vicious circles. And I – I kept the fire out. I brought you everything. To you, up here. I brought everything, peacefully, up here. (*He leaves the burning coals and approaches the statue.*) You look at me. You pierce me with your stinging looks. All you want to do is hurt me. I know that. Beyond those pins, I can see your eyes scanning my face, glowing. I didn't ask for anything. (*He softens.*) I only wanted some warmth, a bit of gratitude. Was that so much?

RUNAWAY CHARACTER (*from his position in the rear*): You wanted her to be a puppet, glowing with the torch of gratitude.

PUPPET MASTER (*ignoring his presence, then remembering*): He told me, but I didn't believe it.

*The voice of the* SUPERVISOR/SCRIPT WRITER *is heard from behind the stage.*

VOICE OF SUPERVISOR/SCRIPT WRITER: They're a rebellious lot. You've barely opened the door, before their existence, and they try and take over.

PUPPET MASTER (*climbs the short ladder, stands on tiptoe and brings his face close to that of the statue*): You should have been different.

VOICE OF SUPERVISOR/SCRIPT WRITER (*still echoing from behind the stage*): When he's finished, I leave someone else to shape the personality, in its mould, subduing it. Then, when I'm sure it's fixed in the mould, I come, and I write the dialogue its author wants. Keeping characters in check – that had become the problem.

PUPPET MASTER: I was positive you'd be different. Now him – (*pointing to the* RUNAWAY CHARACTER *behind him*) he came from paper, he was expected to be fragile. But you, (*polishing the edges of the statue admiringly*) you came from the best wood. I created you, created you from the depths of my knowledge and patience – the essence of quintessence. From the journeyman carpenter I was before, I carried you with me till I was the master I am now. I polished you, day after day. And I found you weren't different after all.

VOICE OF SUPERVISOR/SCRIPT WRITER (*still echoing from behind the stage*): You see!

PUPPET MASTER: My assistant, the Supervisor, and Script Writer – he's an imbecile. I know how low his sights are. He stopped writing, the moment he lost the first and last character he brought to life (*looking at the* RUNAWAY CHARACTER) But I, as you see – you're the last thing I lost. (*Adopts a vaunting air.*) But you're not the last thing I made. Look, (*opening the door wide*) lines of them, ready at my service. And you, you're going to join them, obediently. This is what I schemed, rehearsed, vowed, after I turned my back on you and went off.

RUNAWAY CHARACTER: You should have made up your mind what you wanted – a puppet or a woman.

PUPPET MASTER: I said then, the difference was in the eye.

RUNAWAY CHARACTER: She was just a frame, and a white blotch for a face. A thing like that can't spring to life and put warmth in you.

PUPPET MASTER (*with mingled fury and sarcasm*): Naïve as I was, I thought the eye might send a flame into that cold heart.

RUNAWAY CHARACTER: She did glow –

PUPPET MASTER (*breaking in*): Ingratitude, rebellion. And you're the reason. I would have looked after her. She only had to listen and follow. That's what I wanted. But you had to interfere – and I was desperate enough to listen to you.

RUNAWAY CHARACTER: And she defeated you.

PUPPET MASTER (*in a furious rage*): Who are you, anyway, to be discussing my puppet? You don't even have my permission to be here.

RUNAWAY CHARACTER: I don't stand on anyone's permission. I'm a breakaway, as you can see. Beyond even your control.

PUPPET MASTER (*ignoring him and turning to face the statue directly*): It's the name. (*Feverishly, he pronounces her name backwards.*) Amamayla. Amamayla. Let's erase it. Let's wipe it out. Let her forget. Let's obliterate it for her, make her forget. (*He climbs the ladder and sticks a pin in each eye.*) It was my mistake, right from the start. From the moment this hand of mine stretched out, to draw those clear eyes. I made her a wanderer. I – (*The fire from the coals is extinguished, leaving glowing embers. The* PUPPET MASTER *descends and throws some powder over the embers. Blue clouds of incense begin to fill the room. He moves, with the incense, around the base of the statue.*) Let those two gaping eyes be closed, let the two spaces that suck you into ingratitude be stilled. (*He repeats his circular movement seven times, climbs the ladder, and begins to draw the incense towards the eyes.*) The last thing for them to see is my path. (*With his other hand, he sticks a pin in each eye. Then, descending, he places the censer at the feet of the statue and stands there, viewing the clouds of incense as they creep up the body of the statue.*) She stayed inert till she started leading me on. (*He becomes distracted for a time, then returns to himself.*) She led me on with inertness, and I drew the eyes. She had eyes, and still she was silent, a corpse that affronted my pride. (*furiously*) Cunning, that's what she was! She was leading me on. Till I tried names for her.

RUNAWAY CHARACTER: Two eyes; and the third thing was a name. That was your incantation.

PUPPET MASTER: And she liked her name. I uttered it, within her hearing, so many times. And each time I repeated it, she recognized it. I felt it. I felt her throbbing to the name, whispering it with me, a warmth creeping into her, intoxicating me. I was intoxicated, drunkenly repeating it. Repeating it, with no notion of the hell that was gathering inside her, to consume me.

VOICE OF SUPERVISOR/SCRIPT WRITER (*still echoing from behind the stage*): Bringing her out, that was risky. It was risky.

PUPPET MASTER (*to the statue*): And I didn't listen. Didn't hear anything but this thrill, sweeping through me at your mere pulse.

*The voice of* ZARQA' AL-YAMAMA *is heard from behind the stage.*

VOICE OF ZARQA' AL-YAMAMA: According to experts, true cannibals are themselves the murderers in most cases. They're old or sick animals, who've become accustomed to devouring humans. Some victims, though, have fallen to tigers, whose taste for human flesh is still not understood.

PUPPET MASTER (*clapping his hands in glee*): She imitates me. That day she started imitating me. (*He comes abruptly to his senses.*) She started with imitation and ended with rebellion.

VOICE OF ZARQA' AL-YAMAMA (*from behind the stage*): Do you think your flesh is made from wood?

PUPPET MASTER: I should have heard that dangerous ring in her voice. (*addressing the statue*) You deceived me.

VOICE OF ZARQA' AL-YAMAMA (*sarcastically*): I was curious to know if there was someone with a taste for eating wood.

PUPPET MASTER (*to the* RUNAWAY CHARACTER): You heard that? That's her voice! I always manage to evoke her, and she manages to make me angry. She only comes with that ungrateful voice. (*He gazes at the statue.*) Not a shred of gratitude. You weren't created to be beautiful. That's why I can never evoke you in a state of obedience.

VOICE OF ZARQA' AL-YAMAMA (*the echo resounding across the stage*): I'm so tired of paper. If only I could go out to them!

PUPPET MASTER: Go out? Go out to who?

VOICE OF ZARQA' AL-YAMAMA: To the ones who are dying, living on paper.

PUPPET MASTER: I didn't teach you that. I didn't teach you that, Zarqa'.

VOICE OF ZARQA' AL-YAMAMA: I'll go out, and I'll learn, too, why they die. Why they spill on to paper.

PUPPET MASTER (*angrily*): Who put those words in your programme? I'll go out, I'll go out! You repeat it as if you were a puppet! That was created for them – the firewood, kindling in the earth. Your place was always here.

VOICE OF ZARQA' AL-YAMAMA: When I go out, I'll know.

PUPPET MASTER: I warn you. Don't disobey me, and don't repeat those words.

VOICE OF ZARQA' AL-YAMAMA (*the echo coming serenely across*): Don't you see? I'm not a puppet for you to toy with. Not any more.

PUPPET MASTER (*eyes bulging with fury*): Repeat what you've just said!

VOICE OF ZARQA' AL-YAMAMA (*repeating*): Not for you to toy with. Not for you to toy with any more. (*The* PUPPET MASTER *stands on tiptoe and raises his arms, drawing out a huge pin that he sticks in the nape of her neck.*) I *am* your master, you've no life outside my control. (*A door creaks. He begins to entreat,*

*regretfully.*) Wait. I implore you. You don't need to go out. I – I didn't mean
to hurt you. Your anger's beautiful, but I didn't mean – (*An idea comes to him.*)
Listen, the ones you want to see. I – I'll bring them to you. Here.

VOICE OF ZARQA' AL-YAMAMA (*the echo resounding*): Here?

PUPPET MASTER: Look! (*The* RUNAWAY CHARACTER *hands him the stacks of
newspapers. The* PUPPET MASTER *starts spreading them all around the statue.*)
Here they are. Here. They've always been here. Don't you see?

VOICE OF ZARQA' AL-YAMAMA: I shall know why they've always been here.

PUPPET MASTER (*sarcastically*): You want to know? You? Ridiculous! (*A door is
heard creaking shut. The* PUPPET MASTER *loses all vestige of control.*) Come
back! That's an order! (*then, tensely*) Do something. Don't just stand there,
looking. She wants to know. A dangerous puppet, she's seeking knowledge.
(*He sits down on the ladder, then puts his head between his hands, shaking.*) It's my
fault. I'm the one who let out this genie of expectation in her. (*Bursts out
laughing.*)

RUNAWAY CHARACTER: Don't you get bored, repeating this play of yours
every day? Nothing's going to bring *her* back.

PUPPET MASTER (*springing up and shouting defiantly*): She'll come back! The Puppet
Master knows how to bring her back, in submission. (*Climbing up the ladder, he
plucks some long hairs from the scalp of the statue, winds them around a piece of wood the
thickness of a finger. Then, coming back down, he plunges this into the embers. Yellow
smoke rises and fills the room. He begins to mutter.*) Amamayla. Amamayla.
Extinction, extinction, extinction. You'll return extinguished. (*The echo of his
mutterings resounds around the stage. He climbs the ladder, sticks two pins into the eyes of
the statue, winds the thread around the neck three times. Then, satisfied, he climbs down
the ladder and goes out, shutting the door behind him. The* RUNAWAY
CHARACTER *bursts out laughing.*)

End of Scene One


Scene Two

*The stage is in semi-darkness. A circle of light moves on its right side, exposing a wooden barrier
that starts at the front of the stage and ends at the right wall, making a large square with the
remote right-hand corner of the platform. The barrier is a thin wooden strip. The square formed is
more like a balcony overlooking two sides: the darkness on the left-hand side, and the narrow area
facing the audience.*

*On the farthest wall of the balcony – across the depth of the stage – there is an almost
transparent curtain, behind which coloured light swells in blocks. Every now and then, some of its
rays penetrate into the balcony, then dim out.*

*The circle of light focuses on two stage hands. They go mechanically up and spread beneath the balcony – in the narrow strip facing the audience – a path stretching to the left corner. They set a wooden tree on the side of the path, then exit.*

*A* VENDOR *climbs up, carrying a huge basket of vegetables. Her eyes fall on the tree and the path. Approaching, she spreads out her cloak beneath the tree. We see a baby strapped to her back. She unties him, wraps him carefully in a jute bag, then sets him down by her side and begins arranging the vegetables on the cloak.*

*Out of the darkness, a* MAN *emerges. His features are hidden behind his head-dress. He circles cautiously around the* VENDOR.

MAN (*finally approaching and handling the carrots*): What's fresh today?

VENDOR: They're all fresh. In tip-top condition, and they're cheap too. The whole lot for ten riyals.

MAN (*mechanically*): Cheapness. That's what the economic reports have been underlining.

VENDOR (*astonished*): Reports?

MAN: Everything's so much more interesting now.

VENDOR: I don't understand.

MAN (*mechanically*): Wandering the roads, that brings plenty of excitement.

VENDOR: You're being sarcastic, sir.

MAN (*looks at her in mechanical silence, then goes back to examining the vegetables*): So, you're a real vendor, are you?

VENDOR: You can see I am.

MAN (*repeating*): The whole lot for ten riyals.

VENDOR: Yes. And you won't find any vegetables as cheap and fresh as mine are.

MAN: If I were you, I'd hurry off home.

VENDOR (*astonished*): Hurry off home? Why?

MAN (*not looking at her*): The roads aren't safe any more.

VENDOR: Well, I'm a vendor. For as long as I can remember, I've driven my camels and moved my vegetables along the roads. Fear doesn't put bread on the table.

MAN: Haven't you've heard about the explosive puppet?

VENDOR: I don't stay in one place long enough for rumours to catch up with me.

MAN (*mechanically*): Zarqa' al-Yamama's loose. She's wandering the roads, filled with fury.

VENDOR (*confidently*): You city people have some odd contraptions. A puppet that frightens people! (*She rocks the crying baby, without picking him up.*)

MAN: She's been seen in a lot of places. She might pass by here. So be careful.

ZARQA' AL-YAMAMA *emerges from the darkness, barefoot and dishevelled, wearing a loose, stridently multi-coloured dress. Her face bears a perplexed, fearful expression. The sound of the crying baby attracts her attention, and she moves towards him. The moment the man sees her, he begins to distance himself, leaving the carrots behind.*

VENDOR (*calling after him*): Ten riyals, sir. Didn't you like the price?

ZARQA' AL-YAMAMA (*tentatively approaches the baby; the* VENDOR *smiles at her, and, emboldened, she takes the baby and hugs him, exhilarated*): My God! A real baby! (*She sinks her face into the folds of his clothing.*) Like nothing else in the world!

VENDOR (*surprised*): What? Is this really happening? (*The child's crying begins to abate.*)

ZARQA' AL-YAMAMA (*looking closely into the baby's face*): How fresh he is! And his eyes! Like two spots of light, glittering so brightly! (*She passes her finger tenderly over his cheek.*)

VENDOR (*trying to hide her pride*): That's how they are, babies.

ZARQA' AL-YAMAMA (*in astonishment*): All babies?

VENDOR: Yes, of course. A lovely lass you are. When your children come along, they'll be just as lovely and glowing.

ZARQA' AL-YAMAMA (*stroking her belly*): Do you think this belly will bear?

VENDOR (*staring at her, as if seeing her for the first time*): You put me in mind of that light. (*She points at the light dropping from the balcony.*) It comes down, and yet it doesn't come down.

ZARQA' AL-YAMAMA (*becoming aware of the balcony and curtain, and fixing her gaze on them, then looking back to the* VENDOR *and speaking sadly*): Doesn't come down?

VENDOR (*reassuring*): You're young, though, and young people do bear. (*Looks at her closely.*) I seem to know you. Are you from around here?

ZARQA' AL-YAMAMA: Not from around here, no. And you, (*examining her*) you look different from anyone else I've known.

VENDOR: I'm a vendor. I'm not smartly turned out, the way city people are.

ZARQA' AL-YAMAMA (*interrupting her*): I didn't mean that. It's something in the way your face is so peaceful. Something – (*She fails to find the right word.*) I don't know what it is. But I find it comforting.

VENDOR: Contentment, lass. Contentment.

ZARQA' AL-YAMAMA (*triumphantly*): I know you now. You're one of those who are alive! But (*perplexed*) how do they die, and who do they die among? That's what I don't understand. Who decides which one belongs where?

VENDOR: God save us from all this talk of the dead, and. explosive puppets. (*confidently*) Life's stronger, lass. Life's always stronger.

ZARQA' AL-YAMAMA (*reading out the headlines of the larger newspapers*): Earthquake destroys city. Island dwellers wiped out by nuclear waste. Insecticides serious cancer risk to farmers. (*She gazes at the* VENDOR, *who is listening impassively.*) Why do I get the impression death's stronger? Don't you feel frightened? Don't you feel angry?

VENDOR (*calmly*): In our village, lass, I rent a ground floor room with a terrace, giving on to the road. I've turned the terrace into a small field. The instant the sun rises, I start work, and I stop when it sets. All I need for next season is some fertilizer. I've all the seeds I need, but the soil's weak now. The soil supports us for a good while, then it goes weak for a time. My terrace, my narrow field, has nursed this baby; and next he'll crawl about in it. The green will fill his eyes, and he'll grow up to be a handsome man. Why should I feel angry?

ZARQA' AL-YAMAMA: Grow up handsome? In this ugly world?

VENDOR (*reproving*): Ugly? Ask God's forgiveness for being so ungrateful! (ZARQA' *stares at her in alarm. The* VENDOR'S *face softens.*) Listen. When I was still young, I used to herd camels. There was desert all around, there was drought, and nights of hunger. In the fiercest heat, we used to light our fire and rejoice.

ZARQA' AL-YAMAMA: Limited horizons. Personal aspirations.

VENDOR: I don't understand what you're saying. But let me tell you about my village. If my father did ever leave the desert, he'd still leave me there: "a green spot amid desert and stones." They say the spot was sand too. Till a man came. He harnessed the glitter of the sands, they say, and he drew a well. The well gave birth to other wells, and a village. That green spot led many nomads to settle. The man died, but the village – we – lived on. We grew up with that story. Whenever I feel things getting on top of me, I go to the mountain, where the village is. And from there I look out and spot it – the desert with those accursed stones, just steps from the village, waiting. But it never came any closer. It was as if the man's dream had put up a wall around the village! (*She gazes at the rapt* ZARQA'.) And you talk about ugliness and death? We don't die before we've lived. Not before then.

ZARQA' AL-YAMAMA: But what about the earthquakes? The famines and wars?

VENDOR: The soil has the right to get tired. But it starts flourishing again. With me, with my field.

ZARQA' AL-YAMAMA: Haven't you ever had a flood go through your village? Hasn't it left you hungry? Hasn't anyone ever burned your fields? From what I've heard, the whole earth's scorched fields, pillaged. Why do you go on acting like someone who's never heard of all these things?

VENDOR: Floods? What does someone like you know about floods? If a flood comes, then some are lost, but there are still men there. And the men who are still there don't let bitterness eat them up.

ZARQA' AL-YAMAMA: You're alive. You don't like to hear these disasters talked about. That's the difference.

VENDOR: In our village, the birds and the young ones are liveliest just before they go to sleep. And so, from the time the sun sets, we'd rather lend our ears to the streams. There's soon quiet, over everything.

ZARQA' AL-YAMAMA: So, all these disasters, who do people write about them for? I've never seen a face like yours in any news item!

VENDOR: City people have the faces that suit them. A face like mine, what's that to them?

ZARQA' AL-YAMAMA (*gazing at the baby's palm*): If only I had a baby like this!

VENDOR: As long as there's life, you'll have enough of them. You're young and beautiful. Like my vegetables.

ZARQA' AL-YAMAMA (*after a spell of reflection*): You're right. They don't need a face like yours, or (*to the baby*) like the baby's face – with just the one head, and then he grows to be a man. The news isn't like that. It has a thousand and one heads, they multiply, they split to become a beast – and he comes to attack us. (*raising her head to the* VENDOR) You asked me where I'm from, didn't you? I'm from a heap of old, repeated news. (*The* VENDOR *looks at her, astonished. They exchange looks.* ZARQA'*'S eyes fall on the* VENDOR'S *shawl. She exclaims admiringly.*) Your shawl! It's like a piece of the sun!

VENDOR: And your dress is a field of flowers!

ZARQA' AL-YAMAMA: The loveliest thing I've given. (*She lets her gaze wander around her.*) All the time I'm walking, pursued by papers blotched in black. They force their way in, mix themselves up with everything I see. And you. All the time on the roads. Fresh air, and trees. And you're carrying a real baby.

VENDOR: Don't you have a home to go back to?

ZARQA' AL-YAMAMA: No.

VENDOR: I don't think you're from the city. (*perplexed*) I don't think you come from anywhere! (*Looks at* ZARQA'*'S feet.*) You're delicate, like city girls. But they don't go around without shoes.

ZARQA' AL-YAMAMA (*looking happily down at her feet, then striding about the ground*): It's beautiful, the touch of the ground. Sometimes I shut my eyes and leave it to my feet to find out what things are. They can tell shade, the sunshine and the stones. (*The* VENDOR *nods her head in approbation.*) I used to be afraid of these enclosed places. (*pointing to the scene round about her*) Then I decided it was stupid to leave her cocooned in her darkness, just because they wanted her all for themselves. (*The baby begins to fidget. She rocks him, then raises him to her.*) How fresh his smell is! No newspaper smell here!

VENDOR: He doesn't like the grey city air. But the moment I get him back to our room, he'll forget all this irritation.

ZARQA' AL-YAMAMA: Why do you keep him shut up in this bag? Let him loose, so he can fill the place with his screams and wet swaddling clothes. Let them see him, and they'll see the difference.

VENDOR: Difference?

ZARQA' AL-YAMAMA: Why don't you let him loose?

VENDOR (*astonished*): Here? (*sarcastically*) Even vegetables won't grow here. The air's stagnant.

ZARQA' AL-YAMAMA (*gazing at the ceiling of the theatre*): If we open it, the sunlight will come streaming in.

VENDOR (*despairingly*): I don't think it opens.

ZARQA' AL-YAMAMA: There must be some way.

VENDOR: Yes, there must be. (*changing the subject*) Would you like any of my vegetables?

ZARQA' AL-YAMAMA (*her eyes lighting up with a sudden idea*): You've come from a village where all the men are healthy, a village crammed with real babies. That's right isn't it?

VENDOR: We're mostly a healthy lot in my village, that's true.

ZARQA' AL-YAMAMA (*enthusiastically*): So, why don't they all come here? They could fill this place, open it up. All the closed places. Do you know what it is, this place where you've spread out your vegetables?

VENDOR (*indifferently*): It's a road where I sell.

ZARQA' AL-YAMAMA: It's a theatre.

VENDOR (*shrugging her shoulders*): As long as there are people who buy.

ZARQA' AL-YAMAMA: As long as it's a theatre, no one's going to buy. Everyone sells. (*Seeing the* VENDOR *is disturbed, she changes the subject.*) Would you like me to tell his fortune? (*She points at the baby.*)

VENDOR: What fate's in store for a peasant except farming?

ZARQA' AL-YAMAMA (*fixing her eyes on the darkness to the left*): Unless the bank of green grows greater, the tide of black will spill over to swallow it. Bystanders will be at an end.

VENDOR: You're frightening me. As if you were a real fortune teller! (*hesitating*) I thought I was going to sell my vegetables. (*She hears an approaching commotion.* ZARQA' AL-YAMAMA *puts down the baby and carefully withdraws, towards the darkness. The* VENDOR *calls after her.*) Wait. Let me sell my vegetables, and. I'll go with you to the village. (ZARQA' AL-YAMAMA *hesitates, then vanishes into the darkness.*)

The SUPERVISOR/SCRIPT WRITER *enters, followed by the* RUNAWAY CHARACTER. *The* VENDOR *pays no attention to them, still looking where* ZARQA' AL-YAMAMA *has vanished.*

RUNAWAY CHARACTER (*whispering to the* SUPERVISOR/SCRIPT WRITER): Suppose I were to get to her ahead of you and spoil your scenarios for you?

SUPERVISOR/SCRIPT WRITER (*angrily warning*): Just you try it. You'll end up with some scratches from my pen.

RUNAWAY CHARACTER (*laughing*): Oh, the time for all that's over and past. You can see that. I'm not at the mercy of your pen any more.

SUPERVISOR/SCRIPT WRITER (*looking towards the* VENDOR): She's still here. Just as the latest reports said she would be. We've come in time.

RUNAWAY CHARACTER: Just a puppet, you said. So, let her melt into the great peasant mass. Where's the harm, anyway, in her being together with a baby?

SUPERVISOR/SCRIPT WRITER (*rebuking him*): You just don't understand matters of this sort. She has a knowledge that won't let her melt. You just don't understand this kind of thing. (*He approaches the* VENDOR *and starts handling the vegetables, while she watches him in silence.*) What amazes me is, you never get bored. (*without raising his eyes to her*) You go around with these vegetables, the same old vegetables, as if you supposed they were going to stay fresh for you.

VENDOR (*re-arranging the vegetables*): I'm not saying they're today's pick. But they're better than anything on offer in the big supermarkets.

SUPERVISOR/SCRIPT WRITER: The big supermarkets! (*looking intently at the* VENDOR) It's a good thing vegetables aren't like us. We can carry all the decay inside us and look (*stretching out his fingers to touch her face from a distance*) so beautiful and proud! (*She turns her face away. He smiles at the movement.*) You're hungry, aren't you?

VENDOR (*unthinking*): Not exactly. When buyers don't come along, and the time's up for one sort of vegetable – (*She does not finish, her gaze following the* RUNAWAY CHARACTER *as he picks up a tomato and starts gulping it down.*)

SUPERVISOR/SCRIPT WRITER (*finishing for her*): Aha! You finish it off. The dying, the dying! (*He laughs loudly, and the* RUNAWAY CHARACTER *joins in.*) I can just see it. One day they'll all be dying together, and you'll end up with indigestion. A rare feast!

VENDOR (*somewhat irritated*): What is it you want? You've handled everything. Either buy something, or go away.

RUNAWAY CHARACTER (*wipes his hand on his clothes*): That's just his way. He's a joker. You won't change him.

SUPERVISOR/SCRIPT WRITER: You know, your sitting here, it's illegal. Just like my chatting with you.

VENDOR: I can't go hungry just because I don't own a shop.

SUPERVISOR/SCRIPT WRITER (*smiling coldly*): That's what they all say. Just stick to realistic talk, and I could use you in a play, or for the part of a vendor if I was offered one.

VENDOR (*intensely uncomfortable*): Just what is it you want?

RUNAWAY CHARACTER (*walking around the* VENDOR *and baby*): Their factories don't stop. (*He points to the* SUPERVISOR/SCRIPT WRITER.) You don't stop giving birth. The problem is, you've gone beyond the bounds. You've aroused the appetite of puppets, ahead of their master's. Unless we can find some proper form of disengagement, drastic measures will have to be taken.

SUPERVISOR/SCRIPT WRITER (*paying no attention to him*): You don't know me. That's what makes me feel I want to talk to you.

RUNAWAY CHARACTER: I'll introduce him to you. He's only a drummer's grandson.

VENDOR (*astonished*): A drummer? You?

SUPERVISOR/SCRIPT WRITER (*angrily*): Just a piece of coal. Burned right out. And I can – (*hesitating*) No. Let's find a better word. I'm committed to being your chief representative. For all those who toil, indeed.

VENDOR (*not understanding*): Committed?

RUNAWAY CHARACTER (*sarcastically*): A part that's taken hold of him. From a novel he's been adapting just lately. But he's got the tempo of a real drum, you can't deny it.

SUPERVISOR/SCRIPT WRITER (*bellowing furiously at the* RUNAWAY CHARACTER): You don't believe in me! I set you free, and yet you don't believe in me!

RUNAWAY CHARACTER (*indifferently*): Actually, it's not my business to believe in you or not. Besides – (*sarcastically*) you didn't set me free. You wanted to lock me up in a stupid part. I've decided to be anything I want. Every morning I decide on a part for myself, and I become it. Every morning, I discover a beautiful side to myself. Until – (*beating his chest*) until I fill this gaping void here.

SUPERVISOR/SCRIPT WRITER (*to the* VENDOR): As you can see, he's just a part-formed embryo. Let me explain to you why the Puppet Master –

RUNAWAY CHARACTER (*breaking in*): Can't you see, for God's sake? These are peasants. All they believe in is fertility. And my sort of fertility isn't going to hold her breathless.

SUPERVISOR/SCRIPT WRITER (*trying to stimulate her interest*): You'll understand. You've felt sympathy with a puppet, why not with their master.?

VENDOR: Please, sir. Don't –

SUPERVISOR/SCRIPT WRITER (*interrupting her*): If you can just find time to listen to a story.

VENDOR (*her patience running out*): My vegetables can't find time.

SUPERVISOR/SCRIPT WRITER (*insistently*): Do you know the Puppet Master?

VENDOR: I don't know anyone here.

SUPERVISOR/SCRIPT WRITER: Our relations – the master's and mine – started in the time of our grandfathers. His grandfather was a poet, he was close to a leader who had anyone who opposed him deported from his republic. His words, like my grandfather's drums, would kindle in the spirits of the soldiers a fire that never goes out. The chain of commitment started from there.

RUNAWAY CHARACTER (*sarcastically*): One of them turned his pen into a carrot, which he tied in front of the donkey's nose. As for the other one – (*sadly*) have you heard the sounds of the drums? (*frowning*) The drums have beats that waken *jinn*, beats that draw tears. (*He fixes his eyes on the* SUPERVISOR/SCRIPT WRITER.) His grandfather strangled the *jinn* and the tears in their skins, left them roaring out dry sounds that wakened the donkeys to a frenzy for killing. The day of his assassination, they castrated their better natures and took comfort in croaking. And now – this (*indicating the* SUPERVISOR/SCRIPT WRITER) and his master boast they're going to resurrect everything.

SUPERVISOR/SCRIPT WRITER: The Puppet Master, and we after him, are worthy heirs of that heritage of struggle. (*to the* VENDOR, *who has lost interest in them*) You hear that?

VENDOR (*with annoyance*): What do I have to do with you? Can't you find somewhere else to quarrel? (*The* RUNAWAY CHARACTER *bursts out laughing.*)

SUPERVISOR/SCRIPT WRITER (*contemptuously*): My God! What ignorance! A quarrel – is that the only thing you can see in all this? This is history, you vulgarian! What do I care whether you understand or not? It's in your own interest to believe the Puppet Master is the last of the heroes. That his judgements are sound, and that you've no cause for alarm. Do you understand?

VENDOR: What I understand is, you don't want to buy anything.

SUPERVISOR/SCRIPT WRITER: Do you know the enormity of my viewing myself as ugly? No, you're just a simple woman, you can't face a situation like that. With a little awareness, you can be ugly, and see your ugliness. But you lack awareness.

VENDOR: Perhaps you mean well. Either way, you're interrupting my business.

SUPERVISOR/SCRIPT WRITER: All right then, you don't want to hear about my history and my master's history. Suppose I talk about you? Briefly: you're representative of a type. Your standpoint is an idealized one, of struggle. You want to sell. Have a shop. Wealth. That's what you want, deep down, but you don't come out and say it. None of what you want comes about. You pretend to be content, aloof sometimes. You turn down chances offered by the likes of us. You regard shop owners the way you do ravening beasts. You imagine that, with time, you'll even turn down the chance of a shop, even if it should come your way. (*She wants to break in, but he raises his hand.*) Let me finish. What I'm saying is extremely insightful. I'm not being critical. Take me, for instance. I'm one of a long line of those who adopt standpoints. When those who were fortunate overtook us, we proudly turned our backs on fortune. Then, under pressure of circumstances, we resorted to flattery, and to offering our services to the fortunate. What I want to say is this: you have a perfect right to this pride, as I have to flattery. But the fortunate Puppet Master – he isn't under any obligation to pretend rejection, or contentment. He has the right to take publicly. He has the right to demand blind obedience. Isn't that right?

VENDOR: You seem to be an important man. What's your need to tell me everything you've done? Who are you?

RUNAWAY CHARACTER (*breaking in*): In his present task, he and I are alike: two wanderers pursuing an illusion.

VENDOR: It doesn't look as if I'm going to understand anything.

SUPERVISOR/SCRIPT WRITER: You'll understand. (*He claps his hands. At once a wooden handcart emerges from the darkness, drawn by two men, identically dressed and mechanical in their movements. The* VENDOR *gives a start on seeing them.*)

VENDOR (*stunned*): The municipal supervisor? (*to the* SUPERVISOR/SCRIPT WRITER) You! (*The* SUPERVISOR/SCRIPT WRITER *silently turns his back on her. The two men start collecting the vegetables and dumping them roughly into the cart. The* RUNAWAY CHARACTER *stands indifferently by.*)

VENDOR (*pleading*): Please! I'll go away from here. Let me leave with my vegetables, just this once. They're the last pick of the season. You won't find me on the road after these.

SUPERVISOR/SCRIPT WRITER (*calmly*): It hurts me as much as it hurts you. (*The two men carry off the tree as well, leaving the road.*)

RUNAWAY CHARACTER (*sarcastically*): Leave the tree at least.

SUPERVISOR/SCRIPT WRITER (*gazing at her for the last time*): I'm afraid you're legally bound to get yourself a shop and a proper license. I take it you understand that at least.

VENDOR (*pleading*): And today's meal? (*She tries to hold on to the cart. One of the men pushes her, and she falls on to the road.*)

SUPERVISOR/SCRIPT WRITER (*leaving behind the cart*): These simpletons bring heartache on themselves.

*The* VENDOR *remains there on the road, stunned, till they disappear from sight. After a while she gets up and moves mechanically towards the jute bag in which the baby was lying. She discovers, to her horror, that they have taken him with them too. She rushes, screaming, towards the darkness into which the cart has vanished.*

RUNAWAY CHARACTER (*looking calmly after her*): There's no need to get so worked up. Your part's finished now.

*She disappears.*
*An* ONLOOKER *from the audience shouts out in protest against the contents of the script, making to climb up on to the platform.*

ONLOOKER: They took the baby!

RUNAWAY CHARACTER (*to the* ONLOOKER): Why don't you do something
     then?
ONLOOKER (*protesting*): I'm just an onlooker!
RUNAWAY CHARACTER (*rancorously*): *You* are just an onlooker. And *this* (*pointing
     around him*) is a theatre. And *he* (*pointing to where the* SUPERVISOR/SCRIPT
     WRITER *has disappeared*) is the Supervisor and Script Writer. And *he* – the
     one you're so desperately concerned about – is the new actor. There's no
     place for tolerance with real babies.

*The* ONLOOKER *stares at him in amazement, while the* RUNAWAY CHARACTER
*moves off, following everyone else. From the darkness,* ZARQA' AL-YAMAMA *emerges, then
looks around her, searching for the* VENDOR.

ONLOOKER (*to* ZARQA'): They've kidnapped the baby!

*She freezes in her place, then lets out a stifled scream. She glimpses the curtain and makes a sudden
rush towards it. She goes beyond the wooden barrier, through the coloured curtain, and her shadow
disappears beyond it.*

*Ahmad al-Mulla*

# THE PROMPTER
(al-mulaqqin)

[The play does not have a cast of characters in the normal sense. Visual action is dominated by the interplay of light and shadowy outline, while the different roles are predominantly assumed by a single voice. The format of the text reflects this unconventional arrangement. – EDITOR]

*SCENE: A fabric screen falling across the length and breadth of the space like an empty tableau. The place is enveloped in darkness.*
*The screen is lit from behind. A shadow is highlighted to reveal the form of a man gradually coiling up and shrinking till it becomes a parrot in a cage. The shadow vanishes.*

VOICE: I'm just a tongue – a tongue that hasn't tasted the sweetness of light, or savoured the milk of song, a tongue that hasn't ascended the ladder of desires; content only to savour the crumbs of whispers and regurgitated words, repeating words long extinguished. Yes, I'm just a shrunken tongue, a wasted thing like the appendix, to be removed one day. For such a tongue is like a razor in the throat.

*Abruptly, the light falls on the centre of the fabric screen, to reveal a wooden board bearing a small dome for a theatrical prompter, descending from the ceiling as far as the screen's midpoint. From here emerges the upper part of a man, his hands resting on the board.*
*Sensing the light, the man wakes suddenly, with a shriek, grasping and feeling his neck as though choking.*

What? Did I doze off? Did I fall asleep again? Oh, I'm a man who digs his own grave with his dreams.

If they only knew how I dream, if they got to learn of the dream that stalks me on the threshold of sleep, seizing hold of me, bearing me down paths I've never seen. Oh!

I mustn't fall asleep. That way the dream won't find a way in. But they must know I've dreamed, they must know what I've dreamed, nothing's hidden from them. It's a curse that's afflicted me. I have to wipe it out, before it spreads to my whole body.

If they once get to learn of it, they won't leave any trace of me. How many nights have passed? Night comes, leaving me wakeful in its pit. I wake the moment I sleep, like one who's been bitten, searching for the tell-tale marks of a fang. More than that – searching for the traces of the dream, a dream that's furrowed my head like a plough – that's changed the flow of my life, bearing me over fields whose trees I've never seen before. (*He speaks these words in a dream-like tone.*)

What is this? I'm acting like a man ready to give up his head. What if they knew what I've just said? They know everything, I'm sure they do – yes, because they hear and they see, they monitor everything that happens – because these walls are theirs.

I remember when they built them, to separate the actors one from another. Let each one of you, they said, have a house to shelter him and his family.

They built low ceilings, and so our heads are bowed, our gaze can't scan the horizons. They must have heard me through these walls. You, the dream that's roused me from my torpor; you, the dream that's opened my eyes – how am I going to forestall this? They'll question me, I'm sure they will.

*A scene of interrogation is lit up. A man can be seen tied to a chair; a beam of light is focused on his face. A man is standing directly behind him. A blow falls on the nape of the man's neck.*

Huh?

Your name and address?

M-my name's tongue. M-my address is the dome of the stage. I was an actor in – (*A slap is heard.*)

We know all that. When did you last sleep?

Almost a year ago.

According to our information, in the period since then you've sneaked off to sleep, and you've dreamed.

Huh – huh?

How dare you dream? Who was behind this?

*The* VOICE is silent.

Confess! Don't you know the penalty for this?

What? No – no.

*The shadow vanishes.*

After all those performances, all that hard work and obedience, they spit me out. No. That won't happen, they need me too much. They can't afford to lose me. Who's going to set the actors on the right path if it gets crooked. Who's going to be their guide if they go astray – except me?

How are they going to work without me? I'm the one who restores sense to words – and returns wisdom to dialogue. I'm the invisible watch over the theatre. I'm the one who warns them when they go wrong. No, they won't abandon me. The life of actors is brimful of mistakes, their mistakes are wounds that I heal, and, no, they can't do without my neck. All these years I've mended what they spoiled. They depart from the text, and I bring them back, I make it my business to catch them out. They forget and I remind them – I'm the honest shepherd of words. I won't let them be injured, or destroy their own lives, at the hands of actors who have trouble memorizing things and speaking things. They come and they go, struck with fright, they stumble on a waft of air, they stammer over each letter; while I – I, who remember all, set them straight and guide them to the right path.

*He grows a little calmer, then goes back to his earlier statement, his fear gradually rising.*

But – if they knew what I dream, they'd destroy me. A curse on whoever woke the mania of dreams! It's eating away at my brains. Oh, my head! Here it is at my neck – in my breast, my hand and my heart.

Oh, they're watching me this very moment, I know they are. I'm a castaway who'll be flung overboard – no, I'm not that important to them – that's the truth, the naked truth.

Despite the way I described myself – I'm a small lie that I nurtured till it grew big, I can't hide the truth any more. So what am I?

The shepherd of words – enough of this vanity. I'm not really that. I'm just a failed actor they coaxed into staying on, to be a prompter and monitor words. I watch the actors, fixing them with my eyes; I don't sleep, my eyes are unwinking.

Here I lie at the actors' feet, hidden so no one can see me, like a stigma. I speak in whispers and signs, because my voice isn't allowed. My feet have forgotten how to walk, my body's grown flabby with lack of movement, until I've become just a tongue. And such a tongue! A tongue like a parrot's that repeats, reiterates what it's told, a tongue that doesn't

create, regurgitating what it commits to memory, as though it had no brains.
My very life I've imprinted like that. I don't venture, don't initiate. I just
speak after others have spoken, I've nothing to add except to correct the
words they stumble over, dictating one or two of them. That's my part, the
one I play like a blind nonentity. Everyone ignores me, as though I didn't
exist, as though I hadn't been one of them once. And yet I do exist, and they
can't have their performances unless I'm there.

A nobody, they say. Well, so be it. But I can turn their performances
upside down, I can change a word here or there – stop helping them if they
depart from the text – close my eyes and abandon them. Because those who
take centre stage – they take on parts they're not cut out for, put on faces
that aren't their own. So many times I've been tempted to leap up, thrust
them aside and play their parts instead.

It's like a shadow rebelling against someone who's betrayed himself,
flinging him aside, to live his life in his place.

Yes, I can take on all their parts. They can't fill them, it's as though
they've no connection with what they say. I know they have different ideas
from the ones they speak straight out. Just look at the way they act.

*The lighting reveals the shadow of a woman sitting and quietly sewing.*

Take that woman, for example, who's saying goodbye to her son.

Goodbye – don't forget to write – goodbye. Then she becomes
engrossed with her friends, mending a frayed dress, her pain below the surface, pouring through the threads she sews. Why doesn't she fling that faded
dress from her shoulders, and shriek out at him? (*He takes on the part of the
woman.*)

What, son – you're leaving me here alone, in this emptiness? Let the
breast that fed you dry up! Go off then. May I lose you but not my
livelihood.

*The shadow vanishes. He leaves the part.*

The son goes on his way, his head bowed, as though leaving a house strange
to him. He doesn't hesitate, or pause. Had I been in his place, here's what I
would have said:

*He takes on the part of the son. The shadow of a young man is lit up, with a stick on his back
from which a bundle is hanging.*

O mother, I'm not thankless, or estranged from you. But there's a question
tormenting me. I have to search for an answer to it, there's no other way.

O mother, I'll come back, bearing the mark of longing on my breast, the crown of knowledge on my head. It's the homeland I seek, able to embrace me.

*The shadow is extinguished.*

*He leaves the part.*

And the story-teller. The one who sits in the corner narrating, trying to entertain his listeners, with descriptions of played out corpses into which he tries to breathe life – even though they're decayed and lifeless. In his place I'd cry out at the scene.

*The shadow of a shaikh is picked out, standing on a high platform, one hand gesturing, the other leaning on a cane.*

*He takes the part of the story-teller.*

They halted at another turn of the road – moaning for a time.
Wheels and feet.
The crashing of a tide. Through the waves I could see their eyes peering out, intently, as if expecting some long delayed arrival. We leapt to console them. Don't worry, they said. We've been hearing it for a while now – the echo of his footsteps returning.

*The shadow vanishes.*

*He leaves the part.*

So, what do you think? Aren't I a fine actor? Yes – I know what you're going to say. There's no need to say it anyway – here, from this spot, I can say whatever I like. And when I was one of them, I couldn't say anything.
What's happening? Have I lost my rancour towards them? Yes, I still feel I'm one of them, I still feel pain at their pain – and joy, at their joy. It must be because of that – the spark of the dream that's woken and restored me. Oh, this pain inside my head!
Oh, you dream that's sprouted in my breast. The moment I sleep, you stretch your branches into my head, your roots sprout in my heart – oh –

*The shadow of a child is lit up. He looks up, then starts to run, raising his hands.*

For a year, I've dreamed – the same dream.
I dream of the sun – I dream that I raise my head – and see –

I pluck a bird from my breast, like a stifled sigh, and set it free to
flutter. And I run after it, I run like a child tugged on by a kite.
          Oh, sun, sun, sun!

*Suddenly, he stands on an elevated step, gazing out and singing.*

Approach
There's nothing behind the sands but bygone mountains
Approach
The road invites you
The faint lanterns
Signal you on
Approach
The sand has preserved no similar footprints
It has no memory of them
You'll stumble over twisted necks
Wrapped around ashes lacking warmth
Their murmured elegy
For one dying will follow you
You'll cross wasted fields
That will take you into a void
Search for a sigh that will pierce the darkness
Search for embers that burn up ash
I returned across the fields, trembling with song
Peasants were stooping, scattering seed on the ways
No one sheltered me.

*The shadow vanishes.*

Oh dream that makes them tremble, still I'm quivering.
I quiver with love for actors worn out by the burden
Of their pains – I'm one of them.
The same dream encompasses us all.
Search in the shadows, you'll find us, besieged by darkness
In the corners, till we wilt.
We merit the parts, they steal them from us.
Then it is that the scales are tilted,
Those lacking all glow float on the surface;
They're like bulls blocking the way, like thorns along the road.
You leave with a sense of outrage,
You regret you came, angry with everyone.
But you haven't looked with care.

You haven't plunged in our darkened sea,
Content to stand on the shores, fearful of the water,
Denouncing what you've seen as charade –
Not knowing what passes in the dark, behind the ramparts,
Behind the curtain. What do you know of that?
If you knew that voices rising in song are stifled, muzzled;
That, if an actor wished to utter new words,
The voices would be garbled, reaching you distorted!
Or else the actors would fall dumb,
Communing with each other through signs and gestures.
Then the lights would be switched away from the one dancing
To pick out a scowling face.
Ugliness they expose, hide beauty.
Light is withheld from the place, as though
A bat joyfully sucked in the darkness.
Darkness; the actors feel their way,
Finding just ugly surfaces to rest their hands,
A décor they're not at home with,
That makes them estranged.
They know, more than ever, that someone seeks to mislead them,
Someone reaps profit from the way they're lost.
They say what they're told to say, abject, submissive.
Those who grasp their distress find nowhere to spread it
To dry in the eye of the sun.
Rather, their fingers probe the wound that's still wet,
Powerless to grasp the roots of the fear pulsing deep.
Instead of laying bare and pointing in indictment,
It's they who stand exposed.
Who is it shapes the words that live and grow in us,
Where pain is deep and joy is the fruit?
Tell me, who plays us music
Whose chords catch at our heart?
Oh musicians,
Come let us pool our lost voices.
It's time now.
Oh sin we bear on our shoulders,
Errors along the way,
Who is it plants them within us,
Revealing them as truth?
Who is it did this?
Is it the text? Or the lighting? The décor?
I'm floundering – close to madness – who is it plans all this?

Who stands behind those fingers?
Who sets off this nameless thing, this charade?
Yes,
The same who drove me to monitor
The actors' friends – he it is
Who gave masks to those colluding with him.
I shall expose them all.

*The light goes out abruptly.*

The lighting engineer. Ah, but he's one of them.
I shan't need him, he's the engineer of darkness.

*He lights a candle, grasps the end of it, and cries out.*

This is the start of the thread; and now I'll twine it around your necks,
One by one. Come down, so I can expose you – you won't be able –

*The loudspeaker is switched off.*

You won't be able to shut out my voice.
I'll depart from the text – I'll light my fingers for candles.
I'll cry: Oh you, who depict false burdens to lead us astray,
Who worship the dark, cutting off throbbing voices,
Estranging the place,
Hollowing out the spirit,
Drowning the audience in trivia – and actors,
Actors are jerked like puppets.
Enough – enough – You've made our lives
A hearse – and it's we who draw it,
Moving submissive and blindfold, turning, turning, never arriving.
Oh dream, touch us all – inspiring actors
Who haven't yet seen what lurks behind those skins,
Who haven't discerned who hides behind those masks,
Who haven't seen yet the skeletons, the empty skulls.

*Lights suddenly intersect. There is a sound of laughter rising and a clamour of voices.*

My loved ones, you who play parts that they draw, awake!
They chose you for likeness, for sameness of face.
They tampered with the text, and you swallowed it,
They tamed you till you bore the imprint of their words,

Seeing no other.
Abandon a text that's dead, shake the sand from your buried bodies,
Dig up the past for your chained spirits.
Unchain them, so they can fly, can open up the horizon,
Come out – come out.
You, (*pointing to the shadow*) when you wake from your sleep,
And brush your teeth with the morning brush – don't look down in the
    basin,
Like a fool, at the running water – dare, gaze in the mirror.
Gaze in the mirror, gaze well, you'll be amazed.
You're not as they describe, and you're not what you were.
Don't turn your back on the mirror and bow your head,
As it says in the text – raise your head, leap into your bosom in the mirror,
    bring out,
Bring out what's left in your pocket, of your life's provisions,
And all that's left to you
May suffice for the first step.

*The first shadow ceases to move.*

*The other shadow begins to quiver.*

You, (*pointing to the second shadow*) don't enter.
Entry is only for those who've exited first.
You need so much to exit.
You need your self, search for it outside them.
When they're done with you, they'll discard you like waste.
What are these graves but traps and snares, that they lure you into
With the mighty fanfare
The living believe is homage to the dead?
The dead know
It's just the last mutter over a sacrifice.

*The second shadow ceases to move, and the puppets and dolls begin moving once more.*

They know that one more person is added to those duped.
Come out from your texts – Come out from your graves.
Come out from your homes – Come out from your clothes.
Come out, come out!

*The rope lying alongside him wraps itself around his hands, binding them.*

*All the shadows begin to shake and tremble, and go on doing so.*

You won't need my voice any more,
You won't need any voice but your own.
You'll come out.
You'll reach the road,
Dancing the burning words.
The light's warm.
Between your hands: a child dreaming of the future
A girl seeking hope – a boy helping her.
Wild fields.
There you are crossing – crossing.
I see you, *(with pain)* but I don't see myself among you.
Hey, friends, take me with you,
Take me with you!

*The rope twines completely around him. His head slumps down on the table, extinguished like the candle that had burned for him.*

*Muhammad al-'Utheim*

# THE LEAN YEARS
### (al-sineen al-'ijaf)

*Characters*:
SHAIKH OF THE TRIBE
SOOTHSAYER OF THE TRIBE
'UMAIRA, A NOTABLE OF THE TRIBE
SUBH, A NOTABLE OF THE TRIBE
OTHER NOTABLES
GUARDS FROM THE TRIBE
SOLDIER FROM THE TRIBE
AL-MUHALHIL, CHIEF OF ANOTHER TRIBE
HASIM, AN INTERMEDIARY
SECRETARY TO HASIM
CLIENT OF HASIM
CHORUS
CROWDS OF VARIOUS KINDS

First Tableau:
The Rules of the Game

*The stage should be prepared to represent the encampment of one of the small tribes in existence during the days of the Basous War. Though the war was all around them, the tribe was not in fact a participant. The décor should adopt no descriptive style specific to the tribe; it should rather leave the place abstract, and it should indicate the historical era in a naturalistic fashion, with, however, the possibility of changing the décor quickly to become the luxurious office of an intermediary, furnished in the style of the present century. It may even be changed to a barren desert, or to a conference table filling up the stage. Should the technicians find difficulty in this regard, it will be sufficient to have a fabric screen; connected at the back of the stage, exactly in the centre, to a metre-high upright pole, and at the front to an upright pole mounted on a wheel, making it possible to*

*move the curtain diametrically in all directions of the stage. The length of the curtain will be adjusted by folding or unfolding it around the front pole. (The director is free to adopt this suggestion, or any other he might find better for expressing the intention.)*

*The stage should be lit to depict a mixture of past and present, in a criss-cross that hints at indefinable correspondences between the twentieth century and the days of the Basous War. The* SOOTHSAYER *then stands in the centre to separate the eras, but* HASIM *slips between the eras without the* SOOTHSAYER *seeing him.*

*The present period disappears, and the past remains, after the end of the following song.*

CHORUS (*sings*):
> Kulaib has died to avenge al-Basous,
> Bujair has died to avenge Kulaib.
> The times pass.
> Your quern turns on,
> The quern of war grinds above the heads.
> A stranger comes,
> A man unknown.

*In the tribe's encampment a bloodless contest is in process, the victor of which will be proclaimed Protector of the Howdah and bridegroom to the most beautiful of the tribe's maidens. The contest is attended by the* SHAIKH OF THE TRIBE, *he being the one expert in the game's set of four rules. A various audience is in attendance, made up of knights awaiting their turn to compete, the common people, all who make up a large attendance.*

AUDIENCE (*amid the tumult*):
> Finish the game, Subh!
> Bring him down, Subh!
> Look, he's retreating. Take him from the right flank.
> Keep him away from the colonnade of the tent.
> He's shielding himself from you.
> Bravo! Bravo, Subh!
> Finish before noon, can't you? So we can see the victorious knight.
> The sun's already past noon.

'UMAIRA: Jahsh is the knight. Jahsh, brother, why are you delaying your victory?

SHAIKH (*silencing the audience and striking his sounding plate*): The sun's gone, and here
> we are still, in the afternoon. Stop the contest. Stop the contest!

AUDIENCE (*resentfully*): Oooooh!

SUBH (*stops the contest, approaches the* SHAIKH *and throws his sword down in front of him*):
> No, shaikh, the contest shouldn't be stopped. I'm on the point of finishing it
> off. Let me finish it. It's time it was finished. Let me finish it. It's time it was
> finished.

'UMAIRA: You won't finish it, Subh, if you go on duelling for a year. You must realize, my brother's just stringing things out, for some reason of his own. He'll finish with you sooner or later.

SUBH: You'll see, 'Umaira. This brother of yours won't last long before me. (*striking a pose*) Look! Can he do this? Ha, what do you say? When I've finished him off, it'll be your turn. The gleam of my sword, in the morning sun, will be enough to fill you with terror. You'll see.

'UMAIRA (*unsheathing his sword*): Duel with me and you'll see. Ha! You'll see when my turn comes up.

SHAIKH (*ending the argument between them*): The third rule of the game involves the Parchment of the Secret. And we're in the afternoon now.

SUBH: But the tribe knows, shaikh, I'm the one fit to play the game.

SHAIKH: He'll be a mighty knight who can finish it before noon. Those were the words of our soothsayer in the cave of 'Akraf.

SUBH: I'm a mighty man. Why shouldn't I be the knight to do it? Are these two doing it? Or is there something in the game – (*He leaves his words hanging, and the* SHAIKH *ignores his insinuation.*)

SHAIKH: You're mighty. But you're not the knight. You're not the one.

SUBH (*angrily*): Or maybe that's not the game. Or perhaps you want it for my cousin Kilda.

SHAIKH: Woe to you, Subh. What are you saying?

SUBH: In the days of our ancestors, it finished early in the day. Then we'd devote the rest of our day to the rituals of the Howdah. But now – now, the years pass, the termites devour the edges of the Howdah, and the Parchment of the Great Secret. Nothing changes. And you stop the contest at the decisive moment. Why, shaikh? Look at them, they laugh when I duel.

SHAIKH: Do they laugh with you or at you?

SUBH: I'm simply asking you. Why don't you give me time to finish it?

*The audience appears interested in this argument between the* SHAIKH *and the knight* SUBH.

SHAIKH: Because the knight hasn't appeared. We're waiting for him, in accordance with the rules of the game.

SUBH: Or maybe that isn't the game at all.

'UMAIRA: He's doubting. Did you hear that, shaikh?

SHAIKH: Do you doubt the certainty of the game's rules?

NOTABLES AND AUDIENCE (*murmuring and wondering*):

He deserves death.

He's doubting – doubting the honesty of the game.

Ask the soothsayer.

You need the soothsayer. The soothsayer, he has certain knowledge of this.

The Parchment of the Secret. Bring the Parchment of the Secret and read it to him!

SHAIKH: Be calm. The soothsayer from the cave of 'Akraf will pass judgement on him, if he doubts.

SUBH: No, let reason rule. Why not let the game finish?

SHAIKH: We shall try you in the light of certainty, as made manifest in the Parchment of the Secret.

AUDIENCE (*in turmoil*):

Kill Subh!

No, take away his right to duel. Let him mind the sheep.

You being too kind to him, shaikh.

Devils have taken hold of him.

SHAIKH: Quiet! Quiet, I say! The soothsayer will pass judgement on him. His punishment will serve as a lesson to the knights of the alliances, recounted through the years, from ancestors to descendants. Then you will see the knight who'll protect the domain.

*Two men enter, pulling behind them a man in full modern dress. He has an elegant handsome appearance. The* AUDIENCE *is silent.*

SHAIKH: What's this? Who are you?

GUARDS: We found him wondering in the cave of 'Akraf.

SHAIKH: A disaster. This is infamy, dishonour! Stranger, what are you doing in our domain? Your dress suggests, somehow, my clever grandchildren, a thousand and one years from now. Don't you know, whoever enters the cave of 'Akraf dies?

AUDIENCE: Kill him, shaikh!

SUBH (*unsheathing his sword and adopting the stance of protector of the domain*): God turn you to a monkey, you devil! I shall flay you before cutting you in pieces! The tribe has its knights and protectors. Don't you know that?

'UMAIRA: But you're not one of them, Subh. The tribe's domain will be protected by its knights.

SUBH (*ignoring* 'UMAIRA *and posturing further*): Move aside. Make way for me, so I can cut him straight. (*to the audience*) Where shall I deal his death blow?

AUDIENCE:

Kill him however you want, Subh.

No, he should be crucified.

The traitor should be torn in pieces.

SUBH: So, what is it to be?

SHAIKH: Wait. The soothsayer's coming.

*The* SOOTHSAYER *enters. He is an old, bald-headed man carrying a metal container from which he is sprinkling water. The people freeze, their hands on their chests. In the midst of the general hush, he approaches the guards and, in angry silence, takes the man from them.*

SHAIKH (*his tone apologetic*): We were going to kill him, soothsayer.

SOOTHSAYER (*dealing the* SHAIKH *a kick*): Woe to you, blaspheming wretch! (to the stranger) Why didn't you come to me first? (*to the audience*) Are you about to kill my guest, the Soothsayer of Bani 'Ishreen?6 (*He begins to intone in traditional soothsayer's fashion.*) Turn, turn, by every abandoned way. Good men will come, seeking relics. Move away, move away. Haven't you seen his like, on the television, which dazzles the eye and transmits the news of countries? Don't you know the people of knowledge and wisdom? Slaughter camels for my guest, make him generously comfortable. (*to the stranger*) Have you found your chosen friend?

HASIM: I haven't chosen him yet. (*intoning in soothsayer's fashion*) Prepare for me an abode, a place to stay. I shall come among you at sunset; at night entertainment will be pleasing.

*The stage is quickly darkened, or else lights are played in such a way that the tribe vanishes through moving the colonnade to the left of the stage.* HASIM *appears, sitting in an elegant office in the middle of which is a model of a nuclear rocket. Behind the desk sits the* SECRETARY, *who leaps to his feet on seeing* HASIM.

SECRETARY: Disaster! It's a disaster, by God!

HASIM (*paying no attention to his agitation*): Aren't you going to congratulate me, on my new deals in the Basous alliances?

SECRETARY: I tell you about a disaster, and all you can talk about is the amusing games you're playing.

HASIM: You fool! How can we live without disaster? You talk as though there's a real disaster happening.

SECRETARY: Haven't you read the newspapers?

HASIM (*taking no notice of him and going towards the desk*): Let me finalize these loans, for the purchase of chemical weapons. They're urgent. Then I'll have time for your disasters. (*inquiring*) You didn't tell me if you finalized the bank's liens for the loans.

SECRETARY (*still turning around in an agitated state, holding the newspaper*): Haven't you read the newspapers? They're going to slap an embargo on the spread of nuclear weapons.

HASIM (*without interest, looking at his watch*): I must go. I'm invited for dinner with the Soothsayer of 'Akraf. (*still looking at his watch*) I may be late, time doesn't exist there. Send someone to buy me a watch that can operate in every time, and a radio. And, if Abu Laila al-Muhalhil bin Rabee'a's sent in the guarantees from the World Bank, ship him the swords and spears and arrows.

SECRETARY: Should I convene the scientists for this evening?

HASIM: Yes, convene them. So they can think about the banned weapons, and
    how to use them.

*We overlap to the tribe's encampment.* SUBH *is solitary and depressed.* HASIM *steps confidently
over.*

SUBH (*rising to his feet*): May you be blessed, Soothsayer of Bani 'Ishreen. They've
    prepared food and an abode for you, a place to stay. You are as if among
    your own people.
HASIM: The least you can do. But where are the men of the tribe?
SUBH: They've gone to repel Ghailan's raid against the shepherds.
HASIM: "And why do you stay when the young men are gone?"7
SUBH: They stopped me from duelling, because I argued about a game.
HASIM: What game?
SUBH: The game of duelling for the title Protector of the Howdah. It's mentioned
    in the Parchment of the Great Secret, along with the four rules for the game.
HASIM: That's all very amusing. You still believe there are four rules for the game?
SUBH: There are four, Soothsayer of Bani 'Ishreen.
HASIM: Actually there are five, Subh. There are five rules to the game. If you want
    to win it, that is.
SUBH: May you be blessed, the soothsayer and the shaikh of the tribe say there are
    four.
HASIM: And where's the Parchment of the Secret?
SUBH: In the cave of 'Akraf, in the keeping of the soothsayer.
HASIM: Bring it.
SUBH: May you be blessed – I can't.
HASIM (*in a conspiratorial tone*): If you bring it, I'll mediate for you with the shaikh
    of the tribe and the soothsayer, so you'll be able to duel again. And we'll
    make sure you beat your opponent. Then we'll arrange a loan for you from
    the bank, and we'll have you fight for the rest of your life, the way al-
    Muhalhil does – the master of Rabee'a. Come on, off with you and bring the
    Parchment of the Secret.
SUBH: But – that would be a crime. And I want to be Protector of the Howdah.
    Shall I show you how I duel with my son Kilda? (*with a flourish*) Like that!
    When I've finished with Jahsh, I'll still have to duel against 'Umaira.
    'Umaira's stronger than Jahsh, but he's a short man. I'll have to be faster
    than he is. Look, here's how I'll lay him out on the ground. (*He straddles the
    ground as though he were* 'UMAIRA.) The dust will cover him, and his sister
    Na'isa will laugh. You know, Soothsayer of Bani 'Ishreen, Na'isa isn't the
    most beautiful of the tribe's maidens. It's not her I want, it's 'Alia. We'll duel
    over 'Alia, the loveliest of girls. The victor will become Protector of the
    Howdah. When they read the Parchment of the Secret, with its four rules.

HASIM (*breaking in, apparently annoyed by SUBH'S chatter*): Take my blessing and go, so I can show you there are five rules to the game, not four. Come on, you faint-hearted coward, before they come back. How marvellous it is for me, to find a lad like you in every Arab district.

*The* SHAIKH OF THE TRIBE *enters, agitated and calling out.*

SHAIKH: Soothsayer! Soothsayer, where are you?
HASIM: Come here. What is it you want?
SHAIKH: May you be blessed, I'm looking for our soothsayer.
HASIM: What do you want with him?
SHAIKH (*fearfully*): I've had a frightening dream. I want him to interpret it for me.
HASIM (*sarcastically*): It'll be about a girl. I'll interpret it for you, according to the Freudian school.
SOOTHSAYER (*entering*): Turn, turn.
HASIM: Here he is. Come on, tell us your dream. He'll interpret it.
SHAIKH (*still worried*): I saw, soothsayer, a thing sleepers see: a dream in which you and the Soothsayer of Bani 'Ishreen were uprooting a big tree. When the tree seemed about to fall, you were overjoyed. I came after you and saw a small root you hadn't plucked out; and so I nurtured it and watered it, and the tree became green and straight.
HASIM (*repelled*): That's a pointless dream, shaikh – a chimera. I want no such dreams in the tribe.
SHAIKH: May you be blessed – such beautiful dreams!
HASIM: I, for example, in my waking hours, have seen how I was making nuclear hand grenades, just the size of an apple. Because that was what some genius asked from me.

*The* SOOTHSAYER OF THE TRIBE *begins to take off his priestly garb, and is transformed, before the audience, into someone from the modern age, in elegant white clothes. He begins to act like a broker, and the shaikh goes on gazing at them, dazzled, as though some magic were taking place in front of him.*

SOOTHSAYER: What a marvellous dream! Weapons like that would be useful.
HASIM: The problem lies in financing the studies.
SOOTHSAYER: I have a client who'll finance studies about nuclear hand grenades.
HASIM: You mean someone's thought of bringing it about?
SOOTHSAYER: Yes. He's a man who loves to protect peace and justice.
HASIM: Who is he?
SOOTHSAYER: Let's get him to finance the studies. Then, when the weapons have reached development stage, we'll discuss the matter of selling them to him.

SHAIKH: That's a beautiful dream of yours, soothsayer. But it means nothing to us.

HASIM (*sarcastically*): Like apples. Just like apples.

SOOTHSAYER: Turn, turn. (*He goes back to HASIM, changing his kind of priestly role once more.*) Tell me, what are you going to do about the banned weapons? The long range ones, I mean? And the medium range ones?

HASIM: Simple. We'll cut them down and make them short range. Our clients need weapons to use on their neighbours, not to send overseas.

SOOTHSAYER: Turn, turn.

*He returns to his priestly garb in a son et lumière conference, then leaves. There is a brief passage for the SHAIKH to move with those present to the SOOTHSAYER OF BANI 'ISHREEN, i.e., HASIM.*

SHAIKH: May you be blessed, Soothsayer of Bani 'Ishreen. Our soothsayer in the domain of 'Akraf has agreed to permit Subh one duel.

HASIM: I know that. I've talked to him by satellite phone.

SHAIKH (*to those around him*): What's this he's saying?

EVERYONE:

    What's he saying?

    A priestly rhyme.

    He's talking about the jinn.

HASIM: I forgot, you don't know about the telephone. I mean, the jinn told me. (*He takes from his suitcase two swords and a radio.*) These two swords are a gift to him and the knight he'll be duelling with. You need some blood to know the worth of weapons.

SHAIKH: May you be blessed, soothsayer, what's that you have with you?

HASIM: This thing's called a radio. It lets me know what's happening in the second Basous War. They might invent it for you after a couple of thousand years, if a Marconi happens to be born among you. (*He switches on the radio. As the news broadcast begins, the people flee.*)

HASIM: Don't be afraid. (*He switches off the radio.*) Next time I'll bring you a recorder to entertain you with singing and drums.

SUBH (*entering*): May you be blessed, soothsayer!

HASIM: Take your sword. You'll duel at sunrise tomorrow.

SUBH: But what about 'Umaira? He's strong. (*enacting the scene*) He holds the sword like this, in the middle, and he can cut a fly in the air. So he told me. If he were to fling his sword in the air, he'd cut a bird in mid-flight. (*fearful*) When his turn comes to duel, (*trembling*) I'll stand against him like this, and plant my foot on the ground.

HASIM (*irritated by his chatter*): Off with you now. And don't forget, the game has five rules.

*The lights intersect. We see the* SOOTHSAYER OF THE TRIBE *kneeling in front of* HASIM'S *empty office, appealing to him for prophetic inspiration. As he begins to speak, a film projector switches on and shows the* SOOTHSAYER OF BANI 'ISHREEN *on the screen. At the end of the appeal, the place is transformed to the* SOOTHSAYER'S *cave, to show us that the* SOOTHSAYER *has simply been asking for news from the* SOOTHSAYER OF BANI 'ISHREEN.

SOOTHSAYER (*in his strange garb*): Light, light, eye of the crystal. For joy and delight, the beating of the hearts, hm hm hm hm hm hm. (*The projector is switched on, and the news appears, showing* SUBH *in the garb of Protector of the Howdah.*) She's Subh's, according to the news from al-Muhalhil bin Rabee'a. Turn, turn, eye of the crystal, tar taram tartam tartam. Light, light. Give me light, king of the crystal. (*The light of the crystal goes out.*)
It's Subh they want. I thought they'd choose 'Umaira. I'd better prepare the spells. (*He turns around in his cave.*) From all the ugliness, take Subh, the one who shines like the morning. As for 'Umaira, kill him, or subdue him, or fill him with terror.

End of the First Tableau.


The Second Tableau:
*The same décor. The portico turns to the form of a Bedouin tent. It is early morning. There is a crowing of roosters, together with other such morning effects as an alarm clock ringing, to make clear to the audience the play's overlapping of time.*

HASIM (*waking and shouting into the tent*): Wake up, you credulous fool. Don't you realize I'll be duelling in your place?
SUBH (*coming out of the tent with the radio, which is still sending out a morning song, I suggest "The sun is giving light," by Fairouz*): Isn't it still early?
HASIM: You need some practice before the duel. Come on, repeat for me what we went through yesterday evening. (*He takes the radio from him.*) Didn't I tell you this thing's no use to you? Come on, take the sword and repeat the manoeuvre.
SUBH: Here's how to do it! (*Shows him the manoeuvre.*) And when he leans on the colonnade, my sword will be slanted as if to pass between his ribs. And I should be at an angle to his chest, like so.
HASIM: Marvellous. You have skill. And, when you see the blood gushing out from him, what do you do then?
SUBH: What blood? We're duelling, not fighting. Those are the rules of the game.

HASIM (*showing him a gun*): This thing's called a gun. It will make him explode from inside. His blood will flow out on his chest.

SUBH: You mean you're going to murder my opponent treacherously? With that thing?

HASIM (*sarcastically*): No, I shan't kill him. This thing will deal him a serious wound. Then his blood will flow, and afterwards he'll die.

SUBH: Curse it, soothsayer! Didn't you tell me it was one of the rules of the game, in the Parchment of the Four Secrets? That it was an innocent ploy? (*He begins the cut and thrust of the manoeuvre.*) I can finish it with this – hm, hm – I don't need to kill him. If I were to kill him, then 'Umaira might kill me. This is no innocent ploy, Soothsayer of Bani 'Ishreen.

HASIM: No, I told you. It's the fifth rule of the game.

SUBH (*agitated*): This is shameful, ignominious. No, I'll duel with him till noon and end the game – so. Ha! What would the soothsayer in the domain of 'Akraf say of me? What would 'Alia say of me? And then, what would the tribe say of me?

HASIM: The tribe won't have the chance to say anything about you. You won't be killing the knight, after all. You'll only thrust him to the colonnade, where he'll meet his death. You'll do it plenty more times in the future.

SUBH: And 'Alia, what would she say if she knew I'd done that? I promise you, I'll finish it before noon, with the four rules. Like this. Ha! What devil are you sending to fill my mind, soothsayer of the epochs?

HASIM: It doesn't matter what devil it is. The important thing is, you want to be Protector of the Howdah. To become the obeyed master of the tribe. (*menacingly*) Or would you rather I looked for some other knight? You're all the same. Before you, al-Muhalhil bin Rabee'a didn't want to avenge Kulaib's death. He couldn't even grip a sword, he was so short of practice and sunk in pleasures. I persuaded him with funds from the World Bank, and then we arranged some further loans for him, and we financed military operations for forty years more. "Kulaib's blood," we kept telling him, "is still hot on the rock." The trouble with him is, he doesn't kill women and children – even though they eat up part of the loans. (*In the preceding sentences, he gives the impression of speaking to himself.*) He'll be convinced one day, but by then it will be too late. (*He returns to addressing the other man.*) Come on, fetch me the Parchment of the Secret from the soothsayer's cave in 'Akraf. We have to prepare for the rituals of the Howdah. Here they come.

*As he leaves people and knights come successively to the duelling arena, in the same place as before.*

SHAIKH (*entering*): May you be blessed, soothsayer. You haven't seen that coward Subh?

HASIM: He's gone to seek blessing from the domain of 'Akraf. He'll be back in a short while. But where's the tribe's poet? Where are the drum beaters?

SHAIKH: May you be blessed, soothsayer, we've no poet among us. And we beat the drums only for war, not in time of peace. We're a peaceful tribe, fearful of doing anything to make our enemies suspect we wish them harm, so they start fighting us.

HASIM (*sarcastically*): Woe to you! By God, what you need is television and radio!

AUDIENCE (*in turmoil*):

Television?

Radio?

What does he mean?

Is this priests' talk?

Radio? Radio?

SUBH (*returning and slipping the parchment into* HASIM'S *pocket*): A radio's a thing that talks. And the gun's a thing – (*perplexed*) a thing – what?

HASIM (*breaking in*): Be quiet, you fool. Don't talk about military secrets. Do you want the whole place to be inflamed?

'UMAIRA (*having come among the crowd*): You won't triumph, Subh. You don't have the stomach for it. The Howdah's for the Protector of the Howdah. My brother won't string things out this time. There's no time for playing around.

SUBH (*assuming a weary manner*): Do you hear what 'Umaira's saying, shaikh. Deliver me from him.

'UMAIRA: You're just a sack of straw, Subh.

SUBH (*truculent in the manner of cowards*): You wait till later!

SHAIKH (*intervening and addressing the throng*): This, Subh, is your final duel, expressly to satisfy the Soothsayer of Bani 'Ishreen. Our soothsayer in the domain of 'Akraf, where the Parchment of the Great Secret is, has blessed it.

HASIM *taps his pocket, where the Parchment of the Secret is.*

SHAIKH (*continuing*): As you know, the rules of the game are four.

SUBH (*incautiously*): Five. There are five rules to the game. One, two, three, four, five.

HASIM (*saving the situation by elbowing* SUBH): There are only four. The game has four rules, knight. Come, let's be started, there's no time to lose.

SUBH (*assailing the knight as the latter approaches him*): I'm the Protector of the Howdah, you novice.

SHAIKH: Wait. Let me first announce the beginning of the game.

SUBH: I've no need of that, shaikh. (*He makes a movement.*) I'll finish him, so. You'll see. (*turning to* HASIM, *who is otherwise engaged*) What do I do?

SHAIKH (*coming between the players, trying to separate them*): Wait, wait.

SUBH (*elbows him away and sends him tumbling to the ground, some distance off*): That's enough, out of the way! The soothsayer's blessed me. Out of the way, you! Hm, ha!

*A furious contest takes place. The crowd moves off, leaving the arena. HASIM looks around the tent and remains there behind the colonnade, holding the gun visible to the audience but not to the duellers. The other knight is pushed back till he is finally leaning on the colonnade. HASIM then fires a single shot, muffled by the gun's silencer. The knight staggers and falls.*

AUDIENCE (*appalled*):
> Killed. He's been killed!
> The game hasn't even started!
> Treachery!
> I saw him explode from inside. By God, I saw him!

'UMAIRA (*stunned, and with no real hope*): Jahsh, brother!

HASIM (*approaching, with the gun inadvertently in his hand, then hastily tucking it into his pocket*): Bravo, Subh! Bravo, Subh! Remove the vanquished knight.

SUBH (*amazed*): He's dead. Dead! How is he dead? Huh?

'UMAIRA: My brother's been treacherously killed.

SHAIKH (*keeping the crowd off*): I never announced the start. I never announced the start. The duel is null and void. This is a murder.

HASIM: Let's hear the knight. How did you triumph, Subh?

SUBH (*coming to himself following a kick from HASIM*): He was killed in the duel. He was just going to deal me a fatal blow, so I got in first, and he was killed. The rules of the game. The rules of the game!

HASIM (*placing a hand over his mouth*): The rules of the game are four. Perhaps it's all for the best the vanquished knight should die, rather than live with the ignominy of defeat. This happens often with my people, the Bani 'Ishreen. We see it on television every day.

*There is turmoil, resentment and murmuring among the AUDIENCE.*

'UMAIRA (*advancing*): I shall avenge my brother, Subh, by placing your head beneath my foot. Come! My brother's blood will only be washed away with the blood of a hundred of your father's sons.

HASIM (*confused, as though on the point of madness, he draws his gun, filled with a strange lust to kill*): Yes, vengeance, vengeance! Shame should fall on the one who abandons vengeance! Bravo, the knights of the domain of 'Akraf! See, the wind blowing your way – the horizon filled with dark birds, lured on by the sweet smell of blood and powder!

SUBH: Say it in poetry, Soothsayer of Bani 'Ishreen. Fire my zeal. Let my might soar – my head rise proud in the domain of the tribe!

*A general tussle takes place, mixed with various effects and uproar across the board.* SUBH *is seen to be in difficulties from the knights, whereupon* HASIM, *with his gun, intervenes from behind the knight duelling with* SUBH. *He shoots the knight, and, once he has fallen,* SUBH *follows up swiftly with a cut. The* AUDIENCE *freezes.* 'UMAIRA *throws down his sword and withdraws.*

HASIM: This is unfair. Everyone's duelling with Subh! (*He raises* SUBH'S *hand.*) Thanks be to God, this hero has triumphed! He's triumphed against treachery and treason!

AUDIENCE (*in uproar*):
Treason!
Treachery! This is a foul game!
They're dying at one another's hands!
Stop the duelling!
Destroy the Howdah! Tear up the Parchment of the Secret!
What you're doing isn't honourable!
Alliances! New alliances!

HASIM (*above the din*): I congratulate you. The tribe gives birth to a new hero. Heroes salute heroes, and heroes fight heroes! I give you Shaikh Subh, Protector of the Howdah and the tribe's knight!

SUBH (*dazed*): Me, Shaikh Subh, Protector of the Howdah? Isn't there any challenger? (*to* HASIM) What are we going to do about 'Umaira? I'm afraid of him. You don't know 'Umaira.

HASIM: We'll manage him. If he won't come to his senses.

SHAIKH: The game's gone beyond the bounds set by the rules. Let the notables follow me, to the domain of the Soothsayer of 'Akraf.

SUBH: Don't go, shaikh. Come, let's begin the rituals of the Howdah. And you, summon 'Alia. Tell her Subh is victorious. (*to* HASIM) Look, 'Umaira's vanished.

SHAIKH (*suspiciously, to* SUBH *and* HASIM, *who have been standing to one side*): I remember that same smell from years back, when Kulaib's arrow was planted in the udder of al-Basous's she-camel. I would have cut off my nose before smelling it again.

HASIM: It's the smell of vengeance, shaikh. But your nose, it seems, doesn't relish fragrance.

*The* SHAIKH *and the crowd leave.* HASIM *remains behind with* SUBH, *who, gazing at his bloodstained clothes, is overwhelmed by remorse. He crumples up, weeping.*

HASIM (*noticing him*): Curse it! What's the matter with you, you coward?

SUBH: Can't you see the blood of my tribe? Staining my clothes?

HASIM: That's why you're Protector of the Howdah, according to the fifth rule of the game. Oh, you –

SUBH: I take refuge with you, soothsayer. Protect me. What sort of a knight am I? I'm just a reed, of straw, of despair. Where's the Howdah? Where are the people?

HASIM: Oh yes, that reminds me – the Parchment of the Secret. (*He takes the skin parchment from his pocket.*) Let's read. Ha, hm hm ha. (*He looks at* SUBH.) The four rules here don't apply to you. I'll write down the fifth rule, in my own hand, then return it. That way it will be legitimate. Forgers should work things properly.

SUBH (*who has followed him in a daze*): Woe to me!

HASIM (*striking a pose*): Don't you worry. With the Soothsayer of Bani 'Ishreen, things will always be easy for you. To start with, we'll arrange a loan for you from the bank. I'll just make an estimate – a highly conservative one – of your revenues, then I'll go and finalize the liens. While I'm away, get the rabble together and recruit them on your side. Promise them they'll have plenty of money.

SUBH: I don't know any rabble around here.

HASIM: Then go and look for them somewhere else. Don't bother me with petty details. Just remember, you need them for your own protection. Give them what they ask for. Just sign here, will you?

SUBH (*not understanding*): What?

HASIM: Sign – I mean fix your stamp – here.

SUBH: I don't have any stamp. It's with the shaikh of the tribe.

HASIM (*impatiently taking his thumb and imprinting it on the paper*): Put your print here then.

SUBH: What does it mean?

HASIM: It only means movement of money and arms. And arrangement for your loans at the bank.

SUBH (*feigning concern and adopting a local dialect*): Bank? What's that? You're not setting a trap for me, are you?

HASIM: A bank's a bank. You don't need to understand all that – only that you'll be Protector of the Howdah. Would you like some nuclear grenades as well? The size of apples – just like apples. You put them in your pocket, then you throw them at enemy cities, and they dissolve into thin air! Here, take this gun. In case you need it, before I come back.

SOOTHSAYER (*descending on the frightened* SUBH): Turn, turn. You rat! Have you stolen the Parchment of the Great Secret?

SHAIKH (*entering abruptly*): Have you stolen the Parchment of the Secret.

SUBH (*alarmed, holding the gun*): No, I didn't steal it. It's with the Soothsayer of Bani 'Ishreen.

SOOTHSAYER: How did he come to have it? There must be a traitor in the district.

SHAIKH (*turning around the priest, suspicious of him*): There must be a traitor in the district – a traitor who's stolen it.

SUBH: I was – No, he was, he was – He and I – No, he went and fetched it.

SHAIKH (*angrily*): Can you get it back, Subh?

SUBH: Show me the cave of the Soothsayer of Bani 'Ishreen, and I'll get it back.

SHAIKH: Off with you, Subh. (*emphatically, to the* SOOTHSAYER) We'll get it back.

SOOTHSAYER: We'll get it back, don't upset yourself. Turn, turn.

SHAIKH: Stop all that, and take me to your colleague!

SOOTHSAYER: I'll take you to him.

*He exits to the office, according to the same intersecting action as before, appearing to stumble in the office's darkness. The telephone is ringing incessantly. He switches on the light, then looks at the clock. The following scene is rendered with intense effects if possible, or else kept short to maintain the tempo, this being a scene that shows overlapping of past and present. It might be possible to use a song to start things off. This is a suggestion only, which the director is free to adopt or not.*

HASIM (*annoyed*): Curse it! I've been so involved with that Basous game I forgot our day's their night. (*Turns over the papers.*) Invitation to the International Peace Conference. (*writing down*) We agree to attend. (*reading on*) Saving the ozone layer through joint international effort. (*writing down*) We agree for the sake of appearances. (*reading on*) Wells in the African desert, to mitigate the effects of drought. (*writing down*) To be financed subject to conditions in force for investment in uranium and phosphates. Funding to be solely from profits in excess of the reserves, following eighty years' productive exploitation of the said mines. (*reading on*) Military satellite for the alliance. (*writing down*) To be financed, immediately and without delay, from frozen funds.

SHAIKH (*entering accompanied by the* SOOTHSAYER *and two* KNIGHTS): Soothsayer of Bani 'Ishreen –

HASIM (*surprised*): What on earth brings you here?

SHAIKH: The Parchment of the Secret has been stolen. You're the one who can find it. (HASIM *appears indifferent.*)

SOOTHSAYER: Won't you help us find it?

HASIM: Don't worry, we'll find it. (*Takes out a file with many skin parchments.*) Does it look like any of these? (*Takes the parchment from his pocket and adds it to the file.*) As long as it's like these parchments here, we'll find it – but you'll find the rules of the game are five now. Come on, let's look for it, and appoint a Protector of the Howdah.

SOOTHSAYER (*to the* SHAIKH): It's all over.

*They exit.* End of the tableau.

Third Tableau: The International Meeting.

*The same décor as for the first tableau, i.e., the tribe's encampment.* SUBH *is in difficulties. A group of* RABBLE *are eating and coarsely flinging the leftovers at one another.*

SUBH (*pointing his gun at the group, which appears unconcerned*): They'll come. (*Prowls about, troubled and anxious.*) Yes, they'll come. And they'll appoint me Protector of the Howdah. If they don't, the Soothsayer of Bani 'Ishreen will intervene. (*to the* RABBLE) What do you think? Will they come?
RABBLE: They'll come!
SUBH: Be serious, can't you? I'm most concerned.

*The* RABBLE *leaves.*

SHAIKH (*entering, he and the* SOOTHSAYER *are carrying the Howdah*): We've brought you the Howdah.
SUBH: What took you so long?
SHAIKH: Protector of the Howdah, the Parchment of the Secret had been stolen. We didn't know how to carry out the rituals. But for the Soothsayer of Bani 'Ishreen, we should never have known what to do.
HASIM (*entering abruptly*): There's no need for the rituals any more. He's Protector of the Howdah now. And he instructs you to gather money and prepare to enter the Basous War alongside al-Muhalhil.
SUBH (*breaking in*): Let them install me first.
SHAIKH (*breaking in*): But we can't break our alliance with al-Harith.
HASIM (*insistently*): That was your alliance, not Subh's. It's time for you to go to war. Come on, go and gather the funds.
SHAIKH: If war can't be avoided, then let it be for restoration of our rights.
HASIM: That's another matter entirely. It's a complex issue. Right, off you go.
SUBH: No, don't go. They haven't married me to 'Alia.
HASIM: No, off with you. And gather every penny you own. With the debt obligations you have, you couldn't repay them if your whole land was turned to gold.

*The* SHAIKH, *the* SOOTHSAYER *and the* NOTABLES *exit.*

HASIM (*to* SUBH): Why did you spoil the celebration?
SUBH: You're the one who sent everyone off.
HASIM: But didn't you mention the daughter of the tribe?
SUBH: 'Alia?

HASIM: Her name doesn't matter. She's mine – for me. Don't you understand, you fool? The Howdah's your share. For centuries now, I've been dreaming of a wide-eyed Arab girl.

SUBH (*pointing the gun at* HASIM): What are you saying, soothsayer?

HASIM (*approaches with fearless calm and takes the gun*): Don't do that again, boy. If you were to kill me, who'd lend you money to spend on the war, and go on being Protector of the Howdah?

SUBH (*in helpless fury*): When the war's over, I'll kill you. (*giving a worried glance*) Look, it's 'Umaira. What am I going to do? (*shielding himself behind* HASIM) What does he want?

HASIM: Get a grip on yourself, you imbecile. Just wait to see what he's up to.

'UMAIRA (*surprisingly transformed*): Protector of the Howdah, they say you've summoned the young men of the tribe. Here I am, with my horse, ready at your service.

SUBH (*with somewhat foolish gesturing*): You, 'Umaira. What – (*turning to* HASIM) What – I suppose the Soothsayer of Bani 'Ishreen has lured you here. Shall I kill him?

HASIM (*trying to cover up* SUBH'S *perplexity*): Welcome, 'Umaira. You're to be commander of the rabble, valiant knight that you are. Go and gather them from the district.

'UMAIRA (*leaving*): Your order is obeyed.

HASIM (*to* SUBH, *who is immoderately agitated*): Don't you see, you coward? Once you're Protector of the Howdah, knights will serve you.

*He takes hold of the radio and switches it on. A news broadcast is heard, as put out by the international services.*

BROADCAST (*attracting* HASIM'S *attention and interest*): First the Basous War. Today, Bujair bin al-Harith was killed in individual combat with al-Muhalhil bin Rabee'a. The contest between them lasted a full day, during which each changed his horse several times. Observers from within Rabee'a's encampment say that al-Muhalhil might be prepared to consider a truce, in response to an offer from his uncle, al-Harith, who suggested al-Muhalhil should now be satisfied with Bujair's blood, as avenging Kulaib. According to the Basous Press Agency –

HASIM (*breaking in and silencing the radio*): Curse you, Muhalhil, you philanderer! You've started stalling. What's this truce you're talking about, with your uncle? (*He makes to leave.*)

SUBH: Where are you going?

HASIM: To see that dog Muhalhil. He's started stalling, the way you do sometimes. That's how he does things, when he needs a new loan to finance his war.

(*Goes behind the colonnade – a desert – we see him calling, the radio still with him.*)
Muhalhil! Where are you, you coward?

AL-MUHALHIL (*appearing with his large bulk and exaggeratedly long moustache, riding the dummy of a lion as seen in legends*): At your service, Soothsayer of Bani 'Ishreen.

HASIM: What's all this the radio's saying about you?

AL-MUHALHIL: Have the jinn told you how I killed my cousin Bujair? He was a knight, truly! Look, here's his blood, still on my sword.

HASIM: That's not what I'm talking about. The radio – (*correcting himself*) the jinn, I mean – they say you'll be satisfied with Bujair bin al-Harith's blood, as vengeance for Kulaib.

AL-MUHALHIL (*laughing, and in a modern accent*): These are tendentious rumours. (*reverting to an old Arabic formula*) "I do not accept Bujair for the sole of Kulaib's shoe." For your sake, soothsayer, I shall keep on with this war till none of my cousins are left but the women and children.

HASIM (*deliberately*): Even the women and children, Muhalhil.

AL-MUHALHIL: Even the women and children, if that's your wish.

HASIM: May you be blessed, Abu Laila. I shall send you twenty spears against a soft loan.

AL-MUHALHIL: Make it a hundred, and I'll finish the Basous War for good.

HASIM: That's just what I don't want. Keep this war going as long as you can. It's the war of the epochs. And, if you have any statements to make, send them to the Basous Press Agency, because that has direct links with me. (*Looks at his watch.*) I'll be going now. My instincts tell me Subh's stalling.

*We revert to the tribe's encampment. The* SOOTHSAYER *is kneeling before* SUBH, *who is lashing him with a long whip. The* SOOTHSAYER *is muttering in pain.*

SOOTHSAYER (*raising his hands in pain*): Oh, the agony! Some are killed, and woe to him who lives!

SUBH: You fool of a soothsayer! It's your job to foretell what's happened to that army of outcasts – whether they've defeated the alliances. Just say it straight out. I don't understand soothsayers' rhymes.

SOOTHSAYER: Treachery and lechery. The gullet's torn from the chest. They've broken the alliance – and broken the hoof.

SUBH (*losing patience*): Woe to you, soothsayer! If you don't give me news about my war, and about the Basous – the way the Soothsayer of Bani 'Ishreen does – I'm going to kill you in the most painful way there is. You can see for yourself: I've destroyed your temple, torn up your parchments, and I still haven't suffered any "eclipse from the mountain," the way you used to warn. This is your last chance. Either you speak up, or you die.

SOOTHSAYER (*standing up and speaking normally*): Shaikh Subh, I'm a soothsayer, not a radio. You know well enough the radio isn't invented yet.

SUBH: The radio, yes. You must make me one, soothsayer, like the one with the Soothsayer of Bani 'Ishreen. I want to know the news about Abu Laila al-Muhalhil bin Rabee'a. Come on! Go and make it for me, before night falls. The evening broadcasts come over better.

SOOTHSAYER: I have my doubts, Shaikh Subh. I'm a soothsayer, not Marconi, to make you a radio.

SUBH: Crucify him on a palm trunk, till he invents the radio.

*The* RABBLE *seizes the* SOOTHSAYER *and goes through the motions of tying him up.*

'UMAIRA (*entering in excitement, barely able to gather his breath*): Good news, Protector of the Howdah! Good news, Shaikh Subh!

SUBH (*containing him*): What's happened?

'UMAIRA: We slew them as they were peacefully disarming. As you wished.

SUBH: Leave all that, 'Umaira. Tell me what happened, from the beginning.

SOLDIER: I was present, Protector of the Howdah. We came on them in the early morning. They said, welcome to our allies, and they slaughtered camels and sheep for us.

SUBH (*interrupting*): That's the least they could do, 'Umaira. I want news of the battle.

SOLDIER: We ate and drank, and our men performed the war dance. We stayed with them till evening, when they went peacefully to sleep. Each one of us killed one of them — while they were sleeping there — so that not one remained.

SUBH (*embracing him*): Well done, you valiant heroes. War's an end, after all, and the end justifies the killing. The booty. Where's the booty?

HASIM (*entering*): Yes, the booty. Where's the booty?

SOLDIER: It's on the way, along with the captive women and children.

HASIM: What bank takes women and children? Go and slaughter them all, then bring the booty.

SUBH (*reiterating* HASIM'S *statement*): You're right. We haven't enough to feed them. Kill them, then hurry back with the booty.

SOLDIER (*leaving*): As you command, Protector of the Howdah.

HASIM: Are you sure what they've won in booty will be enough to repay your debt?

SUBH: I don't know.

HASIM: By way of reserve, and until you obtain further loans, collect the last penny from your tribe — even the women's rings. If you want more weapons, that is.

SUBH: I can't stop now. I have to get hold of weapons and funds.

HASIM: If you did stop, someone else would only carry on.

*We revert to* HASIM'S *office. The* SOOTHSAYER OF THE TRIBE *is now in the role of secretary, and there is a* CLIENT *with him.*

HASIM (*entering and hearing the hubbub of the meeting*): Your proposed weaponry isn't
    enough for these rebels. They're like rotten forest wood.
SOOTHSAYER: I told them the forests should be burned.
HASIM (*objecting*): No. What sort of suggestion's that? If you burned the woods,
    where would the First World get its cocoa? Do you want the children to go
    without their chocolate bars? Imagine, you fool, if your own children
    couldn't get chocolate bars.
SOOTHSAYER: So, what's to be done?
HASIM: The practical solution is chemical weapons. We're still waiting for a new
    nuclear weapon. The grenades are the size of an apple. Just like an apple.
CLIENT: Chemical bombs. Poison gases.
HASIM: And the guarantee for the loan. Have you arranged that?
CLIENT: The diamond mine.
HASIM: But isn't the diamond mine in your enemies' hands?
CLIENT: If you'll give us the loans, we'll capture it.
HASIM: When you've captured it, then I'll arrange the loans. As long as it's still in
    your enemies' hands, then they're the ones I'll give weapons to. Don't try
    and negotiate. He who has, borrows.

*The* CLIENT *and* SOOTHSAYER *leave. The* SOOTHSAYER *re-enters.*

SOOTHSAYER: The procedures for financing the nuclear grenade research are
    finalized.
HASIM: Have the funds arrived?
SOOTHSAYER: The transfers are through.
HASIM: Start manufacturing them. And marketing them, away from our vital
    spheres. Are those bankrupts still here.
SOOTHSAYER: Yes.
HASIM: Show them in, so we can get them sorted out.

*They all begin to come in, with* AL-MUHALHIL BIN RABEE'A *at their head, followed by* SUBH *and a number of others. This scene should be characterized by general tumult.*

HASIM: So there you are, Abu Laila.
AL-MUHALHIL: The Bani Murra have been wiped out, to the last one. I've
    nothing to do now.
HASIM: You could have held back from ending the war.
SUBH (*breaking in and addressing* HASIM): Why have you gone back on your
    promise? To install me as master of Rabee'a?

AL-MUHALHIL (*reproving* SUBH): You, you coward? Become master of Rabee'a?

SUBH (*beginning to quarrel with* AL-MUHALHIL): If the Soothsayer of Bani 'Ishreen had kept his word, Abu Laila, I would have cut off your moustache. Made you the laughing stock of the Rabee'a girls!

AL-MUHALHIL (*ready to seize* SUBH): You, you wet bird? Cut off my moustache?

HASIM (*intervening*): Let's stop all this. You can sort out your differences later.

SUBH (*to* HASIM): This man's a spineless coward. He put an end to his feud. Stopped the war.

AL-MUHALHIL: If you don't keep quiet, boy, I'll take you on right here at this table.

SUBH: You don't have a sword any more, Muhalhil. Do you think I don't know that?

AL-MUHALHIL: I'll kill you, Subh, and rightfully.

*Suddenly and unexpectedly, at the other end of the table, a tumult erupts of which nothing can be understood, except that a quarrel is about to develop into a fist fight. This draws general attention and silences the quarrel between* AL-MUHALHIL *and* SUBH. HASIM *bangs on the table with a wooden hammer to put an end to the tumult, while* AL-MUHALHIL *and* SUBH *cross to the middle to see what the matter is.* HASIM *continues banging on the table until those in question, Africans and the people of modern times, are silent.*

HASIM: What is all this, people of Bani 'Ishreen?

SOMEONE: We wanted to mediate in the quarrel between Subh and Abu Laila al-Muhalhil.

HASIM (*to* SUBH *and* AL-MUHALHIL): What are you two doing over here?

AL-MUHALHIL (*with exaggerated benevolence and softness*): We were going to mediate between these brothers, in their dispute.

HASIM (*laughing*): A world where reconciliation rules! (*groaning, then addressing himself to the Old World*) We've decided a new tribe should come into being, a wonderful tribe, one not governed by your clannish traditions, your fundamental points of reference. My private secretary will be soothsayer to this new, international tribe; and he'll provide it with honest advice.

*Everyone appears asleep, or else indifferent.*

SHAIKH (*entering*): Where's the soothsayer?

SOOTHSAYER/SECRETARY: What do you want? Are you still not done with?

HASIM: What on earth is he doing here?

SHAIKH (*disconcerted by his poor reception*): Oh – I want nothing. Or rather, I ask for nothing. But the soothsayer hasn't interpreted that business about the small root. The one you didn't cut off from the giant tree.

HASIM: What tree?

SHAIKH: The tree I had a dream about. I saw it – growing up green from the small root. It grew branches – the branches grew fresh, tender leaves and blossoms. I dream about it every night now.

HASIM: I reckon he must be seeing things!

SOOTHSAYER: Why don't we install him as shaikh of the new tribe?

SHAIKH: No. I'd rather water my small root, and keep the weeds off it, till it's full-blown with blossom.

HASIM: He's not fit to be shaikh of a tribe. He dreams too much!

*All plays were translated by Laith al-Husain and Christopher Tingley*

---

1. The Arabic word commonly used for "artist" bears this meaning. The joke is continued in the two short speeches following, where Bahloul evidently believes that Salim has been insulting him.

2. The original Arabic reads: "When did you get to the palace? Yesterday afternoon, comes the answer!" This is a colloquial retort used when someone has shown himself pompous or boastful (as if only fit for the company of palace people). Since it is meaningless in English as it stands, a free variation has been provided.

3. *Saleeq*: A traditional dish made from rice, chicken, milk and an abundance of cardamom.

4. A *sanjaq* was an administrative unit, equivalent to a county or district, in the old Ottoman Empire.

5. Al-Hajjaj, a key governor under the Umayyad dynasty, was noted for the severity of his methods. When, however, her tribe was suffering dearth, Laila al-Akhyaliyya, a poet and learned woman, was able to secure a large sum of money from him by persuasive appeal combined with some eloquent verses she composed in his praise.

6. Bani 'Ishreen: The people of the twentieth century.

7. This is part of a verse from a well known work about Qais and Laila, two famous lovers of classical times.

# Part V

## AUTOBIOGRAPHICAL LITERATURE

'Abd al-Fattah Abu Madyan

# FROM THE STORY OF YOUNG MUFTAH
(hikayat al-fata Muftah)

I was born in a suburb of the city of Benghazi in Libya. The suburb is called al-Birka, and the part of it where I was born, four kilometres from the centre of Benghazi, is called al-Ruwaisat. It was given this name, so it's said, because of the stones that looked like heads – a reference to the Arabic *ru'us*, meaning "heads."

I was born, almost certainly, at the end of 1926 A.D., corresponding to 1345AH; the date registered on my identity card is 8/3/1344, but I was actually born in 1345. My full name – personal, father's and surname – is Muftah Bin Muhammad Bin 'Abdallah Bou Madyan. When I went to Hijaz with my mother, God rest her soul, my uncle called me 'Abd al-Fattah. Later I dropped the "A" from my father's name to become Muhammad and made a further adaptation to my family's name, to Abu Madyan rather than Bou Madyan. Our surname came from my good grandfather Bou Madyan al-Ghauth. Our roots lay perhaps in Morocco, in western North Africa; we are in any case from one of the connected North African regions. Some of our family members in Benghazi have our family tree. My mother, as she herself told me, came from Algeria, her father having been a scholar called Shaikh Badr al-Din al-Filaiti. When I visited Wahran in Algeria, in 1406AH, I found a family with the name al-Filaiti, the same as that borne by my maternal grandfather.

I came to learn that my father, God rest his soul, had been married to more than one woman; I had two brothers from one wife and one sister from another.

My mother, God rest her soul, had nine children, of whom just two daughters and one son survived: my two full sisters and myself. I was the youngest in the family, my mother having been the last woman my father married. I was the seventh of the nine children borne by my mother.

I was perhaps six when I first became conscious of life. My father was an old man by then, seventy-five years old, and he died at the age of seventy-eight. That at least was what people said then, by reference to the Gregorian calendar. My father owned a shop where he sold coal and firewood by the kilogramme. He had poor eyesight. People in this line of business usually sold kerosene too, but my father, who hated its smell, would never sell it in his own shop. He'd buy the coal in sacks and the firewood by the *qintar* [100 pounds], both from a place called al-Funduq, known locally as the "halqa." He'd chop the wood, which was brought in the form of large trees from the forests of the Green Mountain, seventy kilometres east of Benghazi. The Green Mountain region is two hundred kilometres from east to west and extends eighty kilometres to the south, being bounded in the north by the Mediterranean Sea.

My father, having chopped the firewood, would sell it to people by the kilo, for them to cook their food in that pre-gas era. As for the coal, this was used for making tea and for heating in winter by burning in braziers. Some housewives in fact would cook their food over the coal, which gave a better taste. It was slow, indeed, but mothers woke very early in those days and would start cooking early. Families would have their lunch straight after the midday prayer, at one in the afternoon.

My father, then, was a poor man, selling coal and firewood by the kilo so as to earn enough to support a family of five. He had, though, inherited some land from his father, used for agriculture at that time and watered with buckets of water taken from wells. The water in question, for the vegetables or whatever other plants, was fetched by animals. These wells weren't deep, going no more than twelve metres down. As agriculture declined and construction increased, my father, God rest his soul, started selling the land and spending the money for our support. He'd buy coal and firewood, sell them, then spend the money on his family in a way befitting a poor person. The food was ground barley, from which bread was made, along with kinds of soup, and pastas similar to spaghetti but actually home-made from barley. Sometimes, this barley would be mixed in with wheat — wheat being more expensive and the family poor. Drinking water was brought by the water carrier; he took it around in a barrel on a cart pulled by an animal, and he'd fill our cask. Such few kitchen utensils as we had, like an earthenware cooking pot, a bowl and some tin pots, were washed with non-drinking water; each home had a well for this purpose, and for general cleaning.

Dried meat was made from the meat of lambs, to be consumed during winter. In the morning, or sometimes in the evening, *saweeq* would be made from dates, oil and barley. The barley bread would last from one to three nights, and would sometimes be eaten with water, to help it down, or with a kind of salad made from tomatoes, garlic and oil, along with hot chillis, so as to make a full meal from it. In summer, lunch would consist of watermelon and bread, or grapes and bread. The watermelon was called *habhab* or *dalla'*.

The houses were built out of stones and clay, the ceilings being from boards taken from forest trees. Such a house usually had one bedroom for the family. The father and mother would sleep on raised wooden boards, supported on the two sides by pyramid-shaped legs; it was known as a "donkey's back." On it would be a mattress of stuffed wool with a woollen cover for a blanket, and a cloak would perhaps be added if the weather was especially cold. The bed was concealed (if one can speak of concealment) by a curtain.

As for the children, they'd sleep on straw mats covered with sheep's skin. Even in summer this was all we had, though the straw mats were at any rate preferable despite the hard floor. The pillows were filled with wool, though sometimes poverty meant the filling was old rags instead. Lighting was from a kerosene lamp. Sometimes children, or a guest, would sleep in the open air to escape the heat. If the house had an open ceiling, there would, in addition to the rooms, be a *marbu'a* – what those using more elevated language and enjoying better means would call a reception area or salon – for receiving relations. The furnishing consisted of mats on the floor and nothing else, not even any cushions. The rooms had windows to let in the light and air. The floor was made of sand and lime, to which some richer people might add cement. Tiles could be found, but they were very expensive. It was a primitive life with few means, because resources were so very scanty.

I mentioned earlier that I had two half brothers and a half sister who were older than me. The sister was married and had children. The two brothers each had a grocery shop; one of them, Muhammad, had no children; the other, Mansour, had a son and a daughter, each had their own home and life. They'd never received any education; they lived at a time when there were only *kuttab* schools for memorizing the Quran, or Italian schools after Italy had occupied Libya in 1911. During Ottoman rule there was no education in Arabic. Rich people would send their children to al-Azhar in Egypt, or the Zaitouna Mosque in Tunis, or to Italy and France to follow modern studies.

In these old homes, taking a bath meant a big tub being set down on the bedroom floor after the mats had first been removed. The water would be heated in a copper cauldron over firewood, and would then be accompanied by all the other rudimentary devices: soap, cold water, a sponge made from fibre, and, sometimes, a small wooden chair placed inside the cauldron. Baths would hardly ever be taken at all except in summer. Sometimes a person would stand in the middle of the courtyard and pour over himself a bucket of water fetched from the well, or else he'd stand in the primitive toilet, which had a jute sack as a curtain; there was no money for a wooden door.

When I was almost six years old (I don't recall the date exactly), in the course of this very primitive life of mine, I was taken to a man who gave instruction in memorizing the Quran. His name was *faqeeh*[1] Bou Bakr al-Fazzani. Fazzan was one of the regions of southern Libya, on the edge of the desert, and was a governorate in the days of King Idris al-Sanousi, God rest his soul. Memorization of the precious Book, in one of these *kuttab*s, was carried out according to the old traditional method. Each student would be given a smooth wooden board, cut to a certain shape and with a handle on top. More often than not this handle had a hole through it, so it could be hung up on a nail, out of reverence for the Quranic verses.

The *faqeeh* would write out verses from the Quranic *sura*s, beginning with the *Fatiha*, then followed by "Mankind," "The Break of Day," "Purity of Faith," and so on from there; not from the *Fatiha* and "The Cow," as they do here in the Kingdom. The pupil didn't, of course, know how to read or write; with the *faqeeh*'s help, he'd start pronouncing the toned words, after the *qaloun* fashion, as I remember. In North Africa they placed the dot for the Arabic letter *fa* beneath the letter, and placed only one dot over the top of the Arabic letter *qaf*.

I started going to this *maktab*[2] (or *katateeb*, as those in the Hijaz would say) every morning till noon. Then we'd go to the *faqeeh* six times a week in the evening. On Thursday, as I recall, we used to leave earlier, a little before noon, and didn't go back in the evening.

The *faqeeh* received a modest monthly fee for his efforts. On every Wednesday, each student would bring him a few piastres, according to his means. This was customary, as a token of gratitude and appreciation on the part of the pupil's guardian. It was something that was always done.

I spent three years, maybe four, memorizing God's book. I memorized up to the middle of the *sura* "Pilgrimage." As I said earlier, we began memorizing the *sura*s in an ascending manner. These schools were called the "mosque," perhaps because this was where pupils seeking to memorize the Quran would gather. It was now that my father, God rest his soul, died, and so there was no one to take care of us. Each of my sisters went to live with one of my half brothers, while I remained with my mother.

I remember how the teacher who taught me the Quran would every so often take me with him when he was invited, together with other, similar *shaikh*s, on the death of a citizen, to recite verses from the Quran and to read it through. My teacher used to preside at these occasions. He took me along with him – apart from my classmates – to read, with the other *shaikh*s, parts of the Quran I'd already memorized. Food – rice and meat – would then be served, and I'd eat my fill, because meat rarely entered our home. We might have the chance, once a month, to buy a lamb's head or stomach. On all other days we made do with soup made with the fat we were given from the Eid sacrifices, or bought at the market. We'd roast the fat along with olive oil, with or without dried meat.

I'd earn a few piastres from going with my teacher, and these I'd happily take to my mother. It grieved me that she couldn't eat and feel full like me, from that rich food, but she was happy her son was reading the Quran and eating well. She'd had a lot to eat in her life, she'd tell me, to allay my qualms, and besides, her young ten-year-old son needed the food to strengthen him and build up his frail body. My *faqeeh* used to take me with him because he knew how poor I was; he did it out of sympathy, because he was our neighbour and knew all about our situation. I was quiet and retiring by nature. I didn't mix a lot, even with my classmates and people my own age. I was more of an introvert.

When my father's inheritance was divided up, the share of my mother, two sisters and myself was the home where we lived and a piece of land in front of it, measuring around 500 square metres. I had, reluctantly, to stop going to the *faqeeh* who taught me the Quran. The man regretted this, and wanted me to complete my memorization of the Holy Book. He even told me: "You needn't pay me anything at the end of the month, or any piastres on Wednesdays." I told him, young though I was, that my mother and I needed an income, whatever the situation, to live on and ward off hunger. He understood how our present difficulties had made my capacities even weaker than they'd been before; reluctantly, he accepted my excuse and prayed for God to assist my mother and myself and set our feet on the right path.

But what was a lad like me, a mere child, to do in the face of such hardship? When he was frail and thin, couldn't write his name or do basic arithmetic? What was he to do?

A lot of the children my age went to the Italian schools, where they were provided with an education mostly in Italian, but with some reading and the like taught in Arabic. The teachers at these elementary and secondary schools were Libyans and Italians. The countries that colonized the Arabs, and those in other countries, wanted to spread their language and culture.

My mother was opposed to my studying at the Italian schools; I was her only son, and she was afraid that, if I enrolled at one of these schools, I'd be conscripted and find myself fighting in the army of the colonizing power. My mother, God rest her soul, was illiterate, but she was wise. She saw how Libyans were being sent to Ethiopia, to fight the Ethiopians when Italy invaded the country in 1936. Many Libyans died in the course of the invasion. The war was a very hard fought one, and they were placed in the front lines.

My mother, then, was afraid I might die not fighting for God. That was why she was against sending me to the Italian schools. She was far-sighted in this, even if it did mean I was deprived of a people's culture and language mastered by those who went to their schools, with subsequent access to work where this was available. But all this was according to God's will and the destiny ordained by Him.

Let me return to this matter of work. What could I do? A knotty question indeed! But God, the Enabler and Provider, smoothes all paths. I don't know who it was who arranged for me to go and work at a coffee shop. There I'd take tea, coffee and soda water to the customers, and would also make tea in a large pot, from which I could pour a glass or more. Our teapots in Libya weren't like the ones people have here in Saudi Arabia. I made Turkish coffee, too, and served it to the customers. These coffee shops were usually leased, the lessee providing everything necessary for running them.

The job of waiter at the coffee shop meant that, lad though I still was, I had to wake before sunrise, so as to open the place up. There'd be some embers under the ashes in the stove, and I'd put coal on these and boil the water in the boiler especially made for the purpose, ready to make coffee and tea for those who wanted them.

The owner of the coffee shop would arrive at around eight or eight thirty, to check on the work of this young boy, who was quiet, obedient and none too resourceful. The owner would help me if necessary. By then I would have done everything: cleaned the coffee shop, set out the chairs, sprinkled water on the floor, lit the fire and served the early customers, mostly labourers, their orders for tea and coffee. In winter we'd serve *sahlab*, which was made from sugar, water and ground millet. It would be cooked in a pot during the night and heated up in the morning; it looked like soup, but had a sweet taste. We'd serve it in glasses, having first sprinkled some cinnamon and ginger over it, to help keep the customers warm.

I enjoyed this job, which brought in a few piastres; these I'd hand over to my mother, happy with my success and with the good fortune God had bestowed on me. I worked, at that young age, at more than one coffee shop in my home town, having my lunch, more often than not, at my employer's home. In the evening I'd go home to my mother, and the two of us would eat whatever God had provided for us. I was paid weekly, at the rate of two francs or two Italian liras per day. I spent almost three years working in two coffee shops, before leaving, finally tired of the drudgery involved.

My eldest half brother wanted me to leave my mother and go and live with him, but I refused. I couldn't leave my mother, who was compassionate, loving and warm, and meant the whole world to me. And, apart from God, she had no one but me.

I shall never forget one difficult day, before I went to work at the coffee shop. I was sitting in the front of my brother's shop, where one of his relations worked. He had a Bedouin maid from the desert, who came to work at the shop in the afternoons and would bring lunch with her, from my brother's house. On this particular day she brought a small plate with some stew that was only enough for one person. Bread was taken from what was on sale at the shop. I stayed at the front of the shop, and I was very hungry. The man who worked at the shop invited me to eat, and so I shared his modest meal.

At noon, before I went back home to my mother, my brother came in with a rope in his hand, and he started pulling me with one hand and lashing me with the other. This he went on doing all the way to the house where my mother was, I crying all the while from the pain and beating; upon which he bellowed and scolded me. My fault was to have been hungry, and to have shared the food with the man who worked at my brother's shop.

This was cruel treatment of a kind I'd never known in my life before. It was a lesson, too, that made me turn to honest work, so my mother and I could do without my half brother. I suffered greatly from the incident, which left me sad. I was ten years old, and a child of that age doesn't ever forget, especially hard days and years. But cruelty is a spur to the spirit and imposes discipline. A life of hardship builds a person up, strengthening his will. We should depend on God first, and then on ourselves. A life of luxury may well leave a person weak, lazy, feckless and without goals. The lessons of life are plentiful, and a wise person learns from these lessons, trials and experiences, and adds to his knowledge. "Time," the Arabs say, "is the best teacher." And this usually happens through hardship, which, as the poet Abu al-Tayyeb al-Mutanabbi said, is a factor for rebuke. Al-Mutanabbi, though, wasn't speaking of my situation and the bad conditions I suffered. I thank God life has taught me so many lessons: among them patience in the face of hardship, contentment, and care for those less well off than myself. Islamic teaching calls for endurance, for dependence on God, for hard work; and it teaches that fortune, and the moment of one's death, are in God's hand. A person receives what is destined for him, and he will never receive what was not destined. In the words of the Prophetic teaching: "The pens have stopped and the papers have dried." Thanks be to God in every situation, except for that of the people in hell.

I stopped working at the coffee shops and went to work at a bakery that made white bread at night, then, in the morning, sent it out for sale in the shops. The bakery then worked all day baking home-prepared dough, and the meat and other things on trays which people would send in. These were people who had no gas ovens in their homes, the public bakeries doing the job instead.

I'd be paid three Italian liras per day at this bakery, which welcomed and accepted me. It was the pay of a labourer doing one shift only. The work was hard, but I was young, ambitious and happy, because I was earning a wage sufficient for my mother and myself. Content with the situation I'd reached, I never complained at the quantity of work I had to do night and day, never muttered or grumbled. I was thoroughly happy, and my mother, God rest her soul, was proud of me because I was on the verge of manhood now, though she pitied me on account of the fatigue and the work load. I encouraged her to be patient. Work, I told her consolingly, was for men, and it was only natural for me to pay her back for a little of what she'd done for me. This would make her happy, and tears would well out from her eyes. My mother prayed a good deal that I'd find success, prosperity and a straight path.

My work at the bakery started early in the morning, with the sunrise and sometimes even before. I'd load the trays of bread on the she-ass and take them to the shops, with which I'd already become familiar. Each shop would take the bread ordered from the night before, with none sent back.

After taking around the bread, I'd go, in a cart drawn by the she-ass, to the workshops of the carpenters who made wooden doors, and there I'd pick up sawdust the workshops wanted to get rid of, and which we used for heating the oven. I'd take along jute bags, fill them with the sawdust and be back at the bakery some time before noon, depending on what we needed and how much was available. Sometimes, if there was only a little sawdust available, I'd buy it. It was still much cheaper than firewood.

When I got back to the bakery, I'd start by bringing in the trays of home-prepared dough. I'd find the oven ready and hot; my employer and his family would have seen to that while I was out. Then, after I'd finished baking the bread for sale in the shops, I'd work on till 2.30 in the afternoon, when I'd have my lunch with my employer. My employers at the coffee shops and the bakery regarded me as their son, because I was compliant, obedient, peaceful and mild, simply wanting to make a living. I was also devoted, serious, honest and hard-working, without a trace of pride or arrogance and with no inclination to quarrel. So I've remained throughout my life. I was genuinely fond of my work, which was a blessing from God, and on this account I was popular with my employers and people I worked with. At all events, success comes from Almighty God; thanks be to God for His grace and His favour.

In the afternoon, and on till after sunset, I'd keep taking in home-prepared dough. I'd also spend some time kneading dough for making bread; kneading, at that time, was carried out by hand, not with machines. Then I'd cut the dough into loaves and make them ready. I became so expert that I only had to weigh one portion of dough; one was enough, because my hand was like a scale after that. If I should weigh a tenth portion of dough, I'd find it didn't come to a gram more than the first. Didn't I say how seriously fond I was of my work?

I'd go to the storehouses to buy the flour, carrying the eighty-kilogram bags on my thin back. I never complained, and never asked for help except from God.

My life passed serenely at the bakery. I was happy in my work, and at being close to the mother who was so compassionate and so happy on my account. I took pleasure in my mother's outpouring affection and selflessness, and in her love beside which all else seemed paltry.

I found happiness in my life, for all its hard work and poverty. There was contentment, especially given good health and my mother's blessing and affection. She was there for me, and I was there for her. My elder sister had become married to someone from the family, while my other sister remained with her eldest brother. As for my mother and myself, there we remained in our humble world that was nonetheless both grand and wide-ranging, because we were happy with our lot. My mother was fearful on my account, even from the blowing of the wind. Is she not a true compassionate mother whose heart has mercy enough for the whole world, and still more? It was a blessing from God; from God the Wise, on Whom we can never set value enough, and to Whom we give thanks.

*'Azeez Diya'*

# FROM *MY LIFE WITH HUNGER, LOVE AND WAR*

(hikayati ma' al-ju' wal-hubb wal-harb)

The first morning of my life! Who can remember the first morning of his life, when life's embraced for just one day, before a person goes on with the process of living, welcoming the mornings and evenings, lifting his eyes to the stars, impassioned by the moon as it runs its course from tiny crescent to full?

And yet I can remember that first morning; I'm conscious of it, even after walking so far down the path of life, witnessing those hundreds of morning hours of my childhood, youth and adulthood, along with all the joys and woes of my young years. After rising over all the problems, troubles, losses, retreats from reality in all its sombreness and gloom, I still remember the first morning of my life, as though it were the very first hour even.

I don't recall how old I was that morning; at that hour of the journey on which I found myself embarking. I didn't even know who I belonged to, out of all those around me to whom I found myself attached.

It was in the early morning, as the sun still sought a way into the room, that I found them striving to wake me, everyone yelling at me, telling me to open my eyes, move, get out of bed – not until that morning did I even realize I was sleeping on one. Next to me was a small creature who, like me, stumbled along, getting doggedly up each time he fell, only to walk on unsteadily once more, reaching out to grab at anything he saw. Usually he was carried around at the waist of a black girl, who'd quell his ceaseless cries by stuffing into his mouth a piece of white cloth she'd first dipped in milk – she'd pull it out again if she ever thought he looked like swallowing it. Only that morning did I come to know the tiresome creature alongside me was my brother.

What remains with me of that morning, up to this very day, is the smell of the special food that filled my nose and lungs, which I later found was called *hisa*. It was made from date paste and flour, fried with shortening. Only that morning did I know that the woman making *hisa* was my mother, and that the old man who smacked me on the backside, to make me start calling her "mother" instead of "faffam," was her father; my grandfather, in other words.

That was the first morning I ever knew, the morning I could never forget. And if all those around me – my mother, my grandfather, my aunt, the black girl with my brother at her waist, and that other old black woman who locked up the trunks and the rooms after placing in them such countless items of baggage and furniture, and arranged the keys on a cord of twined black wool – if all those people had been destined to live to this day, they too could surely never have forgotten that morning.

Among my unforgettable memories, of that first morning I knew in my life, I remember how, besides the grandfather who smacked my backside, I knew my mother (known up to that point as "faffam"), my beautiful aunt in the prime of youth, my brother who wrapped his legs around the waist of the black girl, that old black woman who packed the trunks in the rooms, locked them so carefully, and hung the keys on the black woollen cord; I knew the smell of *hisa* that filled my nose and lungs and made my mouth water – but of which I was allowed not one mouthful. I left the house, holding now my mother's hand, now my aunt's. The pot of *hisa* sat on the head of the black girl, my young brother sat on my mother's shoulder. My grandfather carefully locked the door of the house, while the old black woman wailed and cried and spoke some words in Turkish, raising her hands to the sky, and standing there for a while before finally slumping down on the doorstep. The alley along which they walked, so narrow they had to move in single file, was, I now knew, called the Qufl alley and was part of the Saha quarter of Medina. I'd been born in that house, and so had my mother, my aunt and a number of my uncles, one of whose names was constantly on my mother's lips, since he'd died at ten years old. It was difficult for me to remember how I found myself, now, with my old grandfather, my mother with my brother on her shoulder, my aunt taking the pot of *hisa* from the black girl's head. Everyone's eyes were filled with tears, apart from those of my grandfather, who I saw standing by a broad door. This door I took to belong to a house standing next to many other houses with open doors, each looking alike, of the same colour. They all stood on iron wheels. The two of us, along with my mother, aunt and brother, didn't stay there long. The sound of a whistle filled the air. As the sound was repeated, I turned to look, as far as my eyes could reach, and I saw a huge, black object filling the square with noise and commotion, billowing a black smoke that seemed to me to have blocked out the sunlight.

My grandfather reached out to the black girl, took my brother and set him down next to him. Then he reached out again to take me, where my mother was holding me between her arms. He put me down on the ground as if I'd been a piece of luggage. Then he went back to help my mother and aunt climb up to where he was standing. Everyone started to cry as they saw the black girl wailing, standing there on the ground and raising her eyes towards my young brother. With her were many people I later knew to be friends, saying goodbye to my grandfather. I knew, too, that the house they'd climbed into with my grandfather's help was filled not only with dozens of men and women, old and young, and children, but with loads of luggage, bags, bundles and trunks, together with loads of wood, charcoal, stoves, baskets and scuttles. Along with all this was the pot of *hisa*, apparently entrusted to my aunt; there it was between her hands, as she stood in a corner by a window. Next to her stood my mother with my brother on her breast; how he stayed quiet in those moments I didn't know. He wasn't crying the way he usually did, and his mouth was no longer stuffed with the white cloth dipped in milk. As for me, my grandfather, sitting there on a pile of bags, was holding me in his arms so I could see, through the high windows, the great crowds shouting, clustering, calling out. There were tears in their eyes, which were bulging and bloodshot from what I now know was fear and horror, along with a sense of imminent homelessness and loss.

I don't recall how much time passed; I fell asleep, sitting there in my grandfather's lap. But I can never forget how a fierce earthquake woke me. Opening my eyes, I began to stare at something I'd never seen in my life before. The earth was moving, the mountains were moving, the small trees scattered here and there were moving too; and the people I'd seen huddle together, as they fell asleep, had moved back, and those behind them were walking too, but without moving their feet. I looked at my grandfather, and saw he was gazing into the distance; tears, in his eyes and on his beard, were falling on to me. From his lips came murmured prayers to the Prophet and verses from the Holy Quran, which I memorized from the old man's subsequent repetitions: "He who imposed the Quran on you wished to meet with you."

I couldn't understand the reason for the earthquake that had woken me. How could it be that the house with the window I was looking out from could stand still while the earth and the trees, the distant buildings and mountains, were moving? And moving backwards, at that, when I knew that walking always meant moving forwards.

I couldn't ask my old grandfather anything. The tears that filled his eyes, and glistened on his beard, and froze on his cheeks, clearly left him unable to speak, to say anything, beyond those murmurs streaming from his lips, along with prayers for the Prophet and the reciting of verses from the Holy Quran.

I looked to the corner where my aunt was, with the *hisa* pot next to her. I stirred in my grandfather's lap, to draw his attention. The old man knew I wanted to go to where my mother and aunt were sitting. He lifted me in his arms, then put me down till my feet reached the floor. Running over to them, I saw my brother asleep in my mother's lap, beneath her robe, and I saw the two wet veils that covered the faces of my mother and aunt. Each of them was holding a handkerchief she used to dry the tears behind.

I couldn't understand what had made my grandfather cry – he who, before, had only had to set foot in the house for every sound to cease, from fear of his cane and from his concern the neighbours should never hear the voices of the women in his house. And what had made my mother and aunt cry? It struck my young mind that something must be happening in these moments, that it had to do with what we were going through, with all those people on top of all those loads of bags and cases, bundles and trunks.

My imagination began to conceive the sense of horror that had swept over everybody; and I felt ready to shriek out as the smell of the *hisa*, from the pot there between my mother and aunt, stung me with hunger – I'd had nothing to eat since being woken that morning. But I didn't dare, in the face of all that weeping, to ask for anything. I stayed patient, coming closer to my aunt, and she took me in her arms and cradled me on her lap, her soft hand patting my forehead till I was sound asleep.

I don't know just how long I stayed like that, asleep in my aunt's lap. I heard my mother and aunt wake me up; and, opening my eyes, I sat up and saw my grandfather too. My brother was in my mother's arms. Everyone had gathered around a piece of cloth, on which was placed the pot of *hisa*, a plate of cheese and some pieces of bread. Alongside the old man was a teapot, from which he poured tea for my mother and aunt, giving each a piece of sugar. He was still whispering his prayers and reciting that particular verse from the Quran. I was hungry, inclined to reach out and take as much as I wanted from the *hisa* pot, which had been on my mind from the time I saw my mother cooking it, when they'd woken me that morning. But the old man was there, and he never let youngsters take anything; I had to wait till he, or my mother or aunt, gave me my share of any kind of food. I didn't have to wait long. My grandfather reached out to the pot, poured three spoonfuls of *hisa* into a plate, then added a generous piece of cheese, some wheat bread and a cup of tea with a lump of sugar.

My hunger was too strong for me to notice what was going on around me. I saw, even so, that the corner where the family was gathered had a curtain round it, blocking out other people's gaze. My mother and aunt, I noticed, had raised the veils from their faces. But, most striking, the place where they were sitting and eating now, just as they did in the home they'd left earlier that morning, hadn't stopped moving and swaying, and with this there was a noise that deafened the ears.

The old man broke off from his murmured prayers.

"No one's to stay in Medina," he said. "Those are the Pasha's orders. I hear he only gave the order to evacuate the city after getting permission from the Sultan."

"But Uncle Muhammad Saeed," I heard my mother say, "and his wife, aunt Fatima, and uncle 'Abd al-Qayyum and his wife Khatoun, they've all refused to leave. They're still there in their homes."

I saw my grandfather laugh scornfully.

"The Pasha can't make them leave," he said. "But where are they going to find food to eat? They won't find anything in a few months. It'll all be issued to the army."

"That's all very well," my mother said, "but just where are we going, along with all these other people here?"

"To Damascus, of course. I told you that more than a month ago."

"Will we find 'Abd al-Ghani in Damascus?" my aunt asked.

The old man let out his sarcastic laugh.

"'Abd al-Ghani? Where is he, I'd like to know? I don't think he's any different from Zahid."

Zahid had left and was supposed to have come back after three months, but there was still no news of him. His son was four years old now.

"We haven't heard anything. We married you off to 'Abd al-Ghani. He was your cousin, we said, and our own flesh and blood. And he went off, and we've heard nothing from him."

"Perhaps he's been killed in the war," my mother said. "A lot of people have been. We heard that from the people who came to Medina on this train."

"Killed in the war? I only wish he had been! The ones God loves most are those who die in war as Muslim martyrs, fighting the infidel. But Zahid went to Russia, didn't he, to get money from Muslims to set up an Islamic University? He's still there, very likely, and all the roads are closed because of the war. We won't see him till the war's over."

He gave a short, sarcastic laugh, drinking what was left in his teacup.

"As for 'Abd al-Ghani," he went on, "I was always against him marrying Khadija. But it's destiny, I suppose. And your mother Hamida would have it that way, God rest her soul, because he was from her tribe."

With that he took a big handkerchief out from his breast pocket and used it to wipe his mouth.

"No doubt we'll find him in Damascus. Somebody will come and tell us he – "

The old man fell silent. Then he shot a glance at Khadija, full of sympathy, and significant, too, of all the doubts he had about her husband. As my mother went on to gather up the plates and teacups and spoons, and my aunt held my brother to her breast, my grandfather got up, took me by the hand and led me off to my place with him, on the bags by the window. Once there he returned to his prayers, and to gazing dreamily out at the desert and the range of mountains, dark blue and pale red, on the distant horizon. Some of the peaks were partly hidden behind the scattered clouds, others were just visible, as if beckoning their admirers on to a world beyond the distant infinity.

## Our train journey from Medina to Damascus

That day, in spite of all the hardship, I had to disperse the dust of pain settled in my memory. I found myself holding on to my grandfather's hand amid a maelstrom of people hurrying breathlessly towards the covered market, to escape from the rain that started as drops of water, then turned to clear white stones. When we got back home, I learned what these white stones were called. This hail, the old man told his daughters, was a sign of God's wrath. He'd never, he went on, seen hailstones of the size the sky had poured on the people that day. I heard my mother and aunt say: "Oh God, be merciful!"

When my grandfather had finished his talking, he stood on the carpet my mother had laid and began to pray, with deep reverence, my mother and aunt making sure a total silence was preserved. One of them had to take my brother out of the room, while the other prepared dinner.

Round the table sat my grandfather, my mother and my aunt, who had my brother asleep in her lap. Once again the old man started talking about the train he said we'd be taking to "Hama" in two days' time. Nothing has ever made me feel quite so happy as that news did. To this day I recall how enjoyable, how delightful, I found the trip from Medina, aboard that train. The main thing, so striking I'd never forget it, was the number of children I was allowed to play with right through the trip, and especially when we were told the train had reached a station and would be making a long stop there. The grown-ups had the chance to get various chores done, while the youngsters played among the bags and baskets in the carriage, or on the piles of sand and pebbles they found in front of it if ever the grown-ups let them leave the carriage and helped them down.

Another thing, no less important than playing with the other children, was the *hisa*, of which I hadn't had sight since we left the train, not even now, as we sat around the table together. It would, I was sure, re-appear a couple of days later, once we were on the train.

Turning to my aunt Khadija, grandfather told her he'd found no trace of her husband 'Abd al-Ghani in Damascus. He'd been told, though, that 'Abd al-Ghani had been there two weeks before, and had most probably travelled to Aleppo. As for Zahid, no one had heard anything of him. Gazing at me and stroking my head, my grandfather confirmed that the road from Odessa to Constantinople was closed. "Fatima," he went on, "bring me that bag. It's got all the clothes and shoes I've bought."

My mother got up, fetched the bag from a corner of the room and handed it to my grandfather. Then she sat down next to him, helping him take everything out.

"Don't get upset," he said, while they were doing this. "Tomorrow I'll go and buy a pair of shoes for the little one too. I don't know how it slipped my mind today, in the Hamidiyya Market. It must have been the rain and the crowds. All I could think of was holding on to his brother's hand, to make sure he didn't get lost. Who knows, we might never have heard of him again – any more than we've heard of his father ever since he left."

My grandfather took out a good many things from the bag – I realized these were clothes and shoes for the cold weather, and that my mother and aunt were happy with them. The two of them started trying the clothes and coats on my brother and myself.

Eventually my mother gathered up the items scattered about the room. Then I saw her get up, lean over and kiss my grandfather's hand. My aunt followed suit. I saw the old man hug them with tears in his eyes. I was looking at him, but couldn't understand what was making him cry.

My memory of the Hamidiyya Market in Damascus, where my grandfather had bought all those clothes and shoes, was that it was very long, with shops on both sides; and that it was so crammed with people I had difficulty walking along, clutching my grandfather's hand. I haven't forgotten what the old man had to go through, when the bag was filled with all the things he'd bought from the shops on the two sides. It was heavy now, and the old man was carrying it in one hand and holding my hand with the other, till we got out of the market. We went on walking through the muddy streets, under heavy rain and hail, accompanied by thunder and lightning so powerful I'm still reminded of them now, whenever I hear and see these things.

The old man stopped a horse-drawn coach, which I later learned was called a *fitoun*. He flung in the bag, then helped me climb up on to the seat. The moment he'd sat down next to me, he took a handkerchief from his loose robe and started wiping my face and head.

"It's cold," he said, holding me close to him. "It's freezing, isn't it?"

The coach drove down a long road, the rain falling constantly and the people running along the pavements under the downpour and gathering under the shop awnings. For my part, I sat calm in my grandfather's arms, watching the road with sleepy eyes and tempted by the warmth of his chest to fall into a doze. I found myself, even so, opening my eyes, watchful of the columns of soldiers walking along with those things on their shoulders – rifles, as I learned later, which they used to fire bullets to pierce people's bodies and kill them. I also learned that shooting these bullets made fearful sounds, by which people knew the war was still going on. In war soldiers would die just like those being shot at from a distance.

After the columns of soldiers had passed, the coach drove along a different road, by a river bank. On the bank opposite was another street where people were walking and running, under a rain that would stop for a while only to start pouring down all over again.

There were other vehicles on the long road, but they didn't have horses to pull them. Before I had the chance to ask my grandfather how those vehicles moved, a long, uncovered carriage appeared, pulled along by two horses and driven by a soldier. The oddest things the vehicle was carrying were those bodies: human bodies, some with their heads dangling from the carriage, their mouths open, and swarms of flies gathering and buzzing around them. Their eyes were open too, but were unmoving, with a glazed look. And there were feet too, blue or black, dangling and shaking in concert with the heads. I didn't know what made me so frightened, why I almost screamed as I clung on to my grandfather's chest. He, I saw, had covered his mouth and nose with his hand.

"We belong to God," he said, "and to Him we return." No sooner had the carriage passed, than he raised his hands and recited: "Thanks be to Almighty God!"

When I woke during the night, I saw my mother's face as she leaned over me. She had on the *abaya* she only wore to go out in the street, and in her hand was the coat my grandfather had bought for me from the long market. She was, I realized, in a hurry for me to wake up, so I could put on the coat. She'd already put my new shiny black shoes on my feet, while I was still asleep. The small lamp on the wall was still lighting the corners of the dark room.

Where did she want to take me in the middle of the night? Where could my aunt and grandfather and brother be? Eventually, though, I heard my aunt coughing and my brother crying. They were with my grandfather in the other room, all awake, in the night. As I walked in front of my mother, to the other room, I realized they were getting ready to go out. My grandfather was sitting on the prayer mat in a corner of the room, in his hands what I now know to have been the Quran. He'd read from it after finishing his prayer, and my mother and aunt would also read from it occasionally. On the shelf on the wall was a large lamp lighting up a number of bags, among them the big basket in which they kept the food and the pot of *hisa* during our train journeys.

So, it was to be the train again – and the children I'd play with whenever the train made a stop, and even while we were travelling. I was going to find them at last, and play with them among the bags and baskets and trunks.

My grandfather was going to hold me on his lap, to watch, from the window, the distant mountains, the flocks of sheep, the caravans of camels, and the people I'd see standing with pots or baskets in their hands, offering fruit and other foodstuffs, like dates, eggs and tomatoes. The passengers on the train bought from them, including my grandfather. He'd give to me first, then distribute the rest among my mother, aunt and brother; and, if he saw children watching while he was handing things out, he'd call to them and give them some food, stroking their heads or cheeks. Then he'd turn his face to the window, and I'd hear him sigh and say: "Oh God!"

I still haven't forgotten how we stood in the hallway of a house, with a strange man – I had no idea where he'd come from or why he was arguing with my grandfather – when that torch set in a hole in the wall went out. The stranger's shouts grew louder, and so did my grandfather's, and all this was mixed with the crying and wailing of my little brother. There we all were in the midst of a frightening darkness, I standing and holding the hand of my aunt, who, along with my mother, had remained silent.

The situation came to an end when we heard violent knocking on the door. Then, when the door was opened, the dawn light crept into the hallway and we found a soldier asking for my grandfather. Seeing my grandfather, he gave him an envelope and shook hands with him in a friendly manner; then, the moment the soldier had walked out of the door, a *fitoun* appeared. The coachman left his seat, came towards my grandfather, then quickly took the bags and baskets and put them in the coach. My grandfather turned to the stranger who'd been arguing with him, and the stranger, for his part, amicably embraced my grandfather, then swiftly picked up and carried the things left in the hallway.

Once I was settled in my grandfather's lap, in another coach together with my mother, aunt and brother, I fell asleep and didn't wake again till my grandfather carried me into the train. But when I looked around, I didn't see the children I'd been playing with all the way to Damascus. More important still, I couldn't see, among the bags, trunks and baskets, any sign of the beloved *hisa* pot. Even my grandfather, who before had sat on the trunks by the window and put me on his lap to look at the scenery and the various people – even he sat on the floor this time. I was surprised to see a number of men and women sitting on the trunks and bags in such a way their heads almost hit the ceiling. Nor was there any longer the partition between the place where my grandfather, mother and aunt sat and where the other passengers sat. And so my grandfather sat – with me on his lap as usual – and himself acted as a partition between my mother and aunt and the other men and women, the latter with their faces covered with black veils. In front of them, or on their laps, were children who wouldn't stop crying, just like my brother on my aunt's lap. He was screaming too, his small face covered with tears; his screams only growing louder whenever my mother scolded him or pushed his hand away from her breast.

The train's whistle blew at last. I knew it was time to start, and that outside, by the side of the train, there were people standing with tears in their eyes, and others with fruit and sweets they were trying to sell. But this time I didn't see anyone; didn't see them, still though they were, seem to be moving all together, along with everything else the eye could see, even the trees and mountains. I was on my grandfather's lap, and around him were all the people sitting on the floor of the carriage; and alongside these, around these, were the bags and trunks and baskets. I was aware, once more, that there was no sign of the *hisa* pot or the teapot. That meant there was no hope of doing what we usually did at that time of the morning.

Someone closed the wide door in the middle, and the train moved off. As the noise and din of the train rose, the children's screams were drowned, and everything seemed to tremble and shake. My grandfather's murmuring rose as usual, as he recited verses and prayers.

I don't know how long I'd been sound asleep when I felt my grandfather take me off his lap and quickly rise to his feet to open the small box he always kept close by him. He took out a small bottle and went over to the other side where everyone was gathered, their eyes full of questioning and concern. Some were repeating: "There is no strength except in God." Others were saying the woman might die before we reached our destination. If she died before we arrived there, still others were saying, then we'd all be put in quarantine.

All I could grasp was that she was dying; and I knew that anyone who died would be taken to somewhere a long way off, to a place I didn't know. They'd told me, though, that it was called Heaven, and that it was a good place, with trees and flowers, water and birds. So I'd been told when my grandmother Hamida died and was carried off to that faraway place.

As I stood up, I saw my grandfather make his way to where two men, a woman and a little girl were leaning over a woman lying on the floor. I heard my mother say to my aunt:

"Oh God, so many people died in Damascus. They say, once the plague gets into a house, it kills a lot of the people in the family."

"Oh God, be merciful!" my aunt repeated.

After a short while, I saw my grandfather come back to his place, a smile on his face.

"There's nothing wrong with her, thank God," he said. "Just a dizzy spell. She's pregnant, it seems, and the travelling was tiring her."

A short time later I heard my mother whispering in my aunt's ear:

"Are you all right, Khadija?"

"Thank God!"

Having said that, she gave a sigh. Then she leaned down over my brother, there on her lap, and held him close to her breast.

"Thank God!" she repeated.

I began to wonder, in my child's imagination, about this Heaven I'd heard about whenever the dead were recalled to memory. Why, I wondered, didn't everyone go there? And why did they leave the dead there all on their own, and come back without them? I remembered my grandmother Hamida, who'd been carried off to that faraway place – to Heaven, as they kept saying every time I asked about her. But why hadn't she taken her *nargila*[3] with her? I could never forget how I'd been the reason, when I flung myself into my grandmother's arms, for her dropping the *nargila* and scattering the embers all over the living room floor.

## From Damascus to Hama: In search of my father Zahid and my aunt's husband 'Abd al-Ghani

I can't, today, remember anything very special about the trip from Damascus to Hama, apart from the *fitoun* we took from the station to the Sabouni house. The coachman had been a Turk, or at any rate someone who knew Turkish. I had no idea how my grandfather had come to know him, or how the coachman had become acquainted with my grandfather. I gathered later that the *fitoun* was a special carriage owned by the Sabouni family. I'd see it many times, parked there in front of the house where we now found ourselves with my grandfather, living in two of the rooms, along a courtyard with a small garden in the middle. Both rooms had a window overlooking this garden.

There were other rooms off this courtyard, where other people lived. In time I learned they were members of the Sabouni family: men, old women and young people of both sexes. I also knew, from grandfather's remarks to my mother and aunt, that they should be careful to watch my behaviour especially, since we were guests in the house, and should be quiet and not disturb anyone.

I don't remember how much time we spent as guests there. But what I can never forget is a dignified old man named Hajj Bashir. I'd see him return home at sunset; and, the instant he stepped into the courtyard, all the young men and women and children of his family would come out to meet him. They'd kiss his hand, and he'd pat them on the shoulder, and hug the children and laugh with them. Then he'd turn to his eldest daughter and ask:

"Is the shaikh there?"

The shaikh was my grandfather. When Hajj Bashir heard my grandfather had returned from afternoon prayer, he'd hurry off to the room, out of our two, that my grandfather used; and my grandfather, in his turn, would rise to receive him. Then they'd sit and give praise to God, or else exchange small talk in hushed voices. Next I'd see the two old men get up and go to pray the sunset prayer that was led by Hajj Bashir and attended by all the men and boys in the house. When the two old men had finished praying, and the lamp with the long glass and two filaments was lit, everyone else would go out, leaving the two old men alone, and no one would return there till it was time for the evening prayer. Then, once the prayer was over, everyone would go to another room for dinner.

One of the main dishes, which I first encountered in that house and have a relish for to this day, was *kubba*, in all its different variations, and *maghmouma* and *daoud pasha*. Nor have I ever forgotten the brown balls they called *shanklish*, and the strained yoghurt, molasses and olive oil, which were served at breakfast.

I remained in ignorance of the link between the Sabouni family in Hama and my grandfather come with his family from Medina. At that tender age I lacked any background to help explain what was going on around me, or to understand what I heard of the conversation between my mother and aunt, or between my grandfather and some other person. To me everything was a riddle, one I felt no impulse or necessity to try and solve. I heard something my grandfather said about the Pasha in Medina, and about the Sultan in Constantinople. The people of Medina – of whom we were part – had been ordered to leave for Damascus, because there was no food available, all supplies being reserved for the army. I heard people mentioning the "war," this being the reason why we'd boarded the train from Medina to Damascus. But all this, and many other things that were said, failed to stir me to thought. There was nothing for me to do but give my grandfather my hand and go with him wherever he went, from the moment he left the house until he came back.

I also had to obey every command I was given by my mother and aunt, or by anyone who happened to be with us on the train, or in the streets or at the Sabouni house, so long as they were older than I was. This matter of respecting those older than myself was becoming ingrained under the tutelage of my mother, who'd get very cross from time to time if she saw I'd ignored or forgotten something required of me by one of my elders.

And yet, with so much forgetfulness or stupidity, and with all the failure to stop and think about what was happening around me, why was it, even so, that those two words "Pasha" and "Sultan" kept nagging at me? What was the Pasha? What was the Sultan? I didn't perhaps try and form a mental image of the Sultan, but I certainly did for the Pasha – one that would be conjured up every time I heard the word Pasha, any Pasha. This went on happening not only during my childhood, and the times of travelling and wandering, but even when all this was over, up to the time I was a young man. The paramount features of this image were corpulence and splendour, with a hint of limitless power.

This image sprang, no doubt, from what I kept hearing about the Pasha while on the train, and during the conversations between my grandfather and my mother, or among other people. The Pasha was the one who'd ordered the people to leave Medina. He owned the train, along with all the people it carried, and all its deafening noise. He even owned the black smoke that blocked off the sky, and the mighty noise that filled the whole world whenever the train got ready to move its iron wheels, which turned on iron rails. Whenever the sound of the train broke out, everyone would hurry to get back to it. When the train moved, there'd be no other sound heard; only the roaring of the train itself. None of the passengers would move; they'd just sit on the bags and trunks and baskets. And on would go the ceaseless roar, along with the cries of the children scared by the noise, unable to find a haven even in the arms of their mothers, or on their fathers' shoulders.

The creature who owned that terrible train, who could gather all those people and send them from Medina to Damascus, and Hama, and later to other cities and countries known only to God – this was the Pasha. I shaped him, in my imagination, as a huge man, inspiring such enormous awe he could be compared to no other man, no other living creature.

After such a journey, through all that time and all those places, the reader won't, I imagine, expect me to recall just how long we spent as guests at the Sabouni home in Hama. What I do remember is the day I heard my grandfather tell my mother he'd found a house for us to move into. He added something in Turkish, which I couldn't understand, but I saw a smile become etched on my mother's face as she expressed her happiness and gratitude. Then I saw her run to my aunt, apparently to tell her the good news: that we were to move to our own home.

My aunt, now in the final months of her pregnancy, also showed her pleasure at the good news. Even so, the happiness failed to hide her fatigue, poor health and pale colour.

"I wonder," I heard her ask my mother, coughing her barely audible soft cough, "when we'll be able to move?"

"Soon. In three days maybe. I'll go with father to the market; we'll buy carpets, mattresses, covers, pillows and things for the kitchen."

"All right. But have you seen the house?"

"No, not yet. I'm going to see it today. It's near the 'Asi (Orontes) River, father says, and has four rooms. One big room for guests and one for him. And I've some good news for you, Khadija. The house has a small garden, and a well for drinking water with a pump which we can work by hand, just like the one in our orchard in 'Anbariyya, in Medina."

"Don't remind me of Medina. Whenever I hear the sound of the water wheels here, I remember the ones in Medina. Oh, when am I going to hear them again? Dear God, when will we be going back to Medina?"

"God's relief is near, Khadija. In a year, father says, even in seven months maybe, this war will be over. Please pray, Khadija, that God will help the Muslims win over the Christians and infidel."

"Oh, pray God Zahid would come back, and 'Abd al-Ghani too."

"Oh, didn't I tell you? Father says they've heard 'Abd al-Ghani's in Aleppo."

"In Aleppo? Where is it, this Aleppo?"

"I don't know where it is either. But father said they've written him a letter. If he gets it, he'll write back and tell us his news."

"But why did he go to Aleppo?"

"He's a young man, Khadija. The Sultan wants all the men to be with him, so God can help him against the Christians and infidel."

"You mean 'Abd al-Ghani's one of the Sultan's soldiers?"

"No, he isn't a soldier. But he knows about trains, remember. He must be working on a train."

"I hear the train's whistle every day, as it comes in from Damascus. Do you think 'Abd al-Ghani will be able to come and see us?"

"Well, don't forget, he doesn't know we're in Hama."

"Yes, that's true. Maybe he doesn't know we've left Damascus to come here."

"No, I'm sure he doesn't. But I told you, father's written him a letter."

"Do you think father's told him I'm pregnant?"

"Heavens, Khadija, I don't know. Shall I ask him when I see him?"

Abruptly my mother stopped the conversation and turned to look at me.

"What do you think you're doing, sitting there listening? Where's 'Abd al-Ghafour?"

'Abd al-Ghafour was my brother, who'd by now started walking more steadily. He never stayed in one place, except when he was feeding from my mother's breast, or when my aunt stretched out her legs and put a pillow across her feet for him to sleep on, listening to her tender voice as she rocked him this way and that. "Let him rest," she'd sing, "let him sleep, on a pillow of ostrich down." He'd fall asleep then – but only on the bedding of her legs and feet.

My mother had started assigning me the task of watching over him, following him in the corridor between the rooms, or going down to the courtyard, where we'd see him almost tumbling into the flower beds. I don't remember how my days were spent before we moved to our home, as my mother and aunt had started calling it. I'd been luckier than my aunt then, as my grandfather never forgot to take me with him when he went out with my mother to buy furniture for the house. My aunt would have to stay at the Sabouni house, to look after 'Abd al-Ghafour till we got back.

The house was beautiful. Orchards filled with fruit trees divided it from the other houses on the banks of the 'Asi River. The way to these orchards was through a small door, which grandfather didn't approve of: he'd nail it up, he said, to block off the exit. My mother, though, persuaded him just to fix a bolt, promising she'd never let me go out through the door except with her or my grandfather.

The most striking thing about the small garden at the house was that it had roses and another plant called myrtle, whose fruit was sweet and freshened the mouth after eating. There were other flowers, too, like narcissus, and corals, and a plant with flowers called *mud'af*, which filled the garden with their sweet scent in the early morning and at sunset.

As for the fresh water pump over the well, this gripped me from the first moment my grandfather used it, and I saw the water gushing from it into the small basin. It was the toy that enchanted me, and I planned to start playing with it once we were installed in the house.

I still remember the day we left the Sabouni house for our own. Hajj Bashir's eldest daughter, who was called Asma', wept floods of tears, talking constantly to my mother, then looking at my aunt and saying something about the midwife and the delivery, as if to assure my aunt everything would turn out well.

As we walked towards the door, Hajj Bashir and his many daughters and grandchildren were standing there with looks that spoke, I realized, of their great love. I even wondered just why we were moving to our new home. Where was the difference between staying with them and going to our own home?

*Khalid Ben Sultan Ben 'Abd al-'Aziz*

# FROM *A WARRIOR FROM THE DESERT*
(muqatil min al-sahra')

I've loved the military since my childhood, and I realized, from my youth on, that I wasn't born to lead a civilian life. The life I longed for was a rugged, exciting one, in which I could fulfil all my ambitions and perform heroic, unparalleled deeds. That springs, perhaps, from my character – which is still, I think, a tenacious and aggressive one.

As a child I always insisted on doing what I wanted, resisting anyone who tried to impose his views on me. I was proud of never crying, even when I fell on the floor and hurt myself or felt pain. It happened, when I was eleven or twelve years old, that I fell from my horse and broke my leg. My brother Fahd, who was with me, could testify he saw not a tear fall from my eye that day. I was a rough child, one that the other children found hard to get on with. I always insisted on being the leader, not a follower.

The major factor that shaped my personality was, undoubtedly, my being the eldest son of Prince Sultan. My father was, and still is, constantly occupied with his official duties as Minister of Defence, a position he's held unbroken for over thirty years.

The image of him implanted in my memory as a child was that of constant absorption in his work, busy with his papers or talking over the phone. This preoccupation meant I had to fulfil some of the family obligations on his behalf, and this nurtured in me a sense of responsibility, something my father was keen to foster from my childhood on. In a large family like ours, rejoicing in so many brothers and sisters attached to one another by loving and caring bonds, it's natural there should sometimes be minor problems within the family circle, requiring immediate intervention and handling. Such a situation needs someone able to give advice, or reconcile differing points of view, or at least be there for any person needing him. I realized from an early age that this was the role I had to fulfil, as the eldest son of an important dignitary.

At the start of the sixties, I was a lad in the prime of youth, and I remember how very taken I was by the unique, commanding character of King Faisal, God rest his soul, who took over the reins of government in 1964, at a crucial period in the

Kingdom's history. He worked to promote the standing of the royal family and the reputation of the Kingdom. He was a dignified ruler, who won people's respect before he won their love, a man of firmness who made great demands on himself and expected a good deal from others. I was undoubtedly influenced by his personality, as were many other young people in the family.

One other factor made a positive contribution in building my personality, and this was the fact that I was a grandchild of King 'Abd al-'Aziz, known as Ibn Saud. He was the mighty grandfather who united this country through his conviction, his wisdom and his sword, ruling it for half a century and providing it with its name: "The Kingdom of Saudi Arabia." I was just four years old when King 'Abd al-'Aziz died in 1953, and therefore hardly remember him, but I've heard much of him from my father and uncles. I can only sense his austere presence. He was a man of enormous physique, with thick hands and a soft smile.

At the age of fifteen, I wrote an article, which was published in the school's magazine, on King 'Abd al-'Aziz's bold recapture of the city of Riyadh in 1902, when he was twenty-four years old. He launched his attack from the heart of the desert so as to ensure an element of surprise, the kind of tactic known nowadays, in military parlance, as *blitzkrieg*. Having scaled the city walls on palm trunks, he and his men then attacked the garrison. His chief comrades in this expedition were four men from the Jalawi family, which is a branch of the family of Saud. These comprised three of the sons of Prince Jalawi, namely 'Abdallah, 'Abd al-'Aziz and Fahd, together with his grandchild 'Abd al-'Aziz Bin Musa'id, who was then a young boy and later became my maternal grandfather. The Jalawis were renowned for their bravery in war. 'Abdallah Bin Jalawi was, in fact, the one who pursued 'Ajlan, the governor of Medina, in the courtyard of his fortress, plunging his sword into him and so deciding the battle in al-Saud's favour. King 'Abd al-'Aziz was proclaimed governor of Riyadh the very same morning.

Over the following decades, the Jalawis gained a wide reputation for their conspicuous loyalty to the Saudi Kingdom. They fought against the Turks, and likewise against those opposing the regime within the country. In return for their loyalty they were appointed to rule over various regions once the Saudi regime had become established throughout the Kingdom. King 'Abd al-'Aziz appointed members of the Jalawi family as governors of the Eastern Province, and that post continued to be reserved to them until recently. The Jalawis were strong men; and, indeed, that age needed a strong hand to keep a grip on matters, and to impose and implement the law in the Ihsa' region, at a time when the oil industry was still in its infancy there.

In 1922, my maternal grandfather Prince 'Abd al-'Aziz Bin Musa'id Bin Jalawi, following notable achievements as a military leader, was appointed Prince of Hail, the main centre of the north-western parts of the Peninsula. A year earlier, King 'Abd al-'Aziz had captured the city of Hail from the Rashid family, who had been among the fiercest adversaries of the Saud family. 'Abd al-'Aziz Bin Musa'id ruled

Hail for half a century, until his retirement at the beginning of the seventies; he was then almost ninety years old. It was in that Shummar Mountain region in the northern parts of Najd that my mother grew up. 'Abd al-'Aziz Bin Musa'id had two sons, 'Abdallah and Jalawi, and seven daughters. King Fahd married one of the daughters, who gave birth to my foster brothers, his sons Faisal, Muhammad, Saud, Sultan and Khalid. The other daughter, Princess Muneera, was married to my father Prince Sultan and had four sons and five daughters. I also have step-brothers and step-sisters from the other wives of my father. I have strong ties of love and pride with all of them, and I love them dearly. We grew up, and remain, a happy and close-knit family. My uncle Prince Naif married the third daughter of Prince 'Abd al-'Aziz Bin Musa'id, and he has two sons by her: my cousins and foster brothers, Princes Saud and Muhammad. I thank God our family ties are so very strong and intertwined.

I was born in <u>Mecca</u> on 24 September 1949, and it was King 'Abd al-'Aziz in person who gave me my name Khalid. It was our common tradition that the naming of the child should be celebrated on the seventh day following his birth. But it happened that, in my case, the seventh day was the Day of Attendance at Arafat, the holy day when all the pilgrims stand on Mount Arafat and pray in reverence and humility to Almighty God. King 'Abd al-'Aziz, as a strict Muslim, ordered that my naming day should be postponed to the eighth following my birth. Being related to this great man has left its clear marks on every aspect of my personality. Truly, he is a source of pride and honour for me.

The Saud family is a renowned and esteemed one. I say this not because I myself am related to it, but because it is, in all sincerity, unlike any other royal family, in our own region or in any other part of the world. Its roots go back hundreds of years into the heart of the Arabian desert, which has no parallel elsewhere with regard to its tribes and clans; the desert that has given birth to the bravest men and the finest poets; the desert where God chose to endow the heart of His Prophet Muhammad with the perfect Arabic Holy Book, which is recited day and night, now and until the end of time.

The family of al-Saud is closely linked to other major families that are not dissimilar to it by virtue of blood relation and locale. Some of these families have a noble history, no less noble than that of our own family. But what has given our family a place of prominence for 250 years now may be attributed to the accord made between two great men. In 1744, our ancestor Muhammad Bin Saud made an alliance with Shaikh Muhammad Bin 'Abd al-Wahhab, a religious reformer who had dedicated himself to the task of purifying Islam from the heresy and fables prevalent in those days.

At that time, the Arabian Peninsula, the cradle of Islam, was witnessing a degree of slackness in the application of Islamic doctrine. It was also in a state of chaos due to tribal feuds and rivalry for the acquisition of territories of influence, which led to disturbances in the country and a neglect of religious science.

Such was the situation in the Peninsula, one that Shaikh Muhammad Bin 'Abd al-Wahhab was resolved to correct. But he needed a strong man to help him spread his message of reformation, and to mobilize the armies and rule the tribes; and he found the man he sought in our ancestor Muhammad Bin Saud, governor of al-Dir'iyya (the old capital, whose ruins still stand today in the suburbs of Riyadh). The two men were able, through the Quran and the sword, to return the people of the central Peninsula to righteousness.

In the second half of the eighteenth century, one of the sons of our ancestors, Muhammad Bin Saud, married the daughter of Shaikh Muhammad Bin 'Abd al-Wahhab, and with that marriage the relations between the family of al-Saud and the family of al-Shaikh grew stronger; and intermarriage between the two families has continued to this day. The close friendship existing between 'Abd al-Muhsin Bin 'Abd al-Malik al-Shaikh and myself witnesses to this loyalty from my own personal life. This man has, through all the years, kept me constantly aware of his loyalty and love.

Defending Islam in its true form, devoid of any impurities, was one of the main bases on which the legitimate rule of al-Saud was founded, and was represented in the campaign launched in the eighteenth century.

One of the prime sources of strength of the Saud family was that they were viewed as the protectors of the Arab virtues, which have endured for generations before and since Islam; for they have preserved the ethical code of the desert. By the Arab virtues I mean the characteristics of generosity, courage, protecting women and defending their virtue, upholding honour, and looking after others' welfare. Commitment to these principles was one of the reasons life was able to continue in the harsh environment of the desert; deviation from them spelt death. While modern communications and other means of comfort have, today, reduced much of the hardship of desert life, I nonetheless believe that the history of my family, so rich in preserving these Arab virtues, has a considerable role with regard to the loyalty we enjoy today.

Our family numbers, in all, around five thousand men and women, princes and princesses from different branches, all connected through the sons of King 'Abd al-'Aziz and his grandchildren, who have the sole right to the throne. If I had to mention one principle uniting this large family, then that principle would be respect. Each of us respects the person older than himself, even if the difference in age should be only a few months or weeks. As such, there is a pattern dictated by respect, one that retains its dominance whenever any difference in viewpoint emerges between two members of the family, be the party in question brother, cousin or in-law. Some might make objection to a deep-rooted tradition of this kind, maintaining that the individual has the right to express himself without limit or reservation. Yet mature, prolonged reflection will surely lead to the conclusion that it is only rational, and wise, to have a certain limit beyond which a person cannot pass.

I make no claim that everything within our family is ideal and without defect, or that no differences exist. Nor do I claim that we are infallible. Every family will have its members who compromise others by their errors. This is liable to happen even in a family with four or five members, let alone one with five thousand. It is surely beyond dispute, even so, that the family's cumulative achievements are sufficient for any such lapses to be forgiven. Besides, the respect we have for one another is a guarantee that disputes of this kind will not escalate.

The family is well known for standing together during hard times; and this is one of the reasons for its strength and continuity. Should any trouble occur in the future, then it will doubtless spring from differences among the family. As such, we need to raise our children with a strong belief in the importance of family unity, and a firm conviction that every diligent worker has a share, whether large or small. And, indeed, we raise our children in such a way that they will not envy one another, and so that hatred will not cause division between them.

If I were to summarize the prime characteristics from which al-Saud draw their strength, I would enumerate them as follows:

First and foremost, abiding totally by the principles of Islam and protecting it as the faith, the regime and the law.

Second, respecting and honouring the King as head of the family and father of every one of its members.

Third, a commitment to serving society and to doing our utmost positively to promote the name of the Kingdom in international circles.

Fourth, a concern to achieve optimum exploitation of the Kingdom's resources, to distribute the revenues from these in such a way as to include all citizens, and to dedicate these resources to achieving the overall development of the whole country. This has had a very considerable effect for the cultural leap achieved by the Kingdom over the past years.

Fifth, the respect shown by young members to older members within the family circle, regardless of the precise age difference involved.

Sixth, the commitment to resolve differences within the family and to strengthen relations among its members on the basis of putting the family's interest before that of the individual.

Seventh, application of the rulings of Islamic law to members of the family in the same way as these are applied to Saudi society as a whole.

Eighth, allocation of important government posts to those qualified within the family, in the belief that any member is worthy of respect whatever his position.

Violation of any of the principles cited above would, in my view, imperil the status of the family and weaken the foundation of the regime, bringing down the government.

The Saudi people fully realize – in this I have every confidence – that, were it not for the concern of the Saud family in serving citizens with all their countless resources of experience, talent and family union, then the country would have become divided just as it used to be before it was united by King 'Abd al-'Aziz.

I was very much influenced by the fact that my grandfather, King 'Abd al-'Aziz, was a brave warrior and a skilled horseman, who mastered the arts of hunting and the use of dagger, sword and rifle, together with the art of living in the desert. King 'Abd al-'Aziz has indeed surpassed all those celebrated modern figures in the special forces, such as David Stirling, who pioneered such military operations for Britain, and whose group launched raids behind the German lines in the western desert during the Second World War. It was from him that the British derived the idea of the special forces known as the SAS. King 'Abd al-'Aziz, before any of these, had mastered the art of night raids, like the raid he made in the course of recapturing Riyadh. He successfully repeated raids of this kind in the years to come, against the Turks and against other of his enemies. Such an unforgettable heritage was, perhaps, the source of my admiration for the special forces.

King 'Abd al-'Aziz was prepared to assimilate modern military technology, and he knew the worth of the weapons he had gained from the Turks. He knew that ammunition was one of the keys to victory; I was struck by the account of how he would count out the number of bullets distributed among the riflemen. His concern to improve his men's military skills and upgrade their equipment led him to send his son Faisal to buy weapons from Poland and the Soviet Union in 1930-31. Faisal had won himself a lofty glory in the war in 'Aseer and Yemen in the twenties and thirties, when he was still just twenty-seven years old. King 'Abd al-'Aziz also recruited instructors to train his men, like the Nigerian Tariq the African, who was the first to occupy the post of Chief of Staff in the Kingdom. He also recruited experienced military men from Syria. As money became more abundant in the forties and fifties, training continued at the hands of the British and American Missions. In 1942, King 'Abd al-'Aziz sent his son Mansour, the first Minister of Defence, to visit the Indian forces serving as part of the British Eighth Army in North Africa. King 'Abd al-'Aziz was a ruler who listened to advice and sought knowledge; and he sought, too, the assistance of experienced, imaginative and trustworthy people he had selected both from the Arab world and from outside.

As a child I listened eagerly to stories of King 'Abd al-'Aziz and his two brothers Muhammad and 'Abdallah, and stories of his sons, those fierce warriors, my uncles Turki, Saud, Faisal and Muhammad, would fascinate me. These were figures who fought fiercely in the wars of unification during the first decades of the century. Unfortunately, though, I never had the chance to know my uncle Turki, who died when plague swept the country in 1919, thirty years before I was born. They were all military men, raised in a military environment.

In 1922, King 'Abd al-'Aziz described to the Lebanese-American writer Amin al-Raihani the strict discipline he had imposed on his children:

> We must always be prepared and in the best of shape. I train my sons to walk
> barefoot, to wake two hours before dawn, to eat little, and to ride a horse without

a saddle – because sometimes we have no time to saddle our horses, and so have to leap on and ride.

I derived my strength from this mighty grandfather, living as I do in a world filled with risks, where the highest importance attaches to boldness and courage, together with the acquisition of military skills and the use of the latest military technology.

I spent all my schooldays at a school for teaching the young princes, established by King Saud, God rest his soul, in the early fifties. In its early years, this school was located in King Saud's palace at al-Nasiriyya, within Riyadh, and was called the "Institute of the Sons."

In those days the roads were unpaved, and the journey from our house to the palace took three quarters of an hour. This meant we had a long walk home for lunch, and the same again back to school in the afternoon. When King Saud, who was truly a most generous and loving person, learned of the hardship we were undergoing, he gave orders for my brother Fahd and myself to have lunch at his palace with his son Mansour; an arrangement that made us most happy. In 1964, when King Faisal became monarch, the school was transferred from its quarters at the palace and placed under the supervision of the Ministry of Education.

Initially the school comprised a single class with around 25 students. By the turn of the nineties, however, it had become a sizeable institute, where more than 1,200 had enrolled, with classes from kindergarten to high school. It is no longer exclusive to princes; indeed, students who are not princes are now greatly in the majority. The name of the school was also changed to the "Institute of the Capital." A special section for girls has also been introduced, at different premises.

Over the thirty-one years since the school was established, it has been directed – or rather ruled – by a person of ordinary appearance but strong will named 'Uthman Nasr al-Salih, who had been chosen as principal by King Saud. Once appointed, he resolutely resisted intervention from anyone, even from the King himself. If ever anyone attempted to impose his viewpoint on him, he would threaten to resign forthwith.

Later I came to understand what a great man he was; and, after he had retired, I took care to visit him whenever I had the chance, in acknowledgement of his efforts in teaching me and a whole generation of Saudis.

He was the type of principal described as "old-fashioned": he followed a strict system and prohibited the consumption of food or sweets at school; he emphasized the need to respect teachers at all times and allowed no discussion of politics in the classrooms; students were addressed, and known, by their names only, with no mention of titles.

When I was fourteen years old, it happened that I rebelled against the principal's iron regime. "There's no need to be so strict," I told him. "We're children, after all, not puppets to be jerked about on a string. Let us live our lives." Instead of hitting me with his cane, he gave me a broad smile; he was so struck by my courage that he decided not to punish me.

I regard my brother Fahd, eleven months younger than myself, as the person closest to me. We're like twin brothers. When we were children we'd fight and compete, but, as we approached manhood, our friendship grew stronger. We spent our schooldays together, sitting next to one another in the classroom; there we weren't among the top students but we were above average. One summer Mr 'Uthman al-Salih provided us with extra lessons, and this enabled us to skip a whole academic year. Once my father asked Mr 'Uthman which of us was the better student, and he replied that Fahd was slightly better than I was. I was really happy when the examination results came out, and my father, checking them, found I'd done slightly the better of the two. Truth to tell, Fahd was always better than me; things only changed in the last two years at secondary level, when I was luckily able, with a little study, to do somewhat better than him.

I haven't, in recent years, been able to see as much as I would have liked of my brother Fahd. While I was with the armed forces, he was working at the Ministry of Social Affairs, where he eventually became Deputy Minister, being appointed thereafter Prince of Tabuk, in the extreme north-west of the Kingdom. Over the past eight years, he has established an exemplary administration there.

Another of my close childhood friends was Prince Muhammad Bin Fahd, who for many years now has held, in the most capable possible manner, the important post of Governor of the Eastern Province. As I mentioned earlier, this Muhammad is also a foster brother of mine; we were friends in childhood and still remain so. His father, King Fahd, married my aunt (my mother's sister) before he became Crown Prince. We used to play handball together, and I came to master the game in the defensive role, confronting the attackers and blocking the scoring area. Once it happened that I was nominated to be head of our class and so was Muhammad; and then one of our cousins, Sultan Bin Muhammad (now a highly successful businessman, whom I greatly love and respect), nominated himself for the same position. It was clear the votes were going to be split between us, with Sultan emerging as the winner. I therefore withdrew my nomination, asking my supporters to vote for Muhammad, who duly won.

At times we were regarded as being among the mischievous students of the class. Once, while we were misbehaving with one of our teachers, the principal passed and sternly asked the teacher: "Are you satisfied with the behaviour of these children?" "Except for those two," the teacher replied, pointing at Muhammad and me.

Mr 'Uthman al-Salih accordingly summoned us to his office. I tried to argue with him and justify our behaviour, while Muhammad stood there in silence. My course was decidedly unwise. The principal ordered Muhammad to leave, then dealt me a severe beating – an early lesson not to argue in certain circumstances, though one I haven't, to this day, it seems, really absorbed.

The true value of my friendship with Prince Muhammad became apparent during the Gulf War. Understanding one another so well, we were able, with ease, to resolve every problem facing us; a relief to both of us. I was confident I could depend on him, and he provided the best support to me, especially when I sought his help to overcome bureaucratic procedures or for the prompt finalization of some urgent matter.

Muhammad is six months older than me, and has priority and the right to respect according to our family traditions. In view of this, I was deeply moved by a gesture of goodwill on his part, which he himself may not even remember. By virtue of his position as prince of a province, he reported to the Interior Minister, HRH Prince Nayif Bin 'Abd al-'Aziz. When, though, he wanted to go to Jeddah for two days during the Gulf crisis, he called me and asked if I had any objection – something he was under no obligation to do. It was a truly kind gesture on his part, one showing his appreciation of my leadership.

While memories of my grandfather had a major effect in shaping my personality, my supreme ideal, as I grew up, was my father Prince Sultan; he remains, always, the beacon inspiring my life. During the Gulf War, when I occupied the position of Commander of the Joint Forces and Theatre of Operations – one targeted by all parties – my father was my protective shield, defending me from all sides. Suppose us to be playing American football; I would be the player running with the ball, he the player going ahead of me, knocking over any player who tried to stop me. I had a secure line connecting me directly to my father, and I would call him more than once during the day. His daily guidance helped map out my path, and it pained me to read how analysis of the Gulf War failed to do him justice as a Minister of Defence. He played a role no less important than that of Dick Cheney, the American Secretary for Defence. He really was the unknown soldier behind the victory of the Gulf War.

When I was young, I had a sense that my father didn't love me as much as he loved my brothers; that he preferred them to me. When, though, I became an adult, I came to realize that he loved me a great deal, and that what I had taken for undue severity towards me was merely an attempt on his part to bring me up properly and discipline my character. No wonder, then, that I should feel such unparalleled love for him and respect him above all others. I bow humbly before him in acknowledgement of his gracious qualities.

When I was no more than nine or ten years old, my father began taking me with him on his hunting trips with falcons. The trip might take a whole week. He appointed as my mentor a friend and follower of around his own age or slightly older: Shaikh Muhammad Bin Khalid Hithlain, a prominent figure within his tribe. Shaikh Muhammad was fond of hunting and would take me, together with my brothers Fahd and Bandar, and teach us all about life in the desert.

In those days, before the boom that followed the discovery of oil, the mango fruit was a longed-for luxury. Dessert, for us, was condensed milk in tins. We used to pierce the tins with hunting knives, then suck the contents. Nor were air conditioners known. We'd go into the desert on summer nights and sleep there till dawn, when the sun would wake us. When I grew up, hunting became my favourite pastime; I'd go, for a month or six weeks each year, deep into the desert. We'd travel as a convoy, make a camp, then hunt from dawn till sunset. I took much pleasure in those trips, but stopped them completely towards the end of the seventies; my last was in the winter of 1976-77, when I went to the north and passed by the frontier city of 'Ar'ar, spending a whole month hunting in the Iraqi desert. I came to know the terrain of the region very well, something that stood me in good stead during the Gulf War.

My father is known as a systematic man, whose career in public life goes back to his young days when King 'Abd al-'Aziz appointed him Prince of Riyadh. He is punctual in his ways, something he learned, so it's said, from King Faisal, whom he served for many years as his right hand man. King Faisal was himself punctual in his daily activities; people could, so it was said, set their watches by him. I myself, in turn, developed the habit of punctuality and care, directly from my father and indirectly from King Faisal. Love of discipline and devotion to the performance of duty were nurtured in me.

One thing that has stuck in my memory from my childhood is the way my father would set aside time to sit with us no matter how busy he might be. Lunch was an important event, and we would all gather at the house of my grandmother Hussa, the daughter of Ahmad al-Sidairi and widow of King 'Abd al-'Aziz. She was a highly esteemed woman, called Um Fahd by virtue of the name of her eldest son, King Fahd. All of us would go to her home: the King, my father, my uncles, my aunts and all their sons and daughters. It was a daily, full house meeting that never ceased.

Of all my uncles, perhaps the closest to me is Prince Salman Bin 'Abd al-'Aziz, Prince of Riyadh Province, who has been a good friend and sincere counsellor, helping me to solve many problems, including any personal one. Prince Salman has expended great effort, and made an undeniable mark, in the tremendous development that has taken place in the Kingdom's capital.

Um Fahd was a strong personality, respected by all. In her firmness of character was mingled with feelings of love and compassion. I did not, I regret, listen closely to her as a child, so as to learn lessons from the past. Westerners greatly err in supposing women are not respected in our society; such a belief is, indeed, totally at variance with the true facts. The effect of women in the home environment in our country is considerable, indeed limitless. Following the death of Um Fahd in 1969, my father went on with his custom of having lunch with his family, at my mother's home in Riyadh or Jeddah, where his sons and daughters would gather with their spouses and children should they be there.

By means of this tradition, my father was able to bring us together and foster mutual love, and he encouraged us to talk, to discuss numerous issues, and to express our opinions within the confines of decency and respect. It was truly a wonderful tradition, something that was a joy to witness and take part in. It was a daily opportunity, barring some unforeseen cause, to have the pleasure of seeing my mother and kissing her hand, to have the honour of sitting with her and receiving her blessings, to talk with her and with my brothers and sisters.

My mother, Princess Muneera, also left her clear imprint on my life; she was, as mentioned earlier, the eldest daughter of 'Abd al-'Aziz Bin Musa'id al-Jalawi, cousin to King 'Abd al-'Aziz, and his comrade, who fought alongside him and lived to be around ninety years old. I feel proud that the blood running in my veins comes from two noble origins: my grandfathers King 'Abd al-'Aziz and 'Abd al-'Aziz Bin Musa'id al-Jalawi. Both were prominent military leaders, and they played the major role in regaining the city of Riyadh and uniting the Kingdom.

My mother's heart overflows with tenderness and compassion. She bears no grudge towards any, has no place in her heart for anything but love. At the same time, she is extremely forthright, expressing her feelings without hesitation. It is through this trait that she has raised the ethical level of all around her. I never leave the country without going to bid her farewell, and she is the first person I talk with on my return; she comes first, before my wife and children. My mother is proud to be called Um Khalid, rather than Princess Muneera, but I believe I myself should be the one to feel pride. It is known in the Kingdom that, if anyone wishes for a favour from me and fears rejection, then he should address himself to my mother. He knows well enough that anything she asks of me I shall grant without question.

During the Gulf War, each time my mother heard that a Scud missile had landed on Riyadh, she would get into her car and ask to be driven to the Ministry of Defence, where I worked; and she would drive around the building to make sure the building was still standing and her son was still alive!

Besides my mother, there was my nanny Bushra, who was an important figure of my childhood. She was black, short and so very hot-tempered that even my mother would avoid arguing with her. She was a slave belonging to my mother's family in Hail (before slavery was officially abolished in the Kingdom in 1962). She moved to Riyadh when my mother was married to Prince Sultan. Bushra had previously been married for one or two years before her husband was killed in an accident; whereupon she devoted her life to serving our family. Though unable to read or write, she was a nanny without equal, with a rare talent for raising children, and I was lucky to have her. She took care of me and my sister al-Bandari, then of my young brother Turki till he was ten years old.

Bushra and her son Nadir were part of our family, and I can say without exaggeration that her influence on my life was a considerable one; she took care of me throughout my young years and taught me how to be a man. She had a mind of her own and an unrelenting resolve. Solid bedded rock would move before her opinion would be swayed. When I was five or six years old, my father charged 'Abdallah Bin Mas'ud with the task of being my companion. Bushra gave him some money of hers to buy ammunition for his rifle, then had him teach me to use the rifle and learn to shoot. When I toppled over on account of the recoil, she would tell 'Abdallah to help me up so I could start shooting once more. She also had her son wrestle with me, and would spur us on: "Get into him – come on – be strong!" If she saw me walking loosely, she'd yell: "Stand up straight, or I'll break your neck for you!" When I crept into my father's reception room and behaved in an improper way, she used to leap like a tigress and slap my face. "Don't look down when you're talking to people!" she'd shout. "Look them in the face!"

Bushra's role ended, of course, when I graduated from high school, but the affection between us never ceased. When I joined the Royal Military Academy at Sandhurst, she was suffering from cancer and was transferred to London for medical treatment. I'd run off from Sandhurst at eleven in the evening and go to London, where I'd spend the whole night by her side, returning to the Academy before dawn. She died in the Kingdom shortly after returning from London, and I was told she kept my picture with her during her final death struggle. She truly regarded me as her son.

Events in Yemen, where a civil war broke out in the sixties and lasted for nine years, greatly affected my life. I was a young man at the time. The war was a threat to the Kingdom's security and occupied all my father's time. Perhaps the most important effect of the war was that it played a part in bringing King Faisal to the throne, and it determined my own choice of career.

When Imam Badr was toppled, in the wake of a military coup in Sanaa on 26 September 1962, I was thirteen years old. I still remember the shock the news created within the Kingdom and among the Royal Family: it was the first time a monarchy had been toppled in the Arabian Peninsula, and it was not a welcome development. The new republican regime sought help from Egypt, and President Abdel Nasser, who was a symbol of Arab nationalism, sent his army to protect the new regime. Thus, with no prior warning, a state with which we had had friendly relations for the past thirty years became a direct threat. It was a situation much like that created when Saddam Husain invaded Kuwait. That is not to say that Saddam was a second Abdel Nasser, a man who, for all his faults, remains a national hero in the eyes of his supporters.

The danger was imminent and threatened the very heart of our existence. Having sent its army to Yemen, Egypt was now in a position, geographically, to aid the resistance groups who were spreading chaos through the whole peninsula. Before very long Egyptian planes had started raiding our frontier cities in Jizan and Najran, and we were powerless to protect them. We had no army, air force or defence forces with which to confront the Egyptian forces. I still remember my father's deep concern at our weakness and lack of means. I was young then, but I felt the pain. Our pride, I felt, had been wounded.

Abdel Nasser also presented his own ideological challenges. He was a hero we all looked up to, a man loved without exception by the young princes. We'd fight among ourselves if anyone claimed he loved Nasser more.

We were, then, all Nasserites, as indeed were most Arabs. This tendency was very marked in my family. My father and uncles greatly admired Abdel Nasser and relished his speeches and ideas. His pictures could be seen hanging on the walls, and everyone spoke of him. We in the Kingdom are naturally inclined to love our Egyptian brothers, holding for them feelings of fraternal love. Many Egyptians come to live in the Kingdom, especially in the Hijaz, and Egypt remains the preferred place for Saudis to spend their holidays. Because of this many marriages have taken place between the two peoples.

Nevertheless, Abdel Nasser, having sent his army into Yemen and proclaimed his intention of toppling our family's rule, left us no choice but to confront him. This was something that wounded us to the heart. We could see, though, how the Arab nationalism he constantly praised was in reality just a cover for his political ambitions; it was as clear as day to us that Yemen was not the end of Abdel Nasser's ambitions: he was hoping to become sole leader of the Arabs. It was at this point that our views towards him changed radically, from one extreme to another; from being a hero in the fifties, he became, in our eyes at least, a threat in the sixties. We were children at the time, but we could sense what was going through our fathers' minds. We had to resist the Egyptian forces in Yemen with all our strength, so as to preserve our independence. It was as though history repeated itself, for, barely a generation later, we found ourselves, for the same reason, forced to resist Saddam and his dreams of influence and control. Some people see the war we fought in Yemen in the sixties, by proxy, as the first trial of our national will, before the second trial, the Gulf War, which we fought against Iraq on our own part. In both cases an Arab ruler was threatening to exert intolerable pressure on the decision-makers in our country, and resistance against him was unavoidable. In both cases the Kings of Saudi Arabia – first King Faisal, then, later, King Fahd – had the proper strategic vision to deter the danger swiftly, before it could reach our country.

In the first trial, King Saud passed the reins of power, in October 1962, to the then Crown Prince Faisal; an interim stage before Faisal assumed the throne two years later. Prince Faisal immediately appointed Prince Fahd as Minister of the Interior, Prince 'Abdallah as Head of the National Guard, and Prince Sultan as Minister of Defence. Thus my father was the member of the royal family with the prime responsibility to ward off the military danger coming from Yemen.

Tribal feuding was deep-rooted in Yemen, but Prince Sultan, with his wisdom and intelligence, played a skilled part in uniting the chiefs of the tribes. The Yemeni figures with their turbans, and their curved daggers dangling from their belts, continually sought him in Jeddah and Riyadh.

If unable to listen to what was passing between them, I nonetheless watched closely and learned a good deal from my father's patience and wisdom; and this had a major effect on my own ability to deal with the members of the coalition, with all their different viewpoints, during the Gulf War.

The experience gained from the Yemen war was of great value to my father and uncles, though the main burden of the political and diplomatic conflict with Abdel Nasser naturally fell to King Faisal. The Kingdom fought alone against the Nasserite wave. The Kingdom remained steadfast, until at last the 1967 defeat demonstrated that even Abdel Nasser, with all his charisma and all his reputed abilities, was not immune to failure. What helped tip the scales in favour of King Faisal was that – in contrast to Abdel Nasser – he was knowledgeable about the basic strategies appropriate to Yemen; he was conscious of its powerful tribes, its mountainous terrain and its history rich in events. He had learned a good deal about the country in the course of the military expeditions he himself had led to Yemen in 1926 and 1932, on behalf of his father Ibn Saud.

In the sixties, Princes Fahd, 'Abdallah and Sultan had gained a war experience of the kind we now call "crisis management." They learned in those days that, if things turned bad, then there was no alternative but to fight on; that protection of the country and family was something that could not be delegated to others. I believe that our success in building the strong coalition during the Gulf War was clear proof that we are ready to sacrifice our blood and protect ourselves. The coalition consisted not only of the USA, Britain and France, but also included Egypt, Syria, our partners in the Gulf States, Morocco, Niger, Senegal, Czechoslovakia, Poland, the Philippines and other countries. Confronting Saddam was (whatever spreaders of lies may say) an unavoidable necessity. That was a lesson we had learned in Yemen thirty years before.

During the sixties, under the psychological impact of the war in Yemen, many of the young princes joined the military, and I myself was becoming so inclined, unequivocally, as I saw my father constantly surrounded by the armed forces. Eager to undertake military service on my own account, I began, at the age of fourteen or fifteen, to ask my father to send me to the British Royal Military Academy at Sandhurst. I had heard a good deal about this famous academy and the rigorous training it provided, and I also knew that more than ten Saudi students had previously enrolled there.

When, though, I reflect deeply on the matter, I see that our weak ability to protect our country was the main reason for my joining the military.

*Mansour Ben Muhammad al-Khiraiji*

# FROM *BEYOND THE GLAMOUR OF THE JOB: SNAPS FROM MY EARLIER LIFE*
(ma lam taqulhu al-wazeefa)

A person may sometimes remember very minor details of his childhood, but that's by no means a fixed rule or inviolable truth. I myself, for instance, can remember many events from my life as a child, but the one important, basic thing I can't remember is how and when I learned to read and write. If, today, a child generally starts his education at the age of six, we certainly didn't find our way to the *kuttab* till a year or two after that.

Children in al-Qaryatain and other villages weren't initially enrolled in schools but sent by their parents to one of the shaikhs, who'd teach them to read and also teach or help them to memorize the Holy Quran. There were two shaikhs in al-Qaryatain, and, since one of them lived close to our home, it was natural I should join his *zawiya*,[4] the name given to the room in his house, or to his whole house, where he'd receive the children of the neighbourhood. He was a short man, with a chubby red face. He wore a black robe, and, on his bald head, would put a red fez wrapped with a white cloth. His eyesight was poor, and he was always frowning as if about to fly into a rage, whether with good reason or not. His name was Shaikh Ahmad. He'd come in the morning and sit on a platform slightly above the level of the floor, in a room covered with rough mats, and the children would sit around him. In his hand would be a long bamboo cane, which he'd use to point to the child he wanted to start reading. Sometimes – because the stick was so long and so flexible – the pointing would turn into hitting. I don't, as I said earlier, remember when I started reading and how I learned to read or write. All I do remember was that I was taught to read the Quran by this highly strung shaikh, God rest his soul. We didn't memorize the Quran by heart, but learned to read from the *Mus-haf* without mistakes, and anyone who could finally learn to read the Quran in this fashion was regarded as having completed his education in Shaikh Ahmad's "corner." As those of my generation will recall, it was customary in those days for the child's father to assure the teacher, when enrolling his child at the *kuttab*, that the shaikh was at total liberty to follow any method he found suitable for turning the child into a man his parents would be proud of. The father would further tell the shaikh that he was handing him the child whole, but didn't mind having him back as a skeleton, if that was for the good of the child's education!

It was our misfortune that the shaikhs of those days hardly needed any such authorization – for them, it was as if the wretched pupils didn't have the sense of pain children have today. A child had only to stumble in his speech, or make a grammatical mistake, and he'd get a hit on any part of the body the cane could reach. Shaikh Ahmad had a child of our own age, named Idriss, and this Idriss was blessed with countless invocations to God to protect him from all evil. Whenever Shaikh Ahmad's cane landed on any one of us, the beaten student would hastily, in the midst of his weeping, beg for mercy from Shaikh Ahmad and invoke God's preservation of his son Idriss. Idriss used to study with us, and undoubtedly relished all those prayers, although they did him no good in the face of destiny. He died a few years back, after coming to the Kingdom for medical treatment. I had him admitted to the Military Hospital in Riyadh, but the sickness from which he was suffering had spread through his body, and he returned to al-Qaryatain, where, some time after, he died, God rest his soul and his father's.

To complete the reading of the Quran was regarded as a highly important event, and one warranting a celebration for the pupil, along with his classmates in the kuttab. The shaikh would fix a day, and the pupil would begin his reading with the Sura of the Cow, till he reached the words "God has closed on their hearts." I don't know why these particular words were chosen; probably, I think, because of the word "close," one of whose meanings was "finish" or "complete" – which was what concerned shaikh and pupil alike. It certainly wasn't on account of the clear meaning of the Quranic verse, which meant "make them unable to understand."

The day of completing the Quran was a happy one in the "corner," not just for the pupil being celebrated but for all his classmates too, because it was viewed as a holiday. There'd be smiles and marks of happiness on everyone's face, assured as they felt that there'd be no punishment from the shaikh's cane, no pulling of ears after pebbles had been placed in them, or perhaps the falaka – the beating on the soles which would make the lad's feet swell up. The parents of the child would also make their preparations for the important occasion, providing food for the shaikh and his pupils. On such occasions the shaikh himself would be the happiest of all, because it was the day he'd reap the rewards of all the efforts he'd made in teaching the child, to the point of finishing his reading of the Quran. The precise nature of the celebration, and the shaikh's reward, would depend on the financial circumstances of the pupil's family. These were usually very modest, so that the shaikh received nothing of any great significance.

On the morning of the day of celebration, I got to the kuttab at sunrise. I was happy, exuberant and elated with what I'd achieved, but happy most of all because I was about to leave Shaikh Ahmad's corner never to return. As part of the celebratory rites, the pupil in question would choose one of his classmates to stand behind him, with his robe pulled up above his knees, ready for action. The role of this classmate was to give the graduating pupil a hard slap on the neck, then run off, the moment the pupil pronounced the word "closed," i.e., "completed." The slapped student would get straight up and try and catch his classmate; then, if he got hold of him, would return the slap. If he failed, then he lost his right to slap him back. The chase would be from the shaikh's house to the house of the pupil who'd just completed his reading of the Quran. The slap on the neck I took from my classmate was a very hard one, and I didn't manage to catch him up and return it.

The slap did nothing, though, to reduce the overwhelming joy that swept over me because of what I'd achieved – I was free at last and looking forward to enrolling at the Qaryatain Elementary School. Or so I thought. My days in Shaikh Ahmad's "corner," I believed, were over. But that, I soon discovered, was a major illusion. In al-Qaryatain, as in other villages and indeed throughout the Arab countries, the Quranic teachers were in the habit of requiring certain pupils, the ones they found capable and efficient, to teach their fellow pupils who were younger or less intelligent. Our shaikh was as keen as any other to keep any such pupil he found, so as to have him help shoulder the burden of teaching, to his young fellow pupils, the material he'd so readily and easily learned himself. I had, of course, coached other pupils before I celebrated my graduation from the shaikh's "corner," and only naivety made me think my mission would be over once I'd finished my own reading. I didn't go to the "corner" the day after, or the day after that. Why should I return to the shaikh, after I'd finished my own studies? I was waiting for the school holidays to finish, so I could go to school in my turn. But apparently the shaikh had failed to find any pupil to replace me; his standard requirement was to have as many pupil teachers as there were pupils needing teaching from their classmates. After two days the shaikh came to visit my mother, God rest her soul, and persuaded her I should return to studying rather than play in the streets. My mother hardly needed much persuading; she immediately agreed to my return to Shaikh Ahmad's *kuttab*.

Her decision struck me, as the saying goes, like a flash of lightning. It wasn't that I hated studying, or that I was tired of my old fellow pupils. The reason was quite different. Shaikh Ahmad's pupils were boys and girls mixed, and he'd appointed me to teach a little girl. She was a pretty girl. Her hair, I remember, was chestnut, or more towards black when dyed with henna, very curly like the hair on the statues of the mighty Romans at the glorious height of their empire. She was, though, as stupid as anyone could be. She couldn't understand a thing; I don't think she understood a word, or even a letter, of what the shaikh taught her, or anything afterwards, when he dropped her on to me. I spent months before I'd finished, trying to teach her something at least, but to no avail. I'd start teaching her the moment I got to the *kuttab*. It was a job I utterly loathed. I couldn't wait to finish with it and never return to the "corner" again. But our shaikh wasn't so stupid as to throw away the services of a free teacher. Returning to the shaikh's house, I felt

both sad and angry, because I knew I was going back for one purpose and one
purpose only: to teach that little girl. She was no less eager than I was to be rid of
the agony of being taught. Day after day her mother would drag her to the "corner,"
and time and again I'd tell the shaikh I might be able to plant some words in a small
donkey's brain, but not in that little girl's. Each time I said it, I'd get a hit from the
shaikh's cane, or else a public reprimand. I, in turn, would talk harshly to the little
girl. Any female donkey, I told her, would be able to understand something after it
had been repeated a hundred times over. But she took not the smallest notice that I
could see. You might have thought my scolding was directed at someone else
entirely.

In the end I'd had enough. That little girl, I told myself, was incapable of learning
anything, and I wasn't going to teach her any more. Since I had no other role at the
*kuttab* – just suffering from that creature with the curly chestnut hair – I simply
stayed at home and proclaimed a mutiny. But my sanctuary didn't last for long. The
shaikh sent someone to tell my mother I'd escaped from the *kuttab*, and she took
me back in person and flung me into the hands of the shaikh, whose face was
growing redder and redder as his anger rose. He pointed forthwith to two of the
stronger pupils, who, understanding his meaning, lifted my feet into the air;
whereupon the shaikh started hitting my feet with his cane. It was the first and last
time I ever knew the pain of the *falaka*.

During one of my recent visits to al-Qaryatain, I made inquiries about that little
girl on whose account I'd been punished, but no one was able to tell me anything,
since I couldn't remember her name, or indeed any detail about her, apart from her
utter stupidity and curly hair, and these two traits were hardly enough for me to
locate a woman now over fifty years old and whose hair wouldn't be curly any more.

### An orphan in my uncle's arms

When I made my decision to set down these reminiscences of my life, I resolved
from the start to be honest and truthful in everything I wrote; and, moreover, not to
be satisfied with merely recording events and situations concerning myself and those
close to me. I also wanted to make a substantial record of some of my feelings and
emotions, whether immediate or more enduring, leaving their mark deep within my
soul to this day. A prominent circumstance of my life, one's that's left a lasting
imprint on my personality, is that I was raised as an orphan. My father died when I
was little more than seven years old, too young to take in the enormous disaster of
his death. Let me say here – and I'm not soliciting the reader's sympathy – that the
greatest tragedy that can befall any person is the death of one of his parents when
he's still a child. I don't recall anything of my life with my father, but I do have a
vivid memory of the time he died. I recall how, as we were coming back from the
cemetery, I was talking to some of my comrades who'd attended the funeral with us,
and, quickly forgetting my sad situation, started laughing aloud with my friend. Then
I remembered that my father had just died – I should be looking sad and grave. But

soon after I started laughing and joking again, as if the day were no different from any other.

I hadn't, as I said, reached the age when I could comprehend the enormity of what had befallen us. When my father died, even my eldest brother was still of an age to be termed an orphan. Can the reader, I wonder, imagine what it meant to be an orphan in those difficult times? It's very hard for anyone who hasn't passed through the experience to have a full understanding of the significance and suffering entailed by the hard life and lack of means.

My mother's relatives were far poorer, less prosperous, than we were. The old and young alike had to work to earn a living and keep the wolf from the door. It's told how one of the predecessors (it may have been the wise Caliph 'Ali bin Abi Talib) once said: "If poverty were a man, I would have killed him." I don't doubt for a moment that all the poor of the world would share those sentiments. There's nothing worse in life than poverty; nothing that so turns life to a never-ending nightmare of sadness and misery. For all that's been written and said about the philosophy of patience, of being satisfied with life whether good or bad; for all the claims that wealth doesn't bring happiness – and so on and so forth – poverty remains a dreadful thing. Being unable to provide for the necessities of life is a source of wretchedness to the soul. The reader will understand, I trust, that I'm speaking of true poverty, whereby people suffer deprivation of various kinds, unable to reach even the minimum standards of a decent living, the poverty which leaves the head of the family with nothing with which to feed his children; which condemns the child to a state of permanent deprivation, unable, at any time, to know the happiness of getting new clothes or of a piastre to buy what he wants – a source of constant anguish to the adult himself. This is the kind of poverty I'm talking about, the poverty I knew as a child. The poverty that, whenever I recall it, makes me thank God Who changed my past life for a life filled with blessings. Never can I thank Him sufficiently, however hard I strive. I wanted new clothes to wear for particular occasions, but hardly ever was the wish fulfilled; if it did ever happen, it would be just at one of the two Eid feasts, not at every Eid, or indeed in every year. The clothes I wore had usually been passed down to me from my brother Salih when they'd got too small for him, after being altered in various ways so as to fit me. That didn't worry me too much. What really upset me were the patches my mother, God rest her soul, would make to mend any tears in my clothes, of a different colour from the clothes themselves. The new clothes were made of a thick fabric, so as to last longer.

The real "show" came after the fabric had been brought and soaked, for a number of days or even weeks, in water containing peels of pomegranate. The peels would be collected, then placed in a big container, and water would be poured over to soak the new fabric, which would then take on that amazing colour – nothing like it, I think, can be found anywhere among modern dyes. It was a vivid yellow. But stranger even than the colour was the state of the material after being soaked for a number of days in the liquid – it looked like a piece of land with rugged contours, as seen in a picture from a satellite orbiting high up in the heavens; or, if you prefer, like the scaly part from the intestine of a freshly slaughtered lamb. Since the iron was an invention not yet found in al-Qaryatain, children would wear this cloth unpressed. Great was my joy when, one day, they prepared a gown of that material for me. I put on the dream robe and went proudly out to walk in the quarter. The whole world, I felt, was too small to contain my happiness.

Slowly, little by little, I began to hear the word "orphan" – the fashion in which the name Mansour bin Muhammad al-Khireiji began to appear in people's minds, used sometimes with a true feeling of compassion, sometimes as a fairly neutral reality. If anyone thought the youngster didn't weigh up other people's words, understand their true meaning and preserve them in his memory, then such a person was mistaken. If you need any convincing of the truth of that, just try telling your grandchild, or young daughter, or son, or any young child not more than three years old, that you're upset with them, that you don't love them, and just see what the result will be! The youngster will show the same amount of anger and distress you're claiming on your own side, especially if there's no reason behind your anger. He'll burst into tears. Then you'll have to appease him as best you can and bring back the smile to his face. Learning at a young age is, it's said, like engraving on a stone. That's certainly true, and applies to numerous impressions and experiences preserved in youngsters' memories from their relations with their families and the society around them.

We don't always realize just how vivid a child's memory is. Whatever happens around us when we're young is deeply scored in our memory and remains indelible through the passage of time and years. Our personalities spring, in sum, simply from the accumulated events and experiences we've known as children, added on, of course, to the characteristics born with us and ordained by Almighty God at the moment we're conceived in our mothers' wombs.

My earliest memory of my own life is the cold winter nights, when the whole family would gather around the stove in the corner of the room. We'd huddle together in a semicircle, our small bodies touching in search of warmth. Those were the delightful hours we all used to wait for. This feeling of family union and belonging was what gave us strength to endure the tough, hard life and the meagre means it had to offer. It was this, perhaps, that led me to prefer the winter season to all other seasons, and to prefer the night to the daytime.

With the day came the time to go to school, for those lucky enough to be able to study. As for the less lucky, they'd somehow drag themselves from their warm beds to go to their jobs, which were harder on the body than studying: tough jobs needing an effort that was often beyond a child's capacity to endure. Yes, in the days I'm writing about, half a century ago, there were children who never found their way to school. Life was hard and merciless generally. Even the youngsters in the family had to play their part in providing for mouths that needed food to stay alive.

My family's social circumstances meant that, when I got back from school, I had to pick up a rather large axe and go out beyond the village to chop roots and small branches for use on the stove at night, or to bring back some grass to feed a sheep or donkey. It was a severe ordeal, and I thoroughly disliked it, but there was no escape. I was the second son in my family, and no one expected a girl to go and chop wood or do any difficult task belonging to the men and boys. As the second child, you soon learned it was your place to obey orders without argument, because there was no point in arguing. The younger child had to do the work the older brother found degrading. This, of course, was in accordance with inherited traditions that were accepted without question. No doubt my brother had the lion's share of the hard work, which took him far away from the village, together with his young friends, in search of a livelihood. He might be away for a night or two in search of firewood. Sometimes, indeed, he'd be away for many days, ploughing a piece of land, with oxen or donkeys, when the rain had fallen and it was time to plant the seeds.

I wasn't yet old enough to go with my brother on jobs like these. Once, even so, he did take me along when he was ploughing and preparing the land for planting. Together with the older boys there, he decided I should fetch water from a place a few kilometres away from the land they were ploughing. I'd hop on to the donkey's back at sunrise and head for the spring seven kilometres away. There was nothing about the journey for me or my family to worry about, except that some neighbours also preparing their land had a big, vicious dog. I was afraid of dogs (I still am), and hated going near them, especially when there was a glimmer of evil in their eyes. Since it was regarded as a major defect to be afraid of dogs, I buried my fear inside myself and told no one about it, agreeing to the job without demur.

I started to go every day to fetch the water they needed. I'd fill one or two waterskins, then carry the precious load on the back of the lazy donkey, who plodded along taking most of the day getting there and back. Meanwhile, the boisterous dog would drive me on with his barking and bare his sharp fangs, as if ready to kill his prey. I'd pray to God to protect me from his evil, heaving a deep sigh of relief once I'd passed through what I viewed as his domain. To begin with things went all right, since the dog, as I said earlier, would merely drive me on when he met me.

One day, though, when I was on my way back, walking proudly along behind my donkey as it plodded on with its precious load of water, the dog must have decided the situation had gone beyond bearing. He suddenly attacked me from behind, sinking his fangs into my thigh. The shock of it wasn't as hard as I thought it would be; I'd known something of the sort would happen sooner or later. Earlier, apparently, the dog had been testing me out. Then, when he'd decided he could follow his threat with action, he hesitated no longer. I didn't fight back against the dog, because he ran off once he'd bitten me. Oddly enough, I never saw him again.

Our head and organizer, in this trip as in our other domestic affairs, especially after my father's death, was my maternal uncle Muhammad Fahd al-Mihjel, God rest his soul. If all uncles had been like mine, then no one would have needed a father. Being orphaned is a tragedy that scars a child, one from which he can never escape. But this uncle of ours was absolutely like a father to us, doing his utmost to make it up to my brother and myself for the loss of our own father. He overflowed with love and compassion. He treated us exactly as he did his own daughters (he had no sons), and in a natural, unaffected way, as if it was the normal way for someone like him to feel and behave towards people like us. He encompassed us with his compassion from the moment my father died, God rest his soul. He wasn't rich; wasn't even above the poverty line. He owned nothing apart from his physical strength and the ability to bear hard work only strong men could bear. He was a huge man, around two metres tall, and had a distinctive way of walking, rather like a camel. He shared other characteristics with the camel too, like his broad step, steady movement and patience in the face of adversity – which was why he was actually nicknamed "the camel"! The man must have been born the twin to poverty itself. He was born poor and raised as a poor man; he struggled heroically against poverty; and in the end he died poor. There was nothing so very strange or unusual about his state within his society. Even so, if there was one man poorer than the rest, it must have been my uncle. What made him poorer still was the fact that he bore the responsibility for my mother, who was his sister, and for my brothers and myself, quite apart from his daughters and his wife. Owning neither house nor land, he had to toil to feed all the hungry mouths. My uncle was always on the move, wandering the plains and outlandish places to get firewood, or going to the homes and camps of the Bedouins to barter his modest goods for any extra food and supplies they might have. He'd be overjoyed if he could come back with a few days' provisions to feed the youngsters, who'd await his homecoming with eager eyes.

My uncle was a courageous man of the kind not found nowadays, when people have grown used to an easy, comfortable way of living. Once he was making a trip on his donkey to the Bedouin camps somewhere in the wilderness, and, as he rode along at night, he found an enormous hyena in his path. Usually, when a hyena sees its prey, it starts testing it out to see how much it can resist. The hyena approached my uncle on his donkey, and my uncle made not the smallest movement. The hyena approached closer still, testing his reaction. Still my uncle sat motionless on his donkey, his staff in his hand. This staff, used for self-defence, was very thick with a pointed head; in the hands of a brave man it was the equal of a rifle. My uncle let the hyena come closer and closer, till it was almost touching him, feeling confident of an easy hunt. When my uncle sensed the hyena's certainty, he dealt the animal one swift blow with his staff, killing it at a stroke.

When, next morning, my uncle reached his destination and told some people what had happened, they didn't believe him. How could he have killed the hyena with a single blow of his staff? So he led them off to the place where he'd confronted the hyena, and they saw the dead beast for themselves.

Another time, he was on one of the arduous trips he knew throughout his life. It had been a cold, rainy winter day, and now night had fallen on him and his friends. The group was near the historical palace of al-Heer in the Syrian desert. When they reached the place, they found a small corner that afforded them refuge from the streaming rain. There wasn't, though, room enough for all of them. When the time came to sleep, they were tired out. But they found that, if they all wanted to sleep, then one of them had to lie on top of a deep chasm that had once been a well rich with water. Eyes were cast around, for the man who'd risk his life sleeping on top of the old well mouth; whereupon my uncle stepped up and measured his own length against that of the well. He lay down over the top of the chasm, then straight away sank into a deep sleep till morning.

Once he was travelling with my brother Salih, towards the Bedouin camps. Night fell, with the rain streaming down, and my uncle told my brother to bring some scrub to light a fire to warm them. It was pitch dark, and still the rain poured down. The wilderness was bleak and deserted, everything round about gave rise to fear and apprehension. The boy went to fetch the fuel, not daring to say how afraid he was of the thick darkness on a night of heaven's anger, when it was beating its rain in cascades over the heads of those unlucky enough to face its fury.

When Salih had gone a few metres, he saw a light in the distance, which turned out, eventually, to be from a car heading towards al-Qaryatain. By good luck, this car drove straight towards my brother, who waved to the driver; and the driver, seeing him, stopped to ask him for directions to al-Qaryatain. Unable to believe his ears, my brother asked, was he really saying al-Qaryatain? The driver replied that he was indeed going there, and the boy lost no time in asking if he could go along too; while the driver was naturally delighted to find, in my brother, a companion and a guide in one. Forgetting all about his uncle, and what his uncle had sent him for, the boy jumped into the car. My poor uncle kept searching for my brother all night long, and through to the next evening, when he returned weeping to the village, supposing Salih had been lost or devoured by wild beasts.

Many more stories were told about this brave, hard-working man, who went on struggling against a life that was mostly too strong for him. He saw only life's wretched side, never knew tranquility and a soft bed. His day was a struggle, his night preparation for a new struggle; he'd finish one hard job only to start a far harder one still – and all so as to get enough to feed his children and his sister's children. All this he did with contentment and satisfaction, and with a diligence that knew no despair. He'd leave his home full of hope, as if going in quest of a treasure. He knew beforehand what he was really going to find, but saw it nonetheless as the peak of achievement. He never chased after wealth or fortune, because that was beyond his dreams. He was a practical man, stronger than a lion in getting the barest livelihood, which he regarded as the natural right for himself and his children. He was ready to carve the very rocks to achieve that right – the right to live.

My uncle, God rest his soul, had no boys, as I said; only girls. And that was why he kept on toiling till the very end, till he could no longer stand on his two feet. What a rock of a man he was! I never ceased to wish he'd lived long enough for me to be able to compensate him a little for the pain and hard life he endured for us, when we were young, so as to provide us with a decent life and protect us against the humiliation of poverty.

I often let my thoughts wander, imagining my uncle was still alive and myself travelling to see him in Syria. I'd ask for him, only to be told he was in the wilderness, according to his usual habit, travelling among the Bedouin camps, or collecting wood, or tilling a piece of unirrigated land ready to plant it. I imagine myself going to see him wherever he might be, taking him by surprise by appearing there next to him. Then, before he could wake from his astonishment, I'd invite him to go back to his home with me in a comfortable car. His days of toil, I'd assure him, were over for good. From this day on, his hands would never again touch a plough pulled along by a feeble donkey! These were beautiful dreams, but they were never fulfilled, for my uncle died when I was sent on a scholarship to the USA. May God rest his soul, and reward him with the best reward that may be bestowed on a good person, one that life deprived of its material benefits, but who, for his part, harboured no resentment, dying thankful and satisfied with what God had given him.

**The child of difficult tasks**
Of course, the end of winter, and the beginning of summer, didn't mean the end of work and seeking a livelihood. Each season had its demands and requirements, and the constant endeavour to make a living was what marked out most people's lives in any case. One summer, my brother Salih asked me to get ready to go on a "business" trip with him. The merchandise consisted of two cases filled with grapes, loaded on the back of a lazy donkey. We had to start out at dawn so as to reach the Bedouin camps in the forenoon of the same day. In fact the distance was too great in any case to be travelled in a few hours, so we decided to travel the day before the set date and spend the night at a farm halfway between al-Qaryatain and the camps; we actually left on the afternoon of the previous day. Salih, though, having little experience of such trips, was nervous and jumped up with only part of the night gone, and he woke me too. He thought dawn was about to break, and we had to start out. We didn't know about watches in those days!

I found it difficult to rouse myself, especially as I'd only slept for an hour or two. I flung on my clothes, and soon was ready to start. With the help of some of the farm's owners, my brother set the load on the donkey's back, then we headed it towards our destination, and off we went. The donkey, though, was a sluggish beast, and it was still night, so dark you could see no more than two metres in front of you. The whole atmosphere was fearful and desolate. The donkey itself was afraid, it seemed to me, for it was taking one step forward then one step back. When Salih was unable to make it move faster, he told me to walk in front, in the hope this might encourage the beast to increase its speed and get us to our destination in good time.

Actually, when I think of all this now, I simply have to laugh. The place we were headed for was so close by we only had to cross a few hills to find ourselves among the Bedouin camps. And yet, what with the ghostly night and stillness around us, and the fact that we were in the midst of a desolate landscape, along with a donkey who was even more scared than we were, my brother and I felt we'd embarked on a most perilous venture.

When my brother told me to walk in front of the donkey, I felt helpless. The poor animal was afraid, or so I supposed, when it was in the lead. Now that I'd taken its place, so it could walk in the middle, the fear was transferred to me! And yet I didn't dare refuse or raise any objection; the younger brother's place, after all, was to listen and obey. So we'd been taught, and I only wish our own children would keep up that glorious tradition. So, I walked in front of the donkey and Salih walked behind it. The cold was creeping into my bones, the whole appearance of things was utterly different from the evening, when the sky above us had been lit by countless glittering stars. I'd imagined, when gazing at the stars, that they were winking at me one after the other, in a subtle, reassuring way, trying to allay the suffering of my wretched situation.

There were no clear paths for us to take. We were rather heading towards a particular place we'd had described to us. Hardly had my brother told me to take the lead, when I started, little by little, veering away from our destination. Salih thereupon instructed me to go back to my place behind the donkey while he walked in front, and, needless to say, I complied promptly. Now, though, my fears multiplied, as I kept looking behind me, fearing I might be kidnapped by some passing ghoul. The old women had always warned us children of the fearful ghouls who stalked any children straying from their parents' sight. Perhaps all that might come true!

My brother set us on the proper course, and we moved on towards the Bedouin tents. Promptly at sunrise we were at their camps, distributing our goods and taking the money for them, or else bartering them against provisions we needed, like dates. While we were there, we happened to pass by a woman who was sitting in the front part of her tent with her children around her. The moment she caught sight of me, she reproached my brother for subjecting his younger brother to the hardships of travelling, and she promptly bought all the goods we had left, so that Salih could – as she told him – hurry off and get me back to my mother.

*Hasan Naseef*

# FROM *MEMOIRS OF A STUDENT*
(mudhakkarat talib)

The last beating I had was in 1355 AH; I was sixteen years old and, with a sigh of relief, had just received my graduation certificate. Feeling grown up now, I began thinking of my future career. Only one thought came to disrupt my beautiful dreams: two years before I graduated, the government had dispatched a group of students to Egypt to enroll at the Dar al-ʻUlum and the al-Azhar University, and among the members had been the teachers al-Suwayyil, ʻAbd al-Jabbar and al-Fatani. At the time, my father had had hopes I might have been one of those sent; but he wanted me to finish my school studies, and so the crisis passed.

The future, though, held a different crisis for me. After I graduated, a new factor made its distant appearance: the Ministry of Education was considering opening a preparatory school for those undertaking the *hajj*. My father happened to be in Mecca after the pilgrimage, and he gave my name to the Ministry, with no thought as to my own feelings about the serious risk involved. A relative of mine, who was a supervisor for educational affairs in Jeddah, called and gave me the dreadful news, along with a letter from my father telling me of the preparations I needed to make in the face of the new situation. I returned home under a cloud of depression. I was, my father said in his letter, to buy some cloth and have new clothes made ready to attend the school; and so we bought the material and my mother started sewing the clothes.

I had a younger brother, now studying at university. He was playing in the room, and, when he stepped on the new clothes, I hit him. My mother was mild as a rule; she'd only ever hit us a few times, being rather inclined to comfort us when we'd been beaten by our father. This time, though, she started hitting me with her hand and her fan. I took the treatment in astonishment, saying goodbye to one era and welcoming a new one with a beating that was the last I was ever to know.

### Pilgrimage on donkeys
God bless the time before cars entered our lives, and when radio, tape recorder, electricity and all the other modern inventions were still unknown. Young people

today are luckier than we were, with a brighter future. They have before them, from the start, the radio and other modern cultural devices, which, alongside the school, help them develop their understanding. We, by contrast, lived our early lives in the age of donkeys. As a child, indeed, I twice went on pilgrimage on camels, traversing the route between Jeddah and Mecca in two days. I knew the expressions *al-wisk* and *al-'asim* – which gave way, later on, to the names of new models of American cars.

When I reached adulthood, I longed to perform the prescribed pilgrimage. But how was I to tell my father something like this, when I'd never sat in his company or looked him straight in the eye? He'd taken me with him on pilgrimage each year, but didn't want me to go to Mecca that particular year because money was short. I used my mother as a mediator, though, to inform my father of my wish, and he sent me along with my uncle. We took a car from Jeddah to Mecca, where a donkey was waiting; the beast belonged to us, and was used throughout the year to pull a water cart. Imagine a strong donkey like that, carrying a young lad like me! I couldn't rein in the donkey – or the anger of my uncle, God rest his soul, when I sped ahead of him, though he was supposed to be the one leading. I never found any answer to this, and nor did the malicious donkey. Nowadays, our children, having learned to drive cars, don't need to feel proud of having lived in the "age of donkeys." Performing the pilgrimage then was a pleasure and an adventure, and it had its interesting memories. Donkeys would transport us from one place to the next with total freedom of the road, never having to stop or wait for long hours in queues.

My present work makes quick transportation necessary during the *hajj*. And yet I wait in queues, in my car, for hours, longing for the days of the donkey. I even think, quite seriously, of using that quick, comfortable means of travel. Each year, though, I hesitate. When, I wonder, will I achieve my wish? If I could find a donkey, then perhaps I'd be spurred on to do it. But would I be able to find one?

## The Badkouk loufa

We spent happy years at the boarding home in Mecca. Our means were modest, but the ten riyals would last each one of us more than one or two months. The roads out of Jeddah were unpaved, so we only visited our parents every few months and during the holidays, taking the mail car, which was virtually the only means of transport available.

Of the friends we made at that time, one of the most humorous was Mr Muhammad Badkouk. His mother, God rest her soul, came to Mecca at the start of our school year, speaking to his supervisor Shaikh 'Arif and asking him to liaise with Mr Tahir al-Dabbagh, the Director of Education at the time, to allow her to visit the boarding section at the preparatory school for expeditions. She wanted to be sure of her son's comfort: to hang up the *loufa*, put up the nails for the mosquito net, hang up the towel and see his suitcase was properly packed.

Shaikh 'Arif managed, with much effort, to convince her otherwise. She was, God rest her soul, a good talker. We'd go to Jeddah with Muhammad especially to visit her, and she'd lecture us and talk to us from behind a curtain. We'd meddle between her and her son, telling her things her son used to do and so starting up a quarrel between them.

One of the comic stories about Ustadh Badkouk in <u>Mecca</u> was as follows. There was a deranged man who'd come to the expedition centre at al-Misfala, and who we used to joke with and make fun of. One day, Badkouk was standing at the entrance to the centre, wearing his best clothes and glasses. The deranged man, passing by, flung some dirt into Badkouk's face. Then, realizing it was Badkouk, he said:

"I'm sorry. I thought you were Shabankash [meaning Shaikh Husain Shabakshi, who closely resembled Badkouk]."

"And suppose I had been Shabankash?" Badkouk said. "Would you still have flung that dirt on me?"

And with that he roared with laughter as usual, before going on with his humorous discussion, not in the least offended by the incident.

## Help! Help!

It's common enough for people to say, exaggerating or as a joke, that students have a way of driving their teachers crazy. But one day we students really did manage to drive our teacher crazy, so that he gave up teaching altogether. We were at the Preparatory School for Pilgrimage Expeditions, and behind our classroom was the laboratory room, which contained inflammable chemicals. Once these had been set alight and almost started a fire. The teacher was giving us an Arabic lesson on specification. He was an excellent teacher, well versed in his field, but he was faced with students who were masters of mischief in their own right.

There was one particular group of students who wouldn't stop laughing, whether there was a good reason for it or not. The teacher was giving an example of specification. "We Arabs, etc.," he was saying. What, we asked him then, was the singular form of this "etc." he'd mentioned? We went on to tell him how, at marriages, we ourselves used "etc.," and we gave him its singular form. Perhaps, the teacher said then, "etc." was used to indicate a group of ten people.

The discussion went on, the teacher serious, while our group, myself among them, were simply playing around. We were doing a good job when the teacher suddenly put an end to the interchange.

"Help! Help!" he shouted. "Out of here, quickly!"

He was the first out, and we ran out after him, thinking he'd seen something burning in the laboratory. But we didn't find anything. As for the teacher, he went down to the administrative office, picked up his bag and left the school, never to return. We'd put our principal in a difficult situation. Knowing of the incident, he didn't know who he could choose as a replacement, someone who'd be ready to face the same fate as the earlier teacher.

A short time after that incident, we were at Hamidiyya bidding farewell to prince Faisal, may God cure him, when one of the teachers recited a poem inappropriate to the occasion. Also there was our teacher Ustadh Husain al-Hout, a witty man with whom we had plenty of jokes and skirmishes.

"What sort of a country is this?" Ustadh al-Hout said, when we got back to the school. "It's full of imbeciles!" He went on to specify the poet, and the teacher who'd gone before him.

"But," I said at once, "they're not from this country at all."

He accepted my pointed joke, laughing along with the rest of my classmates. The two he'd criticized were in fact natives of his own country.

## A trip, a trial, a penitence

The English teacher, Ustadh 'Abd al-Raouf al-Afghani, was one of the pleasantest people there. Quite apart from his vast knowledge of the English language, he was a scholar of extensive knowledge. When our art teacher was away, he gave us art lessons and proved to be very good, even though art has its own rules and methods. Some of my classmates, having poor memories, were unable to keep things in their heads. And so he told them of an Indian remedy: they were to shave their heads completely, then anoint them with the oil of seven seeds. How we could use a prescription like that today – apart, that is, from the shaving.

He once suggested we should have a Friday picnic in one of the orchards of Mecca, and we started preparing accordingly. Each of us, he advised, should buy an apple for himself; an apple, at that time, was something hugely prized. Later he explained the importance of having an apple. There was, he told us, a saying in English that an apple a day keeps the doctor away.

Friday arrived, and we went happily off to the orchard, the teacher explaining the various kinds of plants to be found there. In the orchard we discovered a man swimming in the pool, and we started teasing him till he finally came out. We wanted the pool all to ourselves.

We had no idea of the trouble his departure was to bring us. Next day the head of the judiciary system summoned us, along with our teacher, for not attending Friday prayers. We took the matter fairly lightly to start with, but our teacher, umbrella in hand, would go off several times a day to meet with the officials in question, then come back to give us the results of his efforts.

On one occasion he told these officials that we hadn't attended the prayers because Hamid al-Harasani's car, which we used for the trip, was out of order; and he primed us all to tell the same story. Finally the matter went to the court, and we officially briefed our friend al-Harasani to attend the case. I don't recall, now, our specific reason for choosing him. Perhaps it was because we were young, and he was older than we were. At last the judge issued his verdict: that we were to make a formal expression of penitence. One day we were taken, along with our teacher, to the headquarters of the organization established to promote virtue, near the Holy Mosque in Mecca; and there, one by one, we expressed our penitence. Then we walked out, scarcely able to believe we'd escaped so lightly.

All this was thanks to the clever lawyer and his broken car. Without these we should have found ourselves marked down as offenders.

### The modern conservative principal

Ustadh Is-haq 'Azzouz was a decent man, who raised generations in this country; a man who combined the preservation of Arab-Muslim traditions with the modern liberal spirit. We were in the boarding section of the school, and he'd wake us for the morning prayer. When we founded a scout troop at the school, he'd put on a scouts uniform himself and join the troop in marching through the streets, without any embarrassment at what people might say.

We had cotton cushions to sit on in the classrooms, and we used to throw these at one another during the break. On one occasion I was aiming to hit my friend Ahmad with my cushion, but missed and hit Ustadh Is-haq, who'd just come into the classroom to check up on us. It struck him full in the face, but he said not a word. I was fearful of repercussions, but it all passed off peacefully: Ustadh Is-haq took the whole matter in a sporting spirit.

Ustadh Is-haq was a brilliant orator, and often delivered speeches on special occasions, winning the audience's hearts with his simple but effective style. He used to surprise us by appearing in the classroom; we'd turn to find him sitting in one of the rare seats, attending the class and observing the teacher's performance. Later, when he'd given up his principal's post, we arranged a big celebration in his honour, which was attended by the scholars and men of letters in Mecca. The students of Ustadh Is-haq 'Azzouz were proud of him, and became his friends, cherishing his friendship. But his ways as a friend and as a teacher were different. He played many tricks on his friends, and frolicked with them, to the extent that they were wary of the stunts he might pull.

### Absentia prayer for the dead

After I'd published my reminiscence about Badkouk's loufa, Badkouk himself phoned to remind me of the story of the absentia prayer for the dead, and also promised to send me, for publication, a further series of his memories for which I'm still waiting.

Badkouk, though, was a whole series of memories in himself. Had I wanted to write about him further, I would have needed to start a new Saudi genre entitled "Memories of Badkouk" or "Badkoukism." And so I'll try to be brief.

We were in the boarding section after breakfast, getting ready to go to our classrooms, and Badkouk was still polishing his glasses. At this point the postman arrived with a cable addressed to Badkouk, who, opening it, read the news of his mother's death. The cable bore the name of Muhammad 'Ali Abu Dawud, who lived in Jeddah. We were all shocked, and did our best to comfort Badkouk. The cable, we told him, hadn't been sent by one of his relatives. He couldn't be certain the news was true. But our efforts were in vain; Muhammad 'Ali Abu Dawud was his brother's colleague and regarded as one of the family. It wasn't as easy as it is now to get through to Jeddah by phone. Badkouk started crying, and we joined with him, while his teachers and classmates tried to console him. Ustadh 'Abd al-Raouf al-Afghani started giving him religious counsel and reading verses from the Quran, while Shaikh 'Arif hired a car to take Badkouk to Jeddah, paying ten riyals, viewed as a large sum then. Badkouk left for Jeddah before noon, along the unpaved road, but before going to his home he passed by the "Mother Eve" cemetery and asked if anyone had just been buried. Being told that no one had, he supposed he was awaited at home and hurried on there. He went first into the room of his brother 'Abd al-Rahman, who was deaf, and asked him about the funeral and when it was due to take place. His brother told him he knew nothing of the matter and started crying. Then the two brothers went upstairs, 'Abd al-Rahman crying still more bitterly than Badkouk. There before them, to their astonishment, was their mother, getting ready to pray. Muhammad threw himself on her weeping, while 'Abd al-Rahman sat on the floor and cried. The mother, who knew all about it, turned to 'Abd al-Rahman.

"I can forgive Muhammad," she shouted, "because of the cable. But what's the matter with you? Are you crazy?"

After they'd calmed down, they started investigating the matter and made inquiries at the telegraph office. One Muhammad Hasan Asfahani, they discovered, had sent the cable on April the first, using the name of Muhammad 'Ali Abu Dawud.

The night Badkouk left for Jeddah, I prayed the night prayer and the absentia prayer for the dead. As for Badkouk, he lodged a formal complaint against Asfahani, who was ordered to restore to Badkouk the substantial amount of money the trip had cost and warned not to do anything of the kind again. The two remained at odds for a long time. If Badkouk ever caught sight of Asfahani in the market place, he'd turn aside to avoid meeting him. Eventually they made up.

Ustadh Mahmoud 'Arif composed a long and splendid satirical poem to mark the occasion. In it he wrote:

*And another from Karachi* [i.e., our teacher Ustadh al-Afghani],
*Who saw you running for cars,*
*To you he came and consoled you,*
*Soothing your feelings.*

The poem went on to describe the trip to Jeddah:

*The wheels became stuck.*
*You pushed, but had no strength.*

    ...

*He erred, al-Asfahani,*
*And caused so much harm*
*With the cable in which he wrote*

*A lie. (How clever of him!)*

Next he gave advice to Badkouk, after the shock and the tribulation he'd endured:

*This your mother, Badkouk,*
*Well knows the use of censers.*

*For the cost of a piaster,*
*Buy olibanum at 'Abd al-Qadir's*
*And ask her to cense you*
*Against all jinn and sorcerers.*
*The principal we were upset for*

One of our most favourite teachers was the honourable Ustadh Ahmad al-'Arabi. A capable teacher, and an admired principal too, he was well versed in Arabic, both in its grammar and its literature. He made a point of speaking properly even when he wanted to attack his students. He was an excellent educator and set a personal example in his morals, self-respect and impeccable reputation.

When we were in the first academic year at the preparatory school, the Directorate of Education decided to transfer him, as principal, to the Saudi Scientific Institute. This decision upset us so much we decided to suspend our attendance at classes till the Directorate rescinded its decision.

The news annoyed the Directorate and its employees. Ours was the first secondary school they'd had, and they didn't want to see it strangled in its cradle on account of such boyish acts. The principal assembled all the students in one of the rooms of the boarding section, and Mr Muhammad Shatta, the Directorate's first inspector and a man of strong character, feared by the students, came to see us there. It so happened that, as he entered the room, Mr 'Umar 'Aqeel was giving one of his rousing speeches.

The inspector questioned us, then left. We, on our side, were in a quandary; the effect of the rousing speeches had evaporated, and we'd calmed down. Next day we were assembled once more, and the Director of Education, the honourable Ustadh Tahir al-Dabbagh, gave an address that combined advice and threat. Then he informed us of the Directorate's decision: some of the agitators were to be suspended from school, others to have points for merit deducted. Things went back to normal after that, and a few months later the suspended students were allowed to return.

After a while Ustadh Ahmad al-'Arabi returned to the school. Once, when we were in the fourth year, we happened to be late for the noon prayer he was leading; when we did arrive, we prayed under Mr Hasan Shatta. When the prayer was over, the principal, regarding our action as a violation and a challenge to his authority, summoned us all. Our punishment, he decided, should be suspension for varying periods of time. So, in effect, the fourth year was at an end.

What made the whole thing so disastrous was that he'd sent the suspension orders to our parents. I, for my part, started checking on my father's movements between Jeddah and Mecca as if I was following up on news of the Sixth Fleet. The late Salih Shatta and Shaikh Ahmad al-Gazawi, may he live long, both made an attempt to mediate. Shaikh Gazawi told Ustadh Ahmad al-'Arabi:

"These particular students stood by you before, when they were upset over your transfer. Isn't that perhaps a point in their favour?"

It was, and we returned safely to school.

### The prince of coffee makers, and "pressed mail"

Here are some miscellaneous memories of our days at the preparatory school for expeditions in Mecca. There were, for instance, those splendid evenings we so looked forward to, spent in al-Misfala district, where we grew familiar with its coffee shops and came to know their owners personally. On the benches of the Bukhari Café, we became acquainted with the great Ustadh Hamza Shihata, and began listening to his poems and literary anecdotes. He had a literary circle that would meet and sit next to us each day.

So (with apologies to Ustadh Fouad Shakir) began the Literary Forum. Sometimes, when we had no money, we used to go to the municipal café in Upper Mecca, where the Traffic Department's sited today. Its owner was known as the Prince of Café Owners, and, since he liked the title, we took care to call him that when we arrived and show him every mark of esteem; and then he'd call for us to be given our drinks on the house. Badkouk always used to come after the rest of us. Once he was very late getting to the café, and, when he did finally arrive, he was out of breath. Mr 'Umar 'Aqeel, he told us, had intercepted him in al-Joudariyya and assaulted him, and so he'd been to the al-Ma'alat police station and filed a complaint. The police, he went on, now had Mr 'Aqeel in custody. A short while later, we saw Mr 'Umar 'Aqeel walk in humming to himself. The officer at al-Ma'alat station was, it so happened, a friend of his, and the two of them had played a trick on Badkouk. The officer had pretended to lock Mr 'Aqeel up, but actually released him the moment Badkouk left. Even so, 'Umar 'Aqeel never went near Badkouk after that.

It was around that time that the "pressed mail" was invented. This invention we offer as a suggestion to our friends who attend the international Mail Conferences, as something they might be proud of. An ordinary letter would cost one and a quarter piastres. If, though, it was puffed out, the postman would carefully weigh it and ask for an additional fee. How could we avoid rousing the postman's suspicions? Badkouk came up with an amazing idea. He'd write the letters, and they'd all look puffed and heavy. Then, in the afternoon, he'd begin with the pressing, putting each letter under his cotton cushion and sitting down on it. What followed was an extraordinary sight: Badkouk would begin moving to the right, then to the left, leaning now forward, now backward. After half an hour out would come the letter, light-looking and slim.

So we contrived to supplement sea, air and road mail with a new postal creation. We gave it the name "pressed mail."

## God bless her and all who sail in her

The announcement arrived that the government intended to send us on an expedition, at a time when the German bombardment was coming close to Alexandria before the Battle of Al-'Alamain and their aircraft were flying over Cairo and Alexandria. We packed our luggage accordingly. At the time I was a teacher at the Falah School in Jeddah, and, since I needed to keep the job, I was reluctant to leave. Still, I didn't want people to think I was a fool in turning down the expedition. The General Directorate of Education organized a farewell ceremony for us in Jeddah, attended by the Jeddah District Commissioner along with other high-ranking officials and prominent figures from the city. Our principal Ustadh Ahmad al-'Arabi said goodbye to us too.

I shall leave the reader (having been through these memoirs and seen how we'd spend our evenings), to judge whether we took that road for education's sake, and spent the long nights studying. We would, we hoped, manage to do our honest duty. As for the tears we shed, I only wish they could have been real, that they'd drowned the dissolved Canal Company of the time and spared us the troubles of the Canal itself, along with their aftermath. But the fact was, those tears were false and exaggerated, transformed to audible glee and ululation on the ship that took us on the trip. I shall meet with you next Friday, with a new anecdote as we follow that pleasant trip, and so enjoy the glee and the ululations together.

## A trip in the darkness

Before the trip started, Ustadh Tahir al-Dabbagh assembled us. We were in Jeddah, where we'd been waiting for several days for the ship to arrive; because of the war we'd only know the date of this arrival one night in advance.

"It's established practice," Ustadh Tahir told us, "that a travelling group should have an appointed leader. I've chosen 'Alawi al-Jafri to lead this trip of ours."

I was sad at this, because I had the best academic record among those undertaking the expedition. My young age, though, had stood between me and the position of leader. In fact, the task proved to be a burden with such a gracious group! The leader became a figure of fun, and we all looked forward to reaching Suez, so we could throw off the burden of his leadership.

The ship travelled in complete darkness on account of the war. We'd be having fun or enjoying ourselves, during the day or night, then the warning siren would sound, and we and the sailors alike would run to put on our lifejackets – only to find out later that it was just a manoeuvre to train passengers and sailors to act quickly if there was any genuine danger. Al-Harasani was the one most afraid. We used to make him think there was an air raid on, and he'd start running, in a panic to get his lifejacket on. In the end he decided to keep it on day and night. A strange sight he presented attired like that, all the prayers and Quranic verses he'd memorized streaming from his lips. The ship had western-style toilet seats, of a kind we'd never seen before, and we had comical difficulties using them for the first time. We made friends with the ship's officers, and with the captain, and we visited all parts of the vessel, listening to the officers as they explained the machinery and how it worked. On board the ship was the Egyptian preacher Shaikh Ahmad Tulba Saqr, and we spent some marvellous days with him. He was a man of pleasant conversation and extensive knowledge. At last the ship dropped anchor in Suez harbour, and we were received by our honourable teacher and supervisor for the expedition, Mr Waliyy al-Din As'ad. He welcomed us in worthy style, rather the way al-Hajjaj Bin Yusuf[5] welcomed the people of Iraq. This will be the subject of our next story.

## The first night in Egypt

We reached Suez in the evening, and Mr Waliyy al-Din As'ad took us to the Hamidiyya Hotel overlooking the railway station. There, for the first time, we met hosts of a new kind, known as fleas.

We didn't sleep all night long. We were all having fun and laughing, except for Mr Hasan Shatta, who looked scared but wouldn't tell us why till the morning.

"Didn't you," he asked us then, "hear that madman shrieking all night long?"

He was most surprised when we told him we hadn't heard anything. At last, as he went on, the truth struck us: he was talking about the whistle of the trains. Each time a train blew its whistle, he thought it was a madman shrieking, and he became ever more anxious and fearful.

In the morning, the train took us to Cairo, where ululations broke out at the station to welcome the shaikhs of the Arabs who'd thus arrived en masse. We were seized with amazement by all the sights around us.

We finally arrived at the house that had been rented for us in the 'Abdeen quarter. Then, in the afternoon, we went with Mr Waliyy al-Din to Averino Stores, where we bought ready-made suits and left the place all dressed up in our new clothes. Mr Waliyy al-Din insisted we each wear a fez, in keeping with our respectable and dignified appearance. This we wore for a full year, never leaving the expedition home without it, on pain of a deduction from our allowance. Eager to show us, from the very beginning, how serious he was, Mr Waliyy al-Din made a speech full of good advice, concluding with his traditional sentence after the manner of al-Hajjaj: "By God, I shall wrap you like flowers in a bunch, and beat you as a man would the most perverse of camels!" We really feared and respected him at first. Then, little by little, the fear vanished, and we started playing tricks on him, which he was unable to stop. I shall describe some of them here and there in these memoirs.

In the evening we decided to relax by taking a walk. There were fifteen of us, and we stayed together the whole time. The comical story of how we entered the park is worthy of mention.

### How I played the idiot's role

Right from the start of our trip from Jeddah to Cairo, we'd had to give our names on every possible occasion: to the passport officials, to the health quarantine officials, to the ship's staff, at the hotel, and so on. Now, when we went out on our first night in Cairo and headed for one of the public parks in the Sayyida Zainab quarter, we found a ticket kiosk and an employee sitting there waiting to take money. Wanting to show how clever and witty I was, I started telling him the names of my colleagues, so that he could issue the fifteen tickets. The man stared at me, then gazed at my fez and suit, which still sat oddly on me; no doubt the necktie also showed I was a stranger in the country and not used to such clothes and places. The man burst out laughing, and so did my friends, thus showing their kindly feelings towards my monumental idiocy.

One night I went early with Sharaf Kazim, so as to book places for our colleagues and ourselves. Before choosing a place to go, we'd check on the nearest mosque so that we could pray; and, accordingly, we booked the places and went to pray the sunset prayer in a nearby mosque in 'Imadiddin Street (the name meaning "Pillar of Religion"). I should say, incidentally, that Mr Waliyy al-Din always called the street Hadmiddin Street (meaning "Destruction of Religion"). Going back, we missed our way and became lost in streets that looked all alike to us. We ran and reached the right place at last, to find the show already started and our waiting friends heaping offensive abuse on us.

We began our preparations to enter the university, which will be the subject of my next memoir.

### At the university gates

My aggregate grades entitled me to enter the Faculty of Medicine, and there I was enrolled; my wish had been to enroll at the Faculty of Literature, but I reconciled myself with time. Mr Waliyy al-Din took us round the various faculties, some of which regretted being unable to accept us because we'd arrived a month after the start of the academic year, and because they were afraid our educational level would be too weak. The Dean of the Faculty of Commerce accepted my colleagues only after tremendous efforts on the part of Mr Waliyy al-Din. Yet, for all that, my colleagues always figured among the top students – even though they knew no French and had to study the secondary school syllabus and that of the first university year over just a few months.

We'd arrived before the money transfer reached Mr Waliyy al-Din. There was no possibility of enrolling at the Faculty of Medicine without paying the fees in advance, and I didn't myself have enough money for this. Some of my colleagues offered to help me, but I refused. Eventually the transfer reached Mr Waliyy al-Din, and he paid all the necessary expenses.

This still left the matter of Badkouk. He too wished to enter the Faculty of Medicine, but they were prepared to accept only three students; and so Mr Waliyy al-Din applied on his behalf to the Faculty of Agriculture, which upset Badkouk. Ever since his secondary school days, he'd wished to study pharmacy and one day own his own pharmacy at Faisal Street in Jeddah; and to have daily fights with Saeed Tamer.,[6] hurling bottles of citric acid!

He saw his dream vanishing into thin air. His late uncle tried to mediate, but to no avail. This uncle, God rest his soul, had promised to invite us for a turkey meal, but he kept evading this till at last he died. Whenever he visited the expedition home, we used to cluster around him talking of the benefits of turkey; but our hopes vanished just like Badkouk's hopes of entering the Faculty of Medicine. In the end he did enroll at the Faculty of Agriculture. I sometimes wonder: if he could go back in time, would he have chosen something other than agriculture, with its numerous benefits and beautiful fruit at the casino in Kilometre No. 10?

## Tram number 22

Tram number 22 was our only means of getting to the preparatory classes at the Faculty of Medicine in al-'Abbasiyya for half the days of the week. The tram's route took passengers between the slaughterhouse and al-'Abbasiyya, and it would be filled with butchers and with labourers working at the English workshops. We'd leave for college early to be sure of places in the front seats, and because of that we could never find seats in the tram and had to hang on to the steps. We'd endure miseries in winter, our hands freezing as we clung to the iron bars. We couldn't afford the hire of a taxi or to ride in the first class section. On top of that, we all developed itches when we arrived in Egypt; we had to wear woollen clothes for the first time in our lives, and, whenever we were in the sun, we'd feel itchy and start taking them off, there in the street. People laughed at the sight, but the itching was really beyond endurance.

One of our friends used to go on ahead to reserve our places, and we'd locate him by looking for his fez. We weren't allowed, as I said, to leave the home without wearing it; otherwise our allowances would be docked. We were in fact almost the only students to wear them. We'd have our lunch at the college, paying two or three piastres, depending on the state of our finances. Our monthly allowance was one and a half Egyptian pounds. In the middle of the week we'd go to the Faculty of Science at al-Giza, for classes in biology and chemistry. Feeling somewhat unsettled during the first year in Egypt, we'd return home at sunset and go on studying till after midnight. Very often Mr Waliyy al-Din would come to our rooms and force us to stop studying and go to sleep, so we could get some rest and avoid exhaustion.

It was a year filled with sweat and tears. And yet we were all successful despite our late start to the academic year, and the domestic problems, and our estrangement from home. That preparatory year at the Faculty of Medicine was exceptionally difficult, but, thanks be to God, we all passed.

### The pioneers and the successors

My colleagues and I, the members of the first group sent to Egypt from the Preparatory School for Expeditions, could in all modesty be termed the pioneers. We were highly conservative in every respect. We always prayed at the proper time, collectively, at the expedition home. None of us ever missed a prayer for fear of having our allowances docked, as Mr Waliyy al-Din did with subsequent expeditions. The fez, again, we always wore outside, whether going to the college, going shopping or during our excursions. The excursion Mr Waliyy al-Din always recommended above all others was to the bridge of the Nile Palace. This was close to the expedition home, and we'd pass the evening breathing in the fresh air till there was none left for anyone else.

We used to go out in a group, being regularly seen in this way. If we heard of some new place, Mr Waliyy al-Din would never allow us to visit it on our own till he'd first gone there with us, to make sure the place was a suitably decent one. If so, he'd allow us to make future visits. We never stayed late outside the expedition home, except on Friday evenings, when we'd stay out till nine thirty, returning to find Mr Waliyy al-Din waiting for us, to record the time of our return.

I don't recall we were ever late back during the whole year, except just twice, when we were subjected to questioning and threatened with deductions from our allowances. The one day we weren't allowed to leave the expedition house was that of Sham al-Naseem; this, according to Mr Waliyy al-Din, was a day when virtue committed suicide and no Egyptian stayed at home.

Mr Waliyy al-Din had his particular virtues and notions of proper manners, and he was adamant in following the Arabic religious education. By a happy coincidence, I have, just at this stage of setting down my memories, received a newsletter from him about the Manyal al-Rawda Schools, which he supervises, and which are regarded as among the most prestigious private schools in Egypt from the point of view of curriculum and the Arabic religious education he provides for his students.

So much for the pioneers. Then came the second expedition, or more correctly the "backsliding" expedition, and our life entered a new phase. If I simply state that the second expedition included As'ad Jamjoum, 'Abdallah Murad and Husain al-'Attas, this should give a good idea of the scale of the change involved. The incident noted in the following episode might well be viewed as a turning point in our lives at the expedition.

### Riding in a carriage

The members of the second expedition arrived, and we welcomed them, hearing from them news of the homeland for which we'd been longing all through the year. War was still raging at Al-'Alamain, and transport to and from the Kingdom of

Saudi Arabia was very slow and restricted to sea voyages. We went with these new colleagues, and with Mr Waliyy al-Din, to Averino stores, and there went through the expedition rites: helped them put on their ready-made suits, showed them how to tie their neckties, then put the fezes on their heads. The evening they arrived, they wanted to see some of the sights of Cairo, and their leader for the evening was As'ad Jamjoum. What did he plan to do? The distance was a long one, he told the others, and walking would tire them out. He'd arrived (he went on) a few days before and had learned a good deal about the city. He thereupon hailed a carriage of the type used by lower class women, and had his respected colleagues, in their suits and fezes, ride in it. There they were – the sheikhs: Babusail, Salih Jamal, Hasan Faqeeha, 'Abdallah Murad and 'Abd al-Qadir al-Ka'ki, sitting cross-legged in the carriage. As'ad Jamjoum joined them, of course, so as not to arouse their suspicions. He took them for a ride through the streets of Cairo, to the amazement of onlookers – a reaction that naturally left his colleagues bewildered.

I had only one criticism to make of As'ad Jamjoum: that he failed to take a picture of this improbable group riding in its carriage – the photo would have made a splendid addition to this memoir. The incident was a turning point in the history of the expedition. The calm, tranquil home was transformed to a place full of bustle and pranks, as the reader will discover in the following reminiscences.

### The ticket conductors complained...

We had numerous comic encounters, well worth recording, with ticket conductors in Egypt. Some of these incidents naturally involved the art of avoiding buying tickets, something at which we became very skilful. Among our friends was a tram conductor who was a graduate of al-Azhar and had memorized a good deal of poetry and many famous sayings. We had, with him, a mobile literary forum. The bus station near the expedition home was called al-Minayyal, and, for a long time, one of our colleagues insisted on calling it al-Minabbal. Close by also was a tram station called Bir al-Nahhas. One day, Sharaf Kazim arrived complaining about the stupidity of a ticket conductor who hadn't understand when Sharaf told him he wanted to get off at "Zir al-Nahhas" station. Our colleague Rashid Radwan burst out laughing at Sharaf's mistake; and, from that time on, the station's name was transformed, to the bewilderment of the poor conductors.

Badkouk had a comical encounter with one of the tram conductors and with a mayor who was also on board. I'll set down the story with the conductor here. As for the one with the mayor, anyone who'd like to hear it can have it from me orally. (I should say, by the way, that the Mr Badkouk mentioned in these memoirs is Mr Muhammad Badkouk, Director of the Department of Agriculture in Jeddah, and not the Mr Badkouk at the Foreign Ministry. This I make clear at my friend's request.)

The incident with the conductor happened soon after we'd arrived in Egypt, while we were living in the 'Abdeen quarter. We were going out in search of the

university in al-Giza, and, when the tram arrived, Badkouk decided to start getting
on board. He put his bag in the tram, and was just about to get on when the
conductor blew his whistle, and off went the tram with Badkouk's bag on board,
while he sprinted behind it yelling: "Hey – wait, please!" Still the conductor went on
blowing his whistle, laughing together with the people on board. At last the tram
stopped and a breathless Badkouk caught up with it and took his seat. He wiped off
the sweat, then burst out laughing himself; and the laughter went on all the way to
our final destination.

One final incident with the conductors happened when Sulaiman Salama came to
Egypt. His cousin As'ad Jamjoum, who'd been appointed to watch over him, took
him by train to Alexandria to enroll him at the Victoria College, buying a full and a
half ticket for the two of them. Sulaiman was tall and still shy. The train moved on,
and, when the conductor came to check the tickets, he asked who the half ticket was
for. As'ad pointed at Sulaiman. The conductor asked Sulaiman to stand up, then
gazed at him along with all the other passengers.

"Look, everyone," the conductor said. "All that, and only half of it's a
passenger!"

While Sulaiman stood there embarrassed, As'ad just kept on laughing. They paid
the difference for the ticket, along with the penalty, while Suleiman proceeded to
curse guardianship and his conscientious guardian.

### Forming a gang

Some of our colleagues would be sent foodstuffs, while others had none. Equality
was an essential requirement, especially as we were all living together. Cockroaches
were constant visitors at the expedition home, and we found, on investigation, that
the food stored in the cupboards of some of our colleagues was a prime reason for
their growing numbers. All these things inspired Husain al-'Attas and As'ad
Jamjoum to form a gang with the following noble aims:

1.    equality among colleagues;
2.    combating cockroaches;
3.    playing comical tricks to divert colleagues.

Mr Waliyy al-Din, the supervisor of the expedition, helped As'ad form the gang –
quite without realizing it, and even though he subsequently suffered from it a great
deal and made constant efforts to combat it. He told us how the first expedition, in
which he'd been a student, had at one time suffered from lack of resources. One
member, Mr Muhammad Shatta, had been especially concerned about this, and had
developed the habit of storing things up: cheese, olives, sweets and various other
foodstuffs were to be found in his room. Mr Waliyy al-Din and his friends had
attacked Mr Shatta in his room and seized the things he'd hoarded.

Learning of the gang's noble goals, I decided to join it; and the memories I have
of it will occupy a substantial part of these accounts. A good number of other
colleagues joined, and their names will crop up at various points.

Mr Ahmad Shatta was one of those who stood out against the gang – so much so, indeed, that we used to refer to him as the Director of Public Security in the press releases we'd issue and hang up on the walls at various times.

It was strictly forbidden to reveal the secrets and plans of the gang. My own modest role was to help draw up the plans, or modify them, to prevent our being caught. As'ad Jamjoum was the gang's grand head. We'd have an annual meeting, attended by all the members, during which a statement would be read out detailing all the work undertaken by the gang. Following the formula "Dear senators, dear representatives," it would begin: "Dear thieves, dear pickpockets."

The exploits of this gang were innumerable. I shall only, in the following episodes, note some of the prominent acts and noble humanitarian missions carried out by the esteemed body in question.

**The first Saudi radio station**

The following account details the inauguration of the new broadcasting transmitter. By this people may be made aware of the first Saudi radio station, which saw the light of day at the expedition home in Cairo thirteen years ago. The transmission used not the wireless system but a short cable no more than a few metres long. "This is Mecca," the announcer would begin. How did this come about? Mr As'ad Jamjoum had brought to the expedition home a small transmitting device, and this we set up in a room on the third floor and secretly connected, by means of a short cable, to the radio system on the second floor.

Only five of us were in on the secret. While tuning in to the radio (we informed the students), we'd heard an announcement from Radio Mecca, which was to be officially inaugurated that night. We even specified the time. Everyone was eager to hear a voice from the beloved homeland; communications with the Kingdom continued to be difficult due to the circumstances of the Second World War. We planned the inaugural programme. At the appointed time precisely, those colleagues detailed to make the broadcast were standing in front of the microphone, while the others stood among the rest of the expedition members, who were gathered to hear the first ever broadcast from Saudi Arabia.

The voice of the commentator came over, describing the ceremony. "There is Shaikh 'Abdallah Kazim, Director-General of Posts, Telegrams and Telephones, receiving high-ranking officials." At this point, Sharaf Kazim leapt up, clapping joyfully. Subsequently, Rashid Radwan recited some verses from the Quran (having been introduced by name as a Quranic reader from the Hijaz). Then Hamid Damanhoury – introduced as Mr 'Abdallah 'Abd al-Jabbar, Director-General of the Saudi Broadcasting Service – read the inaugural speech. "That's 'Abd al-Jabbar's voice all right," al-Harasani commented. "No doubt about it."

The inaugural ceremony came to an end, and the station began transmitting the programme proper, which included a literary feature by Mr Ahmad al-'Arabi, impersonated by one of our colleagues. Then we presented Rashid Radwan in the role of Hasan Labni, with a rendering of a Hijazi song. The audience was transported, repeating constantly: "Bravo, Abu 'Ali!"

Finally, it was time for the news bulletin. We contrived some interesting news. A main feature was the return from Sudan of Shaikh 'Abd al-Rahman Babusail, God rest his soul, having recovered from his illness. His sons Saeed and Salih, who knew of their father's trip and had been waiting to hear of his recovery and safe return, were instantly overjoyed, hugging one another, while the other colleagues offered them their heartiest congratulations. Eventually colleagues began to find out our secret from those who'd taken part in the scheme – all except Saeed 'Umar and Saeed Babusail, who, late into the night, sat on by the radio, listening to the news bulletin being repeated and the voice of Hasan Labni resounding through the expedition house.

### The signing-in book
In the days of the first expedition, we'd go out only in groups, without being asked to do this by the supervisor. When the second expedition arrived, Mr Waliyy al-Din assigned leaders to head groups in their outings, each group to be made up of not fewer than three persons. In time this system of leaders was ended; instead Mr Waliyy al-Din had us write down, in a special book, the name of the place where we intended to spend the Friday evening – the only evening on which he allowed us to go out. He himself would remain in the expedition home to record our time of return, which should be no later than ten o'clock.

One Friday evening, Mr Waliyy al-Din was at the expedition home watching us leave, and he saw Rashid Radwan and Muhammad Mansouri going out all dressed up.

"Where are you going?" he asked them.

"To the Kit-Kat," they replied innocently. They'd seen an advertisement for this in the newspaper, and knew nothing about Cairo as yet.

"I'll Kit-Kat your heads for you!" Mr Waliyy al-Din rejoined.

Then he launched into a renewed lecture about the benefits of breathing in the fresh air of the Mediterranean Sea.

Signing into the book went on until As'ad Jamjoum arrived; in fact he was the reason for it being discontinued. One night As'ad wrote that he was going to such-and-such a play, starring such-and-such an actor and directed by so-and-so, until he'd filled a whole page of the book. When Mr Waliyy al-Din saw this, he deducted fifty piastres from As'ad's allowance. As'ad took this calmly until the evening, when Mr Waliyy al-Din had to stay up late to prepare letters that were to be sent to the Ministry of Education. As'ad, in return for a special extra allowance, was in charge of maintaining the electricity at the expedition home; and that night he switched the electricity off. The furious Mr Waliyy al-Din summoned As'ad, who bargained with him to have his fifty piastres back in return for fixing the electricity. Mr Waliyy al-Din agreed and gave the money back to As'ad, who immediately fixed the electricity.

As'ad struck the first nail in the coffin of the signing-in book. Other incidents followed, and the book vanished, never to return.

## Gang exploits

The gang was responsible for some noteworthy exploits, each of which would merit a separate section in these memoirs. Let me, though, just mention a few small incidents by way of illustration.

Muhammad Mansouri once received a box of dates stuffed with almonds, weighing almost half a kilo. Hearing of this, we seized the box, and found the dates had sesame sprinkled on them, and were utterly delicious. We put the box in a safe place, so that we could take from it whenever we wanted. This happened in the afternoon. That evening we were having dinner at the expedition home, and the meal of the day was chicken – a noteworthy event in the expedition's calendar.

When we left the dining room, we knew Mr Waliyy al-Din had learned of the incident and was going to check the rooms. We went, straight away, to the place where we'd hidden the box of dates. There were five of us, and, for all our hearty meal, we didn't leave the box till we'd eaten everything in it. Then we threw it out into the street. Mr Waliyy al-Din combed the whole place but found nothing.

Some time later, it so happened that a tin of dates, not stuffed with almonds this time, was sent to 'Abdallah al-Baghdadi,. We seized it, ate some of the dates and distributed some among the other students. This we did secretly, without letting al-Baghdadi see us.

Next day we learned al-Baghdadi had reported the incident to Mr Waliyy al-Din, and, to make the point more dramatic, had told him the dates were stuffed with almonds. The moment we heard this, we got out the tin and started eating in front of al-Baghdadi, who couldn't say a word. Hadn't he, after all, reported a missing tin of dates stuffed with almonds?

*'Abd al-'Aziz al-Rabee'*

FROM *MEMORIES OF A PLIANT CHILD*
(dhikrayat tifl wadee')

### Education and industry

There were only three schools in Medina at the time I'm writing about, one a government school, the other two private. Of these latter one was called the Home for Orphans, the other the School for Juristic Sciences. The name of the first defined the school's status and objectives. It was specifically for orphans; only children who had lost their fathers enrolled there.

This school, or "Home," undertook tremendous, unforgettable work, taking full responsibility for the orphans, who resided, ate, drank, lived and studied there. It followed a highly successful educational policy, with remarkably firm discipline, preparing pupils for the elementary certificate. It engaged all the pupils' time: they'd follow the prescribed studies in the classroom, take part in sports or recreational activities in the afternoon, undertake work in the vocational sections (compulsory for all pupils), or sit in the study hall preparing their next day's lessons. Naturally there were breaks in between for meals, sleep and necessary relaxation. The Home provided our country with generations of young men who were honest, enlightened and hard-working, and who played a part in building our modern renaissance.

What I'd like to discuss here is how the "Home" and those responsible for it embraced a remarkable educational concept whereby theoretical education and practical work were combined. I might almost say the method reflected profound understanding, and extensive experience, were I not aware that the combination was simply designed to help pupils find a useful trade for their future lives and prevent them from becoming a burden on their society.

Yet, if the mix of theoretical and practical education was solely for such a purpose, this should not detract from the method's importance, for the educational aim remained the same: to foster skill in industry or handicraft and to raise youngsters to respect manual work on account of its importance and usefulness in advancing the nation's standing. The natural outcome of all this would be to encourage local and national industries, to promote a spirit of creativity and inventiveness among young people, and to boost the national wealth.

Such was the decisive, constructive path to which the Home for Orphans was geared. The other school was designed with similar aims in mind, but with the difference that manual work was an optional subject and that results in this direction were, in consequence, of limited usefulness.

## I'd never been in a car in Medina

I told my children, while talking to them one day, that I'd never been in a car in Medina; the first car I'd ridden in had been the one that took me, along with my mother and younger brother, to Mecca. My children were astonished, their eyes wide with amazement. But for embarrassment, and the fact that they'd never had a lie from my lips, they would have accused me of exaggeration and embellishment. How could they accept such a thing – they who, from the time they were born, had lived in a city full of cars, a city which hardly knew the meaning of peace and quiet, on account of all the noise, confusion and dust created by cars? But that's the truth, children. In fact, up to the time I left Medina for Jeddah, and then for Mecca, there were only two or three cars in the city.

"So," you might ask yourself, "what did you unfortunate people do?" Well, in the first place, we weren't unfortunate. And second, we didn't "do" anything. Our city was small, surrounded by a wall, and there was no need of any kind of mechanical transportation. The people were healthy by and large, since the diseases of civilization hadn't reached them yet. Besides, we had horses, mules and donkeys. The mules would pull a particular type of carriage we called an 'arabiyya – 'arabiyyat in the plural – which consisted of a fairly large box with a door for the passengers to get in and windows for the light and air to enter. This box would be set on a pair of cartwheels, and the whole thing was tied to one or two mules, or one or two horses, or a single donkey. I never saw any carriage of this kind pulled by two donkeys, and never indeed, until I wrote these words, wondered why that should be. I've no idea of the reason. Perhaps it has something to do with the donkey's nature, which is typically individualistic, stubborn and sulky. Such a nature would be an insuperable barrier to accommodation and cooperative effort.

If that wasn't the reason, then so be it. If it wasn't, we must turn to friends of the donkey like Nasr al-Din Hammad, the Countess de Sigur, Raymond Khaminin and Tawfiq al-Hakim. They're sure to have the answer.

Let's, then, return to the carriage, noting that it played a major part in transporting the sick and old; and had a major role, too, in carrying the bride from her parents' home to her husband's, and in taking people, families especially, from inside the city to nearby suburbs.

Apart from the carriages, there were horses, mules and donkeys to convey males – men, young lads and boys – from one place to another. Riding horses, specifically, was the favoured means of luxury transport for those rich enough to afford it.

There was, it should be noted here, a fundamental difference between the means of transportation I've just mentioned and those invented subsequently, like cars and trains working on coal or electricity: namely, that the first kind didn't stop the body from moving. On the contrary, the body would be in constant motion, right through the journey. As such, riding these animals – whether directly or indirectly, as in a carriage – was a species of physical sport, not at all like being in cars and trains. Riding an animal might be different from walking, but had with it one feature in common: that both provide useful and beneficial exercise.

It's a mistake, don't you agree, to remove ourselves further from nature?

### The first car accident in Medina

Our quarter was located outside the city walls and was perhaps the first to rebel against the wall in question, which embraced Medina, and to go beyond its limits. Yet for all that, our quarter shared the tranquility, stillness and quiet that Medina enjoyed. It was part of Medina, indeed, and nothing separated our quarter from the city itself apart from that wall. Then came the dreadful accident. The car accident.

One of our comrades in the quarter was a lad older than the rest of us, and we used to avoid him because of his mischievous and malicious nature. The days passed, and some devil or other spurred on this mischievous boy to make the acquaintance of one of the very few who owned a car, one of the first models that American devil manufactured for people. The boy apparently borrowed the car from its owner and drove it into the quarter to add one more to his evil glories. Vanity and conceit pushed him on to a kind of recklessness in his driving; and, being a mere novice, he killed one of our friends under the wheels. It was an accident that shook everyone in our quarter, and in Medina – the first such to have happened in our good city. Up to now Medina had known nothing of what came to be called car crash victims. What added to the horror of the accident was that the young boy's family had an elder son who'd died shortly before, so that this rubbed salt into the wound. The accident weighed on people's minds; it haunted their imaginations, stirring their feelings and drawing their tears. For a time the accident dominated people's talk, and was on everyone's mind. Only much later would they come to realize this accident was a mere prelude to a long series of such events, confined not just to cars and crimes related to them, but also involving motorcycles, which caused numerous casualties.

### Riding bicycles was frowned on

Bicycles had just arrived in Medina, but so poorly were they received that it was highly uncommon to see anybody actually riding one. People viewed those who rode bicycles with a sarcastic air – they looked down on them, censuring them as being of low character, badly brought up and lacking in manners. Riders weren't spared harsh words, hurtful comments and ironic remarks. All of this militated strongly against people using this form of transport.

Could these opponents ever, I wonder, have imagined that a day would come when this silly means of transport would be used only by children? Or that the bicycle would be used for adult competitions, patronized by high-ranking officials who'd bestow prizes and gifts on the winners? Strange indeed is the pace of development in our modern world.

## How lack of a car almost cost me my scholarship

After completing my secondary studies in Mecca, I returned to Medina, where I'd been appointed as a teacher at the Nasriyya School. But before my first year as a teacher was out, I received a cable stating that approval had been issued to send me on a scholarship to Egypt. I was to leave at once, so that I could be in Jeddah with my colleagues on the date set by the Directorate of General Education. There was, though, an unforeseen hitch. I went to the post office department and asked to have a seat booked for me in the car belonging to the post office. But the officials told me, regretfully, that there were no seats available; I'd have to wait – for another ten days, twenty days, who could say? The seats were always booked well in advance. I went around soliciting sympathy, and the mediation of those who were well connected, but my efforts were quite fruitless. All the seats were booked, and they absolutely couldn't hold up anyone with a previous booking. I'd simply have to wait – which meant the ship would leave with all the other scholarship holders, who were themselves from Mecca and Jeddah. It was out of the question for either the expedition or the ship to be delayed. I almost lost hope of travelling and being part of the expedition. Then relief came unexpectedly. My colleague Ayyoub Sabri – His Excellency the ex-Deputy Minister of Finance – heard of the matter, and made immediate contact with me, telling me he had a place booked for himself in the post office car, but that, in view of my situation, he'd give me his place and wait for the next scheduled car, or for a supplementary one.

My pen could never set down just how happy that seat made me, especially if I tell the reader the ship was to leave the very next day after my arrival in Jeddah. Had I been late by just one day, I would have missed the whole trip and faced endless problems. The cars of the post office department were the only ones travelling between Medina and Jeddah, and made the trip just three times a month, with supplementary cars now and then.

Let the reader compare this situation, in all its cruelty and bitterness, with the situation found today. More cars now travel between Medina and Jeddah in a single day than in a whole year then. "Great is God, Who is the source of change."

## Road bumps in poetry

The carriages had their stars and celebrities, and so did the post office cars. The most notable, without doubt, was the driver 'Abadi, who was so famed for his diligence and speed that no one could compete with him – he was even mentioned in poetry! A poet from Sudan (I don't recall his name now) visited our country and travelled from Mecca to Medina, with 'Abadi, in the post office car.

On arrival in Medina, he composed a poem which he read during one of the celebrations; and in it he talked of the difficulty of the road and of 'Abadi's driving. In this poem, I remember, the poet spoke of the bumps on the road:

*Of bumps, my God, Thou art aware,*
*And after them I fear no threat.*
*'Abadi, he was a prince among us.*
*Come, get in and be like soldiers.*
*All this is easy next to Taiba,*
*By God I truly swear.*

These bumps will be familiar to all those who travelled that road between Mecca and Medina, and suffered bitterly from them before the road was eventually paved. I still recall, vividly, how for a full week after my arrival I'd start from my sleep, imagining nightly that I was still riding in the post office car, along that road that jerked our bodies ceaselessly, without rest or respite.

'Abadi was the shining star of the post office. His driving of the post office car, or another of the company's cars, was the admiration of all. He was the talk of the city, so much that he was even mentioned in poetry:

*'Abadi, he was a prince among us.*
*Come, get in and be like soldiers.*
*The carpenter who pulled out teeth for one riyal*

The story of the tooth and the carpenter is one that deserves to be told. Extracting – or pulling out – teeth is considered an easy enough job nowadays, requiring no great effort or expense. Public hospitals and private clinics are available, after all. But that was emphatically not the case at the time of which we're speaking. Extracting a tooth – or, again, pulling one out if you prefer – was an important event, for three reasons. First, there was no dental section at the hospital. Second, there was no way of treating the tooth except by extraction or pulling. Third, and most important, taking out a tooth cost a huge sum – a whole riyal. Such a sum represented a fifth of an employee's salary – or a seventh for a grade two employee, and a tenth even for an employee of grade three.

That reminds me of two brief anecdotes. Half a riyal once went missing from a shop in our quarter, and the furious shop owner suspected a small child from among our neighbours. The matter occupied a number of the inhabitants for a whole day, and ended only when the shopkeeper found his half riyal. Had he not found it, things might have been complicated much further.

That was one of the two anecdotes. As for the second, I was the prime hero and my young brother the secondary one – or perhaps it was the other way round. To be brief, I was one day carrying my young brother, who still wasn't able to walk; and circumstances drove me to sit him down at the entrance to a shop, where the owner would place bread for sale. I then seem to have got carried away with my games, and I forgot all about my young brother. When I did get back, the shopkeeper told me my brother had taken a loaf of bread and eaten some; I must, he told me, pay a quarter of a piastre for the loaf. Not having the sum, I asked the shopkeeper to give me some time. I didn't want to go and ask my father for the money; if I did, he'd know I hadn't looked after my young brother properly; that I'd left him on his own while I went off to play. So, I went to an old man, a friend of my father's, and asked him for half a piastre. To my delight he gave me a whole piastre, and back I went to the shopkeeper to pay him his quarter for the loaf. He, though, told me, to my surprise, that my father had passed by a short while before; he'd told my father what had happened and taken the money for the loaf from him. I was expecting a scolding or reprimand from my father, but he did nothing of the kind, merely telling my mother about it.

There's a common underlying theme to these two stories. The first person found the idea of losing half a riyal unbearable, while the second simply couldn't wait for me to go back and pay him his quarter of a piastre.

Such was the purchasing power of the riyal then. And it was in these circumstances that I began to suffer severe toothache from a decayed tooth. No amount of pain-killers had any effect; and my father, realizing the situation, gave me a riyal to have the tooth pulled out. I asked one of my school friends to go with me, and this friend supplied me with some surprising news: Hajj 'Abdallah, he told me, would pull out teeth free of charge, every Friday, at his home. This Hajj 'Abdallah was a master carpenter who combined this trade with the extraction of teeth, and he'd dedicated the Friday of each week to helping Muslims by pulling out their teeth without payment. My friend went on to praise Hajj 'Abdallah, speaking highly of his skills and noting his good qualities. Persuaded by my friend's words, I waited almost a week, enduring a good deal of pain, so that I could keep the vast sum of one whole riyal.

On the Friday, I visited Hajj 'Abdallah together with my friend, and everything happened as I'd been told. God bless Hajj 'Abdallah the carpenter-dentist, and God bless my friend who took me to Hajj 'Abdallah the dentist-carpenter! And God reward my friend and Hajj 'Abdallah together for their efforts in ending my pain and preserving my riyal! And such a riyal!

### There's a reason for toothache

This title might sound absurd, or maybe annoy readers of irritable disposition. Let any such, though, exercise a little patience, and they may find some interest in what I have to say.

Throughout its known history, the city of Medina has been famous for its agricultural produce, and above all for its dates, which have had a sustained effect on the good city's life.

It was only natural, therefore, that the people of Medina should have taken a profound interest in the planting of palm trees; and the experience they acquired enabled them to prune, multiply, and improve and supplement the planting process, till finally they had almost a hundred different types of dates. Nor did it stop there. People became so concerned with the process of preserving dates that they were able to devise different dishes substantially based on them, for different times and seasons.

When we consider that dates contain all the necessary elements for the body, and that their sweetness differs from one type to another – so catering for people of all different tastes – we may readily understand the importance of dates, whether used on their own or mixed with other things.

For this reason the date-picking season was one of the most significant in the life of Medina's citizens; for this was the time the dates were brought into every house, rich and poor alike – the only difference lying in the quantities and types involved.

The arrival of the dates, in any house, was not something to be welcomed quietly, as if greeting some passer-by. It was rather met with the welcome proper for a most important guest. The dates would be scrupulously washed in clean water, then placed in new containers carefully prepared for the purpose; and they'd be mixed with various types of aromatic herb designed to add to the flavour of the dates, giving them a taste beyond the power of words to describe – one that induced people to garnish their tables with platters of dates whatever the occasion.

For some rich people, though, even all this wasn't enough. They'd remove the stones from the dates and put almonds in their place, so reducing the sweetness and making them appetizing to eat, tasty and appealing to the palate.

It's clear from all this how the dates were crucial to the human diet at the time we're speaking of: they were, at one and the same time, a source of nourishment, a means of healing and a sweetmeat. We are, the reader should remember, talking specifically of the dates of Medina, deservedly loved by the people generally and by the children in particular. The reader may by now have guessed the reason for my toothache – the source of a pain, and of subsequent events, without which this whole section (be it absurd or interesting) would never have existed.

Dates have lost their old standing now, and people have ceased to care about them. They've turned their backs on them. No longer is there a season for the harvesting of dates, or a joy in welcoming it. There's no sorrow over its disappearance, no relish for the different types of dates, no climbers to ascend the palms. The old, extensive plantations are in decline; newly constructed buildings have encroached on the lovely swathes of trees. From being an oasis where vibrant green and countless trees met the eye on all sides, Medina's become, now, a city like any other, filled with houses and other buildings, the plantations out of sight beyond the near and distant suburbs.

Here is one of the crimes of modern civilization, that two-edged weapon that provides people with luxury in the same measure as it deprives them of nature. Woe to people, when luxury sucks them in and nature turns from them.

## A market for cage builders

The disappearance of plantations and farms, and the decline in the numbers of palm trees, was followed by the disappearance of particular trades and crafts.

One of Medina's most famous markets was the one where cages were made, the cage-makers being a category of local craftsmen dependent on palm branches. They'd make curtains for windows, and beds which the people of Medina would put on the roofs of their houses for sleeping in the hot summer months. And besides these, they'd make cages, large and small. The small cages were used for attractive or singing birds, the large ones for carrying chickens and pigeons, to sell or to take from place to place.

These cage-makers, then, devised a variety of products from palm branches. So why were they specifically called cage-makers? The likeliest reason, no doubt, is that it's simpler to refer to cages than to "curtains or beds," reference to these other products entailing the use of more than one word. Not that it would be impossible to devise a single word. But talking of cages was simpler all round.

Leaving this linguistic digression, I should mention that nothing now remains of the market but its name. We may well hope, though, that the name itself will remain for the place that was once a cage-makers' market, and that people will thus be reminded of a golden era when the market was an attraction for visitors. Time and again I found myself struck by the skill of these people, who made cages, beds and other things, without ever using a nail, or glue, or ropes.

*Ahmad al-Sibaʻi*

# FROM *MY JOURNAL*
(ayyami)

## My Aunt <u>Hasina</u>

My Aunt <u>Hasina</u> (or Khala <u>Hasina</u>), who lived next door to us, was one of those good ladies handed down by the excellent families of <u>Mecca</u>. She'd been a slave to one of the noble families, and, when she was freed, they married her to another of their slaves and she came to live with him in the house next to ours.

Uncle Mahboub, her husband, was very badly off. Lacking even the basic means of livelihood, he was in need of people's charity, and he had to make his wife work within reasonable limits.

When still at her master's home, Aunt <u>Hasina</u> had read what other women read in those days. She'd read the Quran right through, several times, and had also read the Barzanji version of the *mawlid*[7] celebratory rites and mastered the chanting of this at the special celebrations held for women, in those days, for the Prophet's birthday. She'd also memorized the Burda Poem and the Hamzia Poem,[8] and she excelled in chanting the verses in question whenever a celebration took place.

She was good, furthermore, at reading the signs of goodness and the *joshen*,[9] and other supplications whose names I'm not familiar with. With all this, she was regarded as a leading figure of enlightenment among her friends and peers.

It was only natural that people should seek to benefit from her special expertise. They'd send their young girls to her to learn how to read, and to learn some of the poems and. *mawlid* versions that people were fond of chanting at that time.

She had, in her home, something akin to a *kuttab* – not indeed a true *kuttab*, because she wasn't prepared to take just anyone as pupils. She wouldn't agree to take on young boys because, being afraid (as she said) that they'd be "mischievous," she was concerned for the young girls.

Besides her teaching role, she was busy cleaning her simple house, and – for all her poverty – making the furnishings harmonious; I still, to this day, have a delightful picture of these last etched in my mind. All her rooms were furnished with torn pieces of what had once been mats. And yet Aunt <u>Hasina</u> had been able to turn these pieces into what gave the appearance of clean, well-matching furnishings.

As for the corner of the room she'd made into a kitchen, and the small slab she'd turned into a bathroom, and the other walls, and the individual steps – there wasn't a speck of dirt to be seen anywhere.

Not that all this was exclusive to Aunt Hasina; in fact most houses of the time were exactly as I've described. The housewives would vie with one another in the cleanness of their clothes, or in their furnishings, or in their food. Their homes set an example of cleanliness and elegant harmony.

Living next door to us, Aunt Hasina learned that I could read, and so she agreed, exceptionally, that I should go to her after the girls had left, so she could correct my reading.

Her house was familiar enough to me. I'd play in her hallway with the girls of the *kuttab*, and often my mother would send me to her to run some errands; or else she'd take me with her if she decided to spend the evening there. Things changed, though, when I became one of her pupils.

She started laying down the law. "Don't come in, boy, till you've put on your wooden clogs, and you've washed your face, and your feet, and your hands. Use the pot to wash them. Don't touch the ladle when you're covered in dirt. Not yet, boy – keep your clogs on till your feet are dry."

Whenever I went to her home, I'd climb the steps and stand at the entrance to the rooms, till she'd finished tidying the shelf or polishing the copper samovar. Then she'd pick up the pot, fill it with water, and leave me to wash my hands and feet. I could only go in when my feet were dry.

If I sat down to read, she'd order me to put the '*amma* chapter from the Quran[10] on a special wide-angled stand on which it could rest easily. Then, with an ostrich feather in her hand, she'd start pointing to the word I had to read, having first pronounced it to me with carefully stressed enunciation. Apart from that feather, and the double chair, her method of instruction was no different from the one used at a *kuttab*.

After a few days at her class, I began to grow tired of Aunt Hasina; her lessons, I felt, were becoming a nuisance. My friends, after spending their days with me at the *kuttab*, would play hide-and-seek and other games in the afternoons, in the Marwa area and the Khan al-Sadari. And meanwhile there was I, trapped alone with Aunt Hasina, wearily repeating the things she taught me.

Nothing made my father happier than those lessons I took with Aunt Hasina. "Now," he'd say to my mother, "we can have a rest from all his boasting, and running around in alleyways, and playing tricks on people. Now, perhaps, God will guide our son, and Hasina will help make up for what's missing at that useless *kuttab*. She's a good woman, and she'll make a success of it, God willing."

My father, God rest his soul, wasn't to be blamed for thinking like that. He himself had been brought up illiterate, and this had left him with a great sense of inferiority; he wanted to compensate for it, just as much as he possibly could, in his offspring. He'd also decided that my success depended on a constant, unrelenting attention to study, with no rest, and no playing and running around in the narrow streets. "Wash and pray the afternoon prayer. Then sit down and read till it's time for you to pray the sunset prayers. Then, what after that? Read till it's time for the night prayer. Then have a bite to eat and go and sleep, so you'll wake up and feel everything's still there in your mind."

He never realized, God rest his soul, that his programme of hard work was actually the reason for my slow, dull mind; that the hours I spent at the *kuttab*, poring over the *'amma*, were more than enough for me. With that over, I needed to run in the alleyways and the court, to satisfy my urge to play, so as to shake off the tedium of the *kuttab* and stimulate my mind, ready to start studying once more next day.

In this my father was a reflection of his age, unable to see that playing and running around were means of relieving boredom. For them such things were merely a waste of time and a way of getting into mischief that warranted reprimand and punishment.

This diligence decided on by my father, and approved by my mother and Aunt Hasina, brought just the results you might expect. My mind grew even duller than before, the repression acted adversely on my senses, paralysing their capacities and disabling their functions.

Being barred from play was bad for my general behaviour. Given the smallest relaxation, I'd explode with mischief, acting in a quite fiendish way. As a result, my father, my mother and my learned aunt gained the impression I was the most mischievous child alive, that not even demons with scaled backs could match me for devilry.

My father simply lacked the knowledge to study the escalating problem and to loosen the reins a little. Nor did any of our friends or neighbours have the insight to understand and point out the true source of the danger. Rather, they all agreed I was lacking in manners. "Shaikh Muhammad," they'd say to my father, "you must discipline your son, bring him up properly. He won't die before his time comes."

My father started, accordingly, assembling the plaited ropes, the wood, the springy bamboo canes, with a view to undertaking the noble mission. If ever I lost a *halala*,[11] let a board with bread fall from my head, or broke my pencil, if ever one of the neighbours said he'd seen me leaving my shoes on their doorsteps, and playing or fighting with the lad who worked at the bean seller's shop, my father would refer the matter to the plaited ropes and the hard wooden stick, without allowing me a single word in my defence, whatever my grievance. By the time he left me, I'd turned to a torn body with bleeding ribs.

Brutality of this kind left its mark on me. It led me to become stubborn and headstrong, taught me to be reckless, spurred me on to face all kinds of things others would fear. I was going to be beaten anyway, whether I'd done anything wrong or not. So why shouldn't I be the tyrant, and take my revenge?

These traits stayed with me, I won't deny, for a long period of my life. Had I not, through extensive study and reading, come to understand the weak points of my upbringing, then done my careful best to remedy the effects of these, I'd now be the most wretched of people.

And so Aunt Hasina developed the fixed notion that mischief was an instinctive part of my character. My mother supported her in this, and so did all the neighbours and acquaintances. My father, for his part, gave me a choice: either I mend my ways and start behaving properly, or he'd refer my errant habits to the plaited ropes and the wooden stick.

## Kuttabs and teachers

I spent a long time at the *kuttab*, and in going to Aunt Hasina's. Still, though, I couldn't manage to decipher the letters. My reading (as all my father's acquaintances and neighbours would have been able to testify) was totally mechanical.

Eventually my father was advised to transfer me to a different *kuttab*, and he sent me first to one at Bab Duraiba, then to another at Jabal al-Hindi, then to another, and another still. At last I found myself in a larger *kuttab* set up by that genius of his time, Shaikh Muhammad al-Khayyat at al-Qabban Square next to the Mudda'a. This shaikh divided pupils into different classes according to their level of knowledge. Shaikh 'Abd al-Raouf al-Sabban was a pupil in the senior classes. As for me, I was sent to the beginners' class, where I started to learn spelling all over again.

I had no better luck at the new *kuttab* than at the ones before, but the long endeavours had had some effect even so. I'd passed six years of my life before joining the *kuttab* at al-Qabban, and was able by then to complete my reading of the *'amma*. I was able, too, to read, albeit poorly, some words in the letters my father used to receive, and which he insisted on using to test me.

When he was ruler, al-Husain Bin 'Ali established the first Arabic school in front of the Bab al-Salam, and he appointed Shaikh Muhammad al-Khayyat to run it, instructing him to transfer his pupils at the Qabban *kuttab* to this new school. We were all transferred accordingly, and I joined the primary classes.

We began, in these classes, to learn handwriting and some basic arithmetic, to which were then added lessons in jurisprudence and *tawheed*,[12] dictation and reciting the Quran, plus other basic skills compulsory at a preparatory school. My father was delighted with my new progress, but was avid for greater distinction. His painful sense of his own illiteracy seemed to make him anxious and nervous, turning him into someone with extreme hopes and dreams for me – hopes and dreams that hardly fitted with my dull state, which he himself had brought me to and which could only be lifted, if at all, through the influence of time, and a long time at that.

"Look!" he'd tell me. "The son of the cloth shop owner, who isn't much older than you, may God preserve him – he's looking for education from Shaikh al-Dahhan at the mosque. Look! The son of the man who repairs watches, he's younger than you are, has beautiful handwriting – it looks like a string of pearls. The son of the Mahariji at Bab al-Salam, may God preserve him – he can read the Quran perfectly. You'd think he was inspired. You're the only one God's blinded, and put shades over your eyes!"

I'd have to listen to all this and much more. It never occurred to him to think of the effect this was having on my self-confidence and plummeting morale. If only my father, God rest his soul, and so many other parents like him, had realized how it would have been better to encourage me and, within reasonable limits, praise the things I did; how this would have raised my morale and self-esteem for my life ahead. But he and his like, God rest their souls, saw good only in the things they themselves believed in.

My father, God rest his soul, would ask me to show him my handwriting; and so I'd show him the line written by the teacher, which I had to copy, in the same way students are given handwriting books nowadays. This line, I'd maintain, was in my own writing. He, though, would take one look at it, then fling the paper in my face.

"This is a devil's handwriting," he'd say, "not the writing of someone who goes to school! Let's see tomorrow if you're ever going to make good. If you do, then come and…over my grave."

Then, still furious, he'd ask to see the shaikh's writing, and I'd show him a line in my own dreadful hand. This, I'd say, was the shaikh's. The moment he saw it, he'd calm down.

"Look at this lovely writing," he'd say. "Look how clear it is, just like a string of pearls."

The words would hardly be out of his mouth before I'd start laughing, splitting my sides.

"Well, let me tell you, Father," I'd say rudely, "that handwriting you think is so lovely and wonderful, I swear to God it's mine. And the first one, the one you flung back in my face, that was the shaikh's!"

The moment he heard this, he'd lose his temper and start shouting at me.

"Get out of my sight, curse you!" he'd yell. "Trying to make a fool of me, are you? Well, I can fool twenty like you. Look at this boy, the son of sixty liars! I swear to God, if you don't get out of here, I'll turn you into sixty pieces! Get up and get out."

And so, I'd get up and leave. Inside me were a thousand words I would have liked to say – but he was my father after all.

The reader may perhaps realize how my father's angry reaction, towards my teacher's real handwriting, gave me a boost, and a sense of the true personal identity my father refused to see. For parents in those days, a negative attitude was seen as essential for firmness and a proper upbringing. They meant well, God forgive them, in the course they took.

My father's aspirations for my success increased as the days went by and his anxiety about my education grew. He was forcibly concerned to see me reading or writing without respite, not wasting a moment of my precious time in playing or frolicking. If ever I needed a break, I'd say I had to go to the toilet, and the few minutes I spent there would relieve the tedium. This was the same ploy as I'd used at the *kuttab*.

My educational affairs were a matter for discussion taking up most of my father's time, with most of his acquaintances, friends and neighbours drawn in.

"Look, brother Hamza," he'd say, "the boy's stumbling over his reading. By God, shaikh, I wonder if someone's put a curse on him. Where else did he get that stupid head of his from? What do you think? Would you go with me to Shaikh Khuzami in the Haram, and ask him if the boy could recite the Quran with him after sundown?"

If only my father could have known my continual work was the very reason for my dullness; that I needed more time to play and have fun, rather than having still more lessons in reciting the Quran.

My father liked, on his way to afternoon prayer, to pass by the Bab al-Dariba and discuss my education with a Turkish maker of stamps.

"That boy," he'd say, "still doesn't know how to sharpen a pencil, and his handwriting's terrible. I don't know if he's an idiot, or what. I keep telling him, there are three things that put you ahead of the pack: a sharp pencil, a stamp and a straight line! It's as though somebody's cast a spell on the boy, to make him stupid. What do you think, Mr Sabri? I think perhaps I ought to send the boy along to you for an hour or two every afternoon. Maybe that would improve his handwriting a bit."

And so, a new lesson was added to my heavy programme, where I'd be taught how to sharpen a pencil and get my line straight.

My father would drop, too, by the shop of Uncle Saeed, who sold fish. He'd buy in what he needed, then start talking about me

"Would you mind," he asked, "writing out something for the boy to copy? I'll send him round to you to collect it when he gets back from the Mahariji."

And so, on my father's instructions, I'd go off to the shop of Shaikh Saeed the fish seller and get the sample: a written line, in a slanting hand that started in the upper right corner of the paper and ended at the bottom left. The sample text would read as follows: "The example for the glorious one, the topmost among the cream of society, my dear sir, the dearest, the most upright. May God prolong his life and keep him safe, Amen."

Next day, the moment the Mahariji saw Shaikh Saeed's sample text among my sheets of papers, he'd frown and ask me what this was all about, and I'd tell him the whole story. Thereupon he'd lose his temper.

"Do you call that handwriting?" he'd shout. "What sort of people are you, you and your father?"

With that he'd throw me out of the class, and I'd go back to my father, who'd go to the Mahariji to patch things up with him, then tell me to hide the Mahariji's handwriting from Shaikh Saeed, and vice versa. He'd tell me to profit by both at one and the same time, even though – as I subsequently discovered – the styles and patterns involved were quite different.

If my father met with a friend in the coffee shop, the discussion would soon turn to me. "Do you know anyone who could teach him arithmetic? What do you think of Shakir the Egyptian, who writes next to the column at Bab al-Salam?"

That was the answer, by God! But how was I to find the time to go to Uncle Shakir? All the hours were taken up between the school, the Mahariji, Shaikh Khuzami, the fish seller and studying at home. That, though, didn't stop my father finding time. After all, there was plenty of free time on Fridays.

So there I'd sit alongside Uncle Shakir, my legs half-crossed, and take the multiplication table in the hope of memorizing it. But it was no use. My father would pass and see me holding a single piece of paper, waving it to the right and left, day-dreaming about the Marwa area and the Khan al-Sadari. It would upset him seeing me like that, and Uncle Shakir, noticing this, would tell me to start writing.

A pool has three taps (the question might go). The first, on its own, fills the pool in 15 minutes, the second in 10 minutes, the third in 5 minutes. If we turn on the three taps together, how many minutes will it take to fill the pool?

"We need to add, Uncle Shakir," I'd say.

"All right, then. Add them together."

"I've done it. 30 minutes."

"That would mean it takes 30 minutes for the pool to be filled up. But, boy, if one tap can fill the pool in 5 minutes, how could three taps fill the pool in 30 minutes? Does that make sense?"

My father, sitting a yard away and enjoying the arithmetical problem, would answer before I did:

"No – that doesn't make sense."

By now I'd be back from my daydreams among the players in the Marwa area. I'd be on the alert once more.

"Quite right. How could it take 30 minutes?"

"We subtract then, Uncle Shakir."

"What do we subtract, and from what? There are three numbers there. How can we subtract them?"

"Let's add 10 and 5, then subtract them from 15."

"So, what does that leave?"

"Nought."

"Can the pool be filled in nought minutes?"

"No."

It couldn't be right, Uncle Shakir would say. And my father would nod his head in agreement.

Coming back, once more, from my day-dreaming in the Marwa area, I'd realize he was right.

"We multiply, Uncle Shakir," I'd say.

"What do you multiply? By what, boy?"

"We multiply two numbers. Is that enough?"

"So what do we do with the third number?"

"Leave it as it is."

"You can't be serious, boy."

My father would agree I couldn't be serious. That I was unteachable.

"All right then, multiply. Show me."

"I've got it now. You multiply the numbers, Uncle Shakir."

"Multiply then. Let me see."

"10 times 5 equals 50."

"Why not say 5 times 15? Isn't that better?"

"I don't know how much 5 times 15 is, Uncle Shakir."

"Look, if we multiply 10 by 5, that makes 50."

"So what does that mean?"

"It means we fill the pool fifty times."

Bored by this time, my father would make to hit me, but Uncle Shakir would stop him and ask him to be patient.

"But," my father would yell, "what's all this, boy, about filling it fifty times? We only want to fill it once, and that would take 50 minutes."

"No, father, that's wrong."

"All right, tell us the right answer."

"We divide the numbers, Uncle Shakir."

"What do we divide by what?"

"We divide all the numbers by one another."

"Divide the numbers. Show me."

"I don't know how to divide, but, I swear by God, I've heard of it."

Uncle Shakir, his patience finally exhausted, would grab the paper from my hand and start solving the problem by calculating the proportions involved. Then he'd find the answer, which was 2 minutes and some fractions.

My father's respect for Uncle Shakir would grow.

"That's right enough," he'd say.

I'd see, too, that the answer made sense, but I still couldn't see how it was arrived at. How could someone like me understand proportions, when I hadn't even got as far as mastering multiplication?

Uncle Shakir would turn to my father. "Don't get upset, Uncle Muhammad," he'd say. "It's the poor teaching in the schools. If they can't even calculate something with an answer of a mere two minutes and a fraction, what sort of teaching's that?"

My father would agree. The schools couldn't possibly be teaching properly. He'd swear that by God, three times over.

## With the memorizers of the Quran

At that time, al-Husain Bin 'Ali had started preparing for a revolution against the Ottomans. He'd begun to gather the prominent figures from the quarters of Mecca and the other cities of the Hijaz, so as to persuade them of the need for revolt against the oppression to which they were being subjected and to instruct them in how matters ought to proceed.

"Shaikh Makkawi," he said, "you must assemble all the strong young men who work in the night market. We don't want to turn them into soldiers, we just need their support. This country's yours. We just want you to be your own masters, to govern yourselves by your own means. My sons and I are ready to defend you. Hail to you, people of Zamzam! This is your day, and you are the shaikhs of the quarters from al-Ma'abida to Jarwal. Do you understand the arrangement? Through God's will and your efforts, each quarter will gather its young men for support. The Ottomans seek to establish false ways. They want your women to walk openly like men, when we are a people whose religion demands standards of decency. What do you say?"

There was uproar among the council, whose leaders struck the ground with their cudgels. "By God, sire," they shouted, "we are at your command! Where you stand, we stand also! Anything but see our womenfolk demeaned. What do you say, leaders? You, Abu Sadiq, you, Abu Siraj! What is your view?"

The council was fervent in its stand: "We will take no other course – where our ruler stands, there we will stand also – anything but scandal for our womenfolk!"

The council adjourned, and each shaikh went to make contact with the prominent people in his quarter. There they began their quiet preparations. Some of the Turks heard vague rumours of something afoot in Mecca, but they failed to understand precisely what was happening.

Al-Husain fired his first bullet at dawn on 9 Sha'ban, so proclaiming the start of the revolution. A great throng of young men from the quarters marched to Ajyad and surrounded the fortress there, firing on those inside. Others, meanwhile, marched to Jarwal and surrounded the barracks, while still others marched on al-Hamidiyya and the rest of the police stations, giving the Turkish forces a choice: resistance or surrender. The small police stations in Mecca surrendered during the first three days of the revolution, the fortress a few days later, and the soldiers in the barracks after that. Ottoman soldiers could be seen driven along as prisoners, to a place where they would be expelled from the country.

Soon after, the garrisons at Jeddah, Yanbu' and Rabegh surrendered too. The only place that refused to surrender to the army of supporters was Medina, whose garrison remained steadfast till news came of the fall of Constantinople at the end of the First World War; the garrison then requested clemency.

Al-Husain's army, made up of thousands of young men from the quarters, was now moved northward. Some took part in the siege of Medina, while the rest, supported by allied troops, marched on to Syria, where they finally captured Damascus and Faisal Bin al-Husain was proclaimed King of Syria.

The events that followed, one after the other, are related in detail in the history books of the Arab revolt. What concerns us here is the return of the young men to Mecca, after the Arab armies from the various regions, under the leadership of Faisal Bin al-Husain, had succeeded in driving the Ottomans from the Arab lands, back to the northern borders in Adana; for it was in the wake of these young men's return that al-Husain embarked on his revival policy, which he began by founding schools.

I was, at that time, a regular pupil at my preparatory school in Bab al-Salam – for all my father's belief that the schools were no good. Now we were told our preparatory studies were at an end, and that the government would transfer us to the select school at Jabal al-Hindi citadel to begin our advanced education. I didn't understand everything I was told. What I did know was that the school was very active, and that "Sayyiduna," i.e. our master and sovereign, wanted to further our education. The term "our master" was, it should be said, no longer used to denote the shaikh we'd known earlier at our *kuttab*. It was now, in our new youth, used as a title for al-Husain Bin 'Ali, the sovereign of the country.

My father sent urgently for Aunt Hasina, my old teacher, and I heard him discussing matters with her. "I've had a message," he said, "from Shaikh al-Ghazali, the principal of the boy's school, asking if I'll agree to transfer the boy to the Qal'a citadel to study the sciences. Or should he be kept at the school where he is now, to memorize the Quran?"

"By God, Hasina," he went on, "it's best to memorize the Quran. It'll be good for him. When I die one day, he can recite for my soul. If the boy's in a place where they don't complete the Quran, what's he going to do? Whatever he's got right there under his hand, from the Quran, he can recite whenever he wants to. What do you say, Hasina?"

Aunt Hasina, seeing how very serious the matter was, bowed her head in thought for a time. Then she said:

"There's nothing better than learning to recite the Quran. When you finally pass on, the boy could have his own *kuttab*, and teach the children and make some money. Trust in God, Shaikh Muhammad, and let the boy learn the Quran. Or would you rather he became a scientist?"

My father sat upright in his seat, smoking his cigarette.

"There's plenty of time," he said, "for him to become a scientist. In any case, if he memorizes the whole of the Quran now, and goes on to recite it, he'll end up better than any scientist. Let's put our trust in God."

And so my fate was decided, in a parliamentary session where I was accorded no voice. In fact, if I had been asked, I would have failed to understand the issue involved. And if I had understood, I would simply have begged them to put the discussion off, and give me my full head to enjoy myself in the Marwa area and make up for my long deprivation by running, jumping and fighting with the other children.

*Sultana al-Sidairi*

# FROM AUTOBIOGRAPHY OF A WRITER
(mudhakkarat katiba)

## Apprehensions of childhood

I can never forget that entrancing village in the furthest north of the Arabian Kingdom, lying, in tranquility and peace, in the bosom of the sands, among strands of palm trees and the golden rays of the sun that made it yet more entrancing.

There, in the village of Qurayyat, I was born and spent the days of my childhood, filled with emotions that floated within me, and within which I myself floated. I coloured my entrancing village with dreams that made life appear, to me, full of strange contradictions regarding the feelings with which my small heart was filled. My mind, too, would awake, searching and inquiring, longing to pierce the barriers of rigidity and acquire knowledge. I ask myself now: "Does each one of us have an entrancing village, in his imagination and dreams, which filled his early days and coloured his mind? Or was it just my own entrancing village, my own childhood, that were filled and crowded with my questions, expectations and search?" I don't know. But what I intend to do, frankly and with all the honesty of childhood, is to set down my feelings at that stage of my life, and note what still lingers of this in my mind, beyond the power of the days to erase.

My childhood awoke in a large house in which there was a compassionate, wise father and a mother as hardy and strong as this earth that turns along with us and revolves within our galaxy. She it was who directed our lives; her giving had no limits, and yet she gave no quarter to those who strayed. Her answers to problems were direct, positive and swift, her punishment of the wrongdoer firm.

My father was different in that way. He was one of those with a remarkable power to suppress his anger, letting his agitation surge in tense silence till he grew calm at last. He had, God rest his soul, an extensive education for those days, ahead of his time. He had a grasp of human psychology, knew and detected the weak points in human nature, which he could nevertheless forgive. He never punished anyone till he'd fully understood all the reasons for what had happened, and the circumstances that could lead a person from his true nature. But he was firm and wise in his answers.

I had three brothers. My eldest brother was 'Abdallah, now Ambassador of the Kingdom of Saudi Arabia in Kuwait. He had an extensive knowledge, having begun to read in his early years. A sociable man, he loved being with people and could not abide solitude. He was generous and refined. The next brother, Sultan, who followed directly after 'Abdallah and was also older than me, was the child who most took after my father. He was patient and wise, inclined to face situations in silence, revealing his feelings through practical, decisive answers. He is, at present, Prince of Qurayyat. Then there was my youngest brother Nayif, God rest his soul, who was younger than I was. He was strong, bold and gentle, and highly generous, to the point of extravagance. He was, indeed, too readily liberal. He was inclined to be highly strung, but soon he'd grow calm, apologize and forgive.

I had five sisters. Noura, the eldest, was a model in her tenderness and her manners. She was rational and far-sighted too. But she married and left us while I was still a small girl. Hussa, God rest her soul, was bold, ambitious and highly educated, the first of my sisters who learned to read and write. How she came by her education I don't recall; by the time I was aware of things around me she was already reading and writing. In those days there were no means of education here for girls. Most probably my father had her taught, when she was a small girl, by sending her to one of the Quranic schools.

My sister al-Bandari here was almost the same age as I was; there was just one and a half years between us. We were inseparable as children, like twins. I loved her deeply. She was gentle, always preoccupied with her toys and her never-ending childhood.

Then there was my sister Nouf, quite different from me, obstinate and thoroughly headstrong. There was no place for feeling where right and wrong was concerned. She knew what she wanted, and what to do, as well as she knew herself. She only had relations with others in the sense of dealing with them.

To this day Nouf remains utterly independent in her views: she weighs things up in a balanced way, uninfluenced by those around her. Yet, for all that, she's most sensible and temperate in all her concerns, and patient too.

My youngest sister Lulua has a most distinguished character and an abundance of talents. She views life with the irony of optimism. She's strong and cheerful, very witty, with an answer to every problem. She runs my mother's life now that she's old. She's remarkably forthright in speaking the truth. And she has the purest of hearts, with love enough for all.

I grew up with the rest of my family in a big house with plenty of servants. My father, God rest his soul, was Prince of Qurayyat and inspector for the north-west borders; he played a major part, at that time, in drawing up the frontiers with Jordan and Iraq. The late King 'Abd al-'Aziz [Ibn Saud], God rest his soul, delegated him to negotiate the matter with these two fraternal countries. My father was a far-sighted diplomat in dealing with the political issues of his time.

The thing that most disturbed me, when I'd grown up and come to know more of the world, was the presence of female slaves in our home. The matter made me deeply sad. I'd ponder the humiliation endured by human beings who are the property of others. It was indeed common practice at the time, but my young mind would resist it, even though I certainly never saw my parents mistreat any of them.

I was very delicate as a child and often ill. I suffered from the then common disease of ophthalmia; this indeed I had in common with all the other children in the region. There was no doctor, and I'd cry all night, feeling as though two thorns had been planted in my eyes. My mother would come and scold the slave who nursed me, holding me in her arms and sitting up with me. My mother was under the impression the slave had been mistreating me, but in fact she was compassionate and full of pity.

I used to cry from the pain, which only stopped when my father took us to Damascus and an ophthalmologist there treated me and operated on my eyes. From that day on, thanks be to God, I never suffered from any eye condition again.

### The death of my second mother

When I was seven or eight years old, the woman who nursed me as a child, who I loved deeply and who was the person closest to me, fell ill. She had tuberculosis, and was confined to isolation on the orders of my mother and father for fear we might develop the disease. I was very sad, and I missed her. Why was it, I'd keep asking myself, that people who fell ill should be isolated, a source of fear to others who avoided them in consequence?

At night, when everyone was asleep, I'd creep to where my sick mother was and stand at the door of her room, in a corner of the maids' quarters in our big house; and, when I could, I'd carry small presents for her – her share of sweets and fruit – which I'd hide, leaving them for her, then going back for fear someone might see me. I was sad, missing the loving heart I'd known since I was born. The sadness turned silently in my breast – a moaning I held back, afraid others might blame me.

One sad evening I can never forget, I learned that the mother who'd nursed me was dead. I stood in a corner of our garden, watching from a distance as her humble coffin was carried out in peaceful silence by three men, in time to be prayed over during the evening prayer. No one was weeping for her; she just left quietly. I, though, far off in that corner, wept silent tears and uttered a groan that found an echo in my small heart, and in a sadness that chilled all my limbs. I had vague feelings I can't explain even now; and yet, for all my awareness of death, I felt not the smallest fear. I still feel now that her good soul, God rest her, passed gently and peacefully away, leaving me with a calm sadness. I was left with no sense of fear, despite a childhood filled with stories of genies and spirits, to which we listened constantly.

From that day on, I began to feel a gulf between myself and my sister al-Bandari, who was still enjoying her high-spirited childhood. She'd love to play in the garden with her friends. I, though, had entered a different world.

**Entering a lonely world**

The new world I'd entered was one of confusion, loneliness and reflection. I'd sit by myself in a corner of the house, or else on the roof looking up at the moon on our clear summer nights. I'd gaze too, and wonder, about the stars, feeling them closer to me than the people on earth. I was engulfed by a loneliness whose source I didn't know, nor the reasons behind it. For all the semblance of silence and tranquility, a terrible world existed inside my mind. I'd listen a lot, think deeply, then feel myself lost, unable to find the answers or solve the riddles. Seeking to distance myself from this loneliness and solitude, I'd go in the evening to my mother's living room, where she used to sit together with some other women. My mother liked listening to poetry. At the end of every evening, my sister Hussa was asked to recite from a book of poems containing colloquial poetry by Ibn Sabil, al-Sharif and others. I used to enjoy this, feeling the time fleeting by, and wished I could have more.

But after a while, the war began in the sister state of Palestine, and the poetry evenings disappeared to be replaced by listening to the radio. My mother and other women would switch on to hear news of the war, broadcast by Cairo along with patriotic songs and plays about the war that were deeply moving. A dreadful fear began to take hold of me, made all the worse because the electricity was now switched off in our small village – for fear the Israelis might reach the Saudi borders. My father had installed a generator that supplied light for our home and the government departments, but this would be turned off at four in the afternoon, to be replaced by lanterns and oil lamps.

The Saudi armies had reached al-Joaf, and my uncle Muhammad al-Ahmad al-Sidairi, God rest his soul, was appointed commander of the army that was to take part in the war within Palestine. Talk of the war was on everyone's lips. I'd look around, seeking open arms to protect me and keep me safe. And, though I was among my family, barriers of silence and shyness stood between me and them.

**The first encounter with paper**

One day, a day I'll never forget, I was sitting and watching my brother 'Abdallah, who was back on holiday from his studies in Lebanon. He was reading a book and copying things out on to a piece of paper. Still I watched him, as he deciphered those strange symbols and drew those strange lines, wishing I could do the same. This anxious longing overcame my timidity; my only wish was to have for myself a few sheets of paper and a pen to write with.

"Where did you get those papers, brother?" I asked.

He looked at me, smiling. Then he said a sentence I'd never forget through all the years:

"Money brings the honey," he said. Then he added: "Would you like some paper and a pen?"

I looked down, silent and shy. I don't know what my brother had seen in my face. At any rate, he gave me a sheaf of paper and a pen. I rushed out, flying almost in my joy, and went to tell my sisters of the news. Money, I told them, would bring the honey. They laughed, surprised. I had a small box from Damascus, decorated with mirrors and mother of pearl, in which I kept my toys. I flung out the toys, and, my heart overflowing with joy, put in the papers and pen. Then I locked the box and hid the key. Every now and then I'd open this entrancing box, which, in my eyes, contained everything that was most precious; and I'd take out the paper and pen and start drawing strange lines. I didn't know what these were. For me they were just an endless conversation with the paper – of which I was fearful of running out.

That was the start of my journey with paper and pen; I think I was eight at the time. I stopped playing with my small friends and threw my toys away, no longer feeling the least desire for play and diversion. At the time, no doubt, I would have been hard put to find an explanation. But, going back in my memory, I see now that people are born with special qualities inside them, and a special personality that's unique in its behaviour and ways of thinking. All this is part of God's creation, glory be to Him. He fashioned people different in mind and heart.

Perhaps the one diversion I'd spend the whole of the previous night looking forward to was the weekly Friday picnic. My father, God rest his soul, and my mother, may God grant her long life, would gather the people of Qurayyat and take them for a picnic to some open area or to one of the farms in the villages round about.

## First experience of Cairo

In those days, the people of the village lived as if they were one large family with one heart; and my father, as the head, would embrace them, along with their joys and troubles. There were fewer cars than today, most of them belonging to the principality, with just a small number of other owners. My father would take the men, my mother the women, and we'd all go out after Friday prayers and stay till nightfall. We had a good time with our female friends from the village. But my father, God rest his soul, pondered ways of providing us with an education, concerned that boys and girls should receive one. He suggested to the late King 'Abd al-'Aziz, God rest his soul, to urbanize the bedouin and try to educate their children by providing a financial award for every student enrolling at the school. King 'Abd al-'Aziz, God rest his soul, agreed – the suggestion resulted in unprecedented recruitment from the bedouins, and also from those living around Qurayyat, and from the population of the northern parts generally. Providing education for girls was more problematic, but my father, unwilling to leave us without an education, hired a young female teacher who'd finished her secondary education. This was something beyond my dreams. Almighty God, I felt, had accorded me the means of deciphering those symbols in the book I used to hold and gaze at, seeing before me just a mysterious script.

Yet this teacher didn't, I felt, leave with me the effect I so wished for, even though I was a good student, intent on understanding my lessons. I realize now that her teaching methods left something to be desired. After a year, I began to know how to read and write a lot of words, but, dissatisfied with my teacher's lessons, I started getting hold of any newspapers and magazines I could find and copying, alike, things I understood and things I didn't.

After a year the teacher left us to get married. Then, too, we went to Egypt, after my father had fallen seriously ill during a visit to Riyadh. At that time the Kingdom of Saudi Arabia lacked the hospitals it has now. Egypt, by contrast, was known for its doctors and scientists, and for the high standard of living open to all Arabs seeking education or medical care. My father left aboard a private plane placed at his disposal by order of the late King 'Abd al-'Aziz, and went to the Queen Victoria Hospital in Alexandria, which was one of the best. The plane was later sent to take us from Beirut to Cairo, and so it was that I saw Egypt for the first time.

This was in 1950, and I'd just passed my ninth birthday. We'd visited Lebanon and Damascus before, but I still remember, even so, the astonishment we felt when we arrived in Cairo and saw how big and bustling it was, how beautiful and glistening its buildings were. What most caught my attention was the girls going to school – a sight that filled me with anguish and made me wish I was one of them.

At that time our village, like all the others, was fixated on stories and loved spreading small items of news, from which mountains were made out of molehills. What brought me happiness then were the visits of a woman who'd once nursed me, a woman who lived beyond the walls of our large house. She was of cheerful disposition, and had a graphic way of recounting the news going around the village. We used to call her "the daily newspaper"; her real name, in fact, was al-Zeina. She'd come each morning with her children, and stay right through to the evening. We used to wait till our mother took her sleep in the afternoon, then gather round al-Zeina and the teapot – the very tea took on a different taste in those cosy gatherings. There we'd sit, eager to hear al-Zeina's gossip, and the comically enthralling way she told her stories.

In the normal way I dislike talking about others, and have no taste at all for amusing myself with gossip about other people's affairs – so much so that my sister Hussa, God rest her soul, used to call me "Um Faisal," in reference to a relative of ours who was very pious and always shunned talk about others. But I liked, even so, to sit and listen to al-Zeina's stories because of the comic character she gave them. This innocent pleasure didn't, though, escape the censure of mother Noura, God rest her soul, who was our nanny and had come to live with us when she was a young bride. Unable to have children herself, she took good care of us, and would always keep an eye on us, especially when our mother was asleep. She used to worry about the effect of al-Zeina, who she regarded as an utterly frivolous woman. Frequently mother Noura would interrupt our gatherings with al-Zeina, sending sharp looks that sent us scattering resentfully.

Our life in this mansion, within which we were confined for fear our young souls might be harmed by the world outside, wasn't indeed free from minor cares, but these we coloured with a degree of happiness. We'd discuss the characters of all those living in the world of the mansion.

One important event in our home relieved the monotony of life a little. Mysterious things began to happen: numbers of women came to tailor and prepare the clothes for a bride, who was none other than my eldest sister Noura. Talk of her wedding would always subside into whispers the moment she appeared.

The story of the wedding was being written at a distance from the story's hero; such a thing was no concern of hers until the evening of the wedding itself, when she'd be told: "Tonight's your wedding night." She'd learned the news from my sister Hussa, but I was too young and shy to discuss matters of this kind. I made no comment, though I had a sense of the whole affair as something at once mysterious, sweet and frightening.

I can't precisely express my feelings at that time. No truthful girl will deny the wish for marriage. For me, though, it was a fearful wish; and for that reason I felt pity for my sister, gazing at her face each morning to see if anything in it had changed. And changed it had, having lost its radiant, fresh air. I didn't dare to ask her why, but one day I heard her talking to my sister Hussa, God rest her soul.

"Couldn't my father," she said, "have found me some better husband than that old man?"

"But he doesn't have a wife," Hussa answered. "Isn't that better than a young man with a wife already?" It was very unusual at that time for a man to have only one wife.

"But, sister," Noura said, "I'd rather not be married at all than bury my youth with that old man."

Noura was nineteen years old, regarded, in those remote days, as a fully mature girl who had to get married before the train, as they say, passed her by. A girl of twenty was considered an old maid.

I listened to their conversation in dumb silence, the sunlight touching my chair through the door of the room. I felt, on that lovely winter day, as though the rays of the sun no longer held any warmth; as though their light and warmth alike had been lost. A sense of sorrow and darkness crept over me, turning me from someone sitting comfortably in a chair, enjoying the peace and the warm sunshine, to someone who'd do anything to bring the smile back to her sister's face. But this I wasn't able to do; my feelings went on fermenting inside me. I just sat there, subdued and silent, as if mesmerized.

My sister's objection was a mere faint voice, powerless to pass beyond the walls of the room, and the ears of my other sister and myself.

*All personal account excerpts were translated by Noura Halwani*
*and Christopher Tingley*

1. *Faqeeh*: A religious teacher.
2. *Maktab*: I.e., *kuttab*, or Quranic school.
3. *Nargila*: A kind of pipe in which the tobacco is drawn through water.
4. *Zawiya*: in ordinary usage it means 'corner' but here, as in many Islamic references, it is a place where scholars, students, or worshippers meet, often to learn, sometimes to discuss religious subjects or at other times to worship. Sometimes *zawiyas* house pilgrims arriving from out of town.
5. Al-Hajjaj (died 95 AH [714 A.D.]) was a key provincial governor under the Umayyad dynasty. He was a man of probity, but noted for the severity of his methods.
6. Saeed Tamer was the foremost pharmacist in Saudi Arabia.
7. *Mawlid*: In Islam, the birthday of a holy figure, more specifically that of the Prophet.
8. The Burda and Hamzia poems are celebrated ancient poems in praise of the Prophet.
9. *Joshen*: A system whereby the letters of the Arabic alphabet are related to a numerical sequence, each letter having a fixed number. By this means a date for an event of devotional importance may be indicated through the letters used.
10. *'Amma*: The first part of the Quran, learned first by children.
11. *Halala*: A coin of small value.
12. *Tawheed*: The doctrine of the Oneness of God.

# Part VI

## BIOGRAPHICAL INFORMATION

# BIOGRAPHICAL INFORMATION

## The Authors

## I. THE POETS

### Usama 'Abd al-Rahman (b. 1943)

He obtained his Ph.D. degree in 1970, from the American University in Washington, and became a Professor of Political Science at the King Saud University in Riyadh. He has produced many collections of poetry, including: *A Fathomless Sea* (bahrun lujjiyun), 1987; and *No Protector* (la 'asim), 1988. He has also produced studies in politics, culture and society. His writings, both poetry and prose, are characterized by a markedly critical tone.

### Fawziyya Abu Khalid (b. 1956)

She was born in Riyadh, holds a Ph.D. in Sociology and works as a professor at the King Saud University. In 1974 she became the first to issue a collection of prose poetry, under the title *Till When Will They Abduct You on the Wedding Night?* (ila mata yakhtutifunaki lailat al-'urs). Thereafter she restricted herself to prose poetry, her production in this type including her collection *Mirage Water* (ma' al-sarab), 1995, and other work.

### Faisal Akram (b. 1969)

Born in Mecca, he early won recognition as poet obtaining, in 1996, the poetic prize from the Literary Club in the Eastern section of Saudi Arabia. He has published several poetic collections among which are *Interconnections* (al-tadakhulat), *Poem of Individuals* (qasidat al-afrad) and *Preface to the Last Book* (muqaddmat al-kitab al-akheer).

### Muhammad al-'Ali (b. 1932)

He was born in al-Ahsa' and obtained his B.A. degree in Arabic Language from the University of Baghdad. He worked as a teacher and headed the editing of the newspaper *Al-Yawm* ("the day"). A poet and prose writer, neither his poetry nor his prose have been compiled and published, despite their frequent appearances in the press. His tendency is to free verse, and he is regarded as one of those who established this trend in Saudi poetry. His use of language is distinctive, with a wealth of reflection on heritage and a notable correctness of style. He is eager, in poetry and prose alike, to treat modern issues and subjects.

### Muhammad Sa'id al-'Amoudi (1905-1991)

Born in Mecca, he graduated from the Falah School in 1920. He belonged to the first generation of men of letters in the Kingdom of Saudi Arabia, and combined composition of poetry with writing and supervisory work in journalism, and with commercial activities. He produced one small collection of poetry, *My Quatrains* (ruba'iyyati), 1980; collections of essays including *From Our History* (min tarikhina), 1954, and *From What Books Talk About* (min hadeeth al-kutub), 1979; and a set of short stories entitled *Ramiz and Other Stories* (Ramiz wa qisas ukhra), 1983.

### Muhammad Hasan 'Awwad (1902-1980)

Born in Jeddah, he wrote his first poem at the age of ten and gained a prominent position among his country's poets writing mainly in the inherited two hemistich verse, but exercising much originality and a great sensitivity to human suffering and the human condition in general. After publishing several individual volumes he collected his poetry in three volumes titled Diwan al-'Awwad in 1953.

### 'Adnan al-'Awwami (b. 1938)

Born in al-Qatif in the east of the Kingdom, he obtained his school certificate in 1964 and educated himself through constant reading. He has worked in government offices. He has a collection of poetry entitled *The Beach of Desolation* (sahil al-yabab), published in 1991.

### 'Ali Bafaqeeh (b.1960)

He was born in Southern Yemen and obtained a degree in civil engineering from America. Among his publications is his collection of poems, The Majesty of Trees (jalal al-ashjar).

### Ahmad Bahkali (b. 1955)

Born in Abi 'Areesh in the south of the Kingdom, he has an M.A. degree in Linguistics and works as a teacher at the Intermediate College in the town of Jazan. His poetic works include: *The Earth and Love* (al-ard wa 'l-hub), 1978; and *The First of the Rain* (awwal al-ghaith), 1992.

### Sa'd al-Bawardi (b. 1930)

Born in the city of Ta'if, he issued, in 1956, the monthly magazine *Al-Ish'a* "radiance") in the city of al-Khobar in the east of the Kingdom. He worked in the Ministry of Education and later became Cultural Adviser to the Saudi Embassy, first in Beirut and then in Cairo. He is a poet and prose writer who has also made contributions to journalism. Most of his poetry is about the humanity of man and about love of country. It includes the following collections: *The Song of Return* (ughniyat al-'awda), 1961; *Particles in the Horizon* (dharrat fi 'l-ufuq), 1962; *Coloured Snapshots* (laqtat mulawwana), 1963; *Songs for My Country* (ughniyatun li biladi), 1981; *Poems Addressing Man* (qasa'id tukhatib al-insan), 1989.

### Nasser Bouhaimid (b. 1931)
He was born in Riyadh and received his education in Bahrain. In 1962, he issued his only collection of poetry, *Concern* (qalaq), and devoted himself to commerce thereafter. His poetry reflects the influence of the Arab Nationalist trend that prevailed at the beginning of the 1950s. He was one of those poets who paved the way for the appearance of prose poetry, later called "the poems of prose" within Saudi poetry.

### Lulu Buqshan (b. 1965)
Born in Jeddah, she obtained her degree in English literature at the King Saud University and has emerged as an interesting feminist poet.

### Huda al-Daghfaq (b. 1967)
A sensitive poet and writer, who works as a teacher. She is also active in literary journalism and contributes to local and Arabic newspapers. She has also published studies of Saudi literature. She writes both prose and free verse poetry and has two poetry collections: *The Shadow Thrusting Upwards* (al-zillu ila a'la), 1993; and *A New Yearning* (lahfa jadeeda), 2002.

### Fawzi al-Dahhan (b. 1961)
Born in al-Qateef, he obtained an M.A. in public administration from King Saud University, and is active in the literary field in Saudi Arabia and in the Gulf countries, and participates in literary journalism. Among his published works is his well-acclaimed collection, *The Gates of Love* (abwab al-'ishq)

### 'Ali al-Dumaini (b. 1953)
Born in al-Baha, he studied mechanical engineering which he eventually abandoned in favour of a career in literature, working in literary journalism. He has edited several literary reviews and has published a comprehensive collection of his own poetry titled, *Winds of Places* (riyah al-amakin)

### Muhammad al-Domaini (b. 1958)
He was born in al-Baha in the southern part of the Kingdom. He has a B.A. degree in Library Science and works at ARAMCO (the Arabian American Oil Company). A writer of both prose and free verse poetry, he has a collection of poetry entitled *The Ruins of Joy* (anqad al-ghibta), 1989.

### 'Abdallah al-Faisal Al Saud (b. 1923)

He is the grandson of King 'Abd al-'Aziz, the founder of the Kingdom of Saudi Arabia. He was born in the capital, Riyadh, and assumed a number of government positions, including that of Minister of the Interior. He then devoted himself to commerce. He was rewarded with the State Acknowledgement Award for Literature in 1984. A composer of both classical and colloquial poetry, his works include the collection *The Inspiration of Deprivation* (wahyu 'l-hirman), 1980. A number of singers have sung his poems, including the famous Egyptian singer, Um Kulthoum.

### Muhammad Hasan Faqi (1912-2003)

Born in Mecca, he worked first in teaching then as editor-in-chief of *Saut al-Hijaz* paper, and later occupied various prominent positions in the Saudi government, becoming ambassador to Indonesia. He took early retirement and dedicated his time to reading and writing, publishing several collections of poetry, short stories and many books on other topics ranging from literature to religion to legal issues. He has published his full poetic oeuvre in one book. His *Ruba'iyyat* (quartets), a collection of 474 quatrains, represents some of his best poetry.

### Ahmad al-Fasi (b. 1925)

He was born in Mecca and graduated from the School of Islamic Law at al-Azhar University. He worked as Secretary-General of the International Islamic Association in Cairo. He produced one collection of poetry, *The First Tune* (al-lahn al-awwal), 1960.

### Muhammad Habiby (b. 1968)

He obtained an MA in literature and works as lecturer in the Teachers' Training College in Jizan. He obtained the Abha Cultural Prize in Humanisitc Studies for his book, *Creative Trends in Modern Saudi Poetry*. Among his publications is his poetry collection, *Alone, I was Broken* (inkasartu waheedan).

### Sa'd al-Hamazani (b. 1964)

He was born in the city of Ha'il in the north of the Kingdom and has a B.A. in Islamic Law. He works as a teacher in Riyadh. He has published two poetry collections: *The Centre of Intuition* (muntasaf al-hads), 1984; and *A Seventh Grandfather to Silence* (jaddun sabi'un li 'l-samt), 1997.

### Muhammad 'Ubaid al-Harbi (b. 1955)

He was born in al-Madina and studied civil engineering graduating in 1979. He worked in journalism becoming editor-in-chief of the cultural section of *al-Sharq* Review in Dammam. He writes prose poetry and is one of Saudi Arabia's avant-garde poets.

## Salih al-Harbi (b. 1962)

Holder of the Diploma of the Institute for Artistic Education, he is a plastic artist and calligrapher and participates in poetry evenings. His two poetry collections are: *Asma' and the Anguish of Questions* (Asma' wa hurqat al-as'ila), 1996; and *I See Women Giving Water to Corpses* (ara niswatun yasqeena al-juthath), 2000.

## Ashjan Hindi (b. 1968)

She was born in the city of Jeddah and obtained her M.A. degree in Arabic Literature from King Saud University in Riyadh. She is presently preparing her Ph.D. thesis at the School of Oriental and African Studies at the University of London. She has one collection of poetry, *The Dream Has the Smell of Rain* (lil-hulmi ra'ihat al-matar), 1998, and a book of criticism, *Using Heritage in Saudi Poetry* (tawzeef al-turath fi 'l-shi'r al-Su'udi), 1996.

## Ibrahim al-Husain (b. 1960)

Born in al-Ahsa', he obtained his degree in the Arabic language from the teachers Training College and works in the field of teaching. Among his publications are his poetry collections I Came Out of the Narrow Land (kharajtu min al-ard al-dayyiqa) and Wood that Rubs against Pedestrians (khashabun yatamassahu bil-maarrah).

## Hashim al-Jahdali (b. 1967)

Born in the Jeddah district, he did his higher studies at the Arab College and worked as teacher then as an editor at the Ukaz paper. He is active in the literary field participating in many local and Arab literary meetings and festivals, and writing in the literary journals and in the pages of the literary papers. Among his publications is his poetry collection, Blood as Testimony (dam al-bayyinat).

## Nayif al-Juhni (b. 1963)

He was born in al-Qurayyat in the north of the kingdom, and obtained a degree in the Arabic language. He is both a poet and a novelist, publishing in both genres. Among his publications are his novel, The Boundaries (al-hudoud) and his poetry collection, Quickly, as if He Never Passed (sari'an kaman la yamurr).

## Ghassan al-Khunaizi (b. 1960)

Born in al-Qateef, he is one of Saudi Arabia's foremost avant-garde poets. He studied engineering in America and has lived both in America and in Baghdad. He presently works in ARAMCO. His book of poetry, Small Illusions (awham sagheera) won acclaim in Saudi Arabia and beyond.

## Ghaida' al-Manfa

Real name Haya al-'Urainan. Her fame as a poet was established in the 1980s by virtue of the sheer distinction of her poetry. She published her poems in local papers under the pseudonyms *Ghaida' al-Manfa* ("the lass of exile") and *Ghajariyyat al-Reef* ("the gypsy of the countryside"). Only recently, when she resumed publishing her poems after a long cessation, has she divulged her true name. She does not have a published collection.

### Muhammad al-Mish'an (1933-2000)

He graduated in 1960 from the School of Islamic Law at the Islamic University of Imam Muhammad bin Saud in Riyadh and has held various teaching positions. He writes satirical articles, some of which he published, in 1992, in a book entitled *Sieves* (gharabeel). His works of poetry include: *The Ecstasy of Grief* (nashwat al-huzn), 1978; and *Sparkles* (wamadat), 1989.

### Ahmad al-Mulla (b. 1961)

He was born in al-Ahsa' in the east of the Kingdom and holds a B.A. degree in Sociology. He is among the most prominent prose poets and also writes plays. His works of poetry include: *A Shadow Is Flickering* (zillun yataqassaf), 1995; and *Light and Slanting, Like Forgetfulness* (khafifan wa ma'ilan kanisyan), 1996.

### Ahmad Salih Qandeel (1911-1979)

Born in the city of Jeddah, he studied at the Falah Schools and worked as a teacher there after graduating in 1926. Then, in 1936, he became editor-in-chief of the newspaper *Sawt al-Hijaz* ("Voice of the Hijaz") in Mecca, before taking up a number of government posts. A poet and essay writer, he produced a number of classical poetic works including: *The Towers* (al-abraj), 1951; *The Echoes* (al-asda'), 1951; and *Fire* (nar), 1967; in addition to his composition of poems in the Hijazi colloquial dialect, in which he produced two collections under the title *Al-Mirkaz*. After his retirement, he devoted his time to the production of artistic writings for Saudi Radio and Television.

### 'Abd al-Rahman al-Qa'oud (b. 1940)

He was born in the town of al-Hariq in the centre of the kingdom, and has a Ph.D. in Literature and Criticism. He worked as Professor of Literature at the King 'Abd al-'Aziz Military Academy in Riyadh, and was also editor-in-chief of the Academy's magazine. He has produced a collection of poetry, *A Forgotten Piece of Night* (qit'a min lailin mansiyya), and a research paper entitled "Clarity and Ambiguity in Old Arabic Poetry" (al-wuduh wa al-ghumud fi 'l-shi'r al-'Arabi 'l-qadeem), 1990.

### Lateefa Qari

Born in the city of Ta'if in the west of the Kingdom, she has a B.Sc. in Sciences and works in the field of teaching and education. She has one collection of poetry: *The Pearl of the Difficult Evening* (lu'lu'at al-masa' al-sa'b), 1998.

### Fatima al-Qarni (b. 1964)

Born in a village in the 'Aseer region, she has an MA from the College of Education in Riyadh. She writes both poetry and short stories and has published a collection of short stories titled *Saudi Loyalty* (wafa' al-Su'udiyya).

### Hasan al-Qurashi (1926-2004)

Born in Mecca, he gained his B.A. degree in History from the King Saud University in Riyadh. He held many government positions and was appointed Ambassador to Mauritania. Active in poetry evenings and festivals inside and outside the Kingdom, he was endowed with an exceptional memory for his own poetry and for much of the poetry of others of various epochs. He composed both the traditional two-hemistich poem and free verse poems, and had a profuse poetic output published in many collections, some of them compiled in his *Complete Collected Works*, 1985. He also wrote stories and a one-act play that are included in his book *The Groans of the Waterwheel* (annat al-saqiya), 1956.

### Ghazi al-Qusaibi (b. 1940)

Born in the city of al-Ahsa' in the east of the Kingdom, he obtained a Ph.D. in International Relations from the University of London. He worked as a professor at the King Saud University in Riyadh, then assumed cabinet positions. He later became Ambassador to Bahrain then to the United Kingdom where he stayed for several years and was influential in the literary activity of the large Arab community in London. He then returned to Saudi Arabia where he assumed a new cabinet ministry as Minister of Water and Electricity and later as Minister of Labour. He is a profuse writer of articles, poems and novels. His poetry was later collected in *The Complete Poetic Works* (al-a'mal al-shi'riyya al-kamila), 1987. He published two novels to date: *The Apartment of Freedom* (shuqqat al-hurriyya), 1994, and *The 'Asfuriyya Asylum* (al-'Asfooriyya), 1996.

### Hasan al-Sab' (b. 1945)

He was born in the town of Sihat in the eastern region of the Kingdom, and obtained his M.A. in Public Administration from the United States. He has published many literary contributions in the press. His works of poetry include: *Her Oil and the Wakefulness of Lamps* (zaituha wa sahar al-qanadeel), 1992; and *The Garden of the Rosy Age* (hadeeqat al-zaman al-wardi), 1999.

### 'Abdallah al-Safar (b. 1960)

Born in Ahsa' he writes both poetry and the short story and participates briskly in the cultural activity of Saudi Arabia. His collection of poetry, He Opens the Window and Leaves (yaftahu al-nafidha wa yarhal) won acclaim among the avant-garde circles in the country.

## 'Abdallah al-Saikhan (b. 1956)

Born in the town of Ha'il, in the north of the Kingdom, he worked in journalism as an editor and a partner in publishing. Numbered among the modernist poets, his output is somewhat scanty, and he has only one collection of poetry: *Apprehensions on the Climate of the Homeland* (hawajis fi taqs al-watan), 1988.

## Ahmad al-Salih (b. 1943)

He was born in 'Unaiza in the Qassim region in the centre of the kingdom, and is known as "Musafir" (traveller), under which pseudonym he long published his poetry. He obtained a B.A. in History. His collections of poetry include: *When the Soothsayer Falls* ('indama yasqut al-'arraf), 1978; *Shake Yourself Up, Pretty Girl* (intafidi ayyatuha 'l-maleeha), 1983; *The Homeland Is Reflected in Your Eyes* ('aynaki yatajalla fihima 'l-watan), 1997.

## Husain Sirhan (1916-1992)

Born in Mecca, he enrolled at the Falah School and worked for a short period in government offices. A poet and essay writer, he is regarded as being in the vanguard of the pioneer period in the literary renaissance within the Kingdom. His works of poetry include: *Wings Without Feathers* (ajniha bila reesh), 1977; and *The Alien Bird* (al-ta'ir al-ghareeb), 1977. His essays and studies include: *Of Literature and War* (fi al-adab wa 'l-harb), 1978; and *From the Essays of Husain Sirhan* (min maqalat Husain Sirhan), 1979.

## Husain Suhail (b. 1960)

Born in the Island of Farsan in the south of the Kingdom, he obtained the Diploma of the Teachers' Preparatory Institute and worked as a teacher. He is presently principal of an elementary school in Farasan. He participates in poetry evenings and publishes his poetry in local and Gulf newspapers. He has published two collections of poetry: *The Sails of Silence* (ashri'at al-samt), 1990; and *The Moons Have a Gate* (lil-aqmari babun), 1999.

## Jasim al-Suhayyih (b. 1964)

He was born in al-Ahsa' in the east of the Kingdom and has a B.Sc. in Engineering from the United States. He works as a mechanical engineer with the Arabian American Oil Company. He has many poetic works including: *My Shadow Is My Successor Over You* (zilli khalifati 'alaikum), 1994; *A Dance of Gratitude* (raqsa 'irfaniyya), 1999; *The Wailing of the Alphabet* (naheeb al-abjadiyya), 2003.

## Ahmad Sa'd al-Tayyar (b. 1974)

He was born in the town of al-Baha in the south of the Kingdom. He works at the Arabian American Oil Company in Dhahran, in the east of the country, and has one collection of poetry, *The Lights of the Spirit* (adwa' al-ruh), 1999.

### Muhammad al-Thubaiti (b. 1952)

Born in the city of Ta'if in the west of the Kingdom, he is one of the most prominent modernist poets in the Kingdom of Saudi Arabia. Some of his poems have been awarded local and Arab prizes. He has published three collections of poetry: *The Lover of the Rosy Age* ('ashiqat al-zaman al-wardi), 1982; *I Spelled a Dream, Spelled Illusion* (tahajjaytu huluman...tahajjaytu wahman), 1982; and *The Contours* (al-tadarees), 1986.

### 'Ali al-'Umari (b. 1969)

A very sensitive poet, he was born in al-Madina and obtained a degree in Shari'a Law from the Islamic University. After working in various jobs he left official work and dedicated himself to Islamic Guidance.

### Thurayya al-'Urayyid (b. 1945)

Born in Bahrain to the famous Bahraini poet Ibrahim al-'Urayyid, she has a Ph.D. in Sociology from the United States and works at the Arabian American Oil Company in Dhahran in the east of the Kingdom. Her poetic works include: *Which Way Do the Trees Lean?* (ayna ittijah al-shajar), 1995; and *A Woman Without a Name* (imra'a duna ism), 1998. She is also a researcher and a contributor to Saudi and Arab dailies.

### 'Abdallah al-'Uthaimeen (b. 1937)

Born in 'Unaiza in the Qassim region in the centre of the kingdom, he works as a professor teaching Modern History at the King Saud University in Riyadh In addition, he is a member of the Advisory Council and Trustee of the King Faisal International Award. His works of poetry include *The Return of the Absentee* ('awdat al-gha'ib), 1981. His research and studies include: *The History of the Kingdom of Saudi Arabia* (tarikh al-mamlaka 'l-'Arabiyya 'l-Su'udiyya), two vols., *Jazan,* 1984; and *The Rise of the Principality of Aal Rasheed* (nash'at imarat Aal Rasheed), 1992.

### Ibrahim al-Wazzan (b. 1954)

Born in Zulfi, he obtained his degree in Arabic Language and Literature from Imam Muhammad University in Riyadh and works at the General Youth Institution as Director General for the Saudi Literary Clubs. His best known collection is *You're the Origin of All Directions* (wa innaka asl al-jihat).

## II. THE SHORT STORY WRITERS

### Muhammad 'Alwan (b. 1947)

He was born in Abha and obtained his B.A. in Arabic Language from the School of Literature at the King Saud University. He worked at the Ministry of Information in Riyadh and supervised the cultural extras of the magazine *Al-Yamama* and the newspaper *Al-Riyadh*. He is an author known for his short stories. His collections of short stories include: *Bread and Silence* (al-khubz wa 'l-samt), 1977; *Thus Begins the Story* (al-hikaya tabda' hakadha), 1983; *For the Memory of the Homeland* (lidhakirat al-watan), 1994; *Gloomy* (damisa), 1998.

### 'Abdallah Bakhashwain (b. 1953)

Born in the city of Ta'if, he worked in the cultural department of the magazine Iqra'. He also became Director of the Cultural Department of the Cooperative Council of the Arabian Gulf States. He has published many of his short stories in local and Arab newspapers and magazines. His works include *The Party* (al-hafla) (a collection of stories), 1985.

### Fawziyya al-Bakr (b. 1958)

She was born in Riyadh and obtained her M.A. degree in School Administration and Cultural Supervision from the School of Education at the King Saud University. Then, in 1990, she obtained her Ph.D. in the same subject from the Institute of Education at the University of London. She presently teaches in the Department of Education and Children's Kindergartens at the King Saud University. She is known as an active contributor of essays and short stories to local newspapers. Her works include *The Saudi Woman and Education* (al-mar'a 'l-Su'udiyya wa 'l-ta'leem), 1988.

### Badriyya al-Bishr (b. 1965)

She was born in Riyadh and obtained her B.A. in Social Studies from the College of Arts at the King Saud University in 1989, and her M.A. in the same subject and from the same College in 1994. She worked as a social specialist at the King Fahd Hospital in Riyadh and has participated in story evenings inside the Kingdom and outside it. Her collections of stories include: *The End of the Game* (nihayat al-lu'ba), 1992; and *Wednesday Evening* (masa' al-Arbi'a'), 1994.

### Hamza Muhammad Bogary (1932-1984)

He was born in Mecca and received his elementary and secondary education at the schools there. He then received a scholarship to the then University of Fuad 1st in Cairo, where he obtained, from its College of Arts, a B.A. in Arabic Language and Literature. Upon his return to the Kingdom, he worked as Director of the Coordination Administration at the Directorate of Broadcasting, then as Director General of Publications, and was later appointed Under-Secretary of the Ministry of Information. After retiring, he supervised the magazine issued by the Broadcasting Service and contributed material both to it and to local newspapers. He was a pioneer of story writing in the Kingdom of Saudi Arabia. His works include: *The Short Story in Egypt and Mahmoud Taymour* (al-qissa 'l-qasira fi misr wa Mahmoud Taymour), 1979; *The Tobacco Vendor* (ba'i'u 'l-tabgh) (a translated story collection), 1981; *The Safa Sheltered Quarters* (saqifat al-Safa) (a novel), 1984. This novel was translated for *PROTA* by Olive Kenny and Jeremy Reed, and published by the

Middle East Center of the University of Texas in Austin under the title of *The Sheltered Quarters*.

### Sa'd al-Dosari (b. 1959)

He was born in al-Rass in al-Qassim and obtained his B.A. in English Literature from the College of Arts at the King Saud University in 1981. He has worked in journalism and also as Executive Assistant for Information and Health Education Affairs at the Specialized King Faisal Hospital. His collections of stories include: *The Withering of the Disobedient Son* (intifa'at al-walad al-'asi), 1987; and *The Court of the Last Lady* (balat al-sayyida 'l-akheera), 1989.

### Khaleel al-Fuzai' (b. 1941)

Born in al-Ahsa', he worked first in the teaching sector, then moved on to journalism and, in the period 1984-1991, assumed the chief editorial position of the al-Ahsa' newspaper *The Day* (al-yawm). He has made many contributions in radio and television and has participated in numerous cultural symposiums. His short story collections include: *The Clock and the Palm Tree* (al-sa'a wa 'l-nakhla), 1977; *Women and Love* (al-nisa' wa 'l-hub), 1978; and *The Thursday Market* (suq al-khamis), 1979. His book of essays, *Discourse on Literature* (ahadith fi 'l-adab) appeared in 1966;

### Maryam al-Ghamidi (b. 1947)

Born in Asmara, Eritrea, she obtained her B.A. in English Language and Literature from King 'Abd al-'Aziz University in Jeddah in 1989. She also obtained a diploma in nursing. Since 1962, she has been an announcer, a programme organizer for radio and also takes part in acting on radio shows. Her short story collection, *I Love You, But …* (uhibbuka wa lakin…) appeared in 1988.

### Noura al-Ghamidi (b. 1968)

Born in the town of Bisha in the south of the Kingdom, she obtained her B.A. degree from the College of Education, Department of Arabic Language, then started work in educational guidance. Her works include a collection of stories, *Sorry, I'm Still Dreaming* ('afwan, la ziltu ahlam).

### 'Ashiq 'Issa al-Hadhal (b. 1937)

Born in Ha'il in the north of the Kingdom of Saudi Arabia, he obtained the diploma of the Teachers' Preparatory Institute in Mecca and began work in teaching. Subsequently he became Director of Public Relations at the Directorate of Education in Ha'il, then managed the branch of the Society for Culture and Arts. Aside from his involvement in short story writing, he has genuine interest in popular (Nabati) poetry. He has several short story collections to date: *The Self-Made Man* (al-'isami), 1973; *A Wedding at the Hospital* ('urs fi 'l-mustashfa), 1977; *The Broker of Donkeys* (dallal al-hamir), 1980; and *The Dog and Civilization* (al-kalb wa 'l-hadara),

1983. His book, *Selections from Contemporary Nabati Poetry* (mukhtarat min al-shi'r al-nabati 'l-mu'asir) (folk poetry), was published in 1972

## Husain 'Ali Husain (b. 1950)

He was born in Medina and has a diploma in land surveying. He worked in journalism and as a controller at the Department of Publications in the Ministry of Information. He writes stories and newspaper articles, and has supervised the cultural supplement of *Al-Yamama* magazine. He is a member of the Saudi Club for Short Stories. His collections of short stories include: *The Departure* (al-raheel), 1978; *The Man of High Standing* (kabeer al-maqam), 1987; and *The Queue of Mineral Water* (tabur al-miyah al-ma'daniyya).

## Umaima al-Khamees

Born in Riyadh, she gained her B.A. degree in Arabic Language and Literature from the College of Arts at King Saud University in 1988. She works as a teacher of Arabic Language at a secondary school. Her short story collections include: *And the Rib When It Became Straight* (wa 'l-dil'u heena istawa), 1992; and *The Antidote* (al-tiryaq), 2003.

## Najat Khayyat (b. 1944)

Born in Jeddah, she obtained her elementary certificate in Beirut, Lebanon, and made herself cultivated through reading. She began writing stories and contributed social essays for publication in the press and on the radio. Her works include *The Birth Pangs of Silence* (makhad al-samt) (a collection of stories), 1966.

## Fahd al-Khilaiwi (b. 1947)

He was born in al-Qassim in the centre of the kingdom. He worked at the Ministry of Post, Telephones and Telegrams and supervised the cultural section of the magazine *Iqra'*. He is a short story writer and an essayist.

## Hiyam al-Mifleh

Born in Syria, she obtained her B.Sc. in Agricultural Science from the University of Aleppo in 1985. She works as a journalist at the *Riyadh* newspaper. Her works include a collection of stories, *Pages From a Forgotten Memory* (safahat min dhakira mansiyya).

## 'Abdallah al-Nasser (b. 1953)

He was born in Dir'iyya in the centre of Saudi Arabia, and studied Arabic Literature at al-Imam University, Riyadh. He spent several years in Houston as editor of the educational magazine *Al-Mubta'ath* and in Algiers as cultural attaché, and is at present cultural attaché in London and editor of *Al-Thaqafiyya*, a Saudi quarterly publication concerned with Arabic culture. An uncomplicated yet sophisticated writer, with a vein of satire and humour, he is deeply concerned with the inevitable collision between desert and city. His has to date three Arabic collections of short stories, *The Mirage* (al-sarab), 1988; *The Siege of Snow* (hisar al-thalj), 2002; and *The story of a Shoe* (sirat na'l), 2004. An English language collection, *The Tree and Other Stories* (2003) selected from his published and yet unpublished works was prepared by *PROTA* (with an introduction on his fictional work) and was published by Interlink Books, Northampton and London. He has one published book of essays, *Frankly Speaking* (bi 'l-fasih), 2003, and has in press a new collection of short stories, *The Departure* (al-rahil); a book titled, *The Murderous Democracy* (al-dimuqratiyya 'l-qatila) at Dar al-Marrikh publishers in Cairo; and a critical work on the art of imagery in the poetry of the Umayyad poet, Dhu 'l-Rumma, *The Cinamatographical Image in Dhu 'l-Rumma's Poetry* (Dhu 'l-Rumma , al-musawwir al-sinama'i.)

### Hasan al-Ni'mi (b. 1961)
Born in Tihamat 'Aseer, in the south of the Kingdom, he obtained his B.A. in Arabic Language from the College of Arts at King 'Abd al-Aziz University in Jeddah and his Ph.D. on "The Relation of the Novel to the Cinema" from the University of Indiana in the United States. He presently works as an instructor at the College of Arts and Human Sciences at King 'Abd al-Aziz University. His collections of short stories include: *The Time of Boisterous Love* (zaman al-'ishq al-sakhib), 1984; *The Last Word in Village Interpretation* ('akhiru ma ja'a fi 'l-ta'weel al-qurawi), 1987; *Kathib Recounted, He Said* (haddatha kathib qal), 1999.

### 'Abdallah al-Salmi (b. 1950)
Born in Riyadh, he obtained his B.Sc. in Engineering from the United States in 1980. After graduating, he worked as an engineer with the Frontier Force. His collection of short stories, *Cubes of Humidity* (muka''abat min al-rutuba) appeared in 1980.

### 'Abd al-'Aziz al-Saq'abi (b. 1958)
Born in the city of Ta'if, he obtained his B.A. in Literature from the King Saud University in 1981, and worked as Financial and Administrative Director of the King Fahd National Library. He is engaged in cultural and journalistic activities. His works include: *Your Night Isn't Mine – And You're Not Me!* (la lailuka laili wala anta ana) (a collection of stories), 1983; *A Slap in the Mirror* (saf'a fi 'l-mir'at) (a play), 1984; *The Smell of Coal* (ra'ihat al-fahm) (a novel), 1988; *The Story Narrator Loses His Voice* (al-hakawati yafqidu sawtah) (a collection of stories), 1990.

### Khairiya Ibrahim al-Saqqaf (b. 1950)
Born in Mecca, she obtained her Ph.D. in 1988 from the School of Social Sciences at the Islamic University of Imam Muhammad bin Saud. Her subject was the Curricula for Studying Arabic Literature at Universities. She worked as an instructor

at the King Saud University in Riyadh. A well known journalist, she is considered to be the first female editor-in-chief of a newspaper in the Arab Peninsula and the region of the Arabian Gulf. Her works include: *To Sail Towards the Far Horizons* (an tubhira nahwa 'l-ab'ad) (a collection of stories), 1982; and *A Crisis in the Equation* (ma'zaq fi 'l-mu'adala) (essays).

### Ruqayya al-Shabeeb (b. 1957)

She was born in Ha'il in the north of the Kingdom and holds a B.A. in History awarded in 1980 by the Islamic University of Imam Muhammad bin Saud. She is the officer in charge for erasing illiteracy at the Chief Public Office for the Education of Girls. She writes essays and short stories. Her works include two collections of short stories: *A Dream* (hulm), 1984; and *The Grey Grief* (al-huzn al-ramadi), 1987; *Short Dreams* (ahlam qasira), 1992.

### Shareefa al-Shamlan (b. 1948)

She was born in al-Zubair in Iraq and obtained her B.A. in Literature, Journalism Section, from Baghdad University. After graduation, she was employed by the Ministry of Labour and Social Affairs in the Kingdom of Saudi Arabia. She writes short stories and essays. Her collections of stories include: *The Utmost Calm* (muntaha 'l-hudu'), 1989; *Sections From a Life* (maqati' min hayat).

### Hussa Muhammad al-Tuwaijri

She was born in Riyadh and obtained her M.A. in Social Services from the University of St. Louis in the United States. She presently works as Director General of the Care and Guidance Department at the Ministry of Labour and Social Affairs. She has a prominent social presence, being a founding member of the Women's Wafa' Charitable Society in Riyadh and takes a substantial part in literary activities.

### Layla al-Uhaidib (b. 1964)

She was born in al-Ahsa' in the east of the Kingdom and obtained her B.A. in Arabic Language from the College of Education. She then began work as a secondary school teacher. She writes essays and short stories and has participated in the Fourth Festival of Arabian Gulf Stories, held in Muscat, Oman, in 1988. Her works include a collection of stories, *In Search of a Seventh Day* (al-bahth 'an yawm sabi').

### Qumasha al-'Ulayyan

She was born in Riyadh and holds a B.Sc. in Chemistry from the King Saud University (1991). She was engaged as an instructor and student adviser, and also works as a journalist for the Kuwaiti magazine *Al-Majalis al-Kuwaitiyya*. She is a story writer and has published many of her stories in the local press, in *Al-Majalis al-Kuwaitiyya* and in the magazine *Kullu 'l-Usra* ("All the Family"), which is published in the United Arab Emirates. Her works include: *A Mistake in My Life* (khata' fi hayati), 1992; Two collections of stories: *The Virgin Wife* (al-zawja 'l-'adhra'), 1993; and *Tears on the Wedding Night* (dumu' fi lailat al-zafaf), 1997; and three novels: *Eyes on the Sky* ('uyun 'la 'l-sama'), 1999; *Weeping in the Rain* (buka' tahta 'l-matar), 2000; and *The Female of the Spider* (untha 'l-'ankabut), 2000.

## III. THE NOVELISTS

### Hamza Muhammad Bogary
(Please see his entry under "Short Story Writers.")

### Hamid Damanhury (1922-1965)
He was born in Mecca and obtained his B.A. in Literature from the University of Alexandria in 1943. He worked as an inspector with the Viceroy's Bureau in Mecca, then as under-secretary for cultural affairs at the Ministry of Education. His works include the following novels: *The Price of Sacrifice* (thaman al-tadhiya), 1958; *And the Days Passed By* (wa marrat al-ayyam), 1963.

### Turki al-Hamad (b. 1952)
Born in Buraida, he obtained his Ph.D. in 1985 from the University of Southern California. He taught in the Department of Political Science at King Saud University in Riyadh and has produced a number of cogent intellectual studies. He has written the following novels: *Al-Adama* (al-'adama), 1997 (title referring to a neighbourhood in the city of Dammam); *Al-Shamaisi* (al-shamaisi), 1997 (title referring to a neighbourhood in the city of Riyadh); *Al-Karadeeb* (al-Karadeeb) 1998 (title referring to a neighbourhood in the city of Jeddah). His works also include: *Ideological Studies on the Arab Situation* (dirasa ideologiyya fi 'l-hala 'l-'Arabiyya), 1962; and *Contemporary Revolutionary Movements* (al-harakat al-thawriyya 'l-mu'asira) (a translation), 1986.

### Laila al-Juhani (b. 1969)
Born in the city of Tabuk, she obtained her B.A. degree in English Language and Literature from the Medina branch of King 'Abd al-'Aziz University. She writes short stories and novels and has made contributions to the press. Her novel *Always, Love Will Remain* (da'iman sayabqa 'l-hub) was awarded second prize at the Abha Competition for Novels. Some of her short stories won high praise at the Ta'if and the Medina Literary Clubs. Her novel *The Barren Paradise* (al-firdaws al-yabab) won first prize at the Shariqa Competition for Creativity, First Session, 1997, and was published in 1998.

### Abdu Khal (b. 1962)
He was born in Jazan in the south west of the kingdom, and obtained his B.A. degree in Political Science from the King 'Abd al-'Aziz University in Jeddah. He is a

writer on culture with the newspaper *Okaz* ('Ukaz) and has made cultural contributions within literary clubs. He has written the following novels: *Death Walks Here* (al-mawt yamurru min huna), 1995; *Cities That Eat the Grass* (mudun ta'kul al-'ushb), 1998; *The Days Hide No One* (al-ayyam la tukhbi'u ahadan), 2002; *The Clay* (al-teen), 2002; and the following short story collections: *Dialogue at the Gate of the Earth* (hiwar 'la bawwabat al-ard), 1987; *No One* (la ahad), 1991.

### 'Abd al-'Aziz al-Mishri (1955-2000)

He was born in the village of Baha in the south west of the Kingdom, and obtained the Intermediate Certificate. He wrote short stories, novels, poetry and essays in numerous local and Arab newspapers and magazines. His works include the following short story collections: *Death on the Water* (mawt 'ala 'l-ma'), 1979; *The Travels of the Chief* (asfar al-sarawi), 1986; *The Confessions of Sprouting Wheat* (bawh al-sanabil), 1987. He has also written the following novels: *The Clouds and the Thrusting Trees* (al-ghuyum wa manabit al-shajar), 1989; *The Forts* (al-husoun), 1991.

### Ibrahim al-Nasser (b. 1932)

Born in Riyadh, he obtained his Intermediate Certificate, then engaged in work of various kinds. He has subscribed material to a number of local and Arab newspapers and magazines and has presented numerous radio and television series. His works include the following novels: *A Split in the Night's Attire* (thuqub fi rida' al-layl), 1961; *The Virgin of the Exile* ('adhra' al-manfa), 1978; *Autumn Clouds* (ghuyum al-khareef), 1988. He has also written the following short story collections: *Our Mothers and Struggle* (ummahatuna wa 'l-nidal), 1962; *A Land Without Rain* (ard bila matar), 1967; *The Girls' Creek* (ghadeer al-banat), 1977.

## IV. THE PLAYWRIGHTS

### Milha 'Abdallah

Born in the town of Abha in the south of the Kingdom, she now lives in Cairo, where, in 1990, she graduated with a B.A. in Criticism and Drama from the Academy of Fine Arts. She is a prolific contributor to the Saudi theatre, both as a writer and scholar. She has produced, among other things: *Plays* (masrahiyyat), 1995; and a research paper entitled *The Influence of Bedouin Life on the Saudi Theatre* (athar al-badawa 'ala 'l-masrah al-Sa'udi), 1994.

### 'Abdallah 'Abd al-Jabbar (b. 1920)

He was born in Mecca and graduated in Cairo with a B.A. in Arabic Language. He then worked as a teacher in Mecca, before subsequently becoming Head of the Saudi Educational Mission in the Arab Republic of Egypt. One of the early serious scholars in Saudi Literature, he has written many critical essays on the subject of poetry and prose in the Kingdom, and is himself a writer of short stories and plays.

His works include the play *The Dumb Devils* (al-shayatin al-khurs), 1954; and the following critical works: *The Story of Literature in the Hijaz in the Pre-Islamic Period* (qissat al-adab fi 'l-Hijaz fi 'l-'asr al-jahili) (in collaboration with others), 1958; and *Modern Literary Trends in the Heart of the Arabian Peninsula* (al-tayyarat al-adabiyya 'l-haditha fi qalb al-jazira 'l-'Arabiyya), 1959.

### Raja' 'Alem (b. 1963)

Born in Mecca, she has a B.A. in English Literature and works in teaching. She is a prolific novelist and has assumed a prominent role in modernizing this literary genre in the Kingdom. She also writes plays and essays. Her novels include: *Four Zero* (arba'a sifr), 1987; *The Silk Road* (tariq al-harir), 1995; *O Censor, a Nocturnal Walk* (masra ya raqib), 1997; *My Master Alone* (sayyidi wahdanahu), 1998; and *A Ring* (khatam), 2001. She has written two plays: *Punctures in the Back,* (thuqub fi 'l-dhahr), 1978; and *The Actor's Last Death* (al-mawt al-akhir li 'l-mumathil), 1987.

### Ahmad al-Mulla (b. 1961)

(Please see his entry under "Poets.")

### Muhammad al-'Uthaim (b. 1948)

He was born in the town of Brida in the Qassim region and, in 1985, gained an M.A. in Journalism from the United States. He subsequently worked as a lecturer in the Information Department of the King Saud University. A prominent playwright, his plays have featured at a number of local and international festivals. His works show a marked inclination to employ the traditional classical and the popular. He has written a number of plays, including: *The Dome of Rashid* (qubbat Rasheed); *The Lean Years* (al-sinin al-'ijaf); and *The Blue Melon* (al-battikh al-azraq).

# V. PERSONAL ACCOUNT WRITERS:

### 'Abd al-Fattah Abu Madyan (b. 1922)

Born in Benghazi, Libya, he studied Islamic Juristic Science in Medina. He issued the newspaper *Al-Adwa'* ("the lights") in Jeddah in 1957, then the magazine *Al-Ra'id* ("the pioneer") in 1959. He also issued the monthly *Kitab al-Adwa'* ("the book of lights"), and has made many literary and cultural contributions in Saudi newspapers and magazines, and to the Saudi Broadcasting Service. He currently works as Chairman of the Literary and Cultural Club in Jeddah. His works include the following books of essays: *Waves and Peaks* (amwaj wa adhbaj), 1959; *In the Battleground of Life* (fi mu'tarak al-hayat), 1982; and *The Rock and the Nails* (al-sakhra wa 'l-azafir), 1997; his autobiography, *The Story of Young Muftah* (hikayat al-fata miftah), 1996; and his work *And Those Days* (wa tilka 'l-ayyam), 1986.

### 'Aziz Diya' (1914-1998)

He was born in Medina and received his education at the Advanced Hashimite School (*al-Madrasa 'l-Hashimiyya 'l-Raqiya*). He then enrolled at the School of Sanitation and, later, at the American University of Beirut. He worked at the Najah School in Medina, then in various government positions. He issued the newspaper *Okaz* in the city of Jeddah in 1960 and headed its editorial staff. He then became editor-in-chief of the newspaper *Al-Madina 'l-Munawwara*. He was a founding member of the Cultural Literary Club in the city of Jeddah. His works include: a collection of stories, *Mamma Zubaida* (mama Zubaida), 1984; *The Stories of Somerset Maugham* (qisas Somerset Maugham), translated into Arabic, 1981; other translations: *The Age of Youth in the Desert* ('ahd al-siba fi 'l-badiya), 1980; and *Stories from Taghur* (qisas min Taghur), 1983; and *Hamza Shihata, a Peak that Was Known but Not Discovered* (Hamza Shihata – qimma 'urifat wa lam tuktashaf), 1977.

### Khalid bin Sultan (b. 1949)

He was born in Mecca, the son of Prince Sultan bin Abd al-Aziz Al Saud, the Crown Prince of the Kingdom of Saudi Arabia. He obtained his B.A. in Military Sciences from Sandhurst College in Britain, worked as Commander of the Royal Saudi Air Defence Forces, and was Commander of the Allied Forces and military operations during the First Gulf War in 1990. He is presently Deputy Defence Minister for Military Affairs. His major work is *A Warrior from the Desert* – facts, reminiscences and an outlook for the future (muqatil min al-sahra'), 1995.

### Mansour al-Khiraiji (b. 1935)

He was born in Syria and received his basic education at its schools, then in Medina and at the Preparatory School for Missions in Mecca. He obtained his B.A. in English Language and Literatures in 1958, from the Faculty of Arts at Cairo University. He then obtained the degree for Advanced Studies in English Literature from the University of Leeds, England, in 1961, and his M.A. in the same specialization from the University of Nebraska in the United States in 1964. He worked at the King Saud University and is presently Deputy Chief of Royal Protocol at the Royal Bureau. His works include: a novel, *Additional Lessons* (durus idafiyya), 1998; and *What the Job Description Didn't Tell Me - Leaves from My Life* (ma lam taqulhu 'l-wazifa – safahat min hayati), 1977.

### Hasan Naseef (b. 1922)

Born in Jeddah, he enrolled at the Falah School there, then the Preparatory School for Missions in Mecca, following which he joined the Faculty of Medicine at Cairo University. After graduating, he obtained a degree in tropical diseases, then a degree in dermatology from the University of London in 1949. He worked at the Ministry of Health, being appointed Minister of Health in 1960. His works include two book of poetry: *Diversions* (tasali), 2nd edition, 1982; and *The Smiles* (al-basamat) 1984; and his autobiographical *Memoirs of a Student* (mudhakkirat talib), 1959.

### 'Abd al-'Aziz al-Rabee' (1928-1982)

Born in Medina, he graduated in 1951 with a degree in Arabic Language from the Faculty of Sciences at Cairo University. He occupied a number of positions in the field of education and took part in the establishment of the Medina Literary Club, of which he remained Chairman until his death. He was awarded the Gold Medal at the first Conference for Saudi Men of Letters in 1974, and also obtained the Certificate as a Pioneering Figure in Literary Criticism. He participated in a number of conferences inside and outside the Kingdom. Apart from his *Memories of a Pliant Child* (dhikrayat tifl wadee'), appearing in this book, his works include: *Virtuous Character in Islam,* (al-khulq al-fadhil fi 'l-Islam), 1961; and *The Care of Youth in Islam,* (ri'ayat al-shabab fi 'l-Islam), 1980.

### Ahmad al-Siba'i (1905-1984)

Born in Mecca, he received his education at its schools during the Hashimite era, then worked as a teacher at the Fa'izeen School ("School of the Winners") and later became its principal. During the Saudi era, he became editor-in-chief of the newspaper *Sawt al-Hijaz* ("Voice of the Hijaz"); then he published the newspaper *Al-Nadwa* in 1957, and the magazine *Quraish* in 1959. In 1984, he received the State Award for Merit in Literature. He is regarded as one of the pioneers of thinking and literature in the Kingdom of Saudi Arabia. His works include: the novel *An Idea* (fikra), 1948; the following story collections: *The Guide to the Hajj and the Visit* [to the holy places] (al-murshid ila 'l-hajj wa 'l-ziyara), 1948; and *My Aunt Kadrajan* (khalati Kadrajan), 1967; an essay collection, *He Said and I Said* (qala wa qultu), 1968; an autobiography, *Abu Zamil* (Abu Zamil), 1954; and *The Philosophy of the Jinn* (falsafatu 'l-jinn), 1948.

### Sultana al-Sidairi

She was born in al-Qurayyat in the northern region of the Kingdom. Her poetry was published in Beirut under pseudonyms such as "Nida,'" "'Uhud" and "al-Khansa'." She has won many testimonials of acknowledgement and medals of honour from cultural societies and institutions inside and outside the Kingdom. Her works include the following poetry collections: *The Fragrance of the Desert* ('abir al-sahra'), 1956; *My Eyes, in Sacrifice for You* ('aynaya fidak), 1960; *A Cloud Without Rain* (sahaba bila matar), 1984; and *Subjugation* (qahr), 1984; and a story collection, *Images from Society,* (suwar min al-mujtama'), 1975.

## Members of the Academic Committee

PRESIDENT

**Professor Mansour Ibrahim al-Hazimi**

Born in Mecca in 1935, he graduated with a B.A. from the Department of Arabic Langauage, Faculty of Arts, Cairo University in 1958, and obtained his Ph.D. from the School of Oriental and African Studies at the University of London in 1966. He taught in the Department of Arabic Language in the School of Arts at King Saud University, and occupied the following positions: Chair of the Department of the Arabic Language and its Literatures; Dean of the School of Arts; and Dean of the Centre for University Studies for Women. He was elected a member of the prestigious Shura Council in its first session (1414-1418 A.H.), and presently works as a part-time emeritus professor at the School of Arts, King Saud University.

In 1390 H./1970 A.D., he established the first academic magazine for the School of Arts at King Saud University. He is a member of the editorial board of *Al-Darah* magazine, a member of the Board of Trustees for the 'Abd al-'Aziz al-Babtain award for poetic creativity, and has been a member of the Literary Club of Riyadh, of the Higher Committee for the State Award for Merit in Literature, and of the League of Arab States Higher Committee for Comprehensive Planning for Arabic Culture.

His writings and papers include: Muhammad Farid Abu Hadid, Novelist, Riyadh: al-Jazira, 1970; A Dictionary of Journalistic Source Material, Riyadh: 1974; The Art of the Novel in Modern Saudi Literature, Riyadh: 1981; Critical Statements, Riyadh: 1989; Illusion and the Axes of Vision, Riyadh: 2000 A.D.

He has received the following decorations and awards: the Royal Medal for Merit, First Class; the Grand Gold Medal from the Arab Organization for Education, Culture and Sciences; the Medal in Appreciation from the Joint Council of the Arab Gulf States; the King Faisal International Award for Arabic Literature.

MEMBERS

**Ustadh 'Abd al-Rahim bin Mutlaq al-Ahmadi**

He was born in Wadi 'l-Safra in 1938 and graduated with a B.A. in History from the Islamic University of Imam Muhammad bin Saud in Riyadh in 1978. He also gained a Masters degree in the Social Science of Literature from the King Saud University in Riyadh in 1988. After a period of teaching, he devoted himself to social work: first, as Manager of the Centre for Social Development in Wadi Fatima; then as Manager of the Centre for Social Development in al-Dir'iyya; then as Manager of the Youth and Sports Department at the Secretary General's Office of the Joint Council of the Arab Gulf States.

His writings include: *From the Poetry of Ibn Qabil*, Riyadh: Maramir, 1987; *A Thousand and One Remnants*, Riyadh: Al-Mufradat, 1988; *Oh Poet, I Apologize*, Riyadh: Al-Mufradat, 1996; *From the Narrations of Ibn Qabil*, Riyadh: Al-Mufradat, 1998; *The*

*People of the Remnant*, Riyadh: Al-Mufradat, 1998; *Social Trends in the Contemporary Short Story in the Kingdom of Saudi Arabia*, Riyadh: Al-Mufradat, 2004.

He has been awarded the Medal of the Joint Council of the Arab Gulf States (Olympic gold distinction in administration and organization).

### Professor 'Abd al-Rahman al-Tayyib al-Ansari

Born in Medina in 1354 H./1935 A.D., he graduated with a B.A. degree from the Department of Arabic Language, Faculty of Arts, at Cairo University in 1960, and gained his Ph.D. from Leeds University in England in 1966. He taught in the Department of History, then in the Department of Archaeology and Museums at the Faculty of Arts, King Saud University, and occupied the following positions: Deputy Dean, then Dean of the Faculty of Arts; Chairman of the Department of History, then of Archaeology; supervisor of the Centre for Social Services and Ongoing Education at the King Saud University. He supervised the establishment of the Archaeology Division in the Department of History at the Faculty of Arts, King Saud University, and established the Society for History and Archaeology in 1966. He chaired three international seminars at the University for studying the history of the Arabian Peninsula. He was also Chairman of the Saudi Society for Archaeological Studies at the King Saud University and Manager of Archaeological Technologies for the al-Fao district. He was elected to membership of the prestigious Shura Council for both its first and second sessions, and is a member of numerous academic committees, local, Arab and international: such as the Higher Council for Archaeology in the Kingdom; the Arab Organization for Education, Culture and Sciences; and the UNESCO International Agency for Writing the History of Humanity.

His writings and papers include: Transport and Communications in the Kingdom of Saudi Arabia During the Years 1319-1419 H., Dammam: 1999; The Village of al-Fao, a Picture of Ancient Pre-Islamic Arab Culture, Riyadh, 1982; "Writings from the Village of al-Fao" (kitabat min qaryat al-Fao), Journal of the Faculty of Arts, King Saud University, 1974; "Al-Jawf District in the Pre-Islamic Ages" Al-Jawwiyya, 1416 H.

He has received the following medals and awards: the Medal for Merit, First Class, from the Kingdom of Saudi Arabia, 1982; the Award of the Kuwait Institute for Scientific Advancement, 1984; the Sash of Culture and the Arts from the Ministry of Culture in the Republic of Yemen, 1998; the Shield of the Union of Arab Archaeologists, the Arab League, Cairo, 2001.

### Professor 'Ezzat 'Abd al-Majid Khattab

Born in Medina in 1936, he obtained his B.A. from Cairo University, Department of the English Language and Literatures, in 1958, and gained his Ph.D. in Nineteenth-Century English Poetry from the University of New Mexico, U.S.A., in 1969. He then taught at the Faculty of Arts at King Saud University, occupying the following positions: Chair of the Department of English Language; Deputy Dean, then Dean of the Faculty of Arts; supervisor of the Research Centre; and editor-in-chief of the magazine of the Faculty of Arts. He is a member of many societies, including the Modern Languages Society in the United States and the International Society for Comparative Literature. He has also been a member of the Board of Directors of the Literary Club of Riyadh.

His writings include: *Features and Poetic Images*, Riyadh: 1983; *A Second Reading, The Book of Riyadh*, Riyadh: 2000; a translation of Louise Rosenblath's *Literature Is a Process of Discovery*, Riyadh: King Saud University, 1419 H./1998 A.D.; "A translation into Arabic of the 'Elegy' of the English poet Thomas Gray," *Magazine of the Faculty of Arts*, Vol. III, 1393-1394 H.; "'Umar Abu Risha and Robert Browning: A Relationship in the Realm of Dramatic Monologue" *Dirasat Review*, Jordan University, 1984.

### Dr 'Abd Allah bin Hamid al-Mu'aiqil

Born in Yanbu' al-Nakhl in 1950, he graduated with a B.A. in Arabic Literature from the Faculty of Arts at King Saud University in Riyadh in 1975, then gained his Masters and Ph.D. degrees in Modern Arabic Literature from the University of Michigan in the United States. He taught at the Faculty of Arts at King Saud University in Riyadh, then was appointed, during 1977, to teach Saudi Literature at the University of Washington in Seattle, USA. He subsequently worked as a non-full-time Adviser at the Ministry of Post, Telegrams and Telephones, and in the Shura Council.

His research and papers in magazines and at academic conferences include: "Poem Titles in the Poetry of the Countries of the Joint Council"; "The Overtures of Free Verse Poems in Saudi Arabia"; "Prose Poetry in the Kingdom of Saudi Arabia"; "Modern Saudi Poetry" (al-shi'r al-Sa'udi 'l-hadith); "Poetry and enlightenment in al-'Awwad and al-'Urayyid"; *Selections from Saudi Poetry* (in collaboration with others); *A Critical Introduction and Selections from Saudi Poetry* (in collaboration with another); *A Critical Introduction and Selections from Arabic Poetry in the Twentieth Century*; "Searching for the Self in the Novel Saqifat al-Safa."

### Professor Marzouq bin Snaitan bin Tunbak

Born in Medina in 1950, he graduated with a B.A. from the Faculty of Arts, King Saud University, and obtained his Ph.D. from Edinburgh University, Great Britain, in 1982. He taught at the Faculty of Arts, King Saud University, and at one stage was Trustee of the Faculty. He also chaired the Social Committee and the Board of Directors of the Joint Fund at the University, and was a member of many academic committees including: the Committee for Identifying the Roots and Terminology of Arabic Names (Oman); and the Committee for the Guide to European Universities at the Department of Arabic, King Saud University. He has also taken part in academic conferences, such as: the Third Conference for the Festival of Poetry and the Gulf States Novel, in Abha in 1408 H.; the Conference Concerning Social Change in Contemporary Arabic Literature, in India in 1985; and the *Lisan al-'Arab* Conference in Cairo, dealing with Arabic language issues, in 1421 H.

His writings include: Classical Language and the Theory of the Colloquial, Riyadh: 1407 H.; Neighbourly Ethics Among the Arabs, Cairo: Dar al-Ma'arif, 1412 H.; Hospitality and Its Ethics, Cairo: Dar al-Ma'arif, 1413 H.; On the Language of the Quran, Cairo: Dar al-Ma'arif, 1414 H.

He received the award of the Education Bureau of the Arab Gulf States for 1406-1407 H., for his book *Classical Language and the Theory of the Colloquial.*

### Dr Mu'jib Sa'id al-Zahrani

Born in al-Baha in 1954, he obtained his B.A. in the Arabic Language and Literatures from the Faculty of Education at King Saud University in 1976, and his Ph.D. in General and Comparative Literature from the New Sorbonne in Paris in 1989. He has taught at the School of Literature, King Saud University, and is a member of the Committee for Methodology in Literature and Humanistic Sciences, and also a member on the editorial board of the review *'Alamat* ("Signs"), issued by the Literary and Cultural Club in Jeddah. He was a member of the editorial board of *Al-Qawafil* magazine, issued by the Literary Club of Riyadh, and chairman of the Cultural Committee of the Faculty of Arts at King Saud University.

His papers and research published in academic magazines include: "Influences of the Theory of the Western Novel on Arab Criticism of Fiction"; "Aesthetics in Linguistic Criticism"; "On Semiotics – Presentation and Origins"; *The Language of Daily Living in the Language of the Novel.*

## East-West Nexus/Prota

Project for the dissemination of Arabic culture: EAST-WEST NEXUS through the preparation of studies on Arabic history, literature and civilization; and PROTA through the translation of selected material from Arabic literature, classical and modern, into English.

### i. DIRECTOR
### Salma Khadra Jayyusi

Poet, critic, literary and cultural historian, anthologist, and Founder and Director of EAST-WEST NEXUS/PROTA, the Projects for the dissemination of Arabic literature and Arab/Islamic culture and history in the English language, *Salma Khadra Jayyusi* was professor of Arabic literature at several Arab and North American universities before deciding to leave teaching in order to concentrate on the dissemination of Arabic culture and literature in the English language. She has many publications in the various fields, both as an independent scholar and within the programme of her institutions, including ten large anthologies of translated selections from all genres of Arabic literature, classical and modern, with comprehensive introductions written mainly by her. Other publications are her two-volume critical work, *Trends and Movements in Modern Arabic Poetry*, and such edited works as: *The Legacy of Muslim Spain; Human Rights in Arabic Thought; Classical Arabic Narratives*, and *The City in the Islamic World*. She has received many awards the last two of which were the Edward Said "Prize for Career Excellence" from the Organization of Arab/American writers in New York (2005), and the Award of the Higher Council for Culture in Egypt for her work on "Disseminating Arabic Culture in the World" (2006). She lives between the United States, Britain and Jordan.

## ii. THE *PROTA* LITERARY TEAM

*First Translators:*
### Dina Bosio (prose)
Lebanese translator who lives in Cyprus. She has undertaken quite a number of translations for *PROTA*, including *the translation of the short stories in this anthology*.

### Noura Nuweihed Halwani
*Translator of the excerpts from novels in this volume.* She is a short story writer, who published her first collection, *The Winds of the Other Shore*, in 1962. She has edited the women's magazine *Dunya al-Mar'a* for many years, and has worked in journalism for fifteen years and in translation for over twenty years. In 2004 she published her autobiography, *My Sons*.

### Bassam al-Hilu (poetry)
He is one of *PROTA*'s specialised poetry translators from Arabic. Other than *PROTA* work, he has undertaken the translation of a collection of the Saudi poet Hasan ʿAbdallah al-Qurashi, published by Saqi books, London.

### Laith al-Husain (poetry and creative prose)
He is a translator of poetry and prose and a specialist in comparative literature on which he is currently working for a Ph.D. Other than the poetry he has translated for this anthology, he has also translated the excerpts from drama and from personal account literature.

### Reem Yousef Kelani (prose)
Reem Yousef Kelani graduated from Kuwait University with a BSc in Zoology & Computer Sciences in 1986. She worked for four years as a scientific researcher for Kuwait Institute for Scientific Research and Kuwait University. She was brought up as fully bilingual, and in 1980, she assisted her doctor father in revising his translation into Arabic of Manfred Ullman's *Islamic Medicine* (published by the Kuwaiti Ministry of Health). In 1990, Reem turned her attention to Palestinian music, whilst at the same time working as a freelance translator and interpreter for BBC

documentaries and films. Now considered to be one of the foremost researchers and performers of Palestinian music, Reem released her debut album "Sprinting Gazelle: Palestinian Songs from the Motherland and the Diaspora" to critical acclaim (Fuse Records, February 2006). Alongside her husband and business partner, Reem translated the lyrics of her songs into English and published them in the accompanying booklet of the CD.

*Second Translators:*
### Ruanne Abou-Rahme (poetry)
Ruanne Abou-Rahme is a young Palestinian/ American poet writing in English. Born in Boston, USA, she studied Media and Communication Studies at Goldsmith College, University of London, graduating in 2004 with First Class Honours. Her group graduation film about an autistic child won the Royal Television Society Awards for Best Student Fiction Film for the London Region in 2004. She is working now on her MA in Independent Film, Video and New Screen Media at the University of East London. Interests: Film, Photography, literature, and writing poetry. She is at present preparing her first poetry collection for publication.

### Alan Brownjohn (poetry)
English poet. He worked first as a schoolteacher then lectured at Battersea College of Education and South Bank Polytechnic, before leaving to become a full-time freelance writer in 1979. A regular broadcaster, reviewer and contributor to journals, including the *Times Literary Supplement, Encounter* and the *Sunday Times*, Alan Brownjohn was poetry critic for the *New Statesman* and was Chairman of the Poetry Society between 1982 and 1988. His first collection of poetry, *The Railings*, was published in 1961. Other books of poetry include *Collected Poems 1952-1983* and *The Observation Car* (1990). He is also the author of three novels, *The Way You Tell Them: A Yarn of the Nineties* (1990), *The Long Shadows* (1997) and *A Funny Old Year* (2001), as well as two books for children and a critical study of the poet Philip Larkin. Alan Brownjohn's most recent collection of poetry is *The Men Around Her Bed* (2004).

### Patricia Alanah Byrne (poetry)
American poet and literary editor who lives in Massachusetts. She taught literature and writing at Wellesley School, before leaving to live in Gardner, Mass., with her husband. She is an active member of the prestigious New England Poetry Club in greater Boston and has published three books of poetry: *The Cat in the Mirror* (1970); *Whetstone* (1987); and *Always Being There* (2004). She also edits *Tapestry*, a quarterly international anthology of literature.

### Christopher Somes-Charlton (prose)
Graduated from St Andrews University in 1982 with an MA Honours in Arabic & Islamic Studies. He worked for the Foreign Office and the Overseas Development

Administration, before becoming Middle East Business Development Manager for Crown Agents. Later, he moved to the United Bank of Kuwait as senior fund manager, Arab Capital Markets, and from there to Barclays Global Investors as Director, Middle East Client Relations. In recent years, Christopher has worked as a freelance consultant on the Middle East.

### Jinan M. Coulter (poetry)

Jinan May Coulter obtained her B.A. (Honours) in Drama and Theatre Arts from Goldsmiths College at London University, then obtained a Diploma in Media Arts from the London College of Printing. Born in the USA to a Palestinian mother and an English father, her work and interests display a highly gifted and creative diversity: poetry, painting, music and video. She was co-director and co-producer on three video films; *Bushoff* (2003); *To Whom It May Concern* which won the Best First Short Film award at the Greenwich Film Festival (2004) and *What's Going On* (2005). At present, she is pursuing an M.A. in Documentary Film at Royal Holloway College of the University of London.

### Christopher Tingley (creative prose)

Christopher Tingley was born in Brighton, England, and studied English at the universities of London and Leeds. For many years he lectured in English and Linguistics at various African universities. He has been extensively published, in connection with East-West Nexus–PROTA, as a co-translator of Arabic novels, short story collections, folk tales and other individual short stories, notably of Yusuf al-Qa'id's novel, *War in the Land of Egypt* (1986), Liyana Badr's collection, *A Balcony over the Fakihani* (1993), Zayd Mutee' Dammaj's novel, *The Hostage* (1994), Yahya Yakhlif's novel, *A Lake Beyond the Wind* (1999), and most recently, Laila al-Atrash's novel, *A Woman of Five Seasons* (2002), Ibrahim al-Koni's novel, *The Bleeding of the Stone* (2002), Jamal Sleem Nuweihed's collection of folk tales, *Abu Jmeel's Daughter and Other Stories* (2002), and Abdallah al-Nasser's collection of short stories, *The Tree and Other Stories* (2004).